Advanced Excel Reporting for Management Accountants

Founded in 1807, John Wiley & Sons is the oldest independent publishing company in the United States. With offices in North America, Europe, Asia, and Australia, Wiley is globally committed to developing and marketing print and electronic products and services for our customers' professional and personal knowledge and understanding.

The Wiley Corporate F&A series provides information, tools, and insights to corporate professionals responsible for issues affecting the profitability of their company, from accounting and finance to internal controls and performance management.

Advanced Excel Reporting for Management Accountants

NEALE BLACKWOOD

WILEY

Cover image: © iStockphoto/Jess_Yu
Cover design: Wiley

Published by John Wiley & Sons, Inc., Hoboken, New Jersey.
Published simultaneously in Canada.

For general information on our other products and services or for technical support, please contact our Customer Care Department within the United States at (800) 762-2974, outside the United States at (317) 572-3993 or fax (317) 572-4002.

Wiley publishes in a variety of print and electronic formats and by print-on-demand. Some material included with standard print versions of this book may not be included in e-books or in print-on-demand. If this book refers to media such as a CD or DVD that is not included in the version you purchased, you may download this material at http://booksupport.wiley.com. For more information about Wiley products, visit www.wiley.com.

Library of Congress Cataloging-in-Publication Data:

Blackwood, Neale.
Advanced Excel reporting for management accountants / Neale Blackwood.
pages cm. — (Wiley corporate F & A ; 651)
ISBN 978-1-118-65772-0 (paperback)—ISBN 978-1-118-65818-5 (ePDF)—
ISBN 978-1-118-65819-2 (ePub)—ISBN 978-1-118-77716-9 (o-Book) 1. Managerial accounting—Computer programs. 2. Electronic spreadsheets—Computer programs. 3. Microsoft Excel (Computer file) I. Title.
HF5657.4.B59 2014
005.54024'6581511—dc23

2013046695

Printed in the United States of America

10 9 8 7 6 5 4 3 2 1

Thank you to the two women who have helped shape the person I am today.

To my mother, who instilled in me a love of books.

To my wife, Jan, you filled in all the missing colours in my paint-by-numbers dreams.

Contents

Preface

SPREADSHEETS HAVE BEEN A MAJOR part of my work life for nearly 25 years, and most of that time has been spent using Excel. Throughout that period I have learned many techniques that can simplify the reporting process. This book captures that knowledge and shares it in a format that you can learn and then apply to your reporting needs. You can benefit from my successes and, just as important, avoid my mistakes.

Of course, how long you have been using a piece of software isn't always a good indicator of how good you are with it. I've heard it said, "He's used Excel for 10 years, but it's been the same year repeated 10 times."

Unfortunately, when Excel gets upgraded these days, you get little training in the new features. The training you do get always focuses on showing you how to do the things you were doing in the old version. That's a good start, but it's like giving a man a two-story house and not showing him the stairs because their old house was a single-story house and didn't have stairs.

I've been lucky in my career, because I have been given the opportunity to train and share my knowledge for many years. Training is a great way to improve the trainer's knowledge. I love training, and I love answering questions and sharing my knowledge. Questions tend to open one's mind to how differently people think about the same topic.

Being a fairly persistent person has helped me in my Excel journey. I don't give up easily. That's a very useful trait for any spreadsheet developer. Excel can be frustrating at times, and I hope this book will help to remove some of the frustration for you.

Having an enquiring mind has led me to always look for better ways to do things. I don't like to waste my time, so if a task is repeatedly taking me a long time, I will look for a better way to do it. Typically I will look for a built-in method to improve the task. If that fails, I will usually resort to a macro.

I've answered thousands of questions from Australian CPAs over the years, and I must admit that some of the solutions can be achieved only through macros. A macro is necessary when the data set or the report has been built in a way that doesn't permit the use of Excel's built-in features.

For the purposes of this book, macros are mentioned only as a side issue. The models and examples in this book are macro-free. The companion website has a file that includes some helpful macros. These are meant to simplify and speed up the developmental process.

Acknowledgments

I'D LIKE TO ACKNOWLEDGE A few people whose books and websites have helped me along my Excel journey.

John Walkenbach: What can I say that hasn't already been said about the man? His books set the benchmark for Excel books. Thank you for your huge contribution to the Excel knowledge base. Your books gave me the confidence to experiment, and that is when my skills started to expand.

David and Raina Hawley: These are the people behind the Ozgrid.com website. I learned many great techniques there.

Michael Alexander: Another great Excel author with far-reaching knowledge and a relaxed and entertaining writing style.

Bill Jellen: Thanks for the MrExcel website, your podcasts, and your books.

Once the Internet became more available, my skills were boosted by the Excel-G and Excel-L e-mail lists. These lists are like a forum via e-mail. Lots of knowledgeable contributors freely help others and share their knowledge.

Thanks to CPA Australia, which published my first Excel article in its monthly magazine in May 2002. This started my love of writing, and I have been contributing to this magazine for more than 11 years. Thanks to the magazine's staff over the years: Jackie Blondell, Prue Moodie, Matthew Dillon, and John Hampshire. You supported me and allowed me to do a few feature articles that let me cover Excel topics in more depth. One of those articles was the inspiration for this book.

Thanks also to CPA Australia for allowing me to present Excel sessions at its events, where I could teach large audiences.

Thanks to my former bosses, Richard Hyland and Jeff Robson. They both supported me and encouraged me to push Excel to its limits.

To all the CPAs over the years who have e-mailed me questions, thanks. Besides providing material for my articles, you also expanded my Excel knowledge by asking things I had never thought of.

To Wiley, thanks for the opportunity to write this book, and a big thanks to the editing team for improving the finished product.

Finally, a special thanks to my wife, Jan, who has always loved, supported, and encouraged me. Her patience whilst I wrote this book was legendary.

Introduction

If you only have a hammer, you tend to see every problem as a nail.

—*Abraham Maslow*

THE FOCUS OF THIS BOOK is to provide you with a blueprint that allows you to build spreadsheet reporting models. The techniques are advanced, but they are explained and demonstrated so that you can easily apply them to your particular situation. This is not a beginner's book; it assumes you have a good working knowledge of Microsoft Excel.

The book is aimed at management accountants and business analysts because they tend to have to report on many different aspects of a business, and they also frequently perform ad hoc reporting.

The reports created are finance-based reports. The techniques used can be applied to any type of reporting. My background is in accounting, and that is what I focus on.

In terms of versions, the examples and pictures are all based on Excel 2010 unless otherwise specified. The content applies directly to Excel 2007 and Excel 2013. Many of the techniques covered can also be achieved in Excel 2003. Indeed many of the Excel 2003 models that I built using these techniques are still running at the time of this writing.

If you know how to use only a few basic functions, then the reporting models you build will be basic and likely to have many manual steps.

I provide you with many different tools to improve your reporting spreadsheets. These tools are extremely flexible, and as you learn and implement them, you will no doubt develop your own applications for them. These tools can also be used for budgeting and financial modeling.

One of my greatest satisfactions as an Excel developer is when a user takes a model I have built and uses it to do something I had never envisaged (in a good way). This means I have done my job well enough to build in the flexibility to allow users to employ their imaginations in arriving at solutions I had never thought of.

I compare the construction of a spreadsheet to the construction of a building. They have many things in common. One thing that they don't have in common, however, is that buildings are not created by one person, whereas spreadsheets typically are. In this respect you will need to put on different hats at different stages of the development process.

You most likely already have a reporting model, and the ideas in this book provide some renovation ideas for you. Changing an existing spreadsheet, especially one that you have not built, can be a daunting prospect. When you see the advantages of using these advanced techniques, I hope you will be inspired to tackle the renovation project.

Creating a reporting spreadsheet is serious business, and if you do it well it can save you hours of work in creating the monthly report, which then frees up time to spend analysing and adding value to the reporting process.

The spreadsheet designs you will be introduced to address many criticisms of spreadsheets as reporting models. Let's be honest: A spreadsheet is just another piece of software. People make mistakes, and mistakes are part of life. Ideally, you learn from your mistakes and improve. I've made many mistakes, and I've learned from them and improved because of them.

I am passing on my experience here so that you can avoid my mistakes. You will no doubt make your own mistakes, but the validation techniques described will help you identify those mistakes early and allow you to fix them.

I've been lucky enough to have a few supportive bosses over the years who have let me "play" with Excel. By experimenting and trying new things, you can learn a lot. Don't be afraid to experiment, and don't be afraid to make mistakes. The Undo command can fix most things. Saving files regularly and using version numbers can make going back to a previous version easier.

Don't be overwhelmed by the amount of content in the book. As you read, take note of those techniques you can benefit from immediately and start to incorporate them in your Excel files as soon as possible. The sooner you start to use new techniques, the sooner you will master them.

Chapters 14 and 15 each contain a case study. These case studies provide a framework to demonstrate the combination of techniques from the other chapters in providing a reporting solution.

When sharing Excel knowledge, you need to explain techniques in isolation so that you can focus on the important parts of each technique. Unfortunately, it's not always obvious how the techniques can be combined.

The case studies provide a bridge between the individual techniques and how they can be combined to provide a seamless reporting solution.

CHAPTER ONE

Management Accounting and Excel

IT HAS BEEN MY EXPERIENCE that management accountants tend to be the power users of Excel within their organisations. They usually end up being the unofficial Excel help desk. For this reason, I assume the reader has a good working knowledge of Excel and its built-in features.

Position titles vary between organisations, and some of the titles I consider closely related to management accountants are business analysts and cost accountants.

Although many of the topics covered are advanced, I include some basic and intermediate topics when they help explain the more advanced topics. I have found over the years that even advanced Excel users can learn new tips and tricks that improve their Excel productivity.

Many users are self-taught and haven't always learned the best ways to do things. I will share many useful Excel shortcuts in Chapter 3.

ASSUMPTIONS

The premise behind the book is that you have an accounting system but its reporting package does not provide the flexibility you need to create the reports you need. Excel can extract data from most accounting systems and databases. So you can use your existing source data to build your reports.

You may also need to bring together data from other sources and incorporate those values with the financial data. This is an area that has the most scope for providing value-adding reports.

Excel is ideally suited to combining data, financial and non-financial, from different data sources into a single reporting model.

Given that some data resides outside of databases, Excel can also provide the ability to incorporate other small databases that may be held in other spreadsheets.

Please note Excel is not a database. Excel can be used as the data repository for small statistical-type data that may not warrant a database system.

You may also develop your budgets and forecasts in Excel and these can be integrated into your reporting model.

If your database systems do not allow direct connection to Excel, then most database systems have the ability to create files that Excel can read. In general you should aim to have all your data in databases.

Australian Conventions

Examples in this book may include Australian tax terminology, such as GST (goods and services tax).

The Australian financial year is from July 1 to June 30, which spans two calendar years.

Australia has six states and two territories. These are often considered regions for reporting. Laws and holidays can vary amongst the states, and it may be necessary to report differently state by state.

Versions

The instructions and images all relate to Excel 2010 unless otherwise noted. Most instructions will also apply to Excel 2007 and 2013. Some of the new features in Excel 2013 will be noted but not explained in detail.

Many of the techniques can be applied to Excel 2003, but no instructions are included for Excel 2003.

Terminology

There are two terms used frequently in the following chapters that require definition.

1. **Parentheses.** *Parentheses* is the correct term for the symbols used with Excel functions to enclose the function arguments (see the following term). On the Internet and in general conversation, these are commonly referred to as *brackets*. In this book, the term used is *parentheses*.
2. **Arguments.** In this book, the parts of an Excel function are referred to as *arguments*. Many functions accept a single argument, such as the SUM function. Others require more arguments; for instance, the VLOOKUP function requires at least three arguments to return a result. Between the parentheses, arguments are separated by commas. *Argument* is the term Microsoft uses in its Excel help system.

Spelling

The book uses UK spelling, except when referring to Excel features. Excel uses U.S. spelling and all the Excel terms will be spelled as they appear in Excel.

THE GOAL OF REPORTING

Management accounting reports are generally created for performance review. Compliance reports that satisfy a company's legal reporting requirements tend to be reasonably similar across industries. Performance reporting varies depending on the industry and the sector. Excel provides the flexibility to develop performance reports that meet your needs.

Performance Measurement

Measuring your daily, weekly, and monthly performance against the budget, a forecast, or the previous year is the main focus of management reporting. This variance analysis is an important part of the reporting process.

Businesses already have accounting system reporting structures in place. These reports tend to be created by the database system that contains the data and are often limited in their layout structures.

In production systems and other systems in which volumes are important, comparing performance with the total dollar amounts may not be an accurate measure, and per-unit calculations are often required.

Charts can identify relationships and trends and are an important part of the reporting process. Many database systems have limited charting capabilities.

Performance Improvement

Another type of reporting focuses on improving performance. This can involve benchmarking and comparing performance among branches or divisions.

This type of reporting can be ad hoc. Areas may be identified for review and reports created to measure the relevant metrics to assist that review.

The techniques discussed throughout this book can be applied to ad hoc reports. Pivot tables, discussed in Chapter 6, are especially suited to ad hoc reporting.

WHY USE EXCEL?

Excel is the spreadsheet of choice for most accountants. Virtually all accountants use Excel, with various degrees of skill. Excel is the industry's standard spreadsheet, and it is constantly being upgraded and updated to handle today's changing information needs.

Most finance staff members have at least rudimentary skills in Excel.

Excel 2010, which this book is based on, can handle data sets of hundreds of thousands of rows. The built-in data connection systems allow direct connection to most database programs in organisations. Excel 2013 was released in January 2013, and it includes a suite of extra features that can simplify reporting even further.

Excel has the ability to create charts that can summarise large data sets into visual, dashboard reports. There are other reporting packages in the market that can create dashboard reports, but none have the popularity of Excel.

Learning to develop reporting models in Excel is a skill that is transferable between jobs. Other dashboard packages do not have the widespread acceptance of Excel.

Excel has its limitations, but if you are aware of them and build your reporting models accordingly, then you can avoid most issues and create a system that will stand the test of time.

This book encourages you to validate your reports and include validations in all stages of the development process. Reporting models tend to be a work in progress in many organisations. The techniques included in this book make the process of adding to or amending your model easier.

THE GOAL OF THIS BOOK

This book explains and demonstrates many techniques that can be used together to create a reporting system in Excel that has the following characteristics.

Easy to Operate

The reporting model should be easy for the user to operate. This means that there should be a minimum of typing required. The interface should use drop-down selections and check boxes where appropriate to handle selections. Navigation should be straightforward, much like web pages, so you can move quickly and easily between the important sheets.

Easy to Maintain

Reporting models are subject to change. There are the normal day-to-day changes caused by new accounts and new departments; these changes should be easy to handle in your reporting model. Then there are the more drastic changes, in which divisions may be added or removed or the structure of the report has to change to meet new reporting requirements. These changes require more effort but should still be straightforward and logical.

Self-Validating

A number of techniques are demonstrated that make identifying and tracking down errors easier. It's one thing to identify that the balance sheet doesn't balance. It's another to identify *why* it doesn't balance and to provide assistance in tracking down any issues.

Modular

Having a modular approach to creating your file will make achieving the other goals easier. Modular spreadsheets have dedicated sheets for instructions, inputs, settings, data, validations, tables, lists, reports, and charts.

Structured

Structure is achieved by setting and following rules in the developmental process. This book recommends that you use a table structure for much of your data and parameters. The use of lists and range names is also encouraged and is covered in depth in this book.

Flexible

Adding structure allows flexibility. This theme is repeated throughout the book. It seems counterintuitive, but structure provides the framework to incorporate flexibility.

MONTHLY MANAGEMENT REPORTS

These techniques work very well with the standard monthly management reports that management accountants typically create. The techniques can also be applied to virtually any type of report. The monthly management reports tend to be the most time-consuming and offer the most benefits for improving.

The techniques described in this book simplify the reporting process by automating many tasks that in the past had to be done manually.

MACRO POLICY

The techniques described in this book allow you to automate your reporting processes without the use of macros. Formulas and functions are used to automate tasks that had to be done manually in the past. No macro will be used to run the reporting models.

My policy on macros is that you should use Excel's built-in features to their limit and resort to macros only when the built-in features do not provide the functionality that you require.

Macros can be used to replace repetitive tasks, performing those tasks in the blink of an eye and reducing manual processes.

The website for this book includes a number of macros that can assist you in both the model creation phase and the data cleansing phase. I have included instructions on how to install and use the macros. They are not part of the reporting process as such but are basically accessories that can speed up the process of report creation and data cleansing.

Macros are a huge topic in Excel, but this book does not go into depth about them. If you want to learn about macros, I suggest you consult the reading list I have provided on the website.

WARNING: Macros Cannot Be Undone

When you run a macro, you clear Excel's undo list. This means you can't undo what the macro does, and you can't undo anything done before you ran the macro.

Before running a macro it is a good idea to save the file. At least then, if the macro does cause a problem, you can close the file without saving, to revert to the pre-macro version.

CHAPTER TWO

Building Reporting Models

BUILDING A REPORTING MODEL from scratch is much like building a house from scratch. Amending an existing reporting model can be likened to renovating an existing house.

When creating a report, you need to define your requirements and set out your scope. This allows you to design, construct, test, use, and then maintain your report. These are very much like the steps you take in building a house.

You need to identify what type of house you want and then get someone to design it for you. The architect will quiz you on how many bedrooms you need, the type of kitchen you want, and all the other factors he or she needs to know to design the right house for you. Similarly, you need to find out what you or the Excel users need to have in the reporting model. This can include both current requirements and possible future requirements.

You might not have any children, but you may want to build a four-bedroom house because you plan on having children. A similar dynamic is true for reporting. There are current requirements to be met, but there may be plans for future expansion that you can build into the structure of the reporting model now rather than cause a major change in the future.

Just like a house, a report needs a solid foundation. The data forms the foundation of your report. Your reports are built on top of your data. If the data structure is not laid out well or is incomplete, then creating and running the reports will be time-consuming and more difficult.

You need to get the layout of your house right, which means, in spreadsheet terms, laying out your worksheets correctly. Your house has to look good—not too gaudy and not too bland. Similarly, for your reports, your formatting determines how the reports will look. Colour is another important aspect of the report. You need to use both colour and formatting, sparingly and carefully.

Finally, you need to make sure that your house is easy to maintain. Similarly, your reports shouldn't require major rewriting just to add a new department. All common changes should be straightforward.

You need to define the reports that you want, and this definition will determine the data you require. You may have that data in a system already, or you may need to create a system to collect it.

Since data determines the types of reports that you can create, the structure of the data is very important. The data is your foundation, and if your foundation is not sturdy, creating the reports can be problematic or difficult. If your data is well structured, you will find that your reports are easy to create.

In an ideal world you would be able to get all the data you need in the structure you require. Unfortunately, in the real world you often have to make do with the data you can get out of a system. If that is the case, then the data will limit the reports you can create.

In many cases it can be worth spending time cleansing your data (see Chapter 5), which then makes it easier to create your reports.

In many of my consulting jobs, my first task is to get the data right. People like to jump right in and start creating the report, but first spending time getting your data structured correctly makes the report creation process so much easier. Chapter 5 is dedicated to getting your foundation right so that your data is ready to use.

Calculation speed will be affected by the design you choose. This includes the functions you decide to use. There is often more than one way to do something in Excel, so you should choose the fastest calculation option. This could mean avoiding certain functions in large files.

When creating reports, follow these steps:

1. Needs analysis
2. Scope definition
3. Design
4. Construction
5. Testing
6. Operation
7. Maintenance

 NEEDS ANALYSIS

Before starting the design phase, you must define what your report is intended to do. Who is going to read it, and what do they want to use it for? Based on what the report is for, you will have to determine where the data comes from or even whether the data exists.

If the data doesn't exist, you will have to decide whether it is cost-effective to gather and maintain the data.

 SCOPE DEFINITION

The scope of the reporting model is defined by your needs, and it will include such things as the data sources and when and how the report is to be created.

Scoping is one area that tends to be a problem with Excel models. It is common for models to start out meeting one requirement, then other reports are added, like extensions to a house. If you build the original model well enough, these additions can be handled easily.

If you are aware of likely changes to a business, you can incorporate a structure into the model that will assist in creating new reports based on possible changes.

DESIGN

Design is an important step that is often overlooked. Users tend to start creating spreadsheets before they have thought things through. The more time you spend on design, the less time you will have to spend on reworking spreadsheets.

You must think ahead and use your needs analysis and scope to help you figure out the various components you need to build into your spreadsheets. In the design phase, you need to think about using the model on an ongoing basis as well as the maintenance aspect of the model. Depending on your reporting time frame, you need to consider the daily, weekly, or monthly maintenance.

You also have to think about what happens at the end of the year and how easy it is to convert to the next year for the reporting model.

By thinking ahead you can avoid having to make major structural changes to your reporting model in the future. You can also design how to handle structural changes—for example, adding a new department or removing an old department. Normal maintenance processes should be straightforward.

When designing, you need to think about who is going to use the model and how you can make it as easy as possible to use.

Table-driven design is recommended in this book because it provides the flexibility required to handle most situations. The use of range names is also recommended because it provides another way to add structure into your reporting files

CONSTRUCTION

Building the reporting model is much easier when you have already prepared the data and detailed the requirements. Completing the design part of the process then allows you to build your spreadsheets just once.

Part of the construction phase involves creating your instructions, which include the normal day-to-day or month-to-month operation of the model. You also need to add maintenance instructions. These should include what happens when you change a reporting year, what happens when you need to change your forecasts, or any other eventualities that you can think of.

During the construction phase, you usually identify most of the validations you will need to run the reporting model. Building validations into the model during the construction phase helps maintain model integrity throughout the process.

This book provides the tools you need to successfully undertake this construction phase.

TESTING

Testing is another area that is usually overlooked or at least given only a cursory glance. You need to set up your tests and think about what could go wrong, then test for those eventualities. You should lean towards pessimistic thinking in this phase.

Testing is also performed as you build. You need to identify all the issues you have to handle as you go along. Some things become apparent only as you build the model.

You will most likely need to expand your validations as you encounter errors that need to be trapped and identified.

OPERATION

Operation should be the easiest part of the whole process, because you have already designed, constructed, and tested the model.

Make sure you consider the user in the earlier phases so that this step is the easiest. You may need to work a little harder in the design and construction phases to make using the model easier. Remember that you design and construct only once, but you have to use the model regularly.

MAINTENANCE

Maintenance complexity tends to be related to the complexity of the model. How well you build your reporting model will determine how easy it is to maintain. You must consider the maintenance issues during the design phase.

You can spare the user many manual processes if you build the model correctly, but sometimes that means the maintenance processes have to be more complex.

Detailed instructions are usually very important for this phase.

TIME, EFFORT, AND COST

The three considerations of time, effort, and cost are interlinked but can be discussed separately.

Time

The month-end schedule is typically driven by tight deadlines. Time has been pared down to get the report out as soon as possible. During the month-end period, time is your most limited resource.

If your reports are daily, you don't want to spend much of the day creating them, so again, speed is of the essence.

Delegating tasks can help. If you can simplify the processes sufficiently, then delegation can save you vital time. Processes that can be done simultaneously by different people can also save time.

Effort

If a process is difficult or time-consuming, it is a candidate for automation. Automation doesn't always mean macros; it can also mean setting up a file that does a lot of the work for you. All you do is paste a data dump into the file, make a few adjustments, and check the validations; then either your data dump is converted into a finished report or it has created another data dump in the format that you need for the final report. This may involve complex formulas, pivot tables, and, as a last resort, macros.

Automation can simplify a task so that it can be performed by a junior staff member. In addition, properly automated systems are documented, so if that staff member becomes sick or goes on leave, coverage of the task is easier.

This book does not focus on macros, but it does provide sample macros that can be used in the data cleansing phase. This tends to be the time-consuming stage of the process.

The standard of data dumps is improving all the time. Yet there are many legacy systems that are still in existence, and these tend to have data structures and layouts that cannot be changed. In some cases the cost of change is prohibitive, so you have to work with what you are given.

Cost

Time, effort, and cost are, of course, closely related. The month-end schedule is so tight that cost can be the last consideration when you're determining a solution to your reporting requirements. In this respect I am discussing only Excel solutions, although the concept does apply to other systems as well.

Out-of-pocket reporting costs tend to be up front, so once you spend the money to develop the system, very little out-of-pocket expense will be required to run it.

If you have to report to a parent company, you typically are told when to report. There is often little consultation on what is possible; you just have to meet the deadlines. In that case, cost takes a backseat to time.

PRACTICAL CONSIDERATIONS

It has been my experience that the time taken to implement the techniques in this book does not take too much longer than the time taken to perform inefficient manual practices during the month-end cycle. Much of the work of converting or replacing existing models can be performed outside the strict month-end timetable.

The philosophy of this book is as follows:

- You should use existing data sources as inputs for your reporting models as much as possible.
- Avoid rekeying whenever possible (this obviously has cost-benefit implications if the effort required to get a few figures is high; then rekeying them is a worthwhile solution). Rekeying is prone to error and time-consuming.

- You may need to build interim Excel files to handle your data cleansing (see Chapter 5).
- If no data source exists for certain statistics, then you may need to use Excel as a data store, but make sure you use a proper database layout for the data. This is discussed later in the book.
- Data that comes into Excel is not always ready for use by Excel's functions and features. Ideally, the data should be fixed before it comes into Excel, and it is worth the effort to get the data fixed at its source. This is not always practical, since data and data structures can be proprietary and not subject to change.

CHAPTER THREE

Building Tips

I SOMETIMES WATCH THOSE LIFESTYLE PROGRAMS on TV that offer you tips and tricks on doing odd jobs in and around the home. Usually, watching them makes you say, "Why didn't I think of that?" or "I wish I'd known that a few years ago." I hear those same comments when I do training and cover Excel's many shortcuts, tips, and tricks.

This chapter covers shortcuts that I use frequently. It also covers techniques used by other people who work differently from me. People use Excel differently in terms of how they use the keyboard and the mouse. These shortcuts make using Excel easier and also speed up the development process.

I will split up these shortcuts into the following categories:

- **Display.** Tips based on the Excel screen.
- **Keyboard.** Tips associated with shortcut key combinations.
- **Mouse.** Left and right mouse button shortcuts.
- **Keyboard and mouse.** Use of the keyboard and the mouse together for even more shortcuts.
- **General.** All the other tips worth knowing when creating, or using, reporting models.

It is worthwhile to acquaint yourself with these shortcuts and immediately apply those you like. The faster you start using them, the faster you will master them and improve your productivity in Excel. I am still learning new shortcuts and applying them.

I would recommend that you highlight (assuming this is not a library book) the techniques you can use right away and then apply more and more techniques as time goes by.

This chapter contains many shortcut techniques. Don't get overwhelmed; just review each one and see how you can apply it in your particular circumstance. Some will work better with the way you use Excel. Some tips may cause you to experiment, and that's a good thing.

It can be hard to change habits. Repetition is the key. It's usually easier to replace an old habit with a new habit than it is to stop a habit. If there is a better way than your current method, and it works for you, then keep applying it, and in no time you will have replaced the old habit with a new habit.

Don't try applying too many of the techniques at once. Start with the ones that you can see an immediate benefit from and then work your way through the rest.

You will be surprised at how much faster you will be able to complete tasks when you start using these shortcuts.

Many of these shortcuts work in the other Microsoft Office applications of Word, Outlook, PowerPoint, and Access, so don't be afraid to try them in those packages.

DISPLAY TIPS

Excel's screen layout changed radically in Excel 2007. The screen and icons provide many shortcuts. Learning some of these new icons and screen changes can make working in Excel easier.

Wrapped Up with a Ribbon

Excel's ribbon interface was introduced in Excel 2007. It replaced the menu and toolbar system with a ribbon and the Quick Access Toolbar. The reason for the change was to get as many popular options as possible out in plain sight of the user. The ribbon tabs categories were based on common tasks.

The interface was changed because many of Excel's more advanced features were out of sight in the menu structure and were therefore not used. Another problem was that the names Excel used weren't intuitive. A pivot table, as we will see in Chapter 6, is

THE ALT KEY

Keyboard shortcuts usually require pressing two or three keys at once to achieve a shortcut. The Alt key (a key both sides of the keyboard space bar) can work this way but has an alternative method of operation.

There are Alt key shortcuts that require you to press keys in sequence, rather than holding down keys. For example, to open the Excel Options dialog box you press, in sequence, Alt t o. You press the Alt key, then the "t" key, and finally the "o" key.

If you need to hold a key down, the plus symbol is used. To enter the SUM function in a cell, or a range, you can use Alt + =. This means hold the Alt key down and press the = (equal) key.

extremely powerful, but the term *pivot table* means nothing to a new user. So as well as the ribbon being added, the toolbar system has been improved so that when you point the mouse at an icon on the ribbon or the Quick Access Toolbar, a description is displayed to explain what the icon does.

The ribbon can't be customised in Excel 2007 with the user interface. Excel 2010 introduced the ability to customise the ribbon. You can add your own ribbon tabs and modify the existing ribbon tabs.

The ribbon is also context-sensitive. Click on a chart, and you will see three extra ribbon tabs. Depending on what you are working with, there may be a dedicated ribbon tab. Some of the extra tabs for various items are as follows:

Chart: Design, Layout, and Format tabs
Pivot table: Options and Design tabs
Formatted data table: Design tab
Image, shape, or graphic object: Format tab
Slicer: Options tab
Smart art: Design and Format tabs
Sparkline chart: Design tab

There is one hidden ribbon tab that you should display. The Developer tab is hidden when Excel is installed. This tab is dedicated to macros, but it also has an option for adding sheet controls like check boxes and option buttons, which are discussed Chapter 10.

Adding the Developer Tab to the Ribbon

How you add the Developer tab varies by version.

Excel 2007: Press the following keys in sequence: Alt t o. Click Show Developer Tab in Ribbon and click OK.
Excel 2010: Right-click the ribbon and select Customize Ribbon. Click the Developer tab check box on the right and click OK.

Some of the ribbon tab sections have a small arrow icon in the bottom right-hand corner. This icon offers more options. The Clipboard, Font, and Alignment sections all have the extra options icon (see Figure 3.1).

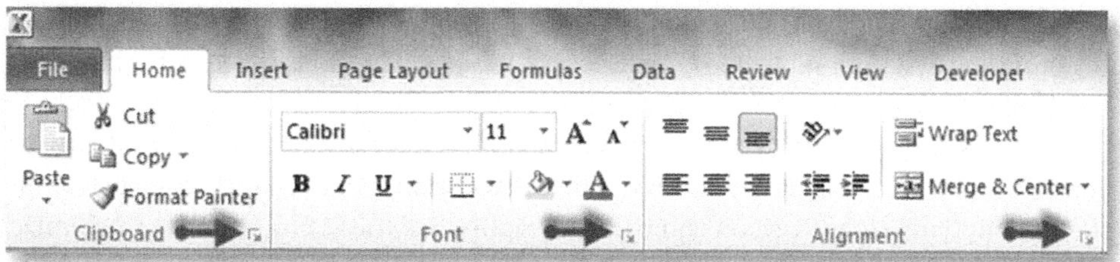

FIGURE 3.1 Extra Options Icon

The extra options icon indicates that there are more options available than are displayed on the ribbon. Not all sections have the icon.

Clicking the icon will open a dialog box that contains all the options. On the Home Ribbon tab, the Font, Alignment, and Number sections each have this icon. Each one opens the corresponding tab in the Format Cells dialog box.

On the Page Layout Ribbon tab, the Page Setup section has the icon, and it opens the Page Setup dialog box. This method of opening the Page Setup dialog box provides access to the Print Titles sections. Some methods of opening the Page Setup dialog box do not provide access to the Print Title options.

Converting from Excel 2003 to 2007 or 2010

In my experience, one of the biggest omissions in the transitional training from Excel 2003 to Excel 2007 or Excel 2010 is the Quick Access Toolbar (a term that means little to new users). This is a toolbar that sits above the ribbon when Excel is installed. It has only a couple of icons visible. I have worked with so many users who still have only those few icons displayed on the toolbar above the ribbon.

The other problem with the transitional training was a result of the ribbon being such a big change. Most of the new features in 2007 were ignored, and the emphasis was placed on where the old options were on the ribbon. People were trained to use Excel 2007 exactly like Excel 2003.

Many of the new features, and even the old features that were brought onto the ribbon, were missed, and most users are still unaware of them. Of course, the more inquisitive users checked out all the options on the ribbon to see what the options could do.

The Quick Access Toolbar

The Quick Access Toolbar (QAT) allows you to customise the interface so that you can display your frequently used icons all the time. This reduces the need to open other ribbon tabs. You should be able to do most of your work with just the Home Ribbon tab and the QAT.

This also allows you to minimise the ribbon, something I do when I want to see as much of the Excel grid as possible. When the ribbon is minimised, the ribbon tab headings are still visible. You can click the tab headings to access the options, but the ribbon itself is hidden and the QAT is still visible.

I recommend displaying the QAT below the ribbon. Right-click the QAT and select Show Quick Access Toolbar Below the Ribbon. This moves the QAT closer to the grid, where you do most of your mouse work.

Adding icons to the QAT is as easy as right-clicking the icon you want to add and selecting the first option, Add to Quick Access Toolbar. This adds the icon to the end of the QAT.

I also advise organising the QAT. Instead of having the icons added randomly to your QAT, place them in a practical sequence. Place similar options together, such as all the print options. To move icons on the QAT, right-click the QAT and select Customize the Quick Access Toolbar. The dialog box shown in Figure 3.2 gives you complete control over the QAT.

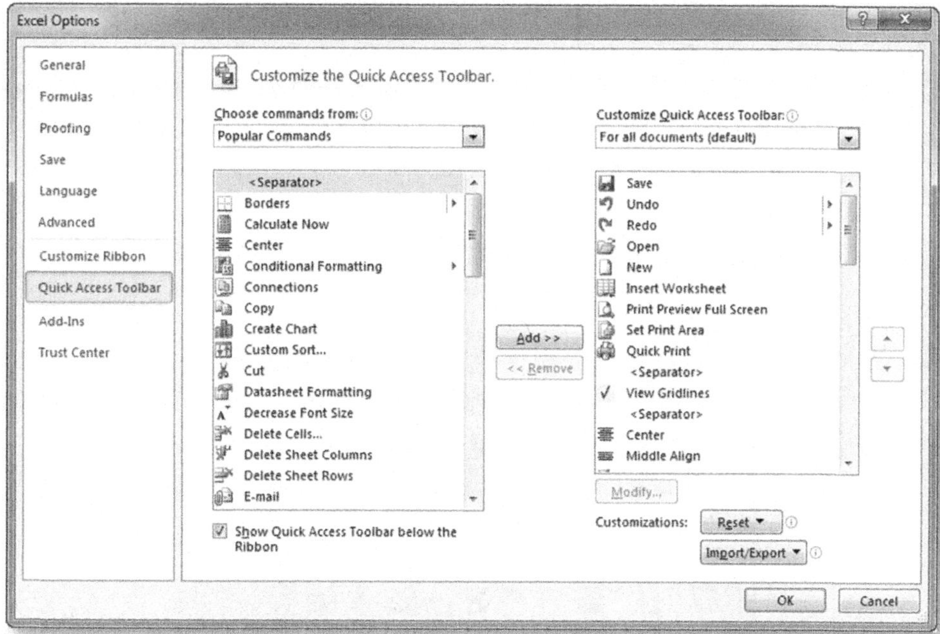

FIGURE 3.2 Customize the Quick Access Toolbar

The Choose commands from drop-down list displays categories of icons you can display below the drop-down list. The first four categories are the most useful (see Figure 3.3). To add an icon to the QAT, either double-click it or select it and click the Add button. If you select an icon on the right and double-click an icon on the left, it will be added to the QAT below the selected icon on the right. To move an icon around on the QAT, select the icon and use the two arrow buttons on the far right of the dialog box to move the icon up or down.

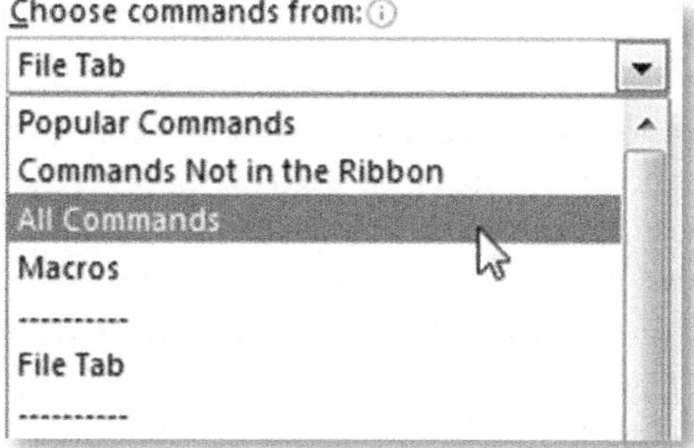

FIGURE 3.3 Categories List

You can add macros to the QAT. When you do, it is a good idea to choose another icon instead of the default macro icon. To change the icon, you first select it on the right-hand side and then click the Modify button. Choose a new icon. You can also change the Display Name to provide a more meaningful description when you point to the icon with the mouse (see Figure 3.4).

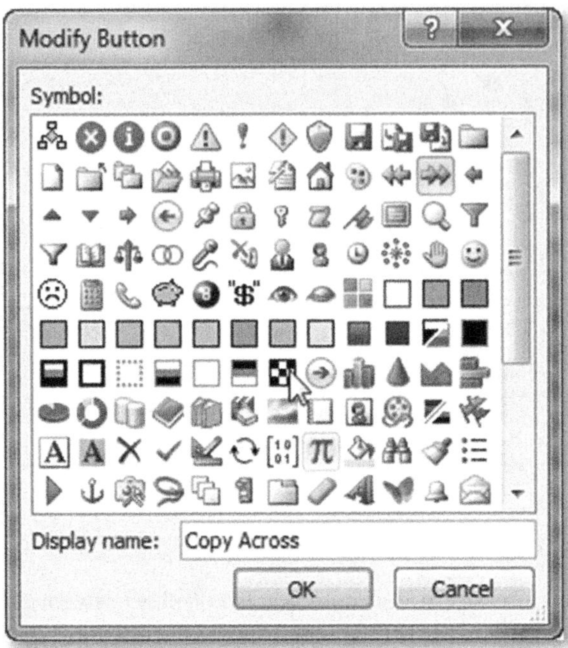

FIGURE 3.4 Modify Button Icon Gallery

Useful Icons to Add to the QAT

Use the All Commands option to find the icons you want to add to your QAT. In my experience, the icons listed here are some of the most useful ones to have on your QAT:

- **Print Preview Full Screen.** Excel 2010 removed the old-fashioned Print Preview window. Many users prefer the older version because all the options are accessible.
- **Set Print Area.** A must-have icon. Define your print area with one click and save paper.
- **Page Setup.** Access all the print options in one click.
- **Gridlines.** Turn sheet gridlines off or on easily and quickly.
- **All Borders.** A format I use frequently, especially when I turn off gridlines.
- **Thick Box Border.** Applies a thick border to the outside of the selected range.
- **Fill Color.** Adds a colour shading to the selected cell background.
- **Center.** Useful for column headings or other cells you want to look different.
- **Format Painter.** Great for copying multiple formats in one step. Double-click it to allow multiple format pasting—press the Esc key to turn off the pasting.
- **AutoSum.** Insert the SUM function,

- **Freeze Panes.** Allows you to set the rows and columns to keep them on the screen at all times.
- **Filter.** Adds the Filter drop-down selection to a table.
- **Clear.** Clears the currently applied filters.
- **Data Validation.** Allows you set validations for cells; the most popular is the drop-down list.
- **Select Objects.** Allows you to select multiple objects (e.g., charts) using the mouse.

Customize the Ribbon (Excel 2010 Only)

You may want to take customisation one step further and create a dedicated ribbon tab for all your reporting options. These could include the toolbar icons you use most during the reporting process as well as any macros that may be involved.

Create a New Ribbon Tab

Right-click the ribbon and choose Customize the Ribbon (see Figure 3.5). Click the last tab and then click the New Tab button (bottom left corner). Click the New Tab (Custom) above and click the Rename button to give it a meaningful name (see Figure 3.6). You can rename the New Group (Custom) using the Rename button. You can also add group sections to your new ribbon tab by using the New Group button. See Figure 3.7 for an example of three groups. You can now drag icons from the left to the new tab on the right (see Figure 3.8). When you are finished, make sure you click the OK button to retain your changes. Figure 3.9 shows an example of a Custom Ribbon tab.

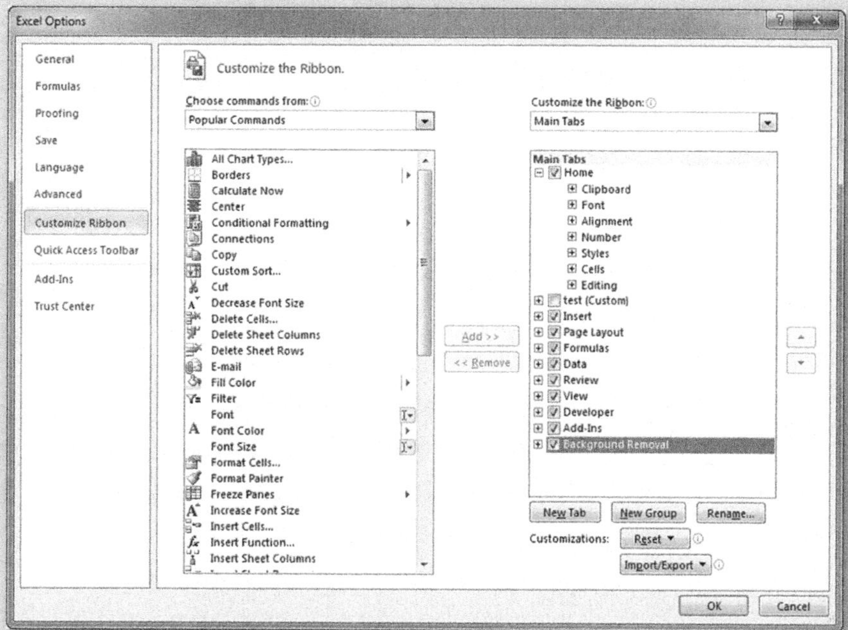

FIGURE 3.5 Customize the Ribbon

(continued)

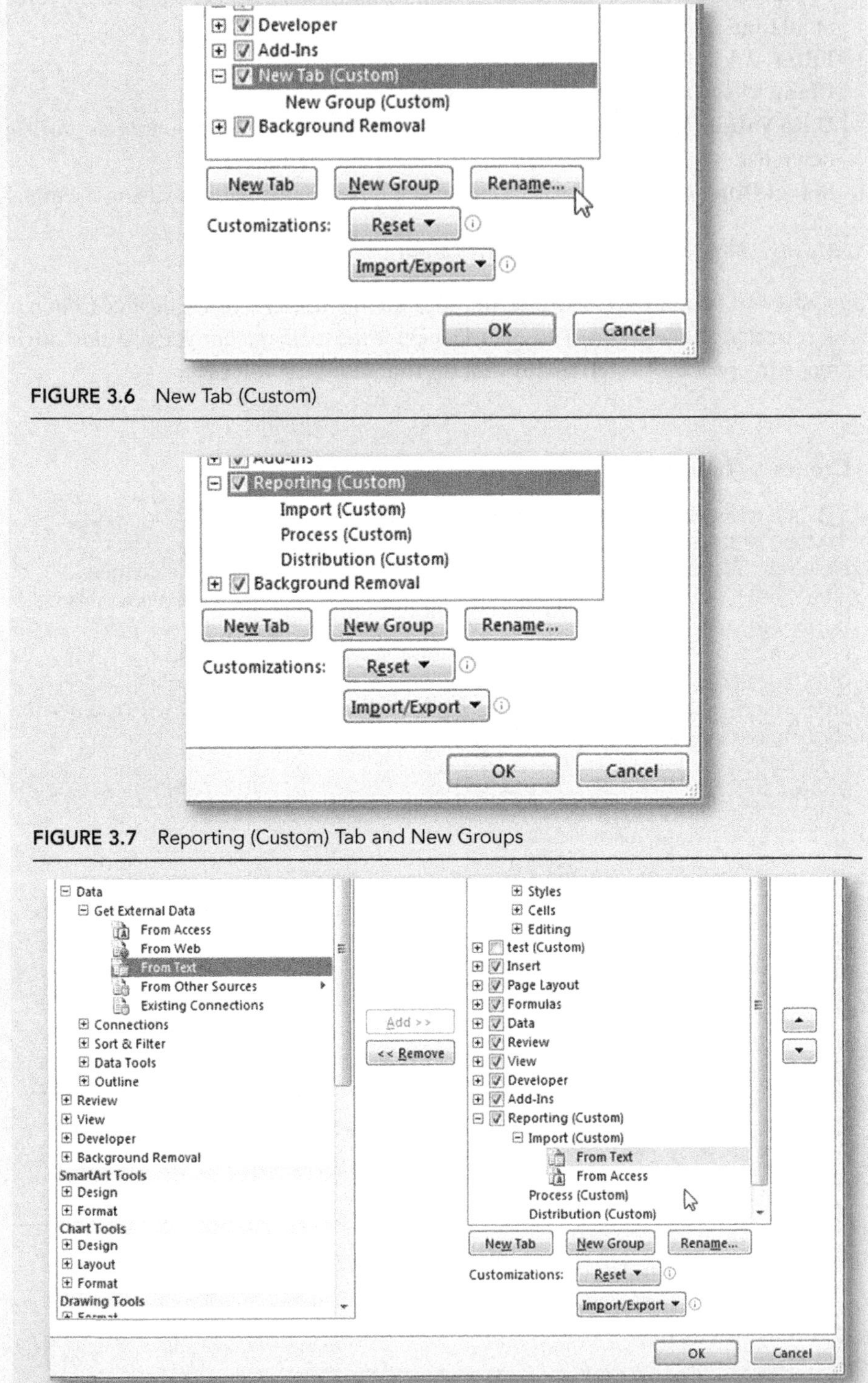

FIGURE 3.6 New Tab (Custom)

FIGURE 3.7 Reporting (Custom) Tab and New Groups

FIGURE 3.8 Adding Icons to a Group

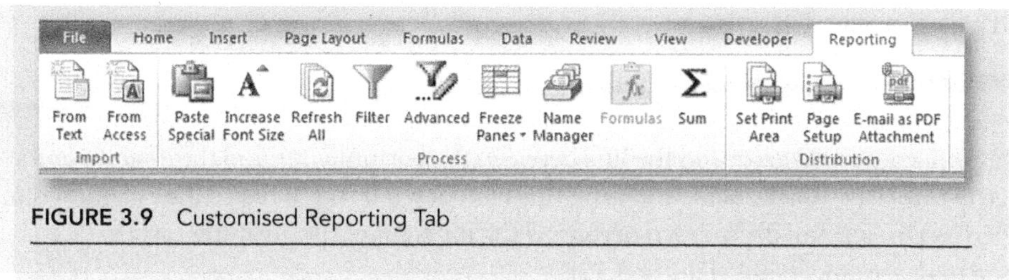

FIGURE 3.9 Customised Reporting Tab

Minimize the Ribbon

Excel 2010 has a new icon, Minimize and Maximize the Ribbon. It is shown on the top right of the screen, to the left of the Help icon (see Figure 3.10).

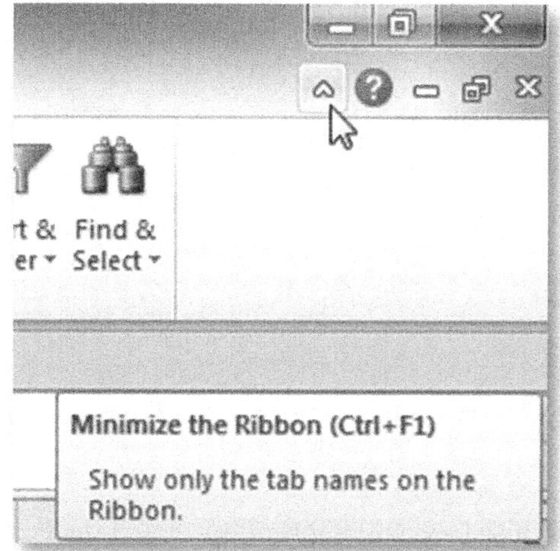

FIGURE 3.10 Minimize Ribbon Icon

The icon changes to Maximize when the ribbon is minimised.

You can also use Ctrl + F1, or right-click the ribbon and choose Minimize the Ribbon. To maximise, use Ctrl + F1 again or right-click and choose Maximize the Ribbon.

Copying Ribbon and QAT Settings

If you use Excel on multiple computers, you may want to transfer your ribbon and QAT settings between computers. On the bottom right of the Excel Options, Quick Access Toolbar dialog box (shown earlier in Figure 3.2), there is an Import/Export drop-down selection that allows you save a file with all the settings. You can copy that file to another computer and then import that file.

Other Screen Changes

Besides the ribbon, a few other changes were made to the Excel screen in Excel 2007.

The Formula Bar can be resized to view multiple rows in a formula or in text. There is a doubled-headed arrow on the line between the Formula Bar and the column letters (see Figure 3.11). Click, hold, and drag this icon down or up to resize the Formula Bar. There is also a small drop-down arrow on the far right of the Formula Bar that can be used to resize quickly (see Figure 3.12).

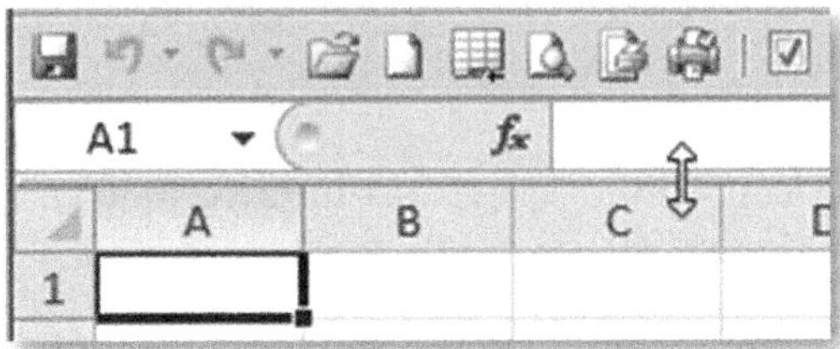

FIGURE 3.11 Formula Bar Resize Double-Headed Arrow

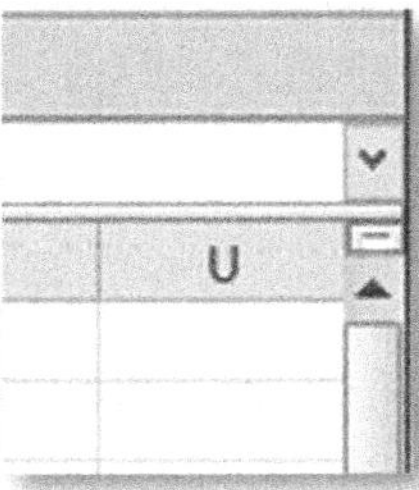

FIGURE 3.12 Formula Bar Resize Drop-Down

The Name Box can also be resized. It is on the left of the Formula Bar and usually displays the currently selected cell reference. The Name Box is associated with range names, which are explained in detail in Chapter 9.

There is a small circle between the Name Box and the Formula Bar. If you point to the circle with the mouse cursor, it changes to a double-headed arrow that you can click, hold, and drag to the right or left to resize the Name Box (see Figure 3.13).

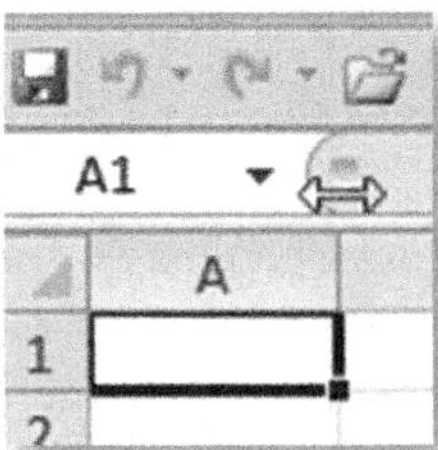

FIGURE 3.13 Name Box Resize Double-Headed Arrow

The Status Bar is at the bottom of the Excel screen, directly below the sheet name tabs. It usually displays the word *Ready* on the far left-hand side. The Status Bar can now display all the Auto Calculation results at once. In previous versions you had to choose the calculation to perform, usually the SUM function. See Figure 3.14 for a list of the options that can be displayed on the Status Bar.

Customize Status Bar

✓	Cell Mode	Ready
✓	Signatures	Off
✓	Information Management Policy	Off
✓	Permissions	Off
✓	Caps Lock	Off
✓	Num Lock	On
✓	Scroll Lock	Off
✓	Fixed Decimal	Off
✓	Overtype Mode	
✓	End Mode	
✓	Macro Recording	Not Recording
✓	Selection Mode	
✓	Page Number	
✓	Average	
✓	Count	
✓	Numerical Count	
✓	Minimum	
✓	Maximum	
✓	Sum	
✓	Upload Status	
✓	View Shortcuts	
✓	Zoom	100%
✓	Zoom Slider	

FIGURE 3.14 Status Bar Options

To the left of the Zoom control on the far right of the Status Bar are three small icons. These are View icons and affect how Excel is displayed (see Figure 3.15).

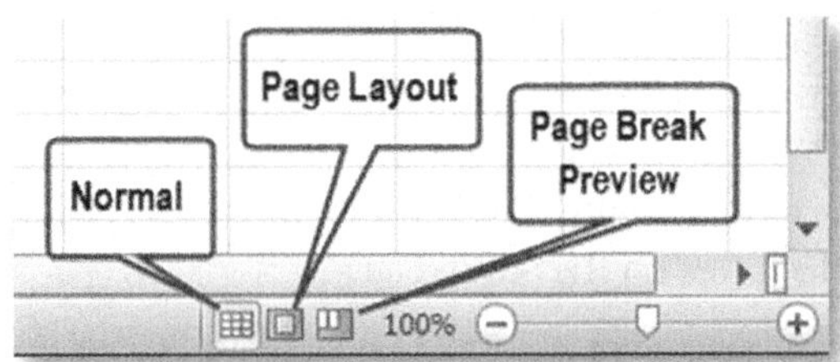

FIGURE 3.15 View Icons on the Status Bar

The first icon represents the normal grid view of Excel.

The third icon is the Page Break Preview view, which displays the grid as it will be printed. This view was available in Excel 2003. The parts of the sheet that won't be printed are displayed with a grey background. This view displays page breaks in blue lines that can be dragged around to amend how the sheet will be printed. A dotted blue line is a calculated page break. A solid blue line is a fixed page break. Dragging a dotted blue line changes it to a solid blue line. The page numbers also display as watermarks on the screen—they do not print out. When you drag a dotted blue line, you may affect the zoom percentage used to print.

The middle icon, called Page Layout, was added in Excel 2007. It displays Excel much like Microsoft Word. It displays the grid as it will print on the page, including header and footer sections and margins. You can amend the header and footer sections by clicking in them. A Design Ribbon tab is displayed when you select the header or footer regions. This tab includes all the header and footer options. You can hide or unhide the page margins by clicking the double-headed arrow that is displayed between the pages. In this view, the Status Bar (bottom left of screen) will display how many pages will print.

KEYBOARD SHORTCUTS

Many users prefer keyboard shortcuts. In some cases I find that keyboard techniques can be faster than their mouse-based alternatives. For some repetitive processes, keyboard shortcuts provide a quick way to repeat changes over large ranges.

The keyboard provides a fixed platform to work from. Mastering keyboard shortcuts allows you to select ranges and apply formats or other features quickly. Using the mouse often requires exact positioning that takes extra time, compared to the keyboard selection process. Some keyboard shortcuts don't have a mouse equivalent.

Some users have wrist injuries and prefer to use the keyboard as much as possible.

WARNING: Page Layout

Clicking the Page Layout icon will clear any Freeze Pane settings you may have, because the view is not compatible with Freeze Panes.

The Control Key

The Control (Ctrl) key has the most keyboard shortcuts associated with it. Table 3.1 shows the shortcuts that I use frequently, with a short description of their uses and benefits. I use keyboard shortcuts if they are quicker or easier to use than the corresponding toolbar icon or dialog entry.

TABLE 3.1 Ctrl Key Keyboard Shortcuts

Key	Description
* (asterisk)	Selects the current region. Great for selecting tables in one step. Use the * key on the numeric keypad.
; (semicolon)	Inserts the current date into a cell as a date entry.
. (period)	In a selected range, each press takes you to a corner of the selected range. Handy for seeing the extent of a large range.
Home	Takes you to the top left of the visible worksheet.
End	Takes you to the intersection of the last-used row and the last-used column. It may be a blank cell.
Page Up	Selects the sheet to the left.
Page Down	Selects the sheet to the right.
Arrow key	Selects a cell in the direction of the arrow. The cell will either be the last cell before a blank cell or the first cell entry after a blank cell.
Tab	Switches between open files.
Enter	Multiple entries—see section below.
Space Bar	Selects the whole column.
1	Opens the Format Cells dialog box.
9	Hides rows.
0	Hides columns.
b	Bold format.
c	Copy.
d	Copies the selected cell down. Select the cell and the range you want to copy to.
f	Find.
h	Find and replace.
k	Inserts a hyperlink.
p	Print.
s	Save. I use this frequently when pausing between tasks. (I don't use the AutoSave option.)
v	Paste.
z	Undo.
F1	Minimises and maximises the ribbon.
F3	Opens Name Manager dialog box (see Chapter 9).

Multiple Entries

You can populate a selected range with the same value or formula by first selecting the range, then typing the entry, and instead of pressing Enter, press Ctrl + Enter. This enters the same value in all the cells, and it is frequently used for populating a range with zeros. When used with a formula, it populates the range with a relative formula. These techniques are discussed in depth in Chapter 5 in terms of their use in data cleansing.

The Shift Key

Shift key shortcuts are mainly associated with selecting ranges in Excel.

Shift + F2 will insert or edit a cell comment.

Selecting ranges is a common task in Excel. In some cases, using the Shift key can simplify and speed up that task.

If you hold the Shift key down and press an arrow key on the keyboard, Excel will select a range. While holding the Shift key down, you can also press the Page Up and Page Down keys to select larger ranges.

Pressing Shift + Home will select the row from the current cell to column A. Pressing Shift + Space Bar will select the whole row.

Sometimes using the keyboard to select ranges can be quicker than using the mouse. See the Ctrl + Shift key shortcuts later in the chapter.

These techniques are also useful if you are on a laptop and you don't have an external mouse. It can be easier to select the range by using the Shift key than by using the laptop's built-in mouse control.

The Alt Key

On either side of the keyboard space bar, the Alt key has a number of useful shortcuts.

Line Break in a Cell

When creating a layout, you sometimes need to have words on separate lines within a cell. One way to achieve this is to use Wrap Text format. This places words on separate lines within the cell when the cell is not wide enough to display all the text on one line.

If you want to ensure that the words are on separate lines regardless of how wide the cell is, you can use Alt + Enter. Pressing Alt + Enter while entering or editing a cell inserts a fixed line break within the cell that is not affected if the cell width is increased.

Visible Cells Only

If you have hidden rows or columns in a range and you copy and paste that range, the hidden entries will also be pasted. If you don't want the hidden cells pasted, you can select Visible Cells Only before you copy the range. The shortcut to select Visible Cells

WARNING: Visible Cells Only

When you paste after using Visible Cells Only to select the range to copy, only the values are pasted; no formulas are pasted.

Only is Alt + ; (Alt plus the semicolon). After you press it, you will see the dotted lines throughout the range that go around the visible cells. You can then copy and paste only the visible cells.

AutoSum

Alt + = (Alt plus the equal sign) enters the SUM function in the selected cell or range in a similar way as clicking the AutoSum icon on the ribbon.

The Alt Key and the Ribbon Commands

If you prefer to use keyboard shortcuts rather than the mouse—and I've met quite a few people over the years who do—then the Alt key may just become your favorite key.

The Alt key was an important key in the early days of personal computers. Before the mouse became commonplace, all the commands had to be done through the keyboard. Selecting menu items was done with the Alt key. In Excel that functionality still exists.

If you press the Alt key, you will see many letters and numbers appear above the ribbon icons and tabs and on the QAT (see Figure 3.16).

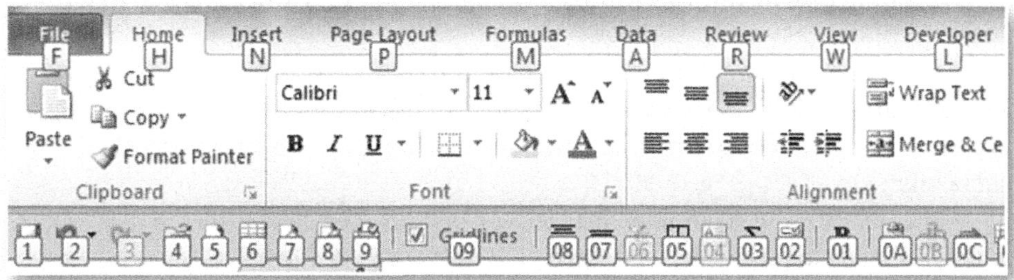

FIGURE 3.16 Alt Key Values on the Ribbon

This allows you to press the relevant key to access that command or tab. Note that the first nine entries on the QAT are accessed with the numbers 1 to 9. This can be a handy shortcut to using those features through the keyboard. Consider moving your more frequently used icons to the first entries on the QAT.

In some Windows menus or dialog boxes, the underlined letter of the option name is the Alt key letter that accesses that option using the keyboard (see Figure 3.17).

FIGURE 3.17 Format Cells (Alignment)—Underlined Options

Alt h will open the Horizontal drop-down selection. Alt w will select the Wrap Text option.

You do not hold down the Alt key to use the shortcuts; you simply press the Alt key once and then press the other relevant key(s). There can be a long sequence to access certain options. You may be surprised how fast you can become using Alt key shortcuts.

Table 3.2 lists some common Paste Special options. Remember that all these shortcuts are a sequence of key presses; you do not hold the keys down.

TABLE 3.2 Alt Key Shortcuts for Paste Special Options

Alt Key Sequence	Result
Alt h v v	Paste Special Values
Alt h v a	Paste Special Values and Number Formats
Alt h v f	Paste Special Formulas

Some other useful Alt key sequences are shown in Table 3.3. If you commonly use an Excel option, check out its Alt key combination; it might be short enough to use.

TABLE 3.3 Useful Alt Key Sequences

Alt Key Sequence	Result
Alt f t	Opens the Excel Options dialog box
Alt a v v	Opens the Data Validation dialog box
Alt p s p	Opens the Page Setup dialog box
Alt w v g	Toggles sheet gridlines
Alt l a s	Opens the Macro Security dialog box
Alt w f f	Freeze Panes

Useful Function Key Shortcuts

F2. Allows you to edit the current cell.

Tip: Editing in Dialog Boxes

There are a number of Excel dialog boxes for which pressing the F2 key will allow you to edit the entry. If you don't press F2 but instead use the arrow keys to navigate within the dialog box, you will actually insert cell references from the sheet into the formula. This is frustrating, and pressing F2 removes that frustration.

F3. Opens the Paste Name dialog box. There are a number of F3 shortcuts; they are all associated with range names, which will be discussed in Chapter 9.

F4. This key has a dual personality. When you are editing a formula in the Formula Bar and other reference dialog boxes, it applies the $ symbol to selected references. Each press of the F4 key changes where the $ symbol is positioned. If you select a group of references, it will apply the $ symbol to all of them.

When not used in the Formula Bar or dialog boxes, the F4 key is a shortcut to repeat the last action. For example, if you use the yellow Fill Color format to a cell and then select another cell or range and press F4, it will apply the yellow format to that cell or range, too. It repeats only the very last action. It doesn't work on all actions.

F5. Opens the Go To dialog box. The Special button in this dialog box displays some useful options (see Figure 3.18).

The Go To Special options allow you to select cells that match certain properties. For example, you could select all the cells containing a formula in one step and then format them with a grey background to identify them.

Some of the options in the Go To Special dialog box appear on the Home Ribbon tab on the far right in the Find & Select icon (see Figure 3.19).

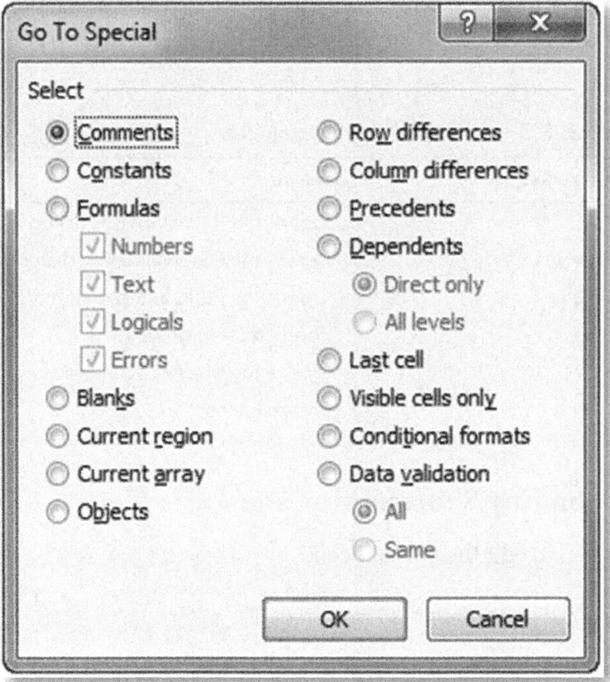

FIGURE 3.18 Go To Special Dialog Box

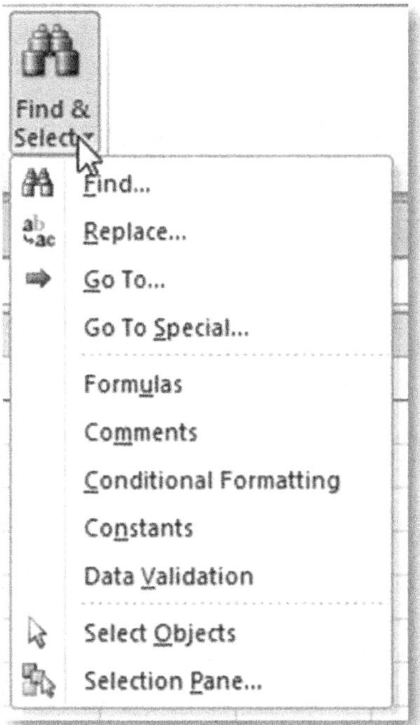

FIGURE 3.19 Find & Select Options—Home Ribbon

> **Tip: Return after Following a Hyperlink**
>
> Pressing F5 and then Enter will return you to a hyperlink that you have followed.

The Go To Special dialog box is used in Chapter 5. There are techniques using the Go To Special dialog box that solve a couple of common data structure issues.

F9. Calculates the current workbook. There is another feature the F9 key provides. When you are editing in the Formula Bar, if you select part of the formula that can be calculated separately and press F9, it will display the result of the selected part of the formula. This can be especially useful when debugging a formula.

F12. Save As.

Ctrl + Shift Shortcuts

Using the Ctrl key and the Shift key in combination can speed up range selections.

As I explained earlier, the Shift key used with the arrow keys selects ranges. The Ctrl key with the arrow keys jumps to the edges of the current range.

When you hold the Ctrl and Shift keys down simultaneously and use the arrow keys, you can select large ranges in a few presses. Using the Shift and the Ctrl keys together, you can select all the cells from the current cell to the edge of the range in the direction of the arrow you press.

Shift + Alt Shortcuts

Grouping is an effective way to hide sections of your sheet. You can quickly hide or unhide rows or columns in your sheet. Icons are added to the sheet that indicate that rows or columns are hidden. These icons also control the hiding and unhiding.

Shift + Alt + right arrow applies groupings to the selected rows or columns.

Shift +Alt + left arrow removes groupings from the selected rows or columns.

MOUSE SHORTCUTS

If you mainly use the mouse to move around and select cells, then the following techniques will interest you. If you are more keyboard-focused, then these may offer some quicker ways to perform certain processes.

The Fill Handle

The Fill Handle is the small plus sign at the bottom right-hand corner of a selected cell or range (see Figure 3.20).

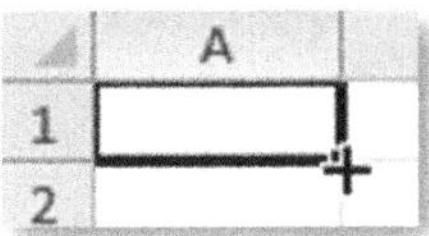

FIGURE 3.20 The Fill Handle

The Fill Handle allows you to copy or increment the selected cell. You can drag the Fill Handle up or down and to the right or to the left (you can't copy diagonally using the Fill Handle). To fill a table, you drag across and then down, or down and then across. It's a two-stage process.

Copying a range with the Fill Handle offers many possibilities to speed up your work. The range you select before using the Fill Handle determines the type of copy or increment result you will achieve.

There are some tricks to copying or incrementing with the Fill Handle. The results you achieve from dragging a single cell with the Fill Handle will depend on the contents of that cell, as follows:

Dates. If the cell has a date in it, then dragging the Fill Handle will result in an incremented date. Dates include names of months and names of days, such as January and Monday.

Numbers. In general, numbers are copied when you drag their cells.

Text. In general, text is also copied when dragged, unless it is the name of a month or a day. The exception to this rule is text that ends with a number. For instance, Booking1, when dragged, will display Booking2, Booking3, and so on.

Controlling the Fill Handle Actions

When you finish dragging the Fill Handle, a small icon is displayed on the bottom right of the range. This is the Auto Fill Options icon (see Figure 3.21).

FIGURE 3.21 Auto Fill Options Icon

Many people complain about this icon and want to know how to remove it. They rarely click the icon. If they did, they would see that it provides control over the Fill Handle results (see Figure 3.22).

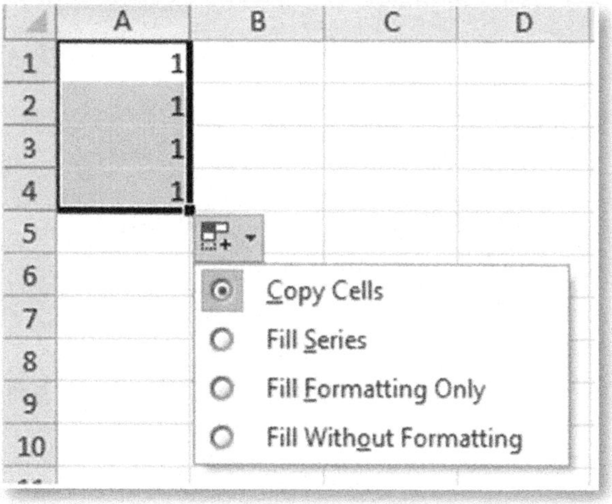

FIGURE 3.22 Auto Fill Options Number Options Displayed

The options displayed will vary, depending on the contents of the cell. Dates have more options (see Figure 3.23).

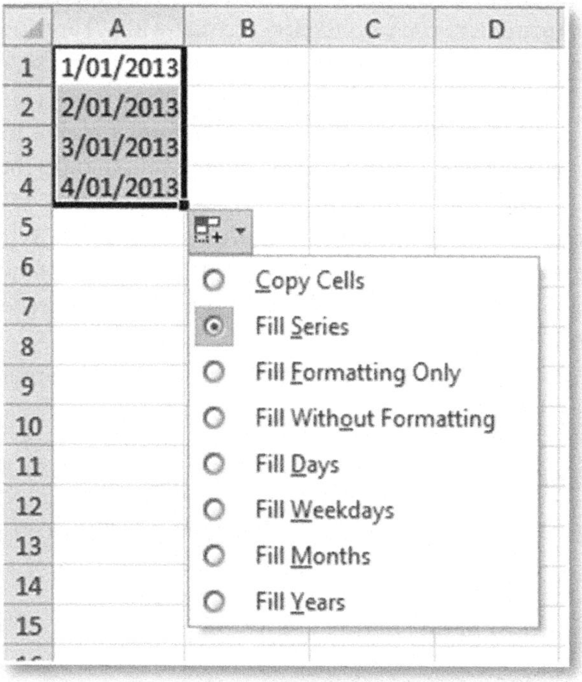

FIGURE 3.23 Auto Fill Options Date Options Displayed

Using the Fill Handle on Multiple Cells

When you select more than one cell and drag the Fill Handle, you can get unusual results, depending on the cells used. You can use this to your advantage. If you have a structure in a range, you can use the Fill Handle to extend that structure (see Figure 3.24).

	A	B
1		
2	North	Opening Balance
3		
4		Stock in
5		Stock Out
6		Sales
7		
8		Closing Balance

FIGURE 3.24 Structure to Copy

The structure in column B has five entries spread over seven cells. To replicate this structure for other regions, you could copy and paste. You could also use the Fill Handle. To copy this structure down, you would select the range B2:B9 and drag the Fill Handle until you see Closing Balance in the tool tip next to the mouse cursor (see Figure 3.25). Then release the mouse.

By including cell B9 in the selected range, you force Excel to insert a blank cell between the ranges. Obviously, the farther you drag the Fill Handle, the more structures you will create.

This technique has an advantage over copying and pasting. When you copy and paste a range, you need to be careful where you paste—that is, how many rows you leave between each structure. When you use the Fill Handle, Excel ensures there are the same number of rows.

This is yet another situation in which implementing and maintaining a structure makes other tasks easier to perform.

Double-Clicking

There are a number of shortcuts involved with double-clicking icons and parts of the Excel screen.

AutoFit Columns and Rows

On the lines between the column letters and the row numbers, there are double-headed arrow mouse cursors (see Figure 3.26).

	A	B	C	D
1				
2	North	Opening Balance		
3				
4		Stock in		
5		Stock Out		
6		Sales		
7				
8		Closing Balance		
9				
10				
11				
12				
13				
14				
15				
16				
17			Closing Balance	
18				

FIGURE 3.25 Closing Balance Tool Tip

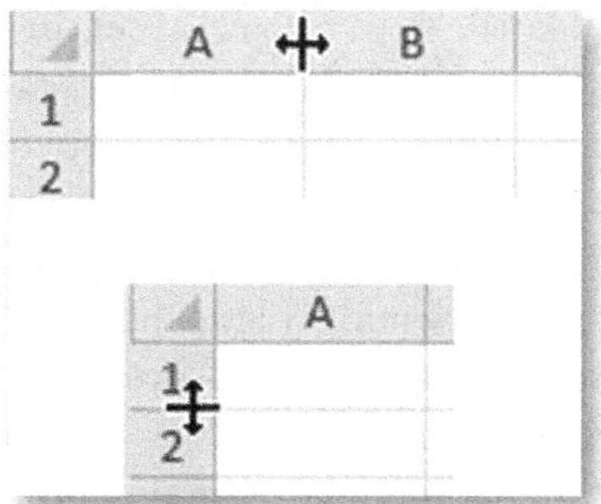

FIGURE 3.26 Column and Row Double-Headed Arrows

You usually click, hold, and drag these cursor shapes to set the width of a column or the height of a row. Double-clicking the icon will automatically change the width or height to fit the contents of the column or row. This is called AutoFit.

You can apply AutoFit to more than one row or column by selecting more rows or columns before double-clicking on any of the lines within the range. You can even apply it to the whole sheet by selecting the whole sheet first. Click the icon where the rows and columns intersect (see Figure 3.27).

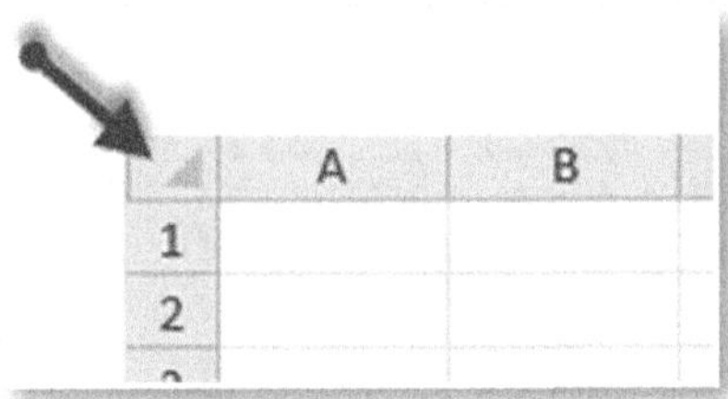

FIGURE 3.27 Whole Sheet Icon

Once you have selected the whole sheet, double-clicking any of the row or column double-headed arrows will apply AutoFit to every row or column in the sheet.

AutoSum

The AutoSum icon is one of the most clicked icons in Excel (it's the Greek letter *sigma*).

Clicking it once inserts the SUM function into the active cell and displays the moving dotted lines around the range that Excel estimates you want to add up.

The formula is in Edit mode, so you can make changes to it with the keyboard or the mouse. Excel usually estimates the range correctly, and most people press Enter to accept the formula.

Double-clicking the AutoSum icon automatically inserts a SUM function into the cell using the estimated range. This can be prone to error if Excel doesn't guess the range correctly. Knowing how Excel estimates the ranges can speed up your formula creation.

How Excel estimates ranges applies to many of Excel's shortcuts and is important knowledge if you want to make the most of Excel's built-in shortcuts.

Excel looks for patterns in your spreadsheet. When a pattern is broken, it is a signal to Excel that something has changed. One of the most common signals of a pattern change is a blank cell.

If Excel is estimating a range and encounters a blank cell, row, or column, it will normally stop at that cell, row, or column. This applies to selecting ranges for AutoSum and for selecting tables or data ranges. It also applies to some selection and navigating shortcuts explained later in the chapter.

A blank cell can affect the automatic selection of ranges. If Excel can correctly select the range automatically, it can save you a lot of effort. Here are a few rules you can employ to ensure that Excel selects the correct range:

Tip: AutoFit Is Not Dynamic

AutoFit does not update when the contents of the cell change. You might need to reapply AutoFit if the entries in the columns or rows change significantly.

- Avoid blank cells in any ranges that contain values.
- Avoid blank cells in any ranges that you intend to do calculations on.
- Avoid blank rows in any table or data range (it is acceptable to have a single entry in a row).
- Avoid blank columns in any table or data range (it is acceptable to have a column heading with no entries below it).
- Insert a blank column between tables of data that are different (this is typically done in the dedicated Table or List sheet that contains the lists used in the file).

In the case of AutoSum, the other types of cells that are signals of a pattern change are date cells, other SUM cells, and text cells. These will all affect the estimated range.

Of course, your data will most likely come from other systems, and avoiding blank cells may be out of your control.

Refer to the Chapter 5 data cleansing topic "Missing or Incomplete Data" for an easy method by which to populate blanks cells with zeros.

Following a Link

When reviewing formulas, you frequently need to find where a cell is linked to. If you double-click a cell, Excel will take you to the cell that it is linked to.

This shortcut requires a setting change. The default setting, when you double-click a cell, is to edit the contents of the cell within the cell. I use editing in the cell only for training purposes. During training it is possible to make the formula larger, so it's easier for students to see a formula as it is created.

In practice, however, I rarely edit a formula in a cell. Instead I use the Formula Bar for all my editing. I find it easier because it is separate from the sheet, so there are no other entries to distract me, which makes focusing on it easier. It also has more space.

There is a setting you can change to stop editing in the cell when you double-click. When you turn off this setting, you enable the double-clicking to follow a link. It's a bit obscure, but it's been around for many versions. The setting is in Excel Options under Advanced. It's called Allow Editing Directly in Cell (see Figure 3.28).

Once you uncheck the setting and click OK, you can double-click a cell to follow a link. This applies throughout Excel, not just the current file. After you follow the link, you can press the F5 function key and then press Enter to return to the original cell where you double-clicked. This technique allows you to quickly check many cell links.

Navigating around the Sheet

You can use your mouse to quickly navigate around large sheets. By double-clicking the arrow cursor (it appears around the border of a selected cell or range), you will move in the direction of the border that you double-click: left, right, top (up), or bottom (down).

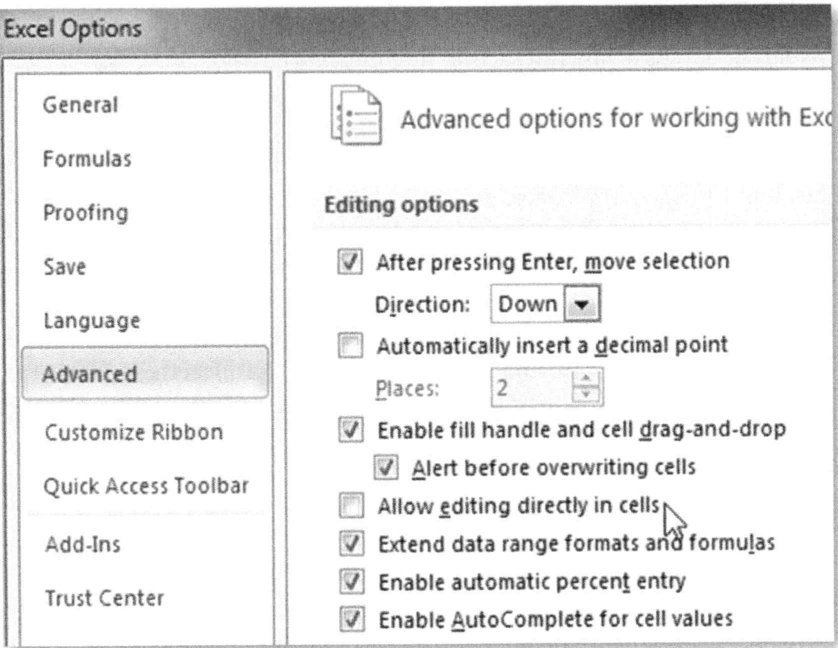

FIGURE 3.28 Editing Cell Option

Copying Down Quickly with the Fill Handle

Double-clicking the Fill Handle is the quickest way to copy down. This is affected by the blanks in the range. How far the copy works depends on a number of factors.

If the cell below has an entry, Excel will copy down in the same column until it encounters a blank cell in the same column.

If the cell has nothing below it, then Excel looks in the column to the left of the cell and checks whether there are entries in the column below the cell. If there are, then Excel will copy down as far as there are entries in the left column. It will copy until it encounters a blank cell.

If there are no entries on the left, Excel will check the column to the right. If there are entries there, it will copy down until it encounters a blank cell.

If there are no entries below, to the right or the left, then nothing happens when you double-click the Fill Handle.

Right-Clicking

In my opinion, the most productive shortcuts in Excel involve the right mouse button. Right-clicking is a common shortcut in all software packages now, and Excel's right-click options have developed over the years to the point that in Excel 2010, almost all your common tasks are now available via the Right Click menu.

Right-clicking is a useful habit to start. It allows you to learn about features in Excel and Windows. If you are unsure about an object or part of a Window, right-clicking it will offer you a hint of what it can be used for or what can be done to it.

Figures 3.29 to 3.33 display some of the most common Right Click menus. As you can see, there are many options available, and using them can save you from having to use the ribbon. This means you can minimise the ribbon and have more screen dedicated to the spreadsheet grid. Note that the image in Figure 3.33 allows you see a list of sheet names and click on the name to open it.

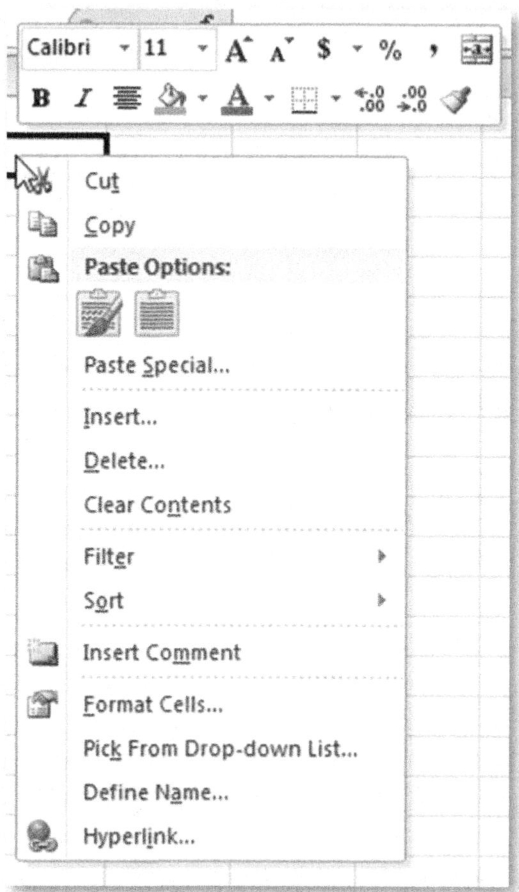

FIGURE 3.29 Cell Right Click Menu

Right-Dragging

Right-dragging is an option that most users have never tried, but those who have and have gotten the hang of it use it all the time. I certainly do.

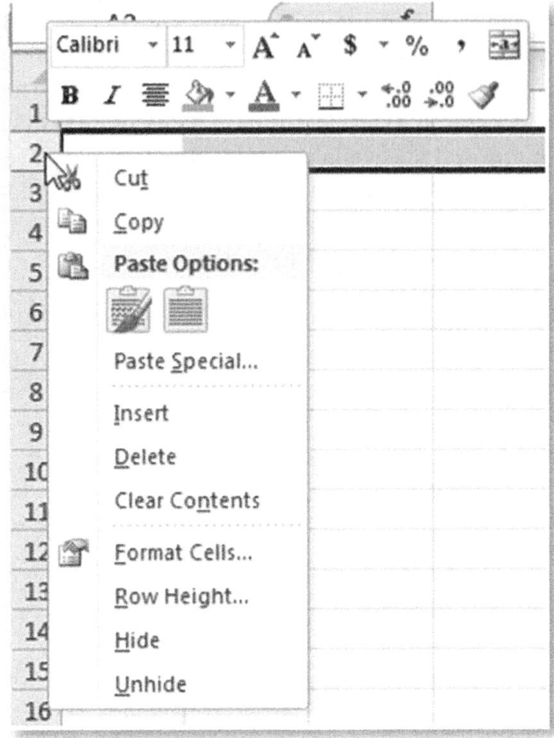

FIGURE 3.30 Row Right Click Menu

Right-dragging refers to using the Arrow icon or the Fill Handle icon, and instead of clicking, holding, and dragging with the left mouse button, you use the right mouse button.

This can take a bit of practice, but it is certainly worth the effort. When you release the right mouse button, a menu is displayed with most of the options you would want to perform (see Figures 3.34 and 3.35).

When right-dragging the Fill Handle, the type of cell you are dragging will affect the options you see. Date cells have different options from most other cells.

KEYBOARD AND MOUSE SHORTCUTS

There are a number of useful techniques that combine the keyboard and the mouse. They involve using the mouse with the Ctrl, Shift, and Alt keys.

Ctrl + Mouse

The arrow-shaped mouse cursor icon appears when you point to the border of a selected cell or a range. If you click hold, drag, and release the mouse using this cursor shape, you are in fact cutting and pasting that cell or range.

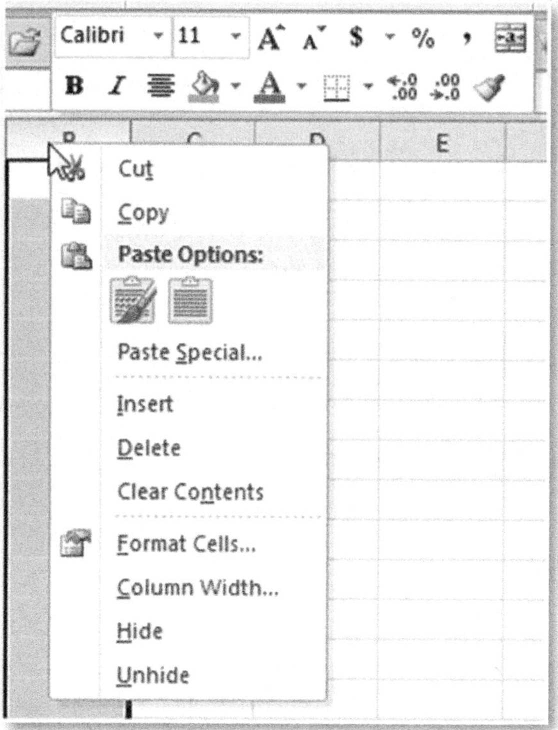

FIGURE 3.31 Column Right Click Menu

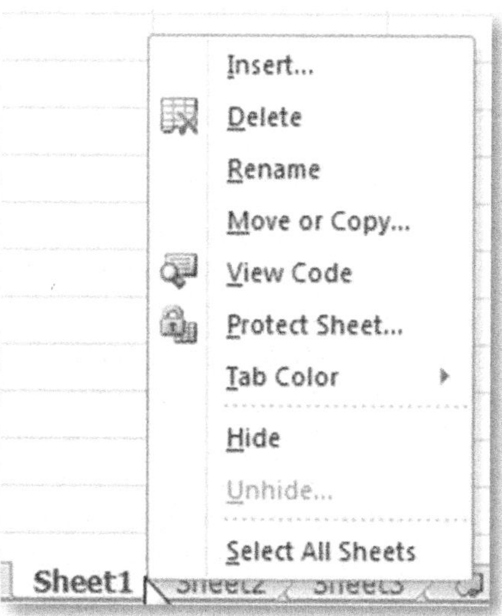

FIGURE 3.32 Sheet Right Click Menu

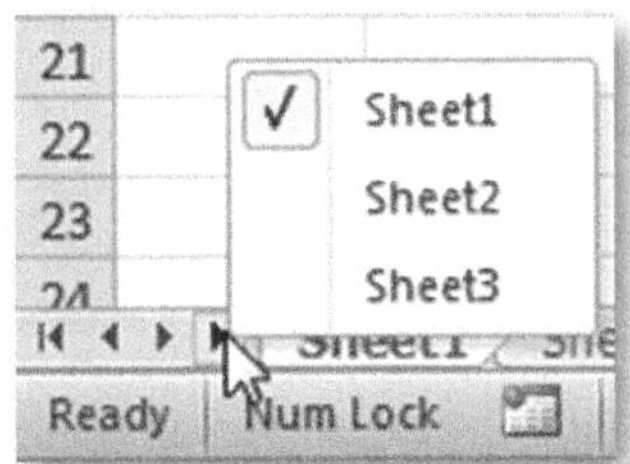

FIGURE 3.33 Sheet Navigation Buttons Right Click Menu

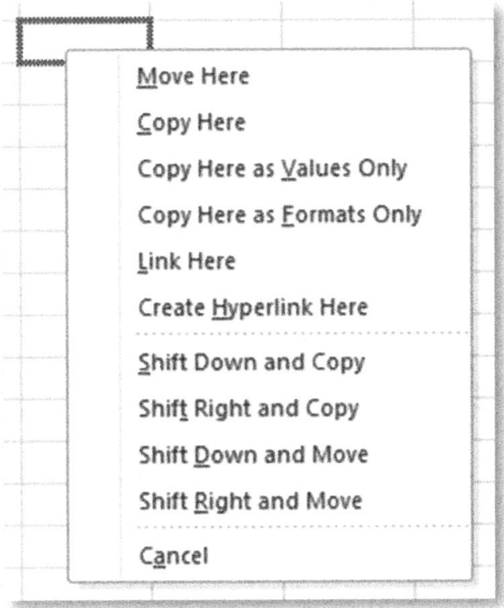

FIGURE 3.34 Right Drag Arrow Menu

Cutting and pasting in Excel can cause problems with formulas that refer to the destination cells. Cutting and pasting is a leading cause of #REF! (reference) errors. #REF! errors can affect all other calculations. A single #REF! error in a SUM range will cause the SUM function to also display the error message.

If you are confident of what you are doing, then cutting and pasting is acceptable and in some cases the easiest way to amend the structure of your file. It is important to include validation cells in most sheets in your reporting file so that you can immediately identify whether a calculation has an error in it.

If you hold the Ctrl key down when you click, hold, drag, and then release the mouse, you will in fact copy the cell or range to the destination. You release the Ctrl key after releasing the mouse. You should notice that a small plus sign displays next to the cursor when you hold the Ctrl key down; this is a visual clue that Excel is doing something different. Examples of the small plus sign are shown in Figure 3.36.

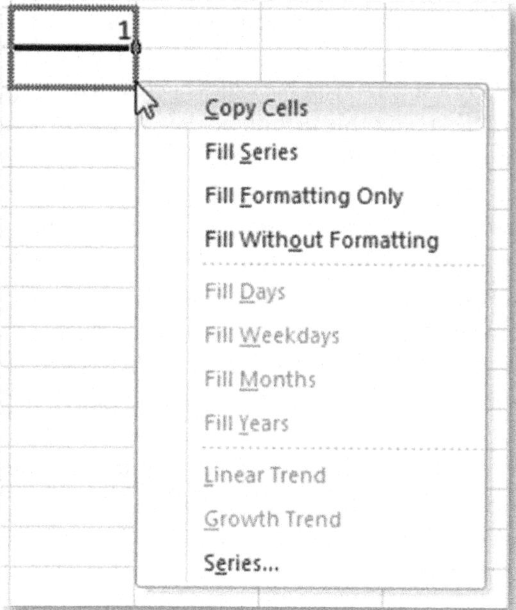

FIGURE 3.35 Right Drag Fill Handle Menu

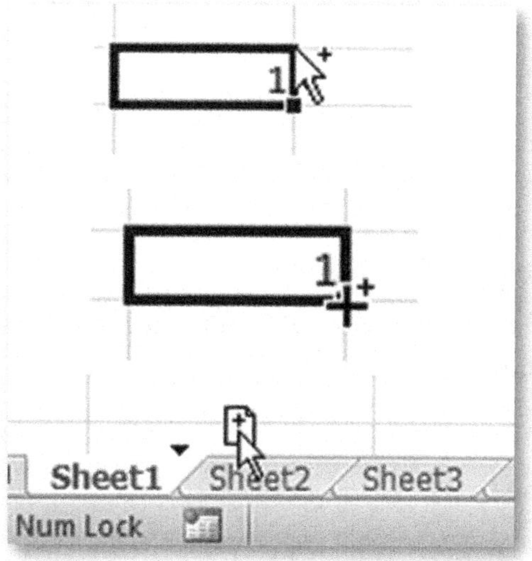

FIGURE 3.36 Ctrl Key Plus Signs

I use this technique all the time. The beauty of it is that it applies to virtually everything in Excel. You can even copy sheets (see the bottom image in Figure 3.36). This is the quickest way to copy a sheet. If you have files open and minimised, you can quickly copy sheets between files using this technique. See the first tip under "General Tips" later in this chapter. It explains how to take advantage of using windows within Excel.

You can copy an image or a chart using this technique. I'm not sure why, but for charts you're required to click, hold, and drag the chart first and then press the Ctrl key.

This brings us to a slight change in the technique that you can use once you are confident with the technique. You only have to hold the Ctrl key down just before releasing the mouse. This means you can drag as normal until you get to the destination, then hold the Ctrl key down, then release the mouse, and then release the Ctrl key.

Figure 3.36 also shows the Ctrl key and the Fill Handle. When you click hold and drag this cursor with the mouse, you either copy or increment, depending on the contents of the cell. Excel has a number of rules for deciding on whether to copy or increment. You may have found those rules frustrating.

Holding the Ctrl key down while dragging the Fill Handle will do the opposite of the default action. Again, you can wait until the end of the process to hold the Ctrl key down. Excel displays a tool tip to show you what the last value will be; if you hold the Ctrl key down, that tool tip will change to show you the alternate result.

Selecting Multiple Ranges

The Ctrl key also allows you to select multiple ranges at once. This is news to many users, who think they can select only one range at a time. When holding down the Ctrl key, you can use the mouse to select as many ranges as you want. Excel's term for this type of selection is a *noncontiguous range*. I think *multiple ranges* is a simpler term. This technique is an efficient method for formatting or deleting ranges in one step instead of several steps.

You can combine this tip with a previous tip. Select multiple ranges using the Ctrl key; type an entry; then, while holding the Ctrl key down, press Enter. All the cells in the multiple ranges will have the same entry. If you type a formula, a relative reference formula will be entered in all the cells.

Shift + Mouse

We saw how well the Shift key works with the arrow keys in selecting ranges. It works just as well with the mouse.

Selecting and Amending Large Ranges

Select a cell. Then hold the Shift key down and click any other cell. Keep holding the Shift key and click another cell.

Tip: Ctrl + Mouse Copy

This copy technique works in most Microsoft products. It's useful in Windows, Word, and PowerPoint.

WARNING: The Tool Tip Updates Only Once

If you press and release the Ctrl key, then the tool tip doesn't update. This is a slight bug, but the developers probably thought that the effort to keep updating the tool tip each time you pressed or released the Ctrl key wasn't worth it.

The first cell you select is an anchor cell, and each time you click another cell, Excel selects a range between the anchor cell and the last cell clicked. This technique allows you to amend the selected range. If you release the Shift key and press and hold it again, you can still amend the range. This can be useful if you have a print range that you need to extend. You can also switch between using the Shift key with the mouse and with the keyboard.

Moving Whole Columns or Rows

A common task is to move a whole column or a whole row to a different location. Most people tend to insert a blank row or column and then use copy or cut and then paste. The Shift key provides a simple process if you are not moving the column or row very far, which is usually the case.

To move a column, first select the column, then point to the edge of the selected range where there is an arrow-shaped cursor, click and hold the arrow-shaped cursor with the mouse, hold the Shift key down, and then drag the column to where you want to place it. Release the mouse, then release the Shift key. Excel will move the whole column and insert it in the position where you release the mouse. You don't need to insert a blank column to do it.

The same technique works for rows. Click the whole row first, then click and hold the arrow-shaped cursor, hold down the Shift key, and drag the row to where you want to place it. Release the mouse, then release the Shift key. Again the row is cut from its source position and inserted into the position you require.

This is a cut-and-paste technique and may therefore cause #REF! errors in certain formulas. Because you are moving whole rows and whole columns, it is less prone to causing #REF! errors than moving only part of a column or row.

Alt + Mouse

The Alt key has a useful and time-saving shortcut. When you need to move or resize charts or other graphic objects, you often use the sheet gridlines to line them up. This can be awkward with the mouse or the keyboard.

Hold the Alt key down when you do this task, and you will see how easy it is. The Alt key uses a "snap to" feature that causes the chart or graphic to move directly to the nearest gridline in the direction you are moving it.

This works the same way if you hold the Alt key while resizing a chart or graphic. It becomes quick and easy to line up many charts on a dashboard and make them all the same size.

GENERAL TIPS

The following tips are more general and cover options that are useful but may take multiple keystrokes or entries to achieve.

Using Windows as They Are Meant to Be Used

The most popular operation system on PCs is Microsoft Windows. Many users are unaware that you can use different windows in Excel.

Some users are aware you can have two or more separate files open in separate windows. Most are unaware that separate sheets can be displayed in separate windows, allowing you to copy and paste or link between sheets in the same file very easily and quickly.

With the large screens that are available now, this is a very powerful technique, because you can have a few windows open at the same time. Switching between sheets is time-consuming; having them open side by side, or above and below, can dramatically speed up many tasks.

In the View Ribbon tab, the New Window option opens a new window for the current workbook. The Arrange All option can fit the open windows neatly into the available screen space (see Figure 3.37).

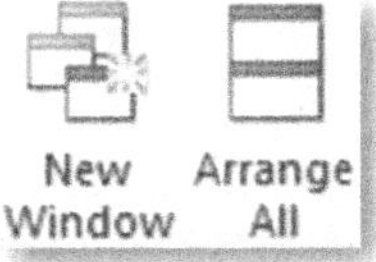

FIGURE 3.37 View Tab Window Options

The New Window option allows you to have separate windows for separate sheets. Clicking this option doesn't change much on the screen. You have to be quite observant to see the difference. Excel places a colon and a number after the title at the top of the screen (see Figure 3.38).

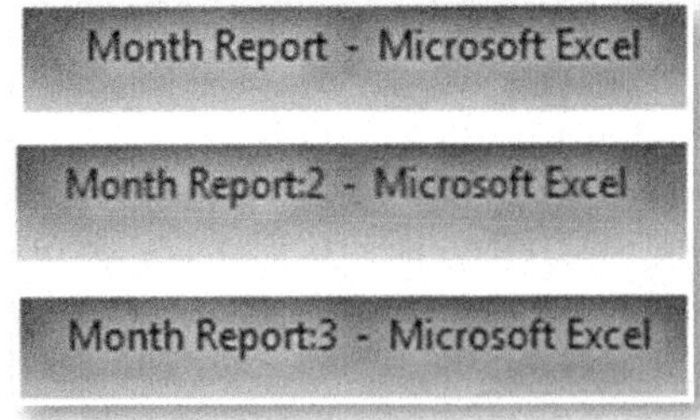

FIGURE 3.38 Screen Name Change

WARNING: Closing Windows

Make sure you close the window with the highest number first. When you open a new window, it has none of the display options of the original window. Hence, it doesn't have the Freeze Panes or the Zoom percentage settings. If you close the original window first (the one with :1 after its name), then you will lose all those display settings. Always close the :3 and :2 windows (when there are three windows) first.

To see the windows next to each other, use the Arrange All icon. It saves you from having to manually resize the windows to get them to fit on the screen.

Data Entry Tips

When designing your reporting interface, you should aim for ease of use and simplicity for the user. Keep in mind that even though you may be the main user initially, this may change over time. Creating an easy-to-use interface makes it easy to hand over or delegate the report creation process in the future.

Data Validation

In terms of the user interface, you should aim to reduce the amount of typing the user has to do. This typically means using a Data Validation List, which inserts an in-cell drop-down list into a cell. This reduces keying errors and makes it obvious what should be entered in a cell.

The Data Validation feature can also be used to assist users with a customisable Error message. Although the list option is the most popular, there are also other types of data validations that can control the entries made in a cell.

With Data Validation List, you can still type the entry in the cell, but it must match one of the entries in the list. Uppercase and lowercase are ignored.

The other data validations concentrate on date and numeric data entry and ensuring that the values and dates entered fall within the parameters that you set. This might mean controlling the number of months to report. A data validation can ensure that entries are not above 12 and can even stop the entry of decimals. The other types of data validation are self-explanatory and easy to create.

Two other tabs in the Data Validation dialog box (shown in Figure 3.39) provide two ways of communicating with the user.

The Input Message tab allows you to customise a dialog box that is displayed to the user every time the cell is selected. It's similar to a cell comment. This sounds like a great idea, but in practice, once you understand what is required, you'll tend to get frustrated that it keeps popping up. I avoid using this tab unless the file is expected to be accessed by new users all the time.

You can define a title and an input message. Figure 3.40 shows a sample message and the dialog box that is displayed.

Creating a Data Validation Drop-Down List

First select a cell.

Click the Data Ribbon tab and then click the Data Validation icon.

In the Settings tab, click Allow: Drop Down and select List.

Click the Source box and navigate on the sheets to select the range to use for the drop-down list. In Excel 2010 you can select a range on any sheet. In Excel 2007 you can select a range only on the current sheet. To select a range on another sheet in Excel 2007, you use a range name (see Chapter 9, which also demonstrates how to create a list that automatically expands or contracts depending on the entries). Ideally, in all versions you should use a range name to define the Source range.

Instead of a range, you can also type entries separated by commas to create the drop-down list (see Figure 3.39).

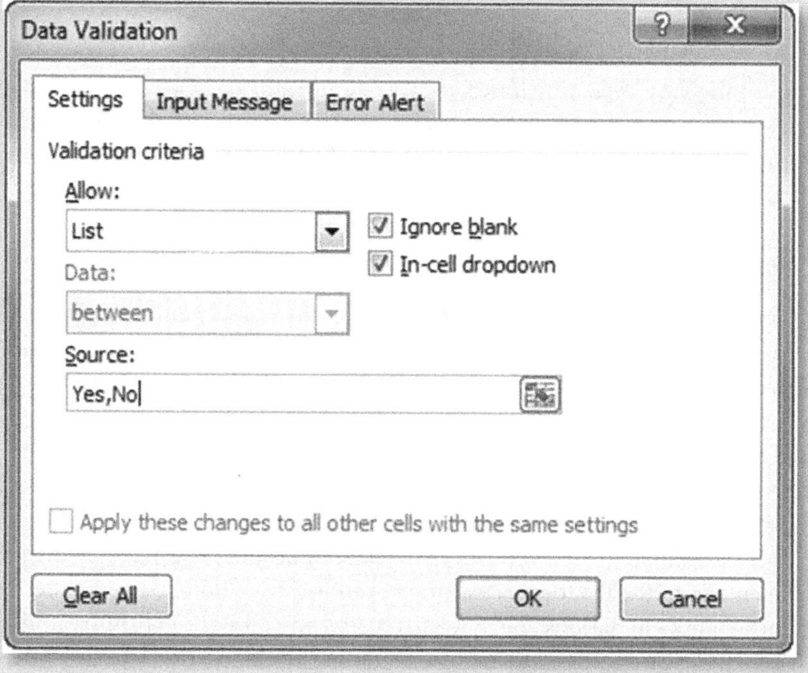

FIGURE 3.39 Data Validation with Entered List

Click OK to complete the process.

This entry technique is used only for short lists and lists that won't change.

Error Alert Tab The Error Alert tab allows you to customise a dialog box that is displayed only when the user doesn't follow the data validation rules. This is more practical, since your cell label and cell comment should describe what the user is required to enter. The error message is a last resort to inform the user exactly what is required. The default error message is not helpful (see Figure 3.41).

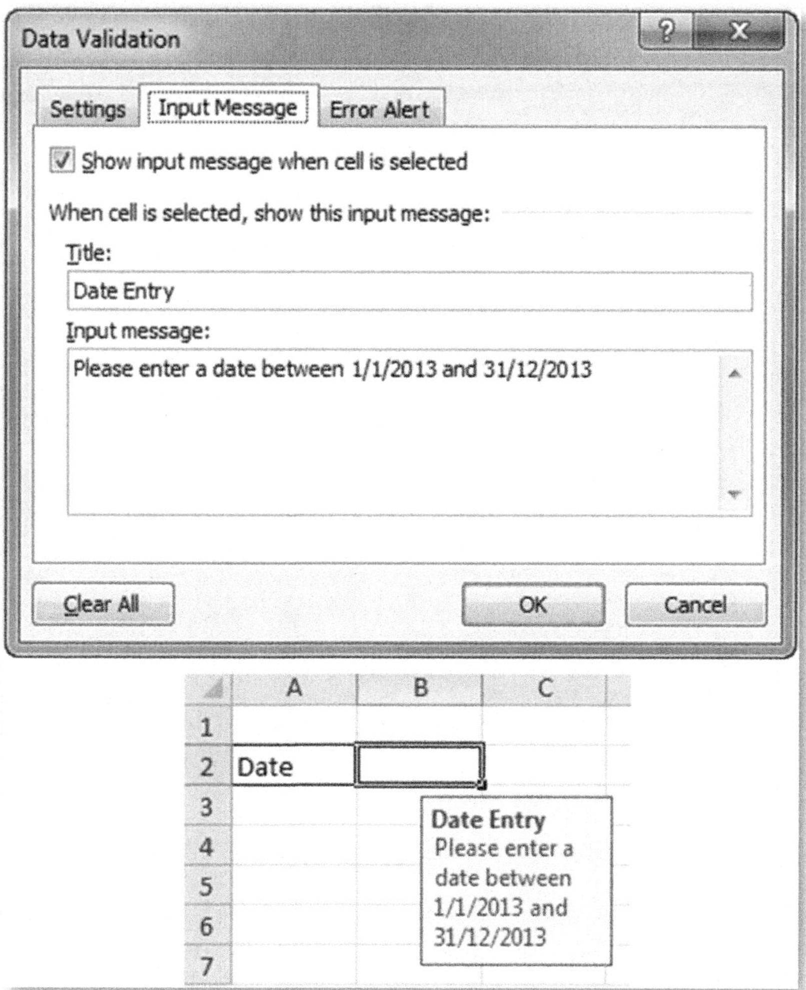

FIGURE 3.40 Example of Input Message Tab

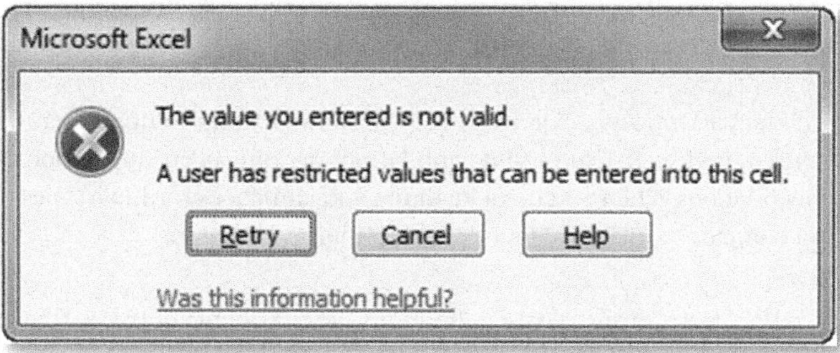

FIGURE 3.41 Default Error Message

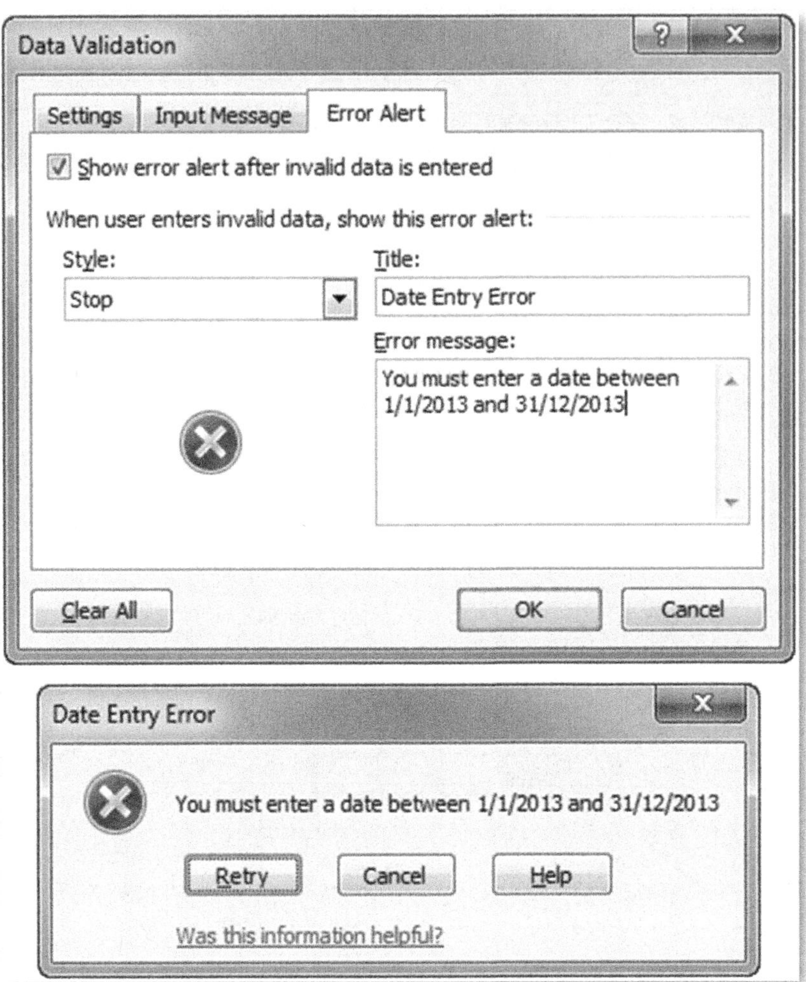

FIGURE 3.42 Customised Error Message

The error message you can customise includes a symbol to display as defined by Style: Drop Down. Typically you use Stop Style, the title, and an error message. Figure 3.42 shows a sample.

Multiple Data Validations You can even create a formula to handle multiple data validations in a single cell. Usually data validations are only of one type, such as a list or a number validation. When you use a formula, you can check multiple types of validation or do a complex validation that is not a standard validation.

Data Validation Limitations Data validations have a couple of issues that you need to be aware of:

- Paste Special Values can insert entries in a data validation cell that do not meet the validation rules.
- If the list changes, it is possible that the entry in the cell will no longer be valid.

There is a Circle Invalid Data option in the Data Validation drop-down list in the Data Ribbon tab. This puts a red circle around any entries that do not meet the validation rules.

I recommend that you add your own validation checks to data validation cells to make sure they only contain what they should. The techniques for doing this are discussed in Chapter 13.

Custom Lists

If you have a list of departments, branches, or any other category, it may be worth creating a Custom List.

A Custom List is treated the same as the months of the year or the days of the week. If you enter one of the list members in a cell and use the Fill Handle to drag the cell, you will populate the other cells with the other members of the Custom List.

The other advantage of a Custom List is that you can sort by it. Without a Custom List, you can sort text fields only in alphabetical order, either ascending or descending. A Custom List allows you to sort data into the order that you want. The order of a Custom List is frequently important, and that order may be used consistently throughout the organisation. If that is the case, being able to sort in the same order can be useful. A Custom List is the only built-in method to apply such a sort.

Creating a Custom List is easy. You will already have the list entered somewhere, so select the list first. The instructions for Excel 2007 and Excel 2010 vary slightly in getting to the Edit Custom List dialog box.

Enter one of the list entries in a cell and use the Fill Handle to drag the entry and see the result. Excel will match the case (uppercase or lowercase) of your entry.

The Custom List exists on your computer. If you e-mail a file to someone, the entries will all be there, but if the other person wants to sort using the Custom List, he or she must first create the Custom List on his or her own computer.

The Clipboard

The Clipboard is the place where what you copy or cut is stored. This can be text, formula, an image, or a chart. In the early days of Microsoft Office, you could copy and paste only one thing at a time. A little-known feature of Microsoft Office, including Excel, is that the Clipboard can hold multiple copies.

As far as Excel is concerned, this is not as exciting as it could be, because the one thing that this multiple copy feature doesn't handle is formulas. The last formula copied is obviously treated as a formula, but previously copied formulas are converted into their respective values.

This lack of ability to copy multiple formulas is a major limitation. The ability to copy multiple formulas would be a handy feature in the development phase of a project. In the data input phase, the clipboard does offer a few useful shortcuts.

Creating a Custom List

Select the list.

Excel 2007
Click the Round Office button.
Click the Excel Options button.
Click the Edit Custom Lists button.

Excel 2010
Click the File tab.
Click the Options button.
Click the Advanced option on the left of the screen.
Scroll down to the bottom of the dialog box.
Click the Edit Custom Lists button.

Both Versions
Click the Import button, and the list should appear in the right section of the dialog box. This section is where you can also edit the list. Click OK, then OK again, and the Custom List is ready to use.

If you are bringing many values together from other sheets or files, this technique can speed up the process by allowing you to do multiple copies in a sequence and then a single paste at the end. Time is frequently taken up by going between the various sources and then back to the destination each time to paste.

To create a sequential set of copies, you need to display the Office Clipboard Task Pane. Click the small arrow icon on the right of the Clipboard section of the Home Ribbon tab (see Figure 3.43).

Clicking the icon again hides the task pane.

The previous copies are listed. They will have a description that describes the value that was copied. Each item has a drop-down selection to paste or delete (see Figure 3.44).

The Paste All button allows you to do a single paste to paste everything that was previously copied in one step.

The Clipboard works in all the Office products, so it lists all the copies from Outlook, Word, and PowerPoint.

Navigation

Reporting models tend to have a large number of sheets. My recommendations for building reporting models are based on a modular design. This means that sheets are dedicated to specific processes, which creates many sheets.

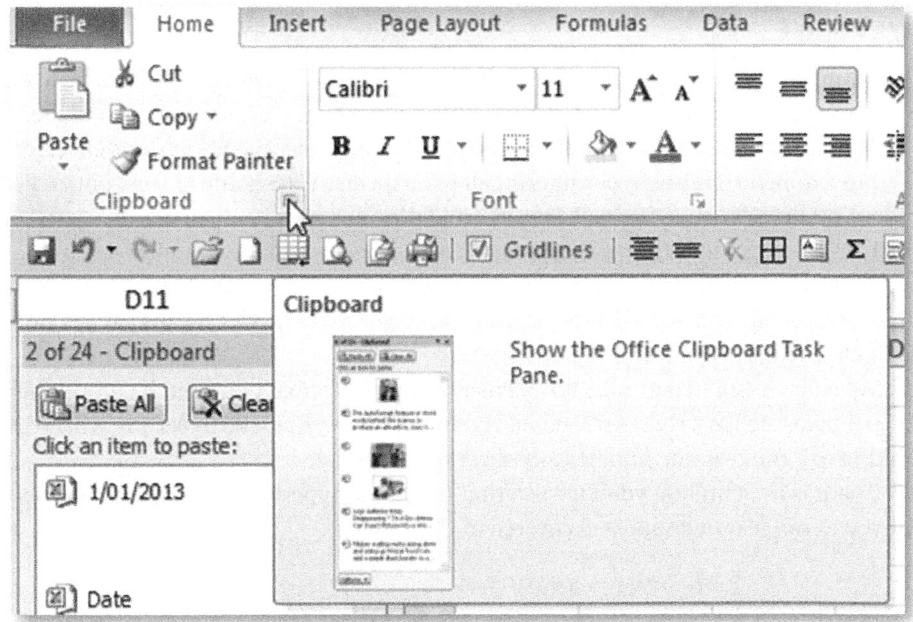

FIGURE 3.43 Display Office Clipboard

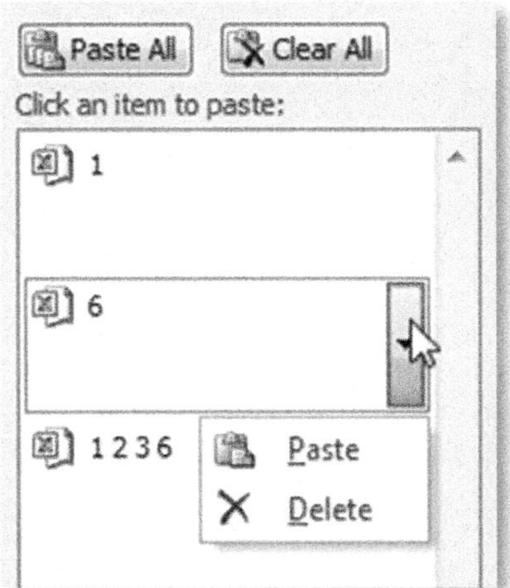

FIGURE 3.44 Clipboard Options

Moving around so many sheets can be time-consuming. To avoid that problem, we can use hyperlinks. These are just like the hyperlinks you encounter on the Internet and can even be used to take you to websites. The hyperlinks that I recommend will move you around the reporting model.

Creating an index of sheets in a structured layout can make it very easy to move around the model and not get lost.

Hyperlinks

I recommend creating a couple of hyperlink indexes: a complete list of sheets sorted by the process and then another list of frequently used sheets, like a favorites list of sheets.

You can also include hyperlinks in your instructions, documentation, and checklists.

I recommend having hyperlinks on all your sheets. You should at least have a link to your main index sheet as well as your validation sheet. When you are on a particular sheet, you may find that going to another sheet is a common practice, so having a hyperlink to that other sheet will save you time.

Have a dedicated row at the top of your sheets for hyperlinks. This area is obviously not included in the print area for the sheet.

When creating hyperlinks, it is advisable to use a range name as the destination. If you link to a cell in a sheet and the sheet name changes, then the hyperlink will break. Linking to a range name handles any sheet name changes.

There is a technique you can use that creates a hyperlink that is hard to break. It involves range names and it is covered in Chapter 9.

CHAPTER FOUR

Design and Structure

STRUCTURE AND FLEXIBILITY, at first glance, seem to be at cross-purposes. Dig a little deeper, though, and you will be surprised how well they can work together.

STRUCTURE = FLEXIBILITY

To say that structure equals flexibility seems counterintuitive. You probably associate structure with restrictions and limitations and think that structure stops you from being flexible. It does, to some extent, but if you create the right structure, it can also allow you to automate much of the reporting process.

In the design of a building, there are laws and standards that must be complied with. There are no such laws or standards for Excel. You must develop and follow your own rules and create your own structure.

Your accounting system is based on a structured chart of accounts. Your databases are also structured. This structure determines how easy or hard it is to extract the data you need. A badly structured database can be frustrating and time-consuming to work with. A well-designed database can be a pleasure to work with.

Database packages are typically very structured, and you have to follow their rules to create new databases. Spreadsheets, in contrast, are more associated with flexibility and individuality than with structure. Most of the problems people face with spreadsheets are a result of a lack of structure in those spreadsheets.

The blank grid of a spreadsheet offers so many possibilities, both good and bad. This chapter will introduce you to some of the structures that will make your reporting model both flexible and robust. The structures will be easy to use and maintain.

There are two important concepts to understand:

1. **Modular sheet design.** The premise with modular sheet design is that one sheet performs one task. You don't mix processes on a sheet. A single sheet shouldn't contain both data and a report. There will be two sheets: one sheet containing the data and another sheet with the report. Some examples in this book may mix data and reports, but only for demonstration purposes.
2. **Table-based systems.** These systems have most of their options defined in tables. They typically have lots of rules and very few exceptions. Fortunately, accounting and finance reporting requirements are perfectly suited to table-based systems. Many of Excel's functions work exceptionally well with tables, and some are specifically designed for tables.

This chapter focuses on the considerations you need to make in creating your design, and it provides suggestions on the types of design to use based on your requirements. Many of these structures are not mutually exclusive, so you can mix and match different components of the design to arrive at a total solution. Designing is the stage in which you need to think ahead so that your design can cope with all your future requirements.

I can't do the design for you, but I can provide you with a number of designs I have used successfully in the past that have stood the test of time and have remained flexible and practical.

MODULAR SHEET DESIGN

A *modular* design in Excel consists of the use of dedicated sheets for separate parts of your model. It also means having the same sheet structure for similar components.

For example, you may have one sheet dedicated to actual statistics and another sheet for budget statistics. It makes sense to have these two sheets laid out identically. This makes it easy to add a new sheet with the same structure for forecast statistics, if the need arises.

Modular design allows you to enter or change something in one place and have the change flow through the whole reporting model. Your goal is to set up the structure to allow this to happen. If you are entering the same data in multiple places, you need to consolidate that information into one place and then refer to it with a formula. This book provides you with the formula tools to do that flexibly and effectively. The more times you enter data, the more chance you have for error.

Range names work well with modular design and are discussed in depth in Chapter 9. They can provide another level of structure to the reporting model that makes maintenance and amendments simpler.

There are many advantages with a modular design. A few of them are listed next. (I use the term *department* to describe a section of your reporting model, but these advantages are just as relevant to divisions, states, branches, business units, or any other way in which you segment your reports.) Here are some of the advantages:

- Navigation is improved because each sheet has a single purpose. It's therefore easier to know where to go when you're using, maintaining, or modifying your model.

- Inserting or deleting rows and columns becomes less of an issue. If you have a mixed-use sheet, inserting and deleting rows or columns can be difficult and cause errors.
- Adding a new department can be as simple as copying an existing department sheet and renaming it.
- Changing the summarisation level of a sheet can be as easy as moving the sheet to a different place within the file.
- Changing the reporting classification of a department can be as simple as changing a single entry in a table.

There can be multiple sheets in each classification. Typically, similar sheets are grouped together. My recommendation is to use colour coding on the sheet tabs for the sheet types. The order of the sheets can be open to individual preference. Some people like to have the sheets they need to work with on the left and work their way across to the right. You can also group similar sheets together; for instance, all the data sheets can be placed together. Here are some typical sheet classifications:

- **Instructions.** These sheets contain the instructions you need to run, modify, and maintain the reporting model. They may also include hyperlinks associated with the individual instructions. These sheets are typically to the left of all the other sheets (except the index sheet; see later).
- **Control.** This sheet is used in the running of the reporting model. It contains options used to produce the desired report. It is typically uses in-cell drop-downs for data entry cells to change the options. It may also use sheet controls such as check boxes or option buttons.
- **Index.** This sheet holds the hyperlinks that are used to navigate around the reporting model. It is typically to the left of all the other sheets. This makes it quick to get to by clicking on the far-left navigation arrow (left of the sheet tabs).
- **Data.** These sheets contain the raw material or building blocks of the reporting models. They may be populated either by copying and pasting or by directly linking to data sources. These sheets typically have columns for the field names and rows for the individual records.
- **Tables.** These sheets hold the tables used to run the reporting models. Tables are the most efficient way to handle different options and are reasonably self-explanatory so that users can update them successfully.
- **Lists.** These sheets contain the various lists that are used throughout the model, such as the lists used in data validation in-cell drop-downs. You can often combine table sheets and list sheets because they do similar work.
- **Validation.** This sheet brings together all the validations that you create throughout your reporting model. Typically, you will have validations in place throughout your reporting model to help you identify where something has gone wrong. However, it is also efficient to bring all these validations into one place so that they can be viewed on a single sheet. This allows you to easily create an overall validation that checks all the validations throughout the model.
- **Workings.** You may need to do some specific global calculations. Rather than have them sprinkled throughout your reporting model, you can have a dedicated sheet that handles these calculations.

- **Reports.** The ultimate goal of our reporting model, of course, is to create reports. In modular reporting you have separate sheets to handle separate types of reports. You may have a hierarchy of reports, so, for example, you may have individual state-level reports that feed into an overall report for the business. By separating the different types of reports into separate sheets, you can achieve the exact layout that you require.
- **Chart data.** When you are creating charts, it is a good idea to centralise all the data for all the charts onto a single sheet. Charts are easy to create when they are based on a table layout. Centralising all your chart data makes it easy to create a chart and then copy it and simply change its data source to produce a new chart. Having all the chart data together makes this a straightforward operation.
- **Charts and dashboards.** Charts are often kept together in a report much like a dashboard rather than included in the standard reports. Again, it is easier to arrange charts when you do not have to worry about the layout of other reports.
- **Inputs.** When creating your reporting models, you may find that some data is not available in any existing system, but they may exist in other spreadsheets or in printed reports. Rather than spending too much time trying to create systems to collect these measures, you may find that it is simpler to create an input section to the reporting model that collects these sundry items. The layout of these input sheets should resemble data tables so that it is easier to work with them.

The case studies in the last two chapters will include most of these sheet types.

STANDARDISED REPORT LAYOUT

Let's say that you have three states to report on. Reasons have developed over the years for state reports to be received in different layouts. You have to combine them into a single summarised report, and the best way to handle this, ideally, is to have a single report layout for all the states that includes all the required information for those states.

This may mean that some states do not have entries in some of the rows or columns, but it also means that the layout is identical for all the states. Achieving this compatibility among all the states will make reporting much easier.

This means that you will have to spend time up-front creating the layout that meets all the requirements from all the states. There may be redundant rows and possibly redundant columns among the state reports. This is easily handled using sheet grouping, discussed later.

Standardising reporting layouts is an important step in the automation of your reporting model. This can be difficult, since many users claim that their state is different and can't be fit into a standardised model. People naturally resist change. Once you explain the advantages of a standardised reporting layout and assure them that their differences will be incorporated, they will usually come on board. If you make the change as effortless as possible for them, then change becomes less of an issue. For instance, provide detailed instructions with the template they will use.

Sometimes you need to compromise to ensure you get the cooperation of all the users. You can utilise a lot of Excel's features to handle the extra values being provided by different states.

As part of your standardisation process, you may recognise that some states are using better practices than others and that rather than compromise, you may need to make sure that the other states accept the best practices.

Obviously, in the standardisation process you are standardising like entities. All states should have the same reporting layout, but that may be different from the layout you use for departments.

Once you have achieved identical layouts for your reports, you then have the ability to use some of Excel's 3D compatible functions (see Chapter 7 for examples). Be aware that when you use 3D formulas, the location of sheets in relation to other sheets is important (this is also explained in more detail in Chapter 7).

Achieving identical layouts can usually be done by inserting blank rows or columns so that everything lines up among all the sheets. Once the sheets are identical, you are able to work on them together.

Sheet Grouping

Excel has a feature that allows you to manipulate multiple sheets in one process. You can use the Ctrl or Shift key to select multiple sheets, then you can then edit any of the selected sheets, and those entries or changes will be made to all the selected sheets.

This is an incredibly useful feature, but it is also an incredibly dangerous one. When you select multiple sheets, Excel will put the word *Grouped* in the title of the window. This is really the only sign that you have selected multiple sheets. The colours of the sheet tabs vary slightly when you select multiple sheets, but this is not always easy to see.

It is important that you get into the habit of grouping the sheets, doing what you need to do, and then ungrouping the sheets right away and saving the file. If you save the file while the sheets are grouped, the sheets will be grouped the next time you open the file. The danger is that when you open the file again, you might not realise that the sheets are grouped, and if you modify one of the sheets, it will affect all of the selected sheets.

The Pros and Cons of Identical Layouts

There are pros and cons with implementing identical sheet layouts. Here are the pros:

- You have a standard template for your reports, which simplifies your reporting requirements.
- You can group the sheets and work on all of them together.
- You can use 3D formulas, which are short and easy to create.

WARNING: Sheet Grouping

Be very careful whenever you use sheet grouping. It has the potential to affect many sheets. You must force yourself to turn off grouping when you are finished each time. If you are interrupted halfway through, you might forget to remove the sheet grouping, which can cause serious issues with your file.

- You can change where the reports are summarised by simply moving the sheets around (this will become clearer when you read the 3D functions section of Chapter 7).
- You can easily create a new report sheet by copying an existing report sheet and renaming it.

Here are the cons:

- You must be vigilant. You have to ungroup the sheets each time as soon as you are done so that you don't open a file later to change it and forget that the sheets are grouped.
- If the entities you are reporting on are too different, then trying to make them all fit the same template may prove difficult.

TABLE-BASED SYSTEMS

Accounting reports work very well with table-based systems. The chart of accounts, on which most reports are based, is a table.

Accounting reports tend to have limited exceptions, which also makes them ideal for table-based systems. If the right structure is in place, handling exceptions can be a straightforward exercise.

Let's assume we have a table of employees that includes the department to which their costs are allocated. We also have a department table that lists the department and the department manager, who may manage more than one department.

By combining these two tables (using techniques you'll learn in Chapter 5), we can create a report by manager, listing all the employees under his or her control.

The complication is that some employees report directly to the general manager or another manager and are not part of the normal departmental structure, even though their costs are allocated to the department.

A table-based system can provide a flexible way to handle this situation. The functions used in the following example will be discussed further in Chapters 7 and 8.

Figure 4.1 shows the separate tables necessary to handle this situation. Column L has to be populated with the employee's relevant manager. A formula will be used to calculate the correct manager.

	J	K	L	M	N	O	P	Q	R
1	Emp_Code	Dept	Manager		Dept	Manager		Emp_Code_Exceptions	Manager
2	1234	Sales			Sales	J Smith		1237	B Boss
3	1235	Sales			Production	L Tan		1240	B Boss
4	1236	Sales			Admin	H Brown			
5	1237	Production			Marketing	J Smith			
6	1238	Production							
7	1239	Marketing							
8	1240	Marketing							
9	1241	Admin							
10	1242	Admin							

FIGURE 4.1 Table-Based Example

The department and manager table is in columns N and O. The exceptions are listed in columns Q and R.

The formula that handles the exceptions in cell L2 is

=IF(COUNTIF(Q:Q, J2)>0, VLOOKUP(J2, Q:R, 2,0), VLOOKUP(K2, N:O, 2,0))

This formula can be copied down.

The table layout shown in Figure 4.2 is easy to use and maintain. A new employee can be added to the bottom of the exception list in column Q with his or her respective manager. You can update column O with a new manager, and that will also flow through to the employee table.

	J	K	L
1	Emp_Code	Dept	Manager
2	1234	Sales	J Smith
3	1235	Sales	J Smith
4	1236	Sales	J Smith
5	1237	Production	B Boss
6	1238	Production	L Tan
7	1239	Marketing	J Smith
8	1240	Marketing	L Boss
9	1241	Admin	H Brown
10	1242	Admin	H Brown

FIGURE 4.2 Completed Employee Table

SPREADSHEET BEST PRACTICES

Because Excel is used for so many different applications, I don't think there are many best practices that apply to all situations. I will provide a list of what I consider spreadsheet best practices based on my 20 years of experience working with spreadsheets.

Some best practices may just be personal preferences. I have successfully used range names for more than 10 years, and Chapter 9 is devoted to the topic.

I have read articles by people who are just as passionate about *not* using range names. They claim that range names add another layer of complexity to spreadsheets and should be avoided. I believe they simplify and create more meaningful formulas. They also can add structure to a model, if used correctly.

There is a valid case for both arguments. The fact that Microsoft has improved the handling and use of range names in recent Excel releases supports the case to use them more, in my opinion.

I have split my best practices between general and reporting. They are further split into practices to follow and those to avoid.

General Practices to Follow

Use the Quick Access Toolbar to speed up your work.

Learn and use keyboard shortcuts—they can be quicker than the mouse.

Use version numbers on your files, and save different versions regularly.

Use descriptive names on all sheets, and use abbreviations where necessary.

Use descriptive names on row and column headings and cell labels.

Provide cell comments where appropriate to give the user extra directions.

Use colour conventions and different styles to identify parts of your sheet and apply them consistently (see Chapter 11).

Provide detailed instructions to users, including operational and maintenance instructions.

Use range names where appropriate. If a cell or range is to be used frequently, create a range name for it.

Include navigation hyperlinks. These can be used as part of an index sheet or as part of the instructions. Consider having a hyperlink back to the control or index pages on each sheet.

Use macros to simplify and speed up repetitive tasks.

General Practices to Avoid

Don't hard-key values into formulas. In programming terms, these values are sometimes called *magic numbers*. They just appear in a formula, and you may not be sure what they mean. The only exception to this rule is a value that will never change. Remember that *never* is a very, very long time. The number of months in the year or days in the week will never change.

Suppose you have a brick-and-mortar retail business that operates seven days a week. There are many average daily sales calculations that are based on the week. After some analysis, it is found that Sunday sales are low and not profitable. A decision is made to close on Sundays. Now your average daily sales calculations based on seven days of trading are wrong. You may be able to use Find and Replace (Ctrl + h) to change /7 to /6.

This is an example in which a number you thought was never going to change did change. If you are looking at Internet sales, then obviously the seven-days-a-week assumption is a lot safer and is unlikely to change. So if you are in any doubt, set up an input cell for the value and give it a range name (see Chapter 9).

Don't use the text format unless you really, really have to. The text format can cause so many formula problems that it should be avoided. The text format is typically used for numbers that may contain leading zeros (e.g., phone numbers, credit card numbers, or account numbers). If you are starting a numbering convention from scratch, please avoid using 0 as the first digit; start with 1. Excel has a lot of issues with leading zeros.

Don't use the Merged Cells format. It might look nice, but it affects too many other processes. There is an alternative called Center Across Selection. It works only with horizontal ranges, but it doesn't have the limitations of the Merged Cells format. Unfortunately, it doesn't have its own icon. You have to create a macro to run it from a toolbar icon. I have included the macro with instructions on the companion website.

Don't rekey existing data. This comes with a cost-benefit waiver. If the rekeying is minimal, and it is complicated or time-consuming to automate the data collection process, then automating might not be worthwhile.

Don't use symbols in sheet names. They can be confusing when you read formulas referring to a sheet that has the +, —, or & symbols in its name.

Don't enter a value twice. Each entry should be done only once; then use links or formulas to refer to the entry.

Reporting Practices to Follow

Use table-based systems.

Use modular sheets designs.

Use flexible reference formulas rather than fixed links (see Chapters 7 and 8).

Use dynamic range names (see Chapter 9).

Use helper cells to simplify complex formulas (see Chapters 7 and 8).

Create a single formula for a report that can be copied down and across. Helper cells and range names can make this possible.

Use the DATE function to handle your date calculations (see Chapter 8).

CHAPTER FIVE

Setting the Foundation

DATA IS BOTH THE FOUNDATION and the building block of your reporting model. If you don't have the data, you can't report on it; it's as simple as that. If you have the data, and its layout or structure is not conducive to using Excel's built-in functions, then it is difficult or even impossible to report on it.

This chapter will focus on getting the data right so that creating the reports is a reasonably straightforward process. I have often gone into businesses to improve their monthly management reports and found that they want to know the magic formulas that can streamline their reporting process.

They are usually disappointed when I initially want to focus on the data that they have and the reports that they want to generate. They are frequently using manual processes to build their reports each month because their data is laid out so badly. This can be because the data is coming out of a system in a poorly laid-out structure. I'm glad to say that this is less of an issue these days, since exporting data to Excel is done well in most new systems. However, there are still legacy systems out there that provide poorly laid-out data to Excel.

This chapter covers techniques that can fix the data, and this process is sometimes referred to as *data cleansing*. Some of these techniques are quick and straightforward; others are a bit more complex.

Once you have your data properly laid out, then using Excel's built-in functions to create your reports becomes a simpler process.

The next chapter covers pivot tables, which offer a quick way to create reports. Pivot tables rely on table-based, structured data. Getting your data right works for both formula-based reports and pivot table reports.

One of the advantages of using Excel to build reporting models is that it can bring together data from different systems into one reporting model. Even if Excel can't link directly into a database, there is usually a way to get the data into Excel. A fallback position is to copy and paste the data into Excel.

Excel has a number of features that allow you to link directly to your data sources. This chapter will introduce you to the concept of linking directly to your data sources, but it will not comprehensively cover the topic. If you want to get more information on this, I recommend reading *Excel 2007 Advanced Report Development* by Timothy Zapawa, which focuses on extracting data into Excel from many different systems.

TERMINOLOGY

It helps to use the right terminology when working with data. There are different ways to refer to data within a database. My definitions may be a bit dated, but they are the ones used by Excel.

A *row* in an Excel data table is the same as a single *record* in a database. They both start with the same letter, so it's easy to remember. In a database there is usually a unique identifier for a record so it can be retrieved easily. The unique identifier may be a single field or a combination of a number of fields (see later for the definition of a field). A single record is made up of a number of fields.

A *column* in an Excel table is the same as a *field* in a database. There are typically column headings in Excel data tables, and these are the same as the field names in databases. Each field usually contains the same type of data. So one field may contain dates, another field may have text entries, and yet another may have dollar values. It is unusual and poor design for a field to have a mixture of data types.

A *cell* is the intersection of a row and a column in a spreadsheet. A *field item* is the intersection of a record and a field in a database.

DATA RULES

If you are using a spreadsheet as your data source for your reports, then follow these rules:

- Use the bold format on your heading row; this helps Excel identify it as the heading row.
- Don't have any blank rows or columns within the data table. It's acceptable to have an empty column as long as it has a field heading. To determine data ranges, Excel stops whenever it encounters a blank row or column. If you have blank rows or columns in a data table, you will have to amend the estimated range each time Excel selects it.
- Populate blank cells in value ranges with zeros. There is a simple technique, explained later in the chapter, to do this in a less than a minute. A macro for doing it is included on the companion website. This, too, improves Excel's ability to guess ranges.
- Keep your data tables on separate sheets. If you are using more than one data source, make sure each is stored on its own sheet. This makes your model more flexible. Having two data sources on one sheet makes filtering them difficult.

DATA STRUCTURES

When dealing with financial, period-based data, there are two structures that are commonly encountered: normalised data and monthly data.

Normalised Data

The normalised data structure is the easier of the two to work with because it is structured like a database and, as such, is more flexible. Figure 5.1 shows an example of a normalised data structure.

	A	B	C	D	E
1	Date	State	Department	Account	Amount
2	1/07/2013	WA	Production	123400	7,762.00
3	1/07/2013	WA	Production	123500	8,247.00
4	1/07/2013	WA	Production	123600	7,589.00
5	1/07/2013	WA	Production	123700	9,370.00
6	1/07/2013	NSW	Production	123400	7,390.00
7	1/07/2013	NSW	Production	123500	8,802.00
8	1/07/2013	NSW	Production	123600	6,799.00
9	1/07/2013	NSW	Production	123700	7,438.00
10	1/07/2013	WA	Sales	123400	5,824.00
11	1/07/2013	WA	Sales	123500	5,355.00
12	1/07/2013	WA	Sales	123600	8,415.00
13	1/07/2013	WA	Sales	123700	7,980.00

FIGURE 5.1 Normalised Data Structure

This type of table typically has many rows (records) with few columns (fields). It can contain summarised data, such as a summary of all the month's accounts, or transactional data, a list of all the transactions for the period.

Excel's summing functions (see Chapter 7) work well with this layout. It is easy to extract monthly and year-to-date data from this structure, and it allows you to have multiple years' data in one data file. This makes it easier to include prior-year results in your reports.

Monthly Data

The monthly data structure is most commonly used when a report is copied and pasted from an accounting package. The layout is a summary report of the current year's results. Figure 5.2 shows an example of this layout.

You can see that the months go across the page and the accounts go down the page. This makes it more difficult to extract monthly and year-to-date data. It is also typically limited to single-year reporting.

You might ask why organisations don't use this layout for their final reports. This is a valid question that I ask when I'm consulting. The typical response is that the

	A	B	C	D	E	F	G	H
1	ABCDE Ltd							
2	Profit & Loss Statement							
3	July 2012 through June 2013							
4								
5			July	August	September	October	November	December
6	4-0000	Sales						
7	4-1010	Sales Retail - Cannington	$127,032.00	$140,645.00	$128,366.00	$138,317.00	$132,421.00	$121,243.00
8	4-1020	Sales Retail - Joondalup	$143,158.00	$129,461.00	$143,479.00	$107,026.00	$126,848.00	$124,332.00
9	4-1030	Sales Retail - Osborne Park	$140,007.00	$116,545.00	$107,381.00	$117,815.00	$111,349.00	$122,912.00
10	4-1200	Sales Wholesale	$344,532.00	$281,858.00	$315,504.00	$212,900.00	$296,886.00	$272,361.00
11	4-1500	Sales Online	$87,894.00	$112,453.00	$105,162.00	$117,690.00	$106,628.00	$112,122.00

FIGURE 5.2 Monthly Data Structure

reporting package can't provide the necessary flexibility to present the reports exactly as the organisation requires. Many reports are not deemed suitable for reporting at board level.

There can be different departmental breakdowns. The chart of accounts might have been created many years ago, before structural changes were made, and the reports need to reflect the new organisational structure. New managers often require new reports in a layout that they are used to, and many reporting packages don't have the flexibility to customise reports.

Excel is seen as a presentation package that can produce the financial information exactly as required. Excel also offers the ability to combine data from multiple sources, like budgets and forecasts, as well as any nonfinancial, statistical data. Excel also has the ability to include charts.

FORMAT AS TABLE

Excel 2007 introduced an updated feature called Format as Table. Many people think this is a new feature to Excel, but parts of it did exist in Excel 2003, where it was called Lists.

Format as Table is much more than just a formatting tool. Although formatting is part of the process, it incorporates many other features to help you work better with your data. There are also a few disadvantages that you need to be aware of.

By using Format as Table, you are instructing Excel to treat a table like a database. Excel is not a database program, but it is excellent at interrogating database programs. When you import data direct from your data source, Excel will automatically apply the Format as Table option to the imported data table.

I recommend using this feature for all your data tables.

Advantages of Format as Table

- The formatting that is applied to the table automatically expands as entries are made to the table. Formats can include alternating row shading, which makes reading the data in the table easier. This format makes it obvious that the range is different from the rest of the sheet.

- Excel's filter option is automatically added to each column heading.
- The table automatically expands to include extra rows (records) and extra columns (fields). This makes it perfect to use as a data source for pivot table reports (see Chapter 6).
- Any formula entered in a column is automatically copied to every other cell in that column within the table. This feature doesn't work if you use the Fill Handle to copy a formula across columns. It does work if you copy and paste the formula.
- Adding a new record to the table will automatically copy down any formulas in all the columns.
- Excel automatically creates table names that work in a similar way to range names. The advantage of table names is that they automatically expand or contract as data is added or removed from the table. Chapter 9 will explain range names and how you can use them in combination with table names.
- You can't use the Merged Cells format within a formatted table. I see this as an advantage, not a disadvantage. Merged Cells is a format that should be avoided in Excel.

Disadvantages of Format as Table

- Some options on the formatted table are affected by sheet protection.
- You can't share a workbook if it has a formatted table in it. Sharing allows multiple users to access and edit a file simultaneously. It simulates a multiuser environment. It has a number of drawbacks and is not widely used.
- You can't use the automated Subtotal feature within a formatted table. The automated Subtotal feature affects the structure of a data table (see Chapter 7).
- You can't copy a sheet to another file if it contains a formatted table.

Format as Table Example

The table shown in Figure 5.3 will be used to demonstrate some of the features of the Format as Table option.

	A	B	C	D	E
1	Part Number	Description	Colour	Price	Cost
2	12345	Widget	Red	15.55	5.65
3	12346	Widget	Green	15.55	5.65
4	12347	Widget	Orange	15.55	5.65
5	12348	Gadget	Red	17.5	6.14
6	12349	Gadget	Green	17.5	6.14
7	12350	Gadget	Orange	17.5	6.14

FIGURE 5.3 Format as Table Example

To use the Format as Table feature, select any cell within the table and click the Format as Table icon on the Home Ribbon tab.

A gallery of table formats is displayed, and you can create your own table format. After you select the format, a small dialog box will appear confirming the range and that the table has headers. Excel will estimate the range correctly providing there are no blank rows or blank columns within the table. Click OK to apply the format.

If you want to use the default table format, then the shortcut Ctrl + t can be used to create the table.

The applied format helps distinguish the table from the rest of the sheet (see Figure 5.4).

	A	B	C	D	E
1	Part Number	Description	Colour	Price	Cost
2	12345	Widget	Red	15.55	5.65
3	12346	Widget	Green	15.55	5.65
4	12347	Widget	Orange	15.55	5.65
5	12348	Gadget	Red	17.5	6.14
6	12349	Gadget	Green	17.5	6.14
7	12350	Gadget	Orange	17.5	6.14
8					

FIGURE 5.4 Formatted Table

Adding a new entry in the row directly below the table will automatically extend the table to incorporate the new row. Making an entry in the column directly to the right of the table will also extend the table (see Figure 5.5).

	A	B	C	D	E	F
1	Part Number	Description	Colour	Price	Cost	Margin
2	12345	Widget	Red	15.55	5.65	
3	12346	Widget	Green	15.55	5.65	
4	12347	Widget	Orange	15.55	5.65	
5	12348	Gadget	Red	17.5	6.14	
6	12349	Gadget	Green	17.5	6.14	
7	12350	Gadget	Orange	17.5	6.14	
8	12351					

FIGURE 5.5 Formatted Table Extended

Entering a formula in any cell in a table column will cause that formula to be copied to all the cells in that column as soon as you press Enter. You can use the Undo option to reverse the copy.

To calculate the margin in cell F2, we deduct Cost from Price. When you click on the cells in the table on the same line, Excel will automatically insert the field name (see Figure 5.6).

D	E	F	G
Price	Cost	Margin	
15.55	5.65	+[@Price]-[@Cost]	
15.55	5.65		
15.55	5.65		

FIGURE 5.6 Formatted Table Formulas

The structure of formatted table formulas has square brackets around the field name and the @ symbol in front of the field name. In Excel 2007 the # symbol is shown in front of the field name. The @ symbol refers to the field item in the same row (record).

When you have a formatted table selected, a Design Ribbon tab is visible. The table name is on the far left of the ribbon. You can change the generic table name and use a descriptive name. I use the prefix tbl for all table names (see Figure 5.7).

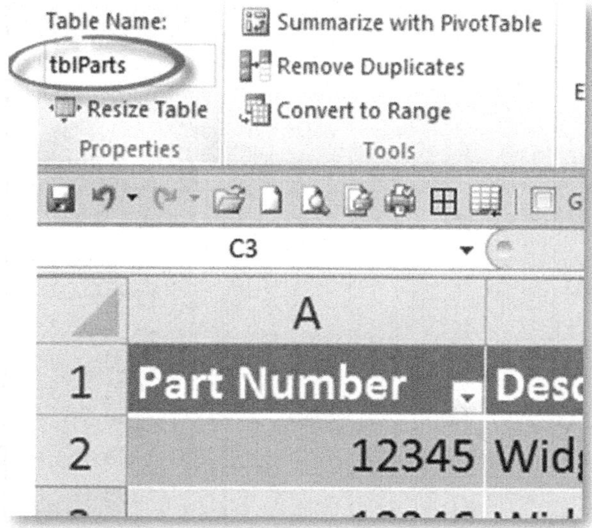

FIGURE 5.7 Table Name on the Design Ribbon

If you use the field names in a cell outside the table, then the table name will also be included in the formula.

```
=AVERAGE(tblParts[Margin])
```

This formula will calculate the average of the Margin field in the tblParts table.

These table names automatically expand as records are added to the table. Table names are discussed further in Chapter 9.

DATA CLEANSING TECHNIQUES

When you import data into Excel, there is a chance that the data will have some issues that reduce your ability to use the data in formula-based or pivot table reports. I have often seen users give up at this point. The data may have one major issue that stops people from using it.

That's where data cleansing techniques come in. *Data cleansing* means modifying or repairing a data set so that it can be used by Excel's functions and other reporting features.

There are a number of common issues with data imported into Excel. It is preferable to get the data fixed at the source before it comes into Excel, but this is not always possible.

The following techniques include a number of functions. They are presented in this chapter as solutions to common data problems. The functions themselves are described in more detail in Chapter 8.

Missing or Incomplete Data

An example of missing or incomplete data is shown in Figure 5.8.

	A	B	C	D	E
1	Date	State	Department	Account	Amount
2	Jul-13	WA	Production	123400	9826
3				123500	9100
4				123600	5601
5				123700	7162
6		NSW	Production	123400	6450
7				123500	9335
8				123600	9919
9				123700	9405
10		WA	Sales	123400	5662
11				123500	7597
12				123600	8975
13				123700	8255

FIGURE 5.8 Missing Data Structure Example

Excel can do little with this type of data layout, which is usually the result of a report or data dump from a system. Neither formulas nor pivot tables can extract reliable information from this layout. It's easy to see why users give up. But this layout is actually easy to fix.

The layout has blank cells below the entries that don't change. The cells below A2 should be populated with Jul-13. The range B3:B5 should contain WA. The challenge is to populate the blank cells with the entries from the cells above.

Follow these steps:

1. Select the range involved: A3:C13, in our case.
2. Press the F5 function key and click the Special button.
3. Select the Blanks option and click OK.
4. Press the = key and click on the cell above the active cell selected. In Figure 5.9, the active cell is B3 (B3 is shown in the Name Box), so click on cell B2.

B3 | *fx*

	A	B	C	D	E
1	Date	State	Department	Account	Amount
2	Jul-13	WA	Production	123400	9826
3				123500	9100
4				123600	5601
5				123700	7162
6		NSW	Production	123400	6450
7				123500	9335
8				123600	9919
9				123700	9405
10		WA	Sales	123400	5662
11				123500	7597
12				123600	8975
13				123700	8255

FIGURE 5.9 Active Cell

5. Here's the important technique: Hold the Ctrl key down and press Enter. That populates every cell in the selected range with a relative formula that refers to the cell above (see Figure 5.10).
6. The data set cannot be left like this, in case it gets sorted. We need to capture the values to finish the process. Copy the whole range A3:C13 and then use Paste Special Values to paste the values back on top of the range.

This process can be done on thousands of cells in a matter of seconds. It actually takes longer to explain it than it does to do it.

Extra Field Required

It is common that after you bring all the data together, you will need to add fields to the data sets. Suppose you bring in your trial balance to the model. It only has Account

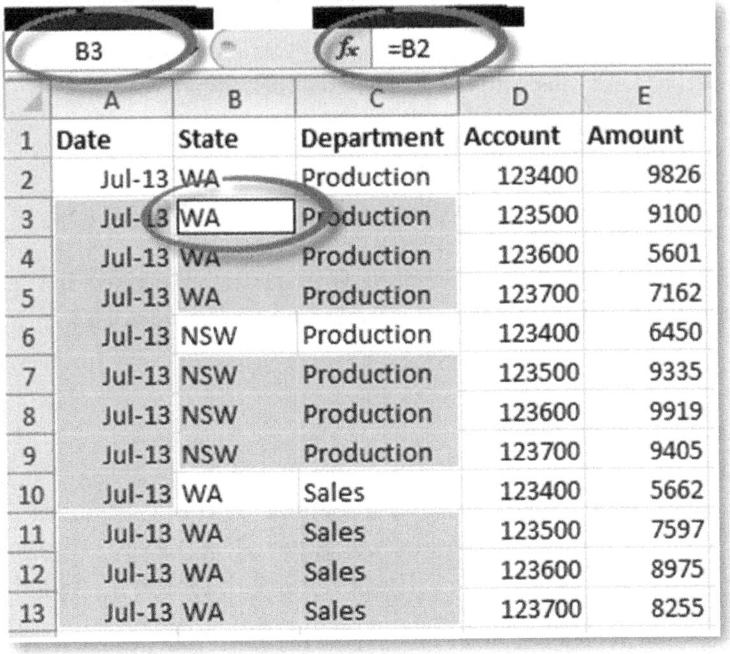

B3 fx =B2

	A	B	C	D	E
1	Date	State	Department	Account	Amount
2	Jul-13	WA	Production	123400	9826
3	Jul-13	WA	Production	123500	9100
4	Jul-13	WA	Production	123600	5601
5	Jul-13	WA	Production	123700	7162
6	Jul-13	NSW	Production	123400	6450
7	Jul-13	NSW	Production	123500	9335
8	Jul-13	NSW	Production	123600	9919
9	Jul-13	NSW	Production	123700	9405
10	Jul-13	WA	Sales	123400	5662
11	Jul-13	WA	Sales	123500	7597
12	Jul-13	WA	Sales	123600	8975
13	Jul-13	WA	Sales	123700	8255

FIGURE 5.10 Formula Entered in Active Cell

Number, Account Name, and Balance. The problem is that you need to create a summarised report based on account categories. Each account number has a category, but it's not in the trial balance. You have a list of account numbers with their categories, but it's on your Tables sheet.

The simple solution is to add a new column to the existing trial balance on the spreadsheet. Always add the column to the right of the existing fields. That makes pasting the new table a simple process. Commonly the VLOOKUP function is used to populate the new column.

In the example shown in Figure 5.11, the required formula in cell D2 of the TB sheet is

```
=VLOOKUP(A2,Tables!$A$2:$C$10,3,0)
```

The VLOOKUP function is designed to look up values in a table based on the entries in the left column of the table. This function is described in detail in Chapter 8.

Date Issues

My examples use the European date convention of placing the day before the month: dd/mm/yy. In Australia we are sometimes confronted with the U.S. date system (month before day) in our downloaded or imported files. Switching from one system to the other can often be handled by adjusting the format.

If dates are entered or formatted as text, Excel won't recognize them as dates. Figure 5.12 contains some text date examples and their conversions.

The conversion formulas all use the DATE function, which is explained in depth in Chapter 8. All the other functions used in the solution formulas are also covered in Chapter 8.

	A	B	C	D
1	Account	Account Name	Amount	Category
2	1000	Bank Account	155071	
3	1100	Debtors	877780	
4	1200	Stock	254980	
5	1300	Prepayments	40815	
6	1500	Plant & Equipment	920955	
7	1510	Accum Depreciation	-398551	
8	2000	Creditors	-730345	
9	2100	Accruals	-84460	
10	2200	Employee Entitlements	-98102	

Missing | TB | Tables

	A	B	C
1	Account	Account Name	Category
2	1000	Bank Account	Current Asset
3	1100	Debtors	Current Asset
4	1200	Stock	Current Asset
5	1300	Prepayments	Current Asset
6	1500	Plant & Equipment	Non Current Assets
7	1510	Accum Depreciation	Non Current Assets
8	2000	Creditors	Current Liabilities
9	2100	Accruals	Current Liabilities
10	2200	Employee Entitlements	Current Liabilities

Missing | TB | Tables

FIGURE 5.11 Missing Field and Lookup Table

	J	K
1	Unusable date format	Corrected Date
2	January 17 2013	17/01/2013
3	2013 08 29	29/08/2013
4	2013 Dec 14	14/12/2013

FIGURE 5.12 Text Dates

The formula in cell K2 is

```
=DATE(RIGHT(J2,4),MONTH(1&LEFT(J2,3)),MID(J2,SEARCH(" ",J2),3))
```

There are two interesting parts of this formula. The first is MONTH(1&LEFT(J2,3)). This uses the LEFT function to extract the first three letters from the month, in this case

Jan. The 1& then converts it to 1Jan. 1Jan is a structure that Excel recognises as a date. The MONTH function extracts the month number from 1Jan.

The second interesting part of the formula is the fact that the month can have various lengths. This makes extracting the day more difficult. The SEARCH function returns the character position of the first space in J2, allowing us to extract the day using the MID function.

The formula in cell K3 is

```
=DATE(LEFT(J3,4),MID(J3,6,2),RIGHT(J3,2))
```

This is a reasonably straightforward conversion because the entries in J3 are all numbers, and they have the structure YYYY MM DD.

The formula in cell K4 is

```
=DATE(LEFT(J4,4),MONTH(1&MID(J4,6,3)),RIGHT(J4,2))
```

This is a combination of the first two solutions.

Spaces

Leading and trailing spaces are a common problem with imported data. If the value you are looking up and the value in the table are different, even by a single space, then the VLOOKUP function will not work. Many systems pad entries with spaces to fill up the number of possible characters in the field. They can fill the beginning or the end of a cell.

Leading spaces are obvious and easily spotted. Trailing spaces are more difficult to spot and account for many questions I receive from accountants about why their VLOOKUP function doesn't work. You can't identify trailing spaces by looking at the entries because the entries will be left-aligned. If you change the format to a right alignment, you can then identify trailing spaces. Figure 5.13 shows examples of leading and trailing spaces.

	K	L	M
1	Leading Spaces	Trailing Spaces	Trailing Spaces Right Aligned
2	WA	WA	WA
3	WA	WA	WA
4	NSW	NSW	NSW
5	NSW	NSW	NSW
6	QLD	QLD	QLD
7	QLD	QLD	QLD

FIGURE 5.13 Leading and Trailing Spaces Examples

Another way to spot trailing spaces is to press F2 and see where the cursor is in the Formula Bar (see Figure 5.14).

FIGURE 5.14 Trailing Spaces in the Formula Bar

Fixing leading and trailing spaces is easy. The TRIM function is specifically designed to remove both leading and trailing spaces. Any spaces within the text are left alone. The syntax is simple:

```
=TRIM(A1)
```

The formula will remove the leading and trailing spaces for the text in A1.

If you need to remove all the spaces within a cell, you can use the SUBSTITUTE function. The following formula will remove all spaces from cell A1:

```
=SUBSTITUTE(A1," ","")
```

Trailing Minus Signs

Some systems place the minus sign to the right of the value. As far as Excel is concerned, that converts the value into text, and Excel won't treat it as a value. The formula to convert a trailing minus into a negative value is

```
=IF(RIGHT(A1)="-",LEFT(A1,LEN(A1)-1)*-1,A1)
```

This leaves positive numbers unchanged.

If the system places DR and CR to the right of the values, you can use the following formula to convert them to positives and negatives, respectively.

```
=LEFT(A1,LEN(A1)-2)*IF(RIGHT(A1,2)="DR",1,-1)
```

Structured Codes

Some system codes have structure built into them. The first two characters may refer to the colour, and the next character may relate to the product size. The last four characters may be the product code. Figure 5.15 shows an example.

	A	B	C	D
1	Code	Colour	Size	Product
2	BKS1234	BK	S	1234
3	WHL4321	WH	L	4321
4				

FIGURE 5.15 Structured Code Examples

Hence, to provide further analysis, you may wish to split up the code into the colour and size. If the code is in A2, the formula to extract colour is

```
=LEFT(A2,2)
```

The formula for the size is

```
=MID(A2,3,1)
```

The formula for the product is

```
=RIGHT(A2,4)
```

Text to Columns

If a code uses a delimiting character, such as the minus sign to separate different sections, Excel has a feature that can split up the code without a formula. Figure 5.16 displays an example using the minus sign as the separator.

	A	B
1	Code	Weight
2	ABC-123-4000	10
3	XYZ-22-50000	15
4	AA-1-400	7
5	X-231-999999	4

FIGURE 5.16 Structured Codes with Delimiters

You can see that the sections of the code have various lengths. The Text to Columns icon in the Data Ribbon tab can separate these sections. Because Text to Columns separates the contents into the columns on the right of the cell, you need to insert two blank columns to the right of column A; otherwise, the Weight column would be overwritten.

Select the range to split, then click the Text to Columns icon. The first step of a three-step Wizard is displayed.

Figure 5.17 shows the first two steps. Note that the minus sign has been entered in the box to the right of the Other check box.

Click the Finish button to complete the process. Click OK in the dialog box regarding replacing the contents of the destination cell.

The third step in the Wizard is not required in this case, but it can be used to format or omit columns.

Figure 5.18 shows the result.

EXTERNAL DATA

Many users are unaware that you can import data directly from an external database into Excel. I will demonstrate using an Access database. Although Access can be used for smaller database requirements, it is rarely used for large, company-wide databases. Most large databases are SQL-based.

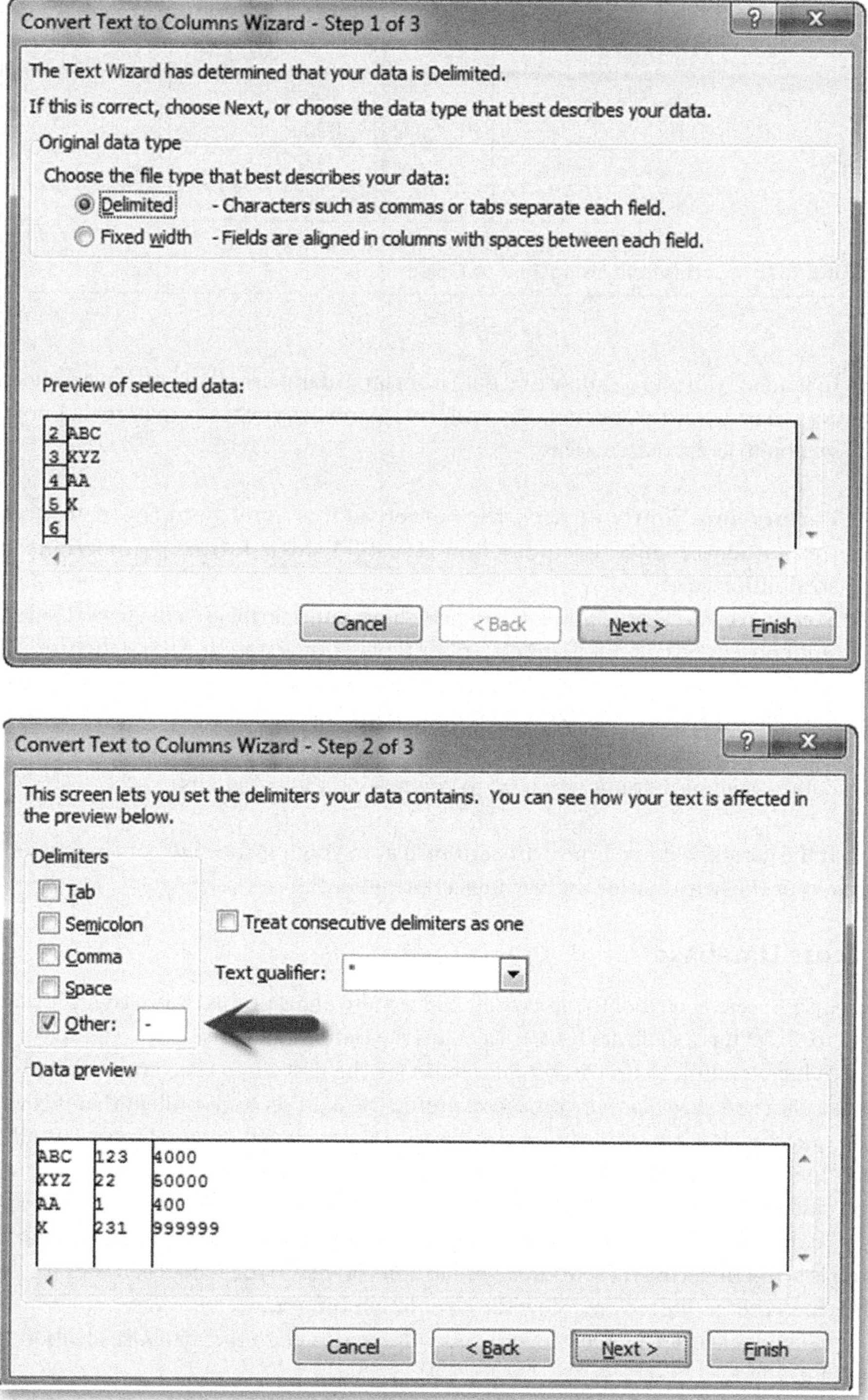

FIGURE 5.17 Convert Text to Columns Wizard Steps 1 and 2

	A	B	C	D
1	Code			Weight
2	ABC	123	4000	10
3	XYZ	22	50000	15
4	AA	1	400	7
5	X	231	999999	4

FIGURE 5.18 Codes Split Using Text to Columns

In practice you will be importing data from large databases that will have dedicated servers and password protection. You will have to involve your information technology (IT) section to assist in two areas:

- **Permission.** You will need the server address and permission to access the database. Once a connection is established, future connections are straightforward.
- **Structure.** Modern relational databases have multiple tables and views. *Views* are summaries and combinations of various tables. Understanding the structure of the database tables is important. You should discuss your requirements with the database administrator. The data you require may exist in a number of tables. If that is the case, you may need to have a view created that has all the data you need. The database administrator will need to create a view for you to use.

If the database doesn't have an administrator, you may need to contact customer support or the help desk for the previous information.

Access Database

Because Access is part of the Microsoft Office suite of programs, it is easy for Excel to link to. Excel has a dedicated Access icon on the Data Ribbon tab.

When you link to an external database for the first time, I recommend bringing in the data to a sheet so that you can examine the data set and confirm that it is what you expected. It is not until you see the data set that you can be sure it provides all the information you need to complete your reports. If a database view has to be amended, you can get it done right away.

In the long run, you may import the data via a pivot table so that only summarised data is being imported rather than a whole table or view, which may be very large and thus increase the file size and slow the calculation time down.

When you click the Access icon, you will have to go to the database location and select it.

The Import Data dialog box is displayed in Figure 5.19, and you can choose to bring the data to a table on a sheet or a pivot table. Pivot tables are discussed in detail in the next chapter.

The Properties button allows you to control how the data is refreshed. Figure 5.20 shows the Refresh options.

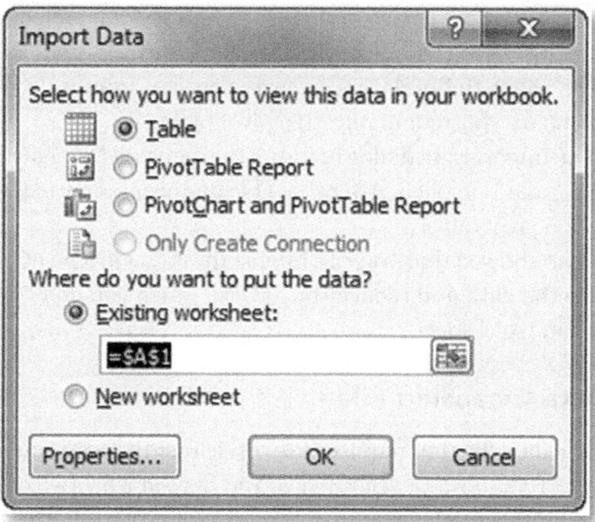

FIGURE 5.19 Import Data Dialog Box

Connection Properties
Connection name: Sales_Data_Base1
Description:
Usage Definition
Refresh control
Last Refreshed:
Enable background refresh
Refresh every 60 minutes
Refresh data when opening the file
Remove data from the external data range before saving the workbook
OLAP Server Formatting
Retrieve the following formats from the server when using this connection:
Number Format Fill Color
Font Style Text Color
OLAP Drill Through
Maximum number of records to retrieve:
Language
Retrieve data and errors in the Office display language when available
OK Cancel

FIGURE 5.20 Connection Properties Dialog Box

Imported data is like a web page and must be refreshed to include the most recent data. In most cases, updating the data when the file is opened is sufficient. If you want more control over when the updating occurs, you can manually refresh the data. Alt + F5 is the keyboard shortcut to refresh a pivot table.

Click OK on the Import Data dialog box, and the data will immediately be imported. The default table format is applied. After the table has been imported, you can use it as the data source for a pivot table.

Figure 5.19 also showed that you can import the data via a pivot table. This allows you to summarise the data and reduce the file size, since you don't have to bring the detailed data into an Excel sheet.

Dedicated Data Cleansing File

Let's say you have a data file that requires a lot of cleansing work. You might need multiple formulas to correct the data deficiencies. You have at least two options.

First, you can build the data cleansing formulas into your reporting model. Our two case studies will use this method.

Second, you can create a dedicated file that handles all the data cleansing processes. This file may use a combination of formula and macros. This would isolate your reporting model from macros and simplify the final reporting model. You would paste the data into the dedicated cleansing file that would then create a cleansed version. You can copy the cleansed data into the reporting model ready to use.

CHAPTER SIX

Pivot Tables (Do-It-Yourself Reporting)

EXCEL'S PIVOT TABLE FEATURE ALLOWS you to convert raw data into a summary report with only a few mouse clicks and without entering a single formula. In my training courses, pivot tables are the second most popular topic after macros. Users seem to have a perception that pivot tables are complex or difficult. This might be because pivot tables are so powerful that users think they must be difficult.

Pivot tables are incredibly easy to use. There are only two concepts you have to understand to effectively use pivot tables:

1. Column headings in your data tables are called *fields*, and these can be reported in the pivot table.
2. Rows are data records and are summarised by the pivot table.

Many users are unaware that pivot tables can extract data directly from an external data source without having to bring any data into an Excel sheet. You can set up a pivot table so that when a file is opened the pivot table automatically extracts the latest data from an external data source and the report is updated—or, in pivot table terminology, *refreshed*.

This chapter focuses on how to use pivot tables for summarising data. It includes some advanced techniques for doing calculations within the pivot table.

THE PROS AND CONS OF A PIVOT TABLE

Pivot tables are perfect for prototyping reports. Because they are so easy, flexible, and fast to create, you can test different layouts in quick succession to help determine your final designs.

You may be able to create all your reports with pivot tables.

Pivot tables have the following advantages:

- In the pivot table's basic form, there are no formulas required to create a report.
- A report can be created in seconds provided the data is structured correctly.
- The layout can be changed in seconds.
- Totals and subtotals are automatically added.
- Reports can be easily filtered (e.g., a report by state).

Pivot tables have several limitations as well:

- Pivot table reports can extract data from only one data table at a time.
- Pivot tables do not refresh dynamically. If you change a value in the data, it won't automatically be updated in the pivot table report. You must refresh a pivot table to update any new data, much like a web page must be refreshed to see the latest version of it.
- The available layouts and structures of pivot tables are limited and might not be suitable for your presentation.
- The terminology used in pivot table headings may not be acceptable for presentation.
- It is easy to exclude values from a pivot table, and that exclusion isn't always obvious.
- Pivot tables do not handle exceptions to rules very well. If you need the ability to be flexible in your reports—for instance, if you need to treat some combinations of department and account codes differently in your reports—then a pivot table probably won't handle that, and you will need to create a formula-based report that can handle exceptions.

Let's examine these limitations first before we look at creating a pivot table.

Single Data Source

The first limitation has been addressed by a free Microsoft add-in called PowerPivot. This remedy is included as standard in some versions of Excel 2013 but is an add-in to Excel 2010. You can build pivot table reports with PowerPivot in Excel 2010 and Excel 2013. There is a PowerPivot reader available for Excel 2007. This feature is not compatible with Excel 2003.

PowerPivot is briefly discussed at the end of this chapter.

Refreshing a Pivot Table

The second limitation of pivot tables is more of a process issue.

When you create a pivot table, Excel initially copies all the data from the source data into memory, into something called a *pivot table cache*. This cache holds the data you are using to create your pivot table report, but the cache is not automatically updated when changes are made to the source data. Figure 6.1 shows the pivot table creation process.

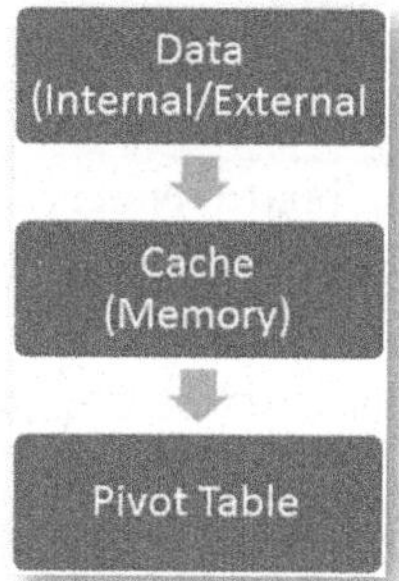

FIGURE 6.1 Pivot Table Data Process

When you refresh the pivot table, you are in effect refreshing the cache that the pivot table report is based on. The cache and the pivot table are dynamic. As soon as the cache is updated, the pivot table updates.

This is an important concept to grasp. Adding rows or columns to the source data will not automatically update the pivot table report. You must refresh the pivot table.

Even though I have listed this as a limitation, it does have a benefit: It allows you to control when the report is updated. As I mentioned, you can link a pivot table report to an external data source. In some instances, if your report changes every five minutes (which is a setting you can change), it would be frustrating to use the pivot table. In other cases, that might be exactly what you require. It is up to you to decide how often to refresh your pivot table.

Sharing the Cache

Each time you create a new pivot table, Excel creates a new pivot table cache of the data, even if you have used that data set before. This duplicates the cache and can cause the file size and memory allocation to increase.

You can share the cache by simply copying a pivot table to another sheet and then making your changes.

Sharing a cache means that the pivot tables will also share a number of features. Data refreshing is one of the shared features. Other features will be mentioned later in the chapter.

Getting the Source Data Right

When creating your pivot table reports on data already in Excel, I highly recommend that you use the Format as Table option discussed in Chapter 5 for the pivot table source data.

This ensures that your pivot table's source data automatically expands and contracts based on the records and fields in your table. It ensures that all the data in the table is updated to the cache and then included in the pivot table report when you refresh the pivot table.

If you don't use Format as Table, you will have to manually adjust the pivot table source data range whenever it changes. This can be tedious and also leads to errors, since new data may be omitted from the pivot table report.

Formatting a Pivot Table

There are many built-in pivot table formats. Unfortunately, most formats are not up to the presentation quality required for board reports or management reports. The layouts are limited, and most of these are not presentation quality, either.

Because a pivot table can change size (rows and columns), applying formats to it can be difficult. Conditional formatting (see Chapter 11) functionality was added to pivot tables in Excel 2010.

Pivot Table Terminology

When Excel creates a pivot table, it automatically inserts words to describe the column values (e.g., Sum of Sales). Some people find this annoying and distracting. In some cases, when you use some of the more advanced features, these descriptions are misleading.

There are macros that will remove this terminology, and if that is your only issue with a pivot table report, it might be worth using such a macro.

I have included macros on the companion website that will remove the "Sum of" terminology from a specific pivot table or from each pivot table in a file.

Filtering

A new feature called Slicers can overcome the issue with filtering by multiple criteria. Slicers are more transparent in applying filters and are covered in more detail later in the chapter.

Pivot Tables and Exceptions

Pivot tables do not handle exceptions very well. Whatever is in the data can be shown in the pivot table. The pivot table is consistent in how it displays the data.

If your exceptions involve filtering, then pivot tables will work, because you can filter by row or column. It would be easy, for instance, to create a pivot table that showed all sales except online sales as long as there was a field (column) that contained "Online" as a field item.

If your exceptions are more complex, you might need to manipulate your data to handle them. You could do this by adding columns to your data that allow you to produce the reports you need. This falls under the topic of data cleansing, discussed in Chapter 5.

CREATING A PIVOT TABLE

The pivot table interface changed in Excel 2007 and changed slightly again in Excel 2010. The Excel 2010 interface and options are the best so far.

If you liked some of the functionality in Excel 2003, there is now a Classic option for a pivot table layout. This replicates some of the Excel 2003 drag-and-drop features.

If you preferred to use the old pivot table Wizard, you may be surprised to learn that it is still available in later versions. You can access it only with the keyboard shortcut Alt d p (pressed in sequence, not held down). I don't recommend that you use this, however, unless you need to use its Multiple Consolidation Range feature, which is not included in the functionality of later versions. Then you use the Wizard; it doesn't recognise Excel's new formatted tables feature, and there are advantages to using formatted tables as the data source for pivot tables.

Pivot tables are really effective only for data that is in a standard data layout, with columns for data fields and rows for data records. The more fields the data set contains, the more useful pivot tables can be. See Chapter 5 for ways of cleansing the data if your data has structural problems.

Internal Data

To create a pivot table based on data already in an Excel sheet, I highly recommend that you use the Format as Table feature on the data first. Using a formatted table as the data source for a pivot table allows the pivot table to automatically include extra records or fields that are added to the data whenever the pivot table is refreshed.

You can select any cell within the data and click the Insert Ribbon tab, then click the Pivot Table icon on the far left.

The dialog box in Figure 6.2 displays the name of the formatted table—in this case, tblSales. (As noted earlier, I use the prefix tbl for my formatted table names.) In most cases you will use the New Worksheet option to create a new pivot table, since this provides the most flexibility.

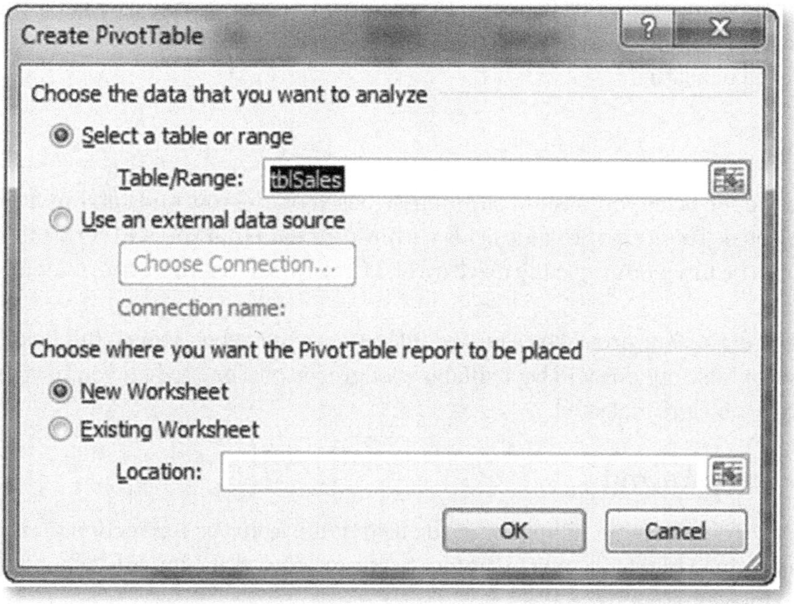

FIGURE 6.2 Create Pivot Table Dialog Box

It is usually preferable to have one pivot table report per sheet. Pivot table report layouts can change as new data is added and the pivot table is refreshed. You can't delete rows or columns within a range containing a pivot table.

Excel will start the pivot table in cell A3. You can see the blank pivot table in Figure 6.3. The PivotTable Field List dialog box is displayed to allow you to select the fields to include in the pivot table. I find it easiest to use the mouse to drag field names to the four areas of the report.

The four areas of the report are described next.

Report Filter

A report filter allows you to filter the report based on the fields you drag to this section. Although this works well for single selections, it does create some issues when you're working with multiple selections, which will be explained later in the chapter.

An alternative to the report filter was added in Excel 2010. The new feature is called Slicers and will also be discussed later in the chapter.

Filters are displayed above the report, from row 1 down.

Row Labels

Row labels are the fields you wish to see as rows in the report. The sequence of the fields is important because it creates a top-down reporting hierarchy. Each field is broken down by the fields listed beneath it.

Column Labels

Column labels are the fields you wish to see as columns in the report. Again, the order is important because it creates a reporting hierarchy. Each field is broken down by the fields listed beneath it.

Values

Values are the fields you wish to summarise based on the row and column field headings selected. These are the value fields within your data that you will perform calculations on. The functions typically used are SUM or COUNT, but there are other functions available.

Each of the four areas has slightly different options when you right-click it. Also, some pivot table options will be available (not greyed out) only when you have the correct pivot table area selected.

Pivot Table Layout

To create the pivot table, simply drag the field name from the top section of the dialog box shown in Figure 6.3 to one of the four area boxes below it. Figure 6.4 shows a report created in a few seconds.

The cells within a pivot table do not contain formulas, just values.

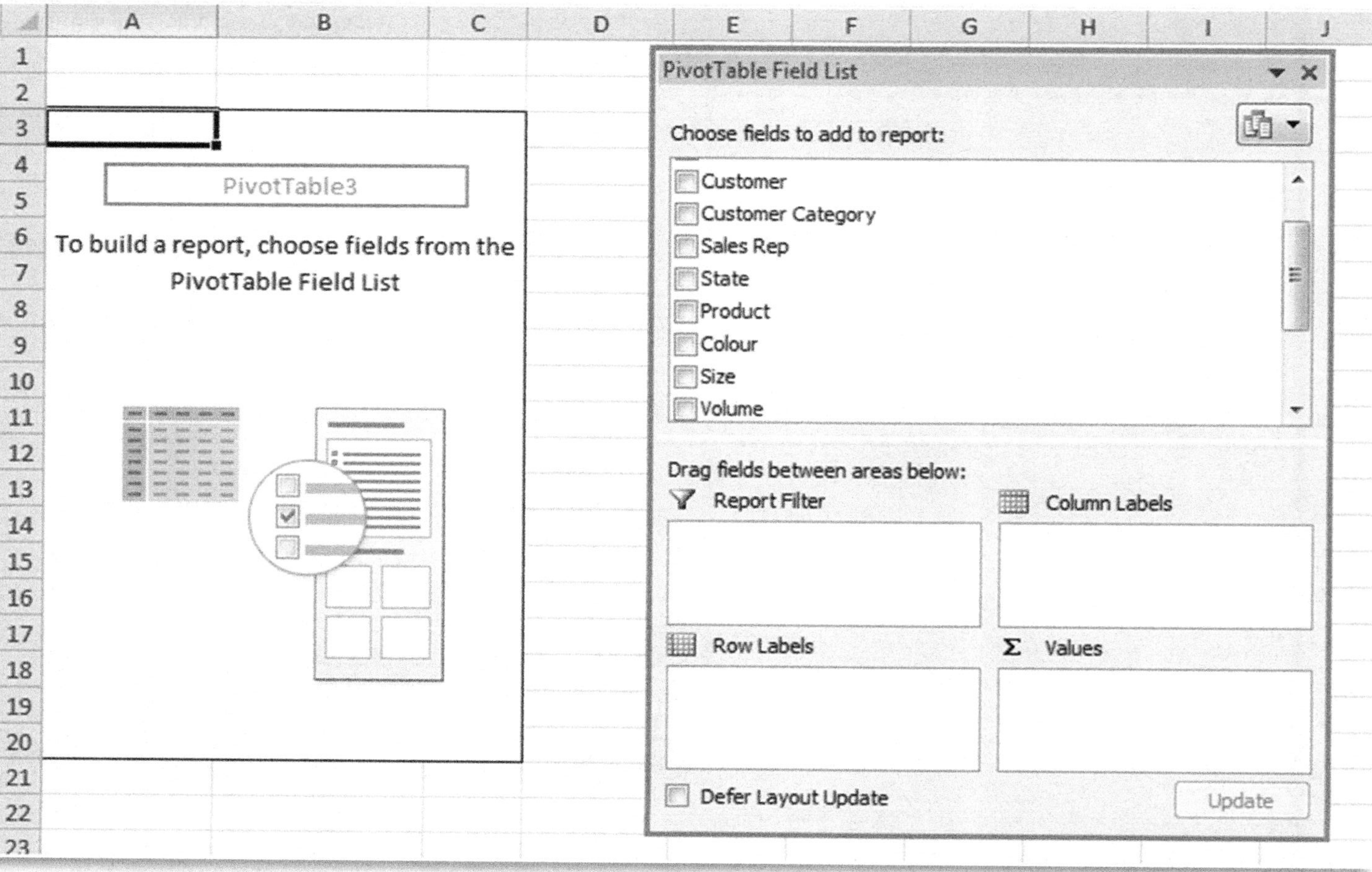

FIGURE 6.3 Blank Pivot Table

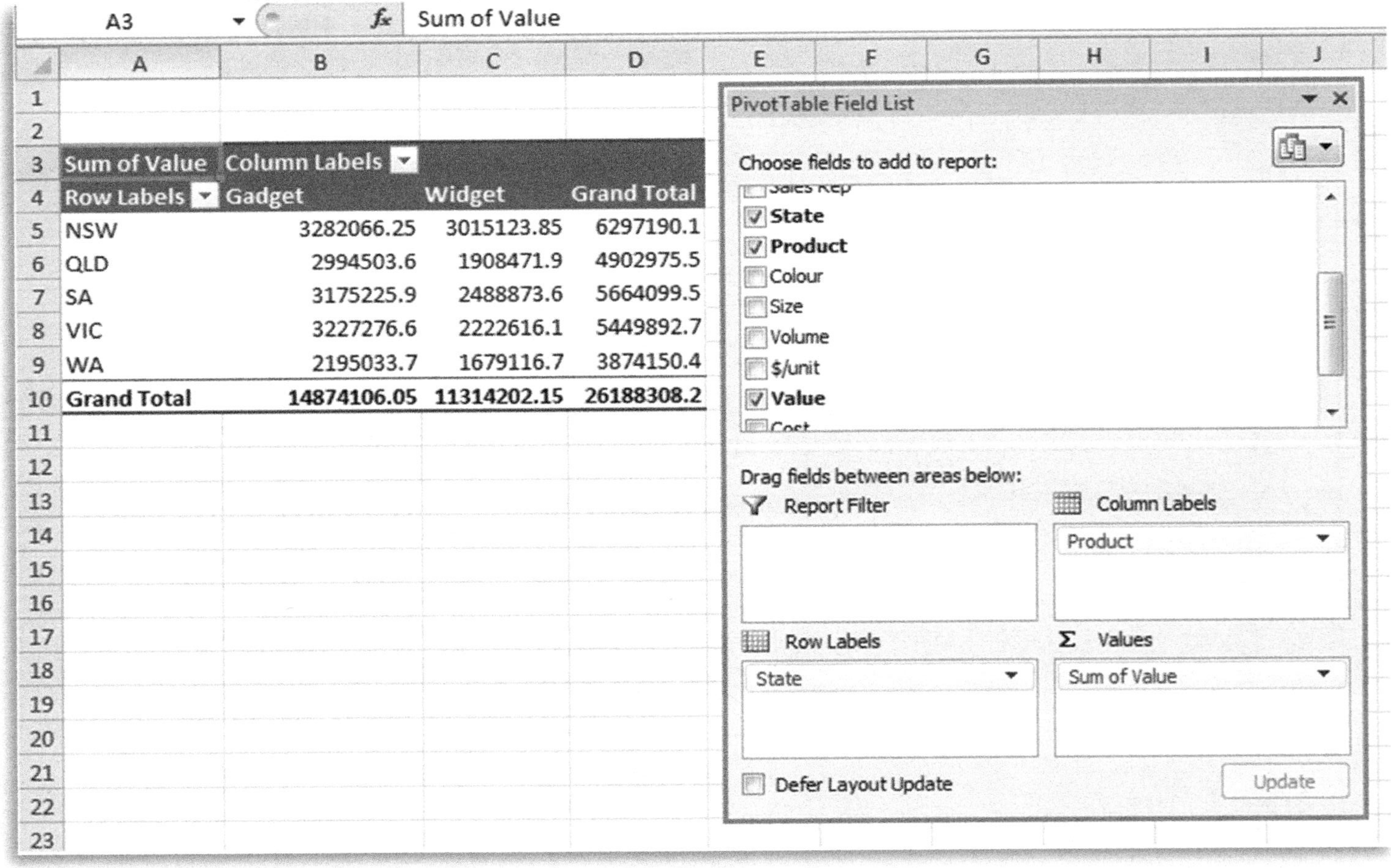

A3 | Sum of Value

Sum of Value	Column Labels		
Row Labels	Gadget	Widget	Grand Total
NSW	3282066.25	3015123.85	6297190.1
QLD	2994503.6	1908471.9	4902975.5
SA	3175225.9	2488873.6	5664099.5
VIC	3227276.6	2222616.1	5449892.7
WA	2195033.7	1679116.7	3874150.4
Grand Total	**14874106.05**	**11314202.15**	**26188308.2**

PivotTable Field List

Choose fields to add to report:

- [x] **State**
- [x] **Product**
- [ ] Colour
- [ ] Size
- [ ] Volume
- [ ] $/unit
- [x] **Value**

Drag fields between areas below:

Report Filter

Column Labels: Product

Row Labels: State

Values: Sum of Value

Defer Layout Update

Update

FIGURE 6.4 Completed Pivot Table

Tip: Blanks in the Data

One of the frustrations with pivot tables is caused by blank entries within value fields. If you have a single blank cell in a column of values, Excel will default to using the COUNT operation rather than the SUM operation. This means you have to manually amend the operation to SUM—an extra step in the process. You can avoid blanks in value fields by using the data cleansing techniques discussed in Chapter 5 to replace blanks with zeros.

Blanks also affect the ability to group dates—see the "Grouping" section later in this chapter.

Blanks will also be shown as a separate item in the pivot table if a blank cell is in a field that has been added to the pivot table.

All the states within the State field are listed, and so are the two products in the Products field. If a new state is added to the data, the new state will automatically be included in the pivot table when it is next refreshed.

The default order of the entries is alphabetical. You have many sorting options. You can even drag the state labels to other rows to get exactly the order you want. This also applies to the column labels.

Pivot Table Headings

The Row Labels and Column Labels headings shown in Figure 6.4 are not popular because they don't add anything to the report. You can turn them off and on by clicking the Field Headers icon on the far right of the Options Ribbon tab. You can also modify them by reverting to the Classic pivot table layout mentioned earlier. This replaces them with their field names, which makes more sense. Figure 6.5 shows the Classic layout.

	A	B	C	D
1	Drop Report Filter Fields Here			
2				
3	Sum of Value	Product		
4	State	Gadget	Widget	Grand Total
5	SA	3175225.9	2488873.6	5664099.5
6	NSW	3282066.25	3015123.85	6297190.1
7	QLD	2994503.6	1908471.9	4902975.5
8	VIC	3227276.6	2222616.1	5449892.7
9	WA	2195033.7	1679116.7	3874150.4
10	Grand Total	14874106.05	11314202.15	26188308.2

FIGURE 6.5 Completed Classic Pivot Table

The drop-down menus on these cells (both standard and classic) contain sorting and filtering options for the field (see Figure 6.6).

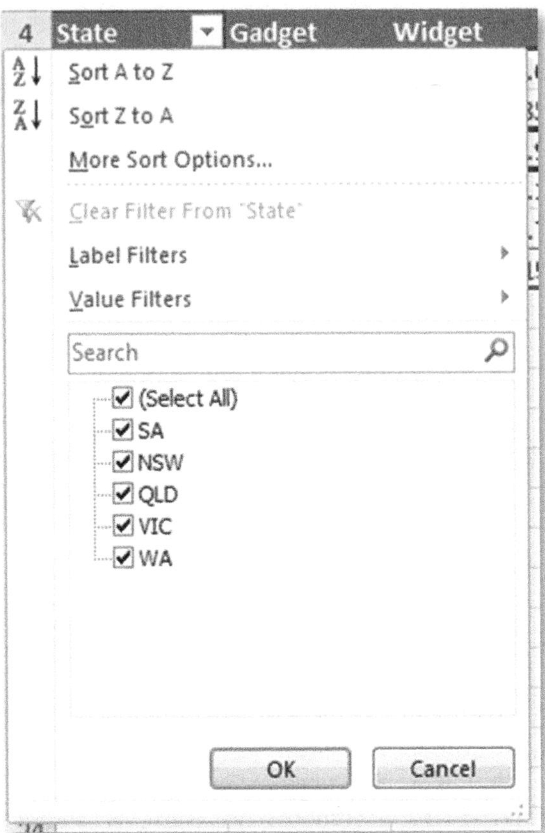

FIGURE 6.6 Pivot Table Sort and Filter Options

When the pivot table is selected in the "Classic" layout, it has thick blue lines around the four pivot table areas. This allows you to drag and drop the fields into the report itself.

Formatting a Pivot Table

In most cases you will need to modify the formatting of your pivot tables. Pivot tables are unusual because you don't have to select a range to apply a format to multiple cells.

To format the values area, you need only select a single cell in the column you want to format. Right-click the cell and choose Number Format (see Figure 6.7).

This opens the Number tab from the Format Cells dialog box (see Figure 6.8).

The format will be applied to all the value cells for the same field as the selected cell. You may have more than one field in the Values area. This allows you to have different formats for the dollar and percentage values displayed in the pivot table.

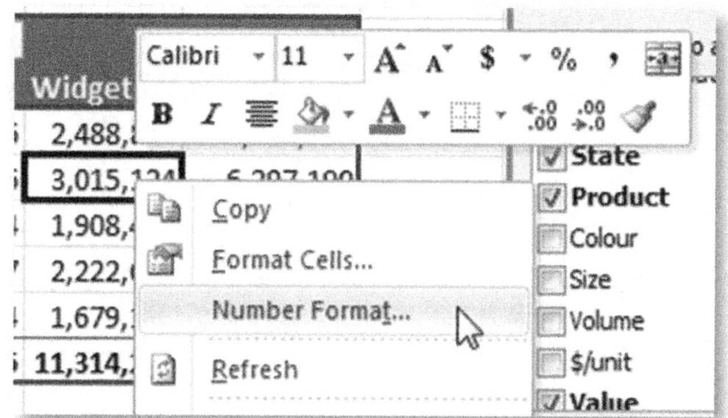

FIGURE 6.7 Number Format Option

Format Cells

Number

Category:

General
Number
Currency
Accounting
Date
Time
Percentage
Fraction
Scientific
Text
Special
Custom

Sample

3,015,124

Decimal places: 0

Use 1000 Separator (,)

Negative numbers:

-1,234
1,234
-1,234
-1,234

FIGURE 6.8 Format Cells—Number Tab

The PivotTable Tools—Options Tab

When the pivot table is selected, the PivotTable Tools—Options tab controls what data is included and excluded. We'll examine some of the most useful features in this tab.

Slicers

The new feature called Slicers was mentioned earlier as an alternative to Report Filters. When you are selecting multiple items, Slicers has two distinct advantages over Report Filters.

The first is that it displays the entries being filtered. A slicer can be added for any field in the data. See Figure 6.9.

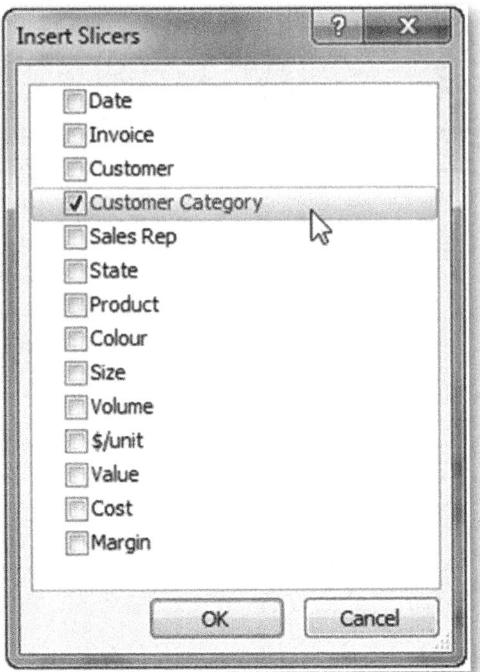

FIGURE 6.9 Insert Slicers Dialog Box

You can hold down the Ctrl key and select multiple items on Slicers (see Figure 6.10). The pivot table is showing state sales for retail and wholesale customers.

Sum of Value	Product		
State	Gadget	Widget	Grand Total
SA	2,039,688	1,634,107	3,673,795
NSW	2,137,825	1,844,465	3,982,291
QLD	2,093,759	1,249,098	3,342,857
VIC	2,411,904	1,717,917	4,129,821
WA	1,470,628	1,037,451	2,508,079
Grand Total	**10,153,805**	**7,483,038**	**17,636,843**

Customer Category
Government
Other
Retail
Wholesale

FIGURE 6.10 Customer Category Slicer—Multiple Items

The second advantage is that one slicer can be used to control the filtering of multiple pivot tables.

When the pivot table is selected, the Slicer Tools Design Ribbon tab is displayed. The Pivot Table Connections icon on that tab allows you to connect a slicer to another pivot table (see Figure 6.11).

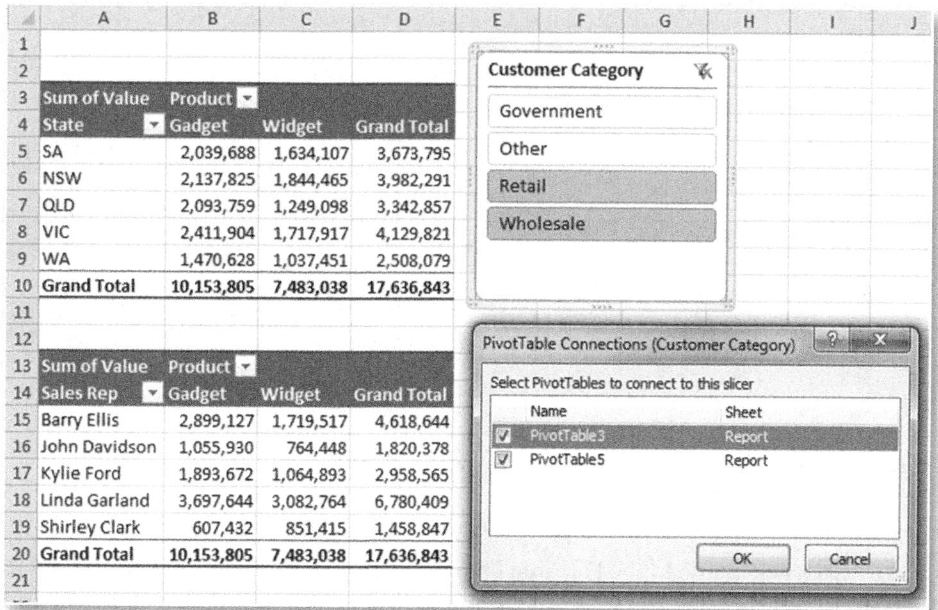

Sum of Value	Product		
State	Gadget	Widget	Grand Total
SA	2,039,688	1,634,107	3,673,795
NSW	2,137,825	1,844,465	3,982,291
QLD	2,093,759	1,249,098	3,342,857
VIC	2,411,904	1,717,917	4,129,821
WA	1,470,628	1,037,451	2,508,079
Grand Total	10,153,805	7,483,038	17,636,843

Sum of Value	Product		
Sales Rep	Gadget	Widget	Grand Total
Barry Ellis	2,899,127	1,719,517	4,618,644
John Davidson	1,055,930	764,448	1,820,378
Kylie Ford	1,893,672	1,064,893	2,958,565
Linda Garland	3,697,644	3,082,764	6,780,409
Shirley Clark	607,432	851,415	1,458,847
Grand Total	10,153,805	7,483,038	17,636,843

FIGURE 6.11 PivotTable Connections Dialog Box

I have added another pivot table (PivotTable5) to the same sheet. This report summarises sales by the Sales Rep field. I can add PivotTable5 to the Customer Category Slicer Connections to control it with the same slicer that was used for the first pivot table.

Pivot Table Calculations

Pivot tables don't contain regular formulas, but you can do calculations within pivot tables. There are two types of calculations. You can access both of them through the Fields, Items & Sets icon on the Options Ribbon tab when the pivot table is selected.

Calculated Field A Calculated Field allows you to create a new field based on other fields. In the sample database, there is a Value field, which contains the sales value, and a Margin field, but there is no Margin % field. Even if there was a Margin % field, you couldn't summarise it in a pivot table because adding up the individual percentages would not make sense. We can add a Margin % field to the pivot table using a Calculated Field. Click the Fields, Items & Sets icon and select Calculated Field (see Figure 6.12).

The Name box is text, and you can name it whatever you want, except for an existing field name.

The Formula box allows you to create the formula using the field headings. You can use all the normal formula operators and some Excel functions in this box. In this example we are dividing the Margin field by the Value field to calculate the Margin %.

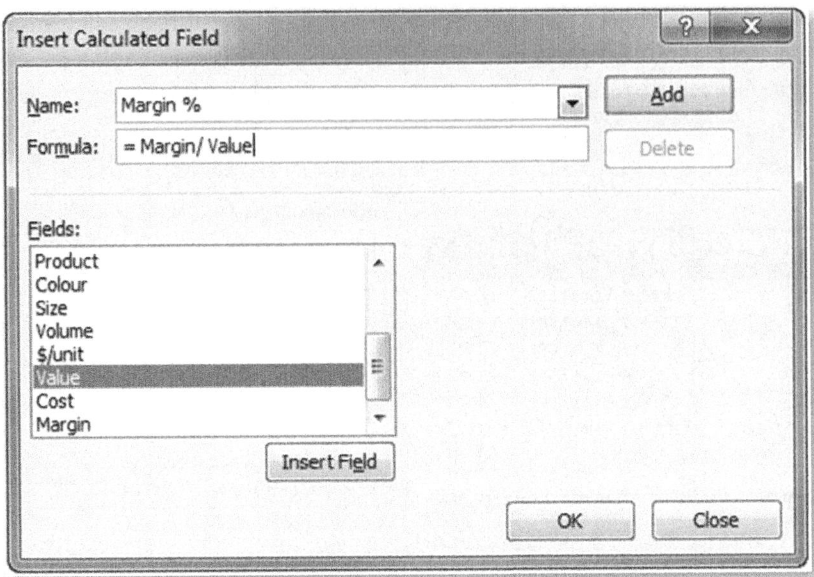

FIGURE 6.12 Insert Calculated Field Dialog Box

To add a field name to the Formula box you can either double-click the field name or select it and click the Insert Field button. Figure 6.13 shows the inserted field and two issues.

	A	B	C	D	E	F	G
1							
2							
3		Column Labels					
4		Gadget		Widget		Total Sum of Value	Total Sum of Margin %
5	Row Labels	Sum of Value	Sum of Margin %	Sum of Value	Sum of Margin %		
6	NSW	3,282,066	0	3,015,124	0	6,297,190	0
7	QLD	2,994,504	0	1,908,472	0	4,902,976	0
8	SA	3,175,226	0	2,488,874	0	5,664,100	0
9	VIC	3,227,277	0	2,222,616	0	5,449,893	0
10	WA	2,195,034	0	1,679,117	0	3,874,150	0
11	**Grand Total**	**14,874,106**	**0**	**11,314,202**	**0**	**26,188,308**	**0**

FIGURE 6.13 Margin % Field

The first issue is simply a formatting problem. The format on the existing field has been applied to the new field. Applying the percentage format fixes this issue (see Figure 6.14).

The second issue is terminology. The column for Margin % has the heading Sum of Margin %. This heading is wrong. Margin % is a calculation, not a sum. You can manually change the heading by removing "Sum of" and adding a space to the end of the heading. You have to add the space to the end because you can't have a column heading with the same name as a field heading. Margin % is now a field heading (see Figure 6.15).

	A	B	C	D	E	F	G
1							
2							
3		Column Labels					
4		Gadget		Widget		Total Sum of Value	Total Sum of Margin %
5	Row Labels	Sum of Value	Sum of Margin %	Sum of Value	Sum of Margin %		
6	NSW	3,282,066	44.6%	3,015,124	48.2%	6,297,190	46.3%
7	QLD	2,994,504	45.5%	1,908,472	44.9%	4,902,976	45.3%
8	SA	3,175,226	46.6%	2,488,874	45.9%	5,664,100	46.3%
9	VIC	3,227,277	43.2%	2,222,616	45.6%	5,449,893	44.2%
10	WA	2,195,034	48.9%	1,679,117	42.6%	3,874,150	46.2%
11	Grand Total	14,874,106	45.5%	11,314,202	45.8%	26,188,308	45.6%

FIGURE 6.14 Margin % Field Formatted

	A	B	C	D	E	F	G
1							
2							
3		Column Labels					
4		Gadget		Widget		Total Sum of Value	Total Margin %
5	Row Labels	Sum of Value	Margin %	Sum of Value	Margin %		
6	NSW	3,282,066	44.6%	3,015,124	48.2%	6,297,190	46.3%
7	QLD	2,994,504	45.5%	1,908,472	44.9%	4,902,976	45.3%
8	SA	3,175,226	46.6%	2,488,874	45.9%	5,664,100	46.3%
9	VIC	3,227,277	43.2%	2,222,616	45.6%	5,449,893	44.2%
10	WA	2,195,034	48.9%	1,679,117	42.6%	3,874,150	46.2%
11	Grand Total	14,874,106	45.5%	11,314,202	45.8%	26,188,308	45.6%

FIGURE 6.15 Corrected Margin % Field

Calculated Fields are shared when a pivot table cache is shared.

I have included a macro on the companion website that removes the "Sum of" prefix from pivot table headings. There is also a macro that removes them from all the pivot tables in a file.

Calculated Item A Calculated Item adds another record to a field. It allows you to do a calculation within a field. It's probably best explained with an example.

The data set used for the pivot table in Figure 6.16 has an account number and an account type. All the values are positive. Hence, a positive revenue value is a credit, and a positive expense value is a debit. This makes it impossible to calculate a profit per department in a standard pivot table. A Calculated Item can solve this problem. The grand total column doesn't work, in this case.

To insert a profit item, you need to select the heading in cell B4 or C4 and then click the Fields, Items & Sets icon in the Options Ribbon tab. This allows you build a new item in a field based on values within the field. Figure 6.17 shows the dialog box used to create the new Item.

The Items selection list contains all the entries within the chosen field. You can then use those items to perform calculations. In our case, we are subtracting the expense values from the revenue values to arrive at a profit. See Figure 6.18 for the result.

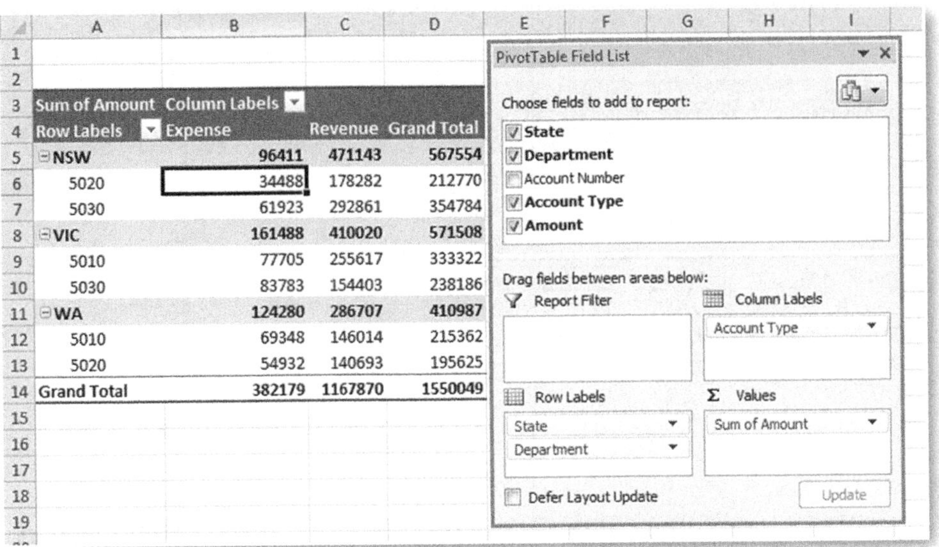

Sum of Amount	Column Labels		
Row Labels	Expense	Revenue	Grand Total
⊟NSW	96411	471143	567554
5020	34488	178282	212770
5030	61923	292861	354784
⊟VIC	161488	410020	571508
5010	77705	255617	333322
5030	83783	154403	238186
⊟WA	124280	286707	410987
5010	69348	146014	215362
5020	54932	140693	195625
Grand Total	382179	1167870	1550049

FIGURE 6.16 Expense and Revenue Data Set

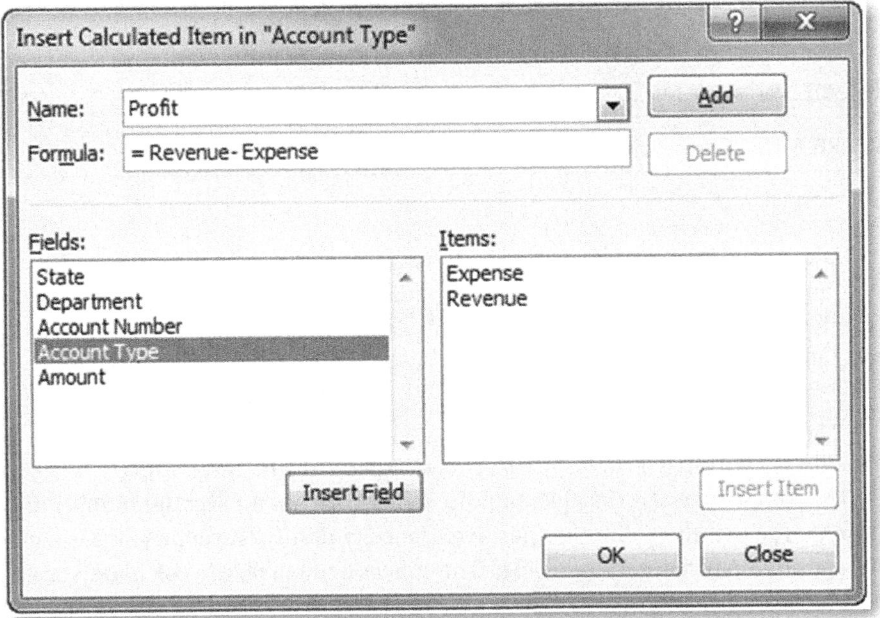

FIGURE 6.17 Insert Calculated Item Dialog Box

The grand total column has been removed. Expense is shown first because the pivot table displays the field items alphabetically.

You can drag the Revenue heading cell and move it to the left of the Expense cell to create a more standard layout (see Figure 6.19).

Calculated Items are shared when a pivot table cache is shared.

	A	B	C	D
1				
2				
3	Sum of Amount	Column Labels		
4	Row Labels	Expense	Revenue	Profit
5	⊟NSW	**96,411**	**471,143**	**374,732**
6	5010			0
7	5020	34,488	178,282	143,794
8	5030	61,923	292,861	230,938
9	⊟VIC	**161,488**	**410,020**	**248,532**
10	5010	77,705	255,617	177,912
11	5020			0
12	5030	83,783	154,403	70,620
13	⊟WA	**124,280**	**286,707**	**162,427**
14	5010	69,348	146,014	76,666
15	5020	54,932	140,693	85,761
16	5030			0
17	**Grand Total**	**382,179**	**1,167,870**	**785,691**

FIGURE 6.18 Profit Calculated via Pivot Table

	A	B	C	D
1				
2				
3	Sum of Amount	Column Labels		
4	Row Labels	Revenue	Expense	Profit
5	⊟NSW	**471,143**	**96,411**	**374,732**
6	5010			0
7	5020	178,282	34,488	143,794
8	5030	292,861	61,923	230,938
9	⊟VIC	**410,020**	**161,488**	**248,532**
10	5010	255,617	77,705	177,912
11	5020			0
12	5030	154,403	83,783	70,620
13	⊟WA	**286,707**	**124,280**	**162,427**
14	5010	146,014	69,348	76,666
15	5020	140,693	54,932	85,761
16	5030			0
17	**Grand Total**	**1,167,870**	**382,179**	**785,691**

FIGURE 6.19 Profit Calculated via Pivot Table Revenue on Left

Grouping

Another useful feature in pivot tables is the Group option. This is most commonly used to group dates. The Group option can also be used to create subtotals for groups of similar entries.

In our earlier example in Figure 6.15, I will add a subtotal for the States NSW, QLD, and VIC; these are commonly called the Eastern States. To create the group, it's as easy as using the Ctrl key with the mouse to select the three cells containing the states and then clicking the Group Selection icon on the Options Ribbon tab.

You can then click the Group cell (A6) and overwrite it with a descriptive name (see Figure 6.20).

Dates are the most commonly grouped items and have many built-in grouping options. Our initial sales database has individual invoice dates. We can summarise them by month.

Placing the Date field in the Rows area will list the daily sales (see Figure 6.21).

	A	B	C	D	E	F	G
1							
2							
3		Column Labels					
4		Gadget		Widget		Total Sum of Value	Total Margin %
5	Row Labels	Sum of Value	Margin %	Sum of Value	Margin %		
6	Eastern States						
7	NSW	3,282,066	44.6%	3,015,124	48.2%	6,297,190	46.3%
8	QLD	2,994,504	45.5%	1,908,472	44.9%	4,902,976	45.3%
9	VIC	3,227,277	43.2%	2,222,616	45.6%	5,449,893	44.2%
10	SA						
11	SA	3,175,226	46.6%	2,488,874	45.9%	5,664,100	46.3%
12	WA						
13	WA	2,195,034	48.9%	1,679,117	42.6%	3,874,150	46.2%
14	Grand Total	14,874,106	45.5%	11,314,202	45.8%	26,188,308	45.6%

FIGURE 6.20 Grouped by States Pivot Table

	A	B	C	D	E	F	G
1							
2							
3	Sum of Value	Column Labels					
4	Row Labels	NSW	QLD	SA	VIC	WA	Grand Total
5	1/01/2014	18,166	13,634	19,458	21,543	1,674	74,475
6	2/01/2014	14,570	13,560	21,852	16,835	6,055	72,872
7	3/01/2014	8,437	15,344	14,015	10,237	4,410	52,443
8	4/01/2014	22,189	7,544	17,837	8,981	21,684	78,235
9	5/01/2014	39,276	9,975	7,969	14,801	21,560	93,582
10	6/01/2014	14,998	25,129	10,295	7,725	11,865	70,011
11	7/01/2014	23,582	12,897	13,961	13,096	2,465	66,001

FIGURE 6.21 Daily Sales by States Pivot Table

Usually you want to summarise by month. To group the date column, right-click on one of the date cells and choose Group. The Grouping dialog box (see Figure 6.22) will display.

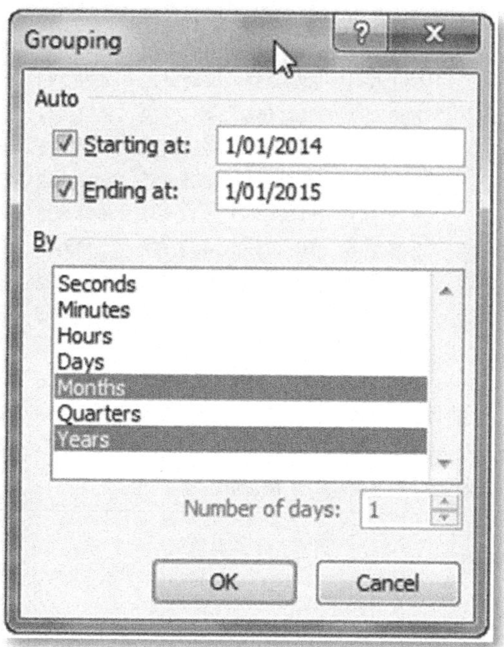

FIGURE 6.22 Grouping Dialog

As you can see, there are lots of options to choose from. If your data might contain more than one year's results, make sure to use the Ctrl key to select both the Months and the Years options, as shown in Figure 6.22. If you just select Months, for example, all the January sales for all the years will be summarised in the January month. Figure 6.23 shows the grouped report.

Grouping is also shared when a pivot table cache is shared.

The PivotTable Tools—Design Tab

When the pivot table is selected, the PivotTable Tools—Design tab controls what the pivot table looks like.

There are built-in formats similar to formatted tables. You can also create your own formats by using the New Pivot Table Style option at the bottom of the Pivot Table Styles drop-down list.

The icons on the left of the Design tab allow you to handle pivot table layout, totals, and blank rows.

	A	B	C	D	E	F	G
1							
2							
3	**Sum of Value**	**Column Labels**					
4	**Row Labels**	**NSW**	**QLD**	**SA**	**VIC**	**WA**	**Grand Total**
5	**⊟2014**						
6	Jan	518,523	465,056	484,134	444,319	321,200	2,233,231
7	Feb	439,382	438,338	460,011	394,085	322,351	2,054,166
8	Mar	561,533	383,453	441,470	459,799	333,703	2,179,958
9	Apr	566,092	408,166	459,712	483,737	273,887	2,191,594
10	May	545,536	418,082	454,884	434,119	367,832	2,220,452
11	Jun	510,194	412,121	505,365	402,488	295,352	2,125,521
12	Jul	518,341	448,474	441,961	464,893	397,432	2,271,102
13	Aug	503,706	393,383	467,713	508,645	280,707	2,154,155
14	Sep	505,708	348,322	457,714	442,707	334,882	2,089,333
15	Oct	473,792	395,209	507,282	541,642	301,233	2,219,158
16	Nov	569,589	444,316	490,270	385,998	353,306	2,243,479
17	Dec	584,794	348,057	493,583	487,460	292,266	2,206,160
18	**Grand Total**	**6,297,190**	**4,902,976**	**5,664,100**	**5,449,893**	**3,874,150**	**26,188,308**

FIGURE 6.23 Grouping by Months and Years

External Data

Excel can extract data from most commonly used databases. This means that the data does not reside in the spreadsheet file.

Excel still creates a cache of the data from the database in memory.

WARNING: Data Tables

Extracting data from modern databases is not always straightforward. Databases are table-based systems, and there are usually many related tables. Not all the data you require may be in a single data table. Remember that a pivot table can work with only one data table at a time.

This can be handled by creating a view. A *view* is a summary of multiple data tables that can be interrogated just like a data table. Sometimes the view you need already exists. If not, then you will need to involve the database administrator to build a view for you to use.

The other problem you may face is understanding all the fields involved and what they contain. Sometimes field names are abbreviated, and their contents may not be obvious from their names. Again, you may need to work with the database administrator, who can usually provide a detailed mapping of what all the fields are and what they contain.

In most cases, getting directly to the data in your organisation will involve your information technology (IT) section. This is because the servers that hold the data will typically be password-protected, and the IT section will also know the paths to get to the data.

You need to establish a link to the data source only once. After that, it is just a question of choosing it when you choose External to create a pivot table.

I will use an Access database to demonstrate using external data to create a pivot table.

Example

Click the Data Ribbon tab and click the From Access icon on the far left. When you go to the Access database file and double-click it to open it, the Import data dialog box will be displayed (see Figure 6.24).

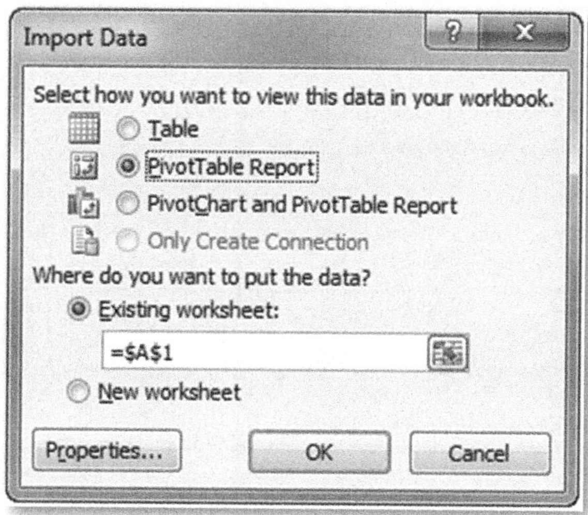

FIGURE 6.24 Import Data Dialog Box

If you are unsure of the data structure, then it can be useful to first use the Table option. This will insert the table of data onto the sheet. You can then review the table to gain a better understanding of the type of data it contains.

The Properties button allows you to set the automatic refreshing options. Figure 6.25 shows the connection options.

Select the Pivot Table Report option and click OK. You can add a pivot chart later, if you wish. We will examine pivot charts later in the chapter.

You will be presented with the same blank pivot table and Pivot Table Field List that you normally see when creating a pivot table; the only difference is that the data is not in the file.

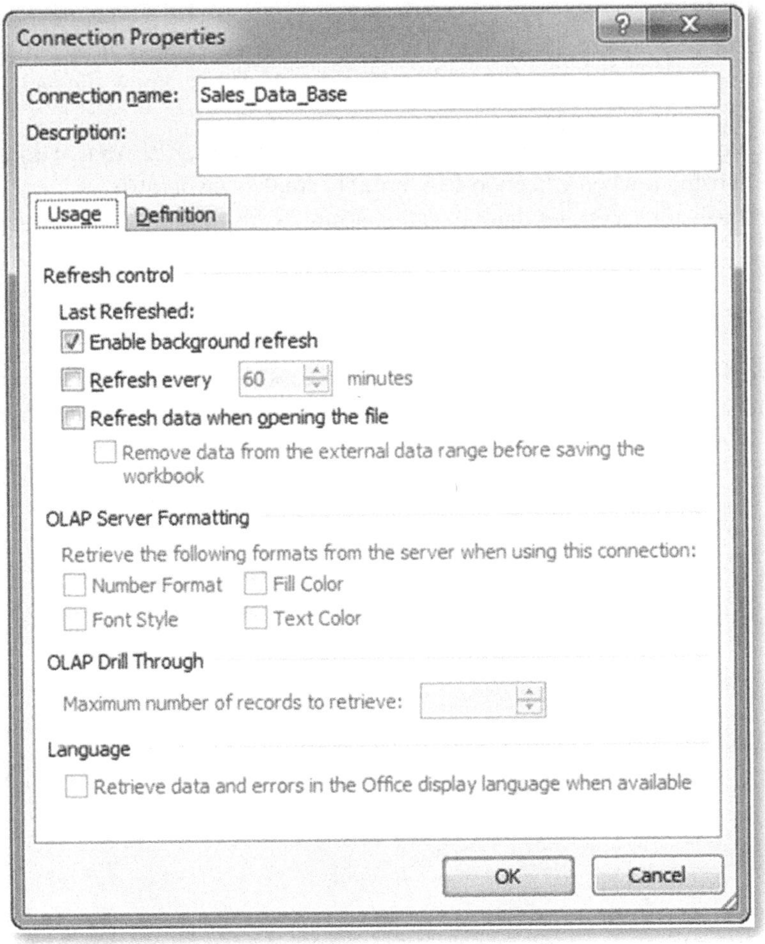

FIGURE 6.25 Connection Properties Dialog

Other Data Sources

The other icons on the left of the Data Ribbon tab provide connections to other data sources.

The From Text icon allows connections to CSV and TXT files.

The From Other Sources icon (see Figure 6.26) allows you to connect to most types of databases. As I mentioned, you will need to involve your IT section to create connections. It is a onetime process. Once established, the connection is then available through the Choose Connection button in the Insert Pivot Table dialog box.

Pivot Charts

A pivot chart requires a pivot table. The pivot chart and the pivot table display the same information. Although you can have more than one pivot chart linked to a pivot table, the data shown on all the pivot charts will be the same.

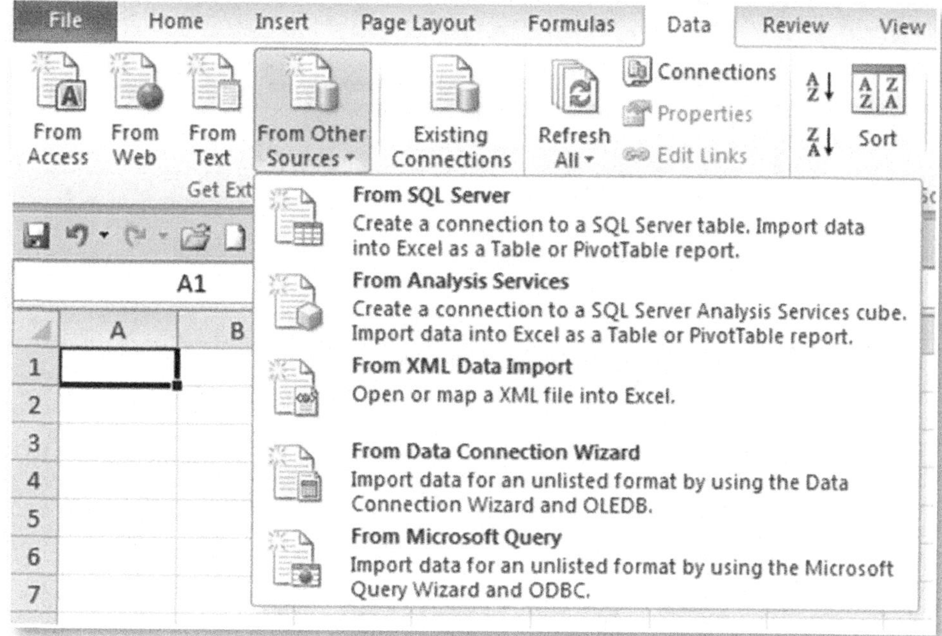

FIGURE 6.26 From Other Sources Drop-Down Selection

Pivot charts allow for easy data selection through the Filter icons on the pivot chart itself. All filter changes made to the chart are mirrored on the pivot table. The pivot chart plots the whole pivot table.

All the common chart types are available to be used as a pivot chart.

Excel 2010 reverted back to displaying the field headings on the pivot chart. Excel 2007 had removed them.

I find pivot charts difficult to work with. To be useful, pivot tables tend to be fairly large. For a chart to be readable, the source data has to be reasonably compact. These two requirements are at cross-purposes. So you probably need one pivot table to provide a useful report and a separate pivot table to provide a readable chart.

The process of creating a pivot chart is easy. Simply select any cell within the pivot table and click the Pivot Chart icon on the Options tab. Select Chart Type and click OK.

The Product and State drop-down selections shown in Figure 6.27 allow you to change what the chart is plotting. Remember that changing the pivot chart changes the pivot table.

Charts are covered in more depth in Chapter 12.

Other Display Options

Pivot tables are predominantly used to add up and summarise large data sets, but they can do much more. The options shown under the Show Values As icon on the Options Ribbon tab offer many other useful reports (see Figure 6.28).

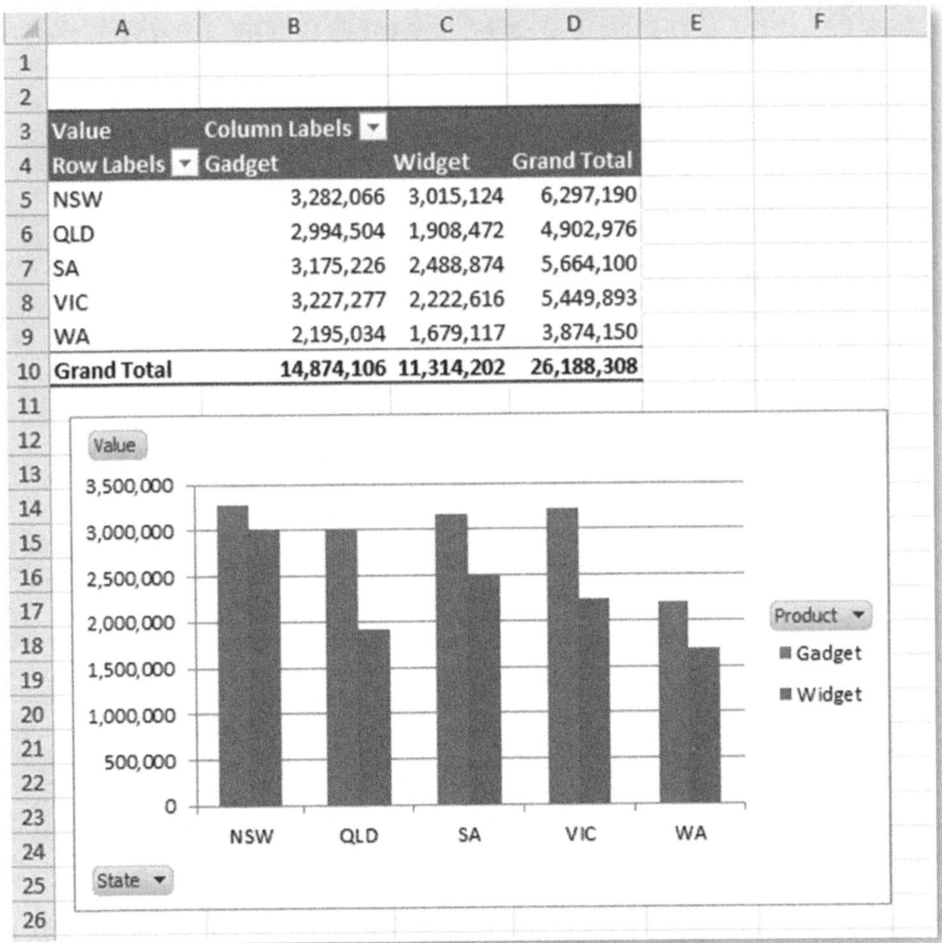

Value	Column Labels		
Row Labels	Gadget	Widget	Grand Total
NSW	3,282,066	3,015,124	6,297,190
QLD	2,994,504	1,908,472	4,902,976
SA	3,175,226	2,488,874	5,664,100
VIC	3,227,277	2,222,616	5,449,893
WA	2,195,034	1,679,117	3,874,150
Grand Total	**14,874,106**	**11,314,202**	**26,188,308**

FIGURE 6.27 Pivot Chart

The Difference options are useful for budget variance reports. Reports based on some of the options are shown in Figure 6.29.

POWERPIVOT

The free PowerPivot add-in for Excel 2010 is easily the most advanced data handling feature Excel has ever had. It has been incorporated in Excel 2013 and improved.

Even though it is a new feature, it is based on software that has a long history and is robust. It provides Excel with features and abilities seen only in advanced database programs.

Power Pivot is a feature-rich add-in that requires study and practice to master. It has its own formula language called DAX. This language is similar to Excel's functions. Many Excel functions can be used in the same way with DAX.

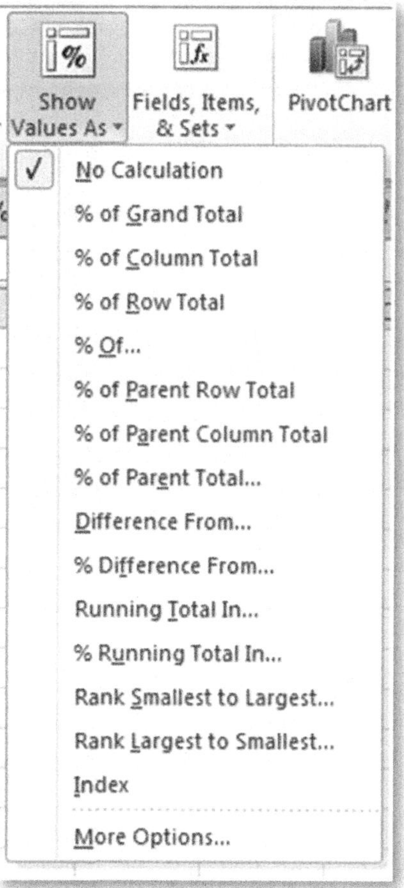

FIGURE 6.28 Show Values As Icon Options

PowerPivot has dedicated functions that have built-in business rules. For example, functions are built to automatically handle month-to-date and year-to-date calculations.

If you do any data analysis or manipulation, the PowerPivot add-in is worth the effort to learn. I have included two books on the companion website's reading list on PowerPivot.

Detailed coverage of the PowerPivot add-in is beyond the scope of this book.

	A	B	C	D
1	% of Grand Total			
2				
3	Value	Column Labels		
4	Row Labels	Gadget	Widget	Grand Total
5	NSW	12.53%	11.51%	24.05%
6	QLD	11.43%	7.29%	18.72%
7	SA	12.12%	9.50%	21.63%
8	VIC	12.32%	8.49%	20.81%
9	WA	8.38%	6.41%	14.79%
10	**Grand Total**	**56.80%**	**43.20%**	**100.00%**

	A	B	C	D
1	% of Column Total			
2				
3	Value	Column Labels		
4	Row Labels	Gadget	Widget	Grand Total
5	NSW	22.07%	26.65%	24.05%
6	QLD	20.13%	16.87%	18.72%
7	SA	21.35%	22.00%	21.63%
8	VIC	21.70%	19.64%	20.81%
9	WA	14.76%	14.84%	14.79%
10	**Grand Total**	**100.00%**	**100.00%**	**100.00%**

	A	B	C	D
1	% of Row Total			
2				
3	Value	Column Labels		
4	Row Labels	Gadget	Widget	Grand Total
5	NSW	52.12%	47.88%	100.00%
6	QLD	61.08%	38.92%	100.00%
7	SA	56.06%	43.94%	100.00%
8	VIC	59.22%	40.78%	100.00%
9	WA	56.66%	43.34%	100.00%
10	**Grand Total**	**56.80%**	**43.20%**	**100.00%**

	A	B	C	D
1	Rank Largest To Smallest			
2				
3	Value	Column Labels		
4	Row Labels	Gadget	Widget	Grand Total
5	NSW	1	1	1
6	QLD	4	4	4
7	SA	3	2	2
8	VIC	2	3	3
9	WA	5	5	5
10	**Grand Total**			

FIGURE 6.29 Show Values As Report Examples

CHAPTER SEVEN

Tools of the Trade: Summing Functions

SUMMING FUNCTIONS WILL BE THE main function tools you use in constructing your report. With the right data structure, building the reports should be reasonably straightforward. If a data set has exceptions or any anomalies, then other functions may be needed.

Before looking at Excel's summing functions, I will first cover a few basics of formula creation to ensure a correct understanding of how you can refer to ranges and the uses of relative, fixed, and mixed references. These apply to all formulas, not just summing functions.

Tip: Formula Entry

You can start any formula with a plus sign. After you press the Enter key, Excel will automatically insert the equal sign for you.

I prefer to use the plus sign because there is a large plus sign key on the far right of your keyboard. (I tend to spend a lot of time on that side of the keyboard. Some people call it the accountant's keypad.) This plus sign key is much easier to use than the equal sign key at the end of the numbers row on the standard keyboard. When you are creating hundreds of formulas, this difference adds up and can save a lot of time.

When training accountants, I don't usually have to convince them to make full use the keyboard's numeric keypad. For developing reports, this keypad has most of the keys you will need to build all your formulas. The large plus sign and Enter keys, combined with the calculator style number layout, are ideal for formula creation.

RANGE NAMES

Range names work well with all types of functions, but they are especially useful when using summing functions to develop reporting models.

I have left the topic of range names until after the coverage of all the functions. Once you have experienced using formulas without range names, you will have a greater appreciation of the advantages of using range names.

Also, having a good grounding in the use of references will assist in creating more useful range names. Range names are covered in depth in Chapter 9.

USING CELLS AND RANGES IN FORMULAS

Many formulas that you create will be copied to other cells. To make sure they remain correct in those other cells, you need a good understanding of relative, fixed, and mixed references.

It is important to make sure you also have a clear understanding of how to use the $ symbol in your cell and range references within a formula.

When copying formulas to the left, right, up, or down, it is important to be aware of the relative nature of formulas.

The ultimate goal of a formula is to be able to copy it across and down as far as necessary without having to change the formula. To achieve this, you have to use a combination of relative, fixed, and mixed references. Helper cells, discussed later in the chapter, can make achieving this goal possible.

Relative References

Relative references are the standard references you see in Excel when you build a formula with the keyboard or the mouse. They serve an important purpose, but in advanced formulas you will usually need to amend some relative references.

The following are examples of relative references:

C:C is a reference to the entire column C. This will change only if you copy it to the left or the right.

10:10 is a reference to the entire row 10. This will vary only as you copy it up or down.

A1:C100 is a reference to a range. It will vary wherever you copy it, unless you copy it to the same cell on another sheet.

Fixed References

The $ symbol fixes whatever it is placed in front of. Fixing a reference means that it doesn't change as you copy it. Fixed references have the $ in front of all their column and row references. You use a fixed reference when you do not want the cell or range to change as you copy the formula to a new cell or cells. Many advanced formulas require fixing some component of the formula to enable it to work. Fixed references are also known as *absolute references*.

Tip: Shortcut for the $ Symbol

When editing a formula in most Excel dialog boxes, you can add the $ symbol to references by clicking on or next to a reference and pressing the F4 function key. Each press changes the reference in the sequence $A$1 > $A1 > A$1 > A1. If you keep pressing, it keeps toggling through that sequence.

If you select a range or more references and then press the F4 key, it will amend all the selected references.

It's easy to remember that the F4 function key is the shortcut for the $ symbol because the number 4 key has the $ above it.

The following are all examples of fixed references:

$C:$C is a reference to the entire column C.
$10:$10 is a reference to the entire row 10.
$A$1:$C$100 is a reference to a range.

Mixed References

Mixed references fix only one part of the reference, leaving the other part to change as it is copied. Formulas in report layouts frequently use mixed references.

The following are all mixed references:

$C:C is a reference to column C. The first reference to column C won't change. The second reference to C will vary if pasted to the left or the right.

$10:10 is a reference to row 10. The first reference to row 10 won't change. The second reference will vary if pasted above or below.

A$1:C$100 is a reference to a range. The row references in this range reference won't vary, but the column references may vary depending on where it is pasted.

Summary of Reference Types

There are four different types of cell references (see Table 7.1).

TABLE 7.1 Cell Reference Types

Reference	Reference Type	Description
A1	Relative	This type of cell reference will vary relative to where it is copied from and to. Both rows and columns may vary.
$A$1	Fixed	This type of cell reference will not vary, no matter where it is copied to.
A$1	Mixed	The row reference will not vary, but the column reference will vary if copied to the right.
$A1	Mixed	The column will not vary, but the row reference will vary if copied down.

Using Fixed and Mixed References

Figure 7.1 shows a report allocating costs across months.

	H	I	J	K	L	M	N	O	P	Q	R	S	T	U	V	W
7	**Allocate costs in Column J between months based on Calendar days**															
8																
9				Jul-13	Aug-13	Sep-13	Oct-13	Nov-13	Dec-13	Jan-14	Feb-14	Mar-14	Apr-14	May-14	Jun-14	Total
10		Calendar Days		31	31	30	31	30	31	31	28	31	30	31	30	365
11																
12		Cost 1	5,000	425	425	411	425	411	425	425	384	425	411	425	411	5,000
13		Cost 2	3,000	255	255	247	255	247	255	255	230	255	247	255	247	3,000
14		Cost 3	10,000	849	849	822	849	822	849	849	767	849	822	849	822	10,000
15		Cost 4	15,000	1,274	1,274	1,233	1,274	1,233	1,274	1,274	1,151	1,274	1,233	1,274	1,233	15,000
16		Cost 5	7,000	595	595	575	595	575	595	595	537	595	575	595	575	7,000
17		Total Costs	40,000	3,397	3,397	3,288	3,397	3,288	3,397	3,397	3,068	3,397	3,288	3,397	3,288	40,000

FIGURE 7.1 Fixed and Mixed Reference Example

Cell K12 contains a formula that does the allocation calculation. The formula is

```
=$J12*K$10/$W$10
```

This formula can be copied across to the range L12:V12 and down to the range K13:V16. It has an example of two mixed references and a fixed reference.

In this example we need to allocate the costs in column J across to columns K to V based on the number of calendar days in row 10.

This means we need to fix the cost reference to column J so that the column reference doesn't change as we copy it across. Hence the $ is placed in front of the J. The row number for the costs has to vary, so it is left relative.

The calendar days in row 10 have to be the same for all rows below, so that row needs to be fixed. The $ goes in front of the 10. The column letter has to vary as we copy it across, so it is left relative.

The total number of days in cell W10 has to remain fixed as cells are copied both down and across, so both column and row references are fixed with the $.

Alternative Fixed and Mixed Formulas

In the previous example, the initial formula in cell K12 referred to specific cells. A little-known technique allows you to refer to ranges and have them be treated like cells.

Two alternative formulas can achieve exactly the same result. The first is

```
=$J$12:$J$16*$K$10:$V$10/$W$10
```

This is a longer formula than the cell-based formula. The two mixed references have been replaced by fixed range references.

When the range reference is used in the above formula, Excel uses the cell's corresponding row from $J$12:$J$16 and the corresponding column from $K$10:$V$10. This means you can fix both ranges without having to consider whether to fix the row or the column.

An advantage of this technique is that all the formulas in the range K12:V16 will be identical. When you use cell-based formulas, the formulas will vary slightly as they are copied across and down.

There is a shorter variation on the above formula, which is

```
=$J:$J*$10:$10/$W$10
```

Alternative Fixed and Mixed Formulas (*Continued*)

This variation fixes the entire column J and the entire row 10. Referring repeatedly to whole rows and columns can affect the calculation speed of your reports.

The last two examples work in a similar fashion to range names, which will be discussed in Chapter 9.

There are three different types of row references (see Table 7.2) and three types of column references (see Table 7.3). Table 7.4 shows the range reference types.

TABLE 7.2 Row Reference Types

Reference	Reference Type	Description
1:1	Relative	This single-row reference will vary when copied down. If copied up, it would result in a #REF! error. When copied across, it will not vary.
$1:$1	Fixed	This single-row reference will not vary no matter where you copy it to.
$1:1	Mixed	This single-row reference will change to a multirow reference as you copy it down. The second 1 in the reference will change relative to the destination cell. Copying up would result in a #REF! error.

TABLE 7.3 Column Reference Types

Reference	Reference Type	Description
A:A	Relative	This single-column reference will vary when copied to the right. If copied to the left, it would result in a #REF! error.
$A:$A	Fixed	This single-column reference will not vary, no matter where you copy it to.
$A:A	Mixed	This single-column reference will change to a multicolumn reference as you copy it to the right. The second A reference will change relative to the destination cell. If copied to the left, it would return a #REF! error.

TABLE 7.4 Range Reference Types

Reference	Reference Type	Description
A1:A100	Relative	The row references will vary relatively if copied down, and the column references will vary if copied across.
$A$1:$A$100	Fixed	None of the references will vary, no matter where they are copied to.
$A$1:A100	Mixed	The reference to A1 won't vary, but the A100 will vary depending on where it is copied to.
A$1:A$100	Mixed	The row references won't vary, but the column references will vary if copied to the right.
$A1:$A100	Mixed	The column references won't vary, but the row references will vary if copied down.

Copying within a Formula

When writing IF functions, you sometimes need to have the same part of the formula duplicated. You can select part of a formula and use Ctrl + c to copy; then move the cursor to where you want, and use Ctrl + v to paste.

If you are referring to references on other sheets, this can save time by reducing the number of times you have to go back to the sheet and select the reference. You could also copy the reference and amend it to refer to another reference on the other sheet to save time.

Techniques for Avoiding Relative Reference Changes

There are two copy techniques in Excel that won't change relative references. They both copy the formula with no modifications. Which one you use depends on where the formula is and where you want to copy it to.

Both of these techniques work with only one cell and cannot be used to copy ranges of formulas.

Copying the Formula Above If the formula you want to copy is in the cell above, use Ctrl + ' (Ctrl + single opening quotation mark, or inverted apostrophe). The formula that is copied down is identical to the one in the cell above. This also works for text and numbers.

Copying to Any Other Cell If you need to copy the formula to any other location, select the whole formula in the Formula Bar, copy it, press Esc, then go to the destination cell and paste.

You press Esc to stop editing in the current cell. If you don't press Esc, you will edit the formula, and if you just click the destination cell, you will overwrite the existing formula with the cell reference. As an alternative to pressing Esc, you can click the checkmark or X to the left of the Formula Bar.

THE HUMBLE SUM FUNCTION

The SUM function is easily the most used function in Excel. It has its own icon and a keyboard shortcut. For use in advanced reports, it has one feature that is not widely known or used. It has another feature that applies to many other functions as well, but many users are unaware of it as well. It's not advanced, but it is useful.

Have you ever seen or written a formula like this?

```
=SUM(A1:A100)+SUM(D1:D100)
```

If so, you can benefit from this little-used technique. The SUM function can accept more than one range within its parentheses. You just separate the ranges with commas. The above formula can be rewritten as

```
=SUM(A1:A100,D1:D100)
```

The ranges can be any length, even whole columns, and can also be individual cells as long as they are separated by commas. This ability applies to most functions that usually just accept a single range within the parentheses, such as COUNT, COUNTA, AVERAGE, MIN, and MAX.

ADVANCED SUM AND 3D FORMULAS

Assume you have a number of sheets that are identically laid out. Each sheet might represent a state. A typical requirement is to add up the same cell on each sheet. Suppose it's a total cost cell and you want to add up all the states. The most common method for doing this is to create a simple formula to add together the same cell on each sheet. It might look like this:

```
=+WA!K20+NT!K20+SA!K20+VIC!K20+NSW!K20+QLD!K20
```

This is a long formula and takes a number of keystrokes and mouse movements to create. The amount of effort is directly related to the number of sheets involved. Double the number of sheets, and the effort is doubled.

There is a much easier way that takes the same time and effort no matter how many sheets are involved. Once created, this technique is extremely flexible and allows you to simply move a sheet to include or exclude it from the calculation.

The SUM function can easily add up the same cell or range in every sheet. It is called a 3D formula, and other functions can also perform 3D calculations. The AVERAGE, COUNTA, MIN, and MAX are some of the other functions that can work with 3D ranges.

This is a powerful feature. The sheets don't have to be completely identical. As long as the range to sum is identical on all the sheets, the technique will work. This means that the top of the sheets (e.g., the first 20 rows and 10 columns) may be identical, but the remaining part of the sheets can be different. In practical terms, this makes the top section a summary and the bottom section the details, where you can have a different layout and calculations.

The typical use for the 3D SUM is when the sheets represent states, departments, divisions, or any other category that you may use to segment your organization.

To see how the 3D SUM works, let's view an example.

Placeholder Sheet Naming

The formulas used in the 3D examples are all short because the blank sheet names are single letters. The naming of the placeholder sheets is a personal preference. I have seen

3D SUM Example

There are six state sheets, named NSW, VIC, QLD, SA, NT, WA. These are the mainland Australian states. There are three regions: West, Central, and East. West contains WA, Central contains NT and SA, and East contains NSW, VIC, and QLD. The state sheets are structured identically.

A summary report is required for all states, and one summary for each region.

When you use a 3D formula, the sequence of the sheets in the file is important. Normally the location of a sheet has no effect on any calculations done to it. With a 3D formula, the location of the sheet in relation to the other sheets is extremely important.

This technique also uses blank sheets as placeholders, like bookends, to increase its flexibility. The benefits of this will become apparent as we go through the example.

(continued)

3D SUM Example (*Continued*)

Examine the layout of the state sheets. Figure 7.2 shows the report for WA.

$'000	YTD		
WA	**Actuals**	**Budget**	**Variance**
Sales	1,550	1,400	150
Costs Of Sales	1,250	1,100	-150
Gross Margin	**300**	**300**	**0**
Overheads	200	175	-25
Net Profit	**100**	**125**	**-25**

FIGURE 7.2 State Report Layout for WA

This technique is possible because all the state sheets are identically structured. The cells we want to summarise are K8, K9, K11, L8, L9, and L11.

The summary sheet has exactly the same layout as the state sheets (see Figure 7.3).

$'000	YTD		
All Regions	**Actuals**	**Budget**	**Variance**
Sales			0
Costs Of Sales			0
Gross Margin	0	0	0
Overheads			0
Net Profit	0	0	0

FIGURE 7.3 Summary Report Layout

There is another part to this technique that makes it more flexible. There are two blank sheets, named *a* and *z*. Their role in this technique will become apparent once we have created the summary sheet. Figure 7.4 shows the current layout of the sheets.

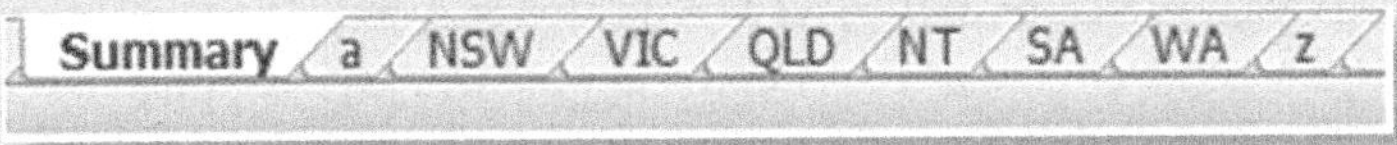

Summary | a | NSW | VIC | QLD | NT | SA | WA | z

FIGURE 7.4 Sheet Tab Structure, a to z

On the summary sheet in cell K8, click the AutoSum button, click sheet tab a, and select cell K8.

Here is the secret to this technique. Hold the Shift key down, click sheet tab z, and then press Enter.

The 3D SUM function has been created. Examine the formula:

```
=SUM(a:z!K8)
```

As you can see, the formula is short. It was also quick to create. It says to sum up cell K8 in every sheet from a to z inclusive. That is why both sheets a and z are

3D SUM Example (*Continued*)

blank, so that they do not affect the calculation. You can copy the formula across and down for all the other required cells.

Because the formula is so short, you could also type it. Using single-letter sheet names makes typing 3D formulas quite easy.

Sheets a and z are placeholder sheets. Their role is to provide the flexibility to move sheets in and out of the SUM range.

3D formulas are based on the position of the sheets in the file. If you moved WA to the right of the z sheet, it would be removed from the above 3D SUM formula and not be included in the result. This is where the flexibility comes in. Simply moving a sheet can amend the summary report.

For another example, let's create a summary report for the East region, which includes three states. To create the East region structure, we can add a blank sheet named *b* between QLD and NT (see Figure 7.5).

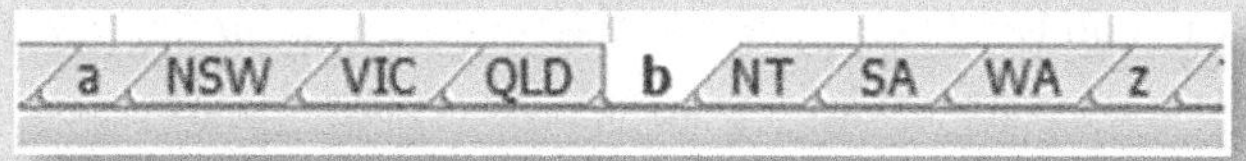

FIGURE 7.5 Summary Report Layout a, b, and z

We can copy the structure of the summary report and paste it below where it was (see Figure 7.6).

	I	J	K	L	M
14					
15		$'000		YTD	
16		**East Region**	**Actuals**	**Budget**	**Variance**
17		Sales			0
18		Costs Of Sales			0
19		**Gross Margin**	0	0	0
20		Overheads			0
21		**Net Profit**	0	0	0

FIGURE 7.6 Summary Report East Region

We can copy the formula from the Formula Bar from cell K8 and paste it in cell K17 and amend the formula to

```
=SUM(a:b!K8)
```

This summarises the East region.

If we add another blank sheet, named c, between sheets SA and WA (see Figure 7.7), we can then create formulas to summarise the Central and West regions, respectively:

```
=SUM(b:c!K8)
=SUM(c:z!K8)
```

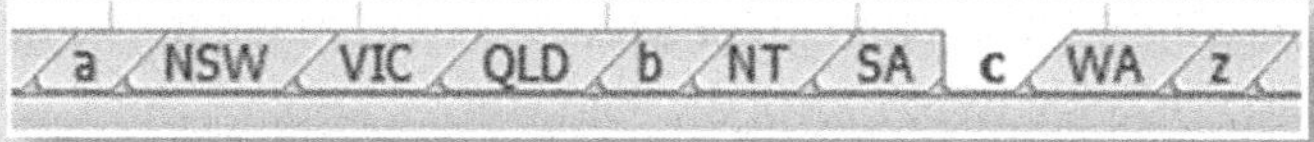

FIGURE 7.7 Summary Report Layout a, b, c, and z

the use of a single period, then two periods, three periods, and so on as the placeholder names. Using single lowercase letters of the alphabet ensures that they are not confused with column references, and you can use the alphabet in sequence. If you are doing only one 3D sum, you can also use names like Start and End, which makes the 3D formula more meaningful.

3D Flexibility

The use of the placeholder sheets means that to move a state from one region to another is as simple as moving the state sheet to a different place in the file. Moving the placeholder sheet will also change the region calculation.

If we need to add a new state sheet for Australia's island state, TAS, in the East region, we can simply copy one of the existing sheets in that region, rename it TAS, and ensure that it is between the a sheet and the b sheet. It will automatically be included in the East region and will be in the total calculation on the summary sheet. No formula change is required.

Without the use of placeholder sheets, certain states would become the placeholder sheet in the 3D SUM formula, and this would reduce the flexibility of the technique.

Let's say you decide to amalgamate the Central region with the West region. All you need to do is move the c sheet to the right of the b sheet, and it is done. The Central region will be zeroed, and the West region will contain SA, NT, and WA.

3D Inflexibility

The fact that the sheet layouts have to be identical for this technique to work is often seen as a drawback. But as I mentioned earlier, only the top section of the sheet has to be identical. This becomes the summary section of the sheet. The detail below that can be in a different layout on each sheet.

Excel's sheet grouping feature, which was discussed in Chapter 4, makes editing multiple identical sheets easy because you can select them all at once and make changes to all of them in one step. Remember to always deselect the grouped sheets when you're finished.

You need to make sure the layout incorporates all the measures you need to collect. This means that the measures will be zero on the sheets that don't use that measure. Otherwise, it is a one-size-fits-all technique to ensure that all measures are on all sheets.

SUBTOTALING

I have found that most people use the SUM function for all their subtotaling formulas. This typically creates a problem when you get to the grand total formula. In Figure 7.8 there are SUM functions in rows 12, 16, and 19.

When you use the SUM function, there are at least three options for the grand total in row 20. In J20 you could use either of the following:

```
=J12+J16+J19
=SUM(J12,J16,J19)
```

	H	I	J	K
6				
7		**Sales $,000**	**Actuals**	**Budget**
8		**East Region**		
9		NSW	2,056	2,000
10		VIC	1,832	1,800
11		QLD	1,562	1,600
12		**Total East**	**5,450**	**5,400**
13		**Central Region**		
14		NT	743	600
15		SA	921	800
16		**Total Central**	**1,664**	**1,400**
17		**West Region**		
18		WA	961	1,000
19		**Total West**	**961**	**1,000**
20		**Total All Regions**		

FIGURE 7.8 Subtotaling Example

The most creative solution, however, is

```
=SUM(J9:J19)/2
```

The last method attempts to handle a problem with the first two methods, which is that they do not handle a category being added. If you insert a new category, you have to modify the grand total row to include it.

The last method handles additional categories as long as the structure is maintained of detail followed by a subtotal. If a single-entry category is added to the list with no subtotal, the last technique doesn't work. In such a case, you are using the wrong tool for the job. Excel has a SUBTOTAL function that is built to handle subtotaling correctly.

THE SUBTOTAL FUNCTION

The SUBTOTAL function does more than just add up. It is a flexible function that can calculate averages, count, and do a few other useful operations. It has two advantages over the SUM function.

The first is that when used as a grand total, it ignores all other SUBTOTAL functions within its range, making it perfect for subtotaling.

The second is that up until Excel 2007, it was the only function that could perform calculations on visible cells only. Excel 2010 added the AGGREGATE function, which also performs calculations on visible cells. AGGREGATE, which is covered later in this chapter, has an advantage over SUBTOTAL.

Performing calculations on visible cells is a very useful ability. If you've ever been given a spreadsheet with hidden rows, you might wonder whether the hidden rows have any values. The SUBTOTAL function can help audit the sheet.

Hidden rows include those rows hidden manually using Hide Rows, rows hidden by Grouping, and rows hidden because of data filters being applied.

Syntax

SUBTOTAL (Function_Number, Range)

Function_Number is a number defining the function to use in the SUBTOTAL. For instance, 9 is used to SUM, and 109 is used to SUM visible cells only. Table 7.5 shows the other values.

Range is the range to use with the function.

TABLE 7.5 SUBTOTAL Function Numbers

Function_Number (Includes Hidden Values)	Function_Number (Excludes Hidden Values)	Function
1	101	AVERAGE
2	102	COUNT
3	103	COUNTA
4	104	MAX
5	105	MIN
6	106	PRODUCT
7	107	STDEV
8	108	STDEVP
9	109	SUM
10	110	VAR
11	111	VARP

Example

The following function will sum the range A2:A10, ignoring any SUBTOTAL cells within the range. The 9 defines the SUM function.

```
=SUBTOTAL(9,A2:A10)
```

Using the SUBTOTAL function is similar to using the SUM function. You just need to add the 9 before the range (see Figure 7.8).

In our example in Figure 7.8, the SUM functions in rows 12, 16, and 19 would be replaced by their corresponding SUBTOTAL functions.

For example, cell J12 would change from

```
=SUM(J9:J11)
```

It would become

```
=SUBTOTAL(9,J9:J11)
```

The grand total formula in row 20 would be

```
=SUBTOTAL(9,J9:J19)
```

This formula will handle any new categories added in the range J9:J19, whether they have a subtotal or not.

Unfortunately, there is no icon by which to insert the SUBTOTAL function. Because I use SUBTOTAL frequently, I wrote a macro that converts a standard SUM function into a standard SUBTOTAL function. This macro assumes a single range in the SUM function.

This allows you to create a number of SUM functions using the AutoSum icon and then select the range and convert all the SUM functions in the range to its corresponding SUBTOTAL function.

I have included the macro on the companion website.

Automated Subtotals

If you have a data list, Excel has a feature that can automatically insert SUBTOTAL functions into the list. Excel also automatically inserts Grouping along with the SUBTOTAL functions.

The only requirement to insert the subtotals is that the list must be sorted by the field (column) that you want to base the subtotal on. You can subtotal as many columns in the list as you want.

WARNING: Formatted Tables and Subtotals

Unfortunately, you can't use the automated subtotal feature on a formatted table.

Add Subtotals Automatically

The first step is to sort the table by the field to be subtotaled. Figure 7.9 has to be sorted by state.

	G	H	I	J
7				
8		State	Post Code	Amount
9		NSW	2000	1,145
10		VIC	3001	1,603
11		NSW	2010	1,681
12		QLD	4000	1,731
13		QLD	4002	1,790
14		QLD	4004	1,805
15		QLD	4008	2,401
16		QLD	4010	2,682
17		VIC	3009	2,773
18		VIC	3100	2,792
19		NSW	2002	2,833
20		VIC	3005	2,902

FIGURE 7.9 Automated Subtotaling Example

(continued)

Add Subtotals Automatically (*Continued*)

Right-click any cell in the table in the State column and choose Sort, then choose Sort A–Z.

With a cell selected in the table, click the Data Ribbon tab, then click the Subtotal icon on the far right, in the Outline section.

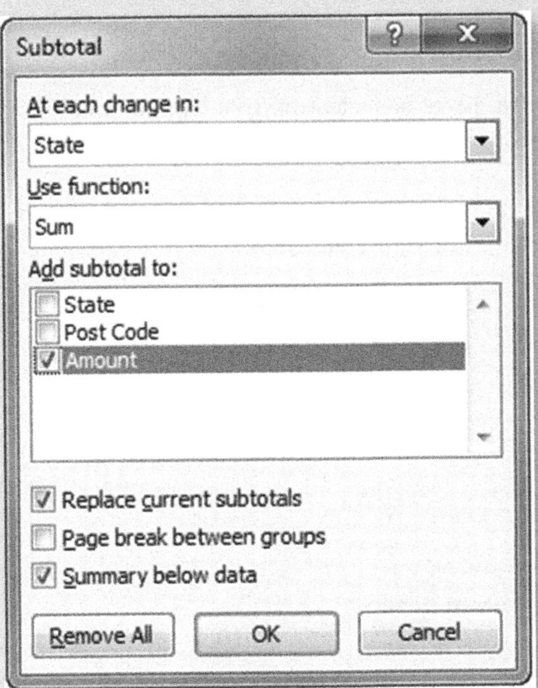

FIGURE 7.10 Subtotal Dialog Box

The keyboard shortcut is Alt a b (pressed in sequence).

Figure 7.10 displays the dialog box.

The first drop-down list displays the fields in the table. This lets you define the field to be subtotaled.

The second drop-down list defines the functions to use. In most cases the function to use is SUM, so that is the default.

The Add Subtotal To section lets you choose the columns to subtotal. Excel has already estimated the Amount column in Figure 7.10. It doesn't always guess correctly, and you use the check boxes to select or deselect the columns to subtotal.

Once you have made your selections, click OK to insert the subtotals.

Add Subtotals Automatically (*Continued*)

Figure 7.11 shows the result.

	G	H	I	J
7				
8		**State**	**Post Code**	**Amount**
9		NSW	2000	1,145
10		NSW	2010	1,681
11		NSW	2002	2,833
12		**NSW Total**		5,659
13		QLD	4000	1,731
14		QLD	4002	1,790
15		QLD	4004	1,805
16		QLD	4008	2,401
17		QLD	4010	2,682
18		**QLD Total**		10,409
19		VIC	3001	1,603
20		VIC	3009	2,773
21		VIC	3100	2,792
22		VIC	3005	2,902
23		**VIC Total**		10,070
24		**Grand Total**		26,138

FIGURE 7.11 Subtotal Inserted

Notice that rows have been inserted and that the grouping controls have been added on the left. Also notice that the border formatting hasn't been extended all the way down the table.

Cells J12, J18, J23, and J24 all contain SUBTOTAL functions.

To remove subtotals, click the table, open the Subtotal dialog box, and use the Remove All button.

THE AGGREGATE FUNCTION

The new AGGREGATE function in Excel 2010 is similar to the SUBTOTAL function and shares some of the function numbers used in the SUBTOTAL function. It has the ability to perform calculations on visible cells only. It can ignore all the other AGGREGATE or SUBTOTAL functions in its range.

The AGGREGATE function can perform more calculations than SUBTOTAL (see Table 7.6). The first 11 functions are the same as in the SUBTOTAL function. AGGREGATE can also ignore error cells within its range, which no other built-in function can do. Its one limitation is that it works only on columns of data; it won't work on rows.

TABLE 7.6 AGGREGATE Function Numbers

Function Number	Function
1	AVERAGE
2	COUNT
3	COUNTA
4	MAX
5	MIN
6	PRODUCT
7	STDEV.S
8	STDEV.P
9	SUM
10	VAR.S
11	VAR.P
12	MEDIAN
13	MODE.SNGL
14	LARGE
15	SMALL
16	PERCENTILE.INC
17	QUARTILE.INC
18	PERCENTILE.EXC
19	QUARTILE.EXC

Syntax

AGGREGATE (Function_Number, Options, Ref1, Ref2, etc.) or
AGGREGATE (Function_Number, Options, Array, k)

Function_Number is the same first 11 numbers as in SUBTOTAL. For example, 9 is SUM. There are more complex functions available, as shown in Table 7.6.

Options determine what cells are to be ignored in the calculations (see Table 7.7). If the option number is omitted, 0 is the default value.

Ref1 and Ref2 are the ranges to calculate.
Array is the range to calculate.
k is used for those functions that require another input to perform their calculations.

Comments on Option Usage

- Options 0, 1, 2, and 3 are used for subtotaling situations.
- Option 4 is not really required, since it doesn't do anything different from normal functions.
- Options 5, 6, and 7 are used for general summing and other calculations.

TABLE 7.7 AGGREGATE Options Descriptions

Option	Ignores
0	SUBTOTAL and AGGREGATE functions in the range
1	Hidden rows and SUBTOTAL and AGGREGATE functions in the range
2	Error values and SUBTOTAL and AGGREGATE functions in the range
3	Hidden rows, error values, and SUBTOTAL and AGGREGATE functions in the range
4	Nothing
5	Hidden rows
6	Error values
7	Hidden rows and error values

FUNCTION WIZARD

When you are using functions for the first few times, it can be worthwhile using the Function Wizard, which uses a dialog box to display and explain the various parts of a function. As well as providing explanations, it has links to the Help system if you need to clarify what part of the function does or what is expected to be inputted.

Since AGGREGATE is a new function in Excel 2010, let's use it as an example of using the Function Wizard to insert a function and to see how AGGREGATE works. The example starts on the following page.

CONDITIONAL SUMMING

In terms of reporting, the most important Excel functions are the conditional sum functions. These functions work on both rows and columns even though they are most commonly used to summarise large columns of data.

SUMIF performs conditional sums based on a single condition.
SUMIFS (Excel 2007 onward) performs conditional sums based on multiple conditions.
SUMPRODUCT (all versions) performs conditional sums based on multiple conditions.

These three functions can handle all the summing requirements you will need to build your advanced reports. There are other conditional functions covered in the next chapter that handle conditional counting, which may also be required for your more advanced reports.

Function Wizard and the AGGREGATE Function

Note the following in Figure 7.12. All the values are the same in the columns except row 9, which has values and errors. Row 10 is hidden. It contains the figures for VIC, which has 1,000 in each column. We will compare the different option numbers for AGGREGATE. The option numbers used are shown in row 21.

	H	I	J	K	L	M	N	O	P
6									
7		Sales $,000	Actuals	Actuals	Actuals	Actuals	Actuals	Actuals	Actuals
8		East Region							
9		NSW	3,000	3,000	#DIV/0!	#DIV/0!	3,000	#DIV/0!	#DIV/0!
11		QLD	1,500	1,500	1,500	1,500	1,500	1,500	1,500
12		Total East							
13		Central Region							
14		NT	750	750	750	750	750	750	750
15		SA	500	500	500	500	500	500	500
16		Total Central							
17		West Region							
18		WA	1,750	1,750	1,750	1,750	1,750	1,750	1,750
19		Total West							
20		Total All Regions							
21		Aggregate Function_Number	0	1	2	3	5	6	7

FIGURE 7.12 Range to Apply AGGREGATE Functions

In cell J12, type =agg, then press the Tab key to accept the AGGREGATE function. Click the Insert Function (fx) icon to the left of the Formula Bar (see Figure 7.13).

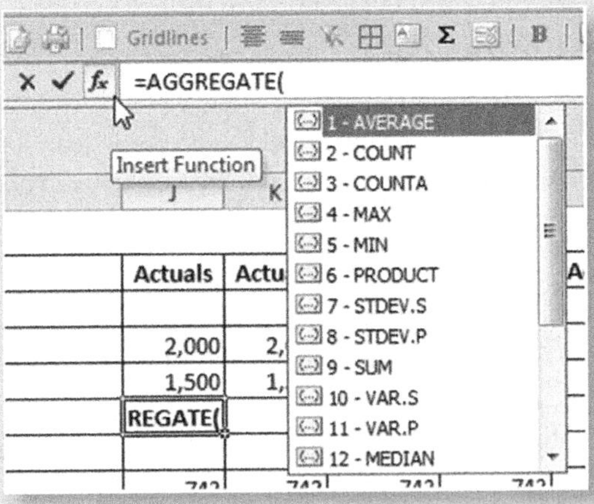

FIGURE 7.13 Insert Function (fx) Icon

Because the AGGREGATE function is used for multiple functions, a dialog box is displayed asking which type you want to use (see Figure 7.14).

Function Wizard and the AGGREGATE Function (*Continued*)

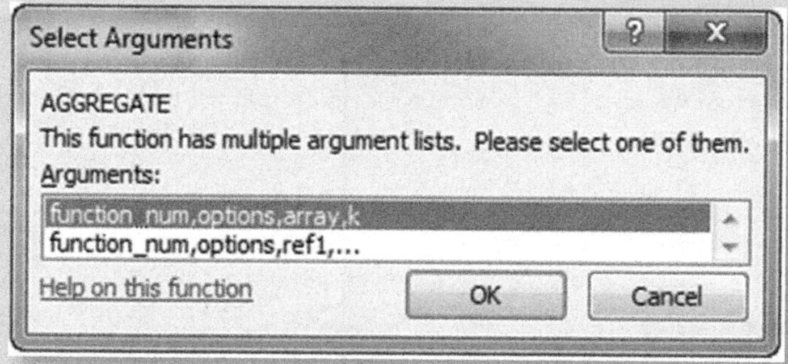

Select Arguments

AGGREGATE

This function has multiple argument lists. Please select one of them.

Arguments:

function_num,options,array,k

function_num,options,ref1,...

Help on this function

OK Cancel

FIGURE 7.14 Select Arguments Dialog Box

The difference is whether you need to use the optional k argument of the function. To be honest, it doesn't matter which one you choose, because if you don't use the optional argument, it won't be included in the formula. In this case, we don't need the optional argument, so we can click the second selection and click OK.

This will display the Function Arguments dialog box (see Figure 7.15).

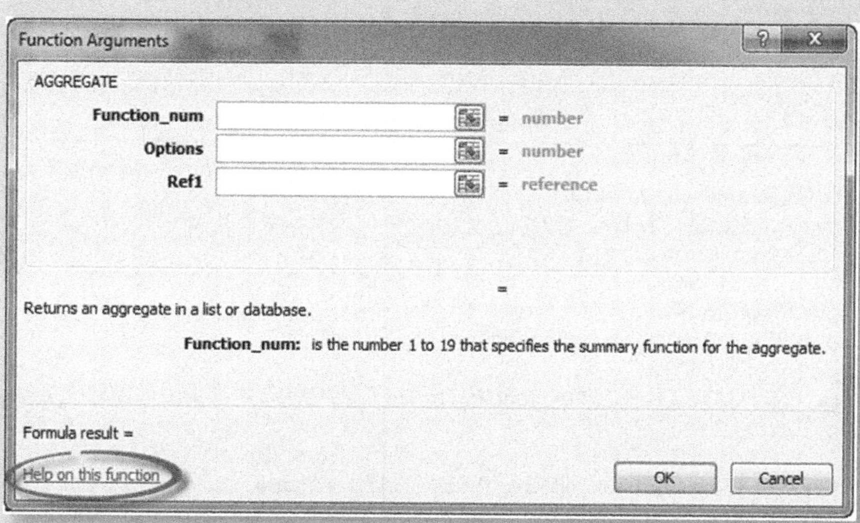

Function Arguments

AGGREGATE

Function_num = number

Options = number

Ref1 = reference

=

Returns an aggregate in a list or database.

Function_num: is the number 1 to 19 that specifies the summary function for the aggregate.

Formula result =

Help on this function

OK Cancel

FIGURE 7.15 Function Arguments Dialog Box

To see the detailed information of the function being created, you can click Help on this function link at the bottom left of the dialog box.

Type 9 in the Function_num box.

Click inside the Options box and click cell J21. Press F4 twice to change it to J$21. This will allow you to copy the formula to different cells and see the difference in the various options results. In practice, you would type in the option number you wanted to use.

Click the Ref1 box and select the range J9:J11. Note that the values in the

(*continued*)

Function Wizard and the AGGREGATE Function (*Continued*)

range are displayed in the right of the dialog box {2000:1000:1500}. It displays the 1000 even though it is in a hidden row.

Also note that the result of the formula is displayed at the bottom left of the dialog box (see Figure 7.16).

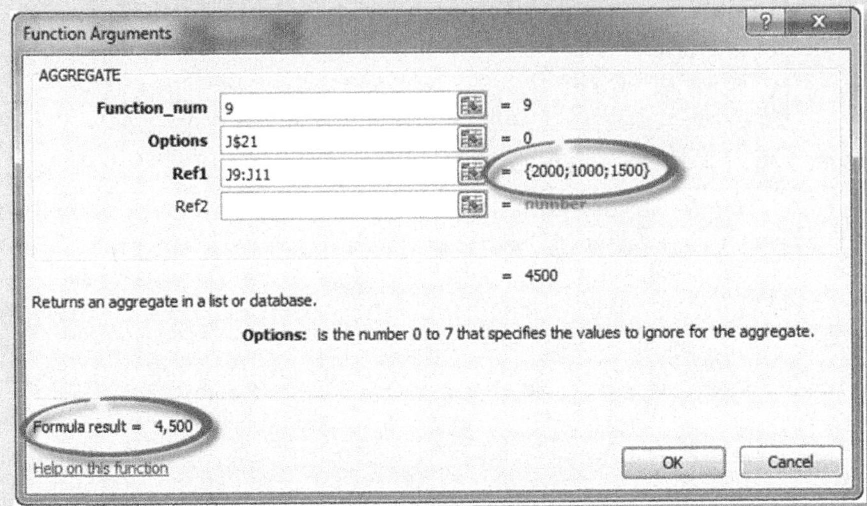

FIGURE 7.16 Completed Function Arguments Dialog Box

Click OK to enter the formula.
Copy cell J12 to K12:M12. Copy only to column M, because options 5, 6, and 7 are not used for subtotaling.
Copy J12 to J16 and amend the function range to J14:J15.
Copy J16 to K16:M16.
Copy J16 to J19 and amend the function range to J18:J18.
Copy J19 to K19:M19.
Copy J19 to J20 and amend the function range to J9:J19.
Copy J20 to K20:P20.

Figure 7.17 shows the completed AGGREGATE example.

Row 20 has different results because of the different option numbers used.

Column J uses option 0, which includes hidden rows and ignores the other AGGREGATE functions in the range. It adds up all the values. This is the benchmark against which we will examine the other options.

Column K uses option 1, which excludes hidden rows and ignores the other AGGREGATE functions in the range. The hidden row contains 1,000, so the result is 1,000 less than the result in column J.

Column L uses option 2, which ignores errors and other AGGREGATE functions. The result is 3,000 less than in column J because the 3,000 on row 9 was replaced with a #DIV/0! error message in column L.

Function Wizard and the AGGREGATE Function (*Continued*)

	H	I	J	K	L	M	N	O	P
6									
7		Sales $,000	Actuals	Actuals	Actuals	Actuals	Actuals	Actuals	Actuals
8		East Region							
9		NSW	3,000	3,000	#DIV/0!	#DIV/0!	3,000	#DIV/0!	#DIV/0!
11		QLD	1,500	1,500	1,500	1,500	1,500	1,500	1,500
12		Total East	5,500	4,500	2,500	1,500			
13		Central Region							
14		NT	750	750	750	750	750	750	750
15		SA	500	500	500	500	500	500	500
16		Total Central	1,250	1,250	1,250	1,250			
17		West Region							
18		WA	1,750	1,750	1,750	1,750	1,750	1,750	1,750
19		Total West	1,750	1,750	1,750	1,750			
20		Total All Regions	8,500	7,500	5,500	4,500	7,500	5,500	4,500
21		Aggregate Function_Number	0	1	2	3	5	6	7

FIGURE 7.17 Completed AGGREGATE Example

Column M uses option 3, which ignores errors and hidden rows and other AGGREGATE functions. The result is 4,000 less than in column J because the 3,000 in row 9 was replaced with a #DIV/0! error message, and the 1,000 in the hidden row is ignored.

Options 5, 6, and 7 are not used in subtotal situations.

Column N just ignores the hidden rows and so is 1,000 less than column J.

Column O ignores errors but includes hidden rows and so is 3,000 less than column J because the 3,000 in row 9 was replaced by a #DIV/0! error message.

Column P ignores hidden rows and error cells and so is 4,000 less than column J because the 3,000 was replaced by a #DIV/0! error message, and row 10 is hidden and contains 1,000.

THE SUMIF FUNCTION

SUMIF is used to add up a range based on values in that range or another range. It can be applied to columns or rows of data. If used on an external file, it will display the #VALUE! error message if the external file is closed.

Syntax

SUMIF (Criteria_Range, Criteria, Range_to_SUM)

Criteria_Range is the range that contains the criteria values you want to base the sum on (e.g., department codes). This can be a whole column or row.

Criteria is typically a cell reference that contains the criteria you want to sum in the Criteria_Range (e.g., department code).

Tip: SUMIF Requirements

Both ranges must line up exactly in terms of row numbers for vertical ranges and column letters for horizontal ranges. If the ranges do not line up, the results may be incorrect.

If there are any errors in the ranges, the SUMIF function will also return an error.

Range_to_SUM (optional) is the range containing the values to sum. It can refer to a whole column or row. Since it is optional, if you omit Range_to_SUM, the Criteria_Range is summed. You could omit Range_to_SUM if you needed to add up all the negative values in a range. In that case, the Criteria_Range is also the Range_to_SUM, since the values themselves are the condition.

Examples

The examples used for the conditional summing functions in Figures 7.18 and 7.19 have reports on the same sheet as the data. This is done only for demonstration and explanation purposes. You should aim to have separate sheets for your data and reports.

	H	I	J	K	L	M	N	O
4								
5							Summary	
6		Date	State	Department	Amount		State	Amount
7		Jul-13	WA	SALES	$8,107		WA	
8		Jul-13	NSW	ADMIN	$3,734		NSW	
9		Jul-13	VIC	PRODUCTION	$4,393		VIC	
10		Jul-13	NSW	SALES	$3,359		Total	$0
11		Aug-13	VIC	PRODUCTION	$9,353			
12		Aug-13	WA	SALES	$5,362		Department	Amount
13		Aug-13	WA	ADMIN	$6,909		PRODUCTION	
14		Sep-13	VIC	PRODUCTION	$8,665		SALES	
15		Sep-13	NSW	ADMIN	$6,893		ADMIN	
16		Sep-13	VIC	SALES	$5,219		Total	$0
17		Sep-13	WA	SALES	$1,124			
18		Oct-13	VIC	SALES	$3,651		Quarter	Amount
19		Oct-13	VIC	ADMIN	$5,560		Sep-13	
20		Oct-13	WA	ADMIN	$3,592			
21		Oct-13	NSW	ADMIN	$9,025		Quarter	Amount
22				Total	$84,946		<=1/9/2013	

FIGURE 7.18 SUMIF Example

	H	I	J	K	L	M	N	O
4								
5							**Summary**	
6		**Date**	**State**	**Department**	**Amount**		**State**	**Amount**
7		Jul-13	WA	SALES	$8,107		WA	$25,094
8		Jul-13	NSW	ADMIN	$3,734		NSW	$23,011
9		Jul-13	VIC	PRODUCTION	$4,393		VIC	$36,841
10		Jul-13	NSW	SALES	$3,359		**Total**	**$84,946**
11		Aug-13	VIC	PRODUCTION	$9,353			
12		Aug-13	WA	SALES	$5,362		**Department**	**Amount**
13		Aug-13	WA	ADMIN	$6,909		PRODUCTION	$22,411
14		Sep-13	VIC	PRODUCTION	$8,665		SALES	$26,822
15		Sep-13	NSW	ADMIN	$6,893		ADMIN	$35,713
16		Sep-13	VIC	SALES	$5,219		**Total**	**$84,946**
17		Sep-13	WA	SALES	$1,124			
18		Oct-13	VIC	SALES	$3,651		**Quarter**	**Amount**
19		Oct-13	VIC	ADMIN	$5,560		Sep-13	$63,118
20		Oct-13	WA	ADMIN	$3,592			
21		Oct-13	NSW	ADMIN	$9,025		**Quarter**	**Amount**
22				**Total**	**$84,946**		<=1/9/2013	$63,118

FIGURE 7.19 SUMIF Example Completed

The following formula is in cell O7. It will add up all the entries in $L$7:$L$21 when the corresponding row in $J$7:$J$21 contains WA, the value in N7. This formula can be copied down because both ranges are fixed.

```
=SUMIF($J$7:$J$21,N7,$L$7:$L$21)
```

The following formula is in cell O13. It will add up all the entries in $L$7:$L$21 when the corresponding row in $K$7:$K$21 contains PRODUCTION, the value in N13. This formula can be copied down because both ranges are fixed.

```
=SUMIF($K$7:$K$21,N13,$L$7:$L$21)
```

Using Other Operators with SUMIF

When creating your criteria, you are not limited to using the "equals" comparison; you can also use "greater than" and "less than" with all the criteria-based functions. Table 7.8 shows the comparison symbols you can use.

The first two examples of this are also based on Figures 7.18 and 7.19.

The following formula is in cell O19 and will add up all the entries in $L$7:$L$21 when the corresponding row in $I$7:$I$21 contains a date less than or equal to

WARNING: Using Operators with SUMIF and SUMIFS

When using the operators in formulas, you must enclose them in quotation marks or include them in the cell you are using as the criteria. You typically need to use these symbols when working with date ranges.

TABLE 7.8 Formula Operators

Operators	Description
>	Greater than
>=	Greater than or equal to
<	Less than
<=	Less than or equal to
<>	Not equal to

September 1, 2013. This calculates the September quarter total and ignores the October entries. The & symbol joins text together and is used to combine the <= to the date in cell N19.

```
=SUMIF($I$7:$I$21,"<="&N19,$L$7:$L$21)
```

The following formula in cell O22 calculates the same result as the O19 formula, but it has the <= included in cell N22. This avoids the need to include quotations marks and the & symbol.

```
=SUMIF($I$7:$I$21,N22,$L$7:$L$21)
```

The next two examples are based on Figure 7.20.

	H	I	J	K	L	M
6						
7		Account	Amount			
8		1100	725			
9		1200	431			
10		1300	260			
11		1400	640			Amount
12		1500	458		Positives	2514
13		2100	-82		Negatives	-2514
14		2200	-567		Total	0
15		2300	-348			
16		2400	-839			
17		2500	-457			
18		2600	-221			
19		Total	0			

FIGURE 7.20 SUMIF No Range_to_Sum

The following formula is in cell M12 and adds up all the positive values in the range $J$8:$J$18. It is an example of a SUMIF that doesn't have Range_to_SUM. When you omit the Range_to_SUM, the Criteria_Range is used as the Range_to_SUM.

```
=SUMIF($J$8:$J$18,">0")
```

The following formula is in cell M13 and adds up all the negative values in the range $J$8:$J$18.

```
=SUMIF($J$8:$J$18,"<0")
```

SUMIF USES

Most advanced reports require multiple criteria SUM formulas, which will be covered next, but the SUMIF function still has a number of uses in advanced reports.

SUMIF can provide overall validation checks to ensure that categories that have subcategories have included all the subcategories.

SUMIF is also useful in adding up columns across the page. You can often have a structure that requires you to summarise the columns across the page. SUMIF can provide an easy and flexible way to do that.

The following example is based on Figure 7.21.

	H	I	J	K	L	M	N	O	P	Q
6										
7			North		South		East		Total	
8		$,000	Actuals	Budget	Actuals	Budget	Actuals	Budget	Actuals	Budget
9		Sales	1,500	1,400	1,800	1,900	2,000	2,100	5,300	5,400
10		COS	1,200	1,200	1,500	1,400	1,500	1,700	4,200	4,300
11		**Margin**	**300**	**200**	**300**	**500**	**500**	**400**	**1,100**	**1,100**

FIGURE 7.21 SUMIF Horizontal Example

The following formula is in cell P9 and will add up all the actuals in columns J to O on the left. This formula can be copied to the right and down.

```
=SUMIF($J$8:$O$8,P$8,$J9:$O9)
```

The SUMIF function has an advantage over direct links. If you insert another region, such as West, then the SUMIF function will automatically include the inserted columns, provided they were inserted between columns J and O. Direct links will require changes to the formula in the range P9:Q10.

HELPER CELLS

Helper cells are extra cells you add to the sheet to simplify other formulas. Helper cells also perform a vital service in increasing the ability to copy formulas from one range to another.

WARNING: Leading Zeros

I've previously mentioned that Excel doesn't handle leading zeros very well. This limitation can affect SUMIF, SUMIFS, and other conditional functions if there is a leading zero in your code.

If you have codes 00123, 0123, and 123, the SUMIFS and SUMIFS functions will treat them all the same—as 123.

If you have or could have leading zeros in your codes, then you should use SUMPRODUCT for all your conditional calculations, because it handles leading zeros correctly.

When designing structure, you must always keep in mind how easy or hard it will be to copy formulas between ranges in the reporting model. Creating accurate formulas is the most important part of creating reporting models.

The goal is to write a single formula that can be copied throughout a report. This is not always achievable, but you should minimise the number of different formulas you use in the body of your reports. Helper cells can go a long way in enabling you to achieve this goal.

Helper cells become more useful when handling more criteria. You will see how to make your formulas simpler and easier to copy with the use of helper cells in the examples that follow.

THE SUMIFS FUNCTION

SUMIFS can SUM based on multiple criteria. SUMIFS was introduced in Excel 2007 and works only in that and later versions. To perform multiple criteria SUMs in all Excel versions, use the SUMPRODUCT function, covered later in the chapter.

The important point to note between the syntax for SUMIF and SUMIFS is that Range_to_SUM is the first argument of the function, not the last argument. Both ranges can refer to whole columns or rows. The SUMIFS function can be used instead of a SUMIF to do single condition summing.

SUMIFS cannot return values from closed files.

Syntax

SUMIFS (Range_to_SUM, Criteria_Range1,Criteria1, Criteria_Range2, Criteria2, . . .)

Range_to_SUM is a range containing the values to sum. The range can be a whole column or row.

Criteria_Range1 is a range containing the first set of criteria to SUM. It can be a whole row or column.

Criteria1 is typically a cell reference containing the first condition to be met.

Criteria_Range2 is a range containing the second set of criteria to SUM. It can be a whole row or column.

Criteria2 is typically a cell reference containing the second condition to be met.

In a vertical range, when all the conditions have been met in the criteria ranges, the corresponding row in the Range_to_SUM is summed.

Extra criteria ranges and criteria are paired and inserted on the end of the function. In Excel 2010, the limit is 127 criteria. I have created or seen very few SUMIFS functions with more than 5 criteria.

Examples

The data and layout in Figure 7.22 are similar to the data and layout used in the first example of the SUMIF function. Note that fixed and mixed references are used frequently in SUMIFS functions.

	H	I	J	K	L	M	N	O	P	Q	R	S
5												
6		Date	State	Department	Amount			Total Costs	PRODUCTION	SALES	ADMIN	Total
7		Jul-13	WA	PRODUCTION	$8,107			WA				$0
8		Jul-13	NSW	ADMIN	$3,734			NSW				$0
9		Jul-13	VIC	PRODUCTION	$4,393			VIC				$0
10		Jul-13	NSW	SALES	$3,359			Total	$0	$0	$0	$0
11		Aug-13	VIC	PRODUCTION	$9,353							
12		Aug-13	WA	PRODUCTION	$5,362			Sep-13				
13		Aug-13	WA	ADMIN	$6,909			Costs	PRODUCTION	SALES	ADMIN	Total
14		Sep-13	VIC	ADMIN	$7,411		Sep-13	WA				$0
15		Sep-13	VIC	PRODUCTION	$8,665		Sep-13	NSW				$0
16		Sep-13	NSW	ADMIN	$6,893		Sep-13	VIC				$0
17		Sep-13	VIC	SALES	$5,219			Total	$0	$0	$0	$0
18		Sep-13	WA	PRODUCTION	$1,124							
19		Oct-13	VIC	ADMIN	$6,824			Oct-13				
20		Oct-13	VIC	SALES	$3,651			Costs	PRODUCTION	SALES	ADMIN	Total
21		Oct-13	VIC	PRODUCTION	$5,560		Oct-13	WA				$0
22		Oct-13	WA	PRODUCTION	$3,592		Oct-13	NSW				$0
23		Oct-13	NSW	ADMIN	$9,025		Oct-13	VIC				$0
24		Oct-13	VIC	ADMIN	$6,931			Total	$0	$0	$0	$0
25				Total	$106,112							

FIGURE 7.22 SUMIFS Example

The following formula is in cell P7 and will add up the values in the range L7:L24 when two criteria are met. The first criterion requires that the corresponding row in the range J7:J24 contains WA (the value in cell O7). The second criterion requires that the corresponding row in range K7:K24 contains PRODUCTION (the value in cell P6). This formula can be copied across and down to the rest of the report.

```
=SUMIFS($L$7:$L$24,$J$7:$J$24,$O7,$K$7:$K$24,P$6)
```

The next examples are based on Figure 7.23 in addition to Figure 7.22.

The following formula is in cell P14. It is the same as the previous two-criteria example but has an additional date range and date criteria added to the end. Along with the first two criteria, the corresponding row in the range I7:I24 must equal Sep 13 (the value in cell N14).

	I	J	K	L	N	O	P	Q	R	S
5										
6	Date	State	Department	Amount		Total Costs	PRODUCTION	SALES	ADMIN	Total
7	Jul-13	WA	PRODUCTION	$8,107		WA	$18,185	$0	$6,909	$25,094
8	Jul-13	NSW	ADMIN	$3,734		NSW	$0	$3,359	$19,652	$23,011
9	Jul-13	VIC	PRODUCTION	$4,393		VIC	$27,971	$8,870	$21,166	$58,007
10	Jul-13	NSW	SALES	$3,359		Total	$46,156	$12,229	$47,727	$106,112
11	Aug-13	VIC	PRODUCTION	$9,353						
12	Aug-13	WA	PRODUCTION	$5,362		Sep-13				
13	Aug-13	WA	ADMIN	$6,909		Costs	PRODUCTION	SALES	ADMIN	Total
14	Sep-13	VIC	ADMIN	$7,411	Sep-13	WA	$1,124	$0	$0	$1,124
15	Sep-13	VIC	PRODUCTION	$8,665	Sep-13	NSW	$0	$0	$6,893	$6,893
16	Sep-13	NSW	ADMIN	$6,893	Sep-13	VIC	$8,665	$5,219	$7,411	$21,295
17	Sep-13	VIC	SALES	$5,219		Total	$9,789	$5,219	$14,304	$29,312
18	Sep-13	WA	PRODUCTION	$1,124						
19	Oct-13	VIC	ADMIN	$6,824		Oct-13				
20	Oct-13	VIC	SALES	$3,651		Costs	PRODUCTION	SALES	ADMIN	Total
21	Oct-13	VIC	PRODUCTION	$5,560	Oct-13	WA	$3,592	$0	$0	$3,592
22	Oct-13	WA	PRODUCTION	$3,592	Oct-13	NSW	$0	$0	$9,025	$9,025
23	Oct-13	NSW	ADMIN	$9,025	Oct-13	VIC	$5,560	$3,651	$13,755	$22,966
24	Oct-13	VIC	ADMIN	$6,931		Total	$9,152	$3,651	$22,780	$35,583
25			Total	$106,112						

FIGURE 7.23 SUMIFS Example Completed

```
=SUMIFS($L$7:$L$24,$J$7:$J$24,$O14,$K$7:$K$24,P$6,$I$7:$I$24,$N14)
```

There are two things to note from this formula. One is that there is a built-in assumption in this copied-down formula, and the other is that column N contains helper cells. The assumption is that the column headings are consistent in all three reports. Column P is always Production, column Q is Sales, and column R is Admin. Hence the reference to cell P$6 remains valid as the formula is copied down to the other reports.

The helper cells in column N are linked to the date cells in O12 or O19 and allow us to create a formula in P14 that can be copied within the current Sep 13 report and also copied down to the Oct 13 report below to cell P21.

When you copy cell P14 to P21, no changes are required, and that formula can be copied to the rest of the Oct 13 report. The cell P21 formula is

```
=SUMIFS($L$7:$L$24,$J$7:$J$24,$O21,$K$7:$K$24,P$6,$I$7:$I$24,$N21)
```

THE SUMPRODUCT FUNCTION

The SUMPRODUCT function is the most versatile of Excel's functions. It is the Swiss Army knife of functions. If you were going to be stuck on a desert island with only one function, this is the one you would take.

It can SUM, COUNT, and perform other calculations that usually require an array formula, an advanced formula that is discussed in Chapter 8. It is rather odd that the most useful application of SUMPRODUCT is not included in Excel's Help system.

To understand how SUMPRODUCT works, we'll start with its documented, or standard, use and then look at its undocumented use.

Tip: Helper Cells Creation

In the previous examples we focused on the SUMIFS formula and copying it between reports. In practice you would set up the whole report structure, including all the headings and helper cells, so that you could copy the whole report and paste it below.

There is a tip to creating useful helper cells that can be easily copied. Helper cells tend to repeat entries so that your reporting formulas are easy to create and copy.

When you repeat cells, you tend to use fixed references. Fixed references are not always useful when copying whole ranges down or across. If you need to use a fixed reference but still need to copy and have the references act like relative references, there is a technique you can use.

In our example, I could create the Sep 13 report as a whole and then copy it below and change the date to Oct 13 and have the whole report calculate. To get the helper cells in column N working as I want them to, I need to use a fixed link to cell O12, where the date is entered. So cells in the range N14:N16 all contain =$O$12. That stops me from copying down, because the cells will remain linked to the report above after I paste it. The solution is to create the fixed references and then select the range and use Find and Replace and replace $ with nothing. This converts all the fixed references to relative references (see Figure 7.24).

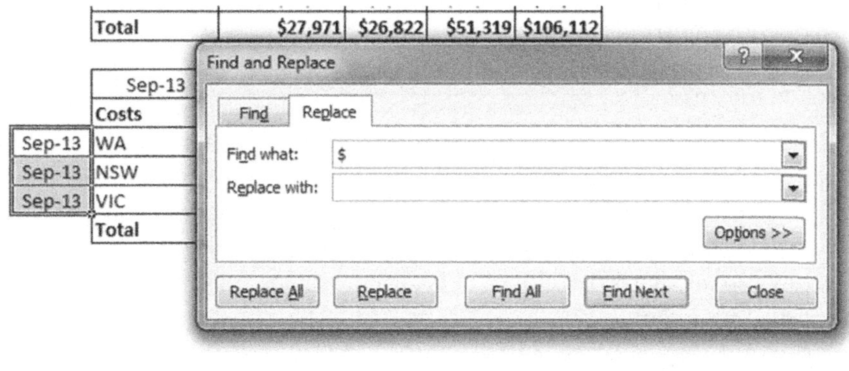

FIGURE 7.24 Find and Replace—Convert Fixed Reference to Relative

Now the whole Sep 13 report range is ready to copy down. All I need to do once it's copied down is change cell O19 to Oct 13, and the report will then calculate for that month.

Standard Use

The SUMPRODUCT function covered in Excel's Help system allows you to multiply values and then sum up the results.

SUMPRODUCT literally means to sum the results (i.e., to find the *product* of two numbers, in mathematical terminology, means to multiply them together) of multiplications.

Syntax

SUMPRODUCT (Range1, Range2)

Range1 and **Range2** must be the same size.

The first cell in Range1 is multiplied by the first cell in Range2, and then the second cell in Range1 is multiplied by the second cell in Range2, and so on. The results of all the multiplications are stored in memory and added up, and the result is displayed.

Example

Figure 7.25 shows an example of SUMPRODUCT's standard use.

	H	I	J	K	L
5					
6		**Region**	**Tonnes**	**$/Tonne**	**Value**
7		North	1,500	$5.36	$8,040
8		South	3,500	$6.48	$22,680
9		East	6,000	$7.58	$45,480
10		West	9,000	$4.12	$37,080
11		**Total**	**20,000**	**$5.66**	**$113,280**
12					
13				Check	**$113,280**

FIGURE 7.25 SUMPRODUCT Standard Use Example

There is a table in the range I6: L11 calculating the total value of all four regions' tonnages. Column L in the table multiplies the tonnes (column J) by the $/tonne (column K) to arrive at a value for the region. Cell L11 sums up the four values above to arrive at the overall total for all four regions. Nothing remarkable there.

Cell L13 also calculates the total value of all four regions, and it does it with a single SUMPRODUCT formula:

```
=SUMPRODUCT(J7:J10,K7:K10)
```

The way this formula works is it multiplies J7 by K7 and stores the result, J8 by K8 and stores that result, J9 by K9 and stores that result, and J10 by K10 and stores that result. It then sums up all the results and displays the total.

Accountants tend to need to see the details, so the standard use of the SUMPRODUCT function is often applied to validate total values rather than used to calculate a single total.

Undocumented Use

The undocumented use of SUMPRODUCT employs the same methodology of multiplying range 1 cell 1 by range 2 cell 1, but it uses a logic technique to handle criteria-based calculations.

TRUE and FALSE

Before we can discuss the most powerful SUMPRODUCT applications, we need to understand the way Excel handles TRUE and FALSE.

We'll look at logic functions like IF in Chapter 8, but before we do, we need to understand that formulas can return TRUE or FALSE as a result.

Figure 7.26 shows cells returning TRUE and FALSE results in column L. The table is comparing the invoice totals from two systems and confirming that they match.

	H	I	J	K	L
5					
6		Invoice	System 1	System 2	Validation
7		1234	156.89	156.89	TRUE
8		1235	15,689.23	15,689.23	TRUE
9		1236	1,289.21	1,289.20	FALSE
10		1237	19,236.00	19,236.00	TRUE
11		1238	12,358.98	12,358.98	TRUE

FIGURE 7.26 TRUE and FALSE Results

We can see that the values in row 9 do not match. The values are different by one cent, which is possibly caused by rounding errors. Cell L9 displays the word FALSE. The formula in cell L9 is

```
=J9=K9
```

This formula has been copied down from cell L7 to the other rows. This formula does not calculate a value; it merely returns TRUE or FALSE depending on whether the two values are equal. If J9 equals K9, then TRUE is displayed. If J9 does not equal K9, it displays FALSE.

You can use the equal sign as well as the other formula operators shown earlier in Table 7.8 when you create these types of formulas. Table 7.9 shows examples.

This type of formula is evaluated by Excel as a statement, which is either TRUE or FALSE. This technique is also discussed in Chapter 13, where it is used to validate reports.

If a cell formula evaluates as TRUE, and you multiply another cell by the TRUE cell, then Excel will treat the TRUE result as having a value of 1. FALSE is treated as having a value of 0 by Excel.

TABLE 7.9 Examples of Logic Formulas

Logic Formula	Explanation
=A1>B1	Will display TRUE when the value in A1 is larger than B1. Otherwise it will display FALSE.
=A1<=B1	Will display TRUE when the value in A1 is equal to or smaller than the value in B1. Otherwise it will display FALSE.
=A1<>B1	Will display TRUE when the value in A1 is not equal to the value in B1. Otherwise it will display FALSE.

Tip: Greater Than and Less Than

When you are dealing with values, the concepts of *greater than* and *less than* are easy to grasp. When you are dealing with text, however, it is a bit more of a challenge.

You can use *greater than* and *less than* when comparing text. Excel treats text as it would if it sorted the text in ascending order. So the letter *a* comes before the letter *b*. This means that *b* is greater than *a* and that *a* is less than *b*.

Excel looks at the letters in the text from left to right, so *azzz* is less than *baaa* but greater than *ayyy*.

Tip: TRUE and FALSE

TRUE and FALSE are both keywords in Excel. They are not text. You do not have to enclose them in quotation marks. They are automatically capitalised by Excel when you use them in formulas. When displayed as the result of a formula, they are also capitalised, as in Figure 7.26.

We can see this in practice if we add a column to our table in Figure 7.26 and insert the following formula in cell M7.

```
=L7*J7
```

When we copy this down, the results are as shown in Figure 7.27.

	H	I	J	K	L	M
5						
6		Invoice	System 1	System 2	Validation	Valid Values
7		1234	156.89	156.89	TRUE	156.89
8		1235	15,689.23	15,689.23	TRUE	15,689.23
9		1236	1,289.21	1,289.20	FALSE	-
10		1237	19,236.00	19,236.00	TRUE	19,236.00
11		1238	12,358.98	12,358.98	TRUE	12,358.98

FIGURE 7.27 TRUE and FALSE Used in Calculations

Column M values are the same as column J, except in row 9, where there was a discrepancy between system 1 and system 2 values. Because cell L9 contains FALSE, when it is multiplied by J9, it zeros the value.

The fact that TRUE = 1 and FALSE = 0 is crucial to how we can use the SUMPRODUCT function to perform multiple criteria calculations. Remember that SUMPRODUCT multiplies values together.

The Multicriteria Technique

The syntax of the undocumented SUMPRODUCT technique is slightly different from that of the standard SUMPRODUCT. It has extra parentheses to isolate each criterion's section. I use the asterisk (*) between the parenthetical sections because it makes the most sense to me. You can also use two consecutive minus signs (no space in between): -- I avoid this because it doesn't make sense to me and it looks strange. Apparently that method has a slightly faster calculation time. I prefer the ability to make sense of a formula over a small improvement in calculation time.

This version of SUMPRODUCT acts in a similar way as array formulas, which are discussed in Chapter 8.

I prefer the SUMPRODUCT function because it is easier to use than an array formula. It has the advantage of not being "array entered." "Array entered" means you hold the Ctrl + Shift keys and press the Enter key when entering the array formula. This is often referred to as CSE (Ctrl Shift Enter). This places curly brackets {} around the array formula, thus defining it as an array formula. If you forget to press CSE, then the formula may display an error or return an incorrect value, usually zero.

I mentioned earlier that both SUMIF and SUMIFS cannot return values from closed files. The SUMPRODUCT function can.

Syntax

SUMPRODUCT((Criteria_Range1=Criteria1)*(Criteria_Range2=Criteria2) *(Range_to_SUM))

The argument definitions are identical to the SUMIFS definitions.

The order of the parenthetical sections is actually not fixed. I always use the above order because it makes the most sense to me, and keeping the sequence makes the syntax easier to understand. In fact, you don't need to have parentheses around Range_to_SUM; I included them just to make the layout consistent.

All the ranges must have identical rows—that is, start on the same row number and end on the same row number.

Example

Let's return to our SUMIFS example data and use a SUMPRODUCT function to populate the report (see Figure 7.28). We'll also look at a date range report.

The SUMPRODUCT formula for cell P7 is

```
=SUMPRODUCT(($J$7:$J$24=$O7)*($K$7:$K$24=P$6)*($L$7:$L$24))
```

I prefer the layout of the SUMPRODUCT function to the SUMIFS because it uses the equal sign. This makes it obvious what the criteria range is and what the criteria are.

How and Why Does This SUMPRODUCT Formula Work?

To see how this formula works, we can use a keyboard shortcut to analyse its parts. If you select part of a formula in the Formula Bar and press the F9 key, Excel will calculate just that part of the formula and show you the result.

Date	State	Department	Amount
Jul-13	WA	PRODUCTION	$8,107
Jul-13	NSW	ADMIN	$3,734
Jul-13	VIC	PRODUCTION	$4,393
Jul-13	NSW	SALES	$3,359
Aug-13	VIC	PRODUCTION	$9,353
Aug-13	WA	PRODUCTION	$5,362
Aug-13	WA	ADMIN	$6,909
Sep-13	VIC	ADMIN	$7,411
Sep-13	VIC	PRODUCTION	$8,665
Sep-13	NSW	ADMIN	$6,893
Sep-13	VIC	SALES	$5,219
Sep-13	WA	PRODUCTION	$1,124
Oct-13	VIC	ADMIN	$6,824
Oct-13	VIC	SALES	$3,651
Oct-13	VIC	PRODUCTION	$5,560
Oct-13	WA	PRODUCTION	$3,592
Oct-13	NSW	ADMIN	$9,025
Oct-13	VIC	ADMIN	$6,931
		Total	$106,112

Total Costs	PRODUCTION	SALES	ADMIN	Total
WA				$0
NSW				$0
VIC				$0
Total	$0	$0	$0	$0

Start Month:	Aug-13
End Month:	Oct-13

Total Costs	PRODUCTION	SALES	ADMIN	Total
WA				$0
NSW				$0
VIC				$0
Total	$0	$0	$0	$0

FIGURE 7.28 SUMPRODUCT Multicriteria SUM

Analyzing the above formula with F9, we see the results shown in Figure 7.29.

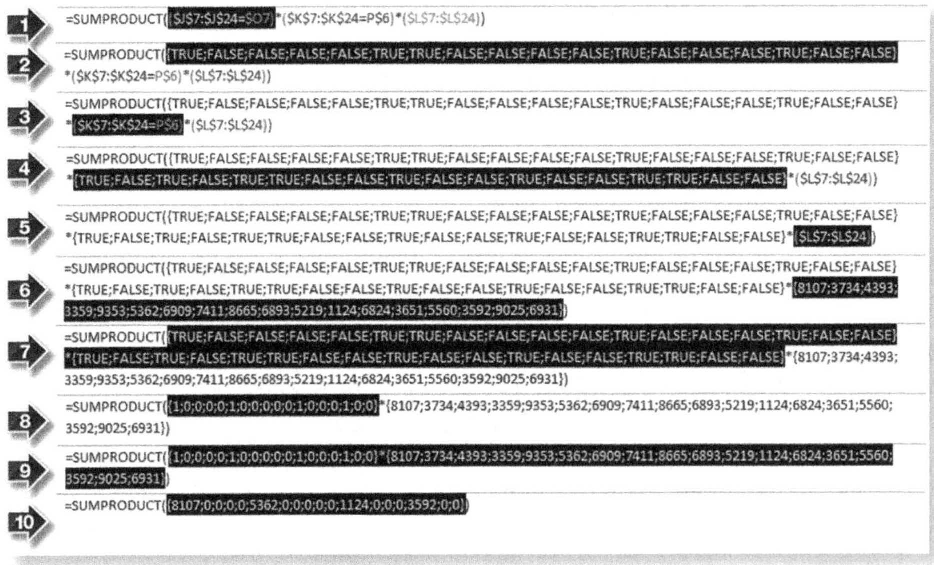

FIGURE 7.29 Analysis of SUMPRODUCT Formula

This is by far the most complex figure in the entire book. Let's review each number on the image. It might take a few passes to grasp how and why this works. We'll look at a couple of other examples to emphasise the power and flexibility of the SUMPRODUCT function. Follow these steps:

1. Highlight the first set of criteria, which is the State criteria. Include the parentheses and press F9.
2. This replaces the highlighted section with the result of all the comparisons. Each TRUE represents WA in the range J7:J24.
3. Highlight the second set of criteria, which is the Department criteria. Include the parentheses and press F9.
4. Each TRUE represents PRODUCTION in the range K7:K24.
5. Highlight the range to sum, including the parentheses, and press F9. The values to SUM are displayed.
6. This shows all the results of all the comparisons plus the values. This is where the SUMPRODUCT does its work. Each TRUE or FALSE in the State criteria is multiplied by its corresponding TRUE or FALSE in the Department criteria.
7. By highlighting both criteria results and pressing F9, you will see the TRUE and FALSE results converted to values.
8. You can now see the values (every 0 and 1) that result from the two criteria being multiplied together. Each 1 represents both criteria being met.
9. Highlight the remaining results and press F9 for the last time to see the final set of values. This will multiply every 1 and 0 by the corresponding value to arrive at the final values to sum.
10. These last values are summed by SUMPRODUCT to provide the result. The values displayed represent the four values where both criteria were met—in this case, cells L7, L12, L18, and L22, or, in terms of the sequence numbers of the 18 cells, the first, sixth, twelfth, and sixteenth cells in the range L7:L24.

As mentioned earlier, the order of the parenthetical sections is not important. The following formula will provide exactly the same result:

```
=SUMPRODUCT(($L$7:$L$24)*($J$7:$J$24=$O7)*($K$7:$K$24=P$6))
```

When referring to ranges on other sheets, the SUMPRODUCT formula can be quite long. This is a good reason to consider using range names (see Chapter 9).

Dates and SUMPRODUCT

SUMPRODUCT handles date ranges better than SUMIF and SUMIFS because it doesn't require the use of quotation marks around the >, >=, <, <=, and <> symbols.

Let's review the SUMPRODUCT and the SUMIFS solution to a date range report. In Figure 7.28 shown above, cells P12 and P13 contain a starting and ending month, respectively. The SUMPRODUCT formula for cell P15 is

```
=SUMPRODUCT(($I$7:$I$24>=$P$12)*($I$7:$I$24<=$P$13)*
($J$7:$J$24=$O15)*($K$7:$K$24=P$14)*($L$7:$L$24))
```

The SUMIFS formula is

```
=SUMIFS($L$7:$L$24,$I$7:$I$24,">="&$P$12,$I$7:$I$24,
"<="&$P$13,$J$7:$J$24,$O15,$K$7:$K$24,P$14)
```

The SUMIFS formula is slightly shorter, but I find it more difficult to read, and it takes more time to create because you need to insert the quotations marks and the & symbols. I find the SUMPRODUCT version much easier to create, read, and understand.

WARNING: SUMPRODUCT Limitations

The SUMPRODUCT function is the slowest, in terms of calculation time, of all the criteria-based SUM functions. With the speed of the latest computers this is less of an issue.

SUMPRODUCT does have two other limitations. Once you know what they are, they can be handled quite easily.

In most versions of Excel, you can't refer to whole columns or rows. You must refer to ranges rather than columns or rows. Using range names can make this easier (see Chapter 9). Some Excel versions allow you to refer to whole columns or rows, but I would advise against this because it will negatively affect spreadsheet performance. There is a technique in Chapter 9 that creates flexible range names that expand as entries are added to your data. I recommend using this technique with SUMPRODUCT functions.

Range_to_SUM must contain only values (i.e., no text); hence no data headings are allowed within the ranges referenced. Table headings in row 1 cannot be included in Range_ to_SUM. This is yet another reason not to use whole-column references in SUMPRODUCT functions.

OR versus AND Calculations

Most SUMPRODUCT calculations that you will do are based on all the criteria being met. This is an AND calculation. You want Criteria_1 AND Criteria_2 AND Criteria_3 to be TRUE. (The AND and OR functions are explained in more detail in Chapter 8.)

If any of the criteria aren't met, then the value isn't summed. You can also do an OR comparison with SUMPRODUCT.

Instead of using the asterisk, which gives you TRUE * TRUE, You can use the plus sign, which gives you TRUE + FALSE or FALSE + TRUE. This means that either criterion can be met for the value to be included.

This is an alternative to adding two SUMPRODUCTS.

The following formula (based on Figure 7.28) will sum the amount in column L if the department is Sales and the state is either NSW or VIC.

```
=SUMPRODUCT(($K$7:$K$24=Q$6)*(($J$7:$J$24=$O8)+($J$7:$J$24=$O9))*
  ($L$7:$L$24))
```

Notice the extra parentheses around the two conditions that are added together:

```
(($J$7:$J$24=$O8)+($J$7:$J$24=$O9))
```

This makes sure the calculations are processed in the correct sequence.

Array Syntax

In cases where you need to compare multiple criteria, you can use the array syntax with the SUMPRODUCT function.

I mentioned array formula earlier in terms of its similarity to the SUMPRODUCT function. Another advantage of the SUMPRODUCT function is its ability to use the array syntax with the curly brackets {} in its arguments. Not all functions can use the array syntax.

You may have noticed that when Excel converted the criteria comparisons to TRUE and FALSE in Figure 7.29, it enclosed all the results in curly brackets. These are used to define arrays.

In the previous section we looked at modifying a SUMPRODUCT formula to add up the NSW and VIC state amounts in a single SUMPRODUCT formula. We can use the array syntax to simplify the formula further:

```
=SUMPRODUCT(($K$7:$K$24=Q$6)*($J$7:$J$24={"NSW","VIC"})*($L$7:$L$24))
```

This formula does the same calculation as the previous version. The downside of the array syntax is that you can't include cell references. The following formula looks as though it would work, but Excel will not accept it as a valid formula:

```
=SUMPRODUCT(($K$7:$K$24=Q$6)*($J$7:$J$24={O8,O9})*($L$7:$L$24))
```

Using Other Functions with SUMPRODUCT

Another feature of the SUMPRODUCT function is that it can use other functions to do other types of calculations. SUMIF and SUMIFS cannot use other functions.

The 80/20 Rule

Pareto analysis is quite common in many organisations. Pareto analysis is based on what is called the 80/20 rule, which states that, for example, 80 percent of your sales or margin will be generated by 20 percent of your clients. This rule actually holds true across many disciplines. It allows you to focus your attention on a small subset of your clients to achieve maximum effect.

Many organisations have reports that are based on the 80/20 rule, so they report on the top 20 percent of their clients. They may even quantify how many clients they want to report on, such as the top 50 clients. The SUMPRODUCT function can then be used to add up the top 50 clients.

The LARGE function can be used for this analysis. It is similar to the MAX function, except that it gives you the choice to specify the position you want to return. MAX always returns the maximum amount from a range; LARGE can, for example, return the third largest value in a range.

Syntax

LARGE (Range, Position_Number)

Range is the range to analyse. If the range is blank or contains only text, the function will return the #NUM! error message. If the range contains any text entries, then the result may be wrong.

Position_Number is a positive whole number: 1 = first, 2 = second, and so forth.

Example

When used in SUMPRODUCT, the LARGE function can accept an array entry in the Position_Number argument. The following formula sums the top three values in the range A1:A10:

```
=SUMPRODUCT(LARGE(A1:A10,{1,2,3}))
```

Obviously, this method doesn't work very well for large numbers, so you can use another technique for them.

The ROW function returns the row number for its argument. If the argument is omitted, the ROW function returns the current row number. We can use the ROW function to generate an array of the top 10 numbers. The following formula will sum the top 10 values in the range A1:A100:

```
=SUMPRODUCT(LARGE(A1:A100,ROW(1:10))
```

ROW(1:10) returns the array {1,2,3,4,5,6,7,8,9,10}.

Day-of-the-Week Sales

If you have a list of dates, such as those shown in Figure 7.30, and you want to summarise them by day-of-the-week sales, you can use the WEEKDAY function with the SUMPRODUCT function.

	J	K	L	M	N	O
1	Date	Amount		Day	Weekday	Amount
2	1/01/2014	1,305		Sunday	1	3,688
3	2/01/2014	1,256		Monday	2	3,189
4	3/01/2014	1,709		Tuesday	3	3,259
5	4/01/2014	1,792		Wednesday	4	2,867
6	5/01/2014	1,879		Thursday	5	2,653
7	6/01/2014	1,392		Friday	6	2,738
8	7/01/2014	1,468		Saturday	7	3,238
9	8/01/2014	1,562			Total	21,632
10	9/01/2014	1,397				
11	10/01/2014	1,029				
12	11/01/2014	1,446				
13	12/01/2014	1,809				
14	13/01/2014	1,797				
15	14/01/2014	1,791				
16	Total	21,632				

FIGURE 7.30 Date List Summarised

The WEEKDAY function returns a 1 if the date is a Sunday and a 2 for Monday, up to a 7 for Saturday. The formula in O2 is

```
=SUMPRODUCT((WEEKDAY($J$2:$J$15)=N2)*($K$2:$K$15))
```

This has been copied down to O8. The weekday number is calculated for each date in the range J2:J15. It is then compared to the value in N2. Sunday (1) will return a TRUE, and all the others will return a FALSE. This is multiplied by the value and summed.

The GETPIVOTDATA Function

Whilst not strictly a summing function, the GETPIVOTDATA function can be used to create summarised reports that are based on values in an existing pivot table. If your reports could be done with a pivot table, but the formats or layout are too limiting, then the GETPIVOTDATA function may offer a solution.

The GETPIVOTDATA function can extract a value from an existing pivot table. If you have ever tried to link to a cell within a pivot table, you may have seen Excel insert this function automatically.

Many users get frustrated with this feature, and you can turn it off on the ribbon. With a pivot table selected, click the drop-down list of the Options icon on the far left of the Design Ribbon tab. Uncheck the Generate GETPIVOTDATA option.

Before you turn this feature off, you should consider using this function for your reports. It has a couple of limitations, but if you know what they are, you can decide whether this function could help you create your whole report.

Limitations of GETPIVOTDATA

- The figures you require must be displayed in a single cell on the pivot table. In practice, this means that the layout of the pivot table should not be changed once it has been established.
- You can't reliably summarise date ranges (e.g., you can't add up three months of values to calculate a quarter). You can get around this with a separate pivot table that does the date summarising for you.

Advantages of GETPIVOTDATA

- The structure of the function is straightforward to use, especially when the function is teamed up with helper cells.
- You don't have to select ranges.
- You can use the field names to extract the figures you want.
- You can combine the ease of use of pivot tables with the flexibility of a formula-based report.

Syntax

GETPIVOTDATA (Data_Field, Pivot_Table, Field1, Item1, Field2, Item2, . . .)

Data_Field is the value field that you want to extract from the body of the pivot table.

Pivot_Table is a cell reference within the pivot table that you want to extract values from.

Field1 is the field name of the value that you want to extract from.

Item1 is the field item name within Field1 that you want to extract.

Fields and items can be paired up to provide more criteria.

Example

Figure 7.31 shows an extract from a pivot table that summarises sales data into states and dates between gadgets and widgets. It includes volume, value, and margin for each product. The pivot table is on a sheet called pivot.

	A	B	C	D	E	F	G	H	I	J
1	Sales Rep	(All)								
2										
3		Column Labels								
4		Gadget			Widget			Total Sum of Volume	Total Sum of Value	Total Sum of Margin
5	Row Labels	Sum of Volume	Sum of Value	Sum of Margin	Sum of Volume	Sum of Value	Sum of Margin			
6	⊟NSW	38,242	1,660,665	743,382	37,260	1,480,594	710,091	75,502	3,141,259	1,453,473
7	1/01/2014	6,689	289,299	127,620	5,735	229,224	108,304	12,424	518,523	235,924
8	1/02/2014	6,266	235,583	104,824	5,658	203,799	93,642	11,924	439,382	198,466
9	1/03/2014	5,770	286,663	130,643	6,871	274,870	132,606	12,641	561,533	263,249
10	1/04/2014	7,308	326,232	145,916	5,874	239,859	114,215	13,182	566,092	260,132
11	1/05/2014	5,886	280,502	131,748	6,779	265,033	129,851	12,665	545,536	261,600
12	1/06/2014	6,323	242,385	102,630	6,343	267,809	131,473	12,666	510,194	234,103
13	⊟QLD	34,839	1,546,753	704,809	27,213	978,461	436,373	62,052	2,525,214	1,141,182
14	1/01/2014	6,398	271,053	121,900	5,151	194,003	86,216	11,549	465,056	208,116
15	1/02/2014	6,598	289,870	130,932	3,764	148,468	67,060	10,362	438,338	197,992
16	1/03/2014	5,743	236,154	104,983	4,005	147,298	66,796	9,748	383,453	171,780
17	1/04/2014	4,301	211,762	99,959	5,534	196,404	86,452	9,835	408,166	186,411
18	1/05/2014	6,455	269,081	118,220	4,405	149,001	68,430	10,860	418,082	186,650
19	1/06/2014	5,344	268,832	128,814	4,354	143,288	61,420	9,698	412,121	190,235
20	⊟SA	35,797	1,590,361	738,283	30,401	1,215,216	558,180	66,198	2,805,577	1,296,463
21	1/01/2014	5,908	271,949	124,476	5,192	212,185	98,844	11,100	484,134	223,320
22	1/02/2014	6,611	291,401	132,363	4,375	168,611	78,075	10,986	460,011	210,437

FIGURE 7.31 Pivot Table Sales Report Extract

In most cases the easiest way to create a GETPIVOTDATA formula is to link to a value cell in the pivot table. This identifies all the components of the function that you need to include from helper cells. Figure 7.32 shows the formula that linked to C12 in the pivot table in Figure 7.31.

```
=GETPIVOTDATA("Sum of Value",Pivot!$A$3,"State","NSW","Product","Gadget","Month",DATE(2014,6,1))
```

FIGURE 7.32 GETPIVOTDATA Function

Figure 7.33 shows the completed report based on the pivot table in Figure 7.31. The report extracts the Value field values for the states, for June 2014, and for both products. The formula in Figure 7.32 has been amended to use the entries in the helper cells in rows 1 and 2 and columns A to D. Helper cells simplify creating the final formula.

The formula in E4 that matches the formula in Figure 7.32 is shown next and has been copied and pasted to the range E4:F8:

```
=GETPIVOTDATA(""&$A$1,pivot!$A$3,$A4,$B4,E$2,E$3,$C4,$D4)
```

The first argument, Data_Field, must be text. For some reason, Excel doesn't accept a text entry in a cell. To force Excel to treat a cell like text, I have used the & symbol to join the cell value from A1 to a blank text string (two quotation marks together signify a blank text string). The & symbol joins text together.

You could include Data_Field as an entry enclosed in quotation marks, as shown in Figure 7.32 above. But that limits the flexibility of the formula. Changing the entry

	A	B	C	D	E	F	G	H	I
1	Value								
2					Product	Product			
3					Gadget	Widget		Total	Check
4	State	NSW	Month	1/06/2014	242,385	267,809		**510,194**	510,194
5	State	QLD	Month	1/06/2014	268,832	143,288		**412,121**	412,121
6	State	SA	Month	1/06/2014	286,682	218,683		**505,365**	505,365
7	State	VIC	Month	1/06/2014	254,362	148,126		**402,488**	402,488
8	State	WA	Month	1/06/2014	156,703	138,649		**295,352**	295,352
9									
10				Total	**1,208,965**	**916,556**		**2,125,521**	**2,125,521**

FIGURE 7.33 GETPIVOTDATA Report

in A1 with the amended formula allows you to change the report to display volume or margin, the other two fields being summed in the pivot table in Figure 7.31.

There are three conditions being applied in the amended formula to specify which cell to extract from the pivot table. The first pair, $A4 and $B4, specify the state. The second pair, E$2 and E$3, specify the product, and the third pair, $C4 and $D4, specify the month.

Column H and row 10 contain SUM functions. Column I contains a check formula. The formula in I4 is

```
=GETPIVOTDATA(""&$A$1,pivot!$A$3,$A4,$B4,C4,D4)
```

This is the same formula as the body of the report except it has the product criteria removed so that it returns the total of all product sales for the state and month.

You can't provide a check for the totals shown in row 10 because those totals do not appear on the pivot table. The pivot table only totals all the sales for all the months by product. It doesn't provide a subtotal for each month. The GETPIVOTDATA function extracts a value that appears in a cell in a pivot table. This means you need to get the pivot table layout correct, to provide all the values you need, before creating your GETPIVOTDATA function.

As you can see, the GETPIVOTDATA function is flexible and allows you to create a formula-based version of a pivot table report in a layout that you can design.

CHAPTER EIGHT

Accessories: Other Reporting Functions and Features

THE SUMMING FUNCTIONS PROVIDE the major tools to create management reports, but there are many other functions and features that need to be combined to complete an automated and integrated reporting solution.

Some of these functions and features were briefly mentioned in the data cleansing section of this book, and they will be examined in more detail in this chapter. Other functions will be used in helper cells, a concept introduced in the last chapter, to make it possible to create and copy formulas to large sections of a report.

HELPER CELLS

Helper cells are used to simplify formulas and enable them to be copied into more ranges. You can create some really impressive, long, and complex formulas in Excel, but most situations don't require you to do everything in one formula. Indeed, it is often more efficient to break up complex formulas into helper cells.

We have seen the use of helper cells in previous chapters. We saw how they can enable you to copy and paste a report layout with less emphasis on fixed references.

Helper cells can also allow you to create shorter formulas by splitting the calculations between cells. This is especially useful when working with the IF function, which is a major reason that formulas can become quite long.

Long formulas can be hard to read and understand. This makes maintaining or changing your reporting model difficult. By splitting up the components of a complex formula into separate cells, it simplifies the final formula. This makes changes to the component parts of the formula easier.

You will find that the components can often be used by other formulas. So instead of repeating the same IF function in multiple formulas, you can use a helper cell to do an IF function comparison and then refer to that cell in your other formulas. This also makes maintenance easier. Should the IF function comparison change, you only have to change the helper cells. Without using the helper cells, you would have to change the individual, more complex formulas.

Using helper cells requires planning. If a particular calculation is to be used a few times, it makes sense to put it in a helper cell so that it can be referred to by other formulas. Sometimes you don't know that a calculation will be repeated, however, so you might have to reengineer parts of your model to take advantage of helper cells.

My basic rule is that if a calculation is to be used more than twice in separate formulas, then it is best to create a separate helper cell for that calculation.

You can also use helper cells to contain sequential numbers, which can be useful for month numbers. In Australia the financial year starts in July. The first month of our financial year is therefore the seventh month of the calendar year, and the seventh month of our financial year is the first month of the calendar year. This means we can't easily use the MONTH function to identify our month numbers in sequence, so using helper cells can simplify some date calculations.

Advantages of Helper Cells

- Helper cells make maintenance easier—they typically have simple formulas, and modifying simple formulas is always easier than working with complex formulas.
- The resulting final formulas are shorter and easier to understand and maintain.
- The spreadsheet is more transparent because the components of the final formulas are displayed on the sheet in the helper cells instead of being included in long, complex formulas. This makes validation and error checking easier.
- They simplify the conditional formatting formulas to be discussed in Chapter 11.

Helper Cells Structure

Dedicating certain rows and columns for helper cells makes sense. Typically you use the first few rows and first few columns on each sheet as helper cells. How many rows and columns will depend on your specific requirements.

You can add structure to your model by specifying certain cells that will perform the same task on all sheets. For instance, maybe cell A1 on all sheets has the full path of the file, and cell A2 has the sheet name. There are formulas that can automate these entries.

Other helper cells or ranges can be included in the body of your report. These are typically hidden in the final model and unhidden only for maintenance or modifications.

The exceptions to this rule are data sheets and table sheets, which are dedicated to a single task and typically don't require helper cells.

Centralising Logic

In the design phase of your model, you need to identify logic arguments that will be used frequently in other formulas. You can perform this logic calculation once and then repeatedly refer to it. This saves you from performing the same logic calculation in multiple formulas. Logic formulas and functions are discussed in the next section of this chapter.

Let's say you are creating a 12-month report that includes actual figures up to the current month and then forecast figures for future months. You will need to identify which months have actuals and which have forecasts. This distinction will be used in many calculations and should be centralised.

By centralising that calculation, you simplify the other calculations and make it easy to amend all of them if you find an error in the method you used to identify the actual and forecast months.

LOGIC FUNCTIONS

Logic functions involve handling logical comparisons that return a TRUE or FALSE result. A logical comparison means comparing values or text using specific operators. If the comparison is correct, then the result is TRUE. If the comparison is incorrect, the result is FALSE.

I introduced the idea of logical comparisons in the previous chapter in the section on the SUMPRODUCT function, which utilises TRUE and FALSE in its calculations.

The IF function is most frequently associated with logical comparisons, but other functions also take advantage of their simplicity.

Table 8.1 contains examples of logical comparisons.

TABLE 8.1 Logical Comparison Examples

Logical Comparison	Result
A1=B1	TRUE is returned if A1 is the same as B1. Otherwise FALSE is returned. In value terms, both cells must be exactly the same. In text terms, uppercase and lowercase is ignored as long as the letters and number are the same. Space characters can cause a difference, especially leading and trailing spaces, as we saw in the data cleansing section of Chapter 5.
A1="Yes"	TRUE is returned if the cell contains the text Yes, yes, or YES. Otherwise, it will return FALSE. When comparing cells to text, you have to enclose the text in quotation marks. The comparison is not case-sensitive.
A1=SUM(B1:B10)	TRUE is returned if the value in A1 equals the SUM of the range B1:B10. Otherwise, it will return FALSE. You can have formulas and functions on either side of the comparison formula.
A1>B1	TRUE is returned only when the value in A1 is greater than the value in B1. Otherwise FALSE is returned. Excel considers alphabetical order when comparing text strings. Hence, the letter *b* is deemed "greater" than the letter *a* because *b* comes after *a* in the alphabet.

(*continued*)

TABLE 8.1 *(Continued)*

Logical Comparison	Result
A1<>B1	TRUE is displayed when A1 is not equal to B1. The "<>" symbolises "not equal to" and is the least-known of the comparisons. This is the opposite of the first entry in this table. Sometimes it can be easier to use this formula in your IF function, but beware: using "not equal to" can get confusing. We tend to understand "equal to" better than "not equal to." "Not equal to" is commonly used to handle exceptions, such as identifying where one department out of several on a list is handled slightly differently.

Each of these formulas can also be entered into a cell starting with an equal sign.

The IF function is the most commonly used function that handles TRUE and FALSE results.

In terms of calculations, Excel treats TRUE as 1 and FALSE as 0. These values can be used in calculations to zero values in certain situations.

Logic Cell Calculation Example

Figure 8.1 has an example in which you can use a logic calculation instead of an IF function. Cell J7 is used to decide whether to apply inflation. There is a data validation list in the cell to select yes or no.

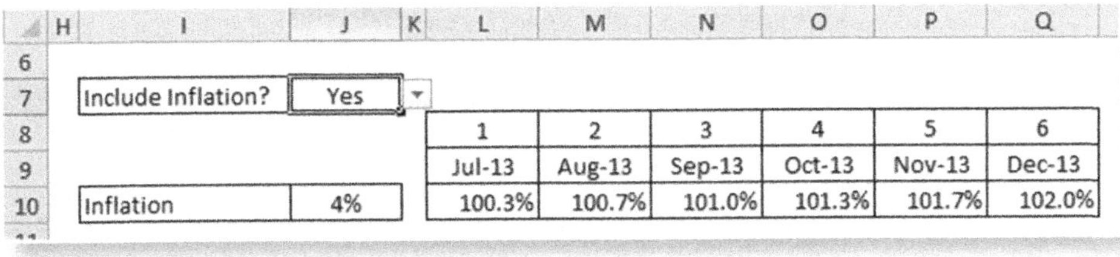

	H	I	J	K	L	M	N	O	P	Q
6										
7		Include Inflation?	Yes							
8					1	2	3	4	5	6
9					Jul-13	Aug-13	Sep-13	Oct-13	Nov-13	Dec-13
10		Inflation	4%		100.3%	100.7%	101.0%	101.3%	101.7%	102.0%

FIGURE 8.1 Logic Calculation Example

Users are more comfortable with selecting yes or no rather than TRUE or FALSE. We'll review the IF function in more detail in the next section. Most people would create a formula like the following to apply inflation. This formula is in cell L10 and can be copied across:

```
=IF($J$7="yes",1+($J10/12*L8),1)
```

This formula will work, and there is nothing wrong with it. However, you could shorten it slightly by using the result of a logical comparison to determine whether to include inflation in the calculation:

```
=1+($J10/12*L8*($J$7="yes"))
```

This technique is useful for zeroing values if a cell meets a certain condition. The part of the formula $J$7="yes" will equate to 1 if cell J7 contains yes, or zero if it doesn't. Multiplying the rest of the formula by 1 will not affect it, but multiplying it by 0 will zero that part of the formula.

In our example, rather than having an inflation formula in each month, we could have an input cell for inflation and a separate cell that contains the inflation to apply (see Figure 8.2).

	H	I	J	K	L	M	N	O	P	Q
6										
7		Include Inflation?	Yes							
8					1	2	3	4	5	6
9		Inflation Input	4%		Jul-13	Aug-13	Sep-13	Oct-13	Nov-13	Dec-13
10		Inflation to Apply	4%		100.3%	100.7%	101.0%	101.3%	101.7%	102.0%

FIGURE 8.2 Logic Calculation Simplified Example

Now cell J9 is the input cell, and cell J10 has a formula to determine whether to use inflation. The J10 formula is now

```
=J9*(J7"yes")
```

The formula in cell L10 is then simplified to

```
=1+($J10/12*L8)
```

This moves the logic calculation into a single cell rather than having it in multiple cells.

You can use logic calculations in validation cells; this will be examined in detail in Chapter 13.

It is important to get a good understanding of logic calculations because they allow you to control how the reporting model copes with different situations.

Logical calculations are also used in conditional formatting, which is discussed in Chapter 11. Conditional formatting automates the formatting of a cell based on the cell's value as well as many other options. For example, a cell that contains TRUE could be shown with a green fill, and a cell with FALSE could display a red fill. This makes tracking down validation errors much easier.

THE IF FUNCTION

The IF function allows you to build decision-making structures into your reporting models and lets your formulas handle many different reporting situations. It is ideal for handling any exceptions that your reports may require. The IF function also makes it easier to create a single formula that can be copied down and across in a report.

Combined with helper cells, the IF function can make your reporting model very flexible.

Syntax

IF (Logical_Test, True_Action, False_Action)

Logical_Test is a statement that must return TRUE or FALSE. These are the same as we saw earlier in the chapter (e.g., A1=B1, A1>0).

True_Action can be a value, text enclosed in quotation marks, a formula, a range, or it can be left blank.

False_Action can be a value, text enclosed in quotation marks, a formula, a range, or it can be left blank.

If True_Action is omitted and Logical_Test is true, the word TRUE is displayed. If False_Action is omitted and the result is false, then the word FALSE is displayed.

Examples

The following formula means that if A1 equals zero (Logical_Test), then display a zero (True_Action), or else display the result of dividing B1 by A1(False_Action). This structure is commonly used to avoid DIV0#! error messages. You check to see if A1 is zero before dividing by it.

```
=IF(A1=0,0,B1/A1)
```

The next formula means that if A1 equals B1, then display the text OK, or else display the text Error. This structure is used for validation purposes: If A1 equals B1, then it is valid and OK is displayed; otherwise, it is an error and the word Error is displayed.

```
=IF(A1=B1,"OK","Error")
```

The next formula means that if A1 contains the text Yes, then display the result of B1 multiplied by 0.1, or else display zero. This is an example of checking an input cell for a value before performing a calculation—in this case, the word Yes before the multiplication by 0.1.

```
=IF(A1="Yes",B1*0.10,0)
```

IF Functions and Helper Cells

If your helper cells have logical tests that display TRUE or FALSE, then this simplifies the IF function. Assume that A1 is a helper cell containing a logical test and that it displays either TRUE or FALSE.

The following two formulas produce exactly the same result:

```
=IF(A1=TRUE,"OK","Error")
=IF(A1,"OK","Error")
```

When a cell contains a logical test, as A1 does, then it is not necessary to test if the cell is equal to TRUE. You can just refer to it, as in the second example. The cell's result becomes the Logical_Test for the IF function.

Obviously, OK and Error are words we understand, so in a validation situation you may need to convert TRUE or FALSE into those words for the final validation check. In the creation of the individual validations, however, you can use simple helper cells that display TRUE or FALSE.

Validations are covered in depth in Chapter 13.

Shorter IF Functions

The True_Action and False_Action parts of the IF function can also contain a range reference. This enables you to create slightly shorter IF functions in certain situations.

Assume that cell A1 is a helper cell and has a logic formula that displays TRUE or FALSE. If A1 is TRUE, we want to SUM one range; if it's FALSE, we want to SUM a different range. The common formula used would be

```
=IF(A1,SUM(B1:B10),SUM(C1:C10))
```

We can shorten this formula because both the True_Action and False_Action contain a SUM function, just with different ranges. So the formula could be rewritten as

```
=SUM(IF(A1,B1:B10,C1:C10))
```

This places the IF function within the SUM function's parentheses, so it will return the range to use with the SUM function. This is a slightly shorter formula by having only one SUM function and having the IF function return a range.

The SUM function has a simple syntax. For more complex functions like the VLOOKUP, this structure can be more efficient.

Nested IF Functions

The True_Action and False_Action parts of the IF function can both contain other formulas, and this includes other IF functions. When you use an IF function within an IF function, this is called nesting IF functions.

There is a limit to how many nested levels you can have. The level limit was 7 in Excel 2003 but was expanded to 64 in Excel 2007 and 2010.

In practice, reading and understanding nested IF functions can be quite difficult. The more nested levels there are, the harder they are to understand. Once the number of IF function levels exceeds four, it becomes difficult to understand the formula.

Figure 8.3 shows a nested IF function example.

	H	I	J	K
5				
6		Cartage charge Rules	Helper Cells	
7		Free when Sales value exceeds	$250	
8		Free when more than 20 items purchased	20	
9		Charge per kilo up to 10kg	$2.00	per kg
10		Charge per kilo above 10kg	$1.75	per kg
11		Weight parameter	10	kg
12				
13			Input	
14		Sales Value	$175.00	
15		Number of Items	15	
16		Weight	11	kg
17				
18			Formula	
19		Cartage Calculation	$19.25	
20				

FIGURE 8.3 Nested IF Example

The rules to calculate cartage are shown in rows 7 to 11. The actual values to compare are in cells J14 to J16.

Cell J19 has the following formula to calculate the cartage cost:

```
=IF(J14>J7,0,IF(J15>J8,0,J16*IF(J16<=J11,J9,J10)))
```

The first two nested IF functions both determine if the cartage is zero. Obviously, this is the best place to start because there are no further calculations required if the cartage is free.

The first IF function checks whether the sales value in cell J14 is greater than the value in helper cell J7. If it is TRUE, then the cartage is zero.

The second IF function is in the FALSE argument of the first IF function. This IF function checks whether the number of items in cell J15 is greater than in the helper cell J8. If it is TRUE, then again the cartage is zero.

The third IF function is in the FALSE argument of the second IF function. This IF function calculates the rate to be multiplied by the weight cell J16. The weight cell J16 is compared to the weight parameter helper cell J11. If it is less than or equal to J11, then the rate from cell J9 is used; otherwise, the rate in J10 is used.

IF Function Complexity

In terms of complexity, there is an argument to keep IF functions to three levels so they can be read and understood. Helper cells can assist with this by breaking down each level of logic into a single formula. In some cases you can then use the AND or the OR function (explained next) to further simplify your IF functions.

In some cases people learn about the IF function and apply it to situations where another formula would be more effective.

If you build a complicated multi-level IF function, it might pay to rethink the problem and see whether there is a better way to handle the situation. A table-based solution can often be used in place of a multi-level, nested IF function.

Excel has a keyboard shortcut that inserts a line break in a cell. It's Alt + Enter when entering or editing in a cell. This is useful for text headings, but it can also be used for formulas. Figure 8.4 shows an amended version of the example formula from Figure 8.3.

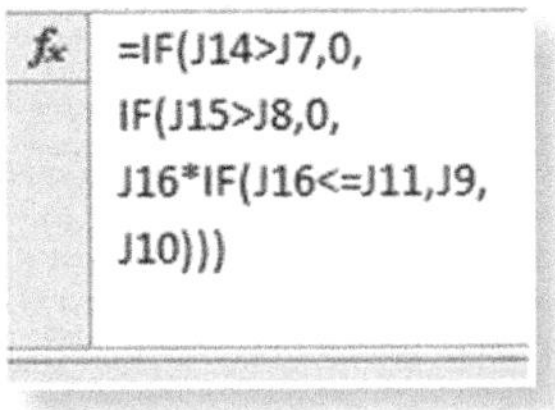

```
fx  =IF(J14>J7,0,
    IF(J15>J8,0,
    J16*IF(J16<=J11,J9,
    J10)))
```

FIGURE 8.4 Alternate IF Function Layout Using Alt + Enter

I don't use this layout, but I have seen it demonstrated and thought it might appeal to some people. It splits the FALSE arguments to the next line.

There are also two other logic functions that can be used to remove levels from IF functions. The AND function and the OR function can help simplify IF functions.

WARNING: IF Functions and Spreadsheet Errors

IF functions are one of the most common sources of errors in Excel spreadsheets. IF functions are like short programming instructions included in your spreadsheet. Programmers need to debug and test their code. In the same way, you must test your IF functions.

Testing involves checking the results using values close to the various parameters used in the arguments: testing with zero values and testing with errors.

Make sure you are using the correct comparison operators (e.g., Should you use the >or the >=?).

Your logic also has to be checked. The sequence of the nested IF functions can often affect the result. You need to make sure the results you achieve are the ones you planned for.

Copied IF functions must be tested in their destination cells to make sure they are still working correctly.

THE AND AND OR FUNCTIONS

The AND and OR functions are best described together. Both allow you to examine multiple logical tests in one step, and both have the same syntax. Each has multiple logical tests separated by commas. Both return either TRUE or FALSE.

Syntax

AND (Logical_Test1, Logical_Test2, . . .)

OR (Logical_Test1, Logical_Test2, . . .)

Logical_Test1, **Logical_Test2**, and so forth can be a single cell or a range containing many logical tests. If the range contains other values, text, or blanks, they are all treated as TRUE. The only exception is zero, which is treated as FALSE.

AND and OR work differently in analyzing the logical tests and returning a result.

The AND function will return TRUE only when every Logical_Test is TRUE. If just one Logical_Test is FALSE, then the AND function will return FALSE. This is useful for validation tests, when all the Logical_Tests have to be TRUE.

The OR function will return TRUE when any of the Logical_Tests are TRUE. The only time the OR function will return FALSE is when all the Logical_Tests are FALSE.

To see how these two functions compare, review the logic table in Figure 8.5. There are three logical tests, so there are eight possible permutations, or 2^3.

You can see that the AND function and the OR function return the same result in only two cases: when all the logical tests are TRUE, and when they are all FALSE. In the other cases they give opposite results.

The AND function is typically used for those situations in which everything must be correct or equal, such as validations.

	H	I	J	K	L	M
6	Logic_Test_1	Logic_Test_2	Logic_Test_3		AND	OR
7	TRUE	TRUE	TRUE		TRUE	TRUE
8	TRUE	TRUE	FALSE		FALSE	TRUE
9	TRUE	FALSE	TRUE		FALSE	TRUE
10	TRUE	FALSE	FALSE		FALSE	TRUE
11	FALSE	TRUE	TRUE		FALSE	TRUE
12	FALSE	TRUE	FALSE		FALSE	TRUE
13	FALSE	FALSE	TRUE		FALSE	TRUE
14	FALSE	FALSE	FALSE		FALSE	FALSE

FIGURE 8.5 Logic Table Comparing AND and OR Functions

The OR function is more suited to those situations in which there are exceptions—when a single TRUE result could mean that a process is to be done.

The functions can also be nested. You can have AND functions within an OR function. You can also have OR functions within an AND function to create complex logic formulas.

Typically, the AND and OR functions are used as the logical test in an IF function. They can, however, be used on their own in a cell, where they will return TRUE or FALSE and can be used as helper cells.

A few examples will help demonstrate the power of using these two functions.

Examples

First, consider a filter we want to apply to the table in Figure 8.6.

	H	I	J	K	L	M	N
4							
5		Accounts	WA	VIC	NSW	SA	QLD
6		1234	$2,817	$2,067	$2,125	$2,873	$2,907
7		1235	$0	$0	$0	$0	$0
8		1236	-$2,859	$2,670	$0	$2,360	$2,649
9		1237	$1,164	$2,619	-$1,480	$1,878	$1,979
10		1238	$0	-$2,403	$2,901	$2,448	$2,532
11		1239	$2,480	$0	$2,984	$2,189	-$1,950
12		1240	$2,127	-$1,954	$0	$2,854	$1,740
13		1241	-$2,467	$0	-$1,265	$1,596	$0
14		1242	$0	$0	$0	$0	$0
15		1243	$1,089	$0	$1,801	$1,857	-$2,647
16		1244	$1,052	$2,798	$1,264	$0	$1,657

FIGURE 8.6 Table to Be Filtered

We want to filter the table so that we see only the rows that contain values. In this case, rows 7 and 14 would be filtered out and hidden. One solution is to add a new column containing an AND function that determines whether there are all zeros in the value columns. You might be able to use a SUM function to total up the values, but there is a chance that there could be positives and negatives that cancel each other out and total zero. Figure 8.7 shows the additional column added to the table.

	I	J	K	L	M	N	O
4							
5	Accounts	WA	VIC	NSW	SA	QLD	Filter
6	1234	$2,817	$2,067	$2,125	$2,873	$2,907	FALSE
7	1235	$0	$0	$0	$0	$0	TRUE
8	1236	-$2,859	$2,670	$0	$2,360	$2,649	FALSE
9	1237	$1,164	$2,619	-$1,480	$1,878	$1,979	FALSE
10	1238	$0	-$2,403	$2,901	$2,448	$2,532	FALSE
11	1239	$2,480	$0	$2,984	$2,189	-$1,950	FALSE
12	1240	$2,127	-$1,954	$0	$2,854	$1,740	FALSE
13	1241	-$2,467	$0	-$1,265	$1,596	$0	FALSE
14	1242	$0	$0	$0	$0	$0	TRUE
15	1243	$1,089	$0	$1,801	$1,857	-$2,647	FALSE
16	1244	$1,052	$2,798	$1,264	$0	$1,657	FALSE

FIGURE 8.7 Table to Be Filtered—Column Added

The formula in cell O6 is

```
=AND(J6=0,K6=0,L6=0,M6=0,N6=0)
```

It has been copied down. It will display TRUE only when all the value cells are zero. If any value cells contain a value that is above or below zero, then it will display FALSE. We could use the FALSE entries to filter out the zero rows.

If we revisit Figure 8.3, we can rewrite the formula in cell J19, which was

```
=IF(J14>J7,0,IF(J15>J8,0,J16*IF(J16<=J11,J9,J10)))
```

There were two conditions that led to free cartage: if the value was over $250 or the number of items was over 20. This is an ideal situation for the OR function because a TRUE in either of two separate conditions results in zero cartage. We can rewrite the above function as

```
=IF(OR(J14>J7,J15>J8),0,J16*IF(J16<=J11,J9,J10))
```

It is only slightly shorter, but it removes one level from the IF function.

Array Syntax

There is a technique mentioned in the previous chapter that you can employ with the OR function that allows you to specify a number of different criteria in one step. If you need to check whether a single cell contains the value 1, 2, or 3, you could write

```
=OR(A1=1,A1=2,A1=3)
```

Another option is to use the array syntax, which involves using curly brackets. Not all functions can use arrays, but the OR function can. So we can rewrite the above formula as

```
=OR(A1={1,2,3})
```

This is exactly the same as the first formula, but it is a shorthand way of writing it.

If you are comparing text—such as whether a cell contains a, b, or c—the formula would look like this:

```
=OR(A1={"a","b","c"})
```

Multiple IF Functions versus a Lookup Function

In many cases, if you are using multiple IF functions, you might find that a lookup function would serve your purposes better and be easier to create and maintain. This may mean creating a table or a list to work with the lookup function.

LOOKUP FUNCTIONS

There are only a few lookup functions, but they can add flexibility to a reporting model by allowing you to use different values for different situations. They are typically based on a table structure. The VLOOKUP function was used in Chapter 5 to add an extra field to a table.

I highly recommend using table structures in Excel to store most of your settings. Tables allow you to set up rules that are easy to create and then maintain. Many of Excel's functions work well with tables.

Lookup functions are usually based on tables that have a field containing unique entries. Lookup functions can also be used to find the first entry in a table that contains duplicated entries. Some of the lookup functions require the table to be sorted, and I tend to avoid those because it is easy in practice for a table to end up being unsorted (e.g., as new entries are added to the bottom of the table).

In the next chapter you will learn techniques for creating autoexpanding tables using range names. Formatted tables, explained in Chapter 5, also provide many advantages when using lookup functions.

THE VLOOKUP FUNCTION

The most widely used lookup function is VLOOKUP. The *V* stands for *vertical*. This function is used to look up values in a traditional table layout with columns for fields and rows for records.

There is another function that works horizontally: HLOOKUP. It works in a similar way to VLOOKUP, but the fields are on rows and the records are in columns.

In general, the number of records is more likely to expand while the number of fields remains reasonably static. Hence, it makes more sense to have the records going down the sheet in rows rather than across the sheet in columns. Excel 2010 is limited to about 16,000 columns (the limit was only 256 in Excel 2003).

In practical terms, HLOOKUP has a problem with sorting the table. Excel has a sort feature, but it only works vertically. So to sort a horizontal table, you have to do it manually or else convert it to a vertical table, sort it, and then convert it back to a horizontal table. Excel has a Transpose option in the Paste Special dialog box that makes that conversion possible.

The use of the VLOOKUP function is often seen as the mark of an Advanced Excel user. I do not agree with that assessment; I tend to put VLOOKUP use on an intermediate level.

I will focus on VLOOKUP here and provide some examples of HLOOKUP in the next section.

Syntax

VLOOKUP (Lookup_Value, Table_Array, Column_Index_Number, Range_Lookup)

Lookup_Value is typically a cell reference that holds the entry to look up in Table_Array.

Table_Array is the range of the table to be looked up. It is usually a fixed reference to a table, a range name, or the name of a formatted table. The left column in the range must contain the lookup value to be searched for. VLOOKUP is not case-sensitive.

Column_Index_Number is a whole number that refers to the column number within Table_Array that contains the value to be extracted from the table. This is commonly a keyed-in entry. If you use a number greater than the number of columns in the table, the #REF! error message is displayed. In many cases a formula can be used for Column_Index_Number to provide a flexible lookup. The function commonly used is the MATCH function, which will be covered later in this chapter.

Range_Lookup (optional) is a logical value TRUE or FALSE, 1 or 0.

TRUE, 1, or omitted means that an exact match is searched for initially. If there is no exact match, then an approximate match is used, which means the next largest value is deemed to match. If you use TRUE or omit Range_Lookup, then Table_Array must be sorted in ascending order by the first column. If it is not sorted in ascending order, incorrect results can be displayed. Ensure you have a zero value in the left column of the table if you are looking up numbers. This helps avoid #N/A error messages.

FALSE or 0 means that an exact match is required. An exact match option requires that the Lookup_Value be in column 1 of the table; if not, the #N/A error message is displayed. An exact match does not require the table to be sorted. Sorting the table by the first column will slightly improve the calculation speed when using exact matches.

In my experience, the exact match method is the most common type of VLOOKUP. The approximate match method is used for lookups that are based on levels or thresholds of values. Their uses are best described by two examples.

Exact Match Example

Figure 8.8 has a table and a range, and we will extract data from the table. In most cases tables are in dedicated sheets and not on the same sheet in which you are extracting the data. The table is not sorted.

	I	J	K	L	M	N	O	P	Q	R	S	T
1		Stock Code	Description	Colour	Cost	Price		1	2	3	4	5
2		ABC123	Widget	Red	$0.20	$0.45		Stock Code	Description	Colour	Cost	Price
3		ABC124	Widget	Green	$0.20	$0.40						
4		XYZ111	Widget	White	$0.90	$1.50						
5		XYZ222	Gadget	Black	$0.10	$0.20						
6		DEF321	Gadget	Blue	$0.80	$1.40						
7		DEF322	Gadget	Yellow	$0.50	$1.00						

FIGURE 8.8 Table and Extraction Range

Stock codes will be entered in cells P3 and P4. Columns Q to T will then populate with data from the table based on the code entered. Cells P1:T1 are helper cells and will enable us to create a single formula in Q3 to copy across and down. The Q3 formula is

```
=VLOOKUP($P3,$J$2:$N$7,Q$1,0)
```

If the entry cells P3 and P4 are empty, then the #N/A error message is displayed. It is common to modify the formula slightly and add an IF function to check for a blank entry cell. The amended formula would be

=IF($P3=" "," ",VLOOKUP($P3,$J$2:$N$7,Q$1,0))

The double quotation marks " " refer to a blank cell. In this case, if cell P3 is blank, then a blank cell is displayed. If P3 is not blank, then the result of the VLOOKUP formula is displayed.

In terms of the VLOOKUP formula, the entry in P3 is looked up in the table J2:N7. The code in cell P3 must be in the range J2:J7, the leftmost column in the table. The reference to Q$1 is the helper cell that contains the column number to extract. The 0 at the end defines the VLOOKUP as an exact match. You can use FALSE or 0. I always use 0 because it requires less typing and shortens the formula.

An exact match VLOOKUP is more likely to display the #N/A error message than an approximate match is.

Figure 8.9 shows an example of entered values.

	I	J	K	L	M	N	O	P	Q	R	S	T
1		Stock Code	Description	Colour	Cost	Price		1	2	3	4	5
2		ABC123	Widget	Red	$0.20	$0.45		Stock Code	Description	Colour	Cost	Price
3		ABC124	Widget	Green	$0.20	$0.40		ABC124	Widget	Green	$0.20	$0.40
4		XYZ111	Widget	White	$0.90	$1.50		DEF321	Gadget	Blue	$0.80	$1.40
5		XYZ222	Gadget	Black	$0.10	$0.20						
6		DEF321	Gadget	Blue	$0.80	$1.40						
7		DEF322	Gadget	Yellow	$0.50	$1.00						

FIGURE 8.9 Table and Populated Extraction Range

Tip: VLOOKUP Approximate Match Table

You should start each table used for approximate matches with zero. This reduces #N/A error messages for values below the first threshold level in the table. Also, blank cells are treated as zero.

In practice, the starting value you use should be below the lowest expected value. If you are likely to have negative numbers, you need to start with a negative value below the lowest expected negative value.

	I	J	K	L	M	N	O
1		Sales $	Commission %		1	2	
2		0	0.00%		Sales $	Comm %	Comm $
3		10,000	1.25%				$0.00
4		50,000	1.50%				$0.00
5		100,000	1.75%				
6		250,000	2.00%				

FIGURE 8.10 Commission Table and Extraction Range

Approximate Match Example

Approximate match VLOOKUPs do not require the value being looked up to be in the table. But they do require the table to be sorted in ascending order by the leftmost column in the table. If the table is not sorted, the formula may return incorrect results.

Figure 8.10 has a sales commission table and an extraction range. The table shows that the more sales there are in a month, the higher the commission percentage.

The formula for cell N3 is

```
=VLOOKUP(M3,$J$2:$K$6,N$1)
```

This formula can be copied down.

A blank cell in M3 doesn't cause the #N/A error message because the blank cell is treated as zero, and zero appears in the table.

This formula uses the approximate match by default because it leaves out the fourth argument in the function.

This version of the VLOOKUP will first look for the value in the leftmost column of the table and extract the relevant column, if found. If it doesn't find the value, it will use the highest value in the left column of the table that is below the value being looked up. Figure 8.11 has the result of two lookups.

The value $75,000 in cell M3 is not in the table. The highest value that is below $75,000 is $50,000, and that is the commission percentage that is extracted in cell N3.

Approximate matches handle lookup values above the highest value in the table by using the highest value, as can be seen with the result in cell N4 in Figure 8.11.

	I	J	K	L	M	N	O
1		Sales $	Commission %		1	2	
2		0	0.00%		Sales $	Comm %	Comm $
3		10,000	1.25%		$75,000.00	1.50%	$1,125.00
4		50,000	1.50%		$255,000.00	2.00%	$5,100.00
5		100,000	1.75%				
6		250,000	2.00%				

FIGURE 8.11 Commission Table and Populated Extraction Range

Whole Columns as Table Range

If you have a long table that is constantly expanding, you may consider referring to the whole columns of the table. It is generally not advisable to do this, since it may affect performance, but it does ensure that the table range includes all the entries.

Avoid using this technique if the table is in another workbook. VLOOKUP functions that refer to external workbooks are notoriously slow.

THE HLOOKUP FUNCTION

As mentioned earlier, the HLOOKUP function is similar to the VLOOKUP but operates across a sheet rather than down a sheet. Its syntax is similar, with only Column_Index_Number being replaced by Row_Index_Number.

Syntax

HLOOKUP (Lookup_Value, Table_Array, Row_Index_Number, Range_Lookup)

The first row in **Table_Array** is the range where the lookup value will be matched.

Row_Index_Number is the same as Column_Index_Number in VLOOKUP.

The topmost row must be sorted in ascending order for approximate matches.

The other components work the same as in VLOOKUP.

Exact Match Example

Figure 8.12 contains monthly values going across the page. The extraction range allows us to extract a certain month's value from the table.

	I	J	K	L	M	N	O	P	Q	R	S	T	U	V
1		Month	Jan-13	Feb-13	Mar-13	Apr-13	May-13	Jun-13		1	2	3	4	5
2		Production	832	414	362	796	733	347		Month	Production	Sales	Marketing	Admin
3		Sales	159	701	283	362	436	798		Feb-13	414	701	797	843
4		Marketing	705	797	655	655	837	352		May-13	733	436	837	395
5		Admin	661	843	352	437	395	808						

FIGURE 8.12 Monthly Table and Populated Extraction Range

The formula to extract the selected month's values in cell S3 is

```
=HLOOKUP($R3,$K$1:$P$5,S$1,0)
```

This formula can be copied down and across. Again, you may need to add an IF function like the following to handle a blank entry cell:

```
=IF($R3="","",HLOOKUP($R3,$K$1:$P$5,S$1,0))
```

The range K1:P1 doesn't have to be sorted. It happens to be sorted because it is date based. If the month being looked up isn't in the range K1:P1, then the #N/A error message will be displayed. The helper cell S1 contains the row number in the table to extract. The 0 specifies an exact match.

Approximate Match Example

Figure 8.13 shows a table that lists interest rates and their active dates.

	H	I	J	K	L	M	N	O	P	Q	R	S	T	U
1		Date	1-Jan-13	17-Jan-13	20-Feb-13	1-Apr-13	7-Apr-13	1-Jun-13	29-Aug-13	1-Nov-13	14-Dec-13			2
2		Interest Rate	6.23%	6.54%	6.27%	6.56%	6.27%	6.58%	6.25%	6.89%	6.27%		Date	Rate
3													18-Jan-13	6.54%
4													06-Sep-13	6.25%

FIGURE 8.13 Interest Rate Table and Populated Extraction Range

The formula in cell U3 is

```
=HLOOKUP(T3,$J$1:$R$2,U$1)
```

The formula can be copied down.

J1:R1 must be sorted in ascending order. As mentioned, that can pose a problem because Excel's sorting feature does not sort rows, it only sorts columns. You have to manually move entries and make sure they are in ascending order.

Again the approximate match looks for the lookup value (the date) first, and if it isn't in the range, it looks for the highest value that is less than the lookup value. It then extracts the row number specified for that column.

WARNING: VLOOKUP and HLOOKUP Problems

There are two major issues you need to consider when using the two lookup functions.

The first is that if a column (VLOOKUP) or a row (HLOOKUP) is inserted in the table, it can affect the accuracy of the extracted data. There is a solution to this issue provided by the MATCH function, to be covered next.

The second is that the code to be used for the lookup must be the leftmost column of the table. If your data table comes from other systems, you may not have control over the layout of the table. Again, there is a solution to this issue. Consider using the INDEX function with the MATCH function. See the section "An Alternative to VLOOKUP."

AN ALTERNATIVE TO VLOOKUP

If you commonly use the VLOOKUP function, there may be a better alternative for extracting values from tables. It is a more complex solution, but it is also more flexible and removes the limitations of the VLOOKUP function.

It involves what is commonly called an INDEX-MATCH solution. Both the INDEX and the MATCH functions have other uses, and both should be added to your functions of choice. INDEX is also used a lot with dynamic range names (see Chapter 9).

THE INDEX AND MATCH FUNCTIONS

If you need to do a two-dimensional lookup on a table, you have a number of options. All these options use the MATCH function, which is rarely used on its own, but is most frequently used with the INDEX function. It can also be used with the VLOOKUP and HLOOKUP functions.

THE MATCH FUNCTION

The MATCH function returns a number representing the relative position of the lookup value within a range of cells. If the lookup value is the third entry in a range, it will return 3. This, by itself, is not that useful, but when combined with other functions it can provide a flexible lookup.

The MATCH function can handle lists sorted in ascending or descending order as well as unsorted lists.

Syntax

MATCH (Lookup_Value, Lookup_Array, Match_Type)

Lookup_Value is the value to be looked up, typically a cell reference.

Lookup_Array is the range of cells that will be searched for Lookup_Value. In practice this tends to be a single-row or single-column range. It is usually a fixed reference or a range or table name.

Match_Type (optional) is similar to the Range_Lookup argument in the VLOOKUP and HLOOKUP functions. There are three options:

1. **1** (default if omitted) assumes Lookup_Array is sorted in ascending order. It finds the highest value that is less than or equal to the lookup value. It will return the #N/A error message if there is no value less than the lookup value in the range.
2. **0** means an exact match is required. If an exact match can't be found, then the #N/A error message is displayed. This is the most common type of MATCH.
3. **–1** assumes Lookup_Array is sorted in descending order. It finds the lowest value that is greater than or equal to the lookup value. It will return the #N/A error message if there is no value greater than the lookup value.

Examples

Figure 8.14 has two ranges, one in ascending order and the other in descending order.

	I	J	K	L	M	N	O
1		Code Ascending	Code Descending		Code	MATCH result	Type and Range
2		1000	9000		3450	3	Ascending J2:J10
3		2000	8000		3450	6	Descending K2:K10
4		3000	7000		7000	7	Exact J2:J10
5		4000	6000				
6		5000	5000				
7		6000	4000				
8		7000	3000				
9		8000	2000				
10		9000	1000				

FIGURE 8.14 Ascending and Descending Range with MATCH Results

The formula in N2 is

```
=MATCH(M2,J2:J10)
```

This is the ascending order (default) version. The result of 3 represents the third cell in the J2:J10 range. The 3000 entry is the highest value less than 3450.

The formula in cell N3 is

```
=MATCH(M3,K2:K10,-1)
```

This is the descending order version (uses –1 as Match_Type). The result of 6 represents the sixth cell in the K2:K10 range. The 4000 entry is the lowest value that is greater than 3450.

The formula in cell N4 is

```
=MATCH(M4,J2:J10,0)
```

This is the exact match version (uses 0 as Match_Type). The result of 7 represents the seventh cell in the range J2:J10 that contains the code 7000.

You can also use a whole column or a whole row reference as the lookup range with the MATCH function. In that way you will return the row number and the column number, respectively, of the lookup value.

VLOOKUP and MATCH

The MATCH function can replace the Column_Index_Number argument in the VLOOKUP function to solve the inserted column issue.

Let's revisit the VLOOKUP example in Figure 8.9. The helper cells in Q1:T1 can be replaced with a MATCH function. The formula for Cell Q1 is

```
=MATCH(Q2,$J$1:$N$1,0)
```

This can be copied across to the other helper cells.

If we now insert a column between columns L and M, it won't break the VLOOKUP formulas (see Figure 8.15).

	I	J	K	L	M	N	O	P	Q	R	S	T	U
1		Stock Code	Description	Colour		Cost	Price			2	3	5	6
2		ABC123	Widget	Red		$0.20	$0.45		Stock Code	Description	Colour	Cost	Price
3		ABC124	Widget	Green		$0.20	$0.40		ABC124	Widget	Green	$0.20	$0.40
4		XYZ111	Widget	White		$0.90	$1.50		DEF321	Gadget	Blue	$0.80	$1.40
5		XYZ222	Gadget	Black		$0.10	$0.20						
6		DEF321	Gadget	Blue		$0.80	$1.40						
7		DEF322	Gadget	Yellow		$0.50	$1.00						

FIGURE 8.15 Lookup Table and MATCH Formula to Calculate Column Numbers

You can see that cells T1 and U1 have updated to extend the column_numbers to cope with the inserted column.

THE INDEX FUNCTION

The INDEX function allows you to extract a cell's value from within a range. It also lets you return a reference to a cell, which can then be used to build ranges for other functions. This technique allows for the creation of dynamic range names (see Chapter 9) and other flexible techniques that work well in reporting situations.

Syntax

INDEX (Range, Row_Number, Column_Number)

Range can be a two-dimensional range or a single-row or single-column range.

Row_Number (optional) is a number that represents the row number within the range to be extracted or referred to. If the range is a single row, then Row_Number is optional.

Column_Number (optional) is a number that represents the column number within the range to be extracted or referred to. If the range is a single column, then Column_Number is optional.

Examples

Figure 8.16 shows statistical data for six months. Columns Q and R extract the current month and the year-to-date (YTD) figures, respectively, based on the entry in cell J1.

	H	I	J	K	L	M	N	O	P	Q	R
1		Number of Months	4								
2											
3		Budget Statistics	Jul-13	Aug-13	Sep-13	Oct-13	Nov-13	Dec-13		Current Month	Current YTD
4		Payroll costs	$620,823	$779,116	$712,215	$619,358	$719,967	$716,904		$619,358	$2,731,512
5		Hours Worked	12,173	14,983	13,965	11,686	14,117	13,276		11,686	52,807

FIGURE 8.16 Statistical Table with Current Month and YTD

Tip: Row and Column References

Whenever you have to refer to a row and a column in Excel (i.e., the INDEX function) it is always in the order of row first and column second.

The only exception to this rule is the A1 cell reference syntax, which has the column letter first and the row number second.

The formula in cell Q4 is

```
=INDEX($J4:$O4,1,$J$1)
```

This formula can be copied down.

This INDEX formula extracts the value from the first row (there is only one row) and the fourth column (cell J1 contains the number 4) from the range J4:O4.

In a single-row range, you can omit the row number from the INDEX, as the following formula shows:

```
=INDEX($J4:$O4,,$J$1)
```

I prefer to include the 1 in this type of INDEX formula so that it is obvious what is being referred to.

The formula in cell R4 is an example of the reference type of INDEX function. The formula in R4 is

```
=SUM(J4:INDEX($J4:$O4,1,$J$1))
```

This formula can be copied down.

In this formula we need a flexible way to add up all the required entries based on the entry in cell J1. The starting cell for the range reference in the SUM function is J4. The ending cell for the range reference is determined by the INDEX function.

In Excel you can build range references like this if a function can return a cell reference, as the INDEX can. We will examine more functions that can return a reference later in this chapter.

You may have noticed that this INDEX function is identical to the one from cell Q4. In these structures you may wish to create the INDEX formula so that it can be copied across and then simply amend it to include in the SUM function to calculate the YTD value.

Value versus Reference

As mentioned, the INDEX function can return a value or a cell reference. Excel will determine which one to use based on how the INDEX function is used in the formula. As you saw in the two examples, the INDEX functions were identical.

The current month's cell was used as a value. The YTD formula was treated as a reference because it was used as a reference in the range for the SUM function. The INDEX function followed a colon in the formula. This forces the INDEX to return a reference.

You could have used HLOOKUP to return the month result, but you couldn't have used it in the YTD formula. HLOOKUP and VLOOKUP return values only, not references.

THE INDEX-MATCH COMBINATION

The INDEX and MATCH functions are made to work together. Using this combination is, in my opinion, an accurate indication of an Advanced Excel user.

Let's review the original VLOOKUP example from Figure 8.9.

We can replace the VLOOKUP formula in cell Q4 with

```
=IF($P3="","",INDEX($J$2:$N$7,MATCH($P3,$J$2:$J$7,0),MATCH(Q$2,$
J$1:$N$1,0)))
```

This is much longer than the VLOOKUP version, but it also doesn't require helper cells in row 1. Let's review how it works.

The table in the INDEX function, $J$2:$N$7, is the same as the one included in the VLOOKUP formula.

The second argument in the INDEX function is the row number. This is supplied by a MATCH function. For this to work, the rows used in MATCH Lookup_Range must be the same as the rows in the INDEX range.

In our example, both ranges start at row 2 and end at row 7.

The third argument in the INDEX function is the column number. This is supplied by another MATCH function. For this to work correctly, the columns of the MATCH function Lookup_Range must be the same as the INDEX range columns.

In our example, both ranges start with column J and finish with column N. Table 8.2 summarises the required ranges and their explanations.

TABLE 8.2 INDEX-MATCH Range Comparisons

INDEX Range	INDEX Argument	MATCH Range	Comments
$J$2:$N$7	Row_Number	$J$2:$J$7	Rows 2 to 7 line up exactly.
$J$2:$N$7	Column_Number	$J$1:$N$1,	Columns J to N line up exactly.

The lining up of the ranges between INDEX and MATCH is vital for this technique to work.

INDEX-MATCH Flexibility

You may have noticed that the table had a colour column. This also has unique entries in it. We can easily convert the stock code lookup into a colour lookup using the INDEX-MATCH method. Figure 8.17 shows the solution.

	J	K	L	M	N
1	Stock Code	Description	Colour	Cost	Price
2	ABC123	Widget	Red	$0.20	$0.45
3	ABC124	Widget	Green	$0.20	$0.40
4	XYZ111	Widget	White	$0.90	$1.50
5	XYZ222	Gadget	Black	$0.10	$0.20
6	DEF321	Gadget	Blue	$0.80	$1.40
7	DEF322	Gadget	Yellow	$0.50	$1.00

	P	Q	R	S	T
1					
2	Colour	Stock Code	Description	Cost	Price
3	Red	ABC123	Widget	$0.20	$0.45
4	Yellow	DEF322	Gadget	$0.50	$1.00

FIGURE 8.17 Colour Lookup Solution Using INDEX-MATCH

The formula in cell Q3 is

```
=IF($P3="","",INDEX($J$2:$N$7,MATCH($P3,$L$2:$L$7,0),
  MATCH(Q$2,$J$1:$N$1,0)))
```

The only difference between the stock code lookup and the colour lookup is that the range for the first MATCH function (the one that determines the row to extract) uses $L$2:$L$7 instead of $J$2:$J$7.

Hence, the column that determines the row to extract can be anywhere within the table, not just in the left column as with VLOOKUP.

The only downside of the INDEX-MATCH combination is that it is more complex to create. However, it is more flexible than a VLOOKUP-MATCH combination.

The INDEX function is used again in Chapters 9 and 10.

ERROR HANDLING FUNCTIONS

As we have seen, there are a number of circumstances when the lookup functions can return an error message. Since error messages will flow through to other calculations, we need to handle any errors when they occur.

Excel has a number of functions to handle the various errors that can occur with Excel's other functions.

THE IFERROR FUNCTION

The newest and easiest to use of the error handling functions is the IFERROR function. It was added in Excel 2007 and replaces the ISERROR function that was commonly used with the IF function in Excel 2003 and earlier versions.

Syntax

IFERROR (Value,Value_If_Error)

Value is another formula, function, or reference.

Value_If_Error is what you want Excel to display or calculate when an error is encountered in the **Value** calculation. This can be another calculation, a value, or a text entry.

Examples

We can convert some of our previous formulas to use the IFERROR function. VLOOKUP, MATCH, and INDEX can all return errors.

The following formula is from Figure 8.8 and cell Q3. It will display a blank cell when an error is encountered with the VLOOKUP calculation. This will handle a blank cell and an invalid entry in the same way.

```
=IFERROR(VLOOKUP($P3,$J$2:$N$7,Q$1,0),"")
```

The following formula is from Figure 8.16 and cell Q4. It will display a zero when an error is encountered with the INDEX calculation.

```
=IFERROR(INDEX($J4:$O4,1,$J$1),0)
```

The IFERROR function handles all the errors that formulas can generate in exactly the same way. This can be viewed as comprehensive, but in some cases you may want to be more selective in your error handling.

When developing a reporting model, you might want to handle specific errors in different ways, rather than use the blanket approach of IFERROR.

As you develop your model, you will identify the calculations that can be affected by dividing by zeros or other errors.

In practice you will want to know about any #N/A error messages that are not caused by blank input cells. If you receive the #N/A error message, it either means the table is not complete or an invalid entry has been made. In both cases you may need to amend the model to correct or at least handle the issue.

Excel's Error Messages

#DIV/0! is generated by a formula trying to divide by 0, which is mathematically impossible. This can be a common error for new users until they find out it's easily handled with a basic IF function. The following are examples of IF functions that stop #DIV/0! errors:

```
=IF(B1=0,0,A1/B1)
=IF((A1+B1)=0,0,C1/(A1+B1))
```

The divisor cell or calculation is tested to see if it equals zero. If it does equal zero, a 0 is displayed; otherwise, the calculation is done.

#N/A is generated by lookup functions when the value being looked up cannot be found or approximated. This error message is usually a warning that your formulas or tables have not been set up correctly. There is a function called ISNA that will be examined later in this chapter that identifies this specific error message.

#VALUE! typically means that text has been entered or encountered in a cell that was expected to contain a numeric value or a logic entry. This may mean you need to add a data validation to an input cell to ensure that only values are entered. It may also be caused by an IF function returning text when it should return a value. There is a function called ISTEXT that can identify text entries, and it is examined later in this chapter. The use of the text format can also lead to this error.

#REF! is the hardest error message to handle because it typically means that someone has deleted rows, columns, or cells or has used cut and paste where they shouldn't have. You basically need to track this back to the source and correct it. Some functions will display this error message and it usually means that there is a structural error with the calculation—for example, it may be trying to refer to a row before row 1 or a column before column A. Both are impossible references.

#NAME? is generated by having any text without quotation marks in a formula that Excel doesn't recognise. The main cause is deleting an existing range name using Name Manager when that range name is still in use in the file. Another cause is incorrectly typing a range name or a function name in a formula. Range names are discussed in detail in the next chapter. Forgetting to put quotation marks around text will also cause this error.

#NUM! can be generated when Excel is expecting a numeric argument and the values are not numeric. It might mean that with the function's current arguments, the resulting number cannot be displayed because it is too large or too small. It can also mean that the formula cannot find a result based on the current arguments.

#NULL! is rarely generated. Typically, it is caused by an error in a range being used. It can also be caused when two ranges don't intersect. See the discussion of range intersection in Chapter 9.

HANDLING SPECIFIC ERRORS

The #N/A error message is the one error message that needs to be handled differently from other errors. There are two functions that work together to cope with the #N/A error message and all other error messages. They are the ISNA and the ISERR functions. The #N/A error message is displayed when a lookup function can't find what it is looking for. To identify #N/A errors, you can use the ISNA function. Used on its own, it returns TRUE if the formula it is examining will display #N/A, and it returns FALSE if the formula will display a value. When you use the ISNA function, it usually results in a long formula. See the following example.

Syntax

ISNA (Value)

Value can be a lookup formula or a cell reference.

Example

In the following formula we have amended the example from Figure 8.8 and cell Q3. If cell P3 is blank, then a blank cell will be displayed. If the code entered is not in the table, ISNA will return TRUE, and the text Missing is displayed in the cell. If the code exists in the table, then the VLOOKUP will return its result.

```
=IF($P3="","",IF(ISNA(VLOOKUP($P3,$J$2:$N$7,Q$1,0)),
 "Missing",VLOOKUP($P3,$J$2:$N$7,Q$1,0)))
```

This formula handles only a blank lookup cell and a code that isn't in the table. If cell P3 contains an error message, then that error message will be displayed. As you can see, the ISNA function structure requires that you repeat the formula you are checking. It is used once within the ISNA parentheses and then again to actually return a result. This does lead to a long formula with nested IF functions, and you may wish to break up the formula into helper cells.

The ISERR Function

The ISNA function has a complementary function: the ISERR function, which handles all of Excel's errors except the #N/A.

Syntax

ISERR (Value)

Value can be a lookup formula or a cell reference.

Example

The following formula will display the text Error, if cell P3 contains any error message or the VLOOKUP function returns any error message apart from #N/A. It will display a blank cell if cell P3 is blank. It will display the text Missing if the code in cell P3 is not in the table. Finally, it will display the result of the VLOOKUP function is no errors are encountered. The ISERROR function returns TRUE for all error messages.

```
=IF(OR(ISERROR($P3),ISERR(VLOOKUP($P3,$J$2:$N$7,Q$1,0))),"Error",
IF($P3="","",IF(ISNA(VLOOKUP($P3,$J$2:$N$7,Q$1,0)),"Missing",
VLOOKUP($P3,$J$2:$N$7,Q$1,0))))
```

As you can see, the length of the formula quickly increases when different errors have to be handled differently. One way to reduce the length of the formula is to place the ISNA and ISERR functions in helper cells and just refer to them.

The IFERROR function is attractive because it can shorten the formula with no helper cells. The above formula could be rewritten as

```
=IFERROR(VLOOKUP($P3,$J$2:$N$7,Q$1,0),"Error")
```

This formula does not display a different message for a different problem. It will display the text Error only if an error is encountered. But it is significantly shorter and much easier to understand.

See the next section on IS functions for an improvement on this formula.

IS Functions

There are a number of other functions that allow you to identify different types of cells. The IS functions work the same as the ISNA and ISERR functions: They return TRUE if they identify their type of cell. See Table 8.3 for a list of some of the IS functions and their use.

TABLE 8.3 IS Functions

Function	Returns True If
ISBLANK(Value)	The value is a blank cell. If a formula in a cell returns "" to display a blank cell, ISBLANK will not treat that cell as a blank cell.
ISNONTEXT(Value)	The value is any item that is not text. Blank cells will return TRUE, since they are not text.
ISTEXT(Value)	The value is text.
ISNUMBER(Value)	The value is a number. Dates are treated as numbers.

An important feature of IS functions is that they handle Excel's error messages. Figure 8.18 has a table that compares values and the results of some of the IS functions. The shaded results are either useful or worth noting; see the following discussion.

	I	J	K	L	M	N	O
1		Value	Value description	ISBLANK	ISNONTEXT	ISTEXT	ISNUMBER
2			Blank Cell	TRUE	TRUE	FALSE	FALSE
3			Formula that returns a blank cell	FALSE	FALSE	TRUE	FALSE
4		1/01/2013	A date	FALSE	TRUE	FALSE	TRUE
5		156	A number	FALSE	TRUE	FALSE	TRUE
6		20	A formula that returns a number	FALSE	TRUE	FALSE	TRUE
7		text	Text	FALSE	FALSE	TRUE	FALSE
8		20	A number entered as text	FALSE	FALSE	TRUE	FALSE
9		ABC123	Text containing a number	FALSE	FALSE	TRUE	FALSE
10		#DIV/0!	Error cell	FALSE	TRUE	FALSE	FALSE
11		#REF!	Error cell	FALSE	TRUE	FALSE	FALSE

FIGURE 8.18 IS Functions Demonstrated

The ISBLANK function will identify blank cells while ignoring errors; see rows 10 and 11 in Figure 8.18. We could rewrite our last IFERROR function and handle a blank cell correctly by displaying a blank cell, if there is one.

```
=IF(ISBLANK($P3),"",IFERROR(VLOOKUP($P3,$J$2:$N$7,Q$1,0),"Error"))
```

There are a few other results that are worth mentioning in Figure 8.18. In cell O4, the ISNUMBER function treats dates as numbers. In cell N8, the ISTEXT function treats the numbers entered as text because the entry in cell J8 has an apostrophe in front of the 20. In cells M10 and M11, the ISNONTEXT function does not treat errors as text.

Structural Errors

The #REF!, #NAME?, and #NULL! error messages typically mean that there is a structural or formula problem that has to be corrected. You can use the Go To Special dialog box in Chapter 3 to identify and format all the error cells in a sheet.

When developing your model, it is a good idea to create the report validations as you go. This enables you to identify and correct the structural and/or formula errors early in the developmental process. Chapter 13 focuses on the techniques you can use to validate your file. Error cells flow through to other cells, so checking an overall validation (as described in Chapter 13) allows you to isolate the changes that have caused an error. Doing this as you go means you can spot errors early and know that your most recent changes caused the error.

Circular Reference Errors

One type of error that is not handled by functions is the circular reference error. This is caused when a formula in a cell refers directly, or indirectly, to that same cell. For instance, if cell A1 contains =A1*2, then a circular reference will be caused. These types of errors are structural, and you need to track them down using the techniques explained in Chapter 13. Excel will alert you immediately to circular reference errors, so fixing it might be as simple as undoing your last action.

Tip: Text Functions Return Text Results

In Excel, text entries are left-aligned. If you use the techniques discussed in this section to extract or create numbers, you will see that they are left-aligned.

You may have to convert text entries to numbers if you need to use them in calculations. Instructions are included at the end of this section.

TEXT-BASED FUNCTIONS

While Excel works well with numbers and calculations, it also has features and functions that can handle text. When working with text, you tend to need to do two operations: join text (e.g., add a first name to a last name to create a full name) and split text (e.g., extract a first name or a last name from a full name).

Joining Text

Excel has a CONCATENATE function that joins text. I don't use it because I find it's easier to use the ampersand (&) to join text. See below for a comparison of the CONCATENATE function and the & methods. Both formulas join the contents of cells A1 and B1:

```
=CONCATENATE(A1,B1)
=A1&B1
```

I find that using the & is usually the quickest way to join text together.

Spaces

When you are creating names or headings using this technique, don't forget to include a space between words or names. To insert a space between text, use quotation marks followed by a space followed by quotation marks, as in the following example:

```
=A1&" "&B1
```

Automating Headings

Some report headings include a date as part of the heading. This is often manually changed. There is a function that can allow you to automate these headings so that they update when a single cell is changed.

Tip: Spaces Are Characters, Too

When working with text, you need to remember that each space is treated as an individual character. We saw in Chapter 5 that both leading and trailing spaces can cause issues with imported data.

Similarly, when working with text, you need to ensure that you are considering not only leading and trailing spaces but also any spaces within the text.

THE TEXT FUNCTION

The TEXT function converts numbers to text. If you have ever tried to join text with a date, you would have seen the issue shown in Figure 8.19.

FIGURE 8.19 Date Shown as a Number in a Heading

Because Excel treats dates as numbers when you join text to a date, Excel uses the underlying number, which is of no use to you. To fix this issue, you use have to use the TEXT function to format that number into the date format you require.

The TEXT function has more uses than just formatting dates. It can also be used to create sentences using formatted numbers, such as the comma format or the dollar format.

Syntax

TEXT (Value, Format_Text)

Value is normally a cell reference to a number or a date.

Format_Text is a text string that must be enclosed in quotation marks. This text string defines the format to be applied to the value. The text used is very similar to the formats used in the Custom option in the Number tab of Format Cells (see Figure 8.20).

Excel's Help system has a good description of the various formats in the help topic on the TEXT function. Some of the most commonly used formats are shown in the examples following.

Examples

Assume that cell A1 contains 1/7/13.

The first formula will display Jul 13:

```
TEXT(A1,"mmm yy")
```

The next formula will display July 2013:

```
TEXT(A1,"mmmm yyyy")
```

See Figure 8.21 for more examples. Column L contains the Format_Text strings used by the TEXT functions in column K. The formula in K2 has been copied down and is

=TEXT(J2, L2)

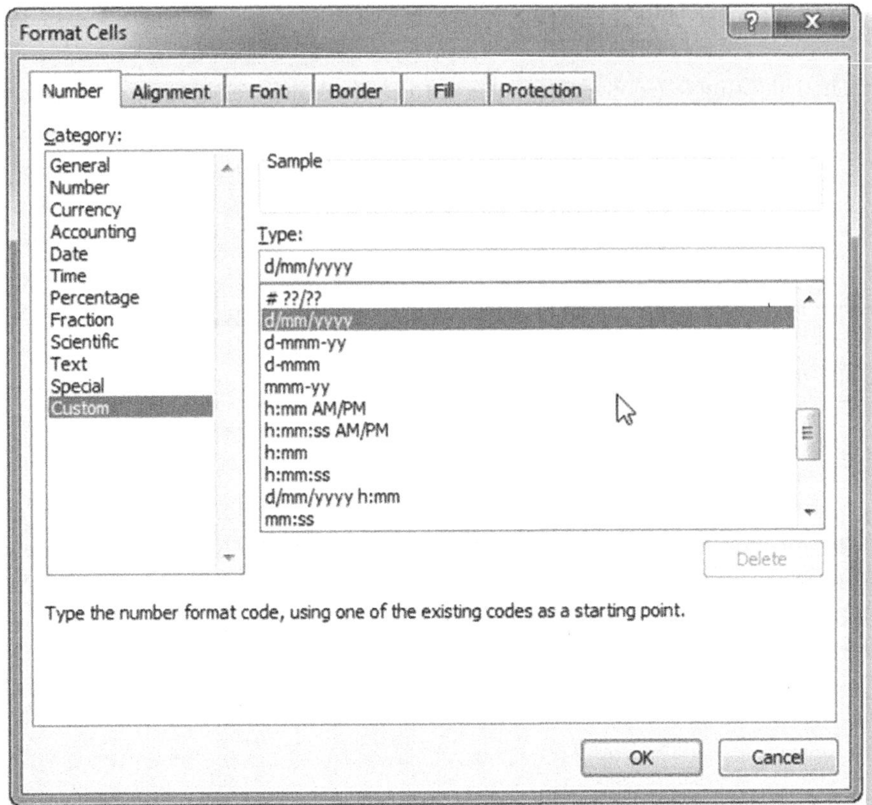

FIGURE 8.20 Formats Cells—Number Tab—Custom Formats

Once the date or value has been converted to text, you can create your headings or narrations (see Figure 8.22).

If you need to make a month uppercase, you can use the UPPER function, as shown in row 4 of the examples in Figure 8.22. Row 6 demonstrates converting a value into millions of dollars and adding an *M* to the end.

	J	K	L	M
1	Value	TEXT result	Format_Text String Used	Description
2	1/07/2013	Jul 13	mmm yy	Abbreviated month and year
3	1/07/2013	July 2013	mmmm yyyy	Full month and year
4	1/07/2013	Monday	dddd	Day of the week
5	1/07/2013	July	mmmm	Full month
6	1/07/2013	2013	yyyy	Full year
7	1/07/2013	01/07/13	dd/mm/yy	Numeric date two digits each
8	12345.67	$12,345.67	$#,###.##	Dollar and two decimals
9	12345.67	$12,346	$#,###	Dollar and no decimals
10	12345.67	$12	$#,	Dollar in thousands

FIGURE 8.21 TEXT Function Examples

	J	K	L	M
1	Text	Value	Combined	Formula in Combined column
2	Report For	1/07/2013	Report For Jul 13	=J2&TEXT(K2,"mmm yy")
3	Report For	1/07/2013	Report For July 2013	=J3&TEXT(K3,"mmmm yyyy")
4	Report For	1/07/2013	Report For JULY 2013	=J4&UPPER(TEXT(K4,"mmmm yyyy"))
5	Profit was	12345679	Profit was $12,345,679	=J5&TEXT(K5,"$#,###")
6	Profit was	12345679	Profit was $12.35M	=J6&TEXT(K6,"$###.##,,")&"M"

FIGURE 8.22 Example of Combining Text and TEXT Functions

Splitting Text

Excel has many functions that allow you to split text strings. These are formula-based alternatives to the Text to Columns feature discussed in Chapter 5.

LEFT AND RIGHT FUNCTIONS

LEFT and RIGHT functions perform much the same process but from different ends of the text in the cell. The LEFT function extracts characters from the left of the text in a cell, and RIGHT extracts characters from the right. This can be useful if you are working with codes that have some structure built into them, such as the first two digits of the code specifying its category.

Syntax

LEFT (Text, Number_of_Characters)

Text is usually a cell reference containing the text string to be manipulated. Numbers are treated as text.

Number_of_Characters (optional) defines how many characters from the left to extract. The number must be a positive whole number. Decimals are truncated. If the number of characters is omitted, the first character will be extracted.

RIGHT (Text, Number_of_Characters)

Text is usually a cell reference containing the text to be manipulated. Numbers are treated as text.

Number_of_Characters (optional) defines how many characters from the right to extract. The number must be a positive whole number. Decimals are truncated. If the number of characters is omitted, the last character will be extracted.

When determining how many characters to extract, remember that spaces are characters, too. The LEFT and RIGHT functions will rarely display an error message as long as the source cell doesn't have an error. If you extract more characters than there are in the cell, then both functions will extract the whole cell text string.

Examples

Figure 8.23 shows a table of results from the LEFT and RIGHT functions.

	J	K	L	M
1	Text	Number of Characters	LEFT Result	RIGHT Result
2	Dog RABBIT cat	3	Dog	cat
3	Dog RABBIT cat	7	Dog RAB	BIT cat
4	Dog RABBIT cat	30	Dog RABBIT cat	Dog RABBIT cat

FIGURE 8.23 LEFT and RIGHT Examples

Row 3 extracts seven characters, but only six letters are displayed because both the LEFT and the RIGHT functions have also extracted a space character. The case of characters is maintained when they are extracted.

Note that in row 4, both functions have extracted all the characters from the cell. When the Number_of_Characters argument is higher than the number of characters in the cell, both functions will extract all the characters.

THE MID FUNCTION

To extract text from the middle of a text string, you use the MID function. For example, if you are working with structured codes, then maybe the third, fourth, and fifth characters of a product code specify the colour of the product.

Syntax

MID (Text, Start_Num, Number_of_Characters)

Text is usually a cell reference containing the text to be manipulated. Numbers are treated as text.

Start_Num specifies the starting character position within Text of the first character to be extracted. It must be a positive whole number. Decimals are truncated. A zero will display the #VALUE! error message. If the value is greater than the number of characters in Text, a blank cell is displayed.

Number_of_Characters specifies how many characters are to be extracted. The characters are extracted from Start_Num to the right. It must be a positive whole number. Decimals are truncated. If you use a number greater than the number of characters remaining in Text, then all the remaining characters are extracted.

Examples

Figure 8.24 shows a table of results from the MID function.

Again, it is important to recognise that spaces have to be counted as characters. The example in row 2 starts at character position 4, which is a space, and that space is included in the extracted text. Hence the result starts with a space and doesn't include the final *T*. Row 3 extracts the middle word of RABBIT correctly, starting at character position 5.

	J	K	L	M
1	Text	Start_Num	Number_Of_Characters	MID Result
2	Dog RABBIT cat	4	6	RABBI
3	Dog RABBIT cat	5	6	RABBIT
4	Dog RABBIT cat	5	30	RABBIT cat

FIGURE 8.24 MID Function Examples

Row 4 shows you can extract all the characters to the right of a character position by using a number larger than the number of characters left in the text.

FLEXIBLE TEXT MANIPULATIONS

The examples above used values in cells to specify the various function arguments. That was acceptable because the character positions were fixed. In practice, codes might not have fixed structures, so you need to have a flexible approach to splitting up parts of a text string. Excel's Text to Columns feature in the Data Ribbon tab (explained in Chapter 5) can also perform these types of flexible text splitting operations.

Let's take the example of the following codes:

123-ABC-45678

23-XY-4567

These might be product codes, and the three parts of the code might all have specific meanings. The hyphen is used to separate the three parts of the code. We can see that the three parts have different lengths. In this case, we couldn't use static values to split up the codes.

Fortunately, Excel has a function that can identify characters within a string. When the placement of symbols is used to separate the parts of a code, we can use the SEARCH function to identify where those symbols are.

THE SEARCH FUNCTION

The SEARCH function returns the starting-character position of the text string being searched for. This allows you to create a flexible formula that can handle varying lengths for the parts of the code. The SEARCH function is not case-sensitive.

If you need to handle uppercase and lowercase differently, use the FIND function, which has exactly the same syntax and operation as the SEARCH function but is case-sensitive.

Syntax

SEARCH (Find_Text, Within_Text, Start_Number)

Find_Text is the text string to be searched for. It is usually a single character but can be a text string of any length. If it is typed into the function, it must be enclosed in quotation marks.

Within_Text is the text string to be searched for—usually a cell reference.

Start_Number (optional) is the character position in the Within_Text string where you want to start the search. If the start number is omitted, the search starts at the first character. This number is used when you try to identify the second or third instance of Find_Text.

The SEARCH function returns the #VALUE! error message when the text being searched for can't be found. You often need to use the error handling functions mentioned earlier with the SEARCH function.

Examples

Figure 8.25 shows a table of results from the SEARCH function.

	J	K	L
1	Text	SEARCH Result	Search Function in column K
2	John Smith	5	=SEARCH(" ",J2)
3	Smith,John	6	=SEARCH(",",J3)
4	ABC-1234	4	=SEARCH("-",J4)
5	ABC1234	#VALUE!	=SEARCH("-",J5)
6	ABC-1234-XY	9	=SEARCH("-",J6,5)

FIGURE 8.25 SEARCH Function Examples

The SEARCH function is one function for which it is acceptable to hard-key entries, since the items being searched for tend to be static. The common characters searched for are a space, a comma, and a hyphen.

Row 5 shows the error when what is being searched for isn't found. It's a pity the function doesn't return a zero in this case, because it would be easier to use. As it stands, you typically have to use the IFERROR or ISERROR function with the SEARCH function.

Row 6 shows an example of finding the character position of the second occurrence of a character.

You may be wondering why there is a Start_Number argument in the function. Wouldn't you always start at the first character? The Start_Number allows you to handle the situation when there are multiple strings in the text string that match the Find_Text string. The code in cell J6 in the figure is an example of that. When multiple matching characters exist, another SEARCH function is used in the Start_Number argument (see the "Flexible Splitting" section).

There is one more function that is commonly used to split up text strings.

THE LEN FUNCTION

The LEN function returns the number of characters, including spaces, in a text string. LEN is short for *length*. This is typically used with the RIGHT function to determine the number of characters to extract from the right.

The syntax is as follows:

LEN (Text)

Text is usually a cell reference containing the text to measure.

FLEXIBLE SPLITTING

If we assume that all our codes have two hyphens to separate the three code sections, then we can ignore error handling. Figure 8.26 shows a table with three codes that we will split into their three sections.

	J	K	L	M
1	Code	First Section	Second Section	Third Section
2	123-ABC-45678			
3	23-XY-4567			
4	1-B-9			

FIGURE 8.26 Codes to Be Split Into Three Sections

The First Section

The following formula is for cell K2 and can be copied down. We use the SEARCH function to calculate how many characters from the left to extract.

```
=LEFT(J2,SEARCH("-",J2)-1)
```

The SEARCH function returns the position of the hyphen. We don't want to include the hyphen in the first section of our code, so we subtract 1 from the result of the SEARCH function.

The Second Section

The next formula is in cell L2. This formula is more complex, because it has to use the SEARCH function within the SEARCH function to identify the second hyphen.

```
=MID(J2,SEARCH("-",J2)+1,SEARCH("-",J2,SEARCH("-",J2)+1)-SEARCH
("-",J2)-1)
```

The first two arguments of the MID function are straightforward. The first specifies the text in J2.

The second argument uses a SEARCH function to determine the starting position of the text to extract. We add 1 to the SEARCH result because we do not want to include the hyphen at the start of the second code section.

The third argument of the MID function, which specifies how many characters to extract, is where the complexity comes in. Let's examine that argument in isolation.

The following calculation uses three SEARCH functions to calculate the number of characters to extract:

```
SEARCH("-",J2,SEARCH("-",J2)+1)-SEARCH("-",J2)-1
```

The first two SEARCH functions are used to calculate the character position of the second hyphen:

```
SEARCH("-",J2,SEARCH("-",J2)+1)
```

The third argument (Start_Number) of this SEARCH function is another SEARCH function. This second SEARCH function sets Start_Number as one more than the character position of the first hyphen found. Because Start_Number is one more than the first hyphen position, it will return the character position of the second hyphen.

We then subtract the first hyphen position to arrive at the number of characters to extract. One is subtracted because we don't want any hyphens in the code.

In our first sample code, the hyphens are in positions four and eight. When you subtract 4 from 8, you get 4, but we want only the characters between the hyphens, so we deduct 1 from the result to determine how many characters to extract.

The Third Section

The following formula is in cell M2:

```
=RIGHT(J2,LEN(J2)-SEARCH("-",J2,SEARCH("-",J2)+1))
```

You may recognise that the nested SEARCH formula to calculate the position of the second hyphen from the second section formula is used within the RIGHT function:

```
SEARCH("-",J2,SEARCH("-",J2)+1)
```

We deduct the second hyphen position from the LEN function result to calculate how many characters from the right to extract.

Figure 8.27 shows the resulting sections. Note that the numbers are left-aligned, signifying they are text entries.

	J	K	L	M
1	Code	First Section	Second Section	Third Section
2	123-ABC-45678	123	ABC	45678
3	23-XY-4567	23	XY	4567
4	1-B-9	1	B	9

FIGURE 8.27 Codes Split into Three Sections

THE SUBSTITUTE FUNCTION

There is one more text-based function that can prove useful in manipulating text. The SUBSTITUTE function allows you to change one text string into another text string, like a find-and-replace function. SUBSTITUTE is case-sensitive.

Syntax

SUBSTITUTE (Text, Old_Text, New_Text, Instance_Number)

Text is usually a cell reference of the text to change.

Old_Text is the text you want to change, and it must be enclosed in quotation marks.

New_Text is the text you want to change Old_Text to, and it must be enclosed in quotation marks.

Instance_Number (optional) specifies which instance of Old_Text is to be changed. This must be a positive whole number. Decimals are truncated. If the number is omitted, all instances are changed.

Examples

Figure 8.28 shows the results of four SUBSTITUTE functions.

	J	K	L	M
1	Text	Old_Text	New_Text	SUBSTITUTE result
2	Dog RABBIT cat	cat	dog	Dog RABBIT dog
3	Dog RABBIT cat	dog	cat	Dog RABBIT cat
4	Dog RABBIT cat	Dog	cat	cat RABBIT cat
5				
6	Dog RABBIT cat			DogRABBITcat

FIGURE 8.28 SUBSTITUTE Examples

The formula in cell M2, which has been copied down to cell M4, is

```
=SUBSTITUTE(J2,K2,L2)
```

Rows 3 and 4 show the case sensitivity. In row 3 the word Dog is unchanged because it starts with an uppercase "D". Row 4 includes the uppercase "D" and adjusts the text.

Row 6 has a different formula. The formula in cell M6 is

```
=SUBSTITUTE(J6," ","")
```

The formula removes all spaces from cell J6.

This technique could be useful if you were working with the same code between two systems. If one system included a hyphen and the other didn't, you could remove the hyphen from the code with the above technique.

Counting Specific Characters

Let's assume we have two types of codes: One has two hyphens, per our previous example, and another has three hyphens. Two different sets of formulas will be necessary to split up these two types of codes. You have to identify how many hyphens are in the code to determine which formula to use.

There is, oddly, no built-in function to count the number of a certain character within a text string (see Figure 8.29).

	J	K
1	Code	Count dashes
2	123-ABC-45678	2
3	23-XY-4567-ABC	3
4	1-B-9	2
5	1-B-10-XYZ	3

FIGURE 8.29 Character Count Examples

The formula in cell K2 is

```
=LEN(J2)-LEN(SUBSTITUTE(J2,"-",""))
```

The first LEN function calculates the total number of characters in the code in cell J2 and then subtracts the length of the resulting text string created by a SUBSTITUTE function that removes all the hyphens. The result is how many hyphens are in the text string.

CONVERTING TEXT TO NUMBERS

The results of text-based functions are text. In many cases you may need to convert a text number into a value. There are two techniques for doing this.

The VALUE function will convert a text number into a number. For example, if cell A1 contains the text ABC100, then the following formula will return 100 as a value:

```
=VALUE(RIGHT(A1,3))
```

An alternative formula is

```
=RIGHT(A1,3))*1
```

Both of these will return the #VALUE! error message when the text cannot be converted into a number.

DATE FUNCTIONS

Dates are an important part of any reporting model. Reports can be daily, weekly, monthly, quarterly, semiannual, and annual. To create automated and flexible dates, you need to use only a few functions. The basic ones are the DAY, MONTH, and YEAR functions. These are all easy to use and simply return values representing their names from dates.

Syntax

YEAR (Date)
MONTH (Date)
DAY (Date)

Date is normally a cell reference that has the date to extract the year, the month, or the day.

Examples

If cell A1 contains the date 25/7/2013 (European style), the following formulas return the numbers 2013, 7, and 25, respectively:

```
=YEAR(A1)
=MONTH(A1)
=DAY(A1)
```

These three functions are commonly used as the arguments for the DATE function.

THE DATE FUNCTION

The DATE function builds a date from three inputs. The three functions above are typically used to supply those three inputs.

Calculations can be done to automatically increment dates through a formula.

Syntax

DATE (Year, Month, Day)

Year is an integer representing the year of the date.

Month is an integer representing the month of the date. The integer can be more than 12. When that is the case, the number is treated as a number of months. For example, the number 13 is treated as January, and 24 is treated as December.

Day is an integer representing the day for the date. If the integer is greater than the highest day in the month involved, it will be treated as though it were a number of days. For instance, using 33 as the day in January will give you the February 2.

Both the Month and the Day arguments can increment the previous argument. Month can increment Year, and Day can increment Month.

Following are some practical examples of the use of the DATE function.

The First and Last Days of the Month

When you are building reports, it is common to have to identify the first and last days of the month. The following two DATE functions handle those two requirements. Assume that cell A1 contains a date.

First day of the month:

```
=DATE(YEAR(A1),MONTH(A1),1)
```

Last day of the month:

```
=DATE(YEAR(A1),MONTH(A1)+1,0)
```

The first day of the month is easy to understand. It uses the year and month from the date in cell A1 and then hard-keys the 1 as the day.

The formula for the last day of the month has a twist. It adds 1 to the month number of the date, and the day is then set to 0. A zero day makes no sense on its own, but it is treated as the number that is one less than 1. Hence the day goes back one day from the first of the month to the last day of the previous month, which is why we incremented the month initially.

When you are referring to months in Excel, the best practice is to use the first day of the month. When you are creating column headings for months, these should also refer to the first day of each month. In most cases, column headings for dates are formatted as mmm yy. Thus 1/1/2013 is displayed as Jan 13. This can hide the fact that the date might not refer to the first of the month.

When creating reports with months as column headings, you should use the following formula to increment the month:

```
=DATE(YEAR(A1),MONTH(A1)+1,1)
```

This ensures that the heading is always referring to the first of the month.

OTHER USEFUL FUNCTIONS

There are two more useful functions, which can be used like a lookup function.

The OFFSET Function

The OFFSET function is very versatile and has typically been used to extract monthly and YTD data from budgets. The typical budget layout has months going across the sheet and cost elements listed down the sheet.

I have seen many reporting models that require the use of Find and Replace to update the current month and YTD figures. Formulas have fixed links to a month column, and every month these links have to be moved one column to the right to link them to the next month.

The OFFSET function can automate this so that no Find and Replace processes are required.

I add columns to the right of a typical budget layout to include OFFSET functions. These columns extract the month and YTD figures for the current month. We saw this layout in one of the examples using the INDEX function earlier in the chapter.

Some businesses include the next month's budget on their reports, and this can also be handled using the OFFSET function.

The OFFSET function, as its name suggests, can refer to a cell or a range by using a starting position and offsetting from that position by a specific number of rows and columns. OFFSET can also refer to a cell or a range reference. It can resize a range reference from a starting cell or a range. Hence, it can be used with functions expecting a single-cell reference or functions expecting a range reference, such as the SUM function.

Syntax

OFFSET (Reference, Rows, Columns, Height, Width)

Reference can be a single-cell reference or a range reference. This is the starting point from which the other arguments will either move or resize Reference. Range references must refer to adjacent cells. Reference can be considered an anchor cell or a range. It's the base from which you move.

Rows is the number of rows to offset the upper-left cell of Reference. Use zero if you are not moving the row reference. The number can be positive, which moves Reference down the sheet, or negative, which moves Reference up the sheet. The #REF! error message is displayed when you try to move Reference above row 1.

Columns is the number of columns to offset the upper-left cell of Reference. Use zero if you are not moving the column reference. The number can be positive, which offsets Reference to the right on the sheet, or negative, which moves Reference to the left on the sheet. The #REF! error message is displayed when you try to move Reference to the left of column A.

Height (optional) is a positive whole number that represents the number of rows in the range to be created. A 2 means Reference will contain 2 rows.

Width (optional) is a positive whole number that represents the number of columns in the range to be created. A 2 means Reference will contain 2 columns.

Examples

The first two examples return a cell reference and can be used in a cell to return a value from a cell.

The following formula refers to cell C2 and will display whatever is in cell C2. C2 is one row below and two columns to the right of cell A1.

```
=OFFSET(A1,1,2)
```

The following formula refers to cell A9 and will display whatever is in cell A9. A9 is one row above (–1) and two columns to the left (–2) of cell C10.

```
=OFFSET(C10,-1,-2)
```

The next three examples are range-based and must be used with a function that uses a range reference. They are not typically used by themselves in a cell.

The following formula refers to the range A1:A10. This range starts at cell A1 because both the rows and columns arguments contain zeros. The height of the range is 10 rows, inclusive of cell A1. The width is 1, which means it is a single-column range.

```
OFFSET(A1,0,0,10,1)
```

The following formula refers to the range A1:F1. This range starts at cell A1 because both the rows and columns arguments contain zeros. The height of the range is one row, inclusive of cell A1. The range has a width of 6, which means it is six columns wide, inclusive of cell A1.

```
OFFSET(A1,0,0,1,6)
```

The following formula refers to the range C2:F4. This range starts at cell C2, which is one row down and two columns to the right of cell A1. The height of the range is three rows, inclusive of cell C2. The range has a width of 4, which means it is four columns wide, inclusive of cell C2.

```
OFFSET(A1,1,2,3,4)
```

In practice, most range-based OFFSET ranges tend to be either one row high or one row wide.

Example

We can use the same layout from Figure 8.16 earlier in the chapter and solve it using an OFFSET function rather than an INDEX function (see Figure 8.30).

	I	J	K	L	M	N	O	P	Q	R
1	Number of Months	4								
2										
3	**Budget Statistics**	**Jul-13**	**Aug-13**	**Sep-13**	**Oct-13**	**Nov-13**	**Dec-13**		**Current Month**	**Current YTD**
4	Payroll costs	$620,823	$779,116	$712,215	$619,358	$719,967	$716,904			
5	Hours Worked	12,173	14,983	13,965	11,686	14,117	13,276			

FIGURE 8.30 Statistical Data Requiring Month and YTD

To the right of the budget layout are two columns: Current Month and Current YTD. These are the two columns that would be referred to by the reports to extract those figures. They will automatically update, so there is no need to use Find and Replace to update the current month's budget.

When using the OFFSET function for this purpose, you need a method to determine the current month. I prefer a data input cell, which allows the user to select the current month. You could also automate the process even further and use a MAX function on the actuals date data to determine the latest month.

Usually the current month is chosen from an in-cell drop-down list. Then you can either use a formula to determine the number of months to report on or use a lookup table.

The formula in cell Q4 will be

```
=OFFSET(I4,0,$J$1)
```

This formula can be copied down.

Cell J1 contains the number of months to offset from I4. I4 is the anchor cell and is not meant to ever be referred to. Cell I4 is chosen because one cell to the right of it is the first month for the budget.

It is important to ensure that there is a control on the number of columns to offset. If more than six are used, in this case, incorrect figures will be returned for the month. A formula method to calculate the number of months is the best technique to ensure this.

To create the YTD calculation in cell R4, there are two methods available using the OFFSET. Both of these formulas produce the same result and they can both be copied down:

```
=SUM(J4:OFFSET(I4,0,$J$1))
=SUM(OFFSET(J4,0,0,1,$J$1))
```

The first formula specifies the start cell J4 for the SUM range and uses the OFFSET to determine the end cell. This is the same technique as the INDEX function example shown earlier in the chapter. It uses the same OFFSET function from the current month column in the SUM function to specify the end cell of the range. The OFFSET function can return the cell value per the Current Month column or a cell reference per this first YTD formula.

The second formula uses the range version of the OFFSET function, which returns the whole range to be used in the SUM function. Remember that you can use this version of the OFFSET function only with a formula that is expecting a range.

The important thing to note in the range version of OFFSET is that the anchor cell is part of the range you create. Cell J4 is the first cell in the range. When you use the last two arguments in the OFFSET function, you are specifying the size of the range, not an offset.

A Secret of the Name Box

The OFFSET function has the ability to reference a range. If you are struggling with understanding how the OFFSET works, you can test your formula visually.

It is a little-known fact that you can enter some formulas into Excel's Name Box. We will look at the Name Box in Chapter 9, but for now you can try something that may help you use trial and error to better understand the OFFSET function.

If you click in the Name Box (it's to the left of the Formula Bar), type OFFSET (A1,1,2,3,4), and press Enter, Excel will select the range C2:F4, which is referred to by OFFSET formula (see Figure 8.31).

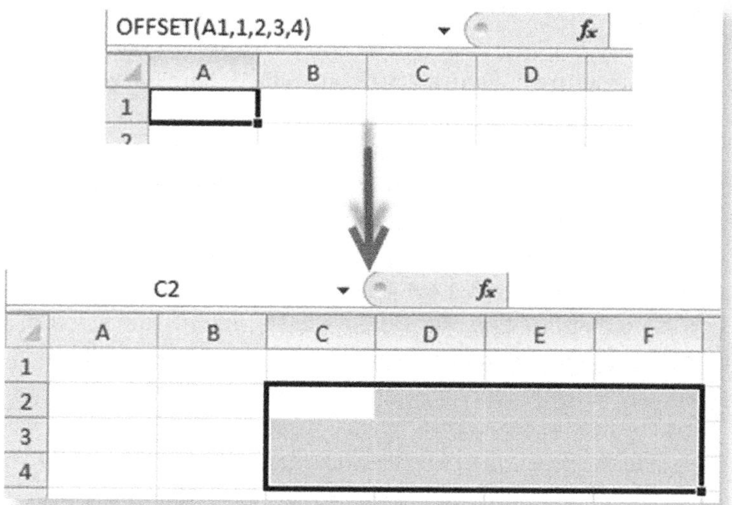

FIGURE 8.31 Name Box Trick—Range Formula

Volatile Functions

OFFSET is a volatile function. A volatile function calculates every time Excel calculates. It also calculates every time the file is opened. Most functions in Excel calculate only when they need to—that is, when the cells that they refer to change. Volatile functions recalculate regardless of whether they need to.

If you use a large number of volatile functions, you will see an effect on your calculation speed. With today's processors and the amount of RAM most computers have, this is less of an issue. It can be annoying to users if there is a delay after entering values while Excel recalculates.

Since OFFSET is a volatile function, I advise using the INDEX function instead wherever possible. INDEX is not volatile, and it can be used to do many of the same calculations as OFFSET.

The CHOOSE Function

The CHOOSE function can be used instead of a lookup function. It can also replace multiple nested IF functions. One advantage of the CHOOSE function over the lookup functions is that whereas a lookup function returns a value, the CHOOSE function can return a value or a range.

Syntax

CHOOSE (Index_Number, Value_1, Value_2, . . .)

Index_Number is a whole positive number between 1 and the number of values listed. It specifies which of the values to choose. To choose the third value from the list of values, enter a 3 for Index_Number.

Value_1, Value_2 can be text, a cell reference, a range or a range name, a formula, or a function. You can list up to 254 values, separated by commas.

Examples

Returning to the structure in Figure 8.30, you will see there is a CHOOSE solution for the Month result. In cell Q4 the formula would be

```
=CHOOSE($J$1,J4,K4,L4,M4,N4,O4)
```

The value in cell J1 determines which cell reference is chosen. With 4 in cell J1, the fourth reference, or cell M4, is extracted.

The YTD formula for the CHOOSE solution is

```
=SUM(J4:CHOOSE($J$1,J4,K4,L4,M4,N4,O4))
```

Let's look at another situation. We want to select a range to sum based on a cell input.

We have three state sheets, and we want to select a state in one cell and have another cell add up a specific range on that state's sheet. The three state sheet names are WA, NSW, and VIC. The range to sum is column K in each sheet. Cell J1 contains the state to sum.

There are at least three ways to do this. The first two involve nested IF functions:

```
=IF(J1=" ",0,IF(J1="WA",SUM(WA!K:K),IF(J1="NSW",SUM(NSW!K:K),SUM(
 VIC!K:K))))
=IF(J1="",0,SUM(IF(J1="WA",WA!K:K,IF(J1="NSW",NSW!K:K,VIC!K:K))))
```

The first formula includes the SUM functions within the IF function arguments. The second formula takes advantage of the fact that the IF function can return a range and so just uses a single SUM function. The IF functions return the range to sum.

The third solution involves the CHOOSE function and four helper cells. Figure 8.32 shows the structure.

	I	J	K	L	M	N
1	State:	WA		States		State Match
2	Total Sales	$43,904.00		WA		1
3				NSW		
4				VIC		
5						

FIGURE 8.32 CHOOSE Function Helper Cells Structure

The CHOOSE function formula for cell J2 is

```
=SUM(IF(N2=0,0,CHOOSE(N2,WA!K:K,NSW!K:K,VIC!K:K)))
```

Cell N2 uses an IFERROR function and a MATCH function to find the state from cell J1 in the range L2:L4. If an error is encountered, a zero is displayed.

The order of the states listed in range L2:L4 must be same as their order in the CHOOSE function list.

I think you will agree that the CHOOSE version is simpler to understand, even though it does rely on helper cells.

There is a fourth solution to this problem that involves the INDIRECT function. See "The INDIRECT Function" section later on.

CHOOSE Function Limitations

Because of the structure of the CHOOSE function, its uses are limited. If you are dealing with a limited number of options, it is useful. It is not as scalable as some other functions when you have to choose from many options.

The COUNTIF Function

The COUNTIF function performs a conditional COUNTA. Just to be clear: The COUNT function counts only numbers or dates. The COUNTA function counts cells containing anything. The COUNTIF function will conditionally count anything in a range that meets the criteria that you set. It is similar to the SUMIF, but with one less argument.

I use the COUNTIF function for one main purpose: to find out whether a value exists within a range. I typically do this for several reasons:

- To check that a value exists in a range before using the MATCH or VLOOKUP function.
- To confirm that a value is in a range as a validation check.
- To find the result of multiple validation checks.
- To compare two separate lists that are supposed to have the same entries.

As you can see, the COUNTIF function isn't used to provide information for the report; although it can be, it is principally used to assist in the validation of reports.

Syntax

COUNTIF (Range, Criteria)

Range is a range that contains the values you want to conditionally count.

Criteria is the criteria that determine whether a value is to be counted. Criteria has the same abilities as noted in the SUMIF function in Chapter 7.

Examples

The following formula will count how many times the value in cell B1 appears in column A:

```
=COUNTIF(A:A,B1)
```

The next formula will count how many positive numbers there are in column A:

=COUNTIF(A:A,">0")

The following formula will count the number of FALSE entries in column A:

=COUNTIF(A:A,FALSE)

I use this example frequently as part of the validation process, which is demonstrated in Chapter 13. I will have a range that includes validation checks that should all be TRUE. If one of them is FALSE, then the overall validation is FALSE.

I use a formula similar to the one below to return TRUE if all the validation cells are TRUE and FALSE if there are any FALSE entries in the range:

=COUNTIF(A:A,FALSE)=0

The INDIRECT Function

The last function fits into no other category. It is badly named, but it allows you to create formulas that can be done no other way in standard Excel without resorting to macros.

The INDIRECT function returns a cell or range reference based on the text between its parentheses. This allows you to create cell and range references from formulas, text, and the contents of cells. The use and power of this function is not apparent until you see a few examples.

Syntax

INDIRECT (Ref_Text, A1)

Ref_Text is text that is analysed in terms of creating a cell or a range reference. See the following examples.

A1 (optional) means you are using the A1 style of cell referencing. Omitting this option means A1 is used, which is the standard reference style for Excel. The other style is R1C1. This book does not cover the use of the R1C1 style.

INDIRECT will return the #REF! error message when Ref_Text cannot be converted into a cell or range reference. That includes range names.

Examples

The following formula refers to cell A1 on the sheet on which it is used:

=INDIRECT("A"&"1")

The next formula refers to the same row in column A of a sheet called WA. If this formula were entered in cell C4, it would refer to cell A4 in the WA sheet. The ROW() function returns the row number of the cell it is used in.

=INDIRECT("WA!A"&ROW())

If we revisit the 3D SUM example from Chapter 7, we can see a perfect example for the use of the INDIRECT function. Remember that the structures of all the sheets in the example were identical. The same cell reference on each sheet referred to the same type of cell on all the sheets.

Another common summary report requirement is to extract a few cells from the each sheet, such as sales and profit figure for actuals. That is typically achieved through direct linking to cells. If the number of sheets exceeds 10, this can be very time-consuming. Wouldn't it be better if we could write one formula that could be copied down and across to create this summary report?

The INDIRECT function allows you to create this formula. There is no other formula-based technique that can create the solution. The solution requires some helper cells. Figure 8.33 shows the structure of the identical state sheets, and Figure 8.34 shows the structure of the summary report.

	I	J	K	L	M
5					
6		$'000	YTD		
7		**NSW**	**Actuals**	**Budget**	**Variance**
8		Sales	1,600	1,500	100
9		Costs Of Sales	1,250	1,100	-150
10		**Gross Margin**	**350**	**400**	**50**
11		Overheads	200	250	50
12		**Net Profit**	**150**	**150**	**0**

FIGURE 8.33 State Sheet Structure

	J	K	L	M
1			K8	L12
2		**Actuals**	**Sales**	**Net Profit**
3		NSW		
4		VIC		
5		QLD		
6		NT		
7		SA		
8		WA		
9		**Total**	**$0**	**$0**

FIGURE 8.34 Summary Sheet Structure

There are several things to note about the structure used in Figure 8.34. The entries in K3:K8 must be identical to the sheet names. The cell references you want to extract from each sheet are entered in cells L1 and M1.

The INDIRECT function for cell L3, which can be copied down and across, is

```
=INDIRECT($K3&"!"&L$1)
```

This formula works only when there are no spaces in the sheet names. If the sheet names have spaces in them, then the following formula would be used:

```
=INDIRECT("'"&$K3&"'!"&L$1)
```

This formula contains double quotation marks followed by a single quotation mark, followed by double quotation marks. Also note the single quotation mark before the exclamation (!) mark.

I recommend using the second formula. This avoids errors when spaces are added to the sheet names. If a space is inserted in a sheet name, the first formula will return the #REF! error message.

The problem is caused because Excel refers to sheet names slightly differently in external cell references. Here are two examples:

```
=Sheet1!A1
='Sheet 1'!A1
```

The second example has a space between the *t* and the 1. Excel surrounds sheet names that contain spaces with single quotation marks.

Figure 8.35 shows the completed report.

	J	K	L	M
1			K8	L12
2		**Actuals**	**Sales**	**Net Profit**
3		NSW	$1,600	$150
4		VIC	$1,800	$115
5		QLD	$1,200	$25
6		NT	$1,300	$75
7		SA	$800	$150
8		WA	$1,550	$125
9		**Total**	**$8,250**	**$640**

FIGURE 8.35 Completed Summary Sheet Structure

Changing cells L1 and M1 would change the cells being extracted from the state sheets. You could change the report to extract the budget figures by changing the cells to L8 and L12, respectively (see Figure 8.36).

	J	K	L	M
1			L8	L12
2		**Budget**	**Sales**	**Net Profit**
3		NSW	$1,500	$150
4		VIC	$1,550	$115
5		QLD	$1,100	$25
6		NT	$1,200	$75
7		SA	$750	$150
8		WA	$1,400	$125
9		**Total**	**$7,500**	**$640**

FIGURE 8.36 Modified Summary Sheet Structure

The INDIRECT function can be especially powerful when used with range names, the topic of the next chapter. More examples of INDIRECT will be used in the following chapter.

There is an INDIRECT solution to the problem from Figure 8.32 that used a CHOOSE function for one solution. The INDIRECT solution in cell J2 is

```
=SUM(INDIRECT("'"&J1&"'!K:K"))
```

This is a much shorter solution, but it does rely on cell J1 containing the exact sheet name.

User Interaction

The INDIRECT function enables you to create formulas that the user can interact with and change. Take this example from the end of the previous chapter, where the SUMPRODUCT function was used to add up the top 10 values in a range. The formula was

```
=SUMPRODUCT(LARGE(A1:A100,ROW(1:10))
```

You can manually change the formula to add up the top 20 values by modifying it as follows:

```
=SUMPRODUCT(LARGE(A1:A100,ROW(1:20))
```

What if you wanted the user to decide how many values to add up? You can replace the 1:20 reference, with an INDIRECT function that refers to an input cell and creates the reference used in the ROW function.

Let's assume that cell B1 contains the input value. The following formula will allow the user to determine how many of the top values to add up:

```
=SUMPRODUCT(LARGE(A1:A100,ROW(INDIRECT("1:"&B1))))
```

The user can change cell B1 to change the number of top values to add up.

INDIRECT Warnings

INDIRECT, like OFFSET, is a volatile function. Its frequent use within a model can affect calculation time.

You can refer to external workbook references using INDIRECT, but the external file must be open for the references to work.

ARRAY FORMULAS

No advanced Excel book would be complete without coverage of array formulas. I use array formulas sparingly, if at all. Other advanced users take full advantage of their flexibility and power.

You may need to reread this section a few times to get a good understanding of array formulas. It is only an introduction; the topic and techniques can be complicated.

I tend to avoid array formulas and opt for nonarray solutions. The SUMPRODUCT function can perform many array-type calculations, and it is my preferred option.

Entering Array Formulas

Array formulas have to be entered in a special way. The only way you can enter an array formula is to use a three-key combination. You hold the Ctrl and Shift keys down and then press the Enter key. This is typically written as Ctrl + Shift + Enter, or CSE.

Curly brackets are added to the start and end of the formula. Whenever you see these brackets, you know you are looking at an array formula. You cannot insert the brackets yourself. You must use the CSE entry method whenever you enter or edit an array formula. This unique input method is one of the reasons people avoid using array formulas. If you are editing the formula and you forget to use the CSE entry, the formula will return an incorrect result. It might return an error value, depending on the formula.

Two Types of Array Formulas

There are two types of array formulas. One type returns a single result, and the other is used to create a range of results.

The Single-Cell Array Formula

The single-cell array formula returns a single result. In many cases it works in a similar fashion to the SUMPRODUCT function, covered in detail in Chapter 7. I use the SUMPRODUCT function in place of an array formula because it doesn't require the CSE entry.

This type of array formula is typically used to include conditions with functions that don't have conditions. The example below will add conditions to the MAX function so you can find the maximum value for a certain condition.

A single-cell array formula is entered in one cell and can be copied to other cells. It is the easier type of array formula to understand and explain.

The Multi-Cell Array Formula

The multi-cell array formula is entered across a range. Sometimes the range is two-dimensional, and at other times it is row-based or column-based. One property of a range-based array formula is that you can't edit or modify a single cell within the range. You have to edit the whole range to make any modifications.

You can't insert or delete rows, columns, or cells within a multi-cell array formula. Each formula in the multi-cell array formula is identical for all the cells.

The results from a multi-cell array formula tend to be sequential or unique. It returns a group of results rather than a single result. The size of the range determines how many results are returned. This type of array formula usually has to handle errors, because the range is typically larger than required to ensure that all results are returned, and some results could generate errors. This will become more apparent when you see the following example.

The multi-cell array formula is more complicated to understand and explain.

Array Syntax

Array formulas perform multiple calculations in one cell or multiple cells. In many cases you could achieve the same result using helper cells, but in some cases an array formula is the only way (apart from resorting to a macro) to perform some calculations.

An *array*, in computing terms, is just a list of entries, which can be either text or numbers. An array can be one-dimensional like a single column or a single row of data, or it can be two-dimensional like a range of data in rows and columns. In computing terms, arrays can also be three-dimensional like a cube, but Excel array formulas can handle only one- and two-dimensional arrays.

The concept of arrays works very well with Excel's grid layout. Array formulas allow you to work with multiple values at once. Let's return to an example used earlier with the OR function, which used an array constant:

```
=OR(A1={1,2,3})
```

This formula was not entered as an array. We will first examine the idea of an array before we look at array formulas. Remember that not all functions can use an array constant. In this case the array constant is used to shorten the formula and create three separate logical tests:

```
A1=1
A1=2
A1=3
```

The array constant, {1,2,3}, is the same as having a row with 1 in the first column, 2 in the second column, and 3 in the third column. To create an array constant that goes down a column, you use a semicolon as a separator {1;2;3}.

In the previous case it makes no difference whether you use a row-based or column-based array constant. The following two formulas return exactly the same results.

```
=OR(A1={1,2,3})
=OR(A1={1;2;3})
```

In both cases the array constant instructs Excel to perform three separate comparisons with cell A1.

Consider the following OR function:

```
=OR({1,2,3}={1,2,3})
```

This formula has the same array constant on both sides of the equal sign. You might think that Excel would perform nine comparisons (3 × 3). But because both array constants have the same structure, Excel still performs just three comparisons. It compares the first item on the left with the first item on the right, the second item on the left with the second item on the right, and the third item on the left with the third item on the right, as shown here:

```
1=1, 2=2, 3=3
```

The next OR formula compares a column-based array on the left (with semicolons) with a row-based array on the right (with commas). This formula will perform nine separate comparisons because the structures on each side of the equal sign are different.

```
=OR({1;2;3}={1,2,3})
```

The first item on the left is compared to the first item on the right, the first item on the left is then compared the second item on the right, and the first item on the left is compared to the third item on the right. This is repeated for both the second and third items on the left, to arrive at nine separate comparisons:

```
1=1, 1=2, 1=3, 2=1, 2=2, 2=3, 3=1, 3=2, 3=3
```

You can confirm this difference by editing the formulas, selecting the entries within the brackets, and pressing the F9 key to calculate the entries. You will see the different number of TRUE and FALSE results.

To create an array range constant that is the same as a range, you use a combination of commas and semicolons. If you select a range of three cells by three cells (e.g., A1:C3) and enter the following formula using CSE, you will see this at work:

```
={1,2,3;4,5,6;7,8,9}
```

The final formula in all cells will be

`={1,2,3;4,5,6;7,8,9}}`

Commas separate cells across columns, and semicolons separate cells down rows.

More on the Single-Cell Array Formula

As noted earlier, I find the single-cell array formula to be easier to understand because they work much like the SUMPRODUCT function discussed in Chapter 7. This type of array formula returns a single result. In most cases, if you are summing, I would recommend using a SUMPRODUCT formula instead of the array formula equivalent, because it doesn't require the CSE entry.

An IF function is normally used in the single-cell array formula because you are usually trying to use a single criterion or multiple criteria with a formula that doesn't have any criteria built into it. Before Excel 2007, you had the option to use an array formula to produce the functionality of a SUMIFS function. Currently, there is no function to conditionally find the maximum value in a range. It would be called MAXIF, if it existed. We can build a MAXIF equivalent using an array function, and this will assist in explaining how this type of formula works.

Figure 8.37 shows a monthly list of amounts by state. The maximum amount from each state is calculated in column O.

	J	K	L	M	N	O
1	Date	State	Amount		State	MAXIF
2	1/07/2014	WA	1,283		WA	4,831
3	1/08/2014	WA	3,094		NSW	4,610
4	1/09/2014	WA	3,492		VIC	4,898
5	1/10/2014	WA	4,831			
6	1/11/2014	WA	1,991			MAXIFS
7	1/12/2014	WA	3,270		State	1/09/2014
8	1/07/2014	NSW	2,470		WA	3,492
9	1/08/2014	NSW	1,587		NSW	2,681
10	1/09/2014	NSW	2,681		VIC	4,067
11	1/10/2014	NSW	2,231			
12	1/11/2014	NSW	4,582			
13	1/12/2014	NSW	4,610			
14	1/07/2014	VIC	3,550			
15	1/08/2014	VIC	4,067			
16	1/09/2014	VIC	1,882			
17	1/10/2014	VIC	2,902			
18	1/11/2014	VIC	4,278			
19	1/12/2014	VIC	4,898			

FIGURE 8.37 MAXIF Results

The formula in cell O2, which has been copied to the cells beneath, is

```
{=MAX(IF($K$2:$K$19=N2,$L$2:$L$19))}
```

Because this has been entered as an array, the IF function compares each cell in the range K2:K19 to cell N2. If the cell equals N2, then the corresponding value in the row in the range L2:L19 is added to an array of values. This final array of values is then used by the MAX function to determine the highest value for WA.

I have used the F9 key to calculate the formula in the Formula Bar, and you can see the results in Figure 8.38. The remaining entries to the right are all FALSE because they relate to other states.

fx =MAX({1283;3094;3492;4831;1991;3270;FALSE;FALSE;FALSE;F

FIGURE 8.38 Formula Bar MAXIF Results

The FALSE entries are ignored by the MAX function, and only the values are used to determine the highest value.

The range in the example is sorted only so it is easier to confirm the highest value. The range does not have to be sorted for this technique to work.

To apply a second condition, you add another IF function. You might think you could add an AND function to achieve a two-condition check, but the AND and OR functions don't work well with array formulas and should be avoided.

Cell O8 is performing a MAX on two conditions: by state and by date. It is finding the MAX value in those months less than or equal to 1/9/14, the value in O7. The formula is

```
{=MAX(IF($K$2:$K$1=N8,IF($J$2:$J$19<=$O$7,$L$2:$L$19)))}
```

This array formula works in a similar way to the first example. The TRUE section of the first IF function contains the second IF function that checks in the same way whether the second condition has also been met. If it has, then the value is added to the array. Figure 8.39 shows the Formula Bar F9 calculation.

=MAX({1283;3094;3492;FALSE;FALSE;FALSE;FALSE;FALS

FIGURE 8.39 Formula Bar MAXIFS Results

When you create multiple conditions, the last condition has the range to work with.

There is a nonarray formula that creates a MAXIF solution. It only works in Excel 2010 and later versions. It uses the AGGREGATE function, introduced in Chapter 7.

The AGGREGATE formula for cell O2 that can be copied down is

```
=AGGREGATE(14,6,($L$2:$L$19)/($K$2:$K$19=N2),1)
```

This uses the LARGE function (14) and ignores errors (6). The LARGE function can accept arrays.

The ($L$2:$L$19)/($K$2:$K$19=N2) part of the formula produces an array of values and #DIV/0! errors. Dividing by TRUE (1) leaves the value unchanged, whereas dividing by FALSE (0) will create a #DIV/0! error. The errors are ignored, leaving only those values that match the criteria.

The 1 at the end of the formula instructs the LARGE function to return the largest value from the array.

The two-criteria (MAXIFS) AGGREGATE formula for cell O8 is

```
=AGGREGATE(14,6,($L$2:$L$19)/(($K$2:$K$19=N8)*($J$2:$J$19<
 =$O$7)),1)
```

Using 15 instead of 14 in the AGGREGATE would perform a MINIF and MINIFS formula.

More on the Multi-Cell Array Formula

In the simplest form of the multi-cell array formula, you can select a range, press =, select a cell, and press CSE. This will array-enter the same formula in every cell in the range, and it stops users from inserting rows or columns within the selected range.

Multi-cell array formulas are very powerful and can perform calculations that can be done no other way except by macros.

I will focus on one particular multi-cell array formula that incorporates a couple of common techniques. If you like this example and find it useful, then I recommend you investigate multi-cell arrays in more depth. This formula is based on one that John Walkenbach included in his book, *Excel 2007 Formulas.*

The formula extracts unique entries from a list. This can be useful in a reporting model because it allows you to easily identify missing entries in a report. The formula works only when there are no blanks in the range.

The final formula we will work towards is flexible and can handle large ranges. To gain an understanding of how the final, flexible formula works and how multi-cell array formulas work in general, we will first look at a formula that works on a fixed range.

The entries in the range are sorted to make it easier to see how the formula works, but the range doesn't have to be sorted for the formula to work.

The array range has to be longer than the expected number of unique entries. The example working columns have been set to the same length as the data range so that you can see the result for each cell.

Figure 8.40 shows the range with the results of the various formulas entered. The range J10:J19 has been named Data. It has 10 entries.

The formula in column K is

```
{=INDEX(Data,SMALL(IF(MATCH(Data,Data,0)=ROW(1:10),
MATCH(Data,Data,0),""),ROW(1:10)))}
```

This formula returns errors, which we will remove in the version in column O. This is too complex a formula to understand in one take. We will break it down to see how the parts work.

Column L contains the first part. This is the simple but powerful formula that is used twice within the main formula:

```
{=MATCH(Data,Data,0)}
```

	J	K	L	M	N	O	P
9	Data	Unique	Part_1	Part_2	Part_2	Fixed	Flexible
10	a	a	1	1	1	a	a
11	a	b	1		4	b	b
12	a	c	1		5	c	c
13	b	d	4	4	8	d	d
14	c	e	5	5	9	e	e
15	c	#NUM!	5		#NUM!		
16	c	#NUM!	5		#NUM!		
17	d	#NUM!	8	8	#NUM!		
18	e	#NUM!	9	9	#NUM!		
19	e	#NUM!	9		#NUM!		

FIGURE 8.40 Unique Array Formula Example

This formula returns the MATCH result for each cell in the Data range. Remember that MATCH returns the position of the first instance of the lookup value. Hence, the values are repeated for the same entry.

Column M contains the next stage in the formula:

```
{=IF(MATCH(Data,Data,0)=ROW(1:10),MATCH(Data,Data,0),"")}
```

The result of this formula is to remove the duplicate row number values. It does this by comparing the result of the MATCH function to a sequential number. When the MATCH result is the same as the sequential number, that number is captured. The ROW(1:10) function provides the sequential numbers 1 to 10. The number of rows has to match the number of rows in the Data range. We will see how to automate that in the final formula. Using the ROW function to provide sequential numbers is common in multi-cell array formulas.

Column N contains the next stage in the formula:

```
{=SMALL(IF(MATCH(Data,Data,0)=ROW(1:10),
MATCH(Data,Data,0),""),ROW(1:10))}
```

The result removes the gaps in the numbers.

The SMALL function is like a flexible MIN function. The MIN function finds the lowest value. The SMALL function allows you to specify the second, third, fourth, or another value. The SMALL function also works well with arrays. For the SMALL function to work correctly, we need unique numbers. The SMALL function wouldn't work on the results in column L because the first, second, and third results would all be 1.

This part of the formula is what was used in column K to provide the INDEX function with the row numbers to extract. Obviously, the #NUM! error messages will flow through into the INDEX results.

Column O handles the error using the IFERROR function:

```
{=IFERROR(INDEX(Data,SMALL(IF(MATCH(Data,Data,0)=
ROW(1:10),MATCH(Data,Data,0),""),ROW(1:10))),"")}
```

This formula would work for up 10 unique items, no matter how long the data list was. The 10 is determined by ROW(1:10). Obviously, the data could contain all unique entries, so you need a way to handle as many rows as the data has.

Adding the INDIRECT function to the formula can provide the flexibility to handle any length of range. The final formula in column P, which handles any length of the Data range, is

```
=IFERROR(INDEX(Data,SMALL(IF(MATCH(Data,Data,0)=
ROW(INDIRECT("1:"&ROWS(Data))),MATCH(Data,Data,0),""),
ROW(INDIRECT("1:"&ROWS(Data))))),"")
```

The INDIRECT function creates the flexible reference to however many rows are in the Data range. The ROWS function returns the number of rows in the range between the parentheses.

This has been an introduction to arrays. I rarely use arrays, as I have already noted, and I have seen many comments over the years about avoiding the use of arrays unless there is no other way to do the calculation.

As I also mentioned previously, it may take a few readings of this section to grasp how arrays work, but I encourage you to investigate array formulas further if they appeal to you.

CHAPTER NINE

Range Names

WHEN YOU CREATE A NEW DOCUMENT or folder in Windows, you usually immediately give it a descriptive name. In Excel, you use meaningful names for both workbooks and worksheets. You rarely leave the name of a sheet as "Sheet1" in your working files.

So we are all comfortable with the concept of applying a descriptive name to a folder, file, or sheet. This concept can be extended further to spreadsheet cells and ranges. In Excel, you can give a name to a cell, column, row, or range. These names are typically called *range names*.

This is actually a misnomer, however, because what you are actually creating is a named formula. The formula refers to the cell or range. The formula can refer to other values as well, which we'll see later in the chapter.

In terms of our building metaphor, using range names is like labeling the areas or containers you are using to hold the components for the building. It makes it easier to identify, control, and then use those components. A name makes it easier to refer to that location. In most businesses it's vital to label the location of physical goods, such as a warehouse or an archive storage unit.

Range names are an exciting topic in Excel, and you can be very creative with them.

In my experience, most spreadsheet users are unaware of range names. They have no idea how to use them or how powerful they can be. If you are not already using range names, I hope to convince you by the end of this chapter to use them, and to do so frequently.

If you are already using range names, I hope to show you some practical techniques later in the chapter that you might never have seen. There are other techniques described later in the book for which range names are an integral part of the process.

Even though the correct term is *formula name* or a *named formula*, I will use the terms *range name* or *named range* throughout the rest of the chapter because it is the most widely used terminology for this feature. Excel calls them Defined Names.

Range names do polarise Excel users. Many users, myself included, are proponents of range names, but there are those who advise against their use.

The argument against range names is that they add another level of complexity to a file. Although I agree that range names add complexity, I believe that if used correctly, they also add structure. I believe the benefits of added structure far outweigh any disadvantages associated with extra complexity.

ADVANTAGES

Here are a few of the advantages to be gained by incorporating range names in your files:

- **Improved worksheet navigation.** You can use a named range like a bookmark. The Name Box (which is discussed later) allows you to go directly to a named range. You can name parts of your file that you go to frequently to speed up navigation.
- **Formulas are easier to understand.** When you see the formulas that are created by using range names, you will see how they can be self-documenting. Formulas created by using range names tend to be more consistent, and if they are done correctly, a single formula in a report range can be identical in every cell.
- **Reduced use of the $ symbol in formulas.** We have seen how important the $ symbol is in creating formulas. Range names can reduce the need to use the $ in references.
- **Easier maintenance of formulas.** By changing a range name, you can automatically update all the formulas that use that range name. There is no need to use Find and Replace to modify references for multiple formulas.
- **More robust macro operation.** Macros that refer to named ranges are more flexible and less likely to crash.
- **Improved linking of worksheets.** Hyperlinks in Excel can cause errors when sheets are renamed. Using a range name as the reference can reduce problems.
- **Additional structure given to files.** By using structured range names—that is, applying consistent prefixes and suffixes—you can add structure to a file, simplify modifications, and speed up development.
- **Improved input range selection.** Ranges can be quickly selected and cleared, ready for new input.

DISADVANTAGES

There are a couple of disadvantages to using range names:

- Cell references are not listed in formulas. When auditing or checking formulas, users are used to seeing cell references and being able to follow them to confirm them.
- Range names can add an extra level of complexity to a reporting model, which can make it difficult for users not familiar with range names to understand.

As with many subjects in Excel, the best way to understand range names is to work with them. Let's create a name.

CREATING A RANGE NAME

The simplest type of range name to both create and use is a single-cell range name. Even though it's simple, it can still be powerful and useful.

Naming a Cell

There are four different ways to create range names. The simplest way to create a single range name is to use the Name Box, which is on the left of the Formula Bar and above the column letters. I briefly demonstrated one of its secrets in the previous chapter. The Name Box usually displays the active cell reference (see Figure 9.1).

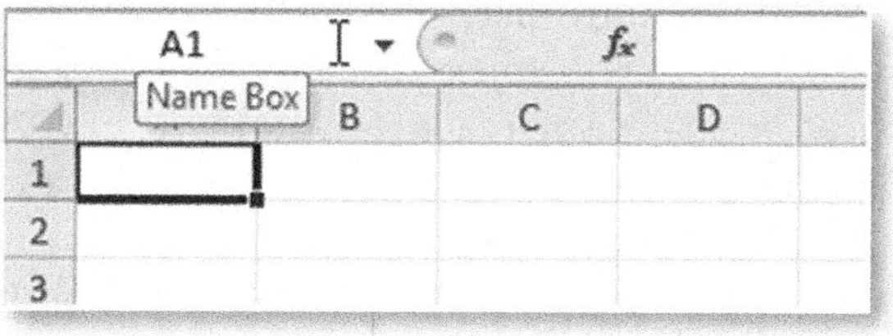

FIGURE 9.1 The Name Box

To name a cell, do the following:

1. Select the cell.
2. Click inside the Name Box and type the name (spaces are not allowed).
3. Press Enter.

You will know whether the name has been accepted because it will be centred in the Name Box. In Figure 9.2, cell B1 has been named GST (short for Goods and Services Tax in Australia).

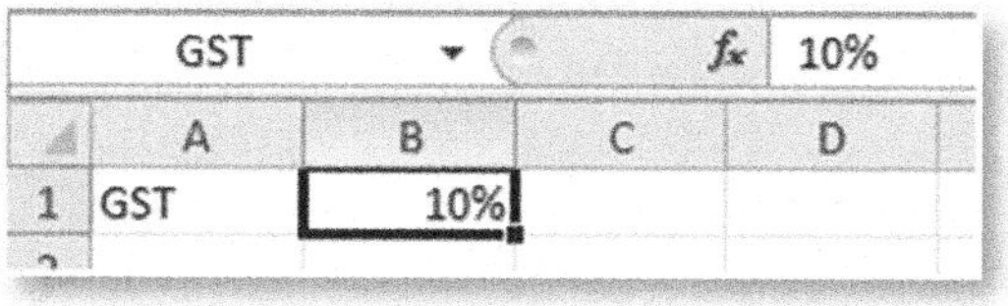

FIGURE 9.2 Named Cell

Tip: Name Box Abilities

Many people are unaware that if you type a cell reference into the Name Box and then press Enter, Excel will take you to that cell and select it.

Typing a range reference into the Name Box and pressing Enter will select that range.

We saw in the previous chapter that you can type certain formulas into the Name Box and press Enter to see the reference that the formula creates or selects.

The same steps apply to naming a range. Select the range you want to name first, then repeat steps 2 and 3.

Naming Rules

There are a number of naming rules associated with creating range names. You can use letters, numbers, and some symbols to create a name. The rules are as follows:

- No spaces are allowed in a name. You can use the underscore character or a period. For instance, Tax Rate is not allowed, but both Tax_Rate and Tax.Rate are acceptable. There is a very good reason that the space character is not allowed in names, which will be covered later in the chapter.
- You cannot create a range name that is also a cell reference. This is more of an issue in the latest versions of Excel, because virtually every three-letter word is now a column reference. For example, you cannot create the name QTR1 because that is a cell reference in all versions from Excel 2007 onwards. You can use the underscore character, so QTR_1 is a valid range name.
- You cannot create a range name that starts with a number, so 1_QTR is not a valid name. You can start a name with the underscore character, so _1QTR is a valid name.
- You cannot create a range name that is a number. Again, you can use the underscore character, so _1 is a valid name.
- You cannot use certain characters in a name such as % or $. You can use the period, however, so Tax.Rate and QTR.1 are both valid names.
- Names are limited to 255 characters. This is obviously not a significant limitation.

Excel will not let you create an invalid range name. It will display the dialog box shown in Figure 9.4 if you break any of the above rules.

Tip: Resizing the Name Box

The Name Box can be resized in Excel 2007 and later versions. Click, hold, and drag the small round icon to the right of the Name Box to resize it. It turns into a double-headed arrow icon when you point to it with the mouse. See Figure 9.3. This is great for longer, more meaningful names.

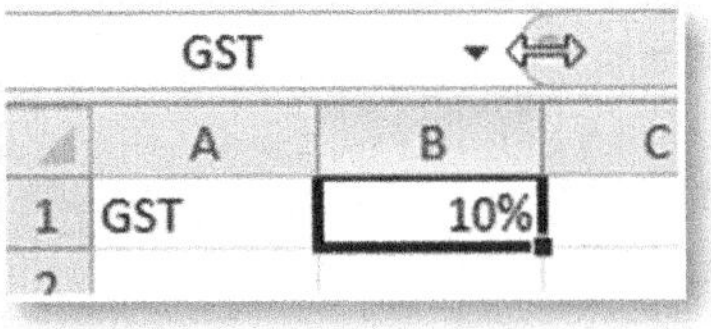

	A	B	C
1	GST	10%	
2			

FIGURE 9.3 Resize the Name Box

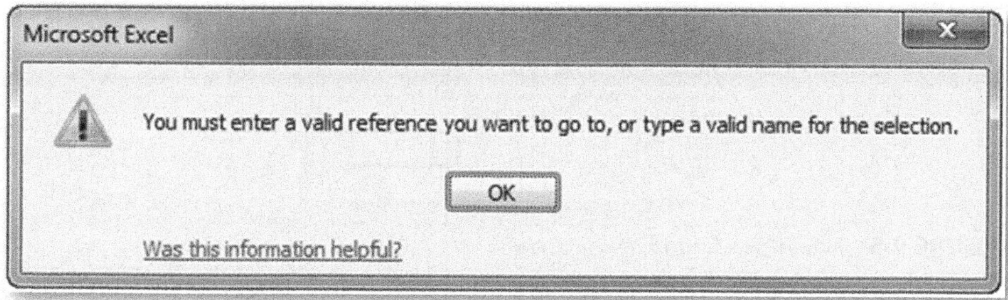

FIGURE 9.4 Range Name Error Dialog Box

Naming Recommendations

I recommend capitalising at least one letter in a range name. I typically capitalise the first letter of each word. So instead of using taxrate, which is a valid name, I would use TaxRate. I find this is easier to read.

It has another advantage. If you type a range name in lowercase and make a spelling mistake, Excel displays the #NAME? error message in the cell. When you use a name in a formula, Excel will use the capitalisation that you used in creating the name. This means you can review any formula returning the #NAME? error and easily spot the misspelled names because they will still be lowercase.

An advantage of range names is that you can create a formula by using a name that doesn't exist yet. You can then create the name, and it will be automatically updated within that formula with the correct capitalization. This can happen if you are creating a calculation and you realise that a value that you need should be a named range, but you haven't created it yet.

I don't recommend capitalising all the letters in all your range names. I used all capitals for the GST example because it is the commonly used abbreviation of a name.

If you make your range name all capital letters, it may get confused with Excel's built-in functions or column references, which are also displayed in all capital letters.

USING RANGE NAMES

Once you have created a range name, there are a number of uses for it.

Navigation

You can navigate back to the range name from anywhere in the file by using the drop-down arrow on the right of the Name Box to select the name, as shown in Figure 9.5.

This will take you to the name and select it, no matter where you are in the file.

The drop-down list gives all the names that are based on ranges within the file. It does not list names that are based on a formula. These are a special type of range names and are explained later in the chapter.

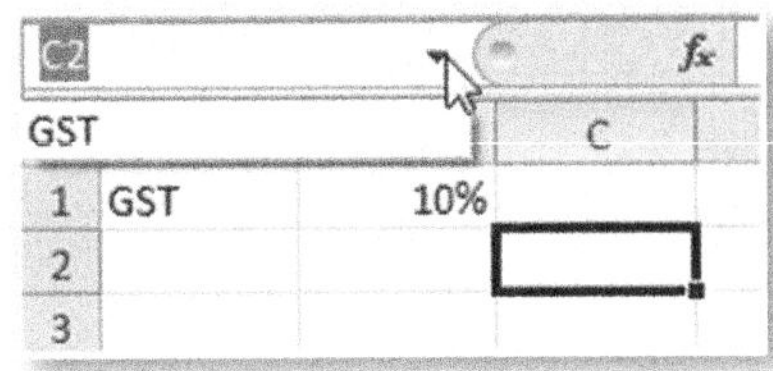

FIGURE 9.5 Name Box Drop-Down Arrow

Formulas

You can use a single-cell range name in a formula in any cell in the file (except the cell itself). For example, the following formula uses the GST range name in cell B4 in Figure 9.6.

```
=A4*GST
```

B4 | f_x =A4*GST

	A	B	C	D
1	GST	10%		
2				
3	Amount $	GST $		
4	100	10		

FIGURE 9.6 Formula with Range Name

Single-cell named ranges are powerful because they can be used in any cell. They are perfect for any values that you use throughout a reporting model. This operates exactly like a fixed reference, so you can copy the formula anywhere, and the range name will still refer to the same cell. Hence, range names reduce the need for fixed references in formulas.

AutoComplete

Excel assists in the creation of formulas by displaying possible functions as you type their names, when creating a formula. This functionality includes table names. It also includes range names. As you start to type a range name, Excel shows you the possible alternatives. As you type more characters, the options reduce (see Figure 9.7). When the range name is highlighted in blue, you can press the Tab key to enter it in the formula. Note that the icon on the left is different for a range name than for a function.

Single-Cell Range Name Uses

Creating a single-cell range name has the following uses.

Fixed References When you create formulas, if you are using a fixed referenced cell, consider naming that cell and using the name rather than the fixed reference. My basic rule is to name cells that you use in more than two separate formulas.

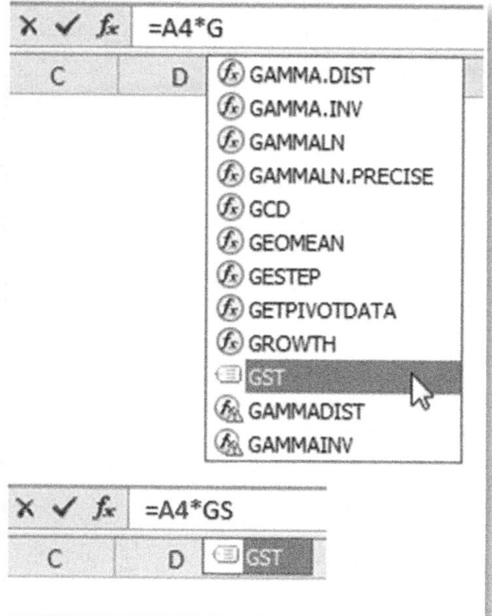

FIGURE 9.7 AutoComplete for a Range Name

Fixed Tax Rates In Australia, our GST is currently a flat 10 percent. Rather than your having to refer to a cell that contains 10 percent, it makes more sense to name that cell GST and use the GST range name in all formulas.

Conversion Rates If you need to convert different dollar values or measuring units, you could create range names to handle the factors used.

Hyperlinks As we have seen, hyperlinks are an effective way to allow the user to move around quickly in large reporting models. Hyperlinks do have one important flaw, however. Renaming a sheet will break all hyperlinks that use that sheet name. To avoid this problem, you can use a range name as the hyperlink reference. This avoids any sheet name issues.

When creating a hyperlink, use the Place in This Document option on the left, and the Defined Names section on the right, to select the reference for the hyperlink (see Figure 9.8).

Changing the sheet name will not affect the hyperlink. You can also modify the range name reference, and that will automatically change all the hyperlinks that use that range name.

Although using a range name handles sheet names changes, the hyperlink can still be broken if the named cell is deleted. If you name cell A1 and then column A is deleted, this will return a #REF! error to the name and cause the hyperlink to break.

Tip: Conversions

Excel has a built-in CONVERT function that can handle common conversions (such as the metric system to U.S. measures).

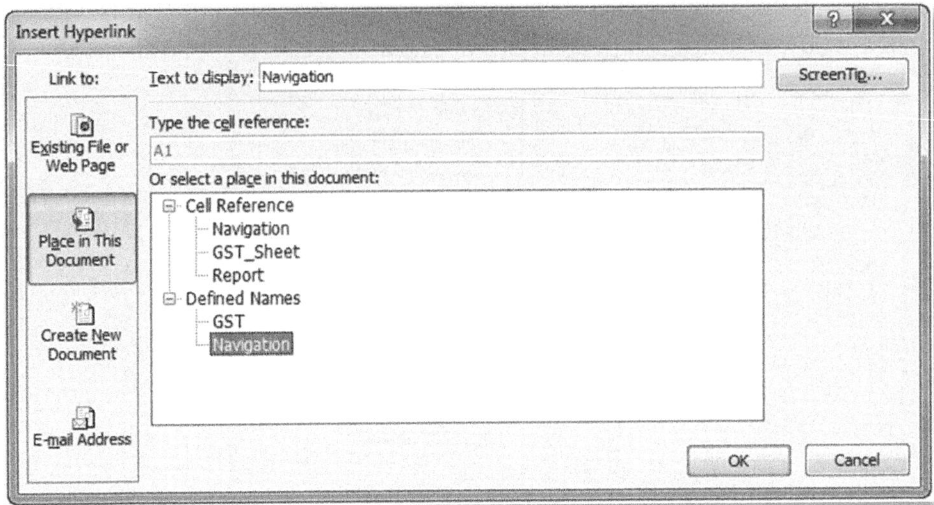

FIGURE 9.8 Insert Hyperlink—Defined Names

A technique to create an unbreakable hyperlink is described later in this chapter.

NAME MANAGER

Before we look at more examples of different types of names and how to create them, I would like to mention Name Manager. This feature was introduced in Excel 2007, and it offers an improvement over the way range names were handled in Excel 2003.

The Name Manager icon is in the middle of the Formulas Ribbon tab, in the Defined Names section (see Figure 9.9).

You can also access the Name Manager using Ctrl + F3. The Name Manager dialog box, shown in Figure 9.10, is resizable, a handy feature when viewing some formula-based range names to be discussed later in the chapter.

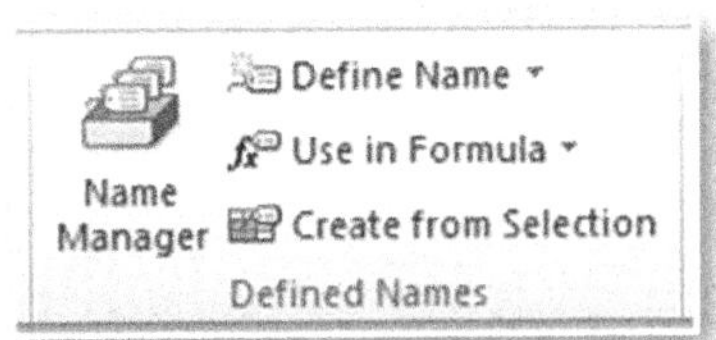

FIGURE 9.9 Formulas Tab—Defined Names Section

The Name Manager dialog box has five columns. You can click a column name to sort by that column. You can even click, hold, and drag the columns to move them. The five column names are as follows:

1. **Name.** This lists the range names as well as any table-based names.
2. **Value.** This displays the current value of the name. It will also show any error values.

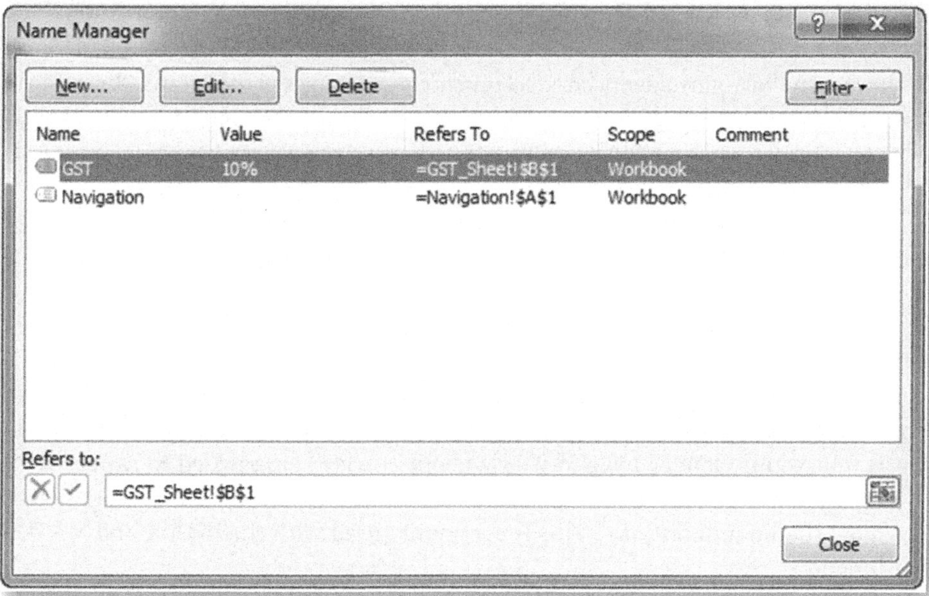

FIGURE 9.10 Name Manager Dialog Box

3. **Refers To.** This displays the reference, or formula, that defines the range name.
4. **Scope.** This is either Workbook (the most common) or Worksheet. Most range names are used throughout a file, and Workbook is the default. You can use the Worksheet option to define the same name on different sheets so that the name has a different value on each sheet.
5. **Comments.** This is a feature that was introduced in Excel 2007 and allows you to add documentation to your names. It is a text field where you can explain the formula or what the name is to be used for, or not used for.

Tip: A Dedicated Function Key

The F3 function key is dedicated to range names. The shortcuts that use this function key will be described later in the chapter.

Tip: Resizable Dialog Boxes

The Name Manager is not the only resizable dialog box. Many of Excel's dialog boxes are now resizable. This can make them easier to use, especially on larger screens.

NAMING A RANGE

We have seen that many advanced Excel functions use ranges in the syntax. Referring to ranges by the actual cell references can be tedious and time-consuming. You constantly have to consider whether to use relative, fixed, or mixed references. Also, manually selecting long ranges can be tedious.

If used correctly, named ranges can eliminate this requirement, since the named range does not change when you copy it. Using named ranges also eliminates the need to move back and forth between sheets.

A named range can refer to the following:

- **A column.** This is used frequently in the SUMIF and SUMIFS functions. You can refer to the entire column or just part of it. The advantage of using an entire column is that you no longer have to worry about entries being added to ranges. This does come at a cost, however, because referring to the entire column can include more than a million rows. This is commonly used with the INDEX and MATCH functions.
- **A row.** This is typically used for dates in multi-month models. You can refer to the whole row or just part of it. This allows you to have a single layout sheet that determines the month to include and then use a range name to refer to that date range throughout the file. This is commonly used with the INDEX and MATCH functions.
- **A two-dimensional range.** This is used for the table in the VLOOKUP and the INDEX functions.
- **A noncontiguous range.** This is a range that has multiple areas, and it is typically used for input ranges that you may want to clear or zero quickly. You can use noncontiguous ranges with some Excel functions, but I will not be covering them in this book.

Using a named range in a formula is not as straightforward as using a single-cell range name. There are a few rules that govern how named ranges are applied in formulas. You can use these rules to your advantage once you know how they work.

To demonstrate these rules, we will create three separate named ranges: a row-based named range, a column-based named range, and a two-dimensional named range.

Row-Based Names

In Figure 9.11, select the range J1:U1, click the Name Box, and name it Months. Remember to press Enter after typing the name.

	I	J	K	L	M	N	O	P	Q	R	S	T	U
1	Months	Jul-13	Aug-13	Sep-13	Oct-13	Nov-13	Dec-13	Jan-14	Feb-14	Mar-14	Apr-14	May-14	Jun-14

FIGURE 9.11 Using a Row-Based Range Name

This name can be used on all the sheets, in columns J to U. When you use the name in a cell, Excel extracts the same column from the named range. For example, if you use the name Months in column K on any sheet, then the value displayed will be Aug-13, which is the value in column K within the named range. Because it is a date, the format may need to be changed so that it displays correctly. The row you use the name in doesn't affect its use.

If you use the name in column G, you will see the #VALUE! error message. This also happens if you use the name in column I. This restricts you from using the range name in a formula in a column outside its designated range. This is one way that range names force a consistent structure throughout a file.

This technique is used frequently in financial models and budgets to standardise the months into columns. You can have a centralised range of months and then use a range name to refer to them throughout the model. This assumes that all the columns in the model are consistent and use the same months. This is a common practice in financial models, and some sheets may have empty columns on the left that are used to line up the month columns and ensure consistency throughout the file.

This technique is useful for reporting models with months across multiple columns. You can also use it to standardise the columns in your reports so that you have a central layout that is replicated throughout the reporting model using named ranges.

You can refer to a specific cell within a row-based name by using the INDEX function. For instance, to refer to the September column in our named range of months, you could use the following formula:

```
=INDEX(Months,1,3)
```

If you wanted a flexible method for extracting the month name, you could use

```
=INDEX(Months,1,A1)
```

In this formula, A1 contains the month number you wish to extract.

Column-Based Names

In Figure 9.12, the range J2:J5 is named Departments.

This name can be used on all the sheets in rows 2 to 5. When you use a name in a cell, Excel extracts the same row number from the named range. For instance, if you use the name Departments in row 3, then the value displayed will be Sales, which is the value in row 3 within the named range.

Column-based names are rarely used by themselves in a formula. They are typically used with an INDEX function to refer to a specific cell within the named range. For example, to refer to the Administration Department in the top example, you could use the following formula

```
=INDEX(Departments,4)
```

You don't have to include the column number in the INDEX function if you are referring to a single-column range like Departments.

When you have lists of entries that you have named, you can replicate that list throughout the model by using sequential numbers in helper cells and the INDEX function.

Figure 9.12 shows an example. The range K8:K11 contains the helper cells with sequential numbers. Cell L8 contains the following formula, which has been copied down:

```
=INDEX(Departments,K8)
```

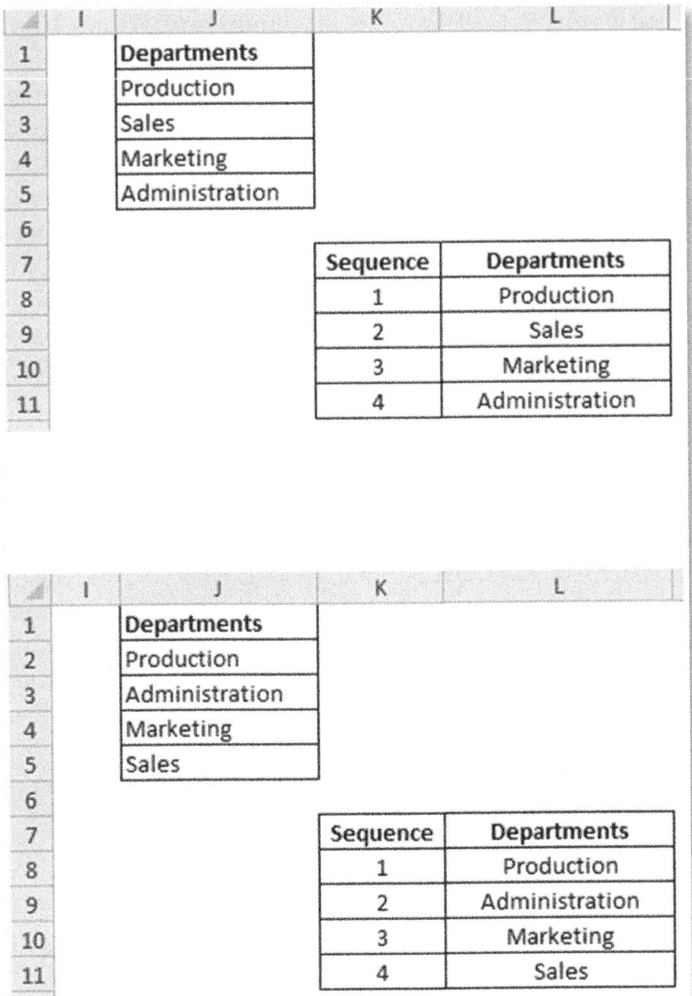

Departments
Production
Sales
Marketing
Administration

Sequence	Departments
1	Production
2	Sales
3	Marketing
4	Administration

Departments
Production
Administration
Marketing
Sales

Sequence	Departments
1	Production
2	Administration
3	Marketing
4	Sales

FIGURE 9.12 Updated Range Name and List

If the sequence of the departments listed changes, as shown in the bottom section of Figure 9.12, then the sequence is automatically updated in the range L8:L11.

Column-based names typically need to be extended as more entries are made to the bottom of them. You can use the Name Manager to extend the specified range.

To add Distribution to the bottom of the list in cell J6, press Ctrl + F3 to open the Name Manager. Select the Departments range name and amend the range at the bottom of the dialog box to

```
=Column_Based!J$2:$J$6
```

Click the checkmark icon on the left to save the change and click the Close button (see Figure 9.13).

If you forget to click the icon, Excel will display a dialog box asking you to confirm the change.

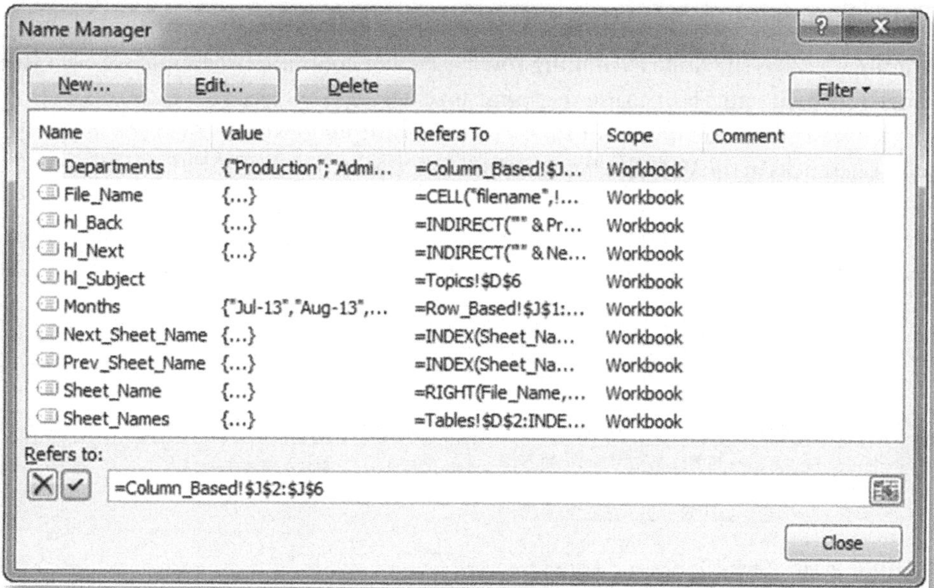

Name	Value	Refers To	Scope	Comment
Departments	{"Production";"Admi...	=Column_Based!$J...	Workbook	
File_Name	{...}	=CELL("filename",!...	Workbook	
hl_Back	{...}	=INDIRECT("" & Pr...	Workbook	
hl_Next	{...}	=INDIRECT("" & Ne...	Workbook	
hl_Subject		=Topics!$D$6	Workbook	
Months	{"Jul-13","Aug-13",...	=Row_Based!$J$1:...	Workbook	
Next_Sheet_Name	{...}	=INDEX(Sheet_Na...	Workbook	
Prev_Sheet_Name	{...}	=INDEX(Sheet_Na...	Workbook	
Sheet_Name	{...}	=RIGHT(File_Name,...	Workbook	
Sheet_Names	{...}	=Tables!$D$2:INDE...	Workbook	

FIGURE 9.13 Departments Range Name Amended

Later in the chapter I will explain two different techniques for creating range names that have ranges that automatically expand and contract.

Having added an entry to the bottom of our Departments range name, we need a mechanism to warn us that our formula-based list in column L is no longer complete. We could use the following formula in cell L6 to warn us:

```
=IF(COUNTA(Departments)>MAX(K8:K13),"Missing Dept","OK")
```

The range K8:K13 is larger than required to include any inserted rows below the list (see Figure 9.14).

	I	J	K	L
1		Departments		
2		Production		
3		Administration		
4		Marketing		
5		Sales		
6		Distribution		Missing Dept
7			Sequence	Departments
8			1	Production
9			2	Administration
10			3	Marketing
11			4	Sales

FIGURE 9.14 Missing Department Noted

Two-Dimensional Names

Naming tables is the same as naming row-based and column-based ranges. Select the range and then name it by using the Name Box.

It is best practice to name any tables you are using for lookups. When you are using table references in the VLOOKUP and INDEX functions, they tend to be fixed references, so using a named range makes sense.

Once created, the names can make your formulas easier to create. We can see this if we revisit an example from the last chapter, shown in Figure 9.15.

	J	K	L	M	N	O	P	Q	R	S	T
1	Stock Code	Description	Colour	Cost	Price						
2	ABC123	Widget	Red	$0.20	$0.45		Stock Code	Description	Colour	Cost	Price
3	ABC124	Widget	Green	$0.20	$0.40		ABC124				
4	XYZ111	Widget	White	$0.90	$1.50		DEF321				
5	XYZ222	Gadget	Black	$0.10	$0.20						
6	DEF321	Gadget	Blue	$0.80	$1.40						
7	DEF322	Gadget	Yellow	$0.50	$1.00						

FIGURE 9.15 Stock Table and Lookup

Select the range J2:N7 and name it tblStock. I use the prefix tbl when naming tables to identify them as tables. It also helps when typing a table name in a formula. When I type tbl, all the named tables in the file are listed.

Then name the range J1:N1 Fields.

Finally, name the range J2:J7 Codes.

Either of the two following formulas in Q3 could now perform our lookups. These can both be copied across and down.

```
=IFERROR(VLOOKUP($P3,tblStock,MATCH(Q$2,Fields,0),0),"")
=IFERROR(INDEX(tblStock,MATCH($P3,Codes,0),MATCH(Q$2,Fields,0)),"")
```

Each of these still has two cell references: $P3 and Q$2. You could name two further ranges and replace those with names.

P2:P5 could be named inpCode.

Q2:T2 could be named inpField.

I use the prefix inp for input cells. When I type inp in a formula, I can see all the input cells listed.

The formulas could be modified as follows:

```
=IFERROR(VLOOKUP(inpCode,tblStock,MATCH(inpField,Fields,0),0),"")
=IFERROR(INDEX(tblStock,MATCH(inpCode,Codes,0),
MATCH(inpField,Fields,0)),"")
```

There are no $ symbols used in either of these formulas, yet they can both be copied down and across to complete the range.

CREATING NAMES AUTOMATICALLY

So far we have used the Name Box to create all our range names. If you have only one or two names to create, then the Name Box is the best alternative.

If you have a lot of names to create, however, you have another option. Excel has a built-in feature that can create range names based on cell labels. This allows you to include the range names in the structures that you use in the developmental phase and then automatically create the range names in one step.

In Australia we have a situation in which each state has some individual public holidays. Most holidays are shared by all the states, but the holidays that are unique to each state have their own dates. In our reporting models, we therefore need to calculate working days for specific states.

Excel has a function that calculates the number of working days between two dates. It accepts a range containing holiday dates as one of its arguments. In a sheet in your model, you can list each state's holiday dates (see Figure 9.16).

	J	K	L	M	N	O	P	Q	R
1	WA Holidays		QLD Holidays		VIC Holidays		SA Holidays		NSW Holidays
2	1/01/2014		1/01/2014		1/01/2014		1/01/2014		1/01/2014
3	27/01/2014		27/01/2014		27/01/2014		27/01/2014		27/01/2014
4	3/03/2014		18/04/2014		10/03/2014		10/03/2014		18/04/2014
5	18/04/2014		21/04/2014		18/04/2014		18/04/2014		21/04/2014
6	21/04/2014		25/04/2014		21/04/2014		21/04/2014		25/04/2014
7	25/04/2014		9/06/2014		25/04/2014		25/04/2014		9/06/2014
8	2/06/2014		13/08/2014		9/06/2014		9/06/2014		6/10/2014
9	29/09/2014		6/10/2014		4/11/2014		6/10/2014		25/12/2014
10	25/12/2014		25/12/2014		25/12/2014		25/12/2014		26/12/2014
11	26/12/2014		26/12/2014		26/12/2014		26/12/2014		

FIGURE 9.16 State Holiday Dates

You could manually create the names for these five state holiday lists, but since they already have names, you can use Excel's built-in creation feature called Create from Selection. This icon is in the Defined Names section of the Formulas Ribbon tab, which was shown earlier in Figure 9.9.

This feature also has a keyboard shortcut: Ctrl + Shift + F3. I use this shortcut frequently.

Notice that NSW has one less holiday than the other states. To create the range names that we need, we can do it in two stages. We'll do NSW dates in the second stage.

First select the range J1:P11. Then press Ctrl + Shift + F3 or use the Create from Selection icon on the Ribbon. The dialog box shown in Figure 9.17 will be displayed.

This dialog box will guess whether the names are in the top row, the left column, or both and check the appropriate box or boxes. In our case it has guessed wrong. Our names are all in the top row so we need to uncheck the left column option and check the top row option (see Figure 9.18).

Clicking OK will create four range names, one for each of the four states.

Before doing anything else, select the range R1:R10 and press the F4 key. Remember that the F4 key repeats your last command. In this case it repeats creating a range name

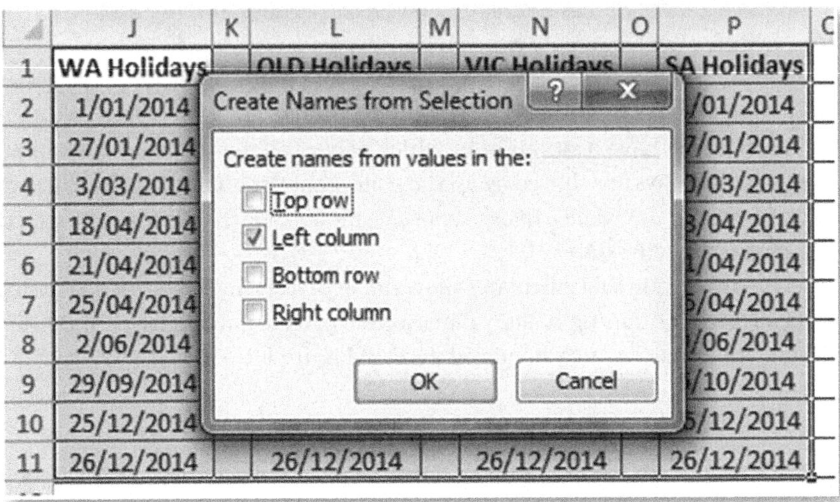

FIGURE 9.17 Create Names from Selection Dialog Box

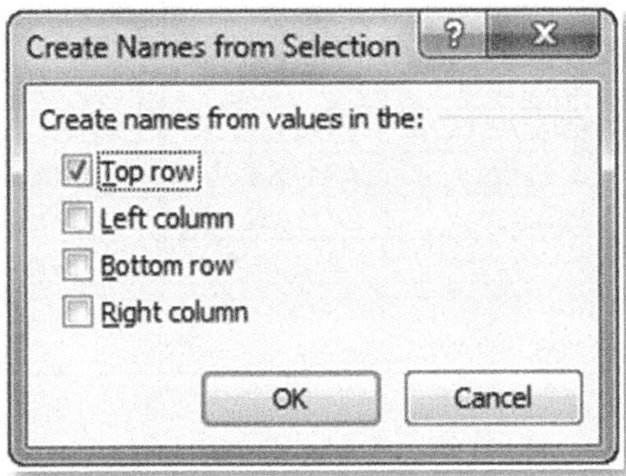

FIGURE 9.18 Amended Create Names from Selection Dialog Box

based on the top row. This allows you to easily create the NSW name, which is one row less than the others. No dialog box is displayed. Excel assumes you are using the same settings as in the previous command.

If you had initially selected the range J1:R11, then the NSW range name would have been one row longer and included a blank cell. Including a blank cell at the bottom of a range can affect its use in data validation in-cell drop-down lists. If you have a blank cell in a range used for a data validation list, it will allow any entry.

If you open Name Manager and sort by the Refers To column, you can see the five new range names (see Figure 9.19).

The NSW_Holidays range name is one row shorter than the others because we created it separately, using the F4 key.

We now have the ranges we need to create a table of working days for each state. We'll use a calendar year example.

Name	Value	Refers To	Scope
WA_Holidays	{"1/01/2014"...	=Holidays!$J$2:$J$11	Workbook
QLD_Holidays	{"1/01/2014"...	=Holidays!$L$2:$L$11	Workbook
VIC_Holidays	{"1/01/2014"...	=Holidays!$N$2:$N$11	Workbook
SA_Holidays	{"1/01/2014"...	=Holidays!$P$2:$P$11	Workbook
NSW_Holidays	{"1/01/2014"...	=Holidays!$R$2:$R$10	Workbook

FIGURE 9.19 Name Manager Listing New Range Names

Figure 9.20 has a table that will be populated with workdays for each month for each state.

Cell T3 is the input cell. The formula in cell U3 is

```
=DATE(YEAR(T3),MONTH(T3)+1,0)
```

This calculates the last day of the month and has been copied down.

	T	U	V	W	X	Y	Z
1	Workdays						
2	Month	End date	WA	QLD	VIC	SA	NSW
3	1/01/2014	31/01/2014					
4	1/02/2014	28/02/2014					
5	1/03/2014	31/03/2014					
6	1/04/2014	30/04/2014					
7	1/05/2014	31/05/2014					
8	1/06/2014	30/06/2014					
9	1/07/2014	31/07/2014					
10	1/08/2014	31/08/2014					
11	1/09/2014	30/09/2014					
12	1/10/2014	31/10/2014					
13	1/11/2014	30/11/2014					
14	1/12/2014	31/12/2014					

FIGURE 9.20 Workday Table by Month and State

Tip: The Underscore Character Replaces a Space

The headings in row 1 in Figure 9.16 all include spaces, but since spaces are not allowed in range names, Excel used the underscore character between the words.

When Excel creates the names automatically, it ensures that the names meet all the naming rules.

The formula in cell T4 is

```
=DATE(YEAR(T3),MONTH(T3)+1,1)
```

This calculates the start of the next month. This saves having to change all the cells in column T when you begin a new year; you just change cell T3.

We will use the NETWORKDAYS function to calculate our workdays.

Syntax

NETWORKDAYS(Start_Date,End_Date,Holidays_Range)

Start_Date and **End_Date** are almost always cell references to dates.

Holidays_Range (optional) contains all the holiday dates you want taken into account in working out your workdays. If you omit the Holidays_Range, you are, in effect, calculating the number of weekdays.

The result of the NETWORKDAYS function is inclusive. That is, it calculates the number of days between two dates and includes both of those dates in the result.

Example

In our example, the formula for V3 is

```
=NETWORKDAYS($T3,$U3,WA_Holidays)
```

I fixed columns T and U, so I can copy the formula across and then simply amend the range name for each state. The other formulas are

```
=NETWORKDAYS($T3,$U3,QLD_Holidays)
=NETWORKDAYS($T3,$U3,VIC_Holidays)
=NETWORKDAYS($T3,$U3,SA_Holidays)
=NETWORKDAYS($T3,$U3,NSW_Holidays)
```

These can all be copied down, and Figure 9.21 shows the results.

	T	U	V	W	X	Y	Z
1	Workdays						
2	Month	End date	WA	QLD	VIC	SA	NSW
3	1/01/2014	31/01/2014	21	21	21	21	21
4	1/02/2014	28/02/2014	20	20	20	20	20
5	1/03/2014	31/03/2014	20	21	20	20	21
6	1/04/2014	30/04/2014	19	19	19	19	19
7	1/05/2014	31/05/2014	22	22	22	22	22
8	1/06/2014	30/06/2014	20	20	20	20	20
9	1/07/2014	31/07/2014	23	23	23	23	23
10	1/08/2014	31/08/2014	21	20	21	21	21
11	1/09/2014	30/09/2014	21	22	22	22	22
12	1/10/2014	31/10/2014	23	22	23	22	22
13	1/11/2014	30/11/2014	20	20	19	20	20
14	1/12/2014	31/12/2014	21	21	21	21	21

FIGURE 9.21 Completed Workday Table by Month and State

We will return to this example when we look at using the INDIRECT function with range names.

NAME INTERSECTIONS

I mentioned earlier that you can't use a space in a range name. We saw that if a cell label has a space and you use it to create a range name, then Excel will substitute the underscore character for the space.

The reason the space is not used in names is that it is used to specify an intersection of two ranges. If you have a vertical (column-based) range name and a horizontal (row-based) range name, then placing a space between the two range names in a formula will return the range intersection of the two ranges.

In a table structure you can use the Create from Selection option to automatically create names for the table, based on the cell labels. You are then able to refer to any cell in the table by using range name intersections.

Consider the table in Figure 9.22.

	J	K	L	M	N	O
1	Head Count	Permanent	Part Time	Casual	Contractors	Total
2	Production	50	11	10	15	86
3	Sales	10	12	16	2	40
4	Administration	5	2	1	1	9

FIGURE 9.22 Head Count Table

If we select the whole table and use Ctrl + Shift + F3 to create the range names using both the top row and left column options, we will create the names shown in Table 9.1.

Having created the named ranges, we can use them to extract specific values from the table.

TABLE 9.1 Range Names to Be Created from Figure 9.22

Range Name	Range
Production	$K$2:$O$2
Sales	$K$3:$O$3
Administration	$K$4:$O$4
Permanent	$K$2:$K$4
Part_Time	$L$2:$L$4
Casual	$M$2:$M$4
Contractors	$N$2:$N$4
Total	$O$2:$O$4

By placing a space between two of the names, we can extract their intersection. The following formula extracts 16, or the value cell M3.

```
=Sales Casual
```

The order doesn't matter, so the following will also return 16:

```
=Casual Sales
```

As long as the two range names intersect, a value will be returned. If they don't intersect, the #NULL! error message is displayed. The following formula will return the #NULL! error message because the names are parallel:

```
=Production Sales
```

Including the Total column allows you to use a formula like the following to extract the total number of workers in Administration:

```
=Administration Total
```

Note that the names remain descriptive and self-documenting while using the intersections.

Column-based names are frequently used for data validation lists, which allow users to select from an in-cell drop-down list. As mentioned earlier, column-based names also typically have to expand as you add entries to the bottom of the list. This can be achieved in two ways.

The first is to define a longer range than you initially need and then gradually fill that range over time. If you define a large enough range, then you may never fill it.

This has a downside for data validation lists: Each list will show a section of blank entries at the bottom. If there is a blank cell in a data validation list, it allows the user to enter anything in the cell. This is usually not acceptable, and so the second method is preferred. This is the topic of the next section.

DYNAMIC RANGE NAMES

The second method involves creating a dynamic range name, a formula-based range name that automatically expands and contracts based on the entries in the range. There are a number of different formulas that achieve a dynamic range name. There is also a technique that uses table names to create dynamic range names.

As we have seen, table names automatically expand based on the number of entries in the table. Unfortunately, you cannot use a table name field as the source for a list in the Data Validation dialog box. To get around this limitation, you can use the table name as the reference for a range name, and this creates a dynamic range name without using a formula.

Table-Based Dynamic Range Names

Table-based dynamic range names are easier to create than the formula-based versions, which will be explained next. Table-based names can handle blank cells within the range and can have entries below the table.

Figure 9.23 shows a list of states that we want to use in a drop-down list.

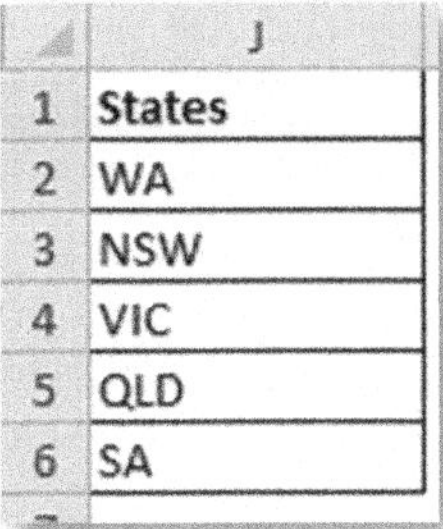

FIGURE 9.23 States List

To create a dynamic name, we must convert the range into a formatted table. Click any cell within the range, press Ctrl + t, confirm the range, and click OK.

This gives the formatted table a generic name like Table1. For the purposes of this example, I will leave the name as Table1, but in practice you can rename the formatted table in the Design Ribbon tab that displays when you select the table. The Table Name box is on the far left side of the Design Ribbon tab (see Figure 9.24).

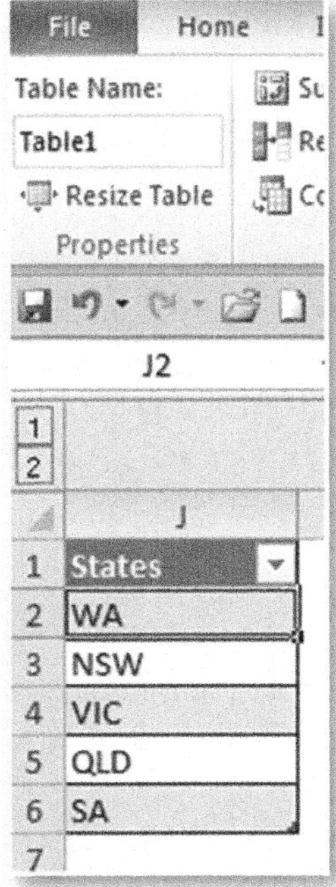

FIGURE 9.24 Table Name Box—Design Ribbon

Click the Define Name button in the Formulas Ribbon tab. (Pressing Alt m m d in sequence also opens the dialog box.) Type the name States in the Name box and use your mouse to select the range J2:J6. Excel will automatically enter the table-based name in the Refers To box. Click OK to complete this dynamic name (see Figure 9.25).

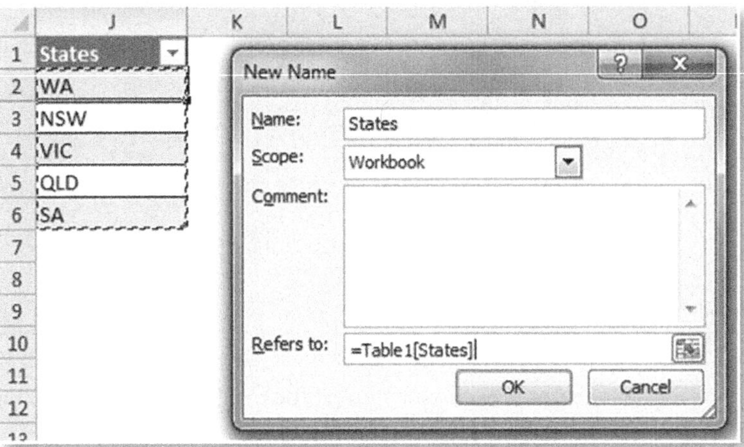

FIGURE 9.25 New Name Dialog Box for States

In another cell, create a data validation list and use =States in the Source box (see Figure 9.26). Pressing Alt a a v in sequence opens the Data Validation dialog box.

Data Validation
Settings | Input Message | Error Alert
Validation criteria
Allow:
List
Ignore blank
In-cell dropdown
Data:
between
Source:
=States
Apply these changes to all other cells with the same settings
Clear All
OK
Cancel

FIGURE 9.26 Data Validation List Using States Range Name

The drop-down list in Figure 9.27 shows the states listed.

Adding TAS to the bottom of the list will automatically update the drop-down list (see Figure 9.28).

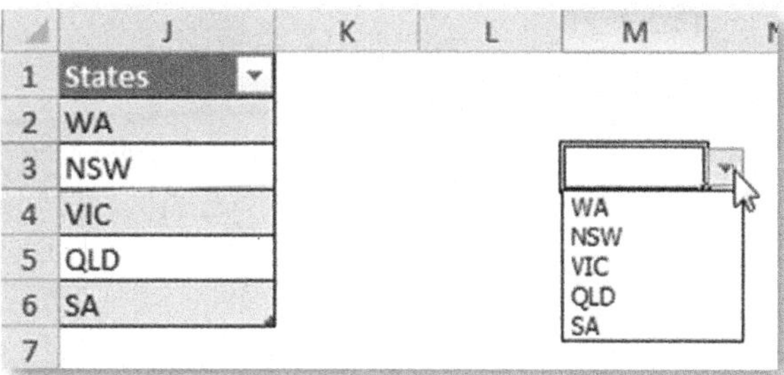

FIGURE 9.27 Drop-Down List Showing States

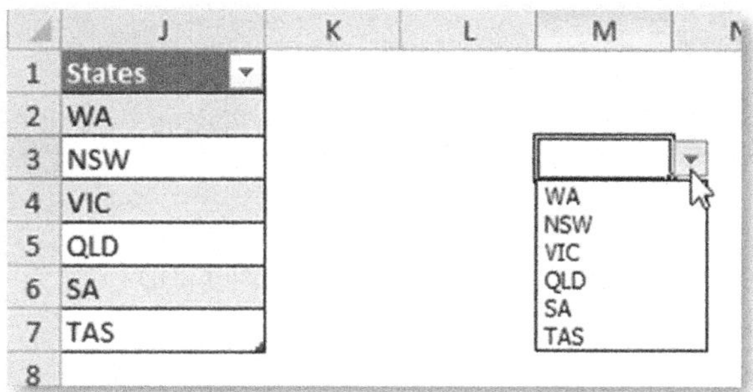

FIGURE 9.28 Drop-Down List with TAS

Formula-Based Dynamic Range Names

I recommend using the INDEX function to create dynamic names. You can also use the OFFSET function, but because it is a volatile function, this adds to the calculation time of your reporting model.

The use of formula-based dynamic range names assumes that there are no blank or empty cells within the range and that there are no other entries below the range.

The dynamic formula defines an anchor cell and then uses the INDEX function to identify the last cell in the range. The COUNTA function is used to count how many cells have entries within the range and, hence, identify the last cell in the range.

Example

Using the same sheet as in the previous example, we can create a formula-based dynamic name.

Click the Define Name button, type the name States_2 in the Name box, and create the following formula in the Refers To box:

```
=Dynamic!$J$2:INDEX(Dynamic!$J:$J,COUNTA(Dynamic!$J:$J))
```

Figure 9.29 shows the formula. Click OK.

This formula uses cell J2 as the anchor cell and then uses the INDEX function that refers to the entire column J, with the COUNTA function determining the last used row. Remember that this technique assumes no blank cells in the list and no other entries below it.

New Name

Name: States_2

Scope: Workbook

Comment:

Refers to: =Dynamic!$J$2:index(Dynamic!$J:$J,counta(Dynamic!$J:$J))

OK Cancel

FIGURE 9.29 New Name Dialog Box Formula-Based Name

If we change the data validation list to use States_2, we can see that the drop-down list still works when we add another state (see Figure 9.30).

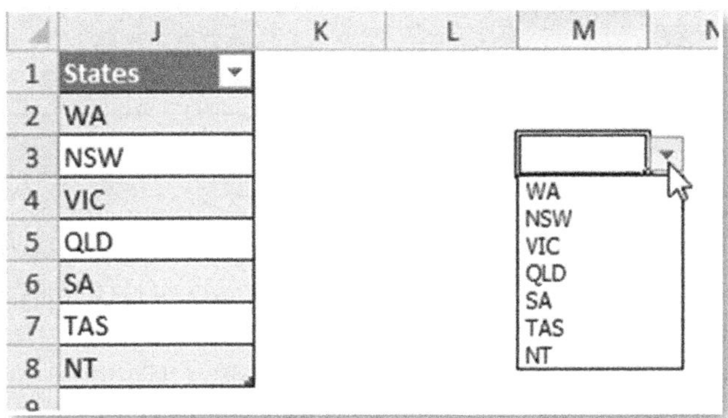

FIGURE 9.30 Drop-Down List with NT

Unbreakable Hyperlinks

Earlier in the chapter, range names were used with hyperlinks to handle sheet name changes. It is possible to create a range name that is very difficult to break.

To create an unbreakable hyperlink, you first use a normal named range as the link, as shown previously. Then you amend the name to use the following formula, using whichever sheet you are linking to:

```
=INDEX(Hyper!$1:$1048576,1,1)
```

The Hyper!$1:$1048576 reference refers to every cell on the Hyper sheet. The 1,1 refers to cell A1 on the sheet. Deleting rows or columns does not affect this reference.

You can't define this name before you associate it with the hyperlink because the dialog box doesn't display formula-based names.

The only way to break this hyperlink is to delete the sheet itself, which means the hyperlink is no longer valid.

USING STRUCTURE IN RANGE NAMES

Range names provide you with a method for applying structure to your reporting models. Whereas other features in Excel are built in, the way you apply structure with range names is based on the names that you use. This means that you are free to create structures that apply to your particular needs. It also means that you must be consistent in your application of those conventions and names.

As an example, let's use a case with three metrics: actuals, budgets, and forecasts. Within each of these metrics, you will no doubt have the same measures. You might have statistics that measure production and sales volumes, so you could use row-based range names like

```
ActProdVol, BudSalesVol, FcastProdVol
```

You might report by current month, last month, and year to date (YTD). These may be column-based names in a statistics sheet, and you could use names like

```
CurrMth, YTD, PrevMth
```

Then, using the intersection method, you could refer to specific statistics with

```
ActProdVol CurrMth
BudSalesVol PrevMth
FcastProdVol YTD
```

This technique retains the descriptive nature of the names and adds another level to the flexibility of the range names. Remember that this is a structure you must create and maintain to make it work and obtain the benefits.

As well as being descriptive, these range names allow you to easily copy and paste and then use Find and Replace to update formulas to build your reports. A formula can be copied and easily modified this way. The find-and-replace process speeds up the developmental stage, but is not required when running the reports.

The table layout in Figure 9.31 has row-based range names created, from labels in column J. The column-based range names are created based on the labels in X1:Z1. I have used the same names that were mentioned earlier.

	I	J	K	L	M	N	O	P	Q	R	S	T	U	V	W	X	Y	Z
1	**Statistics '000**		**Jul-13**	**Aug-13**	**Sep-13**	**Oct-13**	**Nov-13**	**Dec-13**	**Jan-14**	**Feb-14**	**Mar-14**	**Apr-14**	**May-14**	**Jun-14**	**Total**	**CurrMth**	**YTD**	**PrevMth**
2	Current Month	Feb-14																
3																		
4	**Actuals**	**Range Name**																
5	Production Volume	ActProdVol	54	40	75	32	62	25	66	74					428	74	428	66
6	Sales Volume	ActSalesVol	71	16	57	24	19	60	62	42					351	42	351	62
7																		
8	**Budget**	**Range Name**																
9	Production Volume	BudProdVol	13	51	77	37	89	59	75	12	68	83	21	67	652	12	413	75
10	Sales Volume	BudSalesVol	54	24	53	20	38	83	80	60	88	86	59	28	673	60	412	80
11																		
12	**Forecast**	**Range Name**																
13	Production Volume	FcastProdVol	19	21	11	67	49	28	32	59	11	20	45	42	404	59	286	32
14	Sales Volume	FcastSalesVol	33	14	53	70	56	51	60	89	82	42	33	33	616	89	426	60

FIGURE 9.31 Statistics Table

We will use the range names in the statistics table in Figure 9.31 to create reports. Figure 9.32 shows the structure for the report. We will be able to create this report by using just two formulas, which we can copy across and then amend using Find and Replace. Once created, the report will update whenever cell J2 in Figure 9.31 is updated.

	AA	AB	AC	AD	AE	AF	AG	AH	AI	AJ	AK
1		Report	Current Month			Previous Month			YTD		
2			Actuals	Budget	Forecast	Actuals	Budget	Forecast	Actuals	Budget	Forecast
3		Production Volume									
4		Sales Volume									

FIGURE 9.32 Blank Report Structure Table

The formula in cell AC3 is

`=ActProdVol CurrMth`

The formula in cell AC4 is

`=ActSalesVol CurrMth`

We will copy AC3:AC4 to the range AD3:AE4. These will show the same values.

We will use the Find and Replace feature to modify the formula for Budget and Forecast in two steps.

Select AD3:AD4 and press Ctrl + h. Type Act in the Find What box and Bud in the Replace With box. These are the prefixes we have used in our range names. Click the Replace All button (see Figure 9.33). A message box informing you that two replacements have been made will be displayed.

With the Find and Replace dialog box still open, select AE3:AE4, type Fcast in the Replace With box, and click the Replace All button. Two more names will be changed.

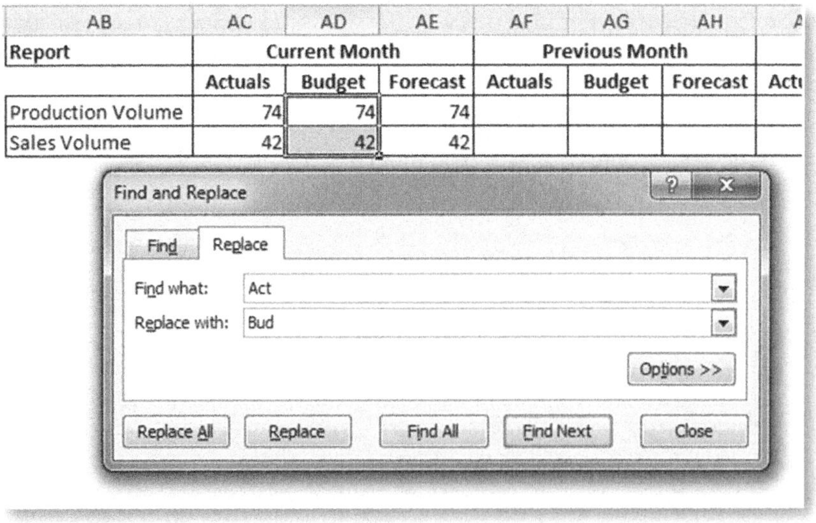

AB	AC	AD	AE	AF	AG	AH	A
Report	Current Month			Previous Month			
	Actuals	Budget	Forecast	Actuals	Budget	Forecast	Actı
Production Volume	74	74	74				
Sales Volume	42	42	42				

FIGURE 9.33 Find and Replace to Amend Formulas

WARNING: Find and Replace

Make sure you select a range before using Find and Replace.

If you have a single cell selected before using Find and Replace, you will make the changes across the whole sheet—not always what you want. You can use Undo to fix it.

WARNING: Choose Your Prefixes and Suffixes Carefully

I have successfully used Act, Bud, and Fcast as prefixes for many years. Something to keep in mind with any prefixes that you use is that they might appear in the main name.

For instance, if I used Manufact as my descriptive name instead of Prod, then using Find and Replace with "Act" would affect my main range name. Hence I would use Act_Manufact rather than ActManufact and replace "Act_" with "Bud_".

The current month figures have been completed (see Figure 9.34). We can use those cells to create the previous month and YTD figures using Find and Replace two more times.

	AA	AB	AC	AD	AE
1		Report	Current Month		
2			Actuals	Budget	Forecast
3		Production Volume	74	12	59
4		Sales Volume	42	60	89

FIGURE 9.34 Current Month Report Complete

Copy AC3:AE4. Paste in AF3, then paste in AI3.

Select range AF3:AH4 and use Find and Replace to replace CurrMth with PrevMth. This will convert each formula to work with the PrevMth range name and change the intersection to column Z. Six changes should be made.

Select range AI3:AK4, then use Find and Replace to replace CurrMth with YTD. This will convert each formula to work with the YTD range name and change the intersection to column Y. Six more changes should be made.

Figure 9.35 shows the completed report.

This report was easy to create because of the structure incorporated into the range names. Prefixes and suffixes allowed you to make the changes easily. Prefixes also group similar range names together in the Name Manager when they are sorted by range name.

	AA	AB	AC	AD	AE	AF	AG	AH	AI	AJ	AK
1		Report	Current Month			Previous Month			YTD		
2			Actuals	Budget	Forecast	Actuals	Budget	Forecast	Actuals	Budget	Forecast
3		Production Volume	74	12	59	66	75	32	428	413	286
4		Sales Volume	42	60	89	62	80	60	351	412	426

FIGURE 9.35 Completed Statistics Report

INDIRECT AND RANGE NAMES

The INDIRECT function explained in the previous chapter can be used with range names to create incredibly flexible reporting models. We can revisit two of our previous examples and convert the formula to use INDIRECT and make them more flexible.

Review Figure 9.20, in which we created a table of working days. Columns V:Z had unique formulas that were copied down. With the INDIRECT function, we can create a single formula in cell V3 that can be copied across and down.

The formula in cell V3 was

```
=NETWORKDAYS($T3,$U3,WA_Holidays)
```

The WA_Holidays range had to be changed because the formula was copied across. The INDIRECT function can be used to replace range names. In the formula above, we could amend it as follows:

```
=NETWORKDAYS($T3,$U3,INDIRECT(V$2&"_Holidays"))
```

This formula can be copied down and across.

Remember that the INDIRECT function uses text entries to create a cell or range reference. A range name is treated as a range reference.

We can use text techniques to build a range name between the INDIRECT parentheses to use that range name in the formula.

The formula above takes advantage of the fact that we have a standard structure for range names. The state is followed by _Holidays. Row 2 has the states, so we just need to join the state from row 2 to the text _Holidays to create the range name we need.

Our statistics report from Figure 9.31 can be created using a single formula with a few helper cells. Figure 9.36 has the amended layout with helper cells. The helper cells contain the three parts of the structured range names. They allow us to build the range names for each cell using the INDIRECT function.

	AA	AB	AC	AD	AE	AF	AG	AH	AI	AJ	AK
1		Report	CurrMth	CurrMth	CurrMth	PrevMth	PrevMth	PrevMth	YTD	YTD	YTD
2			Act	Bud	Fcast	Act	Bud	Fcast	Act	Bud	Fcast
3		ProdVol	74	12	59	66	75	32	428	413	286
4		SalesVol	42	60	89	62	80	60	351	412	426

FIGURE 9.36 Completed Statistics Report with Helper Cells

The following formula can be entered in cell AC3 and copied across and down to complete the report.

```
=INDIRECT(AC$2&$AB3) INDIRECT(AC$1)
```

This replaces each range name with an INDIRECT function. There is a space between the two INDIRECT functions to create the intersection of the two names created by the two INDIRECT functions.

LISTING RANGE NAMES

It is a good practice to list range names used within a file in a Tables or Lists sheet as part of the file documentation process. To paste a list of range names, press the F3 key and click the Paste List button to paste a list of range names along with their respective range references. This list is not dynamic, so you will need to update it manually if you amend or add range names to the file.

CHAPTER TEN

Maintenance Issues

WHEN YOU ARE BUILDING or amending a reporting model, it is important to ensure that you consider its long-term maintenance. By using formatted tables, dynamic range names, and the other techniques described in previous chapters, you can simplify the maintenance process.

MAINTENANCE INSTRUCTIONS

Reporting models should have instructions for all the maintenance procedures. When developing your model, you need to identify the types of maintenance issues that will arise. You then need to develop processes and instructions to deal with all those maintenance issues.

These instructions would include what you have to do to add a new account or department to your model. Many maintenance processes are done only once in a while. Instructions ensure that all the correct steps are taken in the correct order.

It's a good idea to include hyperlinks with the instructions to make it easy for the user to move to the correct area. Include a note in the instructions that pressing F5 and then pressing Enter returns the user to the source of the hyperlink—many users are unaware of this useful shortcut.

You must review the past and also consider the future in terms of what is likely to change. This may mean talking to managers to find out if they have any plans to change the structure of the reporting requirements or the underlying data that drives the reports.

For example, if it is likely that a new division will be added in the foreseeable future, you will need to consider that in your design of the reporting model.

Table-based systems simplify many maintenance issues. They work very well with many of the functions that we have already covered and provide flexibility in handling new accounts and departments.

THE ADVANTAGES OF USING TABLES

There is always a possibility that the structure of your model will have to be amended to handle a change in the business model. When developing a reporting model, you need to consider the types of changes that can be made to your model.

Having standard lists of departments and other categories and then using an INDEX function with sequential numbers to reference them is effective and versatile. It's easy to expand the lists as new entries are added. The order of the departments often has to be consistent. Using the INDEX method can achieve that consistency throughout the reporting model.

Figure 10.1 shows a Reports sheet (left) and a Lists sheet (right). The sequence of departments from the Lists sheet must be maintained in all the reports.

	J	K	L
1	Costs	Departments	Actuals
2	1	Production	285459
3	2	Sales	36449
4	3	Distribution	52845
5	4	Administration	35515
6	5		0
7	6		0
8	7		0
9	8		0
10	9		0
11	10		0
12		Total	410268

Report | Data | Lists | Tables

	A
1	Departments
2	Production
3	Sales
4	Distribution
5	Administration

Data | Lists

FIGURE 10.1 Reports and Lists Sheets

There is a dynamic range name, Departments, which automatically expands to include new names as they are added.

The formula in cell K2 of the Reports sheet is

```
=IFERROR(INDEX(Departments,J2),"")
```

This has been copied down the rest of column to cell K11.

If we need to adjust the order by inserting two new departments, all we have to do is insert the department names onto the Lists sheet. The INDEX function in the report will automatically update (see Figure 10.2).

	J	K	L
1	Costs	Departments	Actuals
2	1	Production	285,459
3	2	Quality Control	26,134
4	3	Sales	36,449
5	4	Distribution	52,845
6	5	Marketing	50,301
7	6	Administration	35,515
8	7		0
9	8		0
10	9		0
11	10		0
12		Total	486,703

Report / Data / Lists / Tables

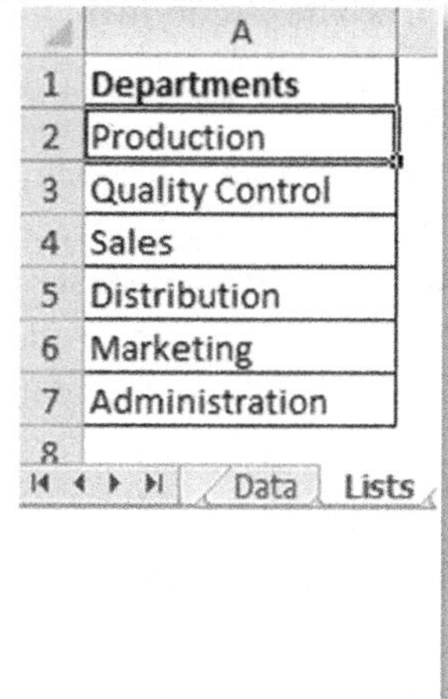

	A
1	Departments
2	Production
3	Quality Control
4	Sales
5	Distribution
6	Marketing
7	Administration
8	

Data / Lists

FIGURE 10.2 Amended Reports and Lists Sheets

COMMON ISSUES

When developing reporting models that are based on external data, the main issue is to keep the reporting model up-to-date with changes in the external data. This means handling such things as adding new account numbers, or new departments, to the reporting model.

Depending on the structure of the reporting model, adding or removing a department could be a major structural change. How likely this is to happen will affect the type of model that you choose to create.

The use of the 3D SUM demonstrated in Chapter 7 allows you to create a sheet for each department. This provides an easy way to either add or remove a department: You can simply add or remove the sheet.

The use of helper cells can make maintenance easier, and your goal should be to simplify the maintenance process as much as possible. Simplifying formulas also makes future maintenance easier.

Adding new account numbers is a common requirement, and it should be as simple as possible to do. Using a table-based layout can make this straightforward.

If a new department is likely to be added, then when you are building your model you should structure it so that adding a new department is not a major change.

Part of the validation process, which is described in Chapter 13, will demonstrate how to identify new accounts and departments so that they can be added to the model.

ROLLING THE YEAR

Rolling over the financial year—that is, ending one year and starting the next—should be a straightforward process. It is typically done when there are many other processes to do involving the previous year's end. Many reports have to be modified for the new reporting year, and making the process straightforward is an important goal.

The main changes for rolling the year are related to date and budget. All dates must be changed for the new year, and the new budget must be incorporated into the reporting model. These two steps should be straightforward.

Dates throughout the model should be based on formulas. As much as possible, any tables for workdays or calendar days should also be formula-driven.

WORKING WITH DAYS

Excel 2010 has a new function that makes it easy to calculate workdays between two dates. This enables you to automate workday calculations. Excel's NETWORKDAYS function, which we used in the previous chapter, handles only the common weekend of Saturday and Sunday. This can't be used when businesses work on Saturday or Sunday.

The NETWORKDAYS function allows the inclusion of a holiday's range that includes dates to be treated as nonworkdays.

The new function NETWORKDAYS.INTL takes into account that some countries have different weekends. Some Middle Eastern countries, for instance, have a Friday and Saturday weekend.

Excel 2010 introduced a number of new functions that use the period to identify a different version of the function. In general, these new functions provide more flexibility or correct deficiencies in the existing functions.

Syntax

NETWORKDAYS.INTL (Start_Date, End_Date, Weekend, Holidays_Range)

Start_Date and **End Date** are typically cell references with the relevant dates. If Start_Date is after End_Date, a negative value will be displayed.

Weekend is a number that represents the weekend to be used in the calculation. See Figure 10.3 for a listing of some of the weekend numbers.

Holidays_Range (optional) is a range containing the holiday dates to be excluded from workday calculations.

Example

Figure 10.4 shows a table of weekdays and working days for the 2014 financial year.

The input cells in this range are J2, which has the starting date for the new year, and Q2:Q11, which is a list of holiday dates to be excluded from the workday calculations. The range Q2:Q11 has been named Holidays.

All the formulas from Table 10.1 have been copied down the rest of their respective columns. Column O applies to businesses that do not open on Sundays.

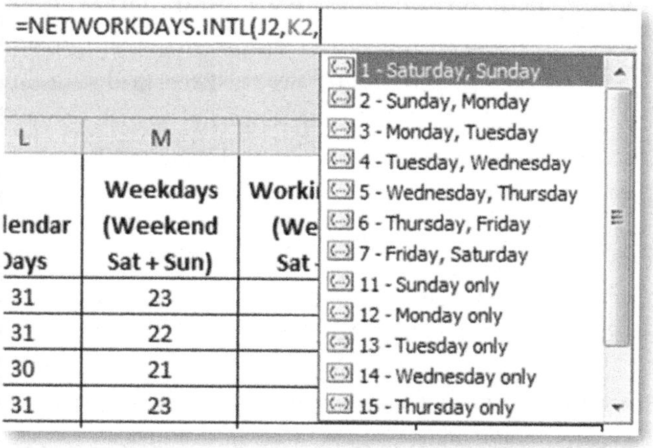

=NETWORKDAYS.INTL(J2,K2,

L	M	
lendar Days	Weekdays (Weekend Sat + Sun)	Worki (We Sat
31	23	
31	22	
30	21	
31	23	

1 - Saturday, Sunday
2 - Sunday, Monday
3 - Monday, Tuesday
4 - Tuesday, Wednesday
5 - Wednesday, Thursday
6 - Thursday, Friday
7 - Friday, Saturday
11 - Sunday only
12 - Monday only
13 - Tuesday only
14 - Wednesday only
15 - Thursday only

FIGURE 10.3 Weekend Numbers for NETWORKDAYS.INTL Function

	I	J	K	L	M	N	O	P	Q
1	Month	Start Date	End Date	Calendar Days	Weekdays (Weekend Sat + Sun)	Workings Days (Weekend Sat + Sun)	Workings Days (Weekend Sun)		Holidays
2	July	1/07/2013	31/07/2013	31	23	23	27		30/09/2013
3	August	1/08/2013	31/08/2013	31	22	22	27		25/12/2013
4	September	1/09/2013	30/09/2013	30	21	20	24		26/12/2013
5	October	1/10/2013	31/10/2013	31	23	23	27		1/01/2014
6	November	1/11/2013	30/11/2013	30	21	21	26		27/01/2014
7	December	1/12/2013	31/12/2013	31	22	20	24		3/03/2014
8	January	1/01/2014	31/01/2014	31	23	21	25		18/04/2014
9	February	1/02/2014	28/02/2014	28	20	20	24		21/04/2014
10	March	1/03/2014	31/03/2014	31	21	20	25		25/04/2014
11	April	1/04/2014	30/04/2014	30	22	19	23		2/06/2014
12	May	1/05/2014	31/05/2014	31	22	22	27		
13	June	1/06/2014	30/06/2014	30	21	20	24		
14			Total	365	261	251	303		

FIGURE 10.4 Weekdays and Workdays Table

TABLE 10.1 Formulas from Figure 10.4

Cell	Formula	Comments
J3	=DATE(YEAR(J2),MONTH(J2)+1,1)	
K2	=DATE(YEAR(J2),MONTH(J2)+1,0)	
L2	=K2-J2+1	When you subtract one date from another, the result is exclusive. You have to add 1 to make it inclusive.
M2	=NETWORKDAYS(J2,K2)	Normal weekdays—no holidays.
N2	=NETWORKDAYS(J2,K2,Holidays)	Workdays equals weekdays minus holidays.
O2	=NETWORKDAYS.INTL(J2,K2,11,Holidays)	The 11 in the formula treats Sunday as the weekend.

SIMPLIFYING THE INTERFACE BY USING CONTROLS

A *control* is a graphic object that is drawn above the Excel grid. Like any other graphic object, it can be moved around without reference to the grid below. These controls are the same as the controls used in Excel's dialog boxes, so users are already familiar with them.

Using spreadsheet controls can improve the user experience, because the user can interact with a control to modify the spreadsheet. Controls can be used in many situations, not just in reporting models.

The following are three popular controls:

1. **Check Box.** This control places a checkmark in a box to turn a calculation on.
2. **Option Buttons.** These allow you to choose one of three to five options.
3. **Combo Box.** This is the name of a drop-down list that is more robust than the Data Validation drop-down list.

To insert controls on the sheet, you have to display the Developer Ribbon (see Chapter 3 for instructions).

The Insert drop-down gallery has two types of controls listed:

1. **Form controls.** These are the controls discussed in the rest of this chapter and are the easiest and most reliable controls to use.
2. **Active-X controls.** These look the same as the Form controls but behave slightly differently. They are more advanced and more complex and can have some compatibility issues. My advice is to avoid using Active-X controls unless you are familiar with their use and limitations. These controls are not covered in this book.

Example

The method of inserting a control is similar for all controls. We'll use the Check Box control as an example, since it is the easiest to create and use.

Open a blank sheet. Click the Insert drop-down item on the Developer Ribbon tab and select Check Box from the Form Controls gallery (see Figure 10.5).

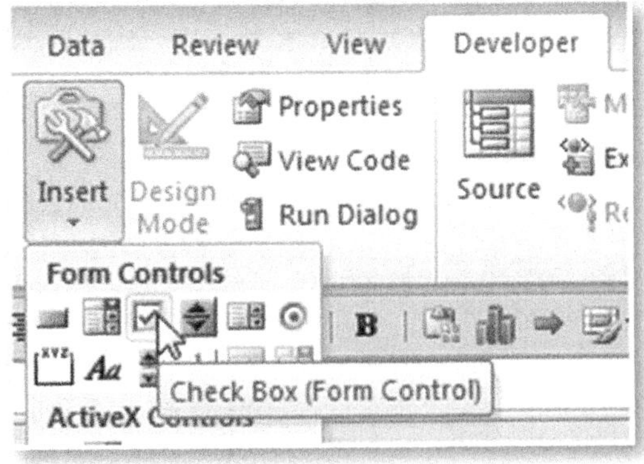

FIGURE 10.5 Insert Check Box Form Control

Use the mouse to draw the control on the sheet. You can draw it as large as you like. The size is set by default.

Once it is drawn, right-click the control and select Format Control from the menu.

The Control tab should display. Click inside the Cell Link box and then click a cell on the sheet to set the linked cell for the control. The cell link is how the control interacts with the sheet. In most cases the cell link is a cell directly below the control itself. In this example we are not concerned where the linked cell is. See the section on cell links later.

By right-clicking the control, you are selecting it rather than using it. Once it has been selected, you can make changes to it. You'll know that a control has been selected by the lines around the control with the drag handles displayed (see Figure 10.6).

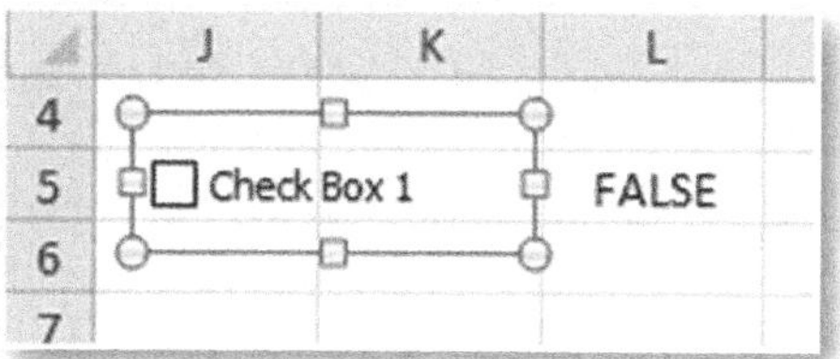

FIGURE 10.6 Selected Check Box Control

To deselect a control, simply click somewhere else on the sheet.

If you left-click the check box, you will see either TRUE or FALSE displayed in the linked cell, depending on whether the control is checked or not. This is the control interacting with the sheet.

Another way to modify the linked cell is to use the Formula Bar when the control is selected (see Figure 10.7).

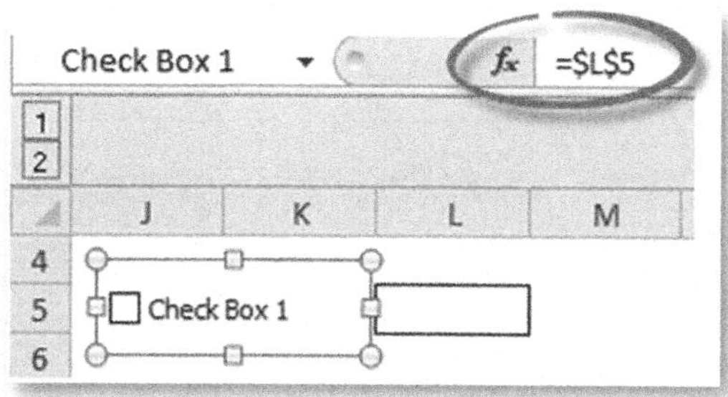

FIGURE 10.7 Linked Cell—Formula Bar

You need to make sure you press the equal sign before you select the linked cell. Figure 10.8 has the checked and unchecked results.

See the section "Check Box" further on for more details on how this can be used.

Cell Links

All of these controls need a cell link to operate. Controls are graphic objects that exist above the Excel sheet grid. They need to link to a cell on the sheet grid so that formulas

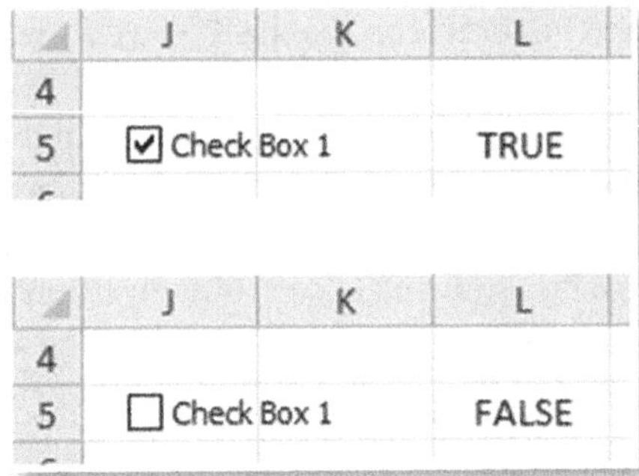

FIGURE 10.8 Check Box Results

and Excel's other features can be changed when the control changes. This provides the interaction with the sheet.

Using the control enters a value into the linked cell based on changes to the control.

It is a good practice to name the linked cell, including a prefix that describes the type of control the cell is linked to. When reviewing or maintaining formulas that refer to the linked cell, you will then be aware that a control is involved.

Common prefixes are chkbx, opt, and combo for the three controls included in this section. Name examples: chkbxInflation, optLarge, comboDepartment.

The Linked-Cell Format

Because entries are made in the linked cell and the control is typically placed above the linked cell, it is common to apply a custom number format to the linked cell to hide the entries. The entries can be distracting to users if left unformatted.

The best custom number format for hiding cell entries is ;;; (three semicolons in a row; see Figure 10.9).

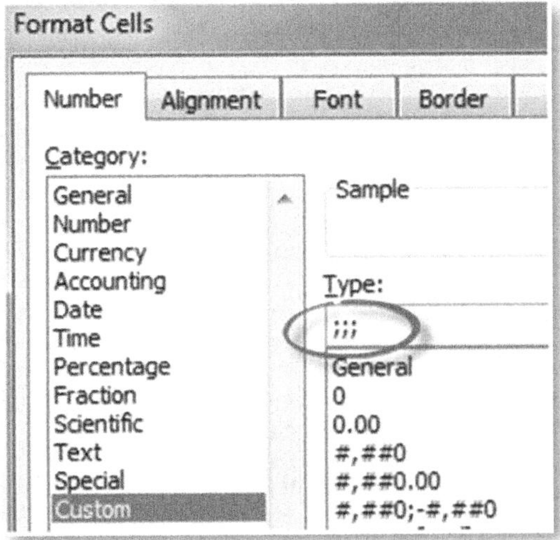

FIGURE 10.9 Custom Number Format to Hide Cell Entries

This format instructs Excel not to display or print anything. This format is preferred to using the white font or the same font colour as the fill colour. A white font can still display the entry in certain circumstances.

If you select a range containing a white font, the contents become faintly visible. Also, if you print a page using the Blank and White option in Print Settings, then the cell will print. The custom number format in Figure 10.9 doesn't display or print.

The linked cell, by its nature, shouldn't be locked. It is possible for the user to select the cell and enter a value via the keyboard. Hence you should have a validation on the linked cell to identify invalid entries. The user could also delete an entry, so don't assume that the linked cell always has an entry.

Check Box

This control is the simplest one for the user to operate and the simplest to create and incorporate into your reporting models.

A check box control can be used to select one of two mutually exclusive actions or to select whether a single option is used. Multiple check boxes can enable more complex selection combinations.

This control returns TRUE or FALSE to its linked cell. A checked box is TRUE, and an unchecked box is FALSE.

As we have already seen in Excel, TRUE = 1 and FALSE = 0. By referring to a check box's linked cell in formulas, we can easily turn certain calculations off and on. By referring to the linked cell in Conditional Formats, we can also control formats using check boxes.

Example

In a budget situation, you may want the ability to quickly turn off various inflation components. Figure 10.10 shows four separate inflation rates.

	J	K	L	M	N	O	P	Q	R
1				1	2	3	4	5	6
2	**Inflation Rates**	**Input**	**Include**	**Jul-13**	**Aug-13**	**Sep-13**	**Oct-13**	**Nov-13**	**Dec-13**
3	Inflation - Wages	3.50%	☑	1.003	1.006	1.009	1.012	1.015	1.018
4	Inflation - Salaries	4.00%	☑	1.003	1.007	1.010	1.013	1.017	1.020
5	Inflation - Energy	7.50%	☑	1.006	1.013	1.019	1.025	1.031	1.038
6	Inflation - General	3.00%	☑	1.003	1.005	1.008	1.010	1.013	1.015

FIGURE 10.10 Inflation Rates

The values in columns M to R are factors that are multiplied by costs to inflate them in the relevant period. The percentages in column K are apportioned over the months. They increase each month. The check boxes in column L allow the user to turn off individual inflation rates. The check boxes are all linked to the cell beneath them in column L. The check boxes have all had their text removed.

Figure 10.11 has two inflation rates turned off.

	J	K	L	M	N	O	P	Q	R
1				1	2	3	4	5	6
2	**Inflation Rates**	**Input**	**Include**	**Jul-13**	**Aug-13**	**Sep-13**	**Oct-13**	**Nov-13**	**Dec-13**
3	Inflation - Wages	3.50%	☑	1.003	1.006	1.009	1.012	1.015	1.018
4	Inflation - Salaries	4.00%	☐	1.000	1.000	1.000	1.000	1.000	1.000
5	Inflation - Energy	7.50%	☑	1.006	1.013	1.019	1.025	1.031	1.038
6	Inflation - General	3.00%	☐	1.000	1.000	1.000	1.000	1.000	1.000

FIGURE 10.11 Amended Inflation Rates

The formula in cell M3, which has been copied down and across, is

```
=1+($K3/12*M$1*$L3)
```

I haven't used a range name in this case because there was a range of inflation rates to work with. Row 1 contains helper cells with the month number. The important reference is $L3, which is the linked cell of the first check box. If this cell contains TRUE, it leaves the inflation factor untouched. If L3 contains FALSE, it will zero the value within the parentheses and leave the final value as 1.

Check Box Text

You can add text to a check box control, or you can delete the text and describe it with a cell label. I tend to use cell labels, such as in Figure 10.10, rather than the text on the control, because there is more flexibility with cell label formatting than with the control formatting.

Check Box Validation

The linked cell validation formula to ensure a correct entry for a check box control is

```
=OR(A1={TRUE,FALSE})
```

This will display TRUE if the cell (A1) is valid; otherwise, it will display FALSE. This ensures that the cell contains either TRUE or FALSE. A blank cell would be invalid.

Option Buttons

Option buttons are easy for the user to make selections with but are slightly more complex to include in a report model. The options used must be mutually exclusive. You can choose only one option from the options listed.

Option buttons work together and are all linked to the same cell. An option button returns a number that identifies the option button chosen. Typically, you have five or fewer option buttons for one selection. If you need to choose between more options, you would use a combo box control.

As you add new option buttons to the sheet, they will all be linked to the same linked cell as the previous option buttons. If you need to use more than one set of option buttons on a sheet, you must group them together using a control called Group Box.

Option buttons are helpful to the user because they display all the possible options at once. A drop-down list has to be used for the user to see what is available. A drop-down box shows the current selection but not the other possibilities.

This control works well with the INDEX, CHOOSE, and OFFSET functions.

Example

Figure 10.12 shows the layout of a sheet that will allow the user to choose a comparison value in a sales chart. The three options are Budget, Forecast, and Last Year. The user can choose just one.

	J	K	L	M	N	O	P	Q
1	**Select**	**Sales**	**Jul-13**	**Aug-13**	**Sep-13**	**Oct-13**	**Nov-13**	**Dec-13**
2		Budget	1,332	1,288	1,174	1,317	1,176	1,350
3		Forecast	1,399	1,404	1,354	1,411	1,445	1,295
4		Last Year	1,051	1,096	1,140	1,078	1,125	1,147
5								
6		Sales	Jul-13	Aug-13	Sep-13	Oct-13	Nov-13	Dec-13
7		Actuals	1,348	1,223	1,271	1,247	1,336	1,350
8								

FIGURE 10.12 Option Button Layout

We will insert three option buttons above cells J2, J3, and J4. When creating option buttons, it is extremely important to create them in the correct sequence. Each option button created has a unique sequential number. The first created is 1, the second is 2, and so on.

We will use the linked cell from the option buttons in an INDEX function to extract the correct comparison from the table in K1:Q4. Hence, we need to put the first option button above J2, the second above J3, and the third above J4.

The option buttons will be linked to cell J2, and that cell will be named optComparison.

As mentioned earlier, option buttons are linked to a single cell, which will be updated with the unique number that refers to the option button chosen. To link an option button to a cell, right-click the option button and choose Format Control. On the Control tab, click inside the Linked Cell box and choose the linked cell, in this case cell J2.

I have not applied the ;;; custom format to J2, so it displays the number in the figures that follow.

The formula in cell K8, which can be copied across, is

`=INDEX(K2:K4,optComparison)`

The charts in Figures 10.13 and 10.14 are linked to the range K6:Q8.

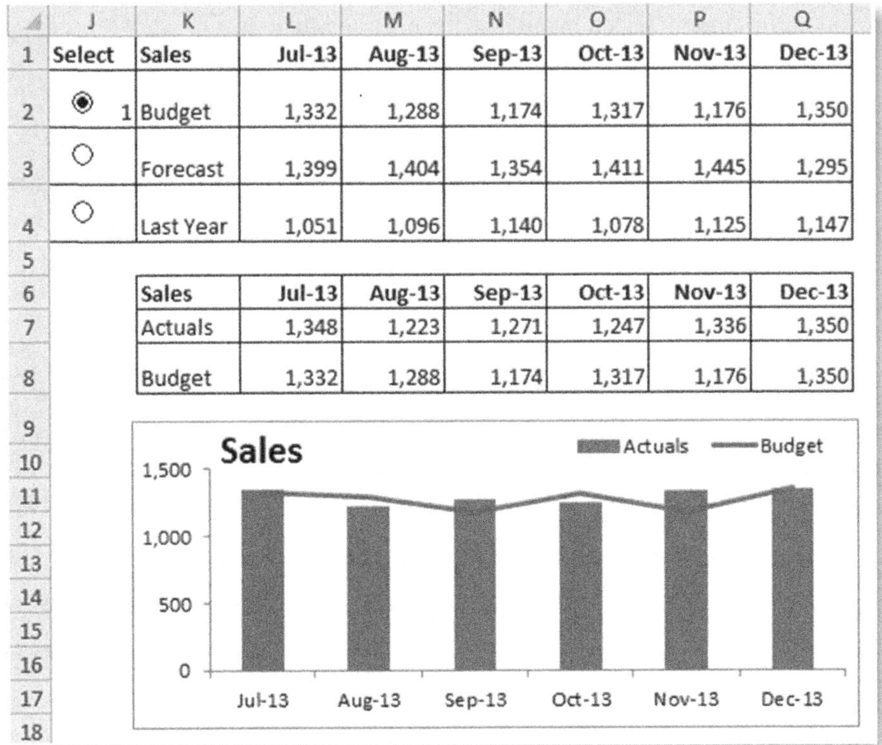

	J	K	L	M	N	O	P	Q
1	Select	Sales	Jul-13	Aug-13	Sep-13	Oct-13	Nov-13	Dec-13
2	◉ 1	Budget	1,332	1,288	1,174	1,317	1,176	1,350
3	○	Forecast	1,399	1,404	1,354	1,411	1,445	1,295
4	○	Last Year	1,051	1,096	1,140	1,078	1,125	1,147
5								
6		Sales	Jul-13	Aug-13	Sep-13	Oct-13	Nov-13	Dec-13
7		Actuals	1,348	1,223	1,271	1,247	1,336	1,350
8		Budget	1,332	1,288	1,174	1,317	1,176	1,350

FIGURE 10.13 Budget Option Button Chosen

Option Button Validation

The linked cell validation formula for three option buttons would be

`=AND(A1>=1,A1<=3,INT(A1)=A1)`

The INT function removes any decimal values. The name is short for integer.

Combo Box

The Data Validation in-cell drop-down option has some limitations (see the "Data Validations Limitations" section in Chapter 3). A more robust solution for drop-down lists is a combo box control. This control returns a number representing the item chosen. If you select the first item, 1 is displayed. Selecting the third item will display a 3.

A combo box control is more dynamic than the Data Validation option.

If you change the list range that the Data Validation option uses, the existing entries do not change. The drop-down list itself will update, but any entries made using the previous list may now have invalid entries.

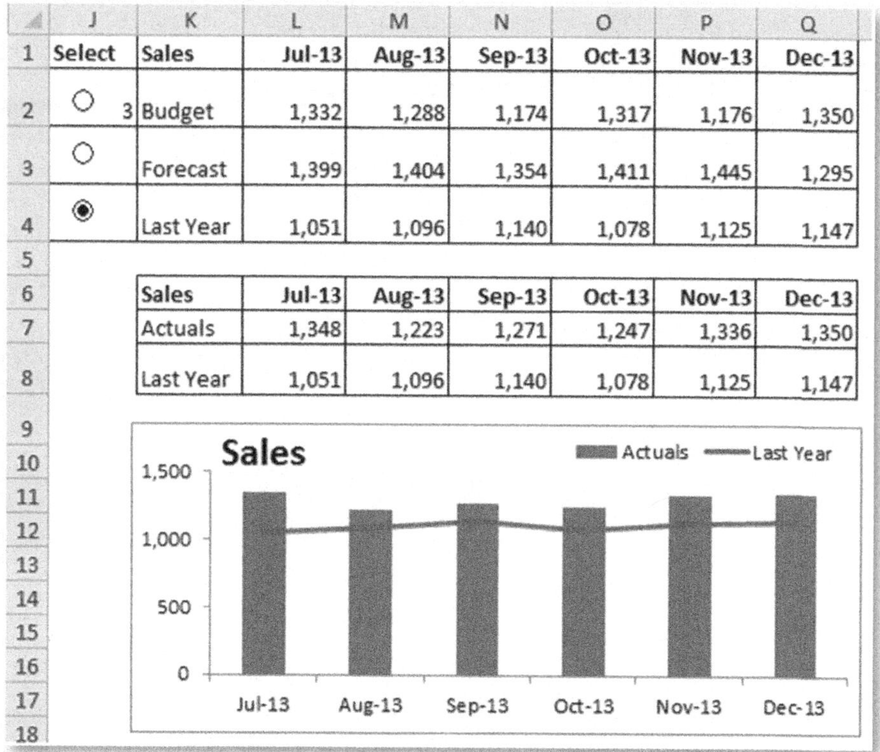

Select	Sales	Jul-13	Aug-13	Sep-13	Oct-13	Nov-13	Dec-13
○ 3	Budget	1,332	1,288	1,174	1,317	1,176	1,350
○	Forecast	1,399	1,404	1,354	1,411	1,445	1,295
◉	Last Year	1,051	1,096	1,140	1,078	1,125	1,147

Sales	Jul-13	Aug-13	Sep-13	Oct-13	Nov-13	Dec-13
Actuals	1,348	1,223	1,271	1,247	1,336	1,350
Last Year	1,051	1,096	1,140	1,078	1,125	1,147

FIGURE 10.14 Last-Year Option Button Chosen

Because a combo box control works by selecting a position on the list rather than an entry on the list, it automatically adjusts to any changes to the list. If you change the list, the selection itself will be a valid choice from the new list.

A combo box control does take a couple of extra steps to install than the Data Validation option.

This control also works well with the INDEX, CHOOSE, and OFFSET functions.

Example

Figure 10.15 shows a layout we will use to compare Data Validation with a combo box control.

The range J2:J6 has been named Fruit. Cell M6 has been named ComboFruit because it will be the linked cell for the combo box control.

A Data Validation List has been used in cell M2 with the name Fruit as the source. This is for comparison purposes.

To insert a combo box control, we first draw the control on the sheet using the Insert icon from the Developer Ribbon tab (see Figure 10.16).

After drawing a combo box control above cell M5, right-click the control, select Format Control, change the Control tab settings as shown in Figure 10.17, and click OK.

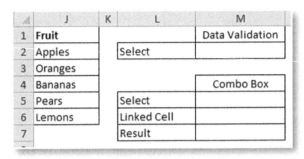

	J	K	L	M
1	**Fruit**			Data Validation
2	Apples		Select	
3	Oranges			
4	Bananas			Combo Box
5	Pears		Select	
6	Lemons		Linked Cell	
7			Result	

FIGURE 10.15 Combo Box and Data Validation Comparison

FIGURE 10.16 Combo Box on the Insert Drop-Down List

Format Control

Size | Protection | Properties | Alt Text | Control

Input range: =fruit

Cell link: $M$6

Drop down lines: 8

☐ 3-D shading

FIGURE 10.17 Format Control Dialog—Completed

The last step is to enter the INDEX function in cell M7. This is the cell that will contain the selection from the combo box control. The formula is

```
=INDEX(Fruit,ComboFruit)
```

Figure 10.18 shows the installed Combo Box.

	J	K	L	M
1	**Fruit**			Data Validation
2	Apples		Select	Apples
3	Oranges			
4	Bananas			Combo Box
5	Pears		Select	Apples ▾
6	Lemons		Linked Cell	1
7			Result	Apples

FIGURE 10.18 Completed Combo Box

The final step with a combo box control is to unlock cell M6 and protect the sheet, which will protect the formula in cell M7 from being overwritten.

Figure 10.19 shows one problem that a combo box control handles better than Data Validation does. If cell A2 in the source list is changed from Apples to Pineapples, then the combo box control will automatically update, as will the INDEX function in cell M7.

	J	K	L	M
1	**Fruit**			Data Validation
2	Pineapples		Select	Apples
3	Oranges			
4	Bananas			Combo Box
5	Pears		Select	Pineapples ▾
6	Lemons		Linked Cell	1
7			Result	Pineapples

FIGURE 10.19 Combo Box Range Change

A Data Validation cell can be overwritten by a paste, which can remove the in-cell drop-down list. A combo box control is more difficult to remove when the sheet is protected.

Combo Box Validation

The linked-cell validation formula for a combo box control, in which the range name for Combo Box is ComboFruit, would be

```
=AND(M6>=1,M6<=COUNTA(ComboFruit),INT(M6)=M6)
```

CHAPTER ELEVEN

Choosing the Right Format

FORMATTING IS AN IMPORTANT PART of a reporting model. A badly formatted report can be difficult to read, which defeats the purpose of creating the report.

Excel has a number of features that allow you to use consistent formatting throughout your reporting model. When considering formatting, you must take into account two main factors:

1. How is the report to be viewed and distributed?
2. Is the report to be printed, and if so, how?

Currently there are many different options for distributing and viewing spreadsheets. These are expanding as the technology for smartphones and tablets improves.

In terms of printing, you need to consider whether the report is going to be printed in black-and-white or colour.

Obviously, if the report is not designed to be printed, you have more scope to develop the report, because you are not limited by A4 and A3 paper sizes.

Personal preferences can determine what formats you use. Be prepared for change requests, because formatting preferences can vary widely among people.

COLOUR BLINDNESS

Until recently I had never considered colour blindness in designing reports. I had a question from a certified practising accountant that alerted me to the issue that some people (mainly men) face. I must admit that in my day-to-day working life I had not encountered any instances of colour blindness.

Apparently, between 5 and 8 percent of males and less than 1 percent of females are colour-blind. The colours that people can't see vary. Red-green colour blindness is the most common, which of course directly affects the effectiveness of traffic light reports commonly used in reporting dashboards.

Conditional formats offer the ability to use icons like checkmarks and Xs. Icons provide the best of both worlds. They provide a visual clue to people affected by colour blindness while providing colour for everyone else.

Also consider how your report could be used. If it is printed in black-and-white, then colours lose their effect, whereas icons retain theirs.

FORMAT PAINTER

The Format Painter icon, shown in Figure 11.1, is in the Clipboard section of the Home Ribbon tab, and it can simplify, and speed up, the formatting process.

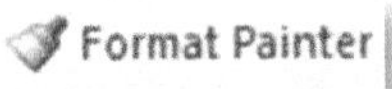

FIGURE 11.1 Format Painter Icon

To use it, select a cell or range with the format you want to apply to another cell or range. Click the Format Painter icon and then use the mouse to select the cell range to apply the format. This will apply all the formats from the source cell or range, including conditional formats.

If you click the Format Painter once, you can apply the format only once. If you double-click the Format Painter icon, you can apply the format as many times as you want. To turn off applying the format, press the Esc key or click on the Format Painter icon again.

This technique provides a quick way to apply multiple formats to multiple ranges.

LESS IS MORE

Excel 2007 and later versions have expanded Excel's formatting capabilities. This is not necessarily an improvement, since it provides many more options for your report formatting. In most cases you should use as little formatting as possible.

You have to be very careful in the use of colour in your reports because it can distract users from the figures. Colour should be used sparingly and for effect.

You should create a colour palette that you use consistently throughout your model. For example, you might use a light-yellow fill color to represent input cells. This means that the users can easily identify where they need to enter data or make selections.

Excel has a feature called Styles that can simplify the formatting process. Styles also allows you to modify the formats globally. Changing a style will modify all the cells that have been formatted with that style.

FONTS

There are hundreds of different fonts available in Excel, and some are much easier to read than others. Be careful with the fonts that you use for text and numbers. Excel's default font is Calibri, which is readable for numbers and text. Arial used to be the default font.

What you deem as easy to read can be affected by your age, in terms of the fonts that you were exposed to growing up.

My recommendation is use Calibri. If you wish to use another font, limit yourself to one or two fonts in a file. One font for text and another one for values is acceptable. Otherwise, avoid using multiple fonts; it will decrease the readability of your file.

CLEAR AND START AGAIN

Sometimes you get to a stage where you just want to clear all the formats and start again. The Clear Formats icon, which allows you to do just that, is in the Clear drop-down list of the Editing section of the Home Ribbon tab (see Figure 11.2).

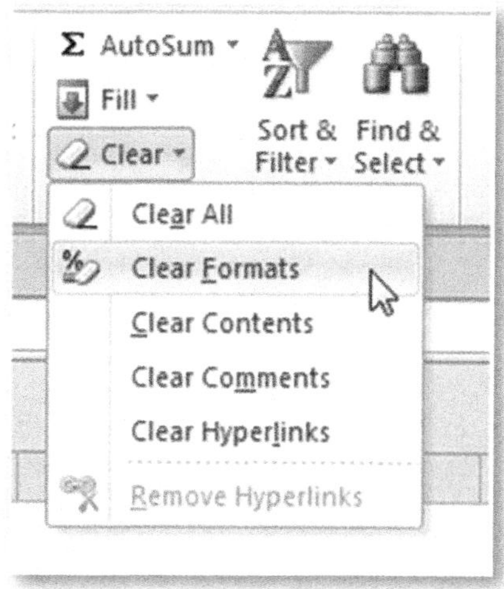

FIGURE 11.2 Clear Formats Icon

THE FORMAT CELLS DIALOG BOX

The common formats are included on the Home Ribbon tab as well as on the right-click menu.

The Format Cells dialog box, which you can access by using Ctrl + 1, gives you complete control over all your formatting. Also, the small arrow icons on the Font, Alignment, and Number sections of the Home Ribbon tab will open the dialog box for the relevant tab (see Figure 11.3).

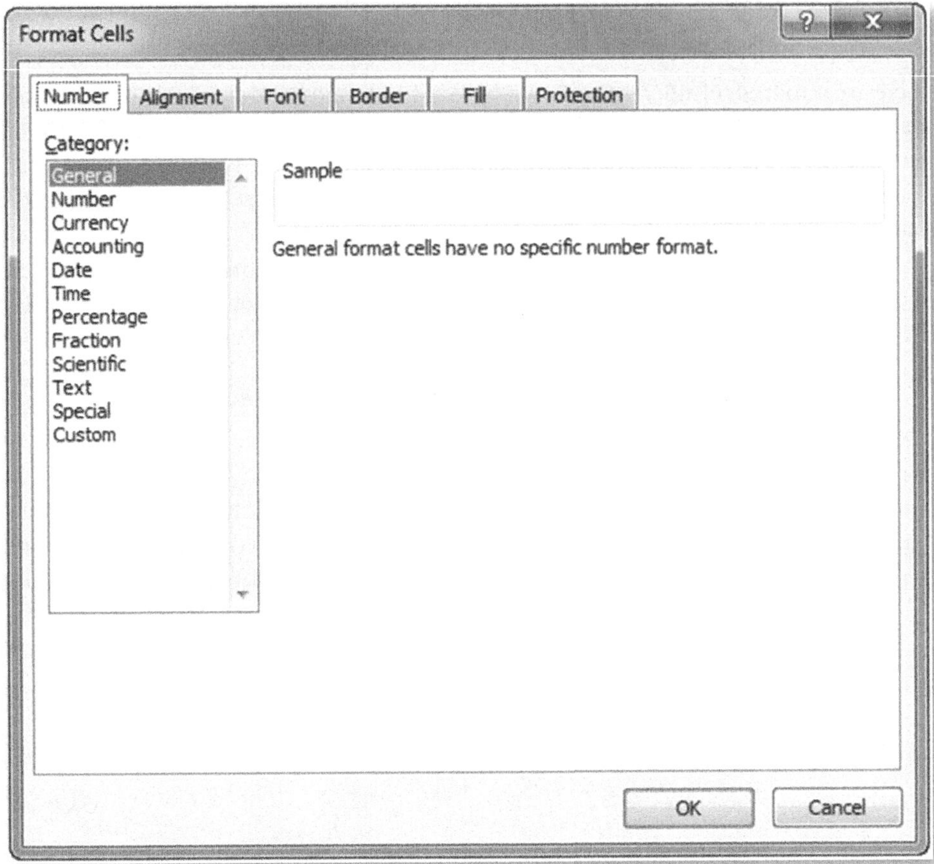

FIGURE 11.3 Format Cells Dialog Box

When you are setting up reports, the Number, Alignment, and Border tabs are the most useful.

Number Formats

Setting the correct number format improves the readability of your reports. The Number section on the Home Ribbon tab has the common formats (see Figure 11.4).

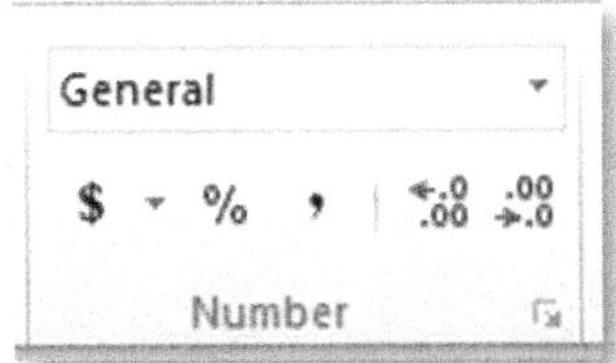

FIGURE 11.4 Number Section—Home Ribbon

The drop-down list, which typically displays General, has even more options (see Figure 11.5).

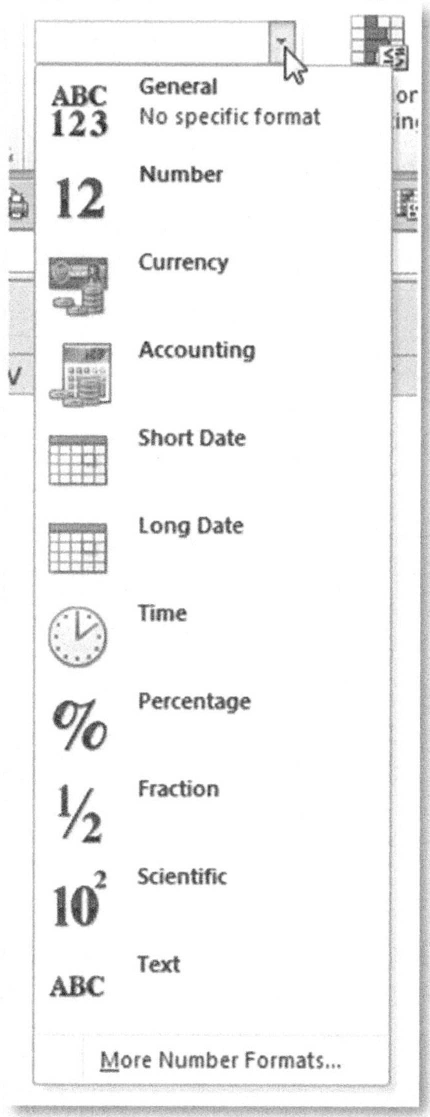

FIGURE 11.5 Number Section—Drop-Down Options

The $ Symbol

As a general rule, don't include the $ symbol in figures in the body of your report. Including $ adds extra characters to the report without adding any meaning. Your report labels should explain what the values represent: $, $000, or $M.

Do use formats that include the $ symbol for input cells. Applying the $ format to an input cell makes it obvious to the users what type of values should be entered.

I prefer the Currency format to the Accounting format when displaying the $ symbol. Figure 11.6 compares the two formats.

Accounting	Currency
$ 1,234.56	$1,234.56
$ 1,234.00	$1,234.00
$ 1,234,567.00	$1,234,567.00
$ -	$0.00
$ 6,543.21	$6,543.21
$ 0.12	$0.12

FIGURE 11.6 Currency versus Accounting Formats

The Comma

Use the comma as thousand separator. It is much easier to read large values when the comma is used. Figure 11.7 shows the comma format compared to no commas.

No Format	Comma Format
12345	12,345
1234	1,234
123456	123,456
1234567	1,234,567
654321	654,321
4321	4,321
12	12
2030256	2,030,256

FIGURE 11.7 Comma Format Comparison

Dates

You are probably aware that Excel treats both dates and times as numbers. You may have seen a date displayed as a number. Excel's calendar started on January 1, 1900; that is day 1. Since then, each day's number has increased by one.

Whereas each day is a whole number, the time of day is a decimal. Since the day begins at midnight, 6 a.m. is 0.25, noon is 0.5, and 6 p.m. is 0.75.

There are two functions that calculate the current date. The TODAY function enters the date, whereas the NOW function enters the current date and time.

If you need to use a date in a text heading, you will have to use the TEXT function to format it correctly (see Chapter 8).

Tip: Keyboard Shortcut for Date Format

To apply a date format, you can use Ctrl + Shift + #.
This applies the d-mmm-yy format. This format avoids any confusion between U.S. and European date style because the month is displayed using three letters rather than as a number (e.g., Mar for March, rather than 3).

Custom Number Formats

Even though Excel has many built-in formats, there are occasions when you need to create your own format. The last category in the Formats Cells dialog box, in the Number tab, is Custom. There are many different types of custom formats for dates, times, and numbers.

You can even use the custom number formats to do basic conditional formatting. I will not delve into those techniques but will just explain the typical custom formats used in accounting reports.

Custom Format Layout There is structure in the layout of a custom number format. You can have up to four sections, separated by semicolons. The first section is for positive numbers, the second section is for negative numbers, the third section handles zeros, and the fourth section handles text. You do not have to define all four sections.

If you define only one custom number format (containing no semicolons), then that format applies to all numbers. Zeros may be hidden.

If the custom number format has two sections (containing one semicolon), then the first section will handle positive numbers and zeros, and the second section will handle negative numbers.

If the custom number format has three sections (containing two semicolons), then the first section will handle positive numbers, the second section will handle negative numbers, and the third section will handle zeros.

Entering Custom Number Formats In the Number tab of the Format Cells dialog box, the Custom option is the last item in the Category list. You can modify an existing Custom format by clicking it on the right-hand side and then making modifications in the Type box. You need to click OK to save that format.

The Sample area of the dialog box shows you what the active cell's value will look like when the selected custom number format is applied. As you change the format in the Type box, the Sample section updates (See Figure 11.8).

The Sample area doesn't display colours.

Rounding When you apply some formats, what is displayed is different from the cell value. See the warning later in the chapter on displaying thousands and millions.

This can cause apparent rounding errors in reports in which the total figure does not equal the sum of the detail figures. In these cases, you need to determine whether to round the cell values through formulas or formats.

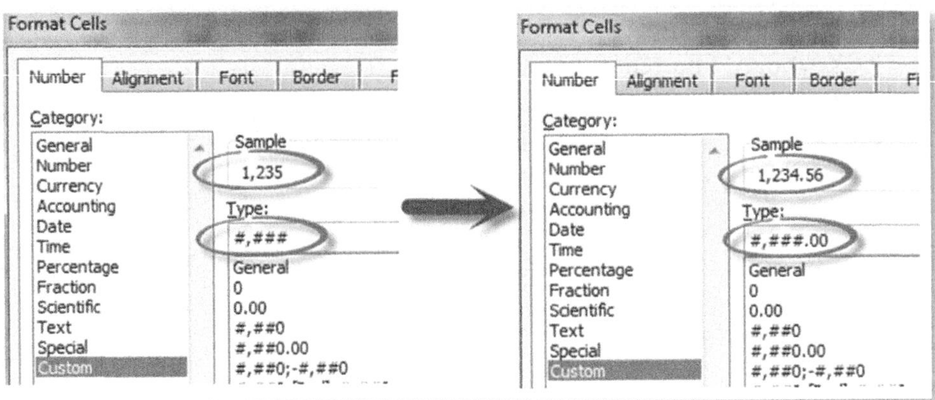

FIGURE 11.8 Entering Custom Number Format

Spaces You may use the space character in custom number formats. This means you must be careful when creating them—a stray space can cause issues. You can also use a space to your advantage when lining up decimals that use parentheses for negative numbers.

Using # and Zeros in a Custom Number Format You can use either the # symbol or 0 to define a number in a custom number format. The two display all nonzero numbers the same but display zeros differently.

When you use 0 in a position, it will display a zero in that position if there is a zero value. The # symbol does not display a zero value.

You can use them together to achieve exactly the right effect for your reports (see Figure 11.9).

	P	Q	R	S	T	U	V	W
2	No Format	#,###	#,##0	#,###.##	#,###.00	#,##0.00	0,000.00	#,##0.00 ;(#,##0.00);"-"
3	1234.56	1,235	1,235	1,234.56	1,234.56	1,234.56	1,234.56	1,234.56
4	1234	1,234	1,234	1,234.	1,234.00	1,234.00	1,234.00	1,234.00
5	12.345	12	12	12.35	12.35	12.35	0,012.35	12.35
6	1.2345	1	1	1.23	1.23	1.23	0,001.23	1.23
7	0.654	1	1	.65	.65	0.65	0,000.65	0.65
8	0.1234		0	.12	.12	0.12	0,000.12	0.12
9	0		0	.	.00	0.00	0,000.00	-
10	-0.1234		0	-.12	-.12	-0.12	-0,000.12	(0.12)
11	-0.654	-1	-1	-.65	-.65	-0.65	-0,000.65	(0.65)
12	-1234.56	-1,235	-1,235	-1,234.56	-1,234.56	-1,234.56	-1,234.56	(1,234.56)
13	-1234	-1,234	-1,234	-1,234.	-1,234.00	-1,234.00	-1,234.00	(1,234.00)
14	-12.345	-12	-12	-12.35	-12.35	-12.35	-0,012.35	(12.35)
15	-1.2345	-1	-1	-1.23	-1.23	-1.23	-0,001.23	(1.23)

FIGURE 11.9 Examples of Custom Number Formats

The entries in rows 3 to 15 in Figure 11.9 are the same across all the columns. The custom number formats applied are shown in row 2 of each column.

Columns Q to V have single custom number formats. Column W has an example of a three-section custom number format that handles positive numbers, negative numbers, and zero values differently.

Useful Custom Number Formats Following are some useful custom number formats that are not standard.

The following hides cell entries:

```
;;;
```

You can't hide an individual cell, only its contents. This format stops cell entries from both displaying and printing. The values remain invisible even when selected in a range. The only time the contents are visible is when you edit them in the cell. This was used in the previous chapter to hide values in linked cells.

You can try to hide a cell by using a white font or the same font colour as the cell background, but this works only in limited situations. If the Print option Black and White is selected, the entries will print. When you select a range including the cell, the values also appear.

This displays numbers as thousands with the comma separator (see the warning sidebar):

```
#,###,
```

This displays numbers as millions with the comma separator (see the warning sidebar):

```
#,###,,
```

This displays negative numbers as red and with parentheses:

```
#,##0 ;[Red](#,##0)
```

Older versions of Excel had this format as a built-in number format, but later versions removed it. There is a space after the first zero to line up the values in the brackets.

Displaying Text with Values If you need to display a value including text and still be able to use the value for calculations, you can use a custom number format to add text to values.

This will display a number followed by m (see Figure 11.10):

```
#,### "m"
```

Avoid using this type of format for input cells, because users are more likely to enter the m and cause #VALUE! errors.

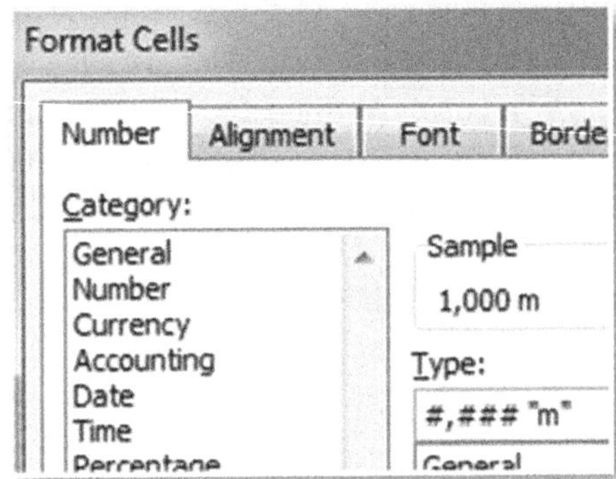

FIGURE 11.10 Example of Text in a Number Format

Stopping the Display of Zeros

I have known a few managers over the years who didn't like zeros being displayed in reports. There are two ways to suppress zeros.

Suppressing Zeros in the Whole Worksheet There is a worksheet setting that stops zeros from being displayed on the whole sheet. Click the File Ribbon tab, click Options, click Advanced, and scroll about two-thirds of the way down the list. You will see the list of worksheet options (see Figure 11.11).

Uncheck the box to stop zeros from showing. Click OK.

This is a sheet-specific setting. You will have to change the setting for each sheet.

Suppressing Zeros in a Range To stop zeros from being displayed within a range, you can use a custom number format. As explained earlier, the third section of the custom number format handles zero values. If you leave that section blank, it might not display

WARNING: Displaying Thousands and Millions

When you use a custom number format to display a cell in thousands, you run the risk of confusing some users about the actual value in the cell.

They may see a number displayed as 15 and assume that it has been rounded via a formula. The cell may contain 15,123, but they may multiply the cell by 1,000 to convert it into dollars.

Hence it is advisable to place some sort of note (e.g., a cell comment or a text box) that warns users that a custom number format has been applied and that the value in the cell may differ from the value displayed.

Of course, the alternative to this particular custom number format is to divide the value in the cell by 1,000 so that it displays and contains the same value.

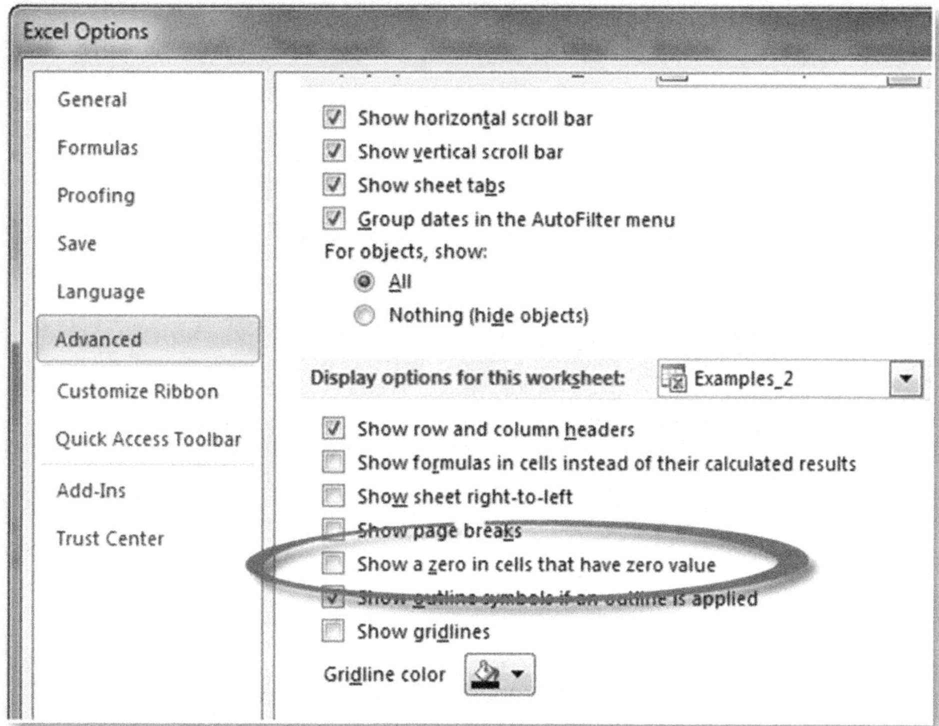

FIGURE 11.11 Excel Option to Suppress Zeros on a Worksheet

zeros. Examples in Figure 11.9 also showed zeros being suppressed. Two examples of custom number formats that will not display zeros are the following:

#,###
#,##0.00;(#,##0.00);

Alignment

The Alignment tab controls how entries are aligned within a cell.

Merged Cells

The Merge Cells option on this tab should be avoided. It causes problems when copying and pasting and can also cause macros to crash.

Unfortunately, because this format has an icon, Merge & Center, on the Home Ribbon tab, it is commonly used for formatting reports (see Figure 11.12).

When you merge cells, you are actually removing cells from the sheet. To see how this affects the structure of a sheet, try this exercise:

On a blank sheet, enter the word Heading in cell A3.
Select the range A3:C3 and click the Merge & Center icon on the Home Ribbon tab.
The resulting format has centred the word Heading across the three cells.

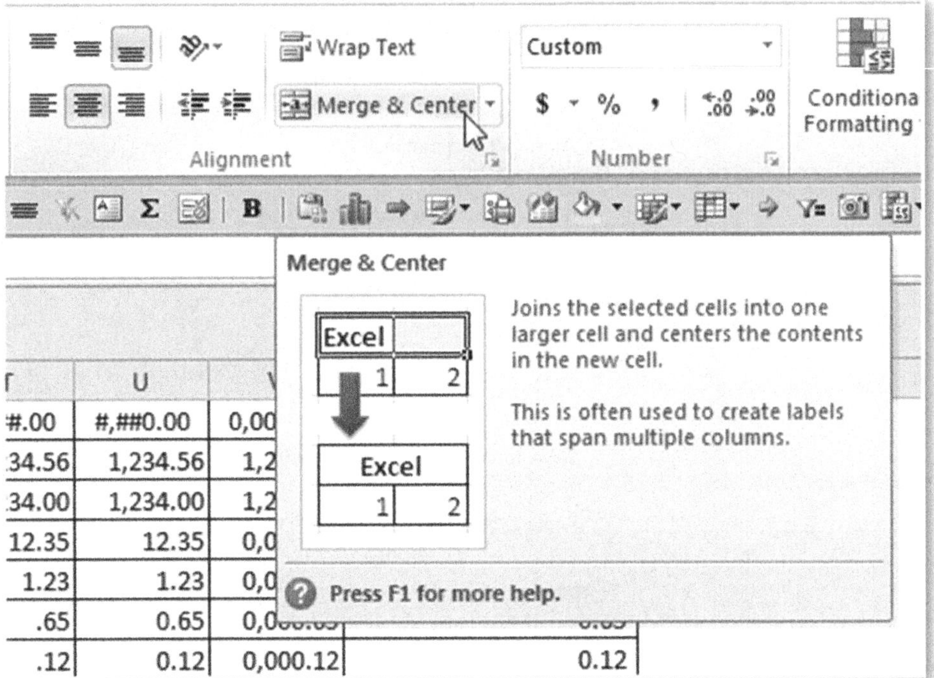

FIGURE 11.12 Merge & Center Icon

Select cell C1 and then press the keyboard down arrow twice, each time noting the cell selected in the Name box.

When you select row 3 you will notice that the Name Box displays A3. The cells B3 and C3 no longer exist because they have been merged with cell A3. This loss of cells is what causes the problems.

Select the range A1:B1 and copy it.

Click on the merged cell and paste.

Figure 11.13 shows the error dialog box that is displayed.

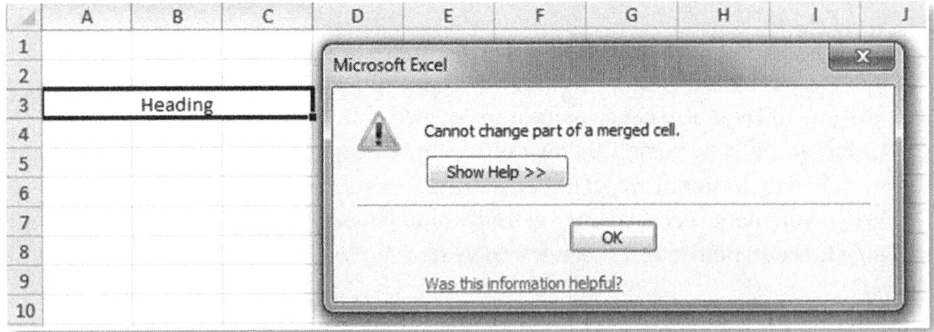

FIGURE 11.13 Merged Cell Error Dialog Box

The error message that is displayed states that you can't change part of a merged cell. This issue can stop you from pasting into ranges that contain a single merged cell.

This error message and the fact that merged cells remove cells from the sheet can affect macros that work with individual cells or that do any copy-and-paste operations.

The Merged-Cells Alternative

There is an alternative to the merged cells format. On the Alignment tab in the Horizontal drop-down list, there is an option called Center Across Selection (see Figure 11.14).

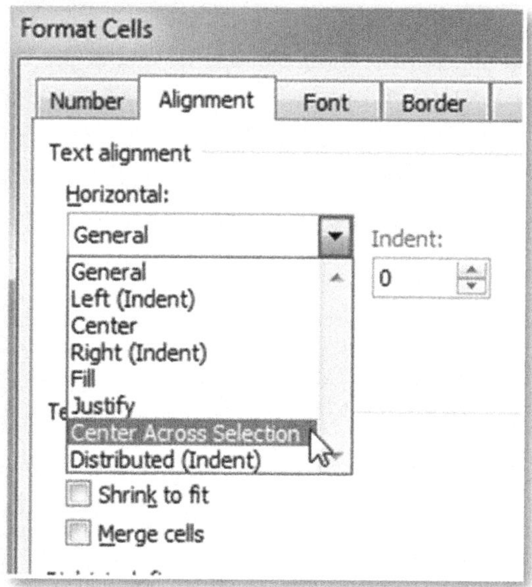

FIGURE 11.14 Center Across Selection

This format achieves the same result, centering the text across multiple cells, but without the problems of removing cells. You will not receive any error messages with this format.

Figure 11.15 shows that you can still select a cell with a range that has Center Across Selection applied.

FIGURE 11.15 Select Cell within Center Across Selection

Center Across Selection Limitations Center Across Selection does not work on vertical ranges (e.g., A3:A5), whereas the Merged Cells format can.

If you hide columns within the range, then the Center Across Selection format does not always display as expected.

Macro I have included a Center Across Selection macro on the companion website that simplifies applying and removing the Center Across Selection format.

The format doesn't have a Quick Access Toolbar (QAT) icon, but you can add this macro to a custom icon on your QAT (see Chapter 3 for instructions).

Wrap Text

The Wrap Text option has an icon on the Home Ribbon tab (see Figure 11.16).

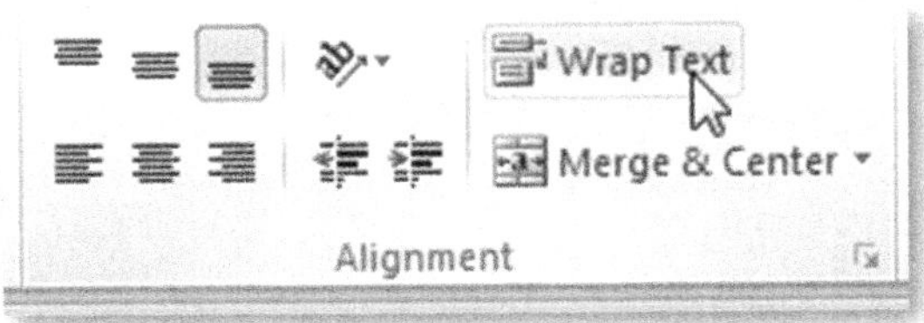

FIGURE 11.16 Wrap Text Icon

This format inserts lines within a cell and wraps the text to the next line to fit the text into the cell. The shortcut key combination for the format, pressed in sequence, is Alt h w.

This format is ideal for column headings that are wider than the contents of the column. It is a useful format for field headings in tables.

You can also use Alt + Enter when entering or editing a cell to insert a fixed line break within the cell.

Borders

Most of the borders you need are included in the Borders icon on the Home Ribbon tab (see Figure 11.17).

This drop-down list allows you to select different line styles, such as dotted lines. You can also change the colour of the lines.

Gridlines

Before using the Borders icon to select the type of borders to apply to your report, you should consider turning off your spreadsheet gridlines. This will make your reports look cleaner on the screen. To turn off the sheet gridlines click the View tab and uncheck the Gridlines option. You can add this icon to your QAT.

The keyboard shortcut is Alt w v g, pressed in sequence. This turns the gridlines on and off.

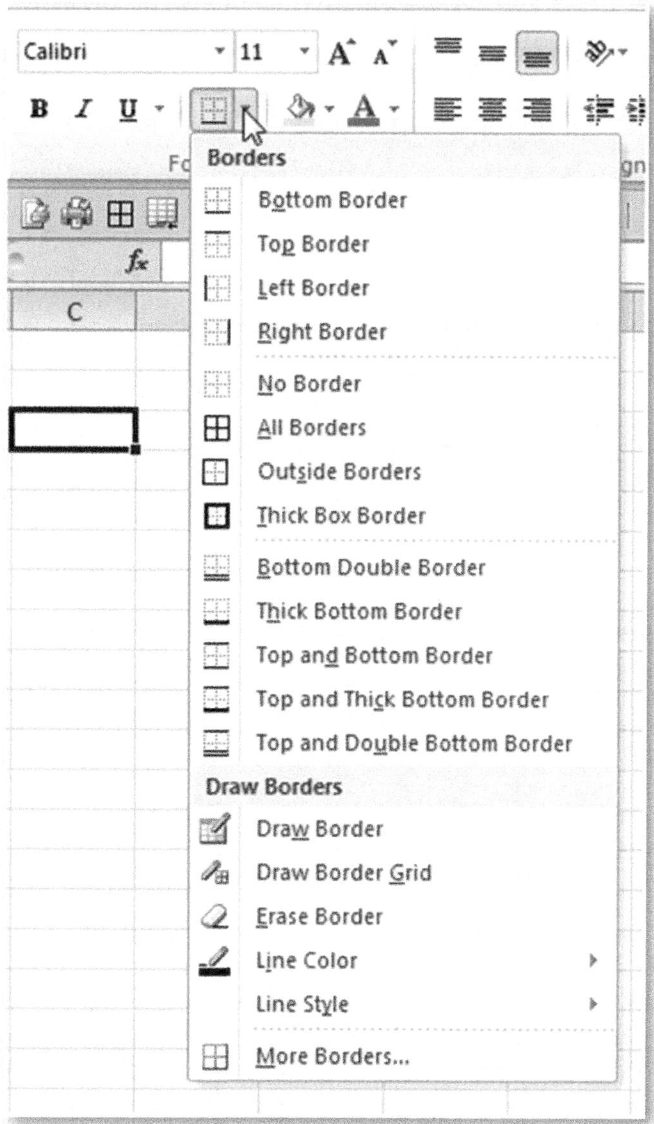

FIGURE 11.17 Border Options on the Ribbon

Displaying or hiding the sheet gridlines in no way affects the gridlines in Excel's Print options. They are controlled separately. If you want to change the print gridlines, use the options on the Page Layout Ribbon tab.

Types of Borders

I include the All Borders icon on my QAT because I use this format frequently for my reports. You can add separate Border formats to your QAT to speed up the selection.

Two border formats that work well together and are commonly used are All Borders and Thick Box Border. All Borders applies a thin line around all the cells in the range. Thick Box Border applies a thick line to the outside of the range (see Figure 11.18).

	A	B	C	D
1				
2				
3				
4				
5				
6				
7				
8				
9				

FIGURE 11.18 All Borders and Thick Box Border

When applying the two formats together, you must apply All Borders first and Thick Box Border last.

STYLES

Styles is an important feature in formatting reports. It allows you to create and apply consistent formatting throughout your reporting model.

A style in Excel is a specific format that you can create and name. Each style can contain multiple formats. You can then easily apply that format combination to a cell or a range of cells by using the style. This allows you to apply consistent formatting throughout your reporting model by using the same style on the same types of cells. Styles have their own section on the Home Ribbon tab (see Figure 11.19).

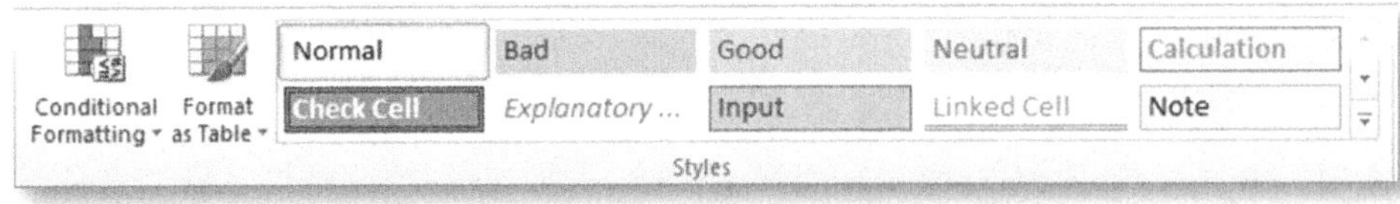

FIGURE 11.19 Styles on the Home Ribbon Tab—Wide Screen

Figure 11.20 shows the Cell Styles icon displayed on a small screen or if you have reduced Excel's Window size.

FIGURE 11.20 Cell Styles on the Home Ribbon Tab—Small Screen

Clicking the icon displays the options (see Figure 11.21).

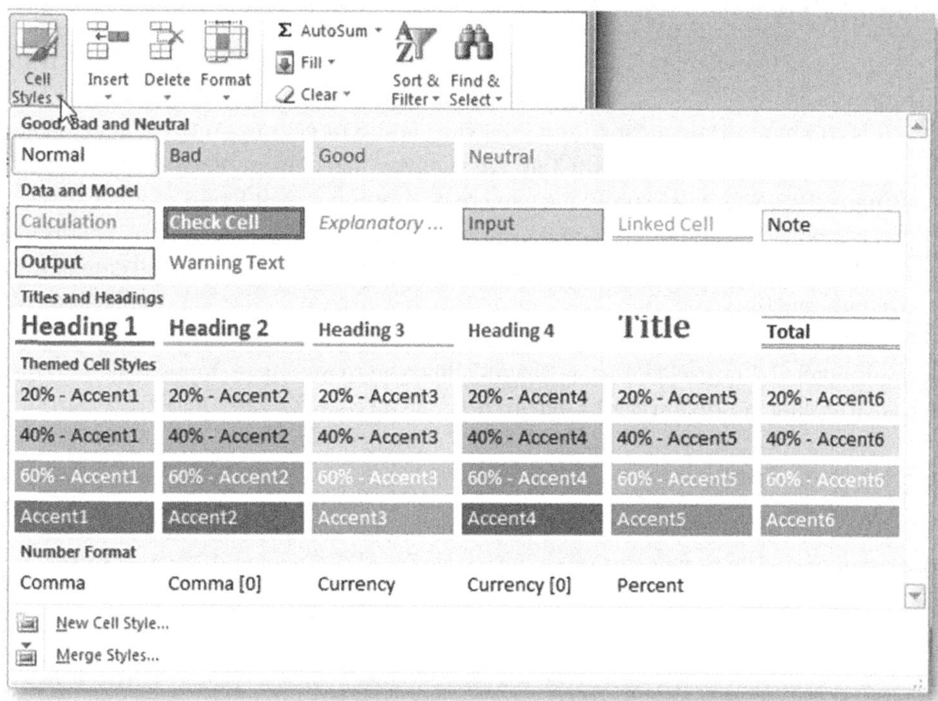

FIGURE 11.21 Styles Options—Small Screen

Excel comes with many built-in styles that can be applied in a single click. You can amend a style or create a new one.

The advantage with using a style for formatting is that if you need to change it, you can change it in just one place, and all the cells that have been formatted with that style will automatically be updated. This makes it easier to maintain consistency in your formats. It is also useful if your manager decides to change a colour used throughout the file.

Tip: Custom Styles Are File-Specific

If you customise an existing style or add a new style, these are added to the file itself, but they are not available in other files.

You can copy a style between files with the Merge Styles option on the Styles drop-down list (see the bottom of Figure 11.21).

I recommend that you save, close, and then reopen the file immediately after you have merged styles. I have had problems saving files after merging styles.

The number of styles can also affect file size, and copying a sheet into another file can bring its styles with it.

Multiple Styles

You may need to create multiple styles for one type of format. Let me explain with an example.

It is common to use a consistent fill colour for input cells in an Excel model. This makes it easier for users to identify the cells that they need to change.

In practice, you will usually have to create a number of different input cell styles because input cells can have different formats in terms of dates, percentages, dollars, or text. Inputting dates can also require more styles if you need to see the full date or just the month and the year.

You might have four input cell styles with the same fill colour but different number formats applied. Right-clicking a style will allow you to modify or duplicate it, making it easy to create multiple styles based on the same fill colour.

Styles and Borders

Styles do not handle outside border formats for ranges. You can only apply the cell border commands. Hence you cannot set up a style for All Borders and Thick Box Border.

CONDITIONAL FORMATTING

Conditional Formatting is another important feature in formatting reports. It allows you to automatically apply different cell formats based on cell values or on cell values in relation to other values in a range. For example, you can change the fill colour of a cell to red if it is negative or green if it is positive. Conditional Formatting also allows you to build formulas to determine what format to apply. It is especially useful for variance reporting.

Once you have set up a conditional format, it will continue to work in the background. Conditional formats, like any other format, can be copied and pasted between cells. The Format Painter option includes conditional formatting. Conditional formats can also be applied to pivot tables and formatted tables.

Excel 2007 greatly expanded the options available for conditional formatting. It added icons that display when cells meet certain criteria. This is especially useful for

Tip: Conditional Formats and Styles

Unfortunately, you can't include a conditional format in a style definition.

dashboard reporting. Many conditional formats that required formulas in previous versions have been included as standard conditional formats in Excel 2007 and later versions.

Excel 2003 had a limit of three conditions. Excel 2007 and later versions removed that limit. There is now no set limit to the number of conditions you can apply. You can also include different types of conditional formats together.

Excel 2010 improved the Conditional Formatting feature and fixed a few bugs with it.

Conditional formats can be used for the following types of reports:

- **Variance reporting.** Using icons and colour to emphasise values outside expected levels.
- **Exception reporting.** Using icons and colour to highlight values outside acceptable levels.
- **Pareto analysis.** Identifying upper and lower values or percentages within a range.
- **Dashboards.** Using icons and data bars (to be explained later) to visualise data in combination with charts
- **Validation.** Automatically highlighting invalid, duplicate. or missing data.

The Conditional Formatting icon is in the middle of the Home Ribbon tab. The built-in options are easy to use, but the results may not always be what you expect. Excel uses default settings to apply many of the built-in conditional formats. You can amend these settings to achieve the conditional format that you want.

There are many useful built-in conditional formats, but you also have the ability to create custom formats based on logic formulas. This gives you more control over the conditions you can apply. These will be discussed after the built-in formats.

Highlight Cells Rules

The Highlight Cells Rules options in the Conditional Formatting drop-down list are self-explanatory (see Figure 11.22).

These options all compare a cell's value to another value or values. The first five options all have similar dialog boxes. There are one or two boxes in which you can either type a value or link to a cell on the sheet that contains a value. You can also enter a range name that refers to a cell (see Figure 11.23).

The formats shown in the drop-down list in Figure 11.23 are standard, and you can use the Custom Format option to access more formats.

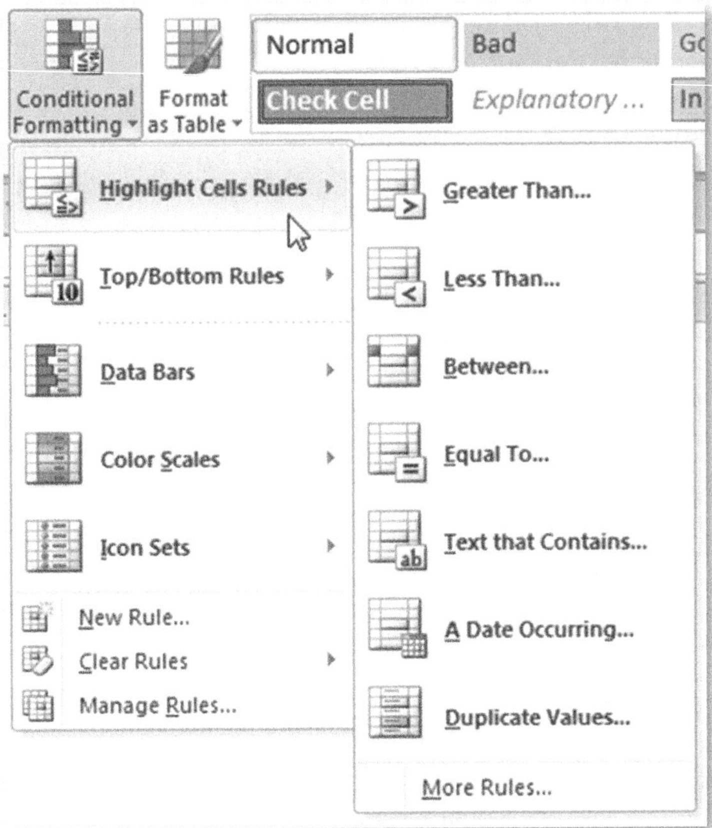

FIGURE 11.22 Highlight Cells Rules Options

The last two built-in options in Figure 11.22, A Date Occurring and Duplicate Values, do not require a value or a cell link. The date option has standard date parameters to choose from (see Figure 11.24).

If you need to apply other date parameters, you can use a formula-based conditional format.

The Duplicate Values option automatically highlights any duplicates within a range. As shown in Figure 11.25, it can also be used to identify unique values.

When creating these types of conditional formats, you need to decide whether you will hard-key in the parameters or link them to a cell on the sheet.

Obviously, using the cell links provides better transparency, more flexibility, and easier maintenance. Most dialog boxes give you the option to link to a cell.

Top/Bottom Rules

Figure 11.26 shows the Top/Bottom Rules options.

These options are more flexible than they appear. You can amend the number of items or the percentages used (see Figure 11.27). These options can go hand in hand with a Pareto analysis.

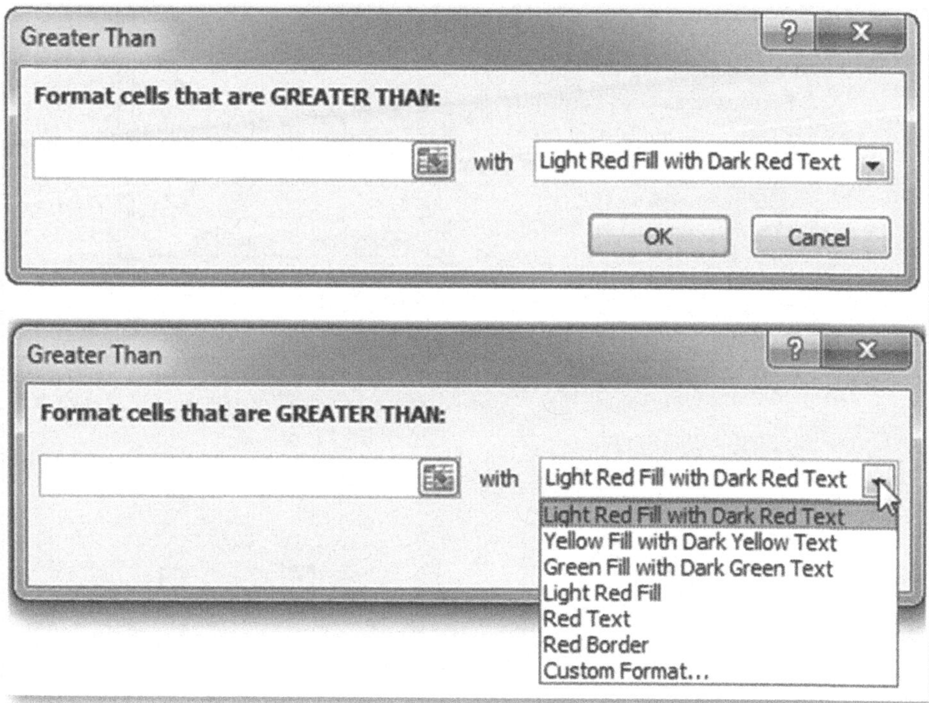

FIGURE 11.23 Greater Than Dialog Box

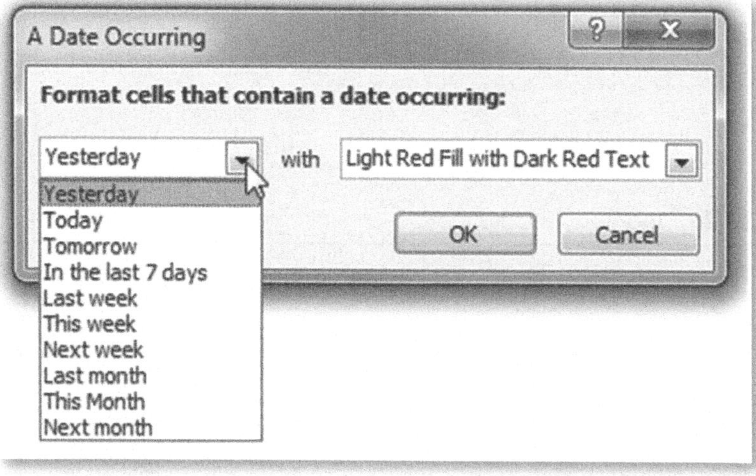

FIGURE 11.24 Date Parameters

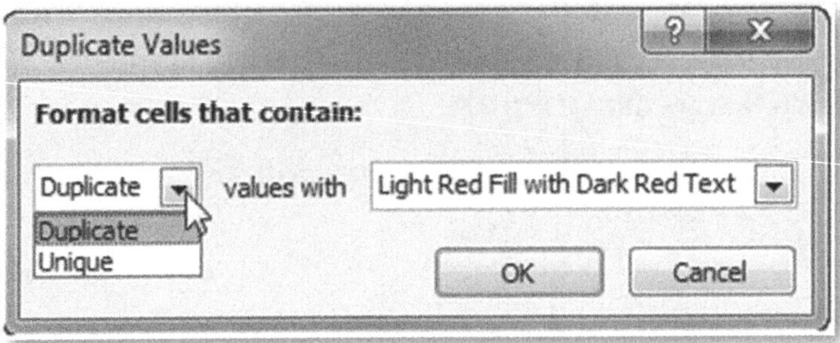

FIGURE 11.25 Duplicate Values Dialog Box

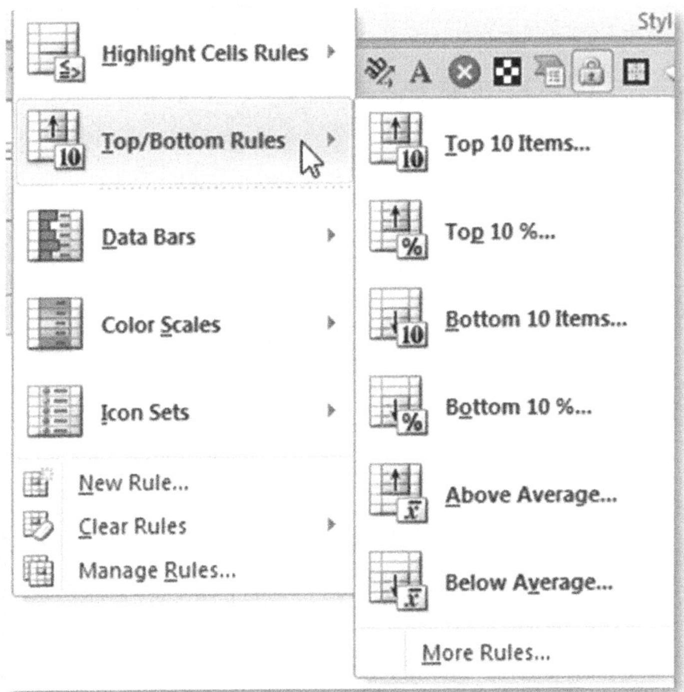

FIGURE 11.26 Top/Bottom Rules Options

The next three types of conditional formats to be discussed were introduced in Excel 2007 and have been improved in Excel 2010. They all are usually applied to a range and use the values in the range to apply settings. If the values are indicative of future values, then the format will probably be acceptable. If the values are not indicative, then the section below on the Manage Rules option will show you how to amend Excel's default settings.

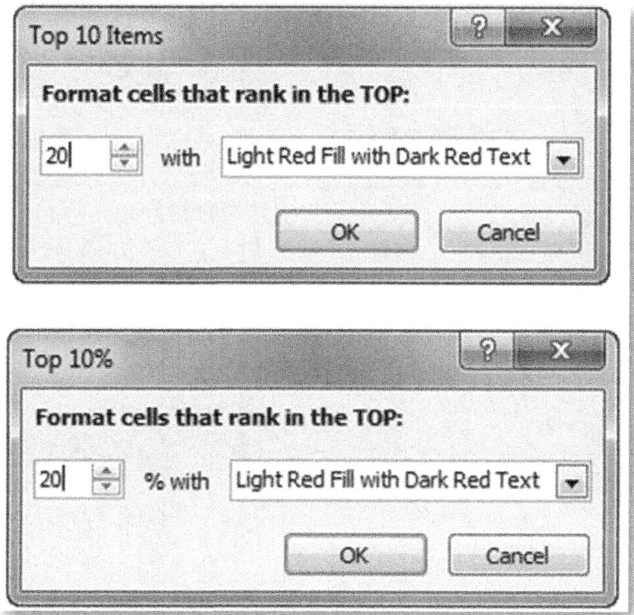

FIGURE 11.27 Items and Percentage Changes

> **Tip: Conditional Formats and Totals**
>
> Be careful how you handle total cells in your conditional formats. If you include a total cell in your range, it can dramatically affect the resulting conditional formats.

Data Bars

The Data Bars format inserts a bar into the cell. The length of the bar represents the size of the cell's value in comparison to the values in the rest of the range. If the bar goes to the far right of the cell, then that cell is the maximum value in the range. Figure 11.28 appears to show more options than there actually are.

In reality, you can choose between only two types of data bars: Gradient Fill or Solid Fill. Gradient Fill was introduced in Excel 2007; the Solid Fill option is new to Excel 2010. The different icons in each section just apply different data bar colours. This enables you to have separate colours for actuals, budgets, and forecasts.

I prefer the Solid Fill format. The two fill formats are compared in Figure 11.29.

Negative numbers and zeros are handled correctly in Excel 2010 (see Figure 11.30). An alternate colour is used for the negative bar, and a dotted line defines zero. These can be amended by changing the settings behind the format (see the section later on the Manage Rules option). See the warning sidebar regarding an issue in Excel 2007.

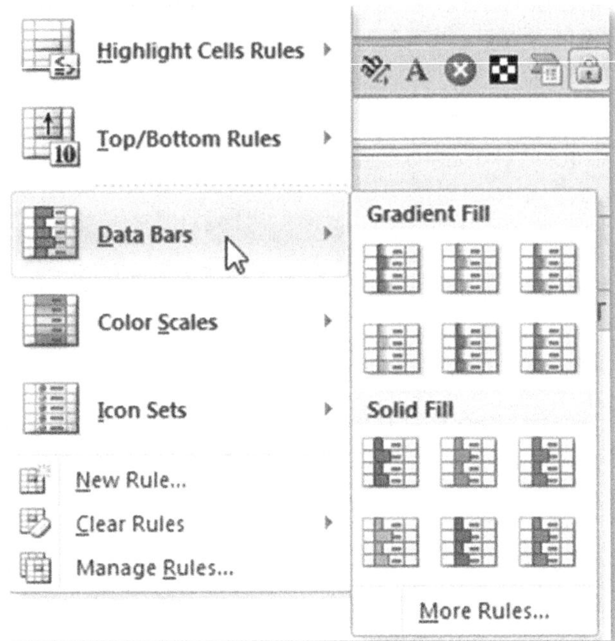

FIGURE 11.28 Data Bars Options

Gradient Fill		Solid Fill	
Sales	Amount	Sales	Amount
East	27,152	East	27,152
West	29,962	West	29,962
North	10,060	North	10,060
South	12,625	South	12,625

FIGURE 11.29 Gradient Fill and Solid Fill Compared

Profit / Loss	Amount
East	20,568
West	15,888
North	-5,687
South	0

FIGURE 11.30 Negative Numbers and Zero Data Bars

WARNING: Excel 2007 Data Bars

The Data Bars feature in Excel 2007 does not handle zeros or negative numbers. A zero cell and a negative value cell will each display a bar starting from the left of the cell. These two results were not intuitive to users.

If there is any likelihood that a range contains negative numbers or zeros, I would recommend that you avoid Data Bars in Excel 2007.

Color Scales

The Color Scales format applies a fill colour to a cell based on its value compared to the other cells in the range. Again, there appear to be more options in Figure 11.31 than there actually are.

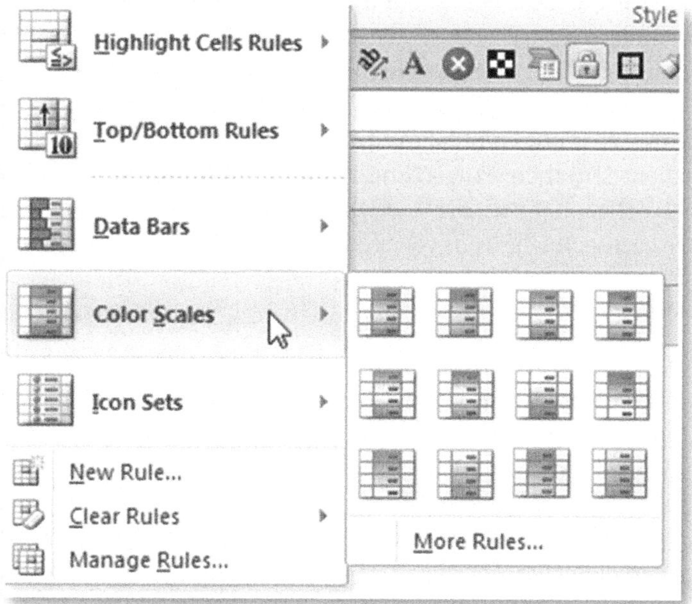

FIGURE 11.31 Color Scales Options

There are two options. Either a high value is good and a low value is bad (e.g., profits or sales), or a high value is bad and a low value is good (e.g., lost-time injuries or your golf score). One colour is applied to good cells, and a different colour is applied to bad cells. The colours are progressively graded, from good to average to bad.

The typical option uses green as good and red as bad (not ideal for colour-blind people), with orange as average. The highest value is bright green, and the lowest value is bright red.

As the values drop from the highest value, they become progressively less green. As they approach average, they become orange.

As the lowest values increase, they become less red, and as they approach average, they also become orange.

You have the option of using two or three colours as well as which colours to use. When you use two colours, the fill colour fades away to no fill as the values approach average.

You can also use just one colour. If you use a two-colour scale and define one of the colours as white, then in effect you create a one-colour scale. The colour will fade as it increases or decreases, depending on the option you choose.

Excel uses the range involved to determine the upper and lower limits used in the format. This doesn't always provide the result you want, so you might need to edit the settings. The section later on the Manage Rules option will take you through some examples and show how you can amend them.

Icon Sets

The Icon Sets format has a lot of options available (see Figure 11.32). These are ideal for use in both standard reports and dashboard reports.

The options basically come down to three, four, or five scale icons. The checkmarks, Xs, and arrows work well with black-and-white printing, whereas the coloured icons work well with screen presentations and colour printing.

You might need to change the settings, as described in the section that follows on the Manage Rules option, if the result is not what you expected. You might also need to use helper cells to get exactly the icons you require, since the options are not very flexible.

Manage Rules

When you initially apply Data Bars, Color Scales, and Icons Sets conditional formats to a range, Excel assumes that the values in the range are indicative of the values that will appear in that range. This may not always be the case, and you might need to amend Excel's default settings to achieve the result you are seeking.

We'll review the settings used for Data Bars, Color Scales, and Icon Sets one by one.

To edit any rule, you use the Manage Rules option at the bottom of the Conditional Formatting drop-down list. The dialog box shown in Figure 11.33 allows you to edit all the conditional formats in the file.

The drop-down list at the top of the dialog box defaults to Current Selection. It has access to all the sheets in the file (see Figure 11.34).

I recommend that you use this dialog box to create your new nonstandard conditional formats. If you use the New Rule option in the Conditional Formatting icon drop-down list, the dialog box closes once you are finished. You have to choose it again to create your next rule.

In my experience, people tend to apply two or three nonstandard conditional formats in succession. When you use the New Rule button (as shown in Figure 11.33), it returns you to the dialog box when you finish, thus making it easier to create successive rules.

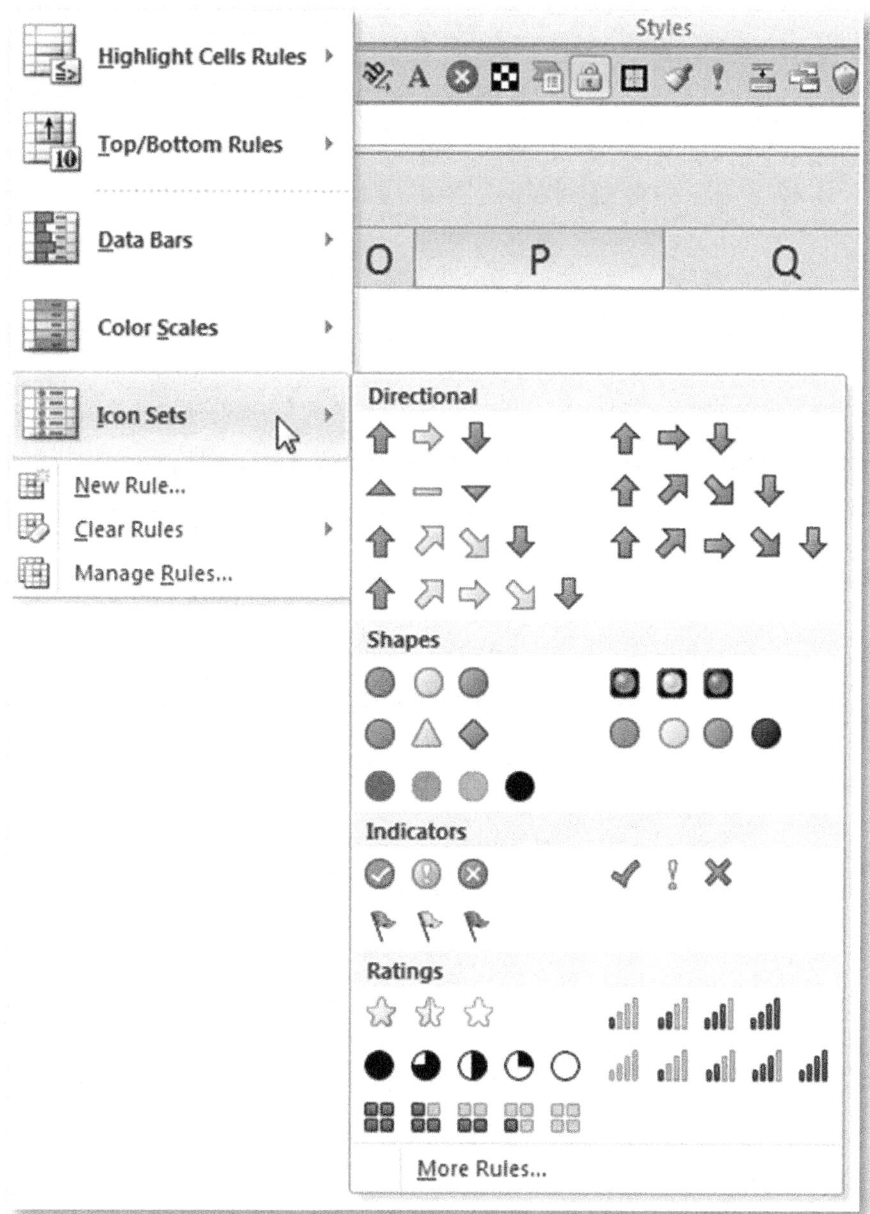

FIGURE 11.32 Icon Sets Options

To edit a rule, you can double-click it or use the Edit Rule button if it is selected. Figure 11.35 shows the dialog box that displays to edit a Data Bar format.

The top part of this dialog box doesn't change, but the bottom section changes depending on the option chosen in the top section and the format style chosen in the bottom section.

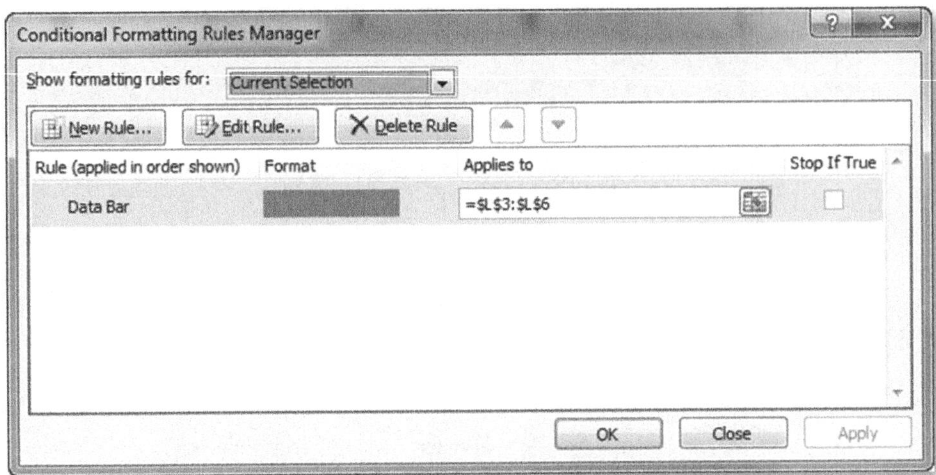

FIGURE 11.33 Conditional Formatting Rules Manager Dialog Box

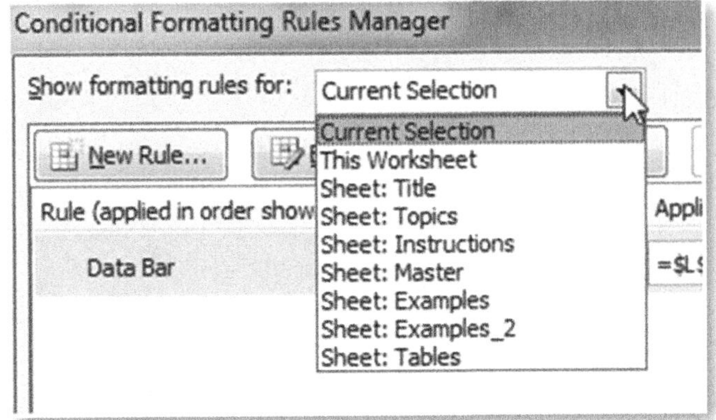

FIGURE 11.34 Conditional Formatting Rules Manager Drop-Down List

Editing Data Bars

Of the three new formats, Data Bars is the most straightforward. There is not a lot you normally will need to change with this format.

The check box Show Bar Only will hide the cell's values and display only the data bar in the cell.

The other options you might want to change are the negative bar colour and where the zero axis is positioned. Click the Negative Value and Axis button to amend these options (see Figure 11.36).

The cell midpoint options are shown in Figure 11.37, which contains modifications based on the report that was shown previously in Figure 11.30.

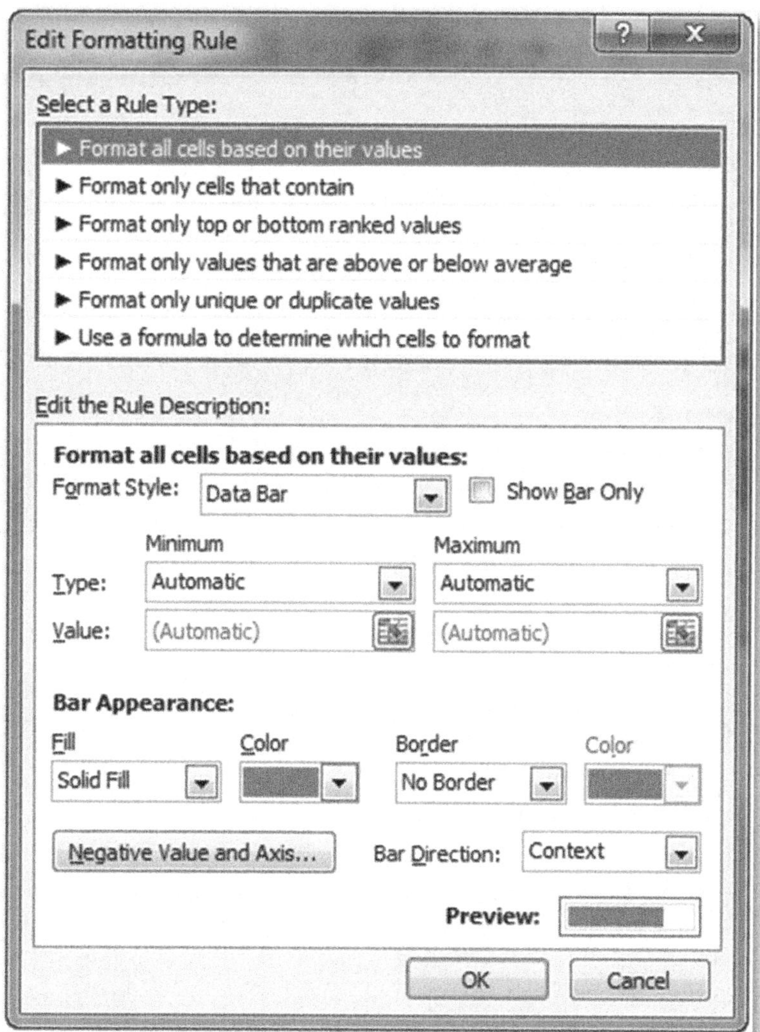

FIGURE 11.35 Edit Formatting Rule Dialog Box—Data Bars

Editing Color Scales

Displaying Color Scales in black-and-white images offers some challenges. I will add some helper cells to aid the discussion of the issues involved.

Figure 11.38 shows a range (K3:K6) that has had the standard three-colour scale applied (green is good, orange is average, and red is bad). Column L contains the colour and description that has been applied to column K.

I don't know about you, but if I got a score of 85 percent, as shown in cell K4, I'd be pleased. This being displayed as red, sets the bar quite high for what is considered bad.

As mentioned, Excel assumes that the range used for the format contains indicative values. Hence the lowest value in the range is deemed to be bad and the highest value is deemed to be good. In our case we need to amend the parameters to make them more realistic.

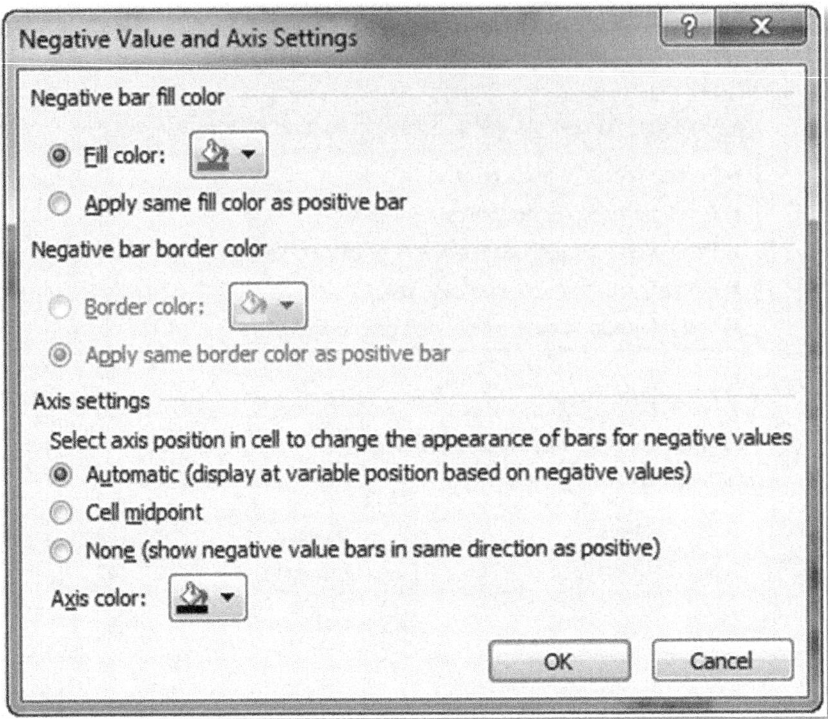

FIGURE 11.36 Negative Value and Axis Settings Dialog Box

Show Bar Only	
Profit / Loss	**Amount**
East	
West	
North	
South	

Axis at Midpoint	
Profit / Loss	**Amount**
East	20,568
West	15,888
North	-5,687
South	0

FIGURE 11.37 Amended Report Examples

	I	J	K	L
1		**Seminar Feedback Scores**		
2		**Region**	**Score**	**Colour applied**
3		East	95%	Green - good
4		West	85%	Red - bad
5		North	91%	Yellow - above average
6		South	89%	Orange - average

FIGURE 11.38 Webinar Feedback Scores

Figures 11.39 through 11.42 show the amendments required. Figure 11.39 shows the default settings that have been applied to the Minimum, Midpoint, and Maximum settings.

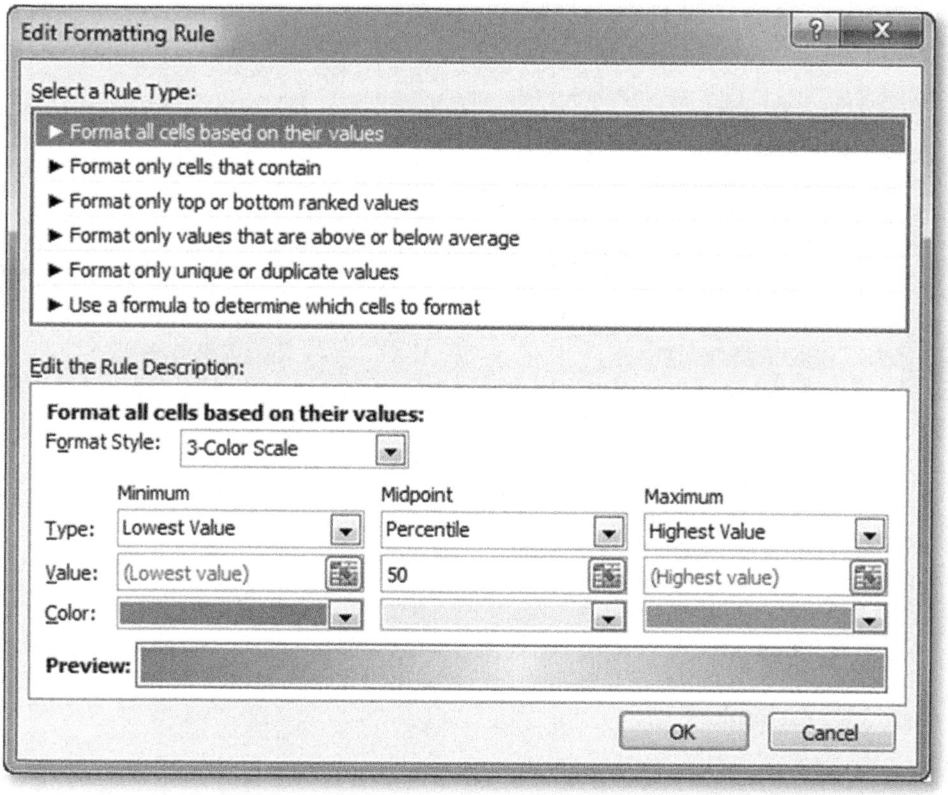

FIGURE 11.39 Editing Formatting Rule—Color Scale

The Minimum, Midpoint, and Maximum drop-down options (see Figure 11.40) allow you to control your parameters.

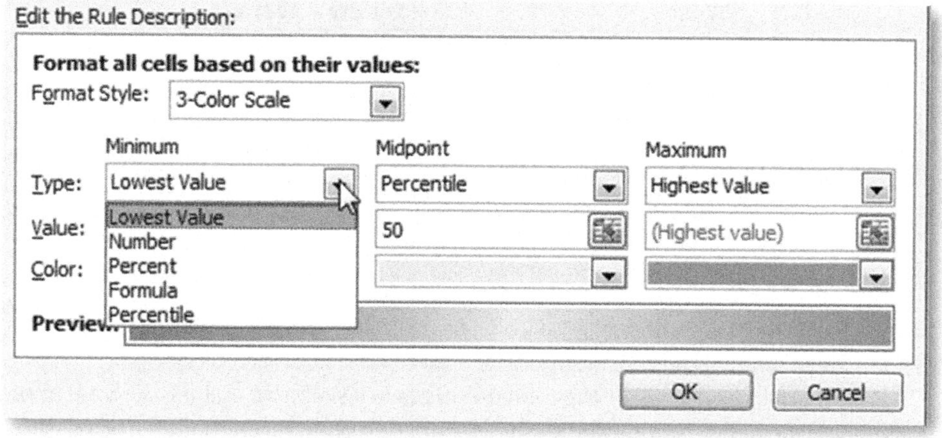

FIGURE 11.40 Parameter Drop-Down Options

In Figure 11.41 you can see how I have used the Number option in all three options to control the three levels used. In this way I am specifying what I deem to be the three levels that determine the colours applied.

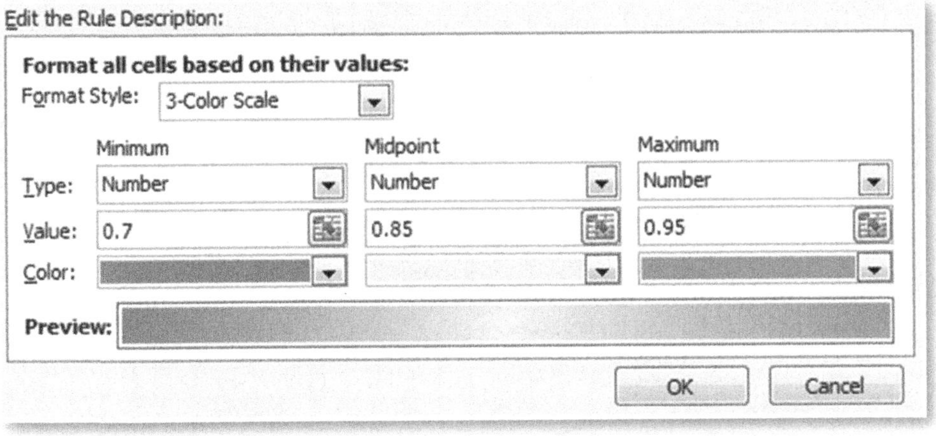

Edit the Rule Description:

Format all cells based on their values:

Format Style: 3-Color Scale

	Minimum	Midpoint	Maximum
Type:	Number	Number	Number
Value:	0.7	0.85	0.95
Color:			

Preview:

OK Cancel

FIGURE 11.41 Amended Parameters

The result in Figure 11.42 is closer to what you would expect for feedback scores. The west score is coloured yellow (average) whilst all the others are a shade of green to signify a good result.

	I	J	K	L
1		**Seminar Feedback Scores**		
2		**Region**	**Score**	**Colour applied**
3		East	95%	Green - good
4		West	85%	Yellow - average
5		North	91%	Light green - good
6		South	89%	Lighter green - good

FIGURE 11.42 Amended Feedback Report

Editing Icon Sets

Icon Sets works in a similar way to Color Scales. The example in Figure 11.44 is the default application of the checkmarks and Xs format.

This looks okay except for the total (in this case it's okay to include the total in the conditional format). The total shows the exclamation point, even though it is a positive (good) variance. Figure 11.44 also shows the standard settings for this format.

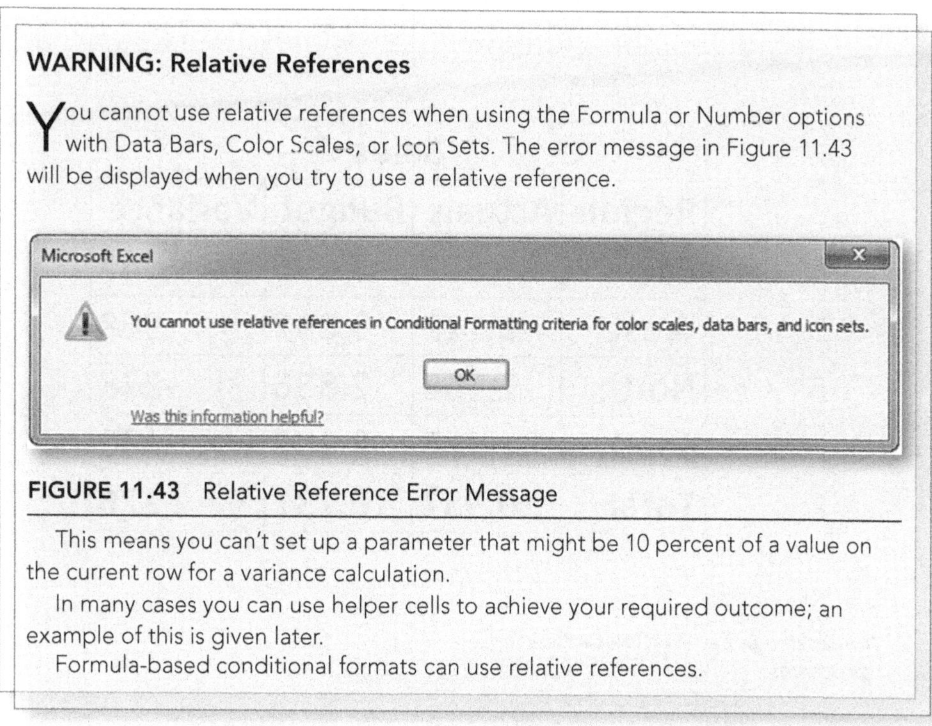

WARNING: Relative References

You cannot use relative references when using the Formula or Number options with Data Bars, Color Scales, or Icon Sets. The error message in Figure 11.43 will be displayed when you try to use a relative reference.

FIGURE 11.43 Relative Reference Error Message

This means you can't set up a parameter that might be 10 percent of a value on the current row for a variance calculation.

In many cases you can use helper cells to achieve your required outcome; an example of this is given later.

Formula-based conditional formats can use relative references.

We can amend this format to use only two icons. Each icon's drop-down list allows you to select any of the icons. We can amend this format as shown in Figure 11.45 to apply just the checkmark and the X, with no exclamation point.

Unfortunately, you can't amend this format to apply the exclamation point to negative variances within 10 percent of the value. You could achieve it with helper cells (see Figure 11.46).

Column O displays 1 when the variance is positive, 0 when it is negative but within 10 percent (cell O1) of the budget figure, and –1 when the negative variance is more than 10 percent of the budget. Having three possible values allows you to use the default settings for the format. The formula in cell O4 is

```
=IF(N4>=0,1,IF(N4>=-M4*$O$1,0,-1))
```

This formula has been copied down.

For demonstration purposes, I have left the values visible in column O. In practice you would check the Show Icon Only option to hide the values.

To use the four- and five-icon sets, you would need to develop a formula that has four and five results, respectively.

Formula-Based Conditional Formats

In most cases, Excel's built-in Conditional Formatting options provide enough flexibility to handle your reporting requirements. As we have seen, you can use helper cells to develop ways to work around some of their limitations.

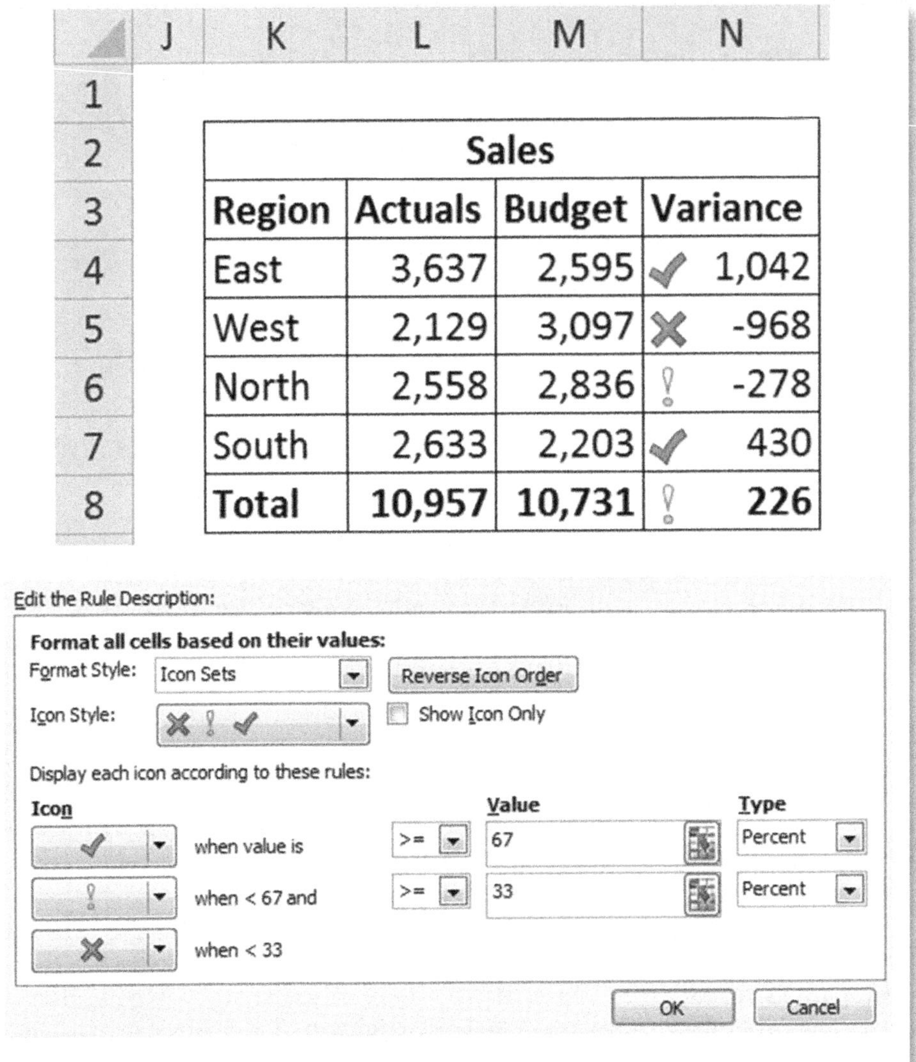

FIGURE 11.44 Variance Report with Format Settings Below

If you can't get the format you require, you can resort to a formula-based conditional format to handle those difficult conditions. Just a reminder: You can't use formula-based conditional formats to apply Data Bars, Color Scales, or Icon Sets.

The formulas used must be logic formulas. You must create the formula to return TRUE if the format is to be applied. In many cases you will have to create a number of formulas to apply multiple formats. As with all logic calculations, you will need to test the logic to see if the formats match your requirements.

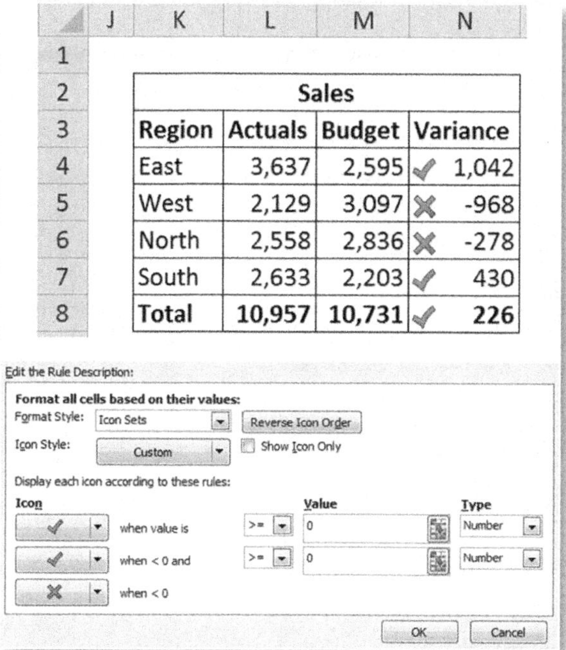

Sales			
Region	Actuals	Budget	Variance
East	3,637	2,595	✔ 1,042
West	2,129	3,097	✖ -968
North	2,558	2,836	✖ -278
South	2,633	2,203	✔ 430
Total	**10,957**	**10,731**	✔ **226**

FIGURE 11.45 Variance Report with Amended Format Settings Below

Sales				10%
Region	Actuals	Budget	Variance	
East	3,637	2,595	1,042	✔ 1
West	2,129	3,097	-968	✖ -1
North	2,558	2,836	-278	! 0
South	2,633	2,203	430	✔ 1
Total	**10,957**	**10,731**	**226**	✔ 1

FIGURE 11.46 Variance Report with Helper Cells

From experience, I can say that it may take a few attempts to get the formula-based conditional format working correctly.

Conditional Formats and Validation Cells

Conditional formats are perfect for validation cells. Figure 11.47 shows a simple balancing check with a before and after report. The values in K4:P4 have to have a red fill if the difference between Net Assets and Equity is greater than 1.

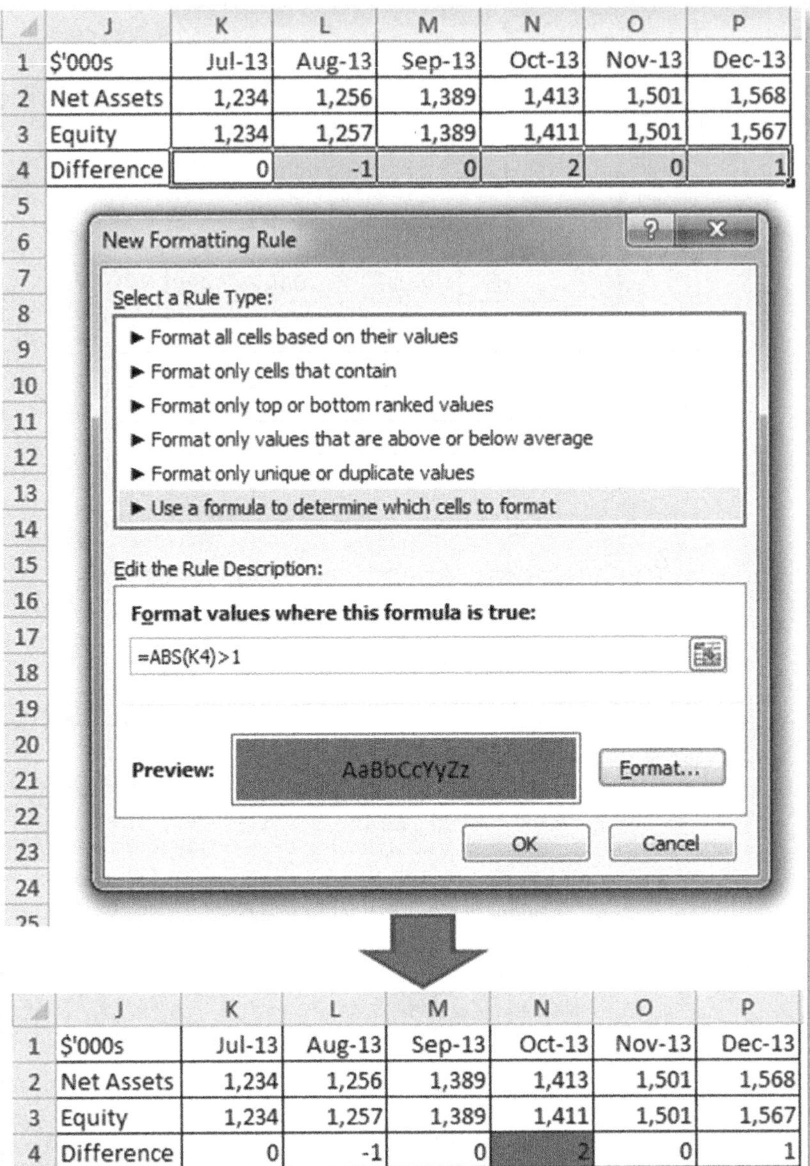

FIGURE 11.47 Report with Conditional Format Settings

The Rule Type to choose in the top section of the New Formatting Rule dialog box is the last option, "Use a formula to determine which cells to format." The formula used is

```
=ABS(K4)>1
```

Two important things to note about this formula are that it uses a relative reference and that the reference used is the top left cell within the range.

When you are creating these formulas and using the mouse to select cells, Excel will default to the fixed reference. You can amend the $ symbols in the references by using the F4 function key.

The ABS function converts all negative numbers to positive numbers and allows us to compare the row 4 values against 1. I have hard-keyed 1 into the formula because it is a common parameter to use to check for rounding errors. This formula will return TRUE when the difference is greater than 1.

The Format button in the New Formatting Rule dialog box opens the Format Cells dialog box, which has only the Number, Font, Border, and Fill tabs visible (see Figure 11.48). These are the only options you can change with a conditional format.

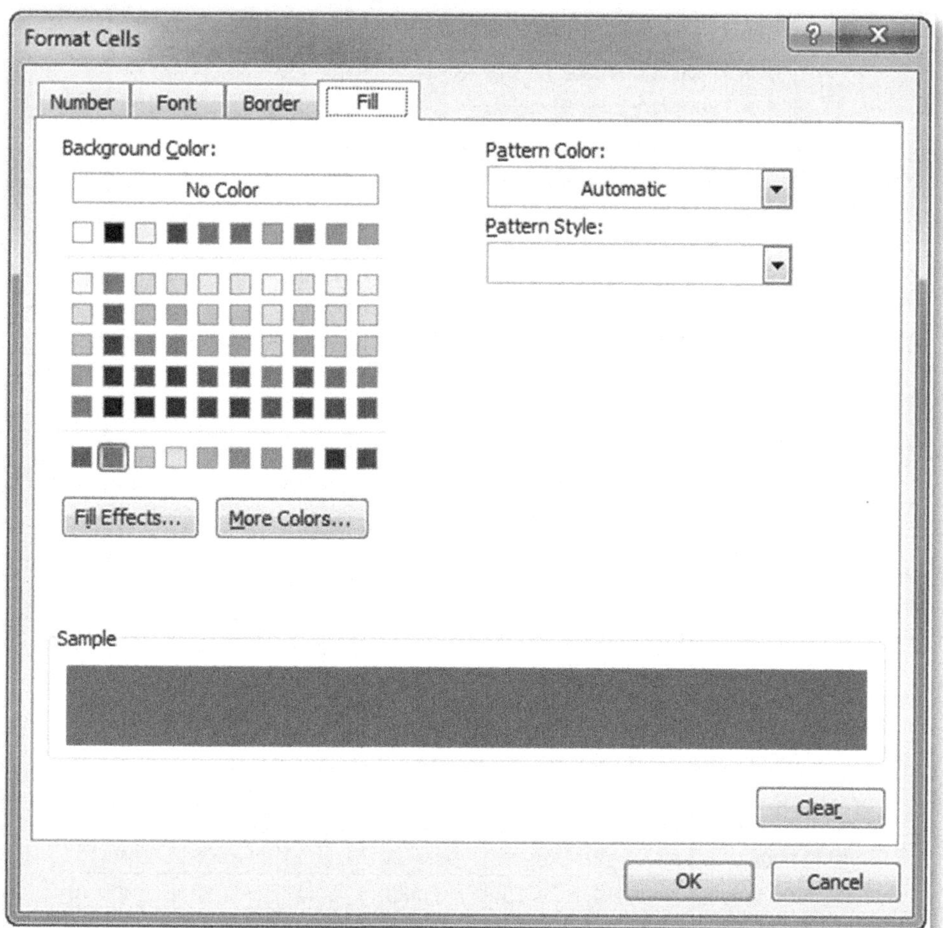

FIGURE 11.48 Format Cells Dialog Box—Limited Tabs

An alternative solution is to use helper cells to handle the logic calculations and then simply refer to those cells in the Rule formula.

The advantage with helper cells is that it displays the logic results on the sheet. This makes what is being done more obvious and also makes maintenance easier, since you have to amend only the cell formula, not the conditional formatting rules.

Figure 11.49 shows the report using helper cells to determine whether to apply the red format.

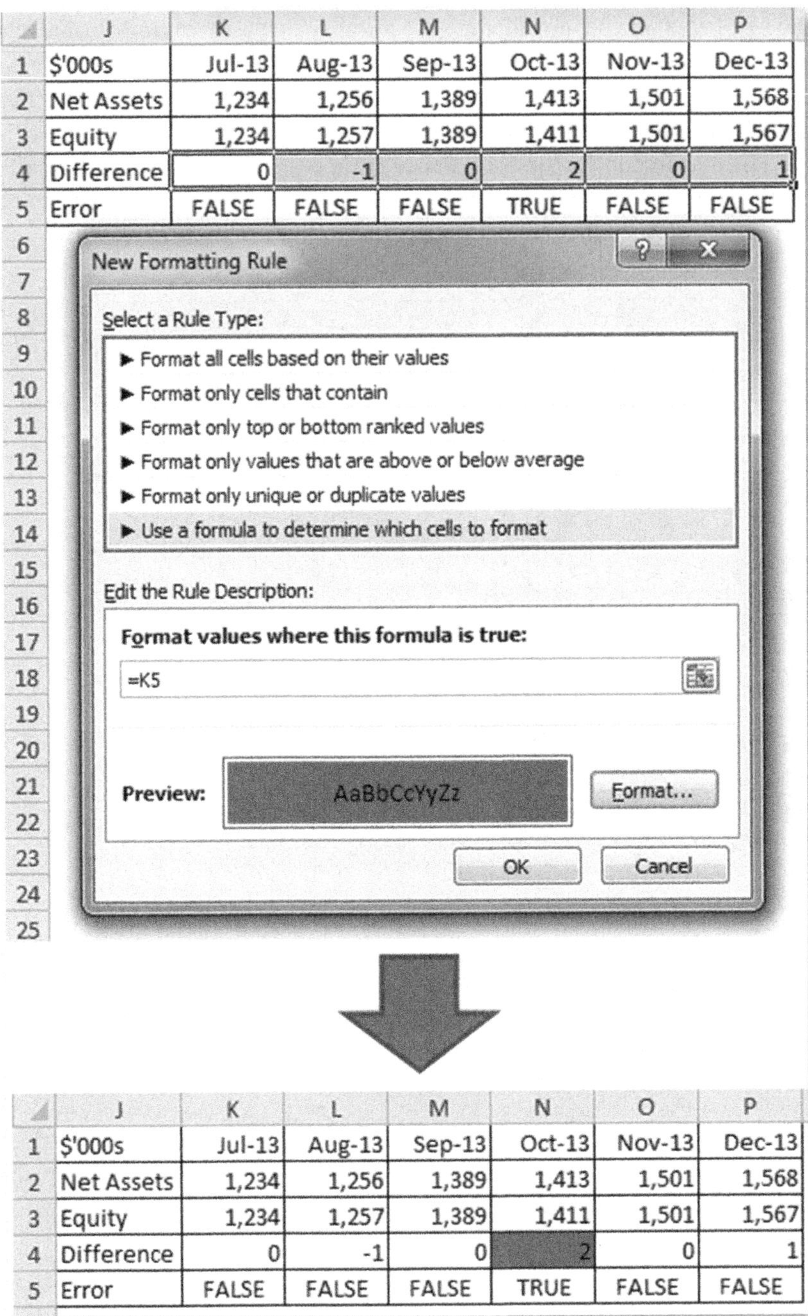

FIGURE 11.49 Report Using Helper Cells

If you need to have a format for the opposite of a formula, you can use the NOT function, which converts TRUE to FALSE and FALSE to TRUE. If you wanted to use a green fill for the TRUE cells, you could use the formula (see Figure 11.50)

```
=NOT(K5)
```

Edit the Rule Description:
Format values where this formula is true:
=NOT(K5)
Preview: AaBbCcYyZz
Format...
OK Cancel

FIGURE 11.50 NOT Function Example Formula

Conditional Formatting and Pivot Tables

Excel 2010 allows you to use conditional formatting on pivot tables. This was not practical in previous versions because changes to the layout of the pivot table could affect the application of the format.

When you apply a conditional format to a pivot table, there is an extra section at the top of the dialog box that allows you to specify what fields you want the format to apply to (see Figure 11.51).

The Selected Cells option is unlikely to be useful. The options below it will vary depending on the actual pivot table and cells chosen. The options allow you to specify the actual fields to apply the format to. Because you are referring to fields, the format becomes flexible when the pivot table is modified.

PRINTING ISSUES

Getting the right printed output from Excel is not always easy. The problem is that the Excel grid is so large. Printing in Microsoft Word or PowerPoint is, by comparison, easy because the pages are already defined.

The Page Layout Ribbon tab has many of the options you need to control your printing. Clicking the small arrow at the bottom left of the Page Setup section on the ribbon will open the Page Setup dialog box, which accesses all the printing options. If you right click the arrow, you can add the option to your QAT.

Excel has three views that can assist you with printing. You are already familiar with the Normal view, since this is the standard view for Excel.

The Page Break Preview view was available in Excel 2003. It can be identified by the grey background on the area that is not going to be printed (see Figure 11.52).

It also places a gray watermark on the sheet to display the page numbers. Page Break Preview displays blue lines on the sheet to identify the page breaks. A dotted blue line is a default page break, and a solid blue line is a fixed page break. If you use the mouse to drag a dotted blue line, it will become a fixed page break.

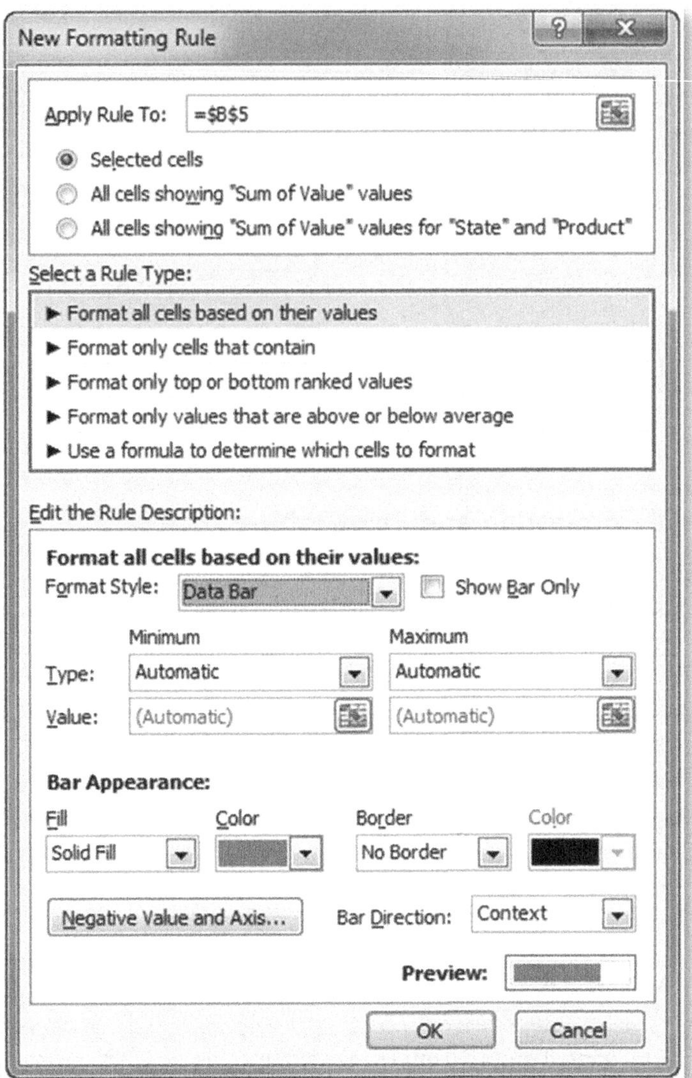

FIGURE 11.51 Pivot Table Conditional Format Options

When using Page Break Preview, there are extra right-click options dedicated to print settings (see Figure 11.52).

Excel 2007 added a new view that makes Excel look like Word. It's called the Page Layout view. I don't use this view much, but it provides direct access to the Header and Footer options (see Figure 11.53).

In this view, the number of pages to be printed is displayed at the bottom left of the screen.

There are a number of steps you can take to make sure you print what you're expecting to print.

FIGURE 11.52 Page Break Preview with Right-Click Menu

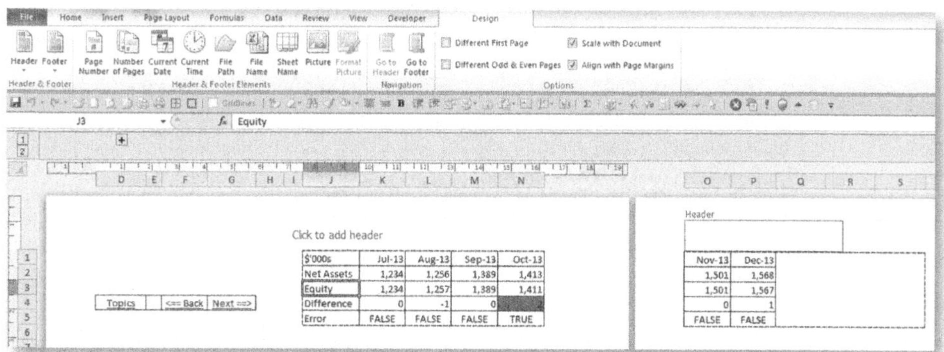

FIGURE 11.53 Page Layout View

Set Print Area

Because Excel is such a helpful piece of software, it will try to print every thing you have entered on the spreadsheet grid. This is not always what you want.

As a standard process, if there is any likelihood that a sheet will be printed, you should set the Print Area for that sheet. This defines the range that will be printed. If you don't set a specific print area, Excel will print everything.

There is an icon for Set Print Area, and I recommend adding it to your QAT. Chapter 3 has instructions on adding icons to your QAT.

Use Print Preview

Excel 2010 added a new Print interface to the File menu, and many people have been disappointed with the result. It displays some of the most common settings but not all of them. Users seem to like the old interface better because it gives you complete control.

Fortunately, the old interface is still there. You can add an icon to your QAT that opens the old Print Preview window rather than the new File Print screen. The icon is called Print Preview Full Screen.

Always check your sheet using Print Preview before printing your document for the first time. Check that all the pages are printing out as you want and that no pages are printing out blank.

Set Print Titles

The titles in Print Titles are the rows and columns you want to repeat on all the printed pages. The icon on the Page Layout Ribbon tab makes setting up Print Titles a simple task.

File Print Options

There are two useful options on the File Print screen. Figure 11.54 shows the Narrow option for margins.

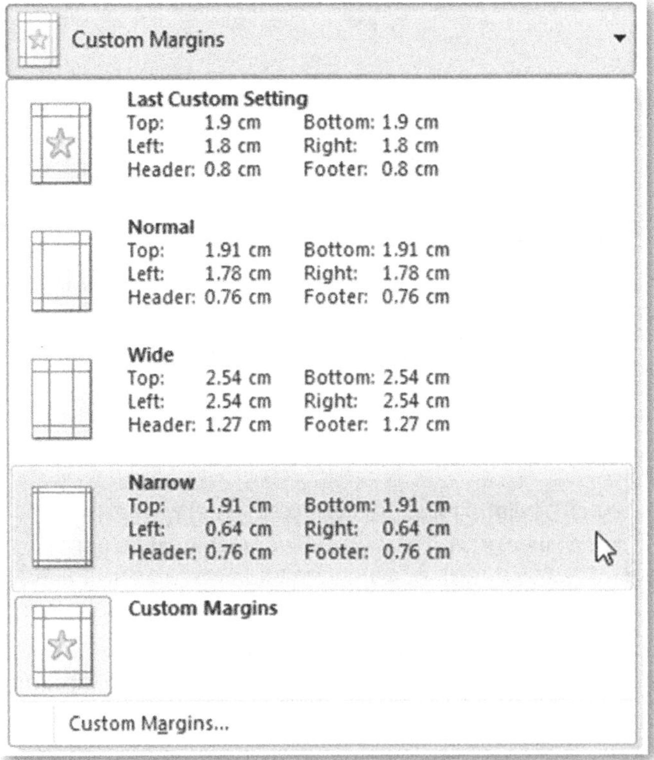

FIGURE 11.54 Print Option—Narrow Custom Margins

The Custom Scaling option of Fit All Columns on One Page is useful because it fits the print area to one page in width (see Figure 11.55).

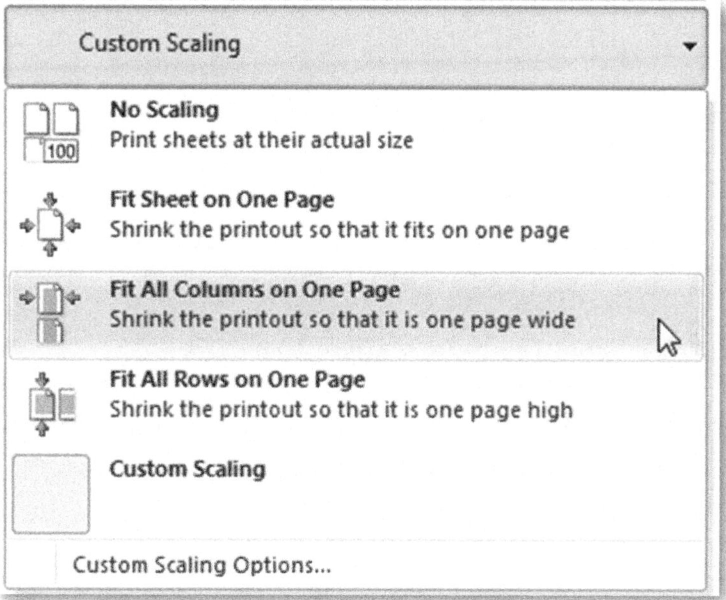

FIGURE 11.55 Print Option—Fit All Columns on One Page

12

CHAPTER TWELVE

Picture Perfect: Charting Techniques

IF A PICTURE IS WORTH 1,000 WORDS, then a chart may well be worth 500 numbers plus 500 words. Charts have the ability to make sense of myriad numbers and turn them into a picture that you can understand, explain, and use to make decisions.

Of course, the flipside of this is that charts can also be used to deceive and manipulate data to promote a particular point of view.

Charts offer an easy way to convert tables of numbers into a visual representation that can be used to identify trends and relationships. We are visual creatures and have the ability to easily spot trends and relationships when they are displayed in charts.

The human brain is adept at pattern recognition. Charts can display numbers in a way that lets us make the most of our pattern-matching abilities.

Reporting dashboards have recently become popular. Displaying important information in small charts is now more common than it used to be, and this chapter will describe the techniques required to create small, useful charts.

Excel 2010 introduced a built-in feature called Sparkline charts. A Sparkline chart is a chart that exists in a cell. As you increase the size of the cell, the chart increases as well.

The name and concept of the Sparkline chart was created by Edward Tufte, an author who specialises in data visualisation. I recommend his books as well as those by Stephen Few, who has written recently about data visualisation.

Excel offers three built-in Sparkline charts, and one of those has only limited usage.

Microsoft is playing catch-up in terms of Sparkline charts. For many years there have been Excel add-ins that allowed you to create Sparkline charts. Indeed, if you want to incorporate more Sparkline charts into your reports, it can be worthwhile investing in a third-party Sparklines add-in.

This chapter will cover the common chart types used in reports and dashboards as well as the techniques required to create and modify them.

CHART VERSUS GRAPH

Strictly speaking, Excel's charts are really graphs. When Microsoft was developing Excel, however, the term *graph* was already used by Lotus, the major spreadsheet package at the time.

To differentiate itself from Lotus, Microsoft decided to use the term *chart* rather than *graph*. This book will use the term *chart* to be consistent with the terminology used in Excel.

CHART BASICS

Creating a chart is incredibly easy. Simply click inside a table of data, click the Insert Ribbon tab, and select the chart type you want to use.

Modifying charts can take some practice. I will share many suggestions and tips to improve your charts. Many of them are based on suggestions made by Tufte and Few.

As with any visual experience, personal preferences come into play. Your manager may hate a chart that you think looks great. Be open to other ideas and don't be afraid to experiment.

Chart Objects

To improve how you work with charts, you need to understand an important concept: A chart is not a single object. It is an object made up of many smaller objects. Each of these smaller objects can be controlled and formatted separately. The controls and options for these objects vary.

Some objects can be controlled as part of a group, whereas others can be controlled and formatted by themselves.

Grasping the multiple-object concept makes it easier for you to modify a chart to meet your requirements.

Each chart object has a name. You can find out what each part of a chart is called by pointing your mouse at the object. A small tool tip will be displayed with the name.

When a chart is selected, three ribbon tabs are displayed: Design, Layout, and Format.

The Design tab contains options that make structural changes to the chart, such as changing the chart data or the chart type. The tab contains the Chart Layouts and Chart Styles sections, which have built-in layout and format options. This tab also has the Save as Template icon, which will be discussed later.

The Layout tab allows you to modify each object in the chart. It has a drop-down menu at the top left that lists each object so that you can select it (see Figure 12.1). The drop-down menu lists only those objects that are being used in the selected chart. As you will see later in the chapter, you can easily remove objects from a chart.

The Format tab has the same drop-down list in the top left corner so you can select part of the chart to format it.

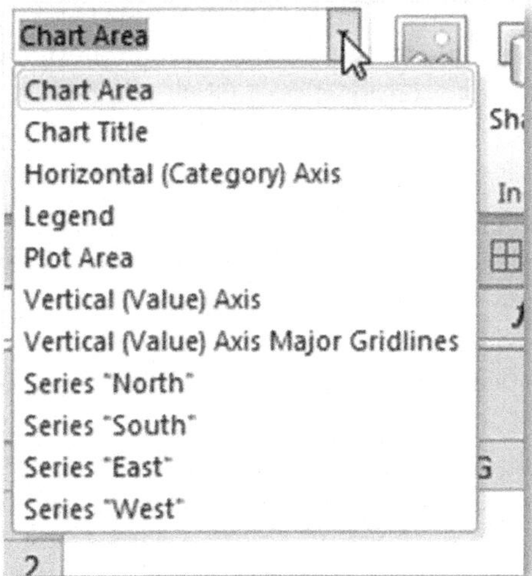

FIGURE 12.1 Drop-Down List Showing Chart Objects

Charts Made Easy

The following techniques and suggestions will simplify the creation and modification process and improve the resulting charts.

Chart Techniques

- Use a table layout for your chart data.
- Double-click objects to open the Format dialog box for that object.
- Right-click objects for a menu with common tasks and formatting options.
- Home Ribbon formatting contains many icons you can use to format chart objects, such as Fill Color, Font Size, and Font Color. These are also displayed on the right-click option.
- Use the Delete key on the keyboard to remove parts of the chart. Experiment and see the effect—you can always undo it.
- Hold the Alt key down when moving or resizing a chart. This automatically lines the chart up with the row and column gridlines, which makes it easier to line up and resize perfectly.
- Use the F4 key to repeat the last action.
- Use the Save as Template (Design tab) feature to capture and reuse a chart layout.

Chart Suggestions

- Have a dedicated sheet for your chart data. The chart data and the charts can be on separate sheets.
- Keep your charts consistent. This is especially applicable to dashboards. Use a consistent colour scheme.
- Remove chart gridlines. Let's face it, a chart is not supposed to supply you with a perfectly accurate value. You don't look at a chart and see that a point is 124.5. You

would see that the point is about 120. Gridlines add visual clutter to a chart without adding any accuracy. Unless they are necessary, remove them.

- If an object doesn't add to the chart's readability, remove it.
- Don't use a colour for the plot area or chart area—leave them both white.
- Avoid all 3D charts. They are gimmicky and can hide data and distort relationships.
- Avoid too many colours or fonts. I can't tell you how many is too many. You have to look critically at the chart and see whether all the colours are required. Use colour sparingly to highlight important parts of the chart.
- Turn off the sheet gridlines.
- Make sure your vertical axes start at zero unless there is an extremely good reason not to.
- When working with column and bar charts, sort the data by values, if possible, to make it easier to read. Sometimes you can't, however, because the order of the items is important.
- If you have a large chart with a lot of information on it, consider converting it to two or three smaller charts.
- Use pie charts sparingly. They take up a lot of space. Unfortunately, they are very popular. If you are going to use a pie chart, make sure it has fewer than five categories. Consider using a 100 percent bar or column chart instead.
- Add labels to parts of the chart that are important; for instance, label the high and low points on a line chart.
- Avoid speedo or gauge-type charts—they are possible in Excel but are inefficient with space and are complicated. There is a more space-efficient alternative called bullet chart, developed by Stephen Few. This is not a standard Excel chart, and I am not covering it in this book. This link has a description of the bullet chart: http://www.perceptualedge.com/articles/misc/Bullet_Graph_Design_Spec.pdf.

CHARTS FOR REPORTS

The most commonly used and understood charts are column and line charts. The pie chart is also popular, but it has limited uses.

Excel charts allow you to combine multiple chart types into one chart. Not all chart types can be combined, however. The most popular combination is a column chart with a line chart. These two chart types work well together.

Another option you have when combining chart types is to use two axes. This is especially useful when plotting two measures that are different in scale, such as Sales $ and Margin %.

AUTOMATING CHARTS

Ideally, you want your charts to automatically plot the right data for your reports. In most cases this involves including the latest month's data in the chart. You may have rolling 12- or 13-month charts. These must be amended every month to add the new month and remove the old month.

You can avoid manually amending charts by using techniques that automate the process. There are a few approaches to this, so you can choose the one that works best for you.

Formula-Based Chart Automation

My preferred technique is to use formulas to create the chart data. We can use formulas that automatically extract the latest data. There is a technique you can employ to stop Excel from displaying entries on a chart.

Excel charts won't plot error cells. You can use this to your advantage and create automatically expanding charts. In many cases you can easily amend existing charts to become automated.

The chart in Figure 12.2 has three empty months. It is based on the range M3:S7. The report uses SUMIFS functions to summarise the data in columns I to K.

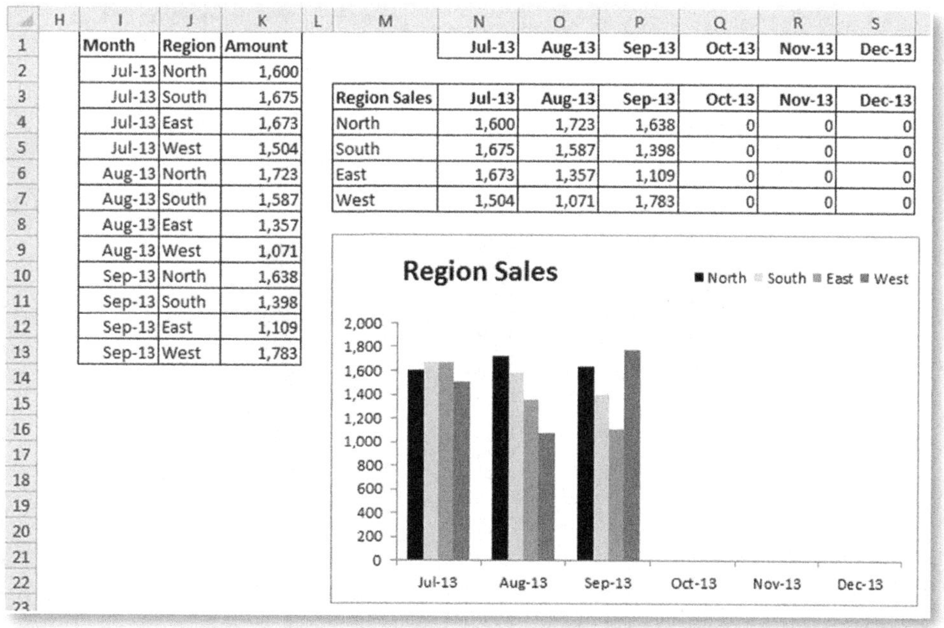

Month	Region	Amount
Jul-13	North	1,600
Jul-13	South	1,675
Jul-13	East	1,673
Jul-13	West	1,504
Aug-13	North	1,723
Aug-13	South	1,587
Aug-13	East	1,357
Aug-13	West	1,071
Sep-13	North	1,638
Sep-13	South	1,398
Sep-13	East	1,109
Sep-13	West	1,783

	Jul-13	Aug-13	Sep-13	Oct-13	Nov-13	Dec-13
Region Sales	Jul-13	Aug-13	Sep-13	Oct-13	Nov-13	Dec-13
North	1,600	1,723	1,638	0	0	0
South	1,675	1,587	1,398	0	0	0
East	1,673	1,357	1,109	0	0	0
West	1,504	1,071	1,783	0	0	0

FIGURE 12.2 Monthly Chart Example

In most cases you don't want to display empty months in a chart. You also don't want to extend the data range for the chart each month as more data is added to columns I to K. The assumption is that the range below the data table is blank.

You can easily amend this report to have the chart automatically hide empty months and display new months. Because charts don't display error cells, you can use a formula that inserts error cells in row 3, where the dates are shown in the report.

The range N1:S1 consists of helper cells, which have all the dates to be charted. The formula we need to add to cell N3 is

```
=IF(N1<=MAX($I:$I),N1,NA())
```

This formula can be copied across.

The NA() function displays the #N/A error message in the cell. The formula will display the date from row 1 as long as the date in row 1 is less than or equal to the maximum (latest) date in column I of the data. If the date is greater than (after) the latest date, the #N/A error message will be displayed. The chart won't display the error dates.

As you can see from Figure 12.3, when the formula is copied across, the chart automatically changes.

Region Sales	Jul-13	Aug-13	Sep-13	#N/A	#N/A	#N/A
North	1,600	1,723	1,638	0	0	0
South	1,675	1,587	1,398	0	0	0
East	1,673	1,357	1,109	0	0	0
West	1,504	1,071	1,783	0	0	0

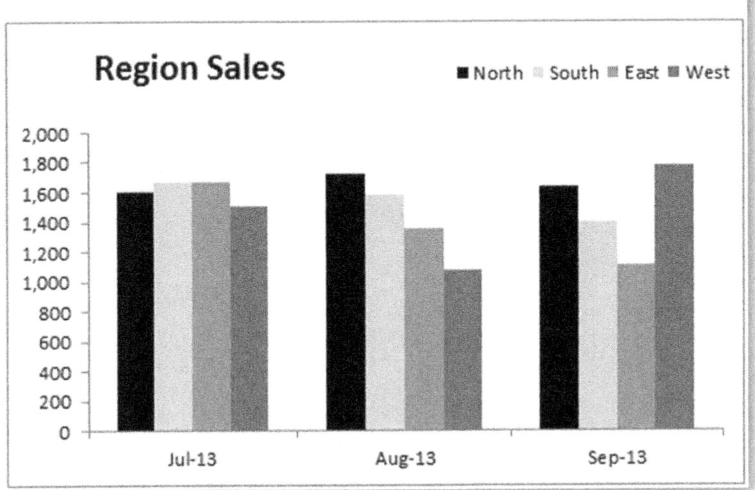

FIGURE 12.3 Updated Monthly Chart Example

When we add the next month's data to the data table, the chart automatically updates (see Figure 12.4).

A rolling 12- or 13-month chart is a common report requirement. Figure 12.5 shows another chart you can automate by using a formula.

Columns J and K contain the data used for the chart. The chart is based on the range M2:N14. Column N has SUMIF formulas that extract the month value from the data columns. The assumption again is that there are no entries below the data in columns J and K. The dates in column J do not have to be in sequence.

Cell M14 extracts the last date in column J using the following formula:

```
=MAX(J:J)
```

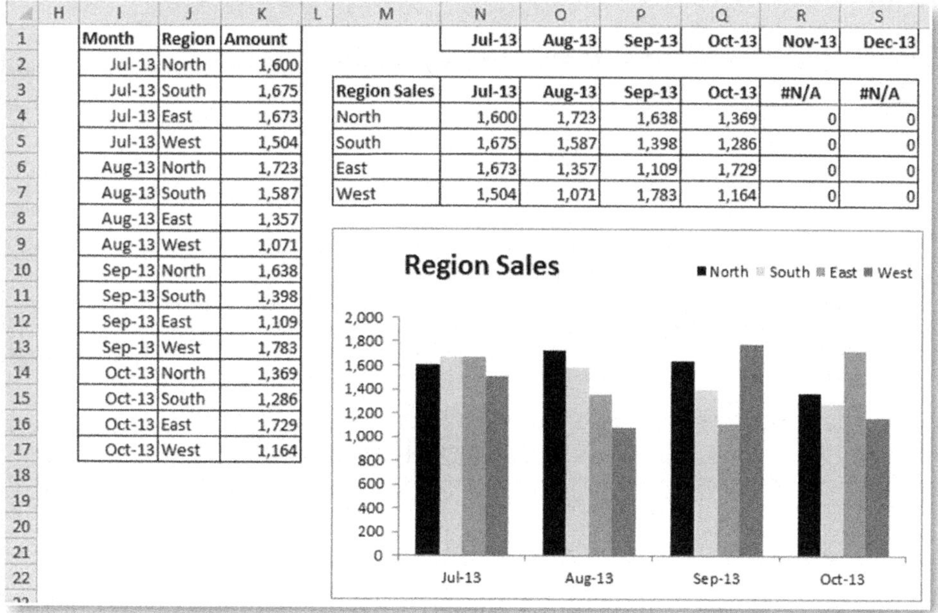

Month	Region	Amount
Jul-13	North	1,600
Jul-13	South	1,675
Jul-13	East	1,673
Jul-13	West	1,504
Aug-13	North	1,723
Aug-13	South	1,587
Aug-13	East	1,357
Aug-13	West	1,071
Sep-13	North	1,638
Sep-13	South	1,398
Sep-13	East	1,109
Sep-13	West	1,783
Oct-13	North	1,369
Oct-13	South	1,286
Oct-13	East	1,729
Oct-13	West	1,164

	Jul-13	Aug-13	Sep-13	Oct-13	Nov-13	Dec-13
Region Sales	**Jul-13**	**Aug-13**	**Sep-13**	**Oct-13**	**#N/A**	**#N/A**
North	1,600	1,723	1,638	1,369	0	0
South	1,675	1,587	1,398	1,286	0	0
East	1,673	1,357	1,109	1,729	0	0
West	1,504	1,071	1,783	1,164	0	0

FIGURE 12.4 Monthly Chart Example—Month Added

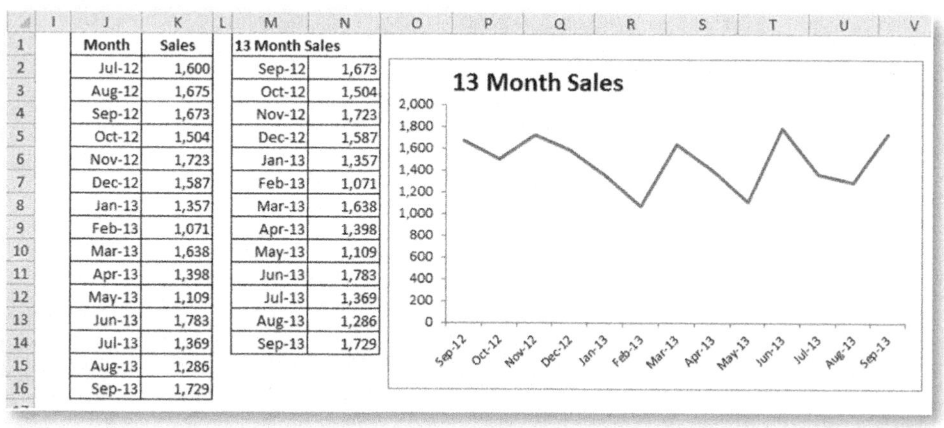

Month	Sales
Jul-12	1,600
Aug-12	1,675
Sep-12	1,673
Oct-12	1,504
Nov-12	1,723
Dec-12	1,587
Jan-13	1,357
Feb-13	1,071
Mar-13	1,638
Apr-13	1,398
May-13	1,109
Jun-13	1,783
Jul-13	1,369
Aug-13	1,286
Sep-13	1,729

13 Month Sales	
Sep-12	1,673
Oct-12	1,504
Nov-12	1,723
Dec-12	1,587
Jan-13	1,357
Feb-13	1,071
Mar-13	1,638
Apr-13	1,398
May-13	1,109
Jun-13	1,783
Jul-13	1,369
Aug-13	1,286
Sep-13	1,729

FIGURE 12.5 Automated Rolling 13-Month Chart

Cell M13 uses a formula to calculate the previous month. The formula is

```
=DATE(YEAR(M14),MONTH(M14)-1,1)
```

This formula has been copied to all the cells up to cell M2.

Adding a new month to the bottom of column J will automatically update cell M14, and the months above will then also update automatically.

Figure 12.6 shows an example in which it is better to use a report as the source data for a chart rather than use the data directly.

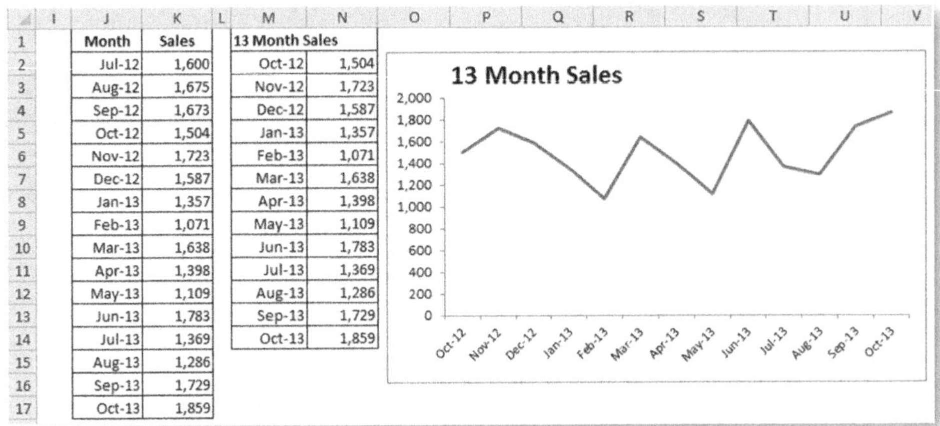

	J	K	L	M	N
1	Month	Sales		13 Month Sales	
2	Jul-12	1,600		Oct-12	1,504
3	Aug-12	1,675		Nov-12	1,723
4	Sep-12	1,673		Dec-12	1,587
5	Oct-12	1,504		Jan-13	1,357
6	Nov-12	1,723		Feb-13	1,071
7	Dec-12	1,587		Mar-13	1,638
8	Jan-13	1,357		Apr-13	1,398
9	Feb-13	1,071		May-13	1,109
10	Mar-13	1,638		Jun-13	1,783
11	Apr-13	1,398		Jul-13	1,369
12	May-13	1,109		Aug-13	1,286
13	Jun-13	1,783		Sep-13	1,729
14	Jul-13	1,369		Oct-13	1,859
15	Aug-13	1,286			
16	Sep-13	1,729			
17	Oct-13	1,859			

FIGURE 12.6 Automated Rolling 13-Month Chart Monthly Update

Avoiding Zeros

In some instances, you might need to plot budget figures for future months but you don't want to plot the actual figures, which will be zeros. This mainly applies to line charts in which the line drops dramatically to zero (see Figure 12.7).

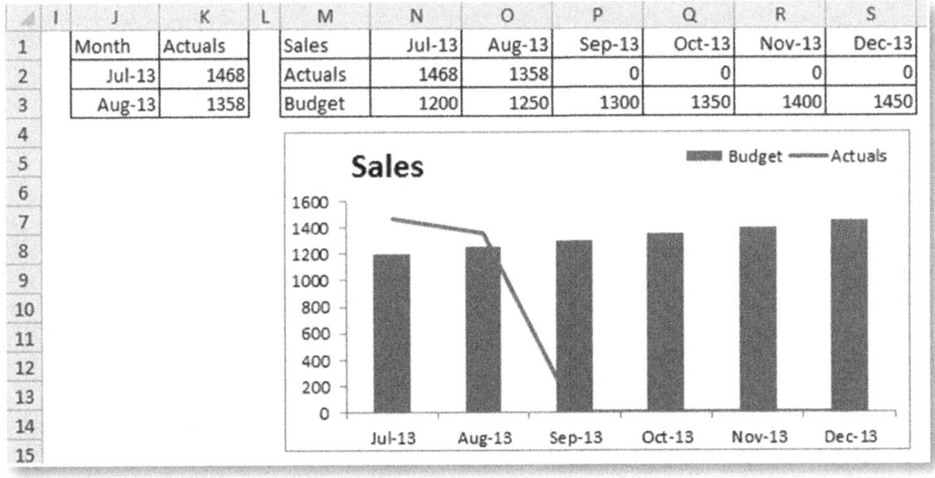

	J	K	L	M	N	O	P	Q	R	S
1	Month	Actuals		Sales	Jul-13	Aug-13	Sep-13	Oct-13	Nov-13	Dec-13
2	Jul-13	1468		Actuals	1468	1358	0	0	0	0
3	Aug-13	1358		Budget	1200	1250	1300	1350	1400	1450

FIGURE 12.7 Line Chart Plotting Zeros

We can also use the #N/A error technique to stop plotting the zeros. Cell N2 has a standard SUMIF formula. We can amend it to display the #N/A error message with the following formula:

```
=IF(N1<=MAX($J:$J),SUMIF($J:$J,N$1,$K:$K),NA())
```

This formula has been copied across. The chart then ignores the error cells and plots only the value cells (see Figure 12.8).

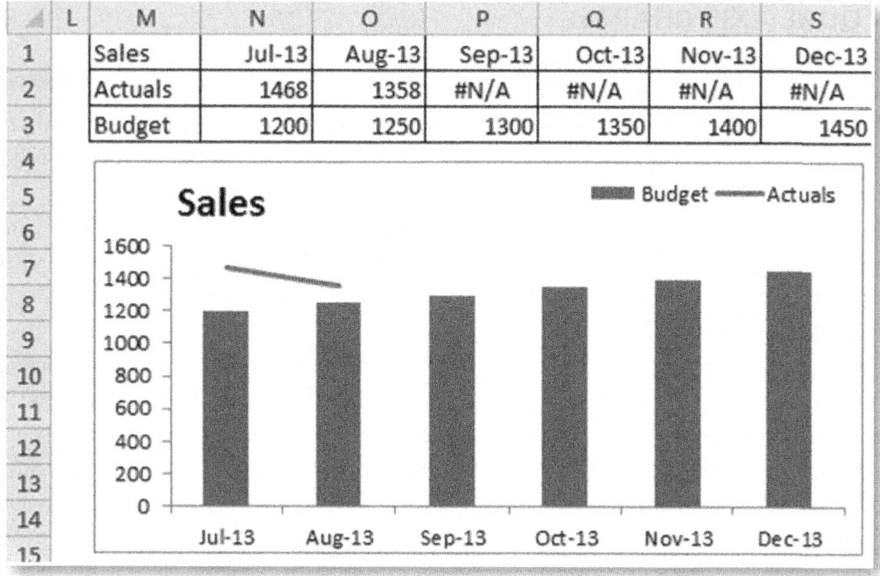

FIGURE 12.8 Line Chart Not Plotting Zeros

MIXING CHART TYPES

Figures 12.7 and 12.8 were examples of combining a line chart with a column chart. This is actually very easy to achieve.

You create the column chart as normal. Then right-click the data series you want to change to a line chart. Select Change Series Chart Type. Then choose the chart type from the dialog box shown in Figure 12.9 and click OK.

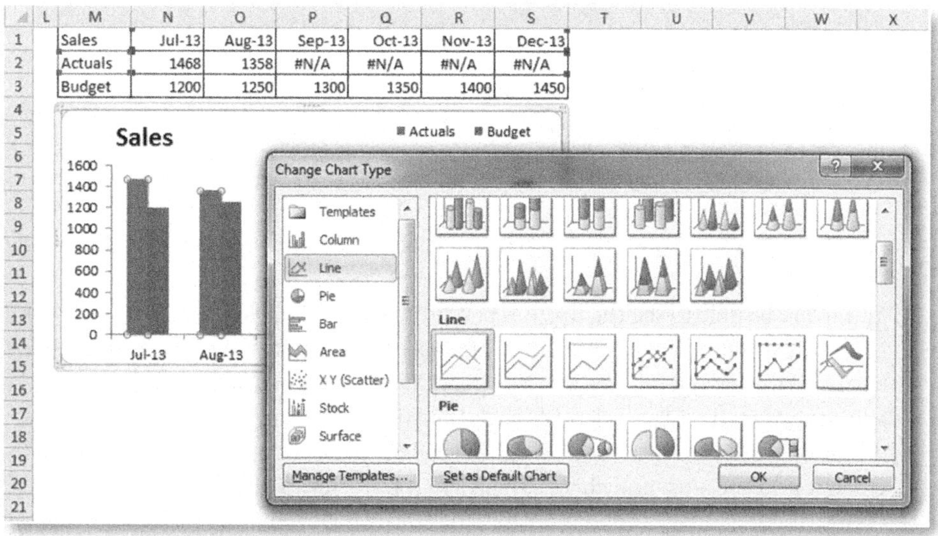

FIGURE 12.9 Changing Chart Type

DUAL-AXIS CHARTS

Plotting different measures together can sometimes highlight the relationships between the measures. Having identified a relationship, you can then investigate further to decide whether it is a causal relationship—that is, the changes in one measure have caused the changes in the other measure.

Suppose an increase in credit note numbers coincides with a decrease in customer complaints and an increase in customer satisfaction scores. This is counterintuitive. Increases in credit notes are usually driven by wrong or bad processes that customers do not like.

Obviously, the credit notes themselves are not the problem. They are simply a measure of the number of errors in the sales process. When you investigate the breakdown of the reasons for the credit note increase, you might find that there are more than the usual pricing reductions. Upon deeper investigation, you might discover that certain sales representatives are matching your competitor's prices and authorising price adjustments after the sale.

Happy, satisfied customers are a good thing, but if this phenomenon is driven by a reduction in your gross margin percentage, it might not be worth celebrating.

The measures you want to compare sometimes cannot be plotted on one axis (e.g., Gross Margin % and Sales $). The answer is to use two axes.

If you are plotting two measures on the one chart and using a different axis for each measure, you would typically also use a different chart type for each measure.

Example

The figures in the report in Figure 12.10 can't be plotted on the same axis. To create a dual axis chart from scratch, use the following instructions:

	I	J	K	L	M	N	O	P
1			Jul-13	Aug-13	Sep-13	Oct-13	Nov-13	Dec-13
2		Sales $	12,963	13,657	12,808	12,456	13,501	11,996
3		Margin %	40.56%	41.90%	41.50%	41.01%	42.34%	41.65%

FIGURE 12.10 Chart Data—Dollars and Percentages

1. Select a cell in the report, click the Insert Ribbon tab. and create a line chart using the first line chart.
2. You won't be able to see the margin percentage line. If you click on the horizontal axis, you should be able to select it. If not, use the drop-down list in the top left corner of the Layout tab (see Figure 12.11) to select Series "Margin %."
3. With the Margin % line selected, click the Format Section option underneath the drop-down list. You can also right-click the selected line chart (which can be tricky when it's on the axis) and choose the Format Data Series option.
4. Choose the Secondary Axis option, and the chart should change. Click Close. Always check your axes to make sure they start at zero. In this case the axis probably won't, as you can see in Figure 12.12. We'll come back to this.

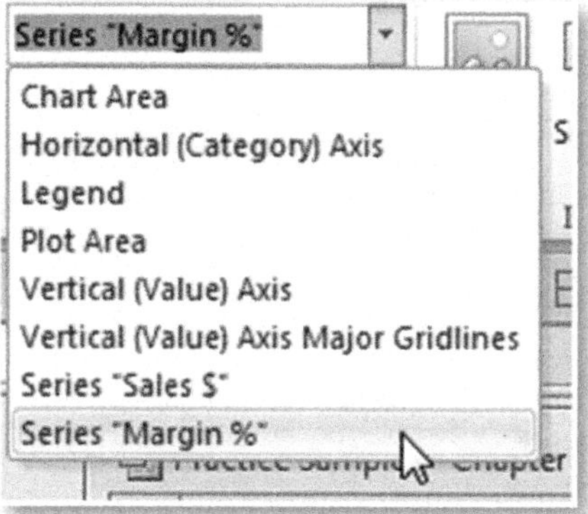

FIGURE 12.11 Select Series from Drop-Down List

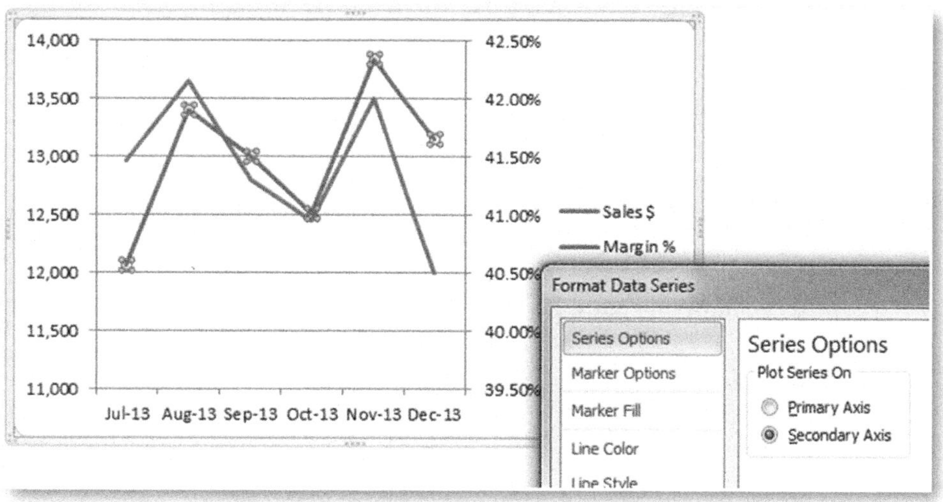

FIGURE 12.12 Axis Change

5. Right-click Sales $ Series and choose Change Series Chart Type. Select Clustered Column Chart (the top left column chart).
6. We now need to adjust the right axis back to zero. Right-click the axis, choose Format Axis, and change Minimum to Fixed and 0. Click the Line Color option on the right and change it to a solid line and the colour red to match the chart line colour. Click Close. Figure 12.13 shows these settings.
7. Right-click the right axis and use the Font Color icon to change the font to red.
8. Set the left axis minimum to zero and its line colour and font colour to blue.
9. Now we can add a chart title. Click the Layout tab and use the Chart Title drop-down list to insert Centered Overlay Title.
10. I usually move the legend to the top right and the title to the left, but this is merely a personal preference.
11. Delete the chart gridlines. Select them and press the Delete key.

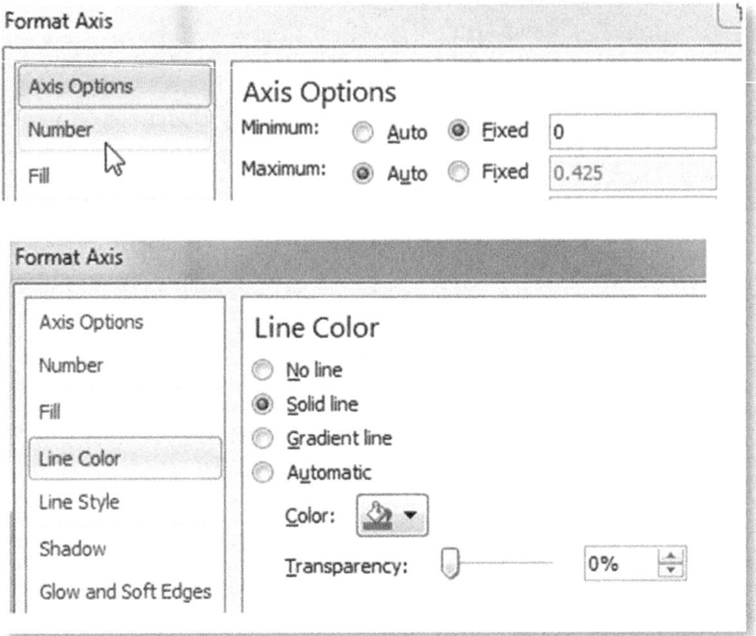

FIGURE 12.13 Axis Settings

The result is shown in Figure 12.14.

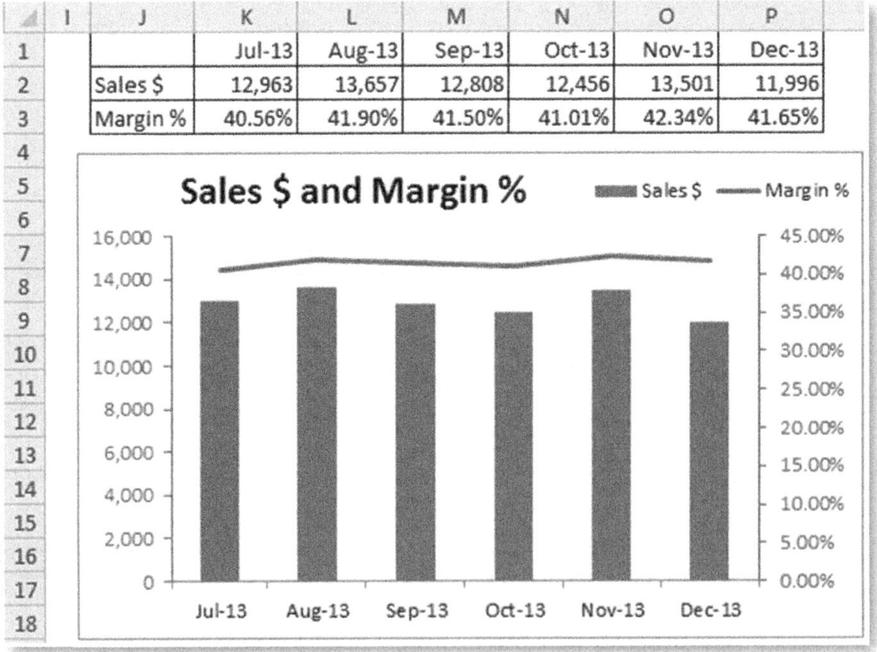

	Jul-13	Aug-13	Sep-13	Oct-13	Nov-13	Dec-13
Sales $	12,963	13,657	12,808	12,456	13,501	11,996
Margin %	40.56%	41.90%	41.50%	41.01%	42.34%	41.65%

FIGURE 12.14 Dual-Axis Chart

HANDLING MISSING DATA

In some cases you may not have all the data you want, but you still want to produce a chart. This applies mainly to line charts. Figure 12.15 shows three options for handling missing data.

In this example, there were no webinars held in December or January.

The first option is to enter a zero as shown in the data on the left of the chart. If you have missing months in a series, then entering a zero will cause the line to fall to zero and then rise back to the next month's value. The zeros entered in the top example caused the drop in the line.

If you leave the cells blank, which is the second option, Excel's default behavior is to leave a gap between the points.

The third option joins the points together. This is created by changing the setting that handles missing or hidden data. This setting is a button in the Select Data Source dialog box.

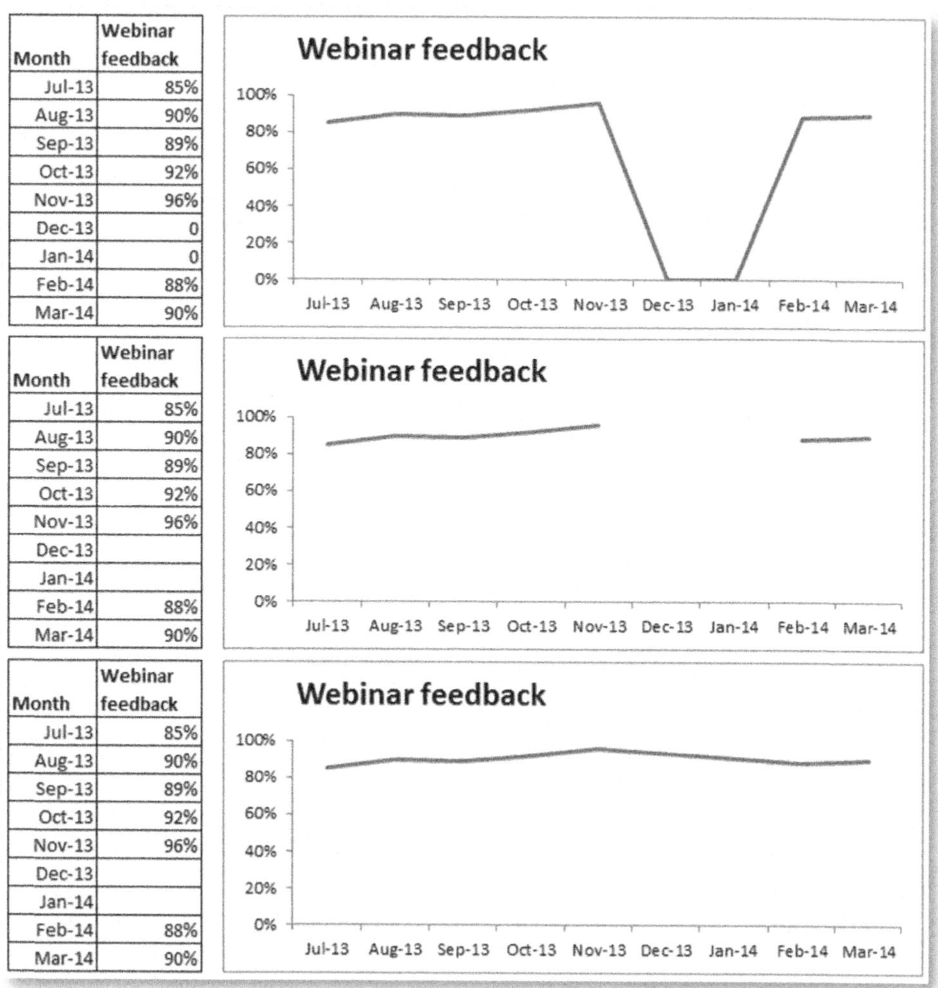

Month	Webinar feedback
Jul-13	85%
Aug-13	90%
Sep-13	89%
Oct-13	92%
Nov-13	96%
Dec-13	0
Jan-14	0
Feb-14	88%
Mar-14	90%

Month	Webinar feedback
Jul-13	85%
Aug-13	90%
Sep-13	89%
Oct-13	92%
Nov-13	96%
Dec-13	
Jan-14	
Feb-14	88%
Mar-14	90%

Month	Webinar feedback
Jul-13	85%
Aug-13	90%
Sep-13	89%
Oct-13	92%
Nov-13	96%
Dec-13	
Jan-14	
Feb-14	88%
Mar-14	90%

FIGURE 12.15 Missing Data Options

You can access this dialog box with a right-click on any object in the chart. Then choose Select Data or click the Select Data icon on the Design Ribbon tab, shown in Figure 12.16.

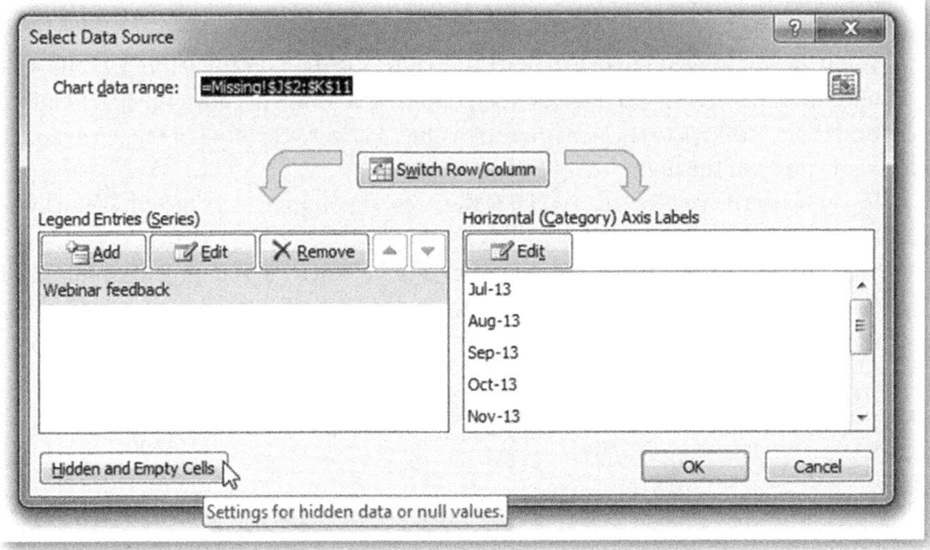

FIGURE 12.16 Select Data Source Dialog Box—Hidden and Empty Cells Button

The settings are shown in Figure 12.17.

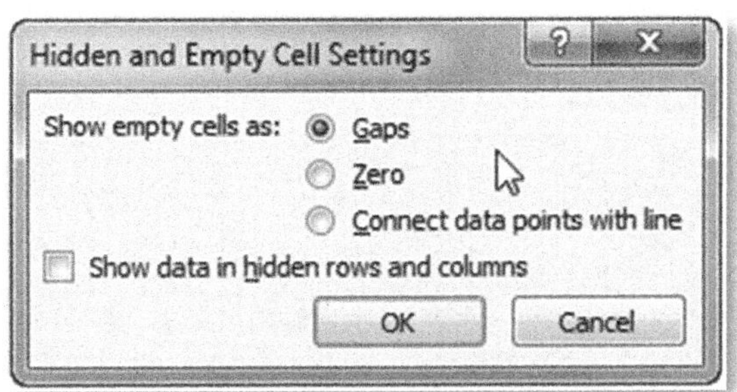

FIGURE 12.17 Hidden and Empty Cell Settings Dialog Box

As you can see, the defaults are to show the gaps and to hide data in hidden rows. The third chart in Figure 12.15 used the third option in Figure 12.17, "Connect data points with a line."

In most cases, I believe the gap method is preferable for displaying such missing data.

There is a fourth alternative: the text axis option. To use it with a date axis, however, you have to change an axis setting (see Figure 12.18).

Format Axis

Axis Options
Number
Fill
Line Color
Line Style
Shadow
Glow and Soft Edges
3-D Format
Alignment

Axis Options
Interval between tick marks: 1
Interval between labels:
Automatic
Specify interval unit: 1
Categories in reverse order
Label distance from axis: 100
Axis Type:
Automatically select based on data
Text axis
Date axis

FIGURE 12.18 Text Axis Option

This will allow you to hide the empty months, as shown in Figure 12.19.

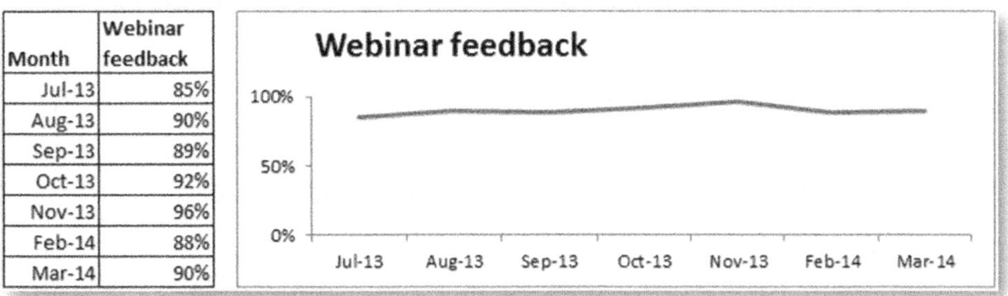

Month	Webinar feedback
Jul-13	85%
Aug-13	90%
Sep-13	89%
Oct-13	92%
Nov-13	96%
Feb-14	88%
Mar-14	90%

FIGURE 12.19 Hidden Date Rows

Excel's default setting is not to display hidden rows or columns. However, when the axis is date-based, it doesn't apply. Hence, you need to tell Excel that the axis is text-based; then the hidden or missing entries won't display.

LABELING HIGHS AND LOWS

An option that is missing in Excel's line charts is the ability to display the high and low values. Sparkline charts have an option to mark the high and low points, but it is not available in the normal line chart.

There is a way to work around this. It involves adding two series to the chart data. Figure 12.20 shows the structure required.

The formula in cell L2 is

```
=IF(K2=MAX($K$2:$K$13),K2,NA())
```

This formula has been copied down the column. This shows the value only when it is the maximum value; otherwise it displays the #N/A error message.

The formula in cell M2 is

```
=IF(K2=MIN($K$2:$K$13),K2,NA())
```

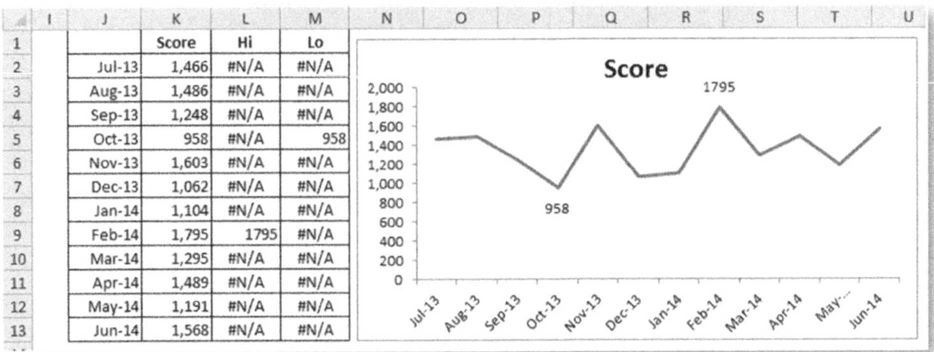

	Score	Hi	Lo
Jul-13	1,466	#N/A	#N/A
Aug-13	1,486	#N/A	#N/A
Sep-13	1,248	#N/A	#N/A
Oct-13	958	#N/A	958
Nov-13	1,603	#N/A	#N/A
Dec-13	1,062	#N/A	#N/A
Jan-14	1,104	#N/A	#N/A
Feb-14	1,795	1795	#N/A
Mar-14	1,295	#N/A	#N/A
Apr-14	1,489	#N/A	#N/A
May-14	1,191	#N/A	#N/A
Jun-14	1,568	#N/A	#N/A

FIGURE 12.20 Show High and Low Labels on a Line Chart

This formula has been copied down the column. This shows the value only when it is the minimum value; otherwise it displays the #N/A error message.

When you plot a single data point on a line chart, it doesn't display anything as a chart, but it does have a single point on the chart.

You can select Hi Data Series in the Chart Elements drop-down list in the Layout Ribbon. Then use the Data Labels icon drop-down list to select the Above option (see Figure 12.21).

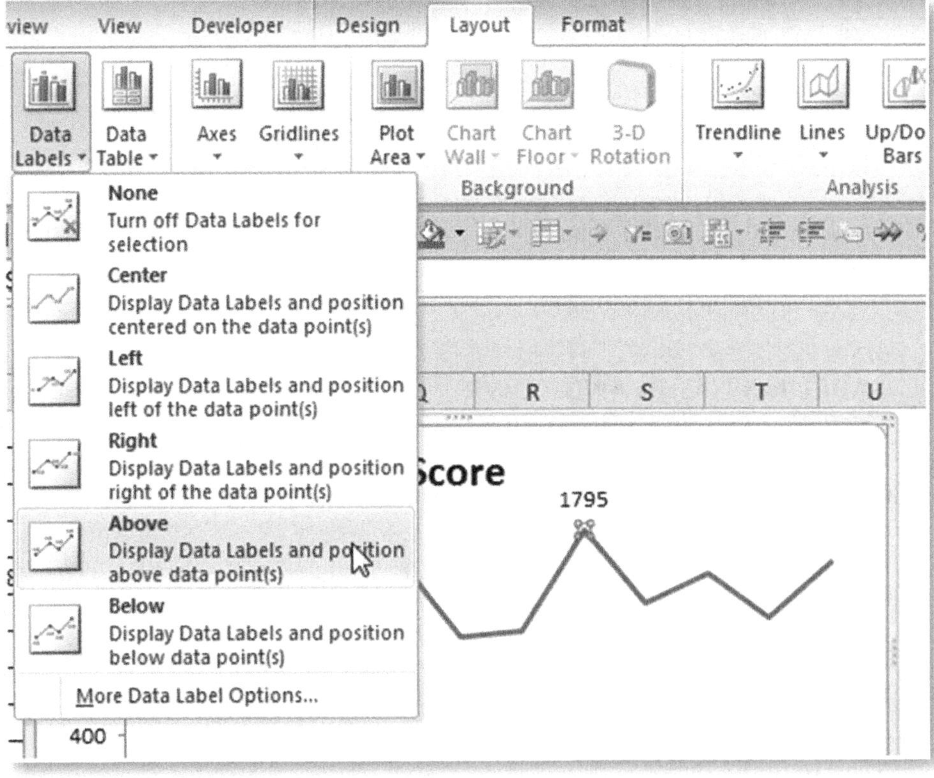

FIGURE 12.21 Selecting a Data Label

Repeat this for Lo Data Series and select the Below option.

The high and low figures are dynamic and will update automatically as the score data change.

TRENDLINES AND MOVING AVERAGES

You may be tempted to use the above technique to plot moving averages instead of high and low points. Excel has its own built-in moving average and trend line options.

To add a trendline or a moving average, right-click the data series and choose Add Trendline. The default is a linear trendline but the others, along with the moving average, are listed in Figure 12.22.

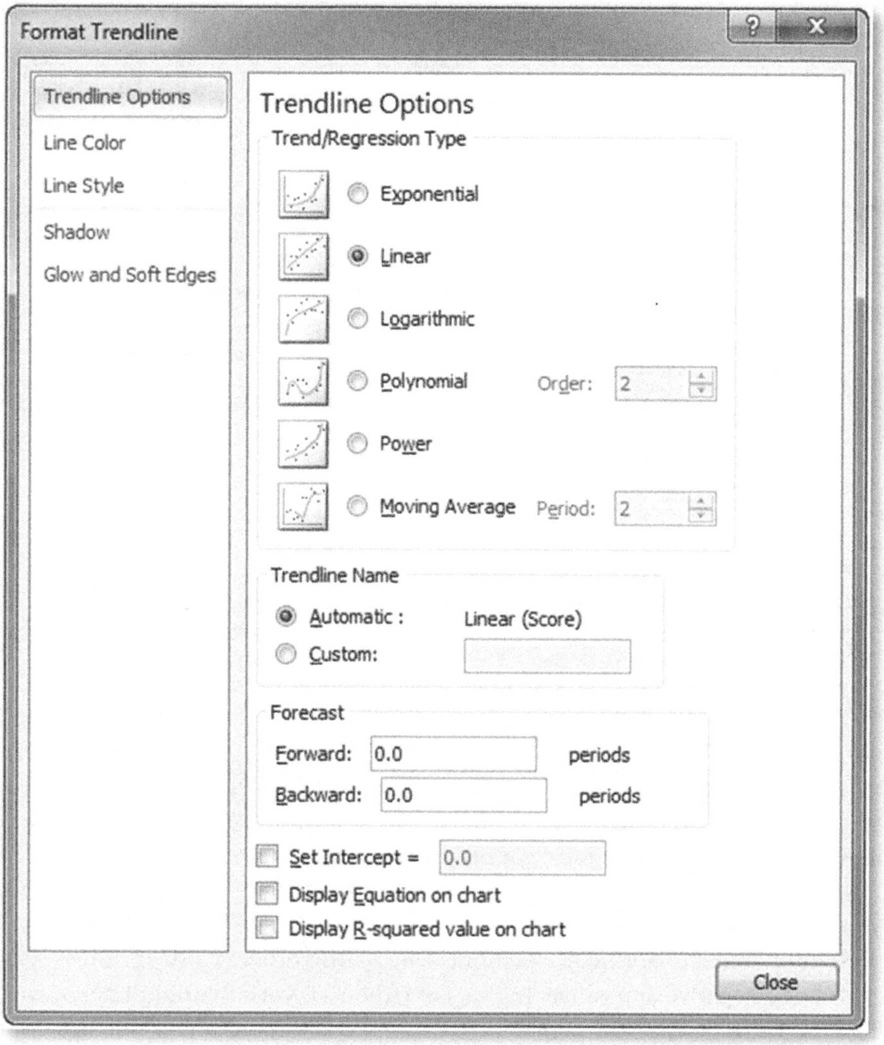

FIGURE 12.22 Format Trendline Dialog Box

The options at the bottom of the dialog box are quite powerful. You can display the formula of the trendline and also extend the trendline into the past or the future.

PLOTTING THE VARIANCE

Many accounting reports include budget variances. In term of charting, rather than plotting both the actuals and the budget, consider whether charting just the variance and the year-to-date (YTD) variance might be easier to understand.

Compare the two charts in Figure 12.23.

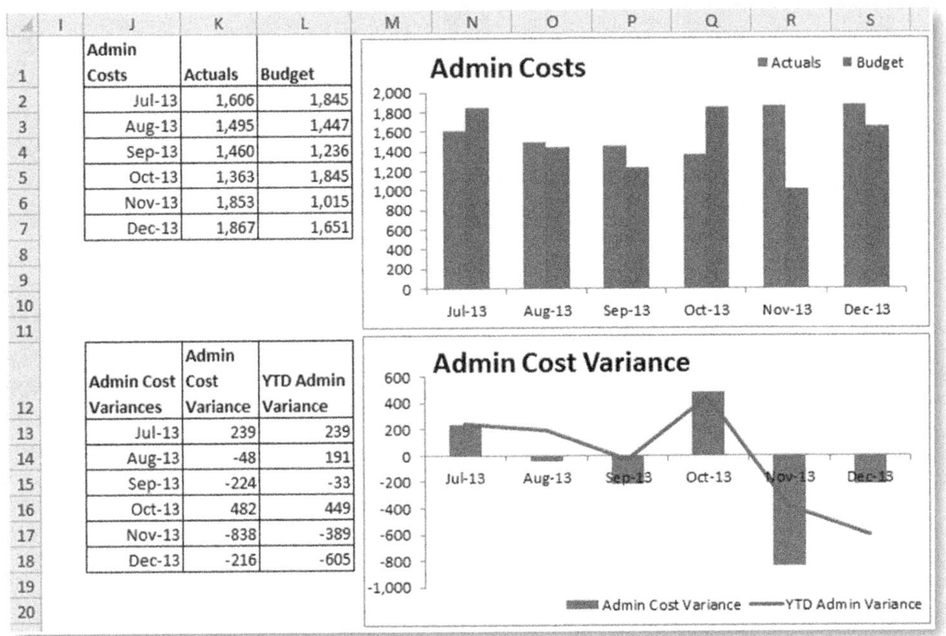

Admin Costs	Actuals	Budget
Jul-13	1,606	1,845
Aug-13	1,495	1,447
Sep-13	1,460	1,236
Oct-13	1,363	1,845
Nov-13	1,853	1,015
Dec-13	1,867	1,651

Admin Cost Variances	Admin Cost Variance	YTD Admin Variance
Jul-13	239	239
Aug-13	-48	191
Sep-13	-224	-33
Oct-13	482	449
Nov-13	-838	-389
Dec-13	-216	-605

FIGURE 12.23 Variance Charts

The top chart shows the month-by-month relationship of actuals to the budget. In most months you can see that the actuals are above budget.

The bottom chart focuses only on the variances. It is easy to see that there are four bars below the line and two above it. Adding the YTD variance quantifies how the year has progressed and what the current situation is.

If your budget is reasonably accurate, you should have both positive and negative variances during the year.

Should your budget be skewed one way or the other, your variance will be consistently negative or positive. In that case, the YTD variance might not be worthwhile, because it will consistently increase over time and affect the scale of the chart.

DASHBOARD TECHNIQUES

Dashboard reports have been around for many years. There are dedicated software packages that can create them. Many business intelligence, enterprise resource planning, and even accounting systems include dashboard modules to create dashboards.

Dashboard reports are supposed to work like a car dashboard. The idea is that you can glance at the dashboard and see whether the business is running well. If there is a problem, the report should tell you which areas are causing it.

In practice, of course, a business is more complicated than a car. A business involves people, and this fact alone increases its complexity. A car is much easier to monitor than an organisation.

In terms of creating a dashboard from the initial idea to the final report, the creation of the report itself is a small part of the whole process. Much of the time is spent determining the following:

- What areas do we need to look at?
- What metrics do we need to measure?
- Can we measure them?
- How often do we need to measure them?
- Who will be responsible?
- Is the data available?
- Is the data reliable?
- How do we display the data?

Once all of those factors have been finalised, you can sit down and design the final dashboard. In this section I will share some techniques that can make creating the dashboard easier.

Remember that the objective of a dashboard is to enable the user to look at the report and gain an immediate understanding of how the organisation is running and where the issues are.

When the oil light on your car dashboard goes on, it doesn't tell you where to put the oil or how much oil to put in. It's just a warning signal that you need to add oil to the engine. In the same way, items on the dashboard report merely signal that part of the organisation requires attention. This means that other reports will be required to identify in detail what has happened.

Paste Picture Link

One of Excel's limitations in terms of presentation and layout is that the placement of reports is limited by the row and column grid. Displaying reports with different column widths above one another is not always possible.

That's where the Paste Picture Link option comes in. You can copy a range and paste a linked picture of that range onto the sheet as a picture. Because it is a picture, it can be placed anywhere on the sheet. Because it is linked, it updates when the range updates.

When using this technique, you typically turn off the sheet gridlines.

Excel has a toolbar icon, Camera, that is worth adding to your Quick Access Toolbar (QAT) if you want to use this technique. See Figure 12.24 to see where you can find it to add to the QAT.

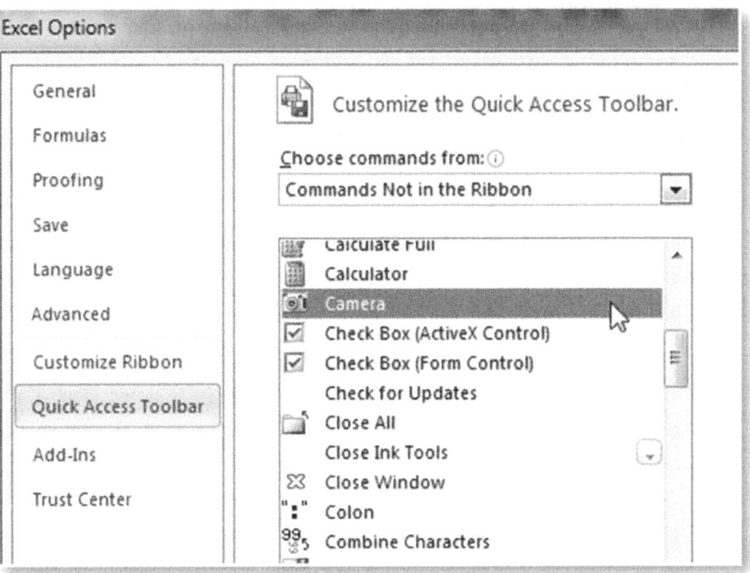

FIGURE 12.24 Excel Options—Camera Icon

Consider the summary report in Figure 12.25.

	J	K	L	M	O	P	Q
1							
2		Month			YTD		
3	Mar-14	Act	Bud	Var	Act	Bud	Var
4	Sales	1,500	1,200	300	12,900	12,500	400
5	COS	1,200	1,000	-200	10,100	10,600	500
6	GM	300	200	100	2,800	1,900	900
7	O/H	175	125	-50	1,650	1,200	-450
8	**NP**	**125**	**75**	**50**	**1,150**	**700**	**1,350**
9	**GM %**	**20.0%**	**16.7%**	**3.3%**	**22%**	**15%**	**7%**
10	**NP %**	**8.3%**	**6.3%**	**2.1%**	**9%**	**6%**	**3%**

FIGURE 12.25 Summary Report

To place this report anywhere on any sheet, you simply select the range J2:Q10 and click the Camera icon. Then go to the sheet where you want to paste the report and draw a small square with the mouse (the cursor is in the crosshair shape). This creates a linked picture. Figure 12.26 shows the picture pasted below the existing report.

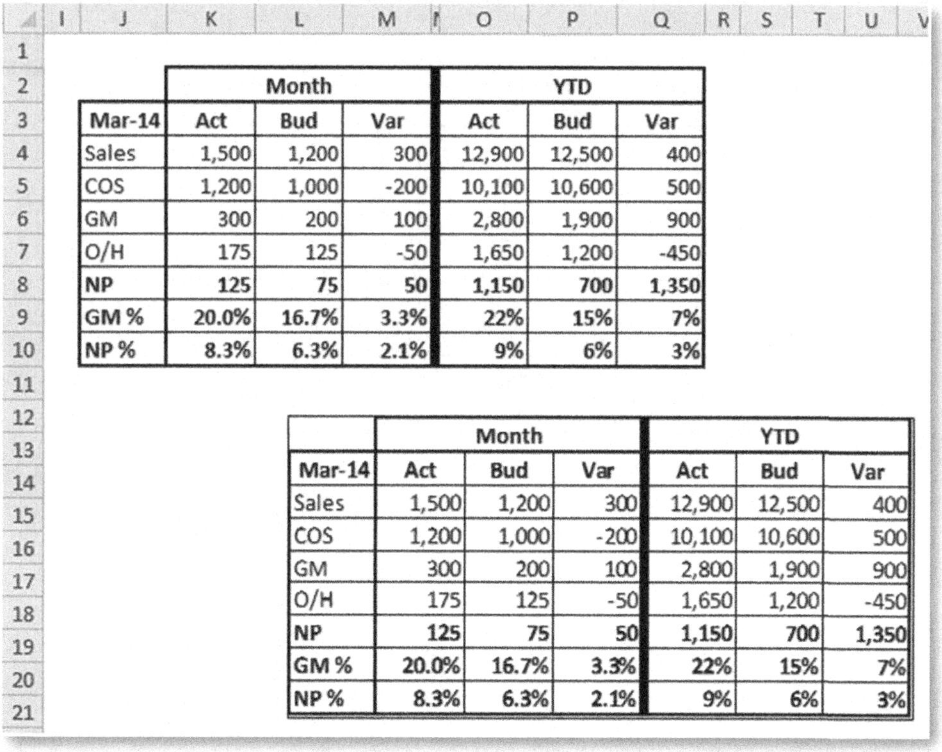

	Month			YTD		
Mar-14	Act	Bud	Var	Act	Bud	Var
Sales	1,500	1,200	300	12,900	12,500	400
COS	1,200	1,000	-200	10,100	10,600	500
GM	300	200	100	2,800	1,900	900
O/H	175	125	-50	1,650	1,200	-450
NP	**125**	**75**	**50**	**1,150**	**700**	**1,350**
GM %	**20.0%**	**16.7%**	**3.3%**	**22%**	**15%**	**7%**
NP %	**8.3%**	**6.3%**	**2.1%**	**9%**	**6%**	**3%**

	Month			YTD		
Mar-14	Act	Bud	Var	Act	Bud	Var
Sales	1,500	1,200	300	12,900	12,500	400
COS	1,200	1,000	-200	10,100	10,600	500
GM	300	200	100	2,800	1,900	900
O/H	175	125	-50	1,650	1,200	-450
NP	**125**	**75**	**50**	**1,150**	**700**	**1,350**
GM %	**20.0%**	**16.7%**	**3.3%**	**22%**	**15%**	**7%**
NP %	**8.3%**	**6.3%**	**2.1%**	**9%**	**6%**	**3%**

FIGURE 12.26 Summary Report Copy

Note that the bottom version doesn't line up with the rows or columns. Also note that there is a line around the whole image. That is the default setting. To remove the line, right-click the image and choose Format Picture, select Line Color on the left and then No line on the right, and click Close.

If you draw the picture on the current sheet, you can't then copy the picture and paste it onto another sheet. You must initially draw it on the sheet you want to use it on.

If you change the sizes of, or insert, columns or rows in the original range, it will affect the linked picture, and you might have to do the paste again to correct it.

You can modify the size of the picture, just like any other image. If you use one of the corner handles to resize the picture, it will maintain its proportions (see Figure 12.27).

When the picture is selected, the Formula Bar displays the range reference of the original report. Modifying that range will modify the image displayed in Figure 12.28.

WARNING: Calculation Issue with Linked Pictures

I have found that using a lot of linked pictures can affect calculation time, even on the latest PCs. Use this feature sparingly.

Whenever you work with images in Excel, it can affect file size as well.

	Month			YTD		
Mar-14	Act	Bud	Var	Act	Bud	Var
Sales	1,500	1,200	300	12,900	12,500	400
COS	1,200	1,000	-200	10,100	10,600	500
GM	300	200	100	2,800	1,900	900
O/H	175	125	-50	1,650	1,200	-450
NP	**125**	**75**	**50**	**1,150**	**700**	**1,350**
GM %	**20.0%**	**16.7%**	**3.3%**	**22%**	**15%**	**7%**
NP %	**8.3%**	**6.3%**	**2.1%**	**9%**	**6%**	**3%**

	Month			YTD		
Mar-14	Act	Bud	Var	Act	Bud	Var
Sales	1,500	1,200	300	12,900	12,500	400
COS	1,200	1,000	-200	10,100	10,600	500
GM	300	200	100	2,800	1,900	900
O/H	175	125	-50	1,650	1,200	-450
NP	125	75	50	1,150	700	1,350
GM %	20.0%	16.7%	3.3%	22%	15%	7%
NP %	8.3%	6.3%	2.1%	9%	6%	3%

FIGURE 12.27 Reduced-Size Picture Report

fx =$J$2:$Q$10

L	M	O	P	Q
16.7%	3.3%	22%	15%	7%
6.3%	2.1%	9%	6%	3%

	Month			YTD		
Mar-14	Act	Bud	Var	Act	Bud	Var
Sales	1,500	1,200	300	12,900	12,500	400
COS	1,200	1,000	-200	10,100	10,600	500
GM	300	200	100	2,800	1,900	900
O/H	175	125	-50	1,650	1,200	-450
NP	125	75	50	1,150	700	1,350
GM %	20.0%	16.7%	3.3%	22%	15%	7%
NP %	8.3%	6.3%	2.1%	9%	6%	3%

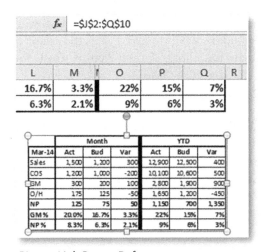

FIGURE 12.28 Paste Picture Link Range Reference

If you delete the range, it will stop the picture from updating and will convert it into a standard image.

When you draw the picture on another sheet, this reference will include the sheet name.

Dynamic Pictures

There is a technique that allows you to create a flexible image. It uses the INDIRECT function and three sets of range names.

Let's say you have eight panels set up on your dashboard sheet to display eight separate reports or charts. You might have a total of 16 possible reports or charts already created, and you want the ability to mix and match these reports or charts on the dashboard sheet.

The first range name is the input cell from which you select the image to display. What you select is the range name for the image.

The second set of range names defines where each of the images is.

The third set of range names uses the INDIRECT function to define the range reference used in the linked picture reference in the Formula Bar.

For the demonstration, I have four reports to choose from and one panel to populate with a report. I have used the Camera icon to create a linked picture of the North report (N2:P5) within the grey panel. Figure 12.29 shows the structure of the example.

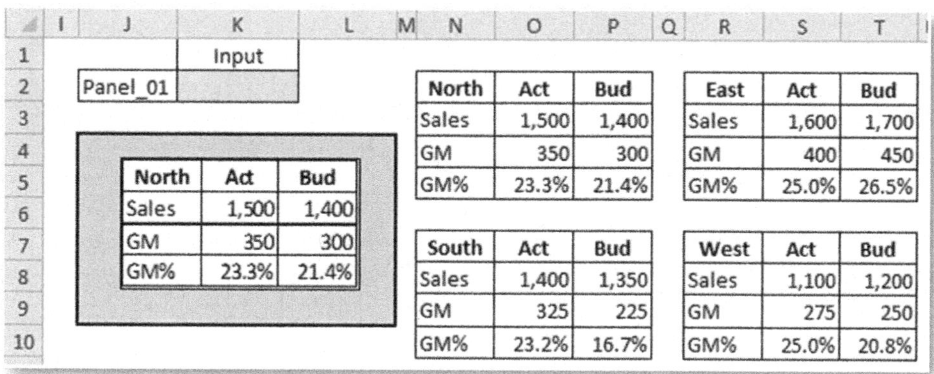

J	K
	Input
Panel_01	

North	Act	Bud
Sales	1,500	1,400
GM	350	300
GM%	23.3%	21.4%

North	Act	Bud
Sales	1,500	1,400
GM	350	300
GM%	23.3%	21.4%

East	Act	Bud
Sales	1,600	1,700
GM	400	450
GM%	25.0%	26.5%

South	Act	Bud
Sales	1,400	1,350
GM	325	225
GM%	23.2%	16.7%

West	Act	Bud
Sales	1,100	1,200
GM	275	250
GM%	25.0%	20.8%

FIGURE 12.29 Dynamic Picture Link System

Each of the small reports on the right is named. The names are rng_North, rng_South, rng_East, and rng_West.

Cell K2 is named Panel_01. In this cell we will type the range name we want displayed in the linked picture. To display the West report, we type rng_West in cell K2.

The final range name we need will convert the entry in K2 into a reference that the linked picture can use. This has to be created by using the Define Name option (see Figure 12.30). The range name is Panel_01_Rng, and the formula is

```
=INDIRECT(Panel_01)
```

The INDIRECT function converts the text from cell K2 (named Panel_01) into the range of the same name.

To complete the report, you select the linked picture and replace the range reference in the Formula Bar with the range name =Panel_01_Rng (see Figure 12.31).

Changing cell K2 updates the linked picture (see Figure 12.32).

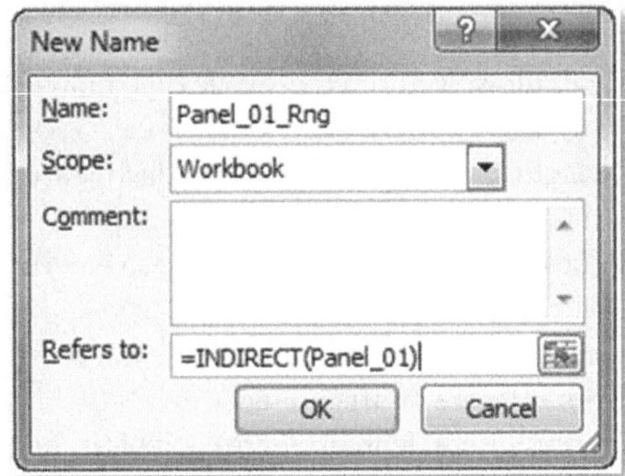

FIGURE 12.30 INDIRECT Function Used with Range Name

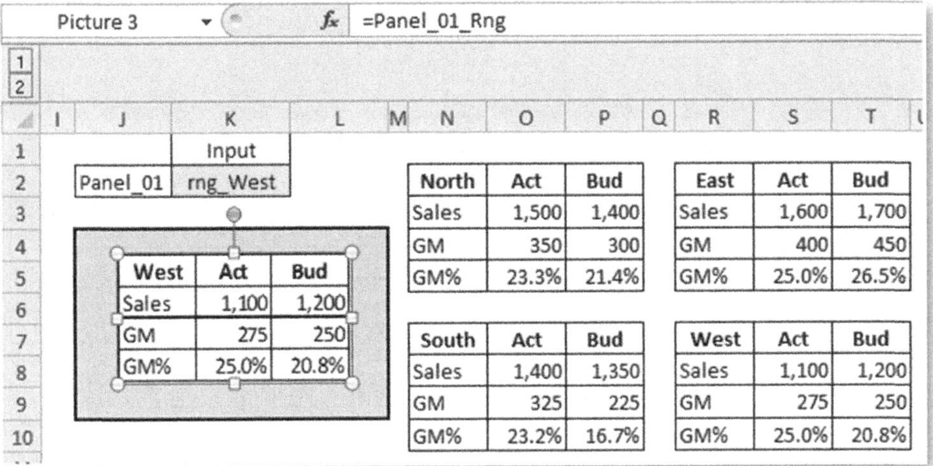

FIGURE 12.31 Completed Dynamic Picture Link System

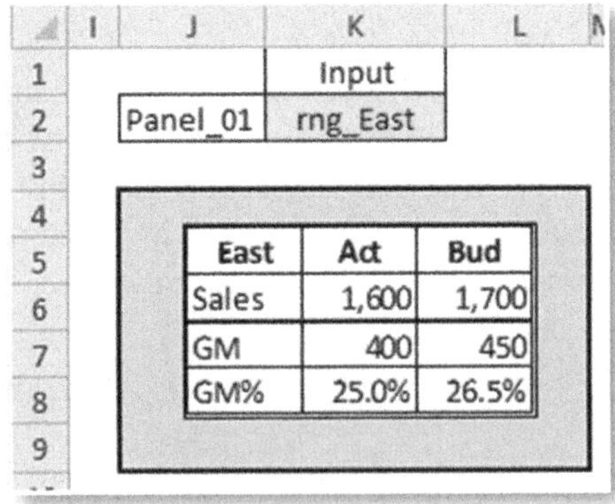

FIGURE 12.32 Dynamic Picture Link Updated

This demonstration used a range that contained a report. If the range had a chart, then the chart would have displayed in the linked picture. Make sure the chart fits completely within the range.

Linked Text Boxes

In the same way that an image can be linked to a range, you can also link a text box to the contents of a cell.

If you have a metric that is best displayed as a number, you can use a text box to make it more prominent on the dashboard without having to change row or column sizes.

To link a text box to a cell, draw the text box, then click inside the Formula Bar while the text box is still selected. Press the equal sign key, use the mouse to select the cell you want to link to, and press Enter. Figure 12.33 shows an example.

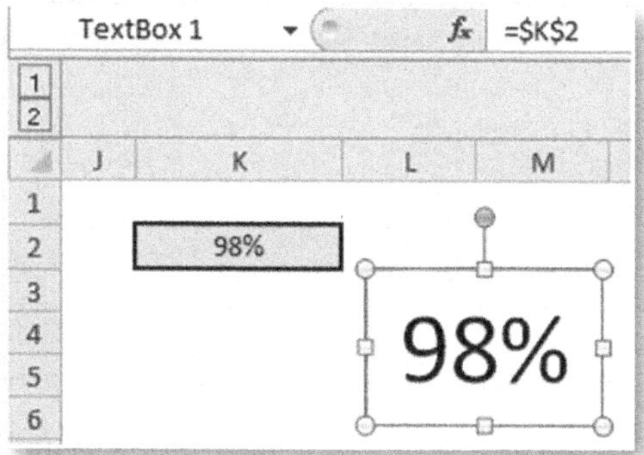

FIGURE 12.33 Linked Text Box

The text box can be resized or moved anywhere on the sheet, and you can amend the font size and colour. You can only link a text box to a cell on the current sheet.

If you use the Alt + Enter shortcut to insert a line break within the cell, it will be duplicated in the text box (see Figure 12.34).

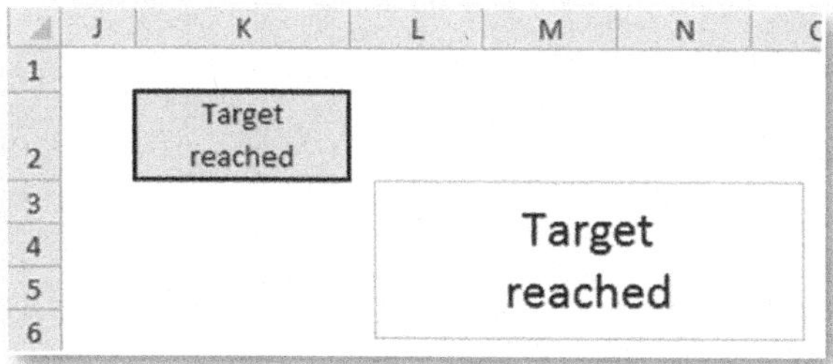

FIGURE 12.34 Linked Text Box with a Line Break

For the placement of text on a dashboard, Excel's grid layout isn't flexible. Row height and column width are fixed, so if you need to place text in specific places, it may be easier to use text boxes. For example, if the left of your dashboard is dedicated to one aspect of the organisation such as sales, and the right side is dedicated to production, there can be a conflict between the layout requirements.

It could be more useful to use the underlying sheet grid more like graph paper, which has columns and rows of the same height and width. You can then use linked text boxes for most of your descriptions. In the next section we will discuss how you can line up and group graphic objects.

Working with Graphics

Charts, text boxes, and images are all graphic objects and can all be controlled with the Format Ribbon tab under Drawing Tools. This displays when a text box is selected or when you select multiple graphic objects.

The useful tools are all on the right side of the tab (see Figure 12.35).

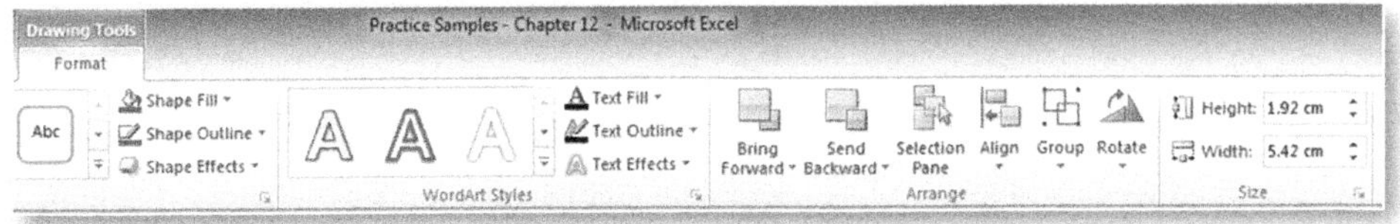

FIGURE 12.35 Drawing Tools Format Ribbon Tab

The Align, Group, and Size icons are all useful when creating the parts of a dashboard.

Let us return to our text box example in Figure 12.33. We can add a heading to the linked text box by using another text box. This allows us to use different font sizes in each text box.

Hold down the Ctrl key and use the mouse to click on the text box. Make sure you click on the border of the text box to select it.

If the border of the text box is a dotted line after you select it, then you have selected the contents of the text box rather than the text box itself. If the border is a solid line, you have selected the text box. Figure 12.36 shows the difference.

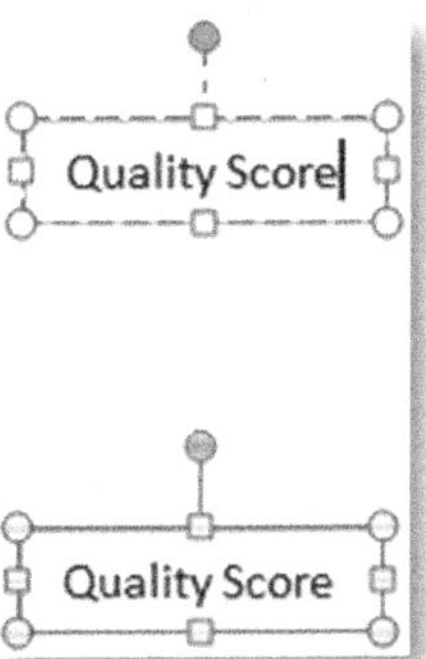

FIGURE 12.36 Text Box Contents (Top), Text Box (Bottom)

Another way to select a lot of graphics in one step is to use the Select Objects arrow, which is an option in the Find & Select icon drop-down on the far right of the Home Ribbon tab (see Figure 12.37).

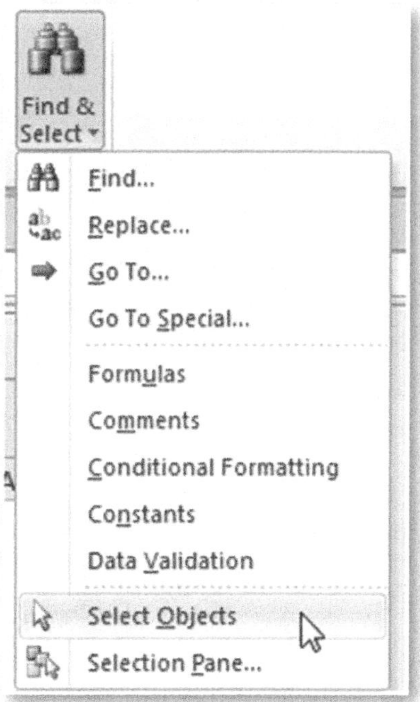

FIGURE 12.37 Select Objects Icon

This arrow mouse cursor allows you to use the mouse to select an area around the objects to select them all. This can be quicker for multiple objects than the Ctrl key.

To use two text boxes to display a Quality Score, follow the steps listed below. All icons relate to the Format tab, as was shown in Figure 12.35. Figure 12.38 shows images of the four steps.

1. Place the heading text box above the linked text box.
2. Line up the text boxes. With both text boxes selected, click the Align icon and select Align Left.
3. Use the Width box and enter 3 (for 3 centimetres). Amend as required.
4. Group the text boxes so that they can be handled as one object. Click the Group icon drop-down list and choose the Group option.

Once the two text boxes are grouped, you can move them around as if they were one.

The Align and Resize options can be used on selected charts to create perfectly aligned and identically sized charts.

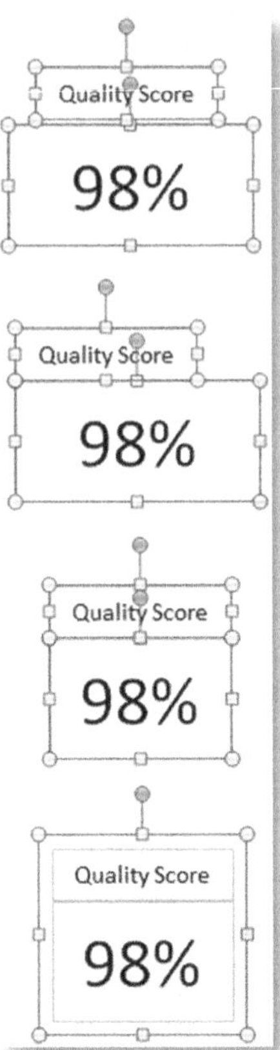

FIGURE 12.38 Grouping Two Text Boxes Together

Conditional Formats

We saw in the previous chapter that conditional formats have a number of features that work well with a dashboard structure. Data Bars, Color Scales, and Icon Sets are all worthwhile additions to your dashboard report toolbox.

Consider whether a measure that uses a chart can be represented by a conditionally formatted cell. If the measure is within acceptable parameters, it could show green or a checkmark. If it is outside those parameters, it could show an X or an exclamation point, which means that further investigation may be required.

There could be more detailed supporting sheets to allow further investigation for any measures that fall outside expected parameters.

Sparkline Charts

Sparkline charts were included as a built-in feature in Excel 2010. Before that, they were available only as third-party add-ins.

A Sparkline is a small cell-based chart. There are three types: column, line, and win/loss.

The column and line types are the same as normal charts. The win/loss Sparkline has an above-the-line column for a positive figure and a below-the-line column for a negative figure. All the columns are exactly the same size. So a positive value of 10 will have the same column height as a positive value of 1,000.

The win/loss is used for simple yes-no or true-false type charting—for example, charting whether a weekly production target was met.

Sparkline charts have very basic and limited options. You can plot only one measure. If the chart you require is a simple column or line chart, you could use a Sparkline chart to display the results. Although Sparkline charts have limited usage, for straightforward results they are easy to create and very small.

Another advantage is that since they are cell-based, it is possible to use a conditional format with them. This can be used to bring attention to the chart if something is wrong.

The report in Figure 12.39 requires charts in Column T.

	I	J	K	L	M	N	O	P	Q	R	S	T
6												
7		Production Volumes	S	M	T	W	T	F	S	Avg	Target	
8		Widgets	100	110	120	150	100	90	70	106	110	
9		Gadgets	100	150	210	220	240	200	50	167	150	
10		Total	200	260	330	370	340	290	120	273	260	

FIGURE 12.39 Weekly Production Report

To insert a Sparkline chart, click the cell you want to insert the chart into, click the Insert Ribbon tab, and choose the Sparkline chart to use. Use the mouse to select the data range (see Figure 12.40).

The range must be one row high or one column wide. The reference can be on another sheet. If you leave the reference as a relative reference, then, as with a relative formula, you will be able to copy the chart down and the references will change. Click OK to accept.

Always check the chart. In Figure 12.41, it is not using a zero-based vertical axis.

The last entry of 70 is shown as a very small column. To fix this, click the Sparkline cell and click the Design Ribbon tab (this is dedicated to Sparklines). Click the Axis drop-down list, select the Custom Value option in Minimum Section, change the value to 0, and click OK (see Figure 12.42).

The maximum value for the vertical axis is determined by the data. If you need two or more Sparkline charts to have the same minimum and maximum axis values, you need to set the values on the first chart and then copy and paste to create the other charts.

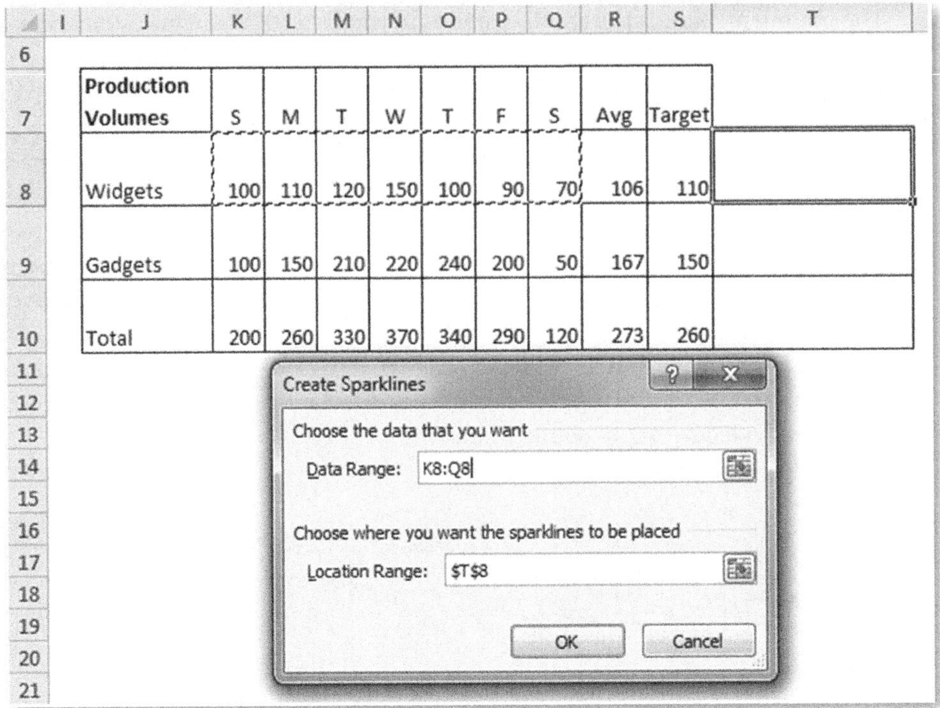

Production Volumes	S	M	T	W	T	F	S	Avg	Target
Widgets	100	110	120	150	100	90	70	106	110
Gadgets	100	150	210	220	240	200	50	167	150
Total	200	260	330	370	340	290	120	273	260

FIGURE 12.40 Create Sparklines Dialog Box

Production Volumes	S	M	T	W	T	F	S	Avg	Target
Widgets	100	110	120	150	100	90	70	106	110

FIGURE 12.41 Sparkline Axis Issue

The Show section of the Design Ribbon tab has the options you can use with the Sparkline chart. The High and Low options are useful.

Similar to the default setting on normal charts, if you hide the data, the Sparkline data will also be hidden. To change this setting for Sparkline charts, click the Edit Data drop-down list on the far left of the Design Ribbon tab and select the Hidden and Empty Cells option. This is the same dialog box that was shown for normal charts in Figure 12.17.

As mentioned earlier, we can add a conditional format to a cell containing a Sparkline chart. In this case, if the daily average in column R is below the target value in column S, we want the cell to have a pink background.

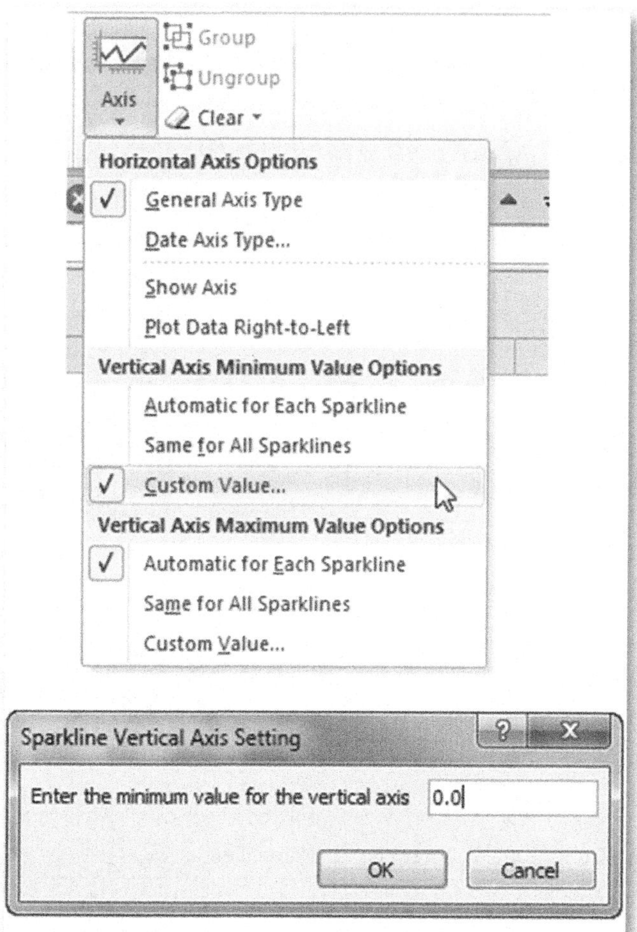

FIGURE 12.42 Sparkline Axis Settings

Figure 12.43 shows the conditional format being applied to a Sparkline cell and the result. Note that the value columns have been hidden and the High and Low options have been applied.

When you right-click a Sparkline cell, there is a Sparklines option on the menu (see Figure 12.44).

You can group Sparkline cells so that changing an option in one cell (chart) changes the others.

Small Charts

If you need a more complicated small chart than a Sparkline chart, then you can use a normal chart. Simply strip away most of the elements to leave a small chart that still delivers a message.

Charts on dashboards tend to be very basic. In most cases you can delete most of the chart elements because there are assumptions inherent in the dashboard.

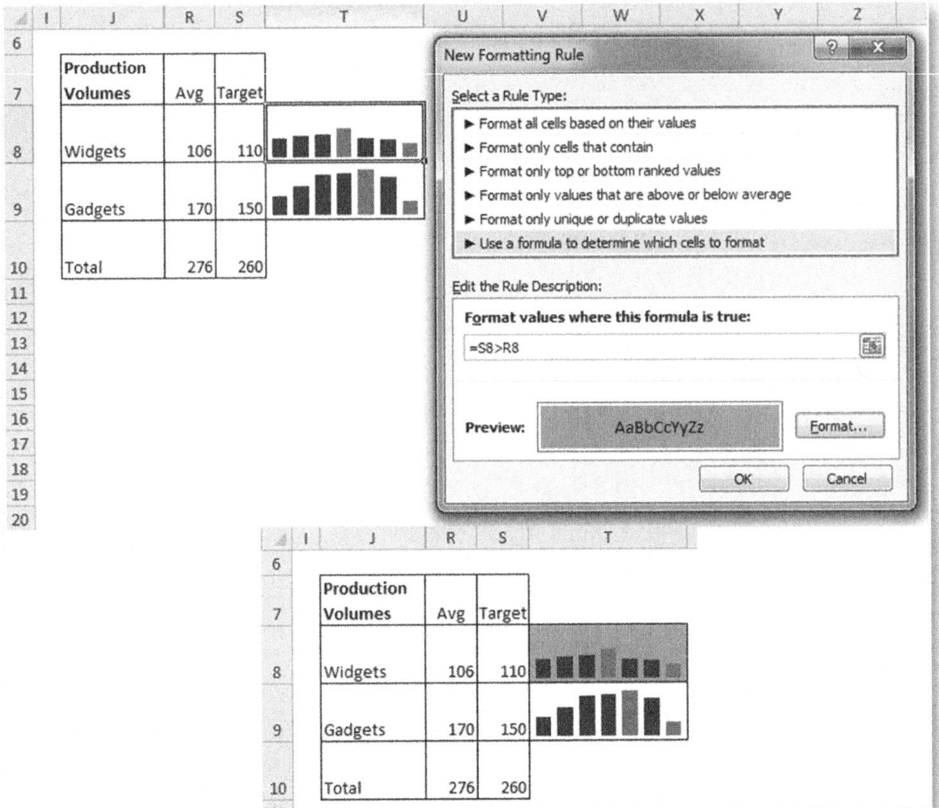

FIGURE 12.43 Conditional Format in a Sparkline Cell

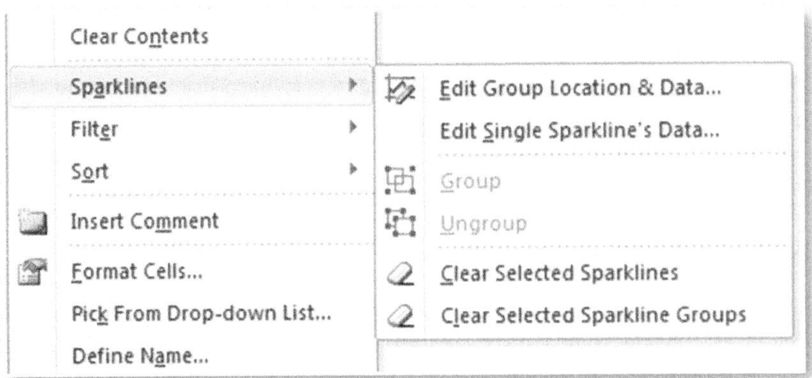

FIGURE 12.44 Sparkline Options—Right-Click

A convention may be set for the whole dashboard that all actuals are blue and all budgets are red. The dashboard could be run weekly so that all charts have seven days of results. You could also have sections of the dashboard dedicated to specific periods or comparison.

This means you can remove the legend, possibly the horizontal axis, and even the vertical axis in many cases. The chart titles can be removed because the chart will be near a cell label describing it. Chart titles are hard to control on small charts.

In many cases you may just be left with the plot area and the data series on the chart.

TEXT IN A CHART

Adding text to a chart is an effective way to draw attention to a specific issue, or to add a note explaining a particular data point or points.

Adding a text message to a chart is a two-stage process. First, draw a text box on the chart and link it to a cell (see Figure 12.45).

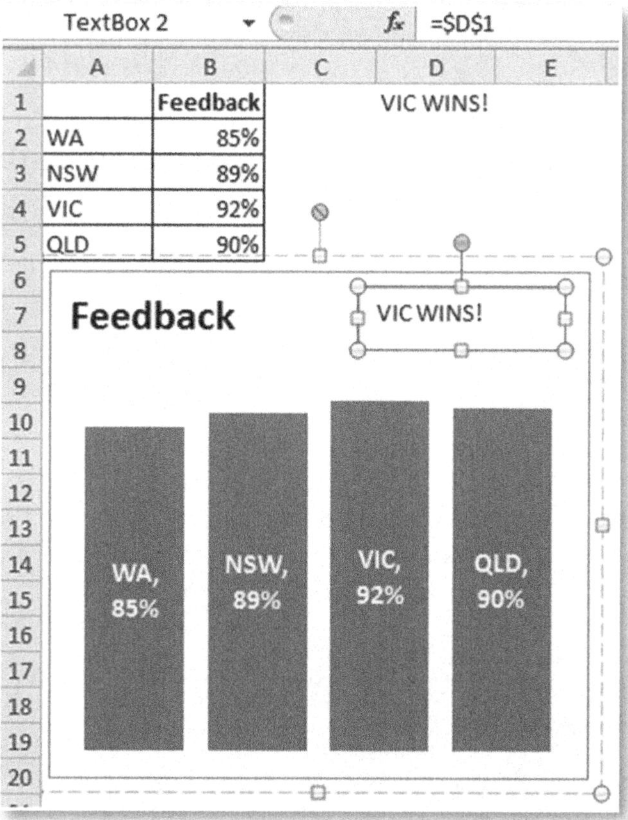

FIGURE 12.45 Chart and Text Box

Use the Select Object icon or the mouse to select both the chart and the text box. Click the Format Ribbon tab, click the Group drop-down list, and select Group.

When you move the chart, the text box will move with it.

THE DATA SERIES FORMULA

When dealing with charts it is important to understand the SERIES formula. The SERIES formula appears in the Formula Bar when a data series is selected. This looks like a function, but it does not always act like a normal function, and you can cause errors in the chart by editing and making a mistake in the SERIES formula. Each data series on the chart has its own SERIES function.

Syntax

=SERIES (Series_Name, Category_Labels, Values, Order, Sizes)
Series_Name (optional) is a reference to a cell that contains the name of the series.
Category_Labels (optional) is a range reference to the value labels.
Values is a range reference to the values to plot.
Order is a positive integer that is the sequence number of the data series within the chart.
Sizes (bubble charts only) is a reference of the value used for the bubble size.

Example

The following SERIES formula is shown in Figure 12.46.

```
=SERIES(Report!$B$1,Report!$A$2:$A$5,Report!$B$2:$B$5,1)
```

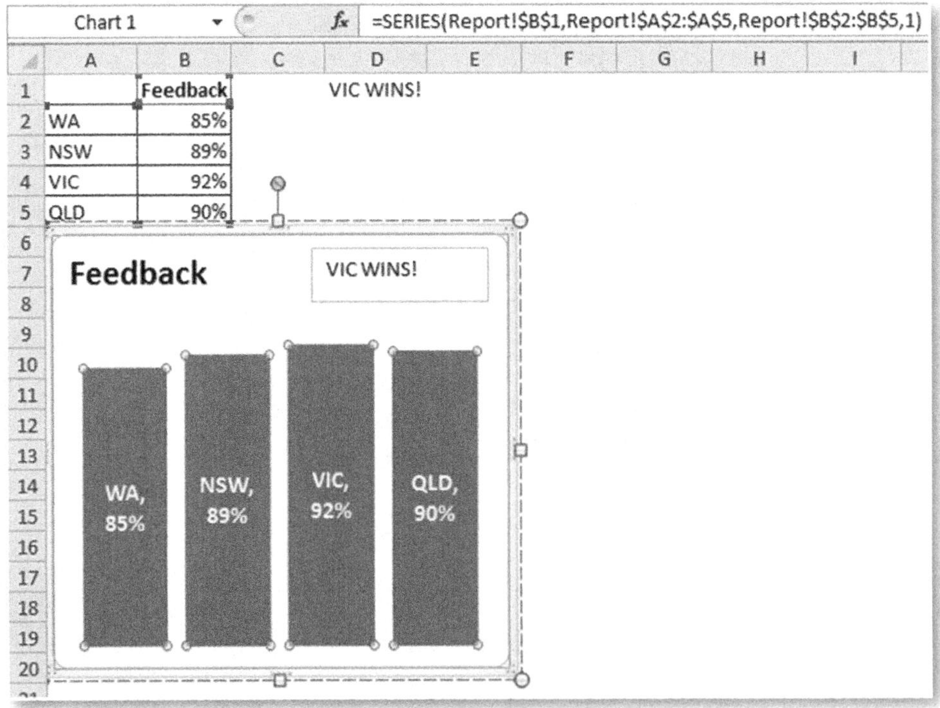

FIGURE 12.46 SERIES Formula Example

- Report!$B$1 (Series_Name)
- Report!$A$2:$A$5 (Category_Labels)
- Report!$B$2:$B$5 (Values)
- 1 (Order)

Note that the sheet names are used in the formula. You must always include the sheet name in the references when dealing with the SERIES formula.

You can amend the data series by amending its SERIES formula in the Formula Bar. In some cases this can be the quickest way to amend a chart linked to another sheet.

BEFORE AND AFTER CHARTS

Following are three comparison charts that demonstrate some of the concepts discussed in this chapter.

Figure 12.47 shows a column chart comparison.

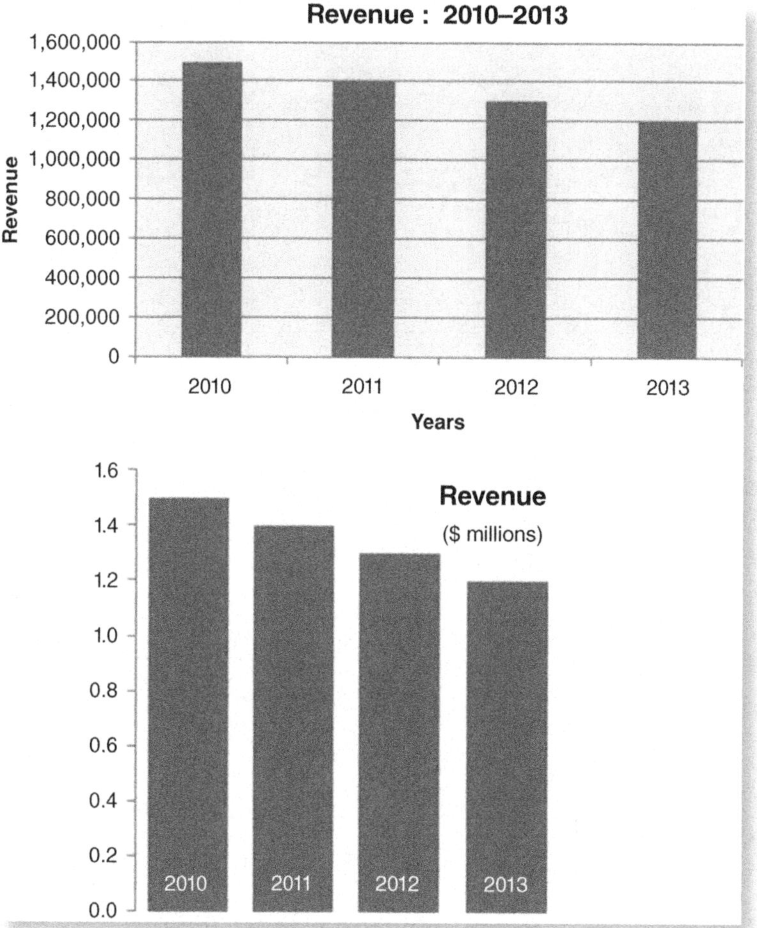

FIGURE 12.47 Column Chart Comparison

Figure 12.47 Commentary

- Remove the plot area colour and the gridlines.
- Reduce the gap between the columns.
- Remove the horizontal axis and use a data label to insert the category name at the base of the column.
- Use a custom number format on the vertical axis to show millions.
- Remove axis titles.

Figure 12.48 shows a line chart comparison.

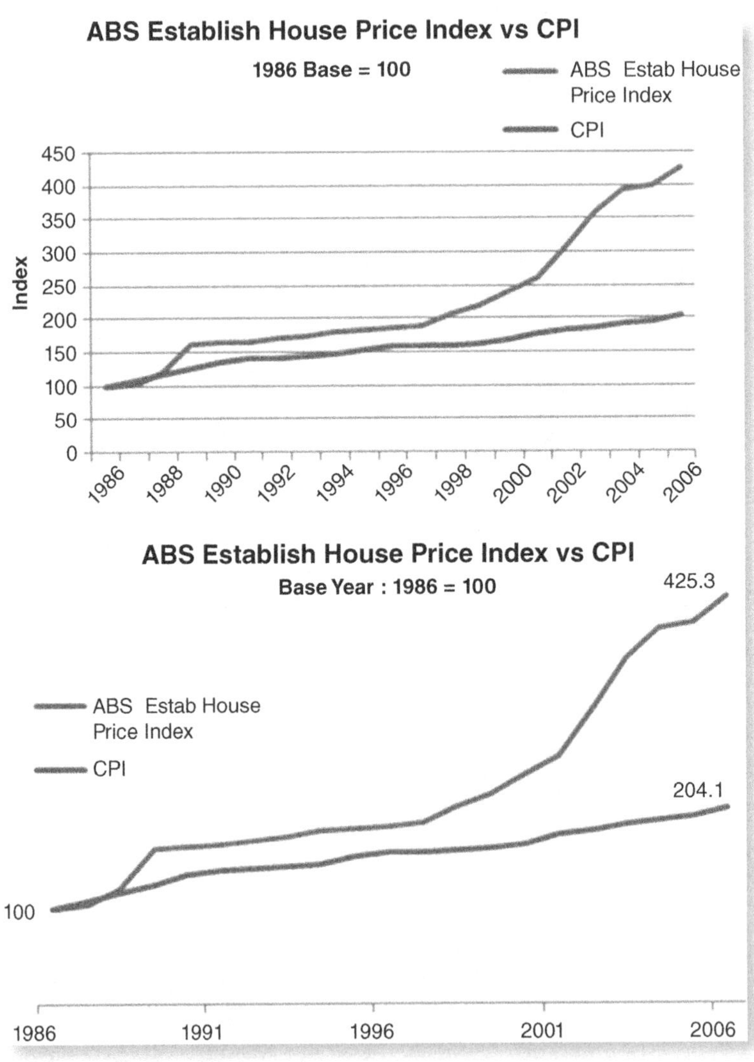

FIGURE 12.48 Line Chart Comparison

Figure 12.48 Commentary

- Remove the vertical axis.
- Remove the gridlines.
- Add data labels for the starting and ending values.
- Change the scale of the horizontal axis to a five-year gap.
- Move the legend to the white space.

Figure 12.49 compares a column chart with a bar chart.

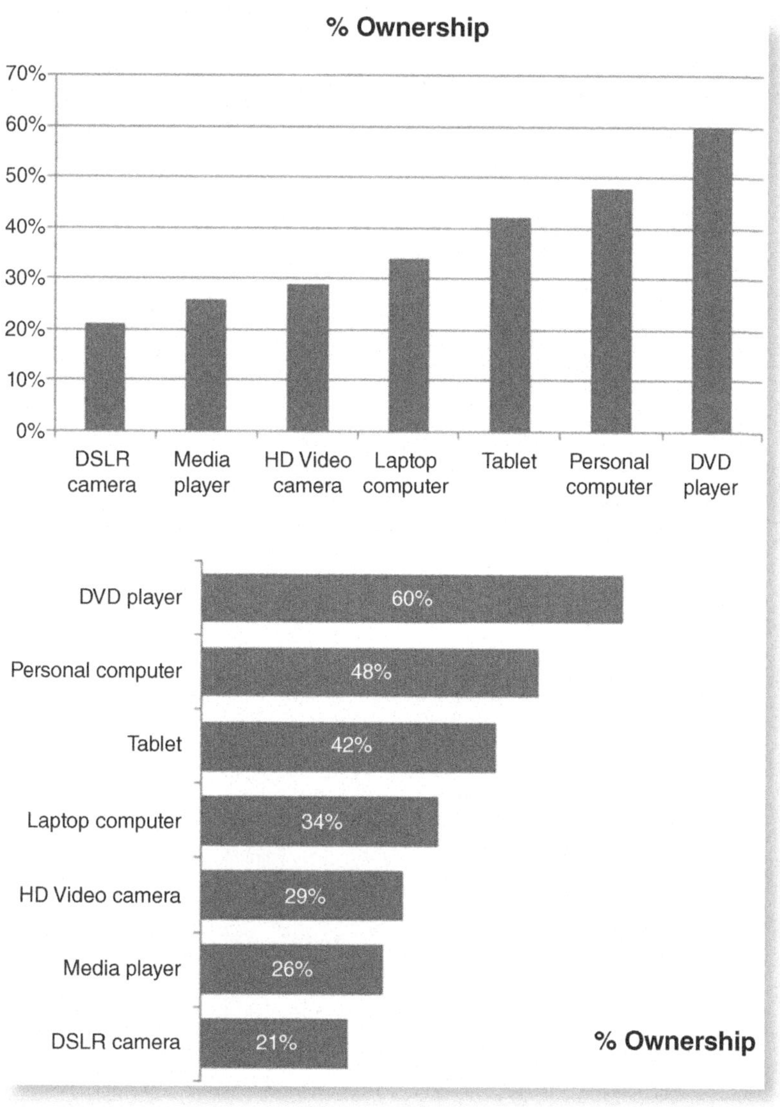

FIGURE 12.49 Column versus Bar Chart

Figure 12.49 Commentary

- Note that both charts use sorted data.
- Switch the chart from a column chart to a bar chart.
- Remove the value percentage axis.
- Insert data labels with values.
- Reduce the gap between the bars.
- Move the chart title to the white space.

CHAPTER THIRTEEN

13 Quality Control: Report Validation

THE CARPENTER'S CREED IS "MEASURE TWICE, cut once." This may be adapted for Excel reporting to "check twice, report once."

Spreadsheets have a reputation for containing errors. Your goal, as a developer, is to reduce or eliminate errors by incorporating validation checks that identify errors and communicate them to the user.

IDENTIFYING ERRORS

Accountants need no convincing to make sure that everything balances. As you are building your reporting model, you will come across balancing points. These are values that should equal another value or that should be the total of a series of values.

These balancing points should become the basis for your validation checks. They will include the standard balance-sheet balance check and the trial-balance balance check. You should also check any detailed values against their overall total from the original data.

TRUE and FALSE

I recommend using standard logic formulas, as explained in Chapter 8, to identify whether a validation has been met. These calculations display TRUE or FALSE. Logic formulas calculate more quickly than their corresponding IF function, which displays OK or Error.

I recommend using TRUE if a validation has been met and FALSE if it hasn't. I tend to use positive labels on my validation cells, such as Balance Sheet Balances or Detail = Total Sales. The word TRUE confirms those statements.

Centralised Validations

I recommend including validations on the sheets where they occur and then centralising them on a single sheet. The validation cells on the sheet become like helper cells, so they can be hidden in the normal display of the report.

In a balancing validation it can be a good idea to have a two-stage validation. Include a cell that calculates the difference between the two values. The validation cell then checks that cell. If it is 0 (or less than 1 if rounding is involved), then TRUE is displayed.

If a balance check is wrong, the first thing you want to know is how much the difference is. There may be multiple entries causing the difference, but knowing the size of the difference gives you a starting point in tracking it down.

I also recommend including validations as you develop the model. Do not leave them to the end of the development process. As you build the model, you need to be thinking about what could go wrong. Then you need to develop a validation to identify when that happens.

Using logic formulas, as discussed in Chapter 8, simplifies the creation of validations and also simplifies the formulas for analysing large numbers of validations.

Consider having a dedicated column in the workings columns on the left side for validations.

When dealing with months going across the page, you will normally have a section of rows that perform the validations. Placing them at the top or the bottom of the report keeps them out of the way. If you need to place them in the middle of the report, use grouping to hide them.

When centralising validations, you can set up a system that groups similar validations in sections and create a hierarchy of validations. This can make it easier to see where the errors are. This also allows you to add instructions to the user to explain what processes have to be taken to investigate and fix certain validation errors.

Some validation errors may flow through to many validations. If a new balance sheet code is included in the data, but not mapped in the tables sheet, this will cause a balance-sheet validation error and a new-code validation error. Fixing the new-code error should fix the balance-sheet validation error.

I also recommend having an overall validation cell that you can link to and display on most of the sheets in the reporting model. This overall validation may use the words OK and Error as well as green or red conditional formatting to increase visibility.

Consider adding the validation message to the report heading if the report is out of balance. This handles the case when a report is printed before the validation has been noticed or rectified.

VALIDATIONS

From experience I have found that the validation section is a very important part of the model. When you are developing a reporting model, it is important to constantly monitor the overall validation.

Rounding

Rounding usually causes issues in Excel when you are confirming that the values balance. Most reports will be rounded to at least dollars, and some reports are rounded to thousands or millions of dollars.

When you are confirming whether a rounded value and a nonrounded value are balancing, the following formula is commonly used:

```
=ABS(B1-A1)=<1
```

Assume that A1 is the balancing value. B1 has been rounded, but it should equal A1. The ABS function converts all negative values to positive values. This means that you can test against a single number instead of worrying whether a value is between 1 and –1. When you use the ABS function to calculate the difference, it doesn't matter whether you subtract A1 from B1, or B1 from A1.

This formula will display TRUE when A1 and B1 are within 1 of each other and FALSE when they are not. The value of 1 may be replaced by a cell reference that contains 1 or a range name.

Tolerances

When you are working with single-month values, rounded results should be within one of the expected values. When you are dealing with values that may have been rounded multiple times, such as checking the year-to-date value total against the rounded month totals over a number of months, you may need to apply a tolerance value.

Tolerance values are commonly used when validating budgets. You may have a total annual expense for a cost item. When the item's value is allocated and rounded across the 12 months, it can be as much as 12 different from the total value.

In these cases, rather than expecting the value to be within 1 of the expected value, you will need to compare it against a tolerance value. You may enter this value in a cell, name that cell, and use the named range in the formula.

The rounding formula for validations shown earlier can be amended to handle tolerances. Assuming that the range name for the tolerance cell is Tolerance, the formula would be

```
=ABS(B1-A1)=<Tolerance
```

Data Validations

Excel's Data Validation feature, which enables in-cell drop-down lists and the ability to limit inputs, does have a major flaw. It is possible to paste a value into a data validation cell without the data validation criteria being triggered. This means that you need a backup system for your data validation cells to identify when one of the cells is not valid.

When using the in-cell drop-down list, you can use the COUNTIF function to confirm whether the cell's entry is in the list's range. If the in-cell drop-down list is in cell B3 and the list is named Departments, the following formula will display TRUE when the cell entry is valid and FALSE when it isn't:

```
=COUNTIF(Departments,B3)>0
```

You will need to develop validations for other types of data validations as well—for example, dates ranges, value ranges, and even to make sure that a cell has a value if it is a required value. The AND function is useful for these types of validations.

ERROR TRACKING

During the developmental phase, an error could be a design error that has to be corrected. During the normal operation of the reporting model, an error should be easily identified and easily corrected.

In the development phase, when your formulas are not final, there are a number of features that can help with the analysis and debugging of the formulas. *Debugging* is usually a software term, but debugging formulas is often required in the development phase. IF functions and logic formulas are the most common formulas that require debugging.

The use of helper cells assists in identifying errors. The simpler a formula is, the easier it is to debug. Splitting up complex formulas into helper cells makes it easier to check for logic errors and then to find and correct those errors.

Helper cells should also be employed when a calculation is to be used by a number of subsequent formulas. This means that you have to get the formula right just once, and all the other formulas can rely on it.

Debugging Techniques

There are three built-in features in Excel that can assist you in identifying errors in your formulas.

The F9 Function Key

The F9 key is typically used to calculate the formulas in a file that has the automatic calculation turned off. You can also use the F9 key on part of a formula within the Formula Bar to display the result of that part of the formula.

If a complex formula is returning an error, identifying which part of the formula is at fault can be difficult. Using the F9 key in the Formula Bar can speed up this process.

You can use the mouse to select part of a formula within the Formula Bar. The part you select must be able to be calculated on its own. If you leave out a bracket or a parenthesis, it might not calculate, and Excel will display an error message.

WARNING: F9 in the Formula Bar

After pressing F9, you must press the Esc key to return the formula to normal. If you press Enter, it will leave the result permanently in the formula. You can use the Undo command to fix it if that happens.

Once the part of the formula is selected, pressing F9 will replace the formula with the result (see Figure 13.1).

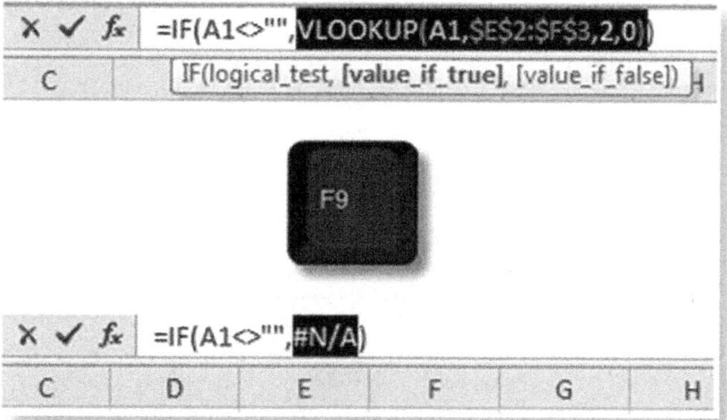

FIGURE 13.1 F9 Used in the Formula Bar

Evaluate Formula

In the Formula Auditing section of the Formulas Ribbon tab, the Evaluate button allows you to step through a formula and monitor the results. It's a more structured method than using the F9 key in the Formula Bar.

You basically work your way through the formula to find errors, check logic assumptions, and confirm that the correct cells are being referred to.

Figure 13.2 shows two tables, which have some duplicated codes. The first table takes precedence when a code is in both tables.

The formula in cell H2 that we will evaluate looks up a value in the first table, and if the code isn't there, it looks it up in the second table. If the code is not in either table, a zero is displayed. The formula in cell H2 is

```
=IFERROR(VLOOKUP(G2,A1:B10,2,0),IFERROR(VLOOKUP(G2,D2:E10,2,0),0))
```

The formula is shown in the Evaluation box. The first reference to cell G2 is underlined. Each time you click the Evaluate button, it works through the formula and evaluates each part in turn. The part of the formula to be evaluated is underlined. The result of the evaluation is shown in italics.

Figure 13.3 shows the six results from the Evaluation box when you click the Evaluate button six times.

Tracing Precedents and Dependents

There are two important concepts to understand when debugging formulas:

1. **Cell precedents.** Only formula cells can have a precedent. Cell precedents are all those cells that are referred to within the formula. A *direct precedent* is a cell that is directly referred to within the formula. An *indirect precedent* is a cell that affects the direct precedent cells but isn't referred to within the formula.

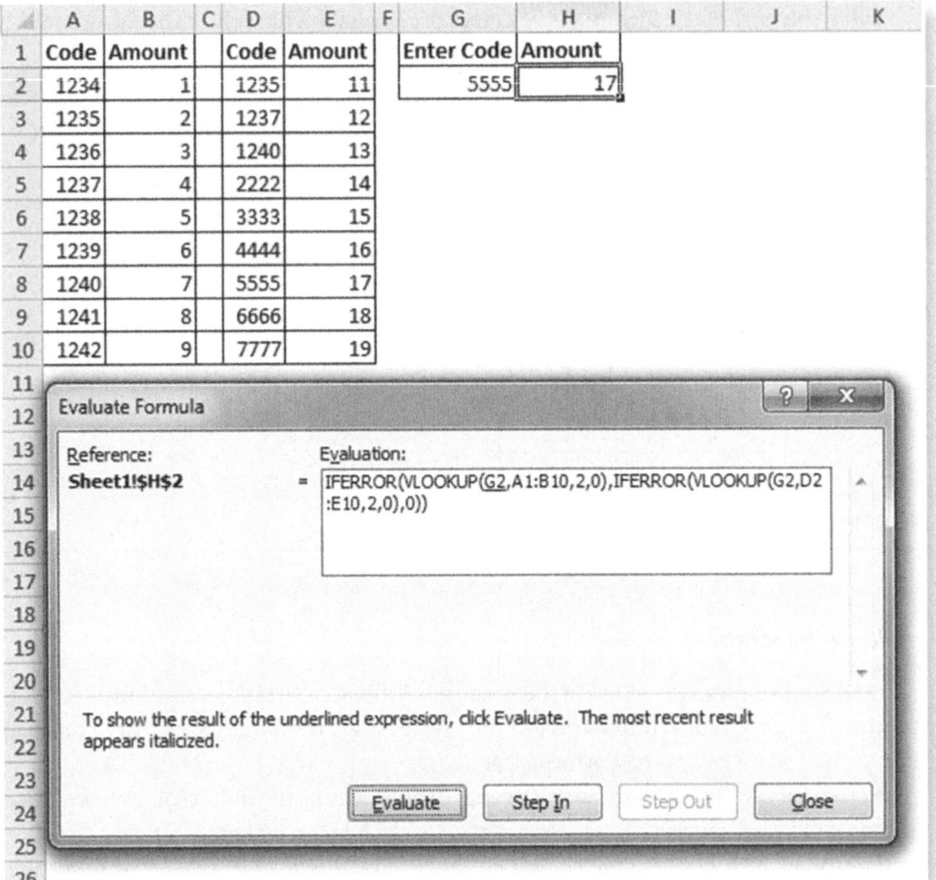

FIGURE 13.2 Evaluate Formula Example

2. **Cell dependents.** These are all the formula cells that refer to the cell being reviewed. There can be a *direct dependent* cell, in which a formula cell refers to the cell being reviewed, or an *indirect dependent* cell, in which one of the dependent cells itself has a dependent cell.

Excel has three buttons in the Formula Auditing section that can help you understand your formulas and their relationships to one another. This can also be useful when you need to modify an existing reporting model that you did not create. These can also help identify where circular reference errors originate. The three buttons are as follows:

1. **Trace Precedents.** This icon will insert blue arrowed lines on the sheet to show you all the cells that the current cell is dependent on. If the cells are on another sheet, then it lists them in a dialog box that allows you to go to those cells.

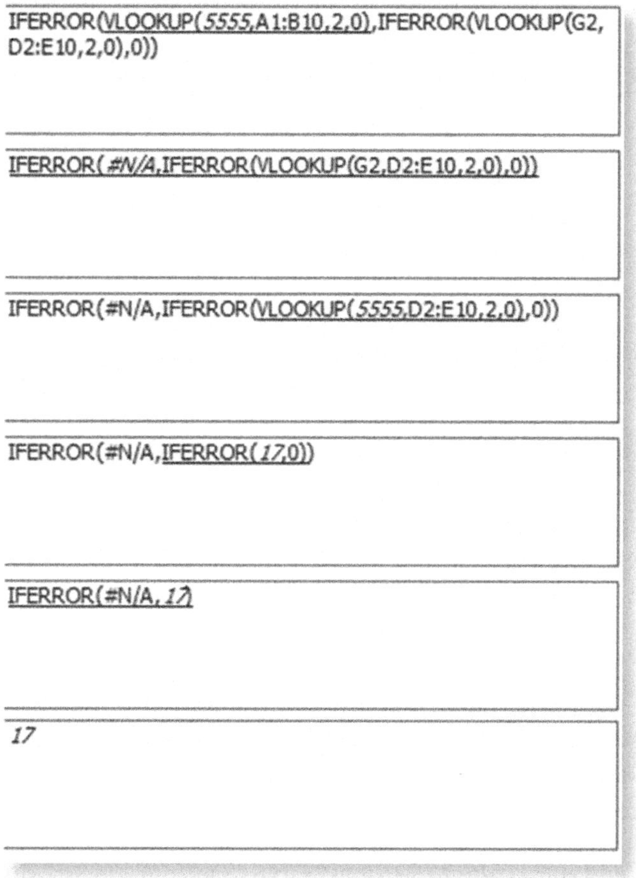

IFERROR(VLOOKUP(5555,A1:B10,2,0),IFERROR(VLOOKUP(G2,D2:E10,2,0),0))

IFERROR(#N/A,IFERROR(VLOOKUP(G2,D2:E10,2,0),0))

IFERROR(#N/A,IFERROR(VLOOKUP(5555,D2:E10,2,0),0))

IFERROR(#N/A,IFERROR(17,0))

IFERROR(#N/A,17)

17

FIGURE 13.3 Evaluate Box Results

2. **Trace Dependents.** This icon will insert blue arrowed lines on the sheet to show you all the cells that are dependent on the current cell. If the cells are on another sheet, then it lists them in a dialog box that allows you to go to those cells. This is handy if you are considering deleting a particular cell.
3. **Remove Arrows.** This icon clears all the blue arrowed lines from the sheet. It is a drop-down item, so you have the option to remove only precedent arrows or only dependents arrows.

WARNING: Deleting Cells

You can use the Trace Dependents icon to identify cells that use a particular cell before deletion. Be aware that this feature doesn't include charts, conditional formats, or data validations that may also refer to the cell.

So even though checking the cell or range before deleting is a good idea, it doesn't cover all the effects of deletion.

In the example from Figure 13.2, I have removed the borders from the ranges. The lines shown in Figure 13.4 are all caused by selecting cell H2 and clicking the Trace Precedents icon.

	A	B	C	D	E	F	G	H
1	Code	Amount		Code	Amount		Enter Code	Amount
2	1234	1		1235	11		5555	17
3	1235	2		1237	12			
4	1236	3		1240	13			
5	1237	4		2222	14			
6	1238	5		3333	15			
7	1239	6		4444	16			
8	1240	7		5555	17			
9	1241	8		6666	18			
10	1242	9		7777	19			

FIGURE 13.4 Trace Precedents Results

There are three small points on cells A1, D2, and G2. These are the starting points of the blue arrowed lines. The formula in H2 refers to two ranges. Cells A1 and D2 are the first cells of each of those ranges, and they are used as the point for starting the line. The ranges are enclosed in blue lines. Cell G2 is a single cell that is referred to and just has the point in the cell.

You can select single cells and click Trace Dependents, as has been done three times in Figure 13.5. This shows three separate lines to the cell that are dependent on those three separate cells.

	A	B	C	D	E	F	G	H
1	Code	Amount		Code	Amount		Enter Code	Amount
2	1234	1		1235	11		5555	17
3	1235	2		1237	12			
4	1236	3		1240	13			
5	1237	4		2222	14			
6	1238	5		3333	15			
7	1239	6		4444	16			
8	1240	7		5555	17			
9	1241	8		6666	18			
10	1242	9		7777	19			

FIGURE 13.5 Trace Dependents Results

You can double-click the blue line to toggle between cells at either end of the line. This is useful when the line goes off the screen.

I amended the formula in cell H2 to also refer to a cell on another sheet. If I click Trace Precedents, it displays a sheet symbol with a black dotted line to show that there is a link outside the sheet. Double-clicking the black dotted line opens the Go To dialog box. You can select the reference and click OK to move to that cell (see Figure 13.6).

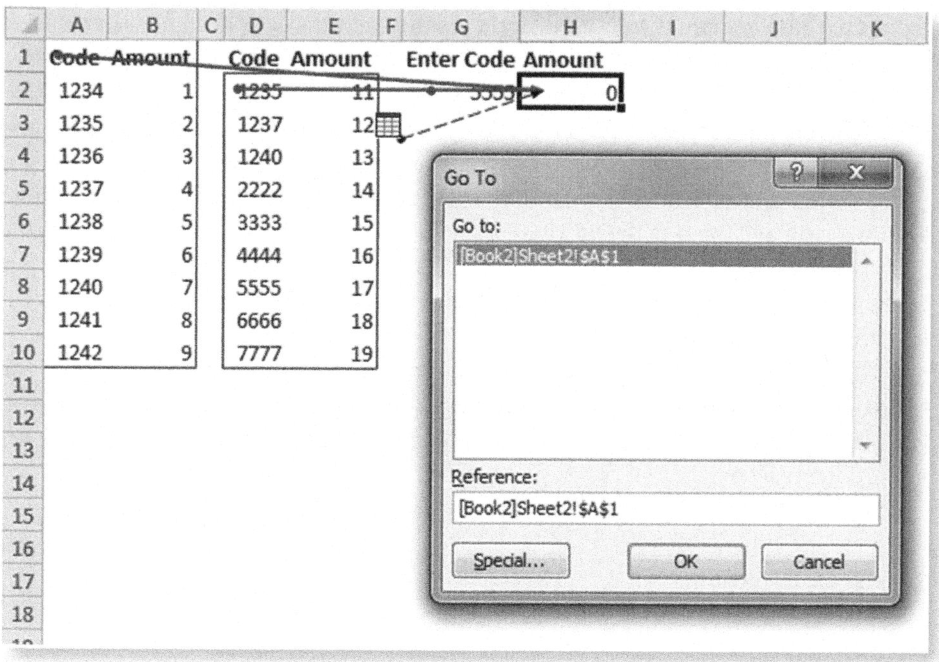

FIGURE 13.6 External Trace Precedents Results

To return to the original cell after following a link to a separate sheet, you can press F5 and then press Enter. This shortcut works for hyperlinks as well.

If your links are on the same sheet, there are some keyboard shortcuts you can use to identify precedents and dependents:

- Ctrl + [will select direct precedent cells on the current sheet.
- Ctrl + Shift +{ will select direct and indirect precedent cells on the current sheet.
- Ctrl +] will select direct dependent cells on the current sheet.
- Ctrl + Shift +} will select direct and indirect dependent cells on the current sheet.

There is also a mouse shortcut you can use to follow single links. This requires a settings change. Depending on how you use Excel, you might not want to make that change.

To make the settings change, you have to turn off editing in the cell, in Excel Options (see Chapter 3). After making the settings change, you can double-click a cell and it will take you to the precedent cell. Pressing F5 and then pressing Enter will also return you to the original cell.

IDENTIFYING NEW CODES

A common requirement in reporting is to identify new codes that have been added in the source data system. If your data might contain new codes or accounts that have to be added to your tables sheet, there is a technique to assist in the listing of the missing items.

This technique makes it reasonably easy for the user to update missing codes and correct the error.

For each column that might contain a new code, you add two columns to the data. Typically you add them to the far right of the table. The first new column identifies the code as new; it displays FALSE for new codes. The other column counts how many new codes there are. You use the MATCH function to identify what those new codes are. You may then display a central list of new codes on your control sheet.

This enables the user to copy the new accounts from the control sheet directly to the tables sheet and then add any necessary details to complete updating the tables sheet. For example, a new account code may need to have a category added so that it appears in the correct section of the report.

Figure 13.7 shows all three components of the system.

	J	K	L	M	N	O	P	Q	R	S	T
1	Department	Code	Amount	Code Exists	Count_New		Seq	New Code		Code	Category
2	Admin	1234	1,515	TRUE	0		1	1239		1234	Revenue
3	Admin	1235	1,863	TRUE	0		2	1240		1235	Revenue
4	Admin	1236	1,830	TRUE	0		3	1238		1236	Expense
5	Admin	1237	1,498	TRUE	0		4			1237	Expense
6	Sales	1234	1,362	TRUE	0						
7	Sales	1235	1,675	TRUE	0						
8	Sales	1236	1,646	TRUE	0						
9	Sales	1237	1,487	TRUE	0						
10	Sales	1239	1,875	FALSE	1						
11	Sales	1240	1,228	FALSE	2						
12	Production	1234	2,000	TRUE	0						
13	Production	1235	1,163	TRUE	0						
14	Production	1236	1,934	TRUE	0						
15	Production	1237	1,741	TRUE	0						
16	Production	1238	1,351	FALSE	3						
17	Production	1239	1,117	FALSE	0						
18	Production	1240	1,149	FALSE	0						

FIGURE 13.7 New Codes Example

Columns J, K, and L contain the source data. Columns M and N have been added to identify and count new codes in column K.

Columns P and Q have the list of new codes (these would normally appear on the control sheet).

Columns S and T are the existing codes that have already been categorised (these would normally be in the tables sheet).

Column M identifies whether the code is new with FALSE. TRUE means the code already exists. The formula in cell M2 is

```
=COUNTIF(S:S,K2)>0
```

This formula has been copied down.

The second column then creates a unique number for all new codes. The formula in cell N2 is

```
=IF(AND(M2=FALSE,COUNTIF($K$2:K2,K2)=1),MAX($N$1:N1)+1,0)
```

This formula has been copied down the column. The AND function determines whether the code is new and whether it is the first time the code has appeared in the column. If that is the case, it adds 1 to the maximum value from the cells above in the same column.

The new-code list in column Q displays the new codes in the order that they are encountered in the data. The user might have to sort the codes once they are added to the existing codes in column S.

This technique doesn't show duplicated new codes.

Adding the new codes to column S will automatically remove them from the new-code list.

CONDITIONAL FORMATTING

When you are using TRUE to confirm a validation and FALSE to identify an invalid entry, it can also be useful to apply Conditional Formatting to show green for valid and red for invalid.

You might want to only show red for invalid entries and leave TRUE validations with no background fill.

Either way, using red identifies invalid entries and makes them easy to see in a validation list.

The conditional format shown in Figure 13.8 will apply the red fill to FALSE entries.

SUGGESTED VALIDATION STRUCTURE

I recommend the following:

- Have your validations near the values you are validating. These may be in hidden rows or columns or outside the report's print area. In this way it is easier to spot the error in place.
- Use a standard convention of TRUE for valid and FALSE for invalid.

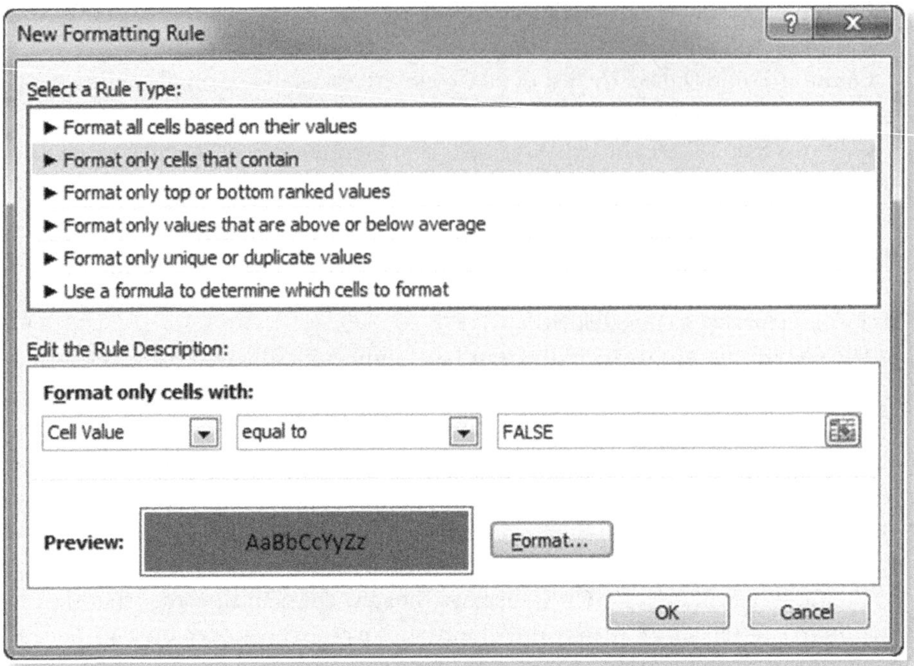

FIGURE 13.8 Red Fill for FALSE Entries

- Apply a conditional format as shown in the previous section to highlight invalid validation cells.
- Centralise all validation cells onto a single sheet via links. This makes it easier to have an overall validation check and to see all the validations together. One validation error can often lead to multiple errors. Fixing one validation may clear multiple validations.
- Have an overall validation cell. All major sheets can then link to this cell so that you can instantly see whether the model has a validation issue.
- Display differences. If you are balancing one value against another, it is common to have two rows. One row will display the difference between the two values, and the other will have the TRUE or FALSE validation. If a value doesn't balance, the first question is always what the difference is. You should calculate that difference to speed up the resolution process.

The layout of your reporting model will determine what validation structure will work best for your situation. The suggested structure that I have just described is flexible and easy to apply over the years. Figure 13.9 shows the structure that I regularly use.

The top of the sheet has the overall validation (cell K2). Other sheets can be linked to this cell to confirm the validation status.

Each row is dedicated to a specific validation. You can have one column for a description and another column for comments. Comments can include the types of issues that could cause an error and the steps to take to resolve it.

	H	I	J	K	L	M	N	O	P	Q
1					Jul-13	Aug-13	Sep-13	Oct-13	Nov-13	Dec
2			Overall Validaton	FALSE						
3										
4		Validation	Comments	Summary						
5		Balance Sheet Balances		TRUE	TRUE	TRUE	TRUE	TRUE	TRUE	TRU
6		Revenue = Detail	Reported Revenue equals detailed revenue report	TRUE	TRUE	TRUE	TRUE	TRUE	TRUE	TRU
7		All Codes Mapped	New codes need to be mapped	FALSE						
8										

FIGURE 13.9 Suggested Validation Structure

One column summarises all the separate validations (column K) for that particular validation. Some validations might not have detailed validations (cell K7) but just a direct link to the validation check.

The individual validation cells on the right side (column L onward) should all be directly linked to the sheet validation cells. This makes it easy to double-click a cell and go directly to the validation cell in question.

The summary validation formulas are based on the COUNTIF function. The formula in cell K2 is

```
=COUNTIF(K5:K100,FALSE)=0
```

This examines all the summary validations below. If the range contains a single FALSE, it will display FALSE. The same idea is used in cell K5; its formula is

```
=COUNTIF(L5:W5,FALSE)=0
```

This examines the validations to the right, and again, a single FALSE will display FALSE in the cell.

The reason for the summary validations in column K is that sometimes the validations on the right may go off the screen. Hence the error cell might not be visible. Having the summary column helps identify which row has the error.

REASONABLENESS CHECKS

The techniques used above for validations can also be used to check certain key report values for reasonableness. Although these checks might not affect the integrity of the reports, they can identify issues that should be investigated further or possibly reported on. You can set up a separate sheet to handle these types of checks and have a cell that displays whether one or more of the values are outside the acceptable parameters.

CHAPTER FOURTEEN

Case Study One: Month and Year-to-Date Reporting

TWO CASE STUDIES WILL EXAMINE the two most commonly used data layout types and produce two common report types.

In the first case study, discussed in this chapter, I will demonstrate the various reporting techniques by using a 12-month data layout to produce a month and year-to-date (YTD) report.

In the second case study, discussed in the next chapter, I will use a database layout to produce a 12-month report.

Swapping the data layouts and reports would have made both case studies easier, but in practice you don't always get the data layout you want, and knowing how to handle different data layouts is an important skill to master.

Both case studies will focus on profit-and-loss (P&L) reporting.

Each case study has two files on the companion website. The first file is a blank file, which has all of the structures required but none of the content. This enables you to follow along with the instructions in this chapter to complete the reporting model. The second file is the completed reporting model for your reference.

SCENARIO

We will examine a manufacturer of two products that operates in three states. The manufacturer uses standard costing, so standard cost variances are expensed each month. We will be reporting for October 2013.

The reports will include values for the month and YTD for actuals, budget, forecasts, and prior year. The forecasted full-year results are also compared to budget and prior year.

The actual figures (this year and last year) are copied into the reporting model in a 12-month system-generated report layout. The budget and forecasts are both created in Excel and are also copied into the model. The budget is updated in July, and forecasts are updated quarterly, in October, January, and April.

The structure of the general ledger (GL) chart of accounts is state, department, and account number. This structure is replicated in the P&L report that is pasted into the reporting model.

The account number has five digits, and the first two digits determine the account category.

Reports are required by state, department, and in total.

There are a number of nonfinancial statistics. Actual statistics will be entered manually into the model. Each of these statistics has budget, forecast, and prior-year figures.

Some reports will utilise these statistics to compare averages.

A one-page dashboard report is required for key measures.

DATA REQUIREMENTS

The budget and forecast data will all be in a similar layout. They have the state, department, and account going down the sheet and the monthly figures going across the sheet, with a total at the end (see Figure 14.1).

No changes are required to the budget or forecast layouts. We will add columns to the right to extract the month and YTD figures.

The actuals require extra columns on the right to correct missing data and to add the account category. We will use formulas for the data cleansing exercise because this will simplify the processes for the user. The user will simply paste the latest P&L report into the GL_Data_Curr sheet, and the formulas will create a data listing that will be used by the formula-based reports.

We will also add columns to the right of the pasted reports to extract the month and YTD figures for the final reports.

PROCESSES

One of the aims of the reporting model is to simplify, and therefore speed up, the reporting process. One of the advantages of simplification is that the report process can be delegated to other staff members.

The monthly reporting process will involve the following:

- Pasting in the latest P&L report
- Keying in the actuals for the statistics
- Changing the current month
- Selecting the comparison metric (budget or forecast)
- Checking validations
- Correcting any validation issues
- Reviewing final reports

	A	B	C	D	E	F	G	H	I	J	K	L	M	N	O	P	Q
1	**State**	**Department**	**Account**	**Category**	1	2	3	4	5	6	7	8	9	10	11	12	
2	*Curr_Bud_State*	*Curr_Bud_Dept*	*Curr_Bud_Acct*	*Curr_Bud_Cat*	**Jul**	**Aug**	**Sep**	**Oct**	**Nov**	**Dec**	**Jan**	**Feb**	**Mar**	**Apr**	**May**	**Jun**	**Total**
3	NSW	SALES	31000	Product Revenue	-1,200	-1,280	-1,260	-1,260	-1,300	-1,290	-1,310	-1,320	-1,330	-1,340	-1,350	-1,360	-15,600
4	NSW	SALES	32000	Product Revenue	-1,430	-1,430	-1,390	-1,460	-1,440	-1,450	-1,480	-1,470	-1,490	-1,500	-1,510	-1,520	-17,570
5	NSW	OTH_REV	33000	Distribution	-250	-260	-270	-260	-270	-270	-270	-280	-280	-280	-290	-290	-3,270
6	NSW	OTH_REV	34000	Other Revenue	-20	-30	-30	-30	-30	-30	-30	-30	-30	-30	-30	-30	-350
7	NSW	OTH_REV	35000	Other Revenue	-30	-30	-30	-30	-30	-30	-30	-30	-30	-30	-30	-30	-360
8	VIC	SALES	31000	Product Revenue	-1,310	-1,280	-1,310	-1,320	-1,320	-1,340	-1,350	-1,360	-1,370	-1,380	-1,390	-1,400	-16,130
9	VIC	SALES	32000	Product Revenue	-1,420	-1,500	-1,660	-1,490	-1,610	-1,610	-1,580	-1,640	-1,630	-1,640	-1,670	-1,670	-19,120
10	VIC	OTH_REV	33000	Distribution	-180	-170	-210	-180	-190	-200	-190	-200	-200	-200	-200	-200	-2,320
11	VIC	OTH_REV	34000	Other Revenue	-20	-20	-20	-20	-20	-20	-20	-20	-20	-20	-20	-20	-240
12	VIC	OTH_REV	35000	Other Revenue	-10	-20	-20	-20	-20	-20	-20	-20	-20	-20	-20	-20	-230
13	WA	SALES	31000	Product Revenue	-920	-870	-920	-910	-910	-930	-930	-940	-950	-950	-960	-970	-11,160
14	WA	SALES	32000	Product Revenue	-1,190	-1,050	-1,160	-1,140	-1,130	-1,170	-1,160	-1,170	-1,190	-1,190	-1,200	-1,210	-13,960
15	WA	OTH_REV	33000	Distribution	-320	-320	-350	-330	-340	-350	-340	-350	-350	-350	-360	-360	-4,120
16	WA	OTH_REV	34000	Other Revenue	-20	-20	-20	-20	-20	-20	-20	-20	-20	-20	-20	-20	-240
17	WA	OTH_REV	35000	Other Revenue	-30	-20	-20	-30	-20	-30	-30	-30	-30	-30	-30	-30	-330

FIGURE 14.1 Budget Layout

The annual reporting process will involve the following:

- Pasting in the new budget for $ values and statistics
- Copying full-year actuals to the prior year's actual sheets for both $ results and statistics values
- Changing the starting month for the year

The quarterly reporting process will involve pasting in the latest forecast for $ values and statistics.

STRUCTURE

We will create separate sheets for each of the data types. Table 14.1 lists the data sheets required.

TABLE 14.1 Required Data Sheets

Sheet Name	Description
GL_Data_Curr	Current-year actual $—latest P&L report pasted in monthly
Statistics	Current-year actual statistics—entered manually monthly
GL_Data_Prev	Prior-year actual $—pasted annually
Statistics_Prev	Prior-year actual statistics—pasted annually
Budget_Data	Current-year budget $—pasted in annually
Budget_Stats	Current-year budget statistics—pasted in annually
Forecast_Data	Current-year forecast $—pasted in quarterly
Forecast_Stats	Current-year forecast statistics—pasted in quarterly

These sheets will have a similar layout, and we will use structured range names on all the sheets to make creating the final reports easier.

The P&L report from the accounting system will require data cleansing.

The budget and forecast data are Excel-based and their structure already meets our requirements.

Because all the layouts have the details going down the page and the month values going across the page, will we add columns on the right to extract the relevant month and YTD values. These will use the INDEX and MATCH functions to extract the current month and YTD figures.

DESIGN

The data will determine the types of reports you can create. Part of the data cleansing exercise may be to add extra fields to an existing data set to make it more useful and to expand the number, and type, of reports you could create.

When designing the file structure, you typically start with your final reports and then work backward toward the data. You might do this on paper first. You must make sure you have all the data you need, in the layout necessary, to extract the values for all the reports. If you don't have all the data necessary, you will have to look at using data cleansing techniques to add more data.

The data structure itself will affect your reports. In our case study, we will require state and department reports, as well as a total report. You also need to consider the level of detail required.

I still work on paper to do some of the designing. It helps me capture my ideas more quickly than jumping straight into a spreadsheet. Obviously, designs will change over time, but I find it easier to do a lot of the trial-and-error work on paper before I start on the spreadsheet.

Your grasp of different data structures will affect your designs and how many iterations it will take you to get to a final report. Experience also plays a large part. Many report layouts are similar, and being able to produce a few common reports stands you in good stead to handle most other reports.

REPORT LAYOUT

You can speed up the creation stage by building the reports with the same layout and then applying different criteria. In this way the total, state, and department reports may have the same layout but report on their respective metrics.

Having a consistent report layout also makes it easier to compare values at various levels.

In this case study, we will create a standard report layout that can then be applied to all the reporting levels.

Each case study has a dashboard report. The techniques used on each case study differ, as do the chart types. The dashboards have been created to provide more examples of the techniques described in Chapter 12. The reporting techniques will be flexible. Flexibility can be used in two ways. The first is to allow you to create a report that can be easily modified between different levels, such as state and department. As the creator, you can then easily change reports. The second is to allow the user to make selections and determine what is to be reported on.

In both cases, you need to define what fields or metrics will be flexible and what will be fixed. In formula-based reports, you must establish the demarcation between variable (what will change) and fixed (what won't change) components.

THE CREATION PROCESS

The various components of the reporting model are described and demonstrated in this section.

The Control Sheet

Here are the first two pieces of information we need to start the creation process:

1. The financial year starting month
2. The current month

Both inputs will be on the control sheet.

Also on the control sheet will be an option for the user to choose the report comparison figure. As the year progresses, the budget often becomes less relevant, and comparing monthly actuals to the forecast may be more worthwhile. The user will be able to choose between budget and forecast comparisons.

These are the only three inputs the user needs to change to create all the reports. On a monthly basis, the user will need only to select the current month.

Structured Range Names

On the $ value data sheets, we will create structured range names. Table 14.2 shows these names. Note their common structure.

TABLE 14.2 Structured Range Names

Columns	Actual Sheet	Budget Sheet	Forecast Sheet	Prior Year Sheet
State	Curr_Act_State	Curr_Bud_State	Curr_For_State	Pyr_Act_State
Department	Curr_Act_Dept	Curr_Bud_Dept	Curr_For_Dept	Pyr_Act_Dept
Account	Curr_Act_Acct	Curr_Bud_Acct	Curr_For_Acct	Pyr_Act_Acct
Category	Curr_Act_Cat	Curr_Bud_Cat	Curr_For_Cat	Pyr_Act_Cat
Month $	Curr_Act_Mth	Curr_Bud_Mth	Curr_For_Mth	Pyr_Act_Mth
Year to Date $	Curr_Act_YTD	Curr_Bud_YTD	Curr_For_YTD	Pyr_Act_YTD
Full Year $		Curr_Bud_Full	Curr_For_Full	Pyr_Act_Full

Having a structure for the range names allows us to define range names for each column of the report so that we can create a single formula in the reports that can be copied across and down to extract data from all the sources.

That is powerful; for the main report we will be able to create a single formula to extract all the data from all the separate sheets.

The actual columns that these relate to will vary among the sheets. By using a consistent naming convention, you can create formulas that use these names to extract the comparison figures from the relevant data sheet.

Within the companion file, range name labels are formatted with a red italic font.

Actual Data

The actual figures are made up of the P&L report from the accounting system and the statistics that will be entered manually each month.

The System P&L Report

The user pastes the latest system-generated P&L report into the GL_Data_Curr sheet in columns A to S. The structure of this report cannot be used as a data source for our reports because of missing data. Figure 14.2 has an extract from the report.

We need to apply data cleansing formulas to convert this structure into a database layout. Figure 14.3 shows the data cleansing columns to the right of the pasted P&L report.

Table 14.3 lists the formulas from cells in row 2 of the data cleansing columns.

TABLE 14.3 Data Cleansing Formulas (All Formulas Copied Down the Column)

Cell	Formula
U2	=E2<>""
V2	=IF(U2,INDEX(G2:R2,1,Curr_Month_Num),"")
W2	=IF(U2,SUM(G2:INDEX(G2:R2,1,Curr_Month_Num)),"")
Y2	=IF(COUNTIF(States,C2)>0,C2,IF(COUNTIF(States,Y1)>0,Y1,""))
Z2	=IF(COUNTIF(Depts,D2)>0,D2,IF(COUNTIF(Depts,Z1)>0,Z1,""))
AA2	=IF(U2,E2,"")
AB2	=IF(U2,INDEX(Account_Category,MATCH(LEFT(AA2,2)*1,Account_Prefix,0)),"")

Column U identifies whether there is an account number in Column E. Only those rows with an account number require extra entries in the other data cleansing columns.

Column E contains only the account number. The formula in column U returns TRUE or FALSE and is referenced by the other data cleansing columns.

Column V first checks column U to see whether the row is an account number row. If it is, it extracts the current month's value from the row based on the range name Curr_Month_Num. This name is defined and calculated on the control sheet. When the user selects the current month's name, the Curr_Month_Num range name updates.

Column W first checks whether the row is an account number row. If it is, it calculates the current YTD value based on the range name Curr_Month_Num.

Column Y first determines whether a state is in column C. If not, it checks the cell above itself to see whether it contains a state. If either has a state, it returns that state; otherwise, it will return a bank cell.

Column Z first determines whether a department is in column D. If not, it checks the cell above itself to see whether it contains a department. If either contains a department, it returns that department; otherwise, it will return a bank cell.

Column AA returns the account number if there is one. There are no other entries in column E, other than account numbers.

Column AB first checks column U to see whether the row is an account row and then looks up the account number in the tables sheet and returns the account category.

Row 1 in Figure 14.3 shows the range names used for each column in the data cleansing section (see also Table 14.2).

	A	B	C	D	E	F	G	H	I	J
1	**Statement of Revenue and Expenses for ABCD Ltd**									
2	**For the period July 2013 to October 2013**									
3					**000s**					
4		**Revenue**					**Jul**	**Aug**	**Sep**	**Oct**
5			NSW							
6				SALES						
7	1000	1500			31000	Gadgets	1,071	1,284	1,232	1,235
8	1200	1700			32000	Widgets	1,338	1,468	1,344	1,390
9				**Total Product Sales**			**2,409**	**2,752**	**2,576**	**2,625**
10										
11				OTH_REV						
12	200	300			33000	Distribution	225	269	238	291
13	20	30			34000	Interest	24	25	25	26
14	20	30			35000	Other	28	30	29	26
15				**Total Other Revenue**			**277**	**324**	**292**	**343**
16										
17			**Total NSW Revenue**				**2,686**	**3,076**	**2,868**	**2,968**

FIGURE 14.2 System-Generated P&L Report Layout

	R	S	T	U	V	W	X	Y	Z	AA	AB
1				Is Account	Curr_Act_Mth	Curr_Act_YTD		Curr_Act_State	Curr_Act_Dept	Curr_Act_Acct	Curr_Act_Cat
2				FALSE							
3				FALSE							
4	Jun	Total		FALSE							
5				FALSE				NSW			
6				FALSE				NSW	SALES		
7		4,822		TRUE	1235	4822		NSW	SALES	31000	Product Revenue
8		5,540		TRUE	1390	5540		NSW	SALES	32000	Product Revenue
9		10,362		FALSE				NSW	SALES		
10				FALSE				NSW	SALES		
11				FALSE				NSW	OTH_REV		
12		1,023		TRUE	291	1023		NSW	OTH_REV	33000	Distribution Revenue
13		100		TRUE	26	100		NSW	OTH_REV	34000	Other Revenue
14		113		TRUE	26	113		NSW	OTH_REV	35000	Other Revenue

FIGURE 14.3 Data Cleansing Columns, P&L Report Layout

The data cleansing columns are the columns used to create the reports.

Prior-Year System P&L Report

The sheet GL_Data_Prev contains last year's full 12-month P&L and has the same structure as the GL_Data_Curr sheet but with an extra column added to the right. The extra column contains the full-year values and is used by reports to compare the current forecast of the full-year result to the previous full-year result.

Cell AD2 contains the formula

```
=IF(U2,S2,"")
```

This formula has been copied down the column. It returns the total for the year when the row contains an account number.

Statistics

The nonfinancial data will be manually entered each month in the statistics sheet. In this sheet, column Q will provide the current month and column R will provide the current YTD figures for statistics.

Figure 14.4 shows the column structure of the statistics sheet.

The range name labels listed in column A were used to create range names using the Create From Selection option (Ctrl + Shift + F3). The names are defined from column B across to column R. Similarly, the range names shown in Q2 and R2 are defined from rows 3 to 34.

This allows us to extract the statistics using range name intersections (a space between range names). For instance, to extract the current month's statistic for sales volume for gadgets in NSW, we would use

```
=Curr_Act_Sales_Vol_Gadget_NSW Curr_Act_Stats_Mth
```

The statistics sheet has totals at the bottom. They use a SUMIF with a wild card character to summarise the statistics above. Figure 14.5 shows the bottom of the statistics sheet.

The formula in cell C27 is

```
=SUMIF($A$3:$A$26,$A27&"*",C$3:C$26)
```

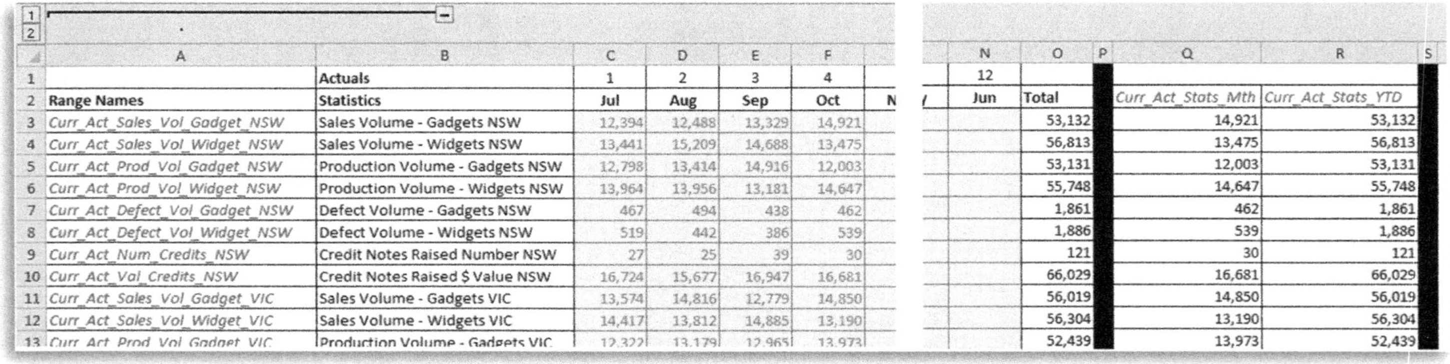

	A	B	C	D	E	F	N	O	P	Q	R	S
1		**Actuals**	1	2	3	4	12					
2	**Range Names**	**Statistics**	**Jul**	**Aug**	**Sep**	**Oct**	**Jun**	**Total**		*Curr_Act_Stats_Mth*	*Curr_Act_Stats_YTD*	
3	*Curr_Act_Sales_Vol_Gadget_NSW*	Sales Volume - Gadgets NSW	12,394	12,488	13,329	14,921		53,132		14,921	53,132	
4	*Curr_Act_Sales_Vol_Widget_NSW*	Sales Volume - Widgets NSW	13,441	15,209	14,688	13,475		56,813		13,475	56,813	
5	*Curr_Act_Prod_Vol_Gadget_NSW*	Production Volume - Gadgets NSW	12,798	13,414	14,916	12,003		53,131		12,003	53,131	
6	*Curr_Act_Prod_Vol_Widget_NSW*	Production Volume - Widgets NSW	13,964	13,956	13,181	14,647		55,748		14,647	55,748	
7	*Curr_Act_Defect_Vol_Gadget_NSW*	Defect Volume - Gadgets NSW	467	494	438	462		1,861		462	1,861	
8	*Curr_Act_Defect_Vol_Widget_NSW*	Defect Volume - Widgets NSW	519	442	386	539		1,886		539	1,886	
9	*Curr_Act_Num_Credits_NSW*	Credit Notes Raised Number NSW	27	25	39	30		121		30	121	
10	*Curr_Act_Val_Credits_NSW*	Credit Notes Raised $ Value NSW	16,724	15,677	16,947	16,681		66,029		16,681	66,029	
11	*Curr_Act_Sales_Vol_Gadget_VIC*	Sales Volume - Gadgets VIC	13,574	14,816	12,779	14,850		56,019		14,850	56,019	
12	*Curr_Act_Sales_Vol_Widget_VIC*	Sales Volume - Widgets VIC	14,417	13,812	14,885	13,190		56,304		13,190	56,304	
13	*Curr_Act_Prod_Vol_Gadget_VIC*	Production Volume - Gadgets VIC	12,322	13,179	12,965	13,973		52,439		13,973	52,439	

FIGURE 14.4 Statistics Sheet Structure

	A	B	C	D
1		Actuals	1	2
2	Range Names	Statistics	Jul	Aug
19	*Curr_Act_Sales_Vol_Gadget_WA*	Sales Volume - Gadgets WA	14,297	13,986
20	*Curr_Act_Sales_Vol_Widget_WA*	Sales Volume - Widgets WA	15,090	13,716
21	*Curr_Act_Prod_Vol_Gadget_WA*	Production Volume - Gadgets WA	13,759	14,090
22	*Curr_Act_Prod_Vol_Widget_WA*	Production Volume - Widgets WA	15,399	13,580
23	*Curr_Act_Defect_Vol_Gadget_WA*	Defect Volume - Gadgets WA	455	430
24	*Curr_Act_Defect_Vol_Widget_WA*	Defect Volume - Widgets WA	451	440
25	*Curr_Act_Num_Credits_WA*	Credit Notes Raised Number WA	36	27
26	*Curr_Act_Val_Credits_WA*	Credit Notes Raised $ Value WA	16,795	15,332
27	*Curr_Act_Sales_Vol_Gadget*	Sales Volume - Gadgets	40,265	41,290
28	*Curr_Act_Sales_Vol_Widget*	Sales Volume - Widgets	42,948	42,737
29	*Curr_Act_Prod_Vol_Gadget*	Production Volume - Gadgets	38,879	40,683
30	*Curr_Act_Prod_Vol_Widget*	Production Volume - Widgets	44,452	42,725
31	*Curr_Act_Defect_Vol_Gadget*	Defect Volume - Gadgets	1,413	1,342
32	*Curr_Act_Defect_Vol_Widget*	Defect Volume - Widgets	1,353	1,355
33	*Curr_Act_Num_Credits*	Credit Notes Raised Number	100	77
34	*Curr_Act_Val_Credits*	Credit Notes Raised $ Value	49,954	47,262
35		Statistics Total Check	TRUE	TRUE

FIGURE 14.5 Statistics Sheet Totals

This formula has been copied across to columns D to N and down to rows 28 to 34.

The statistic range name in column A is the same as the range names above, except is doesn't include the state. Hence, we can use the asterisk wild card to summarise the values in the above cells using the SUMIF. This method is preferable to directly linking because it handles a new state's statistics being inserted above without creating the need to amend the total formula.

When adding a new state's statistics, you insert rows between the existing states rather than below the WA statistics. That way the total formula will not have to be amended.

Row 35 is a validation that confirms that all the state statistics equal the summarised totals. The formula in cell C35 is

```
=SUM(C3:C26)=SUM(C27:C34)
```

This formula has been copied across to columns D to O. These validation cells have been linked to the validation sheet.

The layout of the budget and prior year's statistics sheets are identical to the statistics sheet. The forecast sheet is identical up to column S, but it has extra columns added to the right side to handle calculations for the full-year forecast.

Figure 14.6 shows the right side of the Forecast_Stats sheet.

Columns T to AE extract either the actual statistic or the forecast statistic depending on the current month.

The formula for cell T3 is

```
=IF(T$1<=Curr_Month_Num,INDEX(INDIRECT(SUBSTITUTE($A3,
 "For","Act")),1,T$1+1),C3)
```

	A	B	T	U	V	W	X	Y	Z	AA	AB	AC	AD	AE	AF	AG	AH
1		**Forecast**	1	2	3	4	5	6	7	8	9	10	11	12			
2	**Range Names**	**Statistics**	Jul	Aug	Sep	Oct	Nov	Dec	Jan	Feb	Mar	Apr	May	Jun	Total		*Curr_For_Stats_Full*
3	*Curr_For_Sales_Vol_Gadget_NSW*	Sales Volume - Gadgets NSW	13,084	12,591	14,144	14,088	12,617	13,994	13,212	12,879	13,751	13,352	12,642	12,981	159,335		159,335
4	*Curr_For_Sales_Vol_Widget_NSW*	Sales Volume - Widgets NSW	15,252	13,789	15,073	13,960	14,652	14,224	15,107	15,190	13,860	15,001	14,135	14,031	174,274		174,274
5	*Curr_For_Prod_Vol_Gadget_NSW*	Production Volume - Gadgets NSW	13,189	13,405	13,758	13,931	13,213	13,924	13,760	13,300	13,649	13,450	13,857	13,677	163,113		163,113
6	*Curr_For_Prod_Vol_Widget_NSW*	Production Volume - Widgets NSW	13,633	13,682	13,696	13,544	13,680	13,653	13,561	13,694	13,594	13,629	13,617	13,666	163,649		163,649
7	*Curr_For_Defect_Vol_Gadget_NSW*	Defect Volume - Gadgets NSW	443	420	443	402	436	443	409	410	418	410	427	435	5,096		5,096
8	*Curr_For_Defect_Vol_Widget_NSW*	Defect Volume - Widgets NSW	392	357	444	513	387	420	471	370	420	510	379	478	5,141		5,141
9	*Curr_For_Num_Credits_NSW*	Credit Notes Raised Number NSW	36	34	50	35	39	49	44	37	34	46	36	42	482		482
10	*Curr_For_Val_Credits_NSW*	Credit Notes Raised $ Value NSW	15,721	15,970	16,583	16,829	15,851	16,067	16,153	16,781	16,259	16,414	16,230	16,477	195,335		195,335

FIGURE 14.6 Forecast Statistics Sheet

This uses the SUBSTITUTE function to convert the forecast statistic range name from cell $A3 into the actual statistic range name by replacing For with Act. The INDIRECT function then converts the text string range name into the range name used within the INDEX function.

The reason 1 is added to the T$1 value is that the first cell in the statistic range name is the name description of the statistic in column B. The values start in column C; hence you need to add 1 to the month number to get to the correct month's cell within the range name.

Column AH simply links to column AF. I could have used column AF as the Curr_For_Stats_Full range name, but I have kept a similar structure to the previous columns, separated it, and named it.

THE REPORTS

The reports described in this section are P&L reports. There is a state report and a department report. The state report is then totaled to create the company's total report. We conclude with a look at the dashboard report. You may need to read through this section a few times to obtain a good understanding of the techniques discussed.

The State Report

The state report is reasonably advanced. It has a single formula to extract the data for actuals, budget, forecasts, and prior year. A single formula is possible only because structured range names have been created.

The INDIRECT function has been used in conjunction with helper cells to create the single formula.

The other formulas on the sheet are used for the following:

- Identification of the sheet name
- Helper cells to create the range names required
- Headings
- Variance calculations
- Summing

An extract of the final report is shown in Figure 14.7.

The helper cells are in rows 1 to 8 and columns A to C (see Figure 14.8).

There are seven range names defined on the sheet, and all seven are used by the single formula. Table 14.4 lists the range names with a description of their use.

The entries in column A below row 16 are all linked to cell A2.

The entries in columns B and C below row 16 are all cell entries. The three entries per row define the State, Department, and Account combination to be extracted for that row.

Rows 1, 2, and 3 are the building blocks for the range names created in rows 5 to 8. Rows 1 and 3 contain cell entries. Row 2 contains mainly cell entries but also

State Report for Revenue and Expenses for ABCD Ltd
For the Period 1 July 13 to 31 October 13

STATE	Current Year			Current Year			Current Year			Previous Year			Previous Year			Previous Year		
NSW	Month 000's			YTD 000's			Full Year '000s			Month 000's			YTD 000's			Full Year 000's		
	Actuals	Budget	Var	Actuals	Budget	Var	Forecast	Budget	Var	This Year	Last Year	Var	This Year	Last Year	Var	Forecast	Last Year	Var
Revenue																		
Gadgets	1,235	1,260	-25	4,822	5,000	-178	15,712	15,600	112	1,235	1,361	-126	4,822	4,682	140	15,712	14,684	1,028
Widgets	1,390	1,460	-70	5,540	5,710	-170	17,720	17,570	150	1,390	1,247	143	5,540	5,292	248	17,720	16,592	1,128
Total Product Sales	**2,625**	**2,720**	**-95**	**10,362**	**10,710**	**-348**	**33,432**	**33,170**	**262**	**2,625**	**2,608**	**17**	**10,362**	**9,974**	**388**	**33,432**	**31,276**	**2,156**
Cost of Sale																		
Gadgets	840	900	60	3,397	3,540	143	11,017	10,950	-67	840	939	99	3,397	3,241	-156	11,017	10,130	-887
Widgets	959	990	31	3,780	3,890	110	12,060	11,960	-100	959	873	-86	3,780	3,715	-65	12,060	11,802	-258
Total Product Cost of Sales	**1,799**	**1,890**	**91**	**7,177**	**7,430**	**253**	**23,077**	**22,910**	**-167**	**1,799**	**1,812**	**13**	**7,177**	**6,956**	**-221**	**23,077**	**21,932**	**-1,145**
Product Gross Margin	**826**	**830**	**-4**	**3,185**	**3,280**	**-95**	**10,355**	**10,260**	**95**	**826**	**796**	**30**	**3,185**	**3,018**	**167**	**10,355**	**9,344**	**1,011**

FIGURE 14.7 State Report Extract—Completed

	A	B	C	D	E	F	G	H	I	J	K	L
1	E:\A4\The Book\Excel Files\[Case				Years	Curr	Curr			Curr	Curr	
2	NSW				Metric	Act	Bud			Act	Bud	
3					Period	Mth	Mth			YTD	YTD	
5					*Value_Name*	Curr_Act_Mth	Curr_Bud_Mth			Curr_Act_YTD	Curr_Bud_YTD	
6			State		*State_Name*	Curr_Act_State	Curr_Bud_State			Curr_Act_State	Curr_Bud_State	
7			Dept		*Dept_Name*	Curr_Act_Dept	Curr_Bud_Dept			Curr_Act_Dept	Curr_Bud_Dept	
8			Acct		*Account_Name*	Curr_Act_Acct	Curr_Bud_Acct			Curr_Act_Acct	Curr_Bud_Acct	
9												
10					**State Report for Revenue and Expenses for ABCD Ltd**							
11					**For the Period 1 July 13 to 31 October 13**							
12												
13					STATE	**Current Year**				**Current Year**		
14					NSW	Month 000's				YTD 000's		
15						Actuals	Budget	Var		Actuals	Budget	Var
16	*State*	*Dept*	*Account*		**Revenue**							
17	NSW	SALES	31000		Gadgets	1,235	1,260	-25		4,822	5,000	-178
18	NSW	SALES	32000		Widgets	1,390	1,460	-70		5,540	5,710	-170
19					**Total Product Sales**	**2,625**	**2,720**	**-95**		**10,362**	**10,710**	**-348**
21					**Cost of Sale**							
22	NSW	COS	41000		Gadgets	840	900	60		3,397	3,540	143
23	NSW	COS	42000		Widgets	959	990	31		3,780	3,890	110
24					**Total Product Cost of Sales**	**1,799**	**1,890**	**91**		**7,177**	**7,430**	**253**

FIGURE 14.8 State Report—Helper Cells Displayed

TABLE 14.4 State Sheet Named Ranges

Range Name	Range Reference	Type	Description
State	=NSW!$A$17:$A$73	Column	Contains the state for the report
Dept	=NSW!$B$17:$B$73	Column	Contains the department for the row
Account	=NSW!$C$17:$C$73	Column	Contains the account number for the row
Value_Name	=NSW!$F$5:$AA$5	Row	Contains the range name to be used to extract the value for the column
State_Name	=NSW!$F$6:$AA$6	Row	Contains the range name that has the state entries for the column
Dept_Name	=NSW!$F$7:$AA$7	Row	Contains the range name that has the department entries for the column
Account_Name	=NSW!$F$8:$AA$8	Row	Contains the range name that has the account number entries for the column

formulas to define the comparison metric in cells G2 and K2. The user can choose to compare actuals to budget or forecasts. This is selected on the control sheet. The comparison selection cell is named Curr_Comparison. The formula in cells G2 and K2 is

```
=LEFT(Curr_Comparison,3)
```

This extracts the first three characters from the words Budget or Forecast, which matches the abbreviations used in the range names throughout the file. This simple formula gives the report the flexibility to display budget or forecast comparisons.

Rows 5 to 8 contain the range names required for each column. Table 14.5 contains the formulas that are copied across to the other value columns in rows 5 to 8.

TABLE 14.5 Helper Cells, Rows 5 to 8—Create Range Names

Cell	Formula	Description
F5	=F$1&"_"&F$2&"_"&F3	Creates the range name for the value columns in the various data sets.
F6	=F$1&"_"&F$2&"_"&$C6	Creates the range names in the various data sets for state, department, and account, respectively. Copied down to cells F7 and F8.

Cell A2 extracts the sheet name (NSW) from the full path in cell A1. This means you can copy the NSW sheet and rename it VIC, and this will automatically create the complete state report for VIC. This technique reduces development time because a single sheet name change updates the whole report.

The formula in cell A1 is

```
=CELL("filename",A1)
```

This formula returns the full path of the file, including the current sheet name. The formula in cell A2 is

```
=RIGHT(A1,LEN(A1)-SEARCH("]",A1))
```

This extracts the sheet name from the full path. The sheet name appears after the] in the full path.

The variance formula in cell H17 is

```
=IF(LEFT(Account)*1=3,F17-G17,G17-F17)
```

Positive variances are favorable, whereas negative variances are unfavorable. Revenues and expenses are typically both reported as positive values. Calculating variances usually requires identifying revenue and expenses and treating them differently in terms of their variance calculation.

In our example, all revenue account numbers start with 3. The LEFT function defaults to the first character when the number of characters is omitted. The result of the LEFT function is multiplied by 1 to convert it to a number. Excel treats a text 3 as different from a numeric 3.

The building blocks are now complete, and we can create the following single formula in cell F17:

```
=SUMIFS(INDIRECT(Value_Name),INDIRECT(State_Name),State,
INDIRECT(Dept_Name),Dept,INDIRECT(Account_Name),Account)
```

This formula has been copied to columns G, J, K, N, O, R, S, V, W, Z, and AA.

As you can see, this formula contains no cell references. It uses range names to refer to the correct cells. The four INDIRECT functions all refer to the four helper cells in rows 5 to 8. The three range names refer to the sheet-based names for state, department, and account (helper cells in columns A, B, and C, respectively).

The INDIRECT functions convert the text entries into their respective range names. In cell F17 this converts to

```
=SUMIFS(Curr_Act_Mth,Curr_Act_State,State,Curr_Act_
 Dept,Dept,Curr_Act_Acct,Account)
```

In cell G17 (assuming Budget is the comparison) this converts to

```
=SUMIFS(Curr_Bud_Mth,Curr_Bud_State,State,Curr_Bud_
 Dept,Dept,Curr_Bud_Acct,Account)
```

As the formula is copied across, it is only the range to sum that changes. The criteria ranges and criteria don't change. In cell J17 the formula with the ranges is converted to

```
=SUMIFS(Curr_Act_YTD,Curr_Act_State,State,Curr_Act_
 Dept,Dept,Curr_Act_Acct,Account)
```

The only difference between this formula and the one from cell F17 is the first range name. This formula demonstrates the power of using and applying structured range names. The report layout can be easily modified by changing the helper cell entries and column headings.

The helper cell formulas are all simple and straightforward. The SUMIFS formula itself is more complex, but a single formula has populated the majority of the report.

The flexibility of this structure can be further demonstrated by converting the state report into a department report.

The Department Report

The columns of the department report are identical to those of the state report (see Figure 14.9). The rows on the department report are used to report on the individual state totals.

The helper cells in rows 1 to 7 are the same as the state report and supply the same range names (see Figure 14.10).

Row 8 is used to create the category column range name instead of the account range name.

The helper cells in columns A, B, and C have been amended to provide the different row values. Cells in columns A, B, and C all have entries, not formulas. Column C has been changed to handle the category. The category column uses the asterisk as a wild card. This means that it sums all the categories in the column. In effect, this converts the three-criteria SUMIFS to a two-criteria SUMIF.

I could have left the structure identical and used the asterisk in the account column, but I wanted to demonstrate how the structure could be easily modified to work with different columns.

The single formula in this case in cell F18 is

```
=SUMIFS(INDIRECT(Value_Name),INDIRECT(State_Name),State,
INDIRECT(Dept_Name),Dept,INDIRECT(Category_Name),Category)
```

This formula has been copied across the same columns as in the state report.

The Account_Name and Account range names from the state report have been replaced with Category_Name and Category, respectively.

If we convert the respective ranges to their range names, the formula in cell F18 is

```
=SUMIFS(Curr_Act_Mth,Curr_Act_State,State,Curr_Act_Dept,Dept,
 Curr_Act_Cat,Category)
```

The Total Report

Because the state report sheets have identical layouts, we can use the same layout in another sheet to summarise all the states using 3D SUM formulas. Figure 14.11 shows the Total_State sheet report with the formula from cell F17.

The placeholder sheets a and b have been used to surround the three state sheets. Sheets a and b are both blank. The formula in cell F17 is

```
=SUM(a:b!F17:F17)
```

The flexibility of the state report can be further demonstrated by allowing us to create a Total_Check sheet by amending a copy of the state sheet. You only change cell A2 to convert it to a total report. Delete the formula in A2 and enter an asterisk. That converts the whole report to totals for the whole company (see Figure 14.12).

We can use this sheet to validate the Total_State report, which used the 3D SUM technique.

Department Report for Revenue and Expenses for ABCD Ltd
For the Period 1 July 13 to 31 October 13

DEPARTMENT	Current Year			Current Year			Current Year			Previous Year			Previous Year			Previous Year		
	Month 000's			YTD 000's			Full Year '000s			Month 000's			YTD 000's			Full Year 000's		
	Actuals	Budget	Var	Actuals	Budget	Var	Forecast	Budget	Var	This Year	Last Year	Var	This Year	Last Year	Var	Forecast	Last Year	Var
Revenue																		
Product Sales																		
NSW	2,625	2,720	-95	10,362	10,710	-348	33,432	33,170	262	2,625	2,608	17	10,362	9,974	388	33,432	31,276	2,156
VIC	3,164	2,810	354	11,192	11,290	-98	35,782	35,250	532	3,164	2,592	572	11,192	10,939	253	35,782	33,319	2,463
WA	2,256	2,050	206	8,228	8,160	68	25,658	25,120	538	2,256	1,888	368	8,228	7,496	732	25,658	22,877	2,781
Total Product Sales	**8,045**	**7,580**	**465**	**29,782**	**30,160**	**-378**	**94,872**	**93,540**	**1,332**	**8,045**	**7,088**	**957**	**29,782**	**28,409**	**1,373**	**94,872**	**87,472**	**7,400**
Cost of Sales																		
NSW	1,799	1,890	91	7,177	7,430	253	23,077	22,910	-167	1,799	1,812	13	7,177	6,956	-221	23,077	21,932	-1,145
VIC	2,243	1,950	-293	7,807	7,870	63	24,977	24,600	-377	2,243	1,851	-392	7,807	7,657	-150	24,977	23,016	-1,961
WA	1,585	1,490	-95	5,934	5,890	-44	18,444	18,070	-374	1,585	1,321	-264	5,934	5,444	-490	18,444	16,510	-1,934
Total Product Cost of Sales	**5,627**	**5,330**	**-297**	**20,918**	**21,190**	**272**	**66,498**	**65,580**	**-918**	**5,627**	**4,984**	**-643**	**20,918**	**20,057**	**-861**	**66,498**	**61,458**	**-5,040**
Product Gross Margin	**2,418**	**2,250**	**168**	**8,864**	**8,970**	**-106**	**28,374**	**27,960**	**414**	**2,418**	**2,104**	**314**	**8,864**	**8,352**	**512**	**28,374**	**26,014**	**2,360**

FIGURE 14.9 Department Report—Completed

	A	B	C	D	E	F	G	H
1	E:\A4\The Book\Excel Files\[Case Study 1 - Chapt				Years	Curr	Curr	
2	Departments				Metric	Act	Bud	
3					Period	Mth	Mth	
5					*Value_Name*	Curr_Act_Mth	Curr_Bud_Mth	
6			State		*State_Name*	Curr_Act_State	Curr_Bud_State	
7			Dept		*Dept_Name*	Curr_Act_Dept	Curr_Bud_Dept	
8			Cat		*Category_Name*	Curr_Act_Cat	Curr_Bud_Cat	
9								
10					**Department Report for Revenue and Expenses for ABCD Ltd**			
11					**For the Period 1 July 13 to 31 October 13**			
12								
13					DEPARTMENT	**Current Year**		
14						Month 000's		
15						Actuals	Budget	Var
16	*State*	*Dept*	*Category*		**Revenue**			
17					**Product Sales**			
18	NSW	SALES	*		NSW	2,625	2,720	-95
19	VIC	SALES	*		VIC	3,164	2,810	354
20	WA	SALES	*		WA	2,256	2,050	206
21					**Total Product Sales**	**8,045**	**7,580**	**465**
23					**Cost of Sales**			
24	NSW	COS	*		NSW	1,799	1,890	91
25	VIC	COS	*		VIC	2,243	1,950	-293
26	WA	COS	*		WA	1,585	1,490	-95
27					**Total Product Cost of Sales**	**5,627**	**5,330**	**-297**
29					**Product Gross Margin**	**2,418**	**2,250**	**168**

FIGURE 14.10 Department Report—Helper Cells Displayed

F17 =SUM(a:b!F17:F17)

Case Study 1 - Chapter 14

	D	E	F	G	H	I	J	K
9								
10		**State Report for Revenue and Expenses for ABCD Ltd**						
11		**For the Period 1 July 13 to 31 October 13**						
12								
13		**ALL STATES**	**Current Year**				**Current Y**	
14			Month 000's				YTD 000	
15			Actuals	Budget	Variance		Actuals	Budget
16		**Revenue**						
17		Gadgets	3,605	3,490	115		13,575	13,84
18		Widgets	4,440	4,090	350		16,207	16,32
19		**Total Product Sales**	**8,045**	**7,580**	**465**		**29,782**	**30,16**
21		**Cost of Sale**						
22		Gadgets	2,546	2,490	-56		9,646	9,83
23		Widgets	3,081	2,840	-241		11,272	11,36
24		**Total Product Cost of Sales**	**5,627**	**5,330**	**-297**		**20,918**	**21,19**

Total_Check | **Total State** | a | NSW | VIC | WA | b

FIGURE 14.11 Total_State Report 3D Sum

	A	B	C	D	E	F	G	H
1	E:\A4\The Book\Excel Files\[Case				Years	Curr	Curr	
2	*				Metric	Act	Bud	
3					Period	Mth	Mth	
5					*Value_Name*	Curr_Act	Curr_Bud_Mth	
6			State		*State_Name*	Curr_Act	Curr_Bud_State	
7			Dept		*Dept_Name*	Curr_Act	Curr_Bud_Dept	
8			Acct		*Account_Name*	Curr_Act	Curr_Bud_Acct	
9								
10					**State Report for Revenue and Expenses for ABCD Ltd**			
11					**For the Period 1 July 13 to 31 October 13**			
12								
13					**ALL STATES**	**Current Year**		
14						Month 000's		
15						Actuals	Budget	Variance
16	*State*	*Dept*	*Account*		**Revenue**			
17	*	SALES	31000		Gadgets	3,605	3,490	115
18	*	SALES	32000		Widgets	4,440	4,090	350
19					**Total Product Sales**	**8,045**	**7,580**	**465**

FIGURE 14.12 Total_Check Report Based on State Sheet

The Dashboard Report

The dashboard will report on the statistics and financial data. The formulas used will again make use of structured range names and helper cells.

The dashboard report will use Sparkline charts for rolling 13-month charts. The formulas for the rolling 13-month chart data will have to be able to extract data from both the current year and the previous year.

When you are building multiple charts, I recommend having a dedicated sheet for the chart data. The dashboard sheet will contain charts, text boxes, and linked pictures.

The Chart Data Sheet

The Chart_Data sheet will have to extract monthly data for 13 months. The formulas used so far have focused on month and YTD formulas from the database layouts. The Chart_Data sheet will use a different technique to identify the rows to extract from the current and previous years' data sheets.

The completed Chart_Data sheet is shown in Figure 14.13.

The helper cells at the top of the sheet are shown in Figure 14.14.

The helper cells on the left are shown in Figure 14.15.

The top helper cells identify the months to be extracted and whether to use the current or previous year's data.

Rows 1 and 2 are entries and allow the selection of the current or previous year's range name prefix.

All formulas are copied across, except row 6.

The third row determines the year from which the value will come for that column. The formula in cell J3 is

```
=IF(J6<Start_Month,J1,J2)
```

The fourth row is there to simplify further formulas. It returns TRUE if the column is the current year or FALSE if it isn't. The formula in cell J4 is

```
=J2=J3
```

The fifth row calculates the month number for the column. The formula in cell J5 is

```
=IFERROR(MATCH(TEXT(J6,"mmm"),Months,0),""))
```

Row 6 determines the dates. It has two formulas.

Cell V6 contains the current month date:

```
=Curr_Month_Date
```

This range name is defined on the control sheet.

The other formula subtracts one month from the date on the right. Cell U6 has the formula

```
=DATE(YEAR(V6),MONTH(V6)-1,1)
```

This formula is copied to the range J6:T6.

Row 7 determines the column number in the GL_Data_Curr sheet that matches the month. This assumes that the GL_Data_Curr and GL_Data_Prev have the same column layout, which they do. The formula in cell J7 is

```
=MATCH(TEXT(J6,"mmm"),GL_Data_Curr!4:4,0)
```

ABCD Ltd

13 Month report data

Gadget Sales Volume	Oct-12	Nov-12	Dec-12	Jan-13	Feb-13	Mar-13	Apr-13	May-13	Jun-13	Jul-13	Aug-13	Sep-13	Oct-13
NSW	13,400	14,151	14,665	13,415	14,182	14,385	14,633	14,645	14,445	12,394	12,488	13,329	14,921
VIC	12,109	13,657	13,766	12,986	12,155	13,250	13,058	13,450	13,880	13,574	14,816	12,779	14,850
WA	13,250	13,917	13,468	13,965	14,758	14,229	14,257	13,468	13,669	14,297	13,986	14,016	13,323

Widget Sales Volume	Oct-12	Nov-12	Dec-12	Jan-13	Feb-13	Mar-13	Apr-13	May-13	Jun-13	Jul-13	Aug-13	Sep-13	Oct-13
NSW	13,067	13,767	14,572	14,348	13,464	13,122	13,832	14,398	14,184	13,441	15,209	14,688	13,475
VIC	13,435	15,080	14,516	14,427	14,834	13,820	14,629	13,740	13,589	14,417	13,812	14,885	13,190
WA	13,564	14,872	14,040	15,015	13,640	13,811	14,404	15,039	13,903	15,090	13,716	14,576	13,412

Gadget Sales Value $	Oct-12	Nov-12	Dec-12	Jan-13	Feb-13	Mar-13	Apr-13	May-13	Jun-13	Jul-13	Aug-13	Sep-13	Oct-13
NSW	1,361,000	1,351,000	1,251,000	1,247,000	1,205,000	990,000	1,345,000	1,280,000	1,333,000	1,071,000	1,284,000	1,232,000	1,235,000
VIC	1,117,000	1,169,000	1,209,000	1,266,000	1,284,000	1,334,000	1,169,000	1,269,000	1,357,000	1,233,000	1,330,000	1,171,000	1,407,000
WA	874,000	912,000	825,000	826,000	962,000	1,007,000	1,099,000	771,000	818,000	950,000	861,000	838,000	963,000

Widget Sales Value $	Oct-12	Nov-12	Dec-12	Jan-13	Feb-13	Mar-13	Apr-13	May-13	Jun-13	Jul-13	Aug-13	Sep-13	Oct-13
NSW	1,247,000	1,357,000	1,612,000	1,201,000	1,457,000	1,477,000	1,336,000	1,315,000	1,545,000	1,338,000	1,468,000	1,344,000	1,390,000
VIC	1,475,000	1,537,000	1,419,000	1,310,000	1,720,000	1,523,000	1,467,000	1,682,000	1,665,000	1,361,000	1,433,000	1,500,000	1,757,000
WA	1,014,000	925,000	935,000	1,166,000	1,073,000	1,068,000	853,000	1,069,000	1,072,000	1,266,000	1,070,000	987,000	1,293,000

Gadget Avg $ per Unit	Oct-12	Nov-12	Dec-12	Jan-13	Feb-13	Mar-13	Apr-13	May-13	Jun-13	Jul-13	Aug-13	Sep-13	Oct-13
NSW	101.57	95.47	85.31	92.96	84.97	68.82	91.92	87.40	92.28	86.41	102.82	92.43	82.77
VIC	92.25	85.60	87.83	97.49	105.64	100.68	89.52	94.35	97.77	90.84	89.77	91.63	94.75
WA	65.96	65.53	61.26	59.15	65.18	70.77	77.08	57.25	59.84	66.45	61.56	59.79	72.28

FIGURE 14.13 Chart_Data Sheet

	H	I	J	K	L	M	N	O	P	Q	R	S	T	U	V	W
1		Prev Year Prefix	Pyr	Pyr	Pyr	Pyr	Pyr	Pyr	Pyr	Pyr	Pyr	Pyr	Pyr	Pyr	Pyr	
2		Current Year Prefix	Curr	Curr	Curr	Curr	Curr	Curr	Curr	Curr	Curr	Curr	Curr	Curr	Curr	
3		Year	Pyr	Pyr	Pyr	Pyr	Pyr	Pyr	Pyr	Pyr	Pyr	Curr	Curr	Curr	Curr	
4		Is Current Year	FALSE	FALSE	FALSE	FALSE	FALSE	FALSE	FALSE	FALSE	FALSE	TRUE	TRUE	TRUE	TRUE	
5		Month Numbers	4	5	6	7	8	9	10	11	12	1	2	3	4	
6		Dates	Oct-12	Nov-12	Dec-12	Jan-13	Feb-13	Mar-13	Apr-13	May-13	Jun-13	Jul-13	Aug-13	Sep-13	Oct-13	
7		GL Report Column	10	11	12	13	14	15	16	17	18	7	8	9	10	
8		**ABCD Ltd**														
9		**13 Month report data**														

FIGURE 14.14 Chart_Data Top Helper Cells

	A	B	C	D	E	F	G	H	I
8									**ABCD Ltd**
9									**13 Month report data**
10									
11							Second Part of range name		Gadget Sales Volume
12	Act	Sales	Vol	Gadget	NSW		_Act_Sales_Vol_Gadget_NSW		NSW
13	Act	Sales	Vol	Gadget	VIC		_Act_Sales_Vol_Gadget_VIC		VIC
14	Act	Sales	Vol	Gadget	WA		_Act_Sales_Vol_Gadget_WA		WA
15									
16							Second Part of range name		Widget Sales Volume
17	Act	Sales	Vol	Widget	NSW		_Act_Sales_Vol_Widget_NSW		NSW
18	Act	Sales	Vol	Widget	VIC		_Act_Sales_Vol_Widget_VIC		VIC
19	Act	Sales	Vol	Widget	WA		_Act_Sales_Vol_Widget_WA		WA
20									
21	State	Acct	Acct		Curr	Pyr			Gadget Sales Value $
22	_Act_State	_Act_Acct	31000	Rows =>	7	7			NSW
23	_Act_State	_Act_Acct	31000	Rows =>	21	21			VIC
24	_Act_State	_Act_Acct	31000	Rows =>	35	35			WA
25									
26	State	Acct	Acct		Curr	Pyr			Widget Sales Value $
27	_Act_State	_Act_Acct	32000	Rows =>	8	8			NSW
28	_Act_State	_Act_Acct	32000	Rows =>	22	22			VIC
29	_Act_State	_Act_Acct	32000	Rows =>	36	36			WA
30									

FIGURE 14.15 Chart_Data Left Side Helper Cells

This finds the column number in the GL_Data_Curr sheet by finding the month name in row 4 of the GL_Data_Curr sheet.

The helper cells on the left identify the value to be extracted. There are two types of helper cells. The first set is used for statistics, and the second is used for the financial data.

Rows 12 to 19 in columns A to G are used to build the structured range name used to identify the statistic value to be extracted. The values in the range A12:D19 are all entries. The state entries in E12:E19 are all linked to column I.

Column G creates the structured range name without the year prefix. The formula in cell G12 is

```
="_"&A12&"_"&B12&"_"&C12&"_"&D12&"_"&E12
```

The prefix will be added in the formula in J12, which will be based on the column involved.

The second set of helper cells on the left is devoted to the financial data. The values in the range A22:D29 are all entries. Columns E and F calculate the row numbers in the current and previous years' sheets, respectively.

The formula in cell E22 is

```
=SUMPRODUCT((INDIRECT(E$21&$A22)=$I22)*
```

```
(INDIRECT(E$21&$B22)=$C22)*(ROW(INDIRECT(E$21&$A22))))
```

Converting the INDIRECT functions to their range names, you have

```
=SUMPRODUCT((Curr_Act_State=$I22)*(Curr_Act_State=$C22)*
(ROW(Curr_Act_State)))
```

When the first two criteria return TRUE in the current-year sheet, it is multiplied by the row number of the state range. This is valid because there is only one match. If there is no match, the formula returns a zero.

The formula in cell F22 is

```
=SUMPRODUCT((INDIRECT(F$21&$A22)=$I22)*(INDIRECT(F$21&$B22)=
 $C22)*(ROW(INDIRECT(F$21&$A22))))
```

Converting the INDIRECT functions to their range names, you have

```
=SUMPRODUCT((Pyr_Act_State=$I22)*(Pyr_Act_State=$C22)*
(ROW(Pyr_Act_State)))
```

This works in the same way as in the previous year's data sheet.

That explains all the helper cells. The helper cells' goal is to calculate the row and column numbers in the relevant sheets.

We can now review the two formulas that work in the body of the Chart_Data sheet. Both use the INDEX function.

The Statistics formula in cell J12 is

```
=INDEX(INDIRECT(J$3&$G12),1,J$5+1)
```

Converting the INDIRECT function to its range name it is

```
=INDEX(Pyr_Act_Sales_Vol_Gadget_NSW,1,J$5+1)
```

Remember that the statistics range names all have the statistic descriptive name as their first cell; hence the need to add 1 to the value in cell J5 to extract the correct month column in the range name.

The financials formula first determines whether there is a zero in the relevant column. If there is, it displays a zero. If there is no zero, then an INDEX function is used to extract a row-and-column intersection from the relevant sheet. The formula in cell J22 is

```
=IF(AND(J$4,$E22=0),0,IF(AND(NOT(J$4),$F22=0),0,
INDEX(IF(J$4,GL_Data_Curr!$1:$1000,GL_Data_Prev!$1:$1000),
IF(J$4,$E22,$F22),J$7)*1000))
```

The first IF function within the INDEX function sets the sheet range to use the current or previous year. The reference to $1:$1000 refers to the first 1,000 rows and all the columns. Cell J$7 contains the column number to extract, which is the same on both sheets. The second IF function within the INDEX function determines the row number to use, again based on whether the current or previous year is required.

The *1000 at the end of the formula converts the report values into $.

The bottom of the Chart_Data sheet contains some simple formulas to calculate volumes and sales values and total averages.

These values are used on the Dashboard sheet though a linked picture and a text box.

The Dashboard Sheet

The completed simple dashboard report is shown in Figure 14.16.

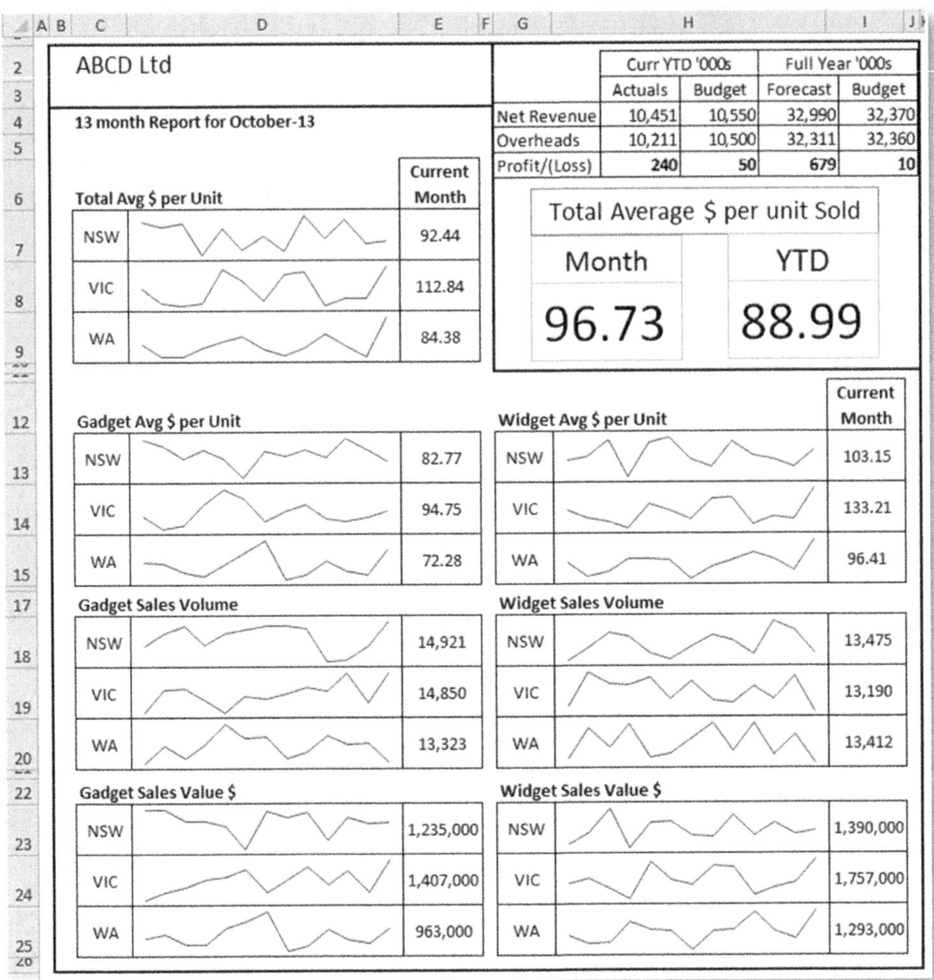

FIGURE 14.16 Dashboard Sheet—Completed

This dashboard uses three separate techniques, which were described in Chapter 12:

1. **Sparkline charts.** These are incredibly easy to insert and can be easily copied down after the first one has been created. I have added the current-month result to the right of each Sparkline chart to provide an indication of the final value. You can standardise the cell size so that all the Sparkline charts are consistent.
2. **Linked picture.** The report at the top right of the dashboard is a linked picture. The report is on the Chart_Data sheet.
3. **Text boxes.** Linking values to text boxes is effective in emphasising important values. You can change the font size without worrying about the underlying row or column sizes.

Sparkline Charts The Sparkline chart in cell D7 on the dashboard sheet was created using the dialog box in Figure 14.17.

Create Sparklines
Choose the data that you want
Data Range: Chart_Data!J42:V42
Choose where you want the sparklines to be placed
Location Range: $D$7
OK Cancel

FIGURE 14.17 Create Sparklines Dialog Box

The data range reference defaults to a relative reference, which allows you to copy the cell down to populate other Sparkline charts. The Sparkline charts on the dashboard sheet were all created in the top cell and copied down to the two cells below.

The cells on either side of the Sparkline charts are directly linked to the chart data sheet.

Linked Picture The reference for the linked picture is shown in Figure 14.18 (top right). This was created using the Camera icon.

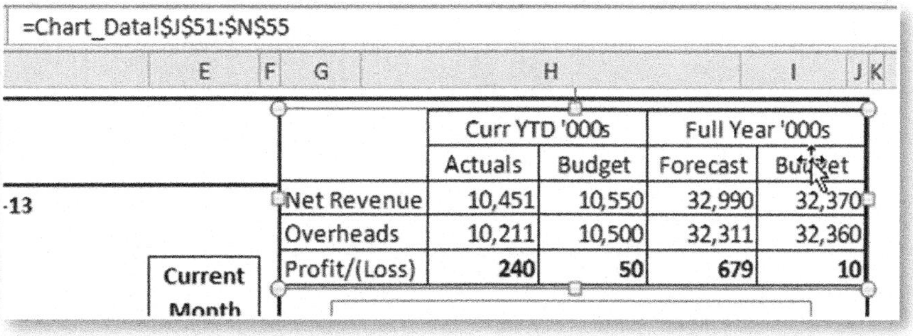

=Chart_Data!$J$51:$N$55

	Curr YTD '000s		Full Year '000s	
	Actuals	Budget	Forecast	Budget
Net Revenue	10,451	10,550	32,990	32,370
Overheads	10,211	10,500	32,311	32,360
Profit/(Loss)	**240**	**50**	**679**	**10**

FIGURE 14.18 Linked Picture Formula

Text Boxes You must link text boxes to a value on the current sheet. I have linked the two values in the text boxes to the values in column T of the dashboard sheet. These in turn are linked to the chart data sheet. Figure 14.19 shows the two text box links plus the linked cells.

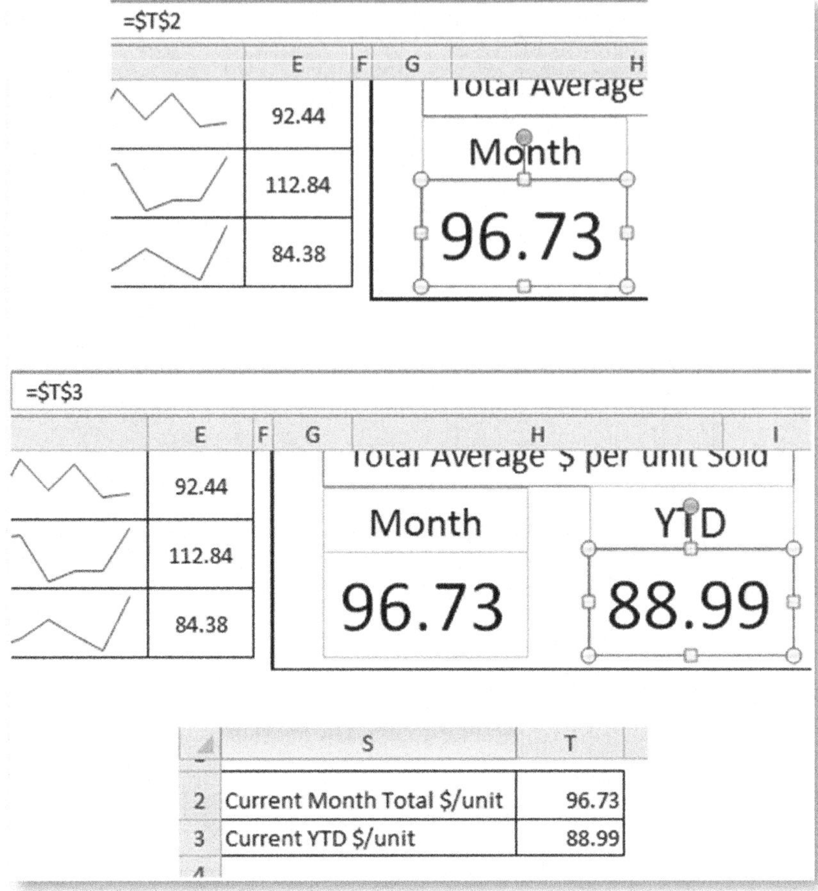

FIGURE 14.19 Text Boxes on the Dashboard Sheet

15

CHAPTER FIFTEEN

Case Study Two: 12-Month Reporting

I WILL USE A SCENARIO FOR the second case study similar to that of the first. The business manufactures the same two products in the same states. There are fewer departments and more accounts.

Each case study has two files on the companion website. The first file is a blank file, which has all the structures required but none of the content. This enables you to follow along with the instructions in this chapter to complete the reporting model. The second file is the completed reporting model for your reference.

SCENARIO

The reports required are 12-month reports and month and year-to-date (YTD) for actuals, budget, and forecasts. Full-year results are also compared to previous-year results.

The actual figures (this year and last year) are copied into the reporting model in a database structure. The budget and forecasts are both created in Excel and are similar to the sheets in Case Study One. The budget is updated in July, and forecasts are updated in October, January, and April.

The structure of the general ledger (GL) chart of accounts is the same as in Case Study One: state, department, and account number. The data set has this structure along with the date.

The account number has four digits. Each account number is allocated an account category. Reports are at account level.

There are a number of nonfinancial statistics. Actuals are in a database structure. Each of these statistics is included in the budget and forecast figures.

Some reports will utilise these statistics to compare averages.

A one-page dashboard report is required for key measures.

DATA REQUIREMENTS

The actuals for both financial and statistics data are in a database layout. They both contain the current and previous years' data (see Figures 15.1 and 15.2).

	A	B	C	D	E
1	Date	State	Department	Account	Amount
2	20120701	WA	TRADING	3100	614934.74-
3	20120701	WA	TRADING	3200	604983.85-
4	20120701	WA	TRADING	3300	9593.84-
5	20120701	WA	TRADING	3400	945-
6	20120701	WA	TRADING	3900	478.42-
7	20120701	NSW	TRADING	3100	828582.03-
8	20120701	NSW	TRADING	3200	769814.81-
9	20120701	NSW	TRADING	3300	19049.82-
10	20120701	NSW	TRADING	3400	1878.78-
11	20120701	NSW	TRADING	3900	955.92-
12	20120701	VIC	TRADING	3100	766129.46-
13	20120701	VIC	TRADING	3200	739825.28-
14	20120701	VIC	TRADING	3300	18524.47-
15	20120701	VIC	TRADING	3400	2792.11-
16	20120701	VIC	TRADING	3900	1373.04-
17	20120701	WA	PRODUCTION	4100	270626.31
18	20120701	WA	PRODUCTION	4110	60107.09

FIGURE 15.1 Actual GL Data Layout

	A	B	C
1	Month	Statistic	Value
2	Jul-11	Production Volume - WA	26097
3	Jul-11	Production Volume - NSW	29439
4	Jul-11	Production Volume - VIC	32693
5	Jul-11	Defect Perc - WA	2.68%
6	Jul-11	Defect Perc - NSW	2.55%
7	Jul-11	Defect Perc - VIC	3.04%
8	Jul-11	Machine Hours - WA	1004
9	Jul-11	Machine Hours - NSW	1186
10	Jul-11	Machine Hours - VIC	1191
11	Jul-11	Maintenance Hours - WA	53

FIGURE 15.2 Actual Statistics Data Layout

The budget and forecasts are in a spreadsheet layout, as in Case Study One.

The actuals database requires data cleansing. The date and the values have to be corrected. An extra field on the right will be added to incorporate the account category, which is not part of the database. New columns will be added to identify new states, departments, and accounts.

Having the data in a database layout will simplify the report formulas.

PROCESSES

The monthly reporting process will involve the following:

- Pasting in the latest actual databases (financial and statistics)
- Refreshing the pivot table
- Checking validations
- Correcting any validation issues
- Reviewing final reports

The annual reporting process will involve the following:

- Pasting in the new budget database
- Changing the start month for the reporting year

The quarterly reporting process will involve pasting in the latest forecast database.

STRUCTURE

We will use separate sheets for each of the data types (see Table 15.1).

TABLE 15.1 Data Sheets Required

Sheet Name	Description	Paste Frequency
Act_GL_Data	Current and previous-year GL data	Monthly
Bud_GL_Data	Current-year budget GL data	Annually
For_GL_Data	Current-quarter forecast GL data	Quarterly
Act_Stats_Data	Current and previous-year statistics data	Monthly
Bud_Stats_Data	Current-year budget statistics data	Annually
For_Stats_Data	Current-quarter forecast statistics data	Quarterly

The data sheets will all have a formatted table structure. We will convert the table field names to range names to make creating the final reports easier. This automatically creates dynamic names that expand as data is added to the tables.

DESIGN

Range names will be used widely again. The prefixes we will use for the range names this time are shown in Table 15.2.

TABLE 15.2 Range Name Prefixes

Prefix	Type of Range Name
a_	Actuals GL
b_	Budget GL
f_	Forecast GL
r_	Report column or rows
s_	Actual statistics

THE CREATION PROCESS

The various components of the reporting model will be described and explained.

The Control Sheet

This control sheet has only one selection: the measure to use to populate the future months. The choice is between budget and forecast. Both the starting date and the current month are determined by formulas. The assumption is that the GL download contains no future month's data.

The formula to determine the current month in cell D6 is

```
=MAX(a_Date)
```

The range name a_Date is the corrected date column in the Act_GL_Data sheet. The current month cell D6 is named Curr_Month.

The formula to determine the starting date in cell D5 is

```
=DATE(YEAR(Curr_Month)-IF(MONTH(Curr_Month)<=6,1,0),7,1)
```

This formula deducts 1 from the year of the current month when the month of the current month is less than or equal to six. Otherwise it uses the current month's year and creates the July 1 date. The financial year's starting month cell is named Start_Month. This formula is based on the Australian financial year that begins in July.

The control sheet lists any missing states, departments, and accounts in the actuals data and also contains the headings cells (see Figure 15.3).

Table Names

Formatted tables are used for both the actuals GL data and the actuals statistics data. I have also used formatted tables for the lists and tables in the tables sheet.

The use of formatted tables allows you to easily create dynamic range names. Formatted tables also provide visual clues to users that certain ranges are used as tables.

	A	B	C	D	E	F	G
1		WXYZ Corporation					
2							
3		Validation		TRUE			
4			Range Names				
5		Financial Year Start Month	*Start_Month*	1/07/2013			
6		Current Month	*Curr_Month*	1/11/2013			
7		Select Measure for Future Months	*Future_Months*	Forecast			
8							
9		**Headings**	Range Names				
10		12 Month Report For	*hdg_Main*	12 Month Report For November 2013			
11		Report For	*hdg_Month*	Report For November 2013			
12							
13		**Missing Codes Listing**		**State**	**Dept**	**Account**	
14		1					
15		2					
16		3					
17		4					
18		5					
19		6					
20		7					
21		8					
22		9					
23		10					

FIGURE 15.3 Control Sheet Layout

Although you can use table names in your formula, it does cause the formulas to be quite long, since the table name is included as well as the field name. We will convert the table fields we use most often into range names. This will shorten the formula and make it easier to select ranges when creating the formula.

As in Case Study One, range name labels are shown in red italics. In Figure 15.3, the range name labels are in cells C5, C6, C7, C10, and C11. The range name cells are on the right of the range name labels.

Actual Data

The Actual GL data and the data for statistics are in a database layout. The GL data dump will have some data cleansing columns added. No changes are required to the statistics data.

GL Data Dump

The sheet Act_GL_Data contains the GL data. The downloaded data is in columns A to E, as was shown in Figure 15.1.

There are two issues that must be fixed in the data. The first is the date column. The format used is not recognised by Excel as a date. It has a text layout with the sequence year, month, and day.

The second issue is that the amount column uses a trailing minus sign for negative numbers. Excel does not recognise this as a value.

The data cleanse exercise will correct both of those issues. We will also add a new field for account category to the data. Figure 15.4 shows the extra three columns to add to the downloaded data.

F	G	H
Correct Amount	Correct Date	Account Category
-614934.74	1/07/2012	Revenue
-604983.85	1/07/2012	Revenue
-9593.84	1/07/2012	Revenue

FIGURE 15.4 Data Cleansing Columns

Finally, we will add six extra columns to identify missing states, departments, and accounts for validation purposes. Figure 15.5 contains the validation columns.

I	J	K	L	M	N
Confirm States	Confirm Dept	Confirm Accounts	New State Seq	New Dept Seq	New Account Seq
TRUE	TRUE	TRUE	0	0	0
TRUE	TRUE	TRUE	0	0	0
TRUE	TRUE	TRUE	0	0	0

FIGURE 15.5 Data Validation Columns

The first three columns confirm that the codes exist. The last three columns allow us to list the missing unique codes on the control sheet.

The formulas for row 2 are shown in Table 15.3. Note that the first six columns use formatted table field names, whereas the last three columns include mixed references.

TABLE 15.3 Formulas Added to Actuals Data

Cell	Formula
F2	=IF(RIGHT([@Amount])="-",(LEFT([@Amount],LEN([@Amount])-1))*-1,[@Amount])
G2	=DATE(LEFT([@Date],4),MID([@Date],5,2),RIGHT([@Date],2))
H2	=IFERROR(INDEX(tblAccounts[Category],MATCH([@Account],tblAccounts[Account Number],0)),"")
I2	=COUNTIF(tblStates[States],[@State])>0
J2	=COUNTIF(tblDepts[Departments],[@Department])>0
K2	=COUNTIF(tblAccounts[Account Number],[@Account])>0
L2	=IF([@[Confirm States]]=FALSE,IF(COUNTIF(B$2:B2,B2)=1,MAX(L$1:L1)+1,0),0)
M2	=IF([@[Confirm Dept]]=FALSE,IF(COUNTIF(C$2:C2,C2)=1,MAX(M$1:M1)+1,0),0)
N2	=IF([@[Confirm Accounts]]=FALSE,IF(COUNTIF(D$2:D2,D2)=1,MAX(N$1:N1)+1,0),0)

> **Tip: The DATE Function and Text Values**
>
> The DATE function accepts text values in its arguments and converts them into values. You don't need to multiply them by 1 to convert them into a value.

Cell F2 identifies when the entry has a minus sign on the right. If it does, then (LEFT([@Amount],LEN([@Amount])-1)) extracts all the characters from the left except the minus sign. The result is then multiplied by −1 to convert it into a negative number. If there is no minus sign, the unchanged amount is displayed.

Cell G2 takes the date format used, yyyymmdd, and converts it to an Excel date through the DATE function using text functions.

Cell H2 uses an INDEX-MATCH combination to extract the account category from the formatted table named tblAccounts on the tables sheet.

Columns I, J, and K use COUNTIF to return FALSE when the state, department, or account is not in its respective table on the tables sheet.

Columns L, M, and N all use the same type of formula to enter a new sequential number for every new state, department, or account. This allows the list on the control sheet to show only unique entries rather than duplicating the same new codes. The COUNTIF function identifies that the row is the first to have the new code. It then creates the next sequential number by adding 1 to the maximum value from the range above it.

The INDEX-MATCH formulas on the control sheet use a sequential number to extract the first 10 new codes in each column.

Structured Range Names

There is an extensive use of range names in this case study. Many of these range names take advantage of the dynamic nature of table names and use them as their reference. The name of the formatted table in the sheet Act_GL_Data is tblAct_Data.

We need to create the range names to use in the rest of the model. In the case of the date field for the GL actuals, we will use the correct date field (column G). To create a name based on a table field, use the Define Name option. Figure 15.6 has the completed New Name dialog box.

Once you have entered the name in the Name box, you can remove the entry in the Refers To box and select the first cell in the column involved—G2, in this case. I use a keyboard shortcut to select the whole range down to the bottom of the column. Hold the Ctrl and Shift keys down and press the down arrow. This keyboard shortcut works when there are no blanks in the column. When you select the range of the field, Excel will automatically insert the table name and field name into the Refers To box, as shown in Figure 15.6. Click OK to finish the naming process. Note the a_prefix is for actuals.

This process must be repeated for the other columns we will use in the model. With practice, this becomes quite a fast procedure.

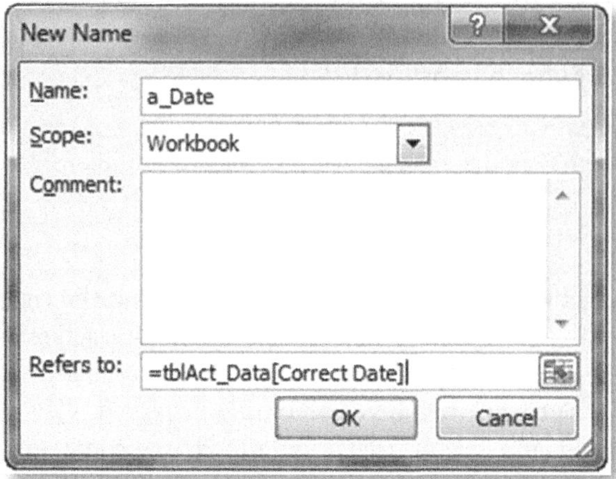

FIGURE 15.6 New Name Dialog Box

The range names required, as well as their definitions, are shown in Table 15.4. I've used some abbreviations in the range names to reduce formula length.

The range names for the actual statistics data are shown in Table 15.5. The table name of the data in the Act_Stats_Data sheet is named tblAct_Stats.

TABLE 15.4 GL Actual Data Range Names

Range Name	Refers To
a_Account	=tblAct_Data[Account]
a_Amt	=tblAct_Data[Correct Amount]
a_Cat	=tblAct_Data[Account Category]
a_Date	=tblAct_Data[Correct Date]
a_Dept	=tblAct_Data[Department]
a_State	=tblAct_Data[State]

TABLE 15.5 Actual Statistics Range Names

Range Name	Refers to
s_Month	=tblAct_Stats[Month]
s_Statistic	=tblAct_Stats[Statistic]
s_Value	=tblAct_Stats[Value]

Budget, Forecast GL, and Statistics Data

The layouts of the budget and forecast GL and statistics data sheets are similar to the first case study sheets, except that there are no helper cells added to the right side of the sheets. The formulas used will take advantage of another technique to extract the correct month's data.

THE REPORTS

The report sheet will contain a 12-month report that has actuals and budget or forecast. There will also be a current-month, YTD, and full-year report.

The reason I have combined reports is that the row layout of the report is already set up, so rather than creating another sheet that has to be maintained, we can use grouping to hide columns and have both reports on the same sheet.

Figure 15.7 shows the current-month and YTD report.

The first six rows and four columns are used for helper cells.

The monthly report is hidden by grouping in columns G to S. Figure 15.8 shows the monthly report.

The helper cell rows and columns are shown in Figure 15.9.

Columns A, B, and C have entries. Column D has a formula that will be explained later in the chapter.

There are multiple formulas used in this report. Case Study One had a single formula using the INDIRECT function; this report will use more common formulas.

There are also three other reports to the right of the current-month and YTD report. These have the same layout as the 12-month report but hold the budget, forecast, and previous year figures respectively.

The 12-Month Report

The monthly report has a single SUMIFS formula for all the account rows. The other rows have SUBTOTAL or simple addition and subtraction formulas.

The formula in cell G13 is

```
=IF(r_Actuals,SUMIFS(a_Amt,a_State,r_State,a_Dept,r_Dept,a_
 Account,r_Account,a_Date,r_Date)*r_Sign,IF(Future_Months=
 "Budget",AD13,AV13))
```

The range names with the r_ prefix are all on the report sheet, and their range name label cells are shown in Figure 15.9.

The r_Actuals range name contains TRUE when the month is an actual or FALSE when it is not. It has a simple formula that compares the month in the r_Date range name to the Curr_Month range name. The formula in cell G3 is

```
=Curr_Month>=r_Date
```

The SUMIFS function uses a_prefix range names for the actual data and r_prefix names from this sheet to extract the correct values. The r_Sign range name in column D handles the fact that the revenue data values are negative but should be reported as positive.

In the tables sheet (see Figure 15.10) there is an account table (tblAcounts) that has the account category and the default sign for the account in column I.

The formula in cell D13 of the report sheet is

```
=INDEX(tblAccounts[Sign],MATCH(r_Account,tblAccounts[Account
 Number],0))
```

This uses the table names from the tblAccount formatted table in the tables sheet.

	F	T	U	V	W	X	Y	Z	AA
7	**WXYZ Corporation**		**Report For November 2013**						
9									
10	**Description**		**Current Month**		**Current YTD**		**Full Year**		
11	**Revenue**		**Actuals**	**Budget**	**Actuals**	**Budget**	**Report**	**Budget**	**Last Year**
12	WA								
13	Trade Sales Gadgets		732,879	756,250	3,529,644	3,539,250	8,404,244	8,379,250	8,037,109
14	Trade Sales Widgets		706,320	731,250	3,367,196	3,422,250	8,079,196	8,102,250	7,775,252
15	Other Sales		10,075	10,000	50,561	50,000	121,061	120,000	115,230
16	Interest Income		1,013	1,000	5,053	5,000	12,053	12,000	11,547
17	Gain / Loss on Sale of Assets		509	500	2,518	2,500	6,018	6,000	5,798
19	**Total WA Revenue**		**1,450,796**	**1,499,000**	**6,954,973**	**7,019,000**	**16,622,573**	**16,619,500**	**15,944,935**
21	**NSW**								
22	Trade Sales Gadgets		946,164	1,003,200	4,640,661	4,699,200	11,106,161	11,121,000	10,620,050
23	Trade Sales Widgets		913,612	930,240	4,353,362	4,357,440	10,348,162	10,312,200	9,880,043
24	Other Sales		19,778	20,000	101,553	100,000	242,553	240,000	232,066
25	Interest Income		2,009	2,000	9,895	10,000	23,895	24,000	23,109
26	Gain / Loss on Sale of Assets		1,005	1,000	4,972	5,000	11,972	12,000	11,521
28	**Total NSW Revenue**		**1,882,567**	**1,956,440**	**9,110,445**	**9,171,640**	**21,732,745**	**21,709,200**	**20,766,789**

FIGURE 15.7 Current-Month, YTD, and Full-Year Report Structure

	F	G	H	I	J	K	L	M	N	O	P	Q	R	S
7	WXYZ Corporation	12 Month Report For November 2013												
9		Actuals	Actuals	Actuals	Actuals	Actuals	Forecast	Forecast	Forecast	Forecast	Forecast	Forecast	Forecast	
10	Description	Jul-13	Aug-13	Sep-13	Oct-13	Nov-13	Dec-13	Jan-14	Feb-14	Mar-14	Apr-14	May-14	Jun-14	Total
11	Revenue													
19	Total WA Revenue	1,333,799	1,313,425	1,428,288	1,428,664	1,450,796	1,573,400	1,543,000	1,468,000	1,353,200	1,213,600	1,303,200	1,213,200	16,622,573
28	Total NSW Revenue	1,733,849	1,779,201	1,843,893	1,870,935	1,882,567	2,050,200	2,015,400	1,916,900	1,767,700	1,584,100	1,704,400	1,583,600	21,732,745
37	Total VIC Revenue	1,621,401	1,667,450	1,698,793	1,776,866	1,738,698	1,918,500	1,889,700	1,792,900	1,660,600	1,488,500	1,599,100	1,479,200	20,331,708
38														
39	Total Revenue	4,689,049	4,760,076	4,970,974	5,076,466	5,072,060	5,542,100	5,448,100	5,177,800	4,781,500	4,286,200	4,606,700	4,276,000	58,687,026
40														
41	Direct Costs													
58	Total WA Direct Costs	958,594	972,280	1,035,989	1,061,304	1,062,370	1,183,200	1,167,600	1,090,350	989,100	878,400	937,650	867,100	12,203,936
59														
76	Total NSW Direct Costs	1,129,534	1,148,459	1,226,557	1,246,595	1,249,029	1,404,668	1,387,568	1,291,636	1,167,004	1,025,754	1,100,164	1,011,394	14,388,362
77														
94	Total VIC Direct Costs	1,266,213	1,285,478	1,336,698	1,389,011	1,379,035	1,542,816	1,524,716	1,429,140	1,307,760	1,152,640	1,236,360	1,139,896	15,989,764
95														
96	Total All Direct Costs	3,354,341	3,406,217	3,599,243	3,696,910	3,690,434	4,130,684	4,079,884	3,811,126	3,463,864	3,056,794	3,274,174	3,018,390	42,582,062
97														
103	Total Gross Margin	1,334,708	1,353,859	1,371,731	1,379,556	1,381,626	1,411,416	1,368,216	1,366,674	1,317,636	1,229,406	1,332,526	1,257,610	16,104,963

FIGURE 15.8 Monthly Report Structure

	A	B	C	D	E	F	G	H
1						r_Month_Nums	1	2
2						r_Date	Jul-13	Aug-13
3						r_Actuals	TRUE	TRUE
4							Actuals	Actuals
5								
6								
7						WXYZ Corporation	12 Month Report For Nc	
9							Actuals	Actuals
10	r_State	r_Dept	r_Account	r_Sign		Description	Jul-13	Aug-13
11						Revenue		
12						WA		
13	WA	TRADING	3100	-1		Trade Sales Gadgets	677,555	663,348
14	WA	TRADING	3200	-1		Trade Sales Widgets	644,444	638,390
15	WA	TRADING	3300	-1		Other Sales	10,286	10,192
16	WA	TRADING	3400	-1		Interest Income	1,017	994
17	WA	TRADING	3900	-1		Gain / Loss on Sale of Assets	497	501
19						Total WA Revenue	1,333,799	1,313,425

FIGURE 15.9 Helper Cells Structure

	A	B	C	D	E	F	G	H	I
1	States		Departments	Statistic		Account Number	Account description	Category	Sign
2	WA		TRADING	Sales Volume		3100	Trade Sales Gadgets	Revenue	-1
3	NSW		SALES	Sales Volume		3200	Trade Sales Widgets	Revenue	-1
4	VIC		PRODUCTION	Production Volume		3300	Other Sales	Revenue	-1
5			ADMIN	Sales Volume		3400	Interest Income	Revenue	-1
6						3900	Gain / Loss on Sale of Assets	Revenue	-1
7						4100	Production Labour	Direct Costs	1
8						4110	Maintenance Labour	Direct Costs	1
9						4130	Payroll Tax Expense	Direct Costs	1

FIGURE 15.10 Tables Sheet

You could use slightly different formulas for revenue and expenses, but it is preferable to use a single formula for both. Using tables in this way allows you to add flexibility to a model and handle exceptions more easily.

In the last IF function in cell G13's formula, the Future_Months range name defines whether the budget or forecast figures are used for the future months within the 12-month report. The Future_Months range name is on the control sheet and it is entered by the user. The cell references AD13 and AV13 are the budget and forecast cells, respectively, that are on the right side of the report sheet. The three reports on the right of the report sheets are shown in Figures 15.11, 15.12, and 15.13.

As you can see, the reports are identically laid out.

The formula for the budget in cell AD13 is

```
=SUMIFS(OFFSET(b_Account,0,r_Month_Nums),b_State,r_State,b_
 Dept,r_Dept,b_Account,r_Account)
```

The b_ prefix is for budgets. The OFFSET function is used to create a dynamic range to sum. The range b_Account is on the left of the budget values on the Bud_GL_Data sheet. By using the month number (r_Month_Nums), the range to sum will move across the sheet as the formula is copied across.

	AB	AC	AD	AE	AF	AG	AH	AI	AJ	AK	AL	AM	AN	AO	AP	AQ	AR	AS
1			1	2	3	4	5	6	7	8	9	10	11	12				
2		Budget	Jul-13	Aug-13	Sep-13	Oct-13	Nov-13	Dec-13	Jan-14	Feb-14	Mar-14	Apr-14	May-14	Jun-14	Total			
3																		
4																		
5																		
6																		
7																		
9			Budget	Budget	Budget	Budget	Budget	Budget	Budget	Budget	Budget	Budget	Budget	Budget			5	5
10			Jul-13	Aug-13	Sep-13	Oct-13	Nov-13	Dec-13	Jan-14	Feb-14	Mar-14	Apr-14	May-14	Jun-14	Total		Current	YTD
11																		
12																		
13			665,500	680,625	710,875	726,000	756,250	786,500	786,500	726,000	665,500	605,000	665,500	605,000	8,379,250		756,250	3,539,250
14			643,500	658,125	687,375	702,000	731,250	760,500	760,500	702,000	643,500	585,000	643,500	585,000	8,102,250		731,250	3,422,250
15			10,000	10,000	10,000	10,000	10,000	10,000	10,000	10,000	10,000	10,000	10,000	10,000	120,000		10,000	50,000
16			1,000	1,000	1,000	1,000	1,000	1,000	1,000	1,000	1,000	1,000	1,000	1,000	12,000		1,000	5,000
17			500	500	500	500	500	500	500	500	500	500	500	500	6,000		500	2,500
18																		
19			**1,320,500**	**1,350,250**	**1,409,750**	**1,439,500**	**1,499,000**	**1,558,500**	**1,558,500**	**1,439,500**	**1,320,500**	**1,201,500**	**1,320,500**	**1,201,500**	**16,619,500**		**1,499,000**	**7,019,000**

FIGURE 15.11 Budget Layout of the Report Sheet

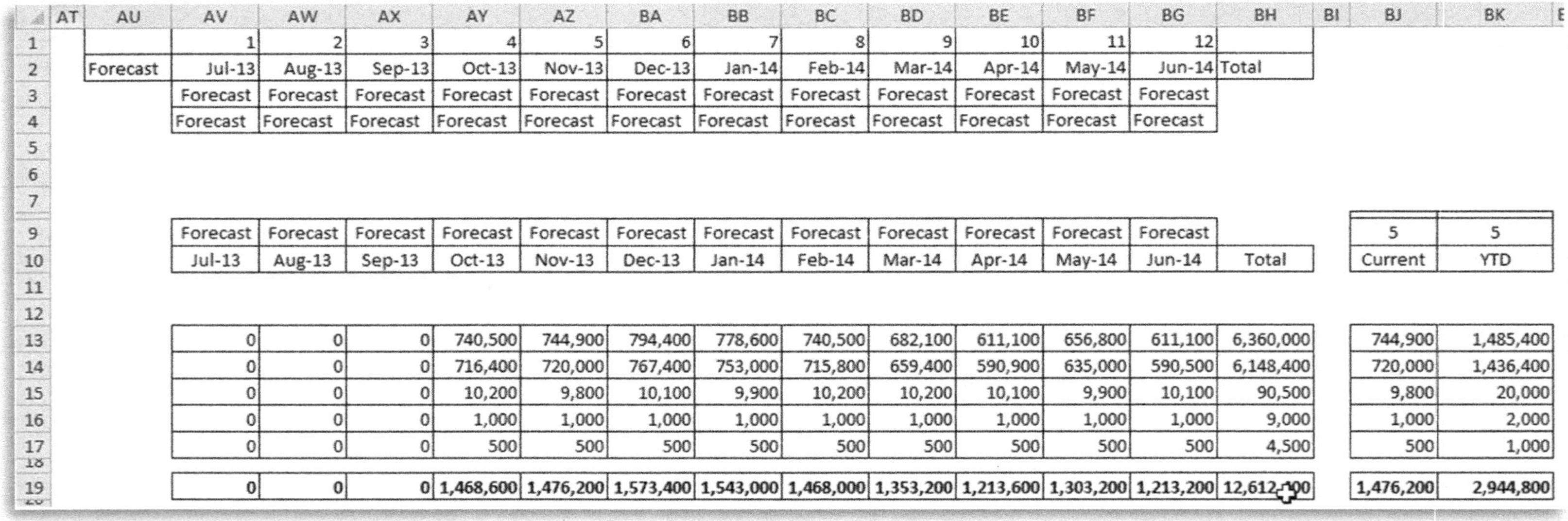

	AT	AU	AV	AW	AX	AY	AZ	BA	BB	BC	BD	BE	BF	BG	BH	BI	BJ	BK
1			1	2	3	4	5	6	7	8	9	10	11	12				
2		Forecast	Jul-13	Aug-13	Sep-13	Oct-13	Nov-13	Dec-13	Jan-14	Feb-14	Mar-14	Apr-14	May-14	Jun-14	Total			
3			Forecast	Forecast	Forecast	Forecast	Forecast	Forecast	Forecast	Forecast	Forecast	Forecast	Forecast	Forecast				
4			Forecast	Forecast	Forecast	Forecast	Forecast	Forecast	Forecast	Forecast	Forecast	Forecast	Forecast	Forecast				
5																		
6																		
7																		
9			Forecast	Forecast	Forecast	Forecast	Forecast	Forecast	Forecast	Forecast	Forecast	Forecast	Forecast	Forecast			5	5
10			Jul-13	Aug-13	Sep-13	Oct-13	Nov-13	Dec-13	Jan-14	Feb-14	Mar-14	Apr-14	May-14	Jun-14	Total		Current	YTD
11																		
12																		
13			0	0	0	740,500	744,900	794,400	778,600	740,500	682,100	611,100	656,800	611,100	6,360,000		744,900	1,485,400
14			0	0	0	716,400	720,000	767,400	753,000	715,800	659,400	590,900	635,000	590,500	6,148,400		720,000	1,436,400
15			0	0	0	10,200	9,800	10,100	9,900	10,200	10,200	10,100	9,900	10,100	90,500		9,800	20,000
16			0	0	0	1,000	1,000	1,000	1,000	1,000	1,000	1,000	1,000	1,000	9,000		1,000	2,000
17			0	0	0	500	500	500	500	500	500	500	500	500	4,500		500	1,000
19			**0**	**0**	**0**	**1,468,600**	**1,476,200**	**1,573,400**	**1,543,000**	**1,468,000**	**1,353,200**	**1,213,600**	**1,303,200**	**1,213,200**	**12,612,[illegible]00**		**1,476,200**	**2,944,800**

FIGURE 15.12 Forecast Layout of the Report Sheet

	BL	BM	BN	BO	BP	BQ	BR	BS	BT	BU	BV	BW	BX	BY	BZ	CA	CB	CC
1																		
2		Prev Yr	Jul-12	Aug-12	Sep-12	Oct-12	Nov-12	Dec-12	Jan-13	Feb-13	Mar-13	Apr-13	May-13	Jun-13				
3																		
4																		
5																		
6																		
7																		
9			Actuals	Actuals	Actuals	Actuals	Actuals	Actuals	Actuals	Actuals	Actuals	Actuals	Actuals	Actuals			5	5
10			Jul-12	Aug-12	Sep-12	Oct-12	Nov-12	Dec-12	Jan-13	Feb-13	Mar-13	Apr-13	May-13	Jun-13	Total		Current	YTD
11																		
12																		
13			614,935	636,761	672,323	694,586	696,496	706,731	772,166	727,135	639,283	604,855	666,748	605,089	8,037,109		696,496	3,315,101
14			604,984	631,435	656,911	670,047	644,422	697,428	761,542	685,242	635,436	571,848	636,536	579,420	7,775,252		644,422	3,207,800
15			9,594	9,584	9,469	9,141	9,144	9,247	9,831	9,897	10,005	9,864	9,648	9,806	115,230		9,144	46,932
16			945	918	950	945	921	959	996	1,006	988	978	979	963	11,547		921	4,679
17			478	456	458	465	479	475	504	501	500	488	490	503	5,798		479	2,337
19			**1,230,936**	**1,279,154**	**1,340,111**	**1,375,185**	**1,351,463**	**1,414,841**	**1,545,039**	**1,423,780**	**1,286,212**	**1,188,033**	**1,314,401**	**1,195,781**	**15,944,935**		**1,351,463**	**6,576,849**

FIGURE 15.13 Previous-Year Layout of the Report Sheet

The forecast section uses the same type of formula because the forecast sheet has the same layout as the budget sheet.

The formula in cell AV13 is

```
=SUMIFS(OFFSET(f_Account,0,r_Month_Nums),f_State,r_State,f_
Dept,r_Dept,f_Account,r_Account)
```

The f_ prefix is used for forecasts.

The budget and forecast formulas are copied to all the account rows.

The previous-year section uses exactly the same SUMIFS function that was used in cell G13 because the current and previous years' data are in the actuals data table.

The formula in cell BN13 is

```
=SUMIFS(a_Amt,a_State,r_State,a_Dept,r_Dept,a_Account,r_
Account,a_Date,r_Date)*r_Sign
```

The Current-Month, YTD, and Full-Year Report

The formula in cell U13 (current-month actuals) of the report sheet is

```
=SUMIFS(a_Amt,a_State,r_State,a_Dept,r_Dept,a_Account,r_
Account,a_Date,r_Date)*r_Sign
```

This is the same SUMIFS function that has been used in cells G13 and BN13. This formula has been amended to handle the YTD calculation required in cell W13.

```
=SUMIFS(a_Amt,a_State,r_State,a_Dept,r_Dept,a_Account,
r_Account,a_Date,"<="&r_Date,a_Date,">="&Start_Month)*
r_Sign
```

The dates criteria have been amended to handle a date range using the <= and >= symbols. Note that they are enclosed in quotation marks.

The other columns in this section are links to the other section on the right of the sheet.

The formula in cell V13 is

```
=AR13
```

The formula in cell X13 is

```
=AS13
```

The formula in cell Y13 is

```
=S13
```

The formula in cell Z13 is

```
=AP13
```

The formula in cell AA13 is

```
=BZ13
```

The current and YTD columns on the right side of the report use a standard INDEX function to calculate the values. The formula in the budget section in cell AR12 (current month) is

```
=INDEX(AD13:AO13,1,AR$9)
```

The formula in cell AS13 (YTD) is

```
=SUM(AD13:INDEX(AD13:AO13,1,AS$9))
```

The grouping buttons on the left allow for the display of summary or detail values (see Figure 15.14).

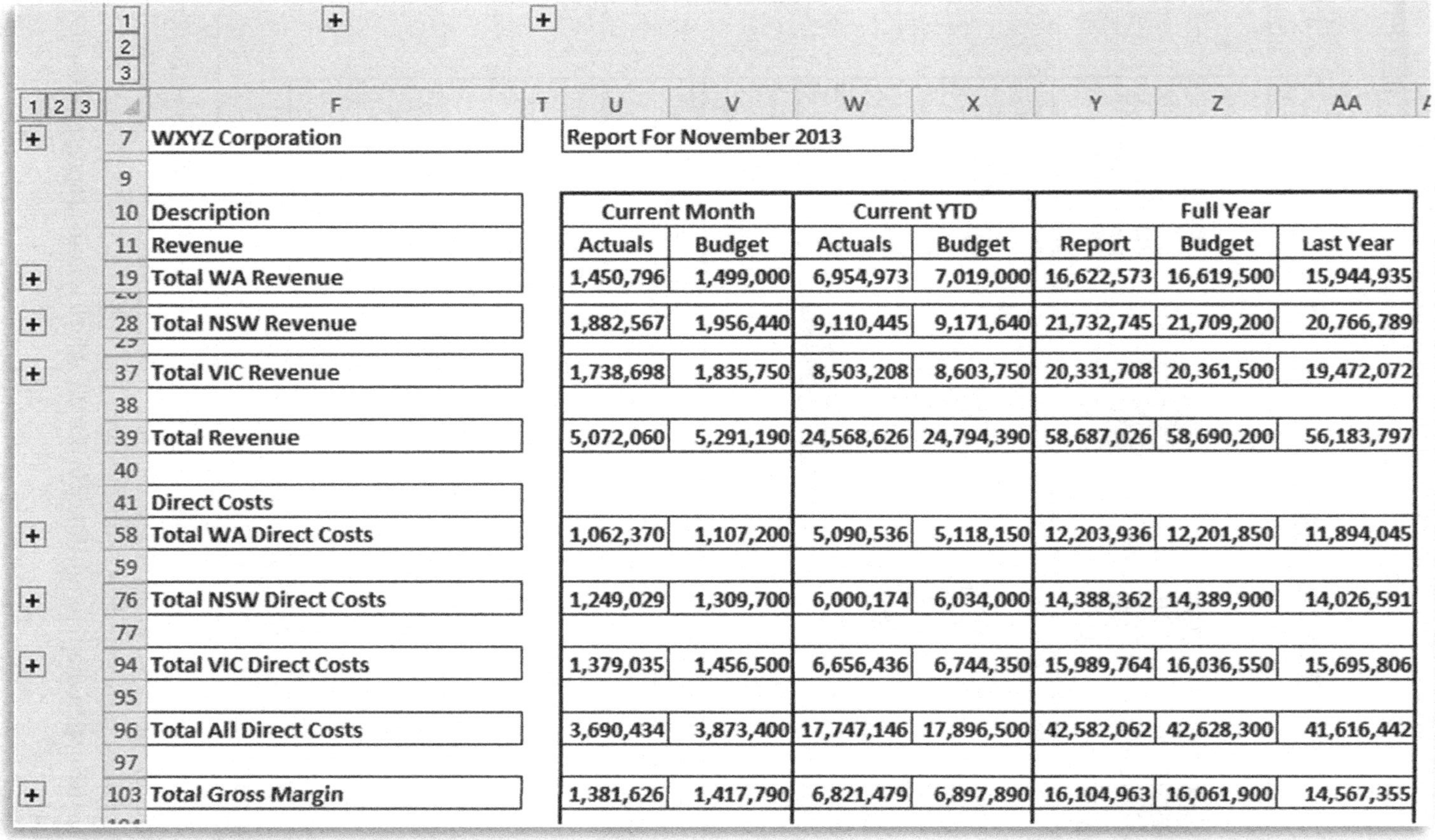

	F	T	U	V	W	X	Y	Z	AA
7	WXYZ Corporation		Report For November 2013						
9									
10	Description		Current Month		Current YTD		Full Year		
11	Revenue		Actuals	Budget	Actuals	Budget	Report	Budget	Last Year
19	Total WA Revenue		1,450,796	1,499,000	6,954,973	7,019,000	16,622,573	16,619,500	15,944,935
28	Total NSW Revenue		1,882,567	1,956,440	9,110,445	9,171,640	21,732,745	21,709,200	20,766,789
37	Total VIC Revenue		1,738,698	1,835,750	8,503,208	8,603,750	20,331,708	20,361,500	19,472,072
38									
39	Total Revenue		5,072,060	5,291,190	24,568,626	24,794,390	58,687,026	58,690,200	56,183,797
40									
41	Direct Costs								
58	Total WA Direct Costs		1,062,370	1,107,200	5,090,536	5,118,150	12,203,936	12,201,850	11,894,045
59									
76	Total NSW Direct Costs		1,249,029	1,309,700	6,000,174	6,034,000	14,388,362	14,389,900	14,026,591
77									
94	Total VIC Direct Costs		1,379,035	1,456,500	6,656,436	6,744,350	15,989,764	16,036,550	15,695,806
95									
96	Total All Direct Costs		3,690,434	3,873,400	17,747,146	17,896,500	42,582,062	42,628,300	41,616,442
97									
103	Total Gross Margin		1,381,626	1,417,790	6,821,479	6,897,890	16,104,963	16,061,900	14,567,355

FIGURE 15.14 Grouping Buttons on Report Sheet

The Dashboard Report

The dashboard uses common Excel charts and conditional formatting. Figure 15.15 shows the dashboard sheet, which can be modified by making changes in column H.

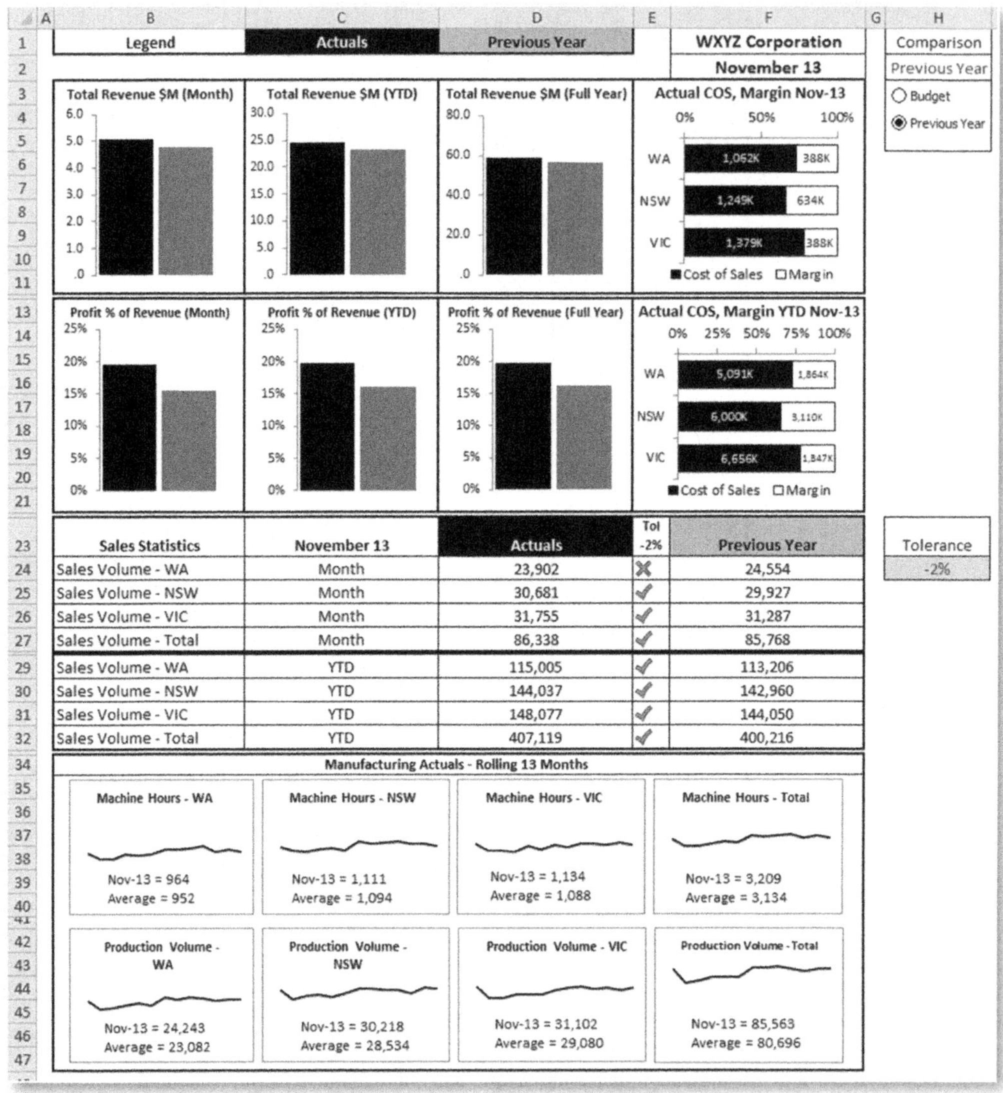

Sales Statistics	November 13	Actuals	Tol -2%	Previous Year
Sales Volume - WA	Month	23,902	✗	24,554
Sales Volume - NSW	Month	30,681	✓	29,927
Sales Volume - VIC	Month	31,755	✓	31,287
Sales Volume - Total	Month	86,338	✓	85,768
Sales Volume - WA	YTD	115,005	✓	113,206
Sales Volume - NSW	YTD	144,037	✓	142,960
Sales Volume - VIC	YTD	148,077	✓	144,050
Sales Volume - Total	YTD	407,119	✓	400,216

FIGURE 15.15 Dashboard Sheet

Cell H2 holds the comparison measure. The user can select the comparison measure using the two options buttons. The comparison is used for the column charts (top left) and the sales statistics (middle) of the dashboard.

The two options buttons are linked to cell H3, which is named optComparison. The formula in H2 is

```
=IF(optComparison="","Budget",CHOOSE(optComparison,"Budget",
 "Previous Year"))
```

The IF function handles the situation when cell H3 is empty.

Cell H24 allows the user to set the tolerance for the conditional formatting used in column E (checkmarks and Xs). The checkmarks and Xs compare the actual figures (column D) to the comparison figures (column F).

A positive tolerance percentage means that the acceptable target value is raised. Hence, a checkmark is harder to achieve. If 2% is entered, then an X will be displayed when the actual figure is less than 102% (100% + 2%) of the comparison figure. A positive percentage increases the value deemed to be acceptable. Figure 15.15 shows the results.

A negative percentage lowers the bar and makes it easier to achieve a checkmark. If –2% is entered, then the acceptable target is 98% (100% – 2%) of the comparison figure. Figure 15.16 shows the change in the report when –2% is entered.

Sales Statistics	November 13	Actuals	Tol -2%	Previous Year
Sales Volume - WA	Month	23,902	✗	24,554
Sales Volume - NSW	Month	30,681	✓	29,927
Sales Volume - VIC	Month	31,755	✓	31,287
Sales Volume - Total	Month	86,338	✓	85,768
Sales Volume - WA	YTD	115,005	✓	113,206
Sales Volume - NSW	YTD	144,037	✓	142,960
Sales Volume - VIC	YTD	148,077	✓	144,050
Sales Volume - Total	YTD	407,119	✓	400,216

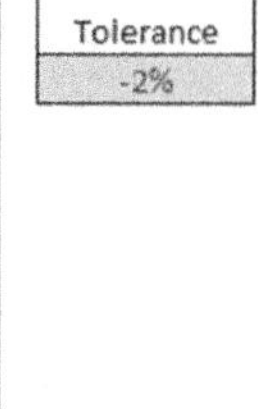

Tolerance
-2%

FIGURE 15.16 Tolerance of –2%

All the charts are based on data in the Dashboard_Data sheet.

Column Charts

Figure 15.17 shows the chart data used for the column charts at the top of the dashboard.

The values in rows 5 to 11 are all extracted using INDEX-MATCH formulas from the helper cells below in rows 16 to 29.

The formula in cell C5 is

```
=INDEX(C$20:C$22,MATCH($B4,$B$20:$B$22,0))
```

The formula in cell C10 is

```
=INDEX(C$27:C$29,MATCH($B10,$B$27:$B$29,0))
```

Both formulas have been copied down and across in their respective ranges.

Rows 17 to 29 are all linked to the respective current-month and YTD columns on the report sheet.

Bar Charts

The bar charts on the top right of the dashboard are based on the data in Figure 15.18.

The values in rows 34 to 42 are all linked to the respective current-month and YTD columns on the report sheet.

	A	B	C	D	E	F	G	H	I	J
1		WXYZ Corporation	Dashboad Data							
3		Column Charts - Top - First Row					Titles			
4		Total Revenue $M	Month	YTD	Full Year		Total Revenue $M (Month)			
5		Actuals	5,072,060	24,568,626	58,687,026		Total Revenue $M (YTD)			
6		Previous Year	4,766,952	23,157,949	56,183,797		Total Revenue $M (Full Year)			
8		Column Charts - Top - Second Row					Titles			
9		Profit % of Revenue	Month	YTD	Full Year		Profit % of Revenue (Month)			
10		Actuals	19.5%	19.8%	19.4%		Profit % of Revenue (YTD)			
11		Previous Year	15.5%	16.1%	17.7%		Profit % of Revenue (Full Year)			
14		Helper Cells for the Column Charts								
16		Total Revenue	Month	YTD	Full Year					
17		Actuals	5,072,060	24,568,626	58,687,026					
18		Budget	5,291,190	24,794,390	58,690,200					
19		Previous year	4,766,952	23,157,949	56,183,797					
21		Total Net Profit Before Tax	Month	YTD	Full Year					
22		Actuals	988,967	4,864,599	11,394,483					
23		Budget	1,026,160	4,939,740	11,362,340					
24		Previous year	736,836	3,737,063	9,925,425					
26		Net Profit % of Sales	Month	YTD	Full Year					
27		Actuals	19.5%	19.8%	19.4%					
28		Budget	19.4%	19.9%	19.4%					
29		Previous year	15.5%	16.1%	17.7%					

FIGURE 15.17 Dashboard _Data Sheet—Column Chart Data

	A	B	C	D	E
32		Bar Charts - Top Right			
33			Actual Margin $		
34		Actual COS, Margin Nov-13	Month	Cost of Sales	Margin
35		Total VIC Direct Costs	VIC	1,379,035	388,426
36		Total NSW Direct Costs	NSW	1,249,029	633,538
37		Total WA Direct Costs	WA	1,062,370	388,426
38					
39		Actual COS, Margin YTD Nov-13	YTD	Cost of Sales	Margin
40		Total VIC Direct Costs	VIC	6,656,436	1,846,772
41		Total NSW Direct Costs	NSW	6,000,174	3,110,270
42		Total WA Direct Costs	WA	5,090,536	1,864,437

FIGURE 15.18 Dashboard _Data Sheet—Bar Charts Data

Line Charts

The line charts at the bottom of the dashboard are all 13-month charts and are based on rows 46 to 57 (see Figure 15.19).

Line Charts - Bottom - Second Last Row

Rolling 13 Month	Nov-12	Dec-12	Jan-13	Feb-13	Mar-13	Apr-13	May-13	Jun-13	Jul-13	Aug-13	Sep-13	Oct-13	Nov-13
Machine Hours - WA	944	807	791	914	880	913	1,024	1,023	1,042	1,085	968	1,022	964
Machine Hours - NSW	1,077	977	967	1,016	1,031	999	1,201	1,163	1,167	1,195	1,162	1,162	1,111
Machine Hours - VIC	1,159	978	985	973	1,098	1,015	1,137	1,077	1,154	1,140	1,116	1,175	1,134
Machine Hours - Total	3,180	2,762	2,743	2,903	3,009	2,927	3,362	3,263	3,363	3,420	3,246	3,359	3,209

Text Boxes
Nov-13 = 964Average = 952
Nov-13 = 1,111Average = 1,094
Nov-13 = 1,134Average = 1,088
Nov-13 = 3,209Average = 3,134

Line Charts - Bottom - Last Row

Rolling 13 Month Defects	Nov-12	Dec-12	Jan-13	Feb-13	Mar-13	Apr-13	May-13	Jun-13	Jul-13	Aug-13	Sep-13	Oct-13	Nov-13
Production Volume - WA	23,635	19,179	19,804	21,014	22,139	20,990	25,997	24,415	25,839	25,064	23,358	24,395	24,243
Production Volume - NSW	29,831	24,089	26,110	27,120	26,080	27,592	30,344	30,446	29,847	30,047	28,006	31,211	30,218
Production Volume - VIC	32,055	24,729	24,794	27,208	26,868	27,078	29,633	31,115	32,066	30,267	31,177	29,947	31,102
Production Volume - Total	85,521	67,997	70,708	75,342	75,087	75,660	85,974	85,976	87,752	85,378	82,541	85,553	85,563

Text Boxes
Nov-13 = 24,243Average = 23,082
Nov-13 = 30,218Average = 28,534
Nov-13 = 31,102Average = 29,080
Nov-13 = 85,563Average = 80,696

Helper Cells for the Line Charts

13 Months Actual Data

Actual Statistics	Nov-12	Dec-12	Jan-13	Feb-13	Mar-13	Apr-13	May-13	Jun-13	Jul-13	Aug-13	Sep-13	Oct-13	Nov-13
Production Volume - WA	23,635	19,179	19,804	21,014	22,139	20,990	25,997	24,415	25,839	25,064	23,358	24,395	24,243
Production Volume - NSW	29,831	24,089	26,110	27,120	26,080	27,592	30,344	30,446	29,847	30,047	28,006	31,211	30,218
Production Volume - VIC	32,055	24,729	24,794	27,208	26,868	27,078	29,633	31,115	32,066	30,267	31,177	29,947	31,102
Defect Perc - WA	2.6%	2.3%	2.4%	2.4%	2.2%	2.2%	2.3%	2.1%	2.8%	2.5%	2.7%	2.4%	2.6%
Defect Perc - NSW	2.4%	2.3%	2.2%	2.2%	2.1%	2.1%	2.1%	2.0%	2.6%	2.3%	2.5%	2.3%	3.1%
Defect Perc - VIC	2.9%	2.8%	2.7%	2.6%	2.5%	2.7%	2.4%	2.5%	3.0%	2.9%	3.0%	2.6%	2.8%
Machine Hours - WA	944	807	791	914	880	913	1,024	1,023	1,042	1,085	968	1,022	964
Machine Hours - NSW	1,077	977	967	1,016	1,031	999	1,201	1,163	1,167	1,195	1,162	1,162	1,111
Machine Hours - VIC	1,159	978	985	973	1,098	1,015	1,137	1,077	1,154	1,140	1,116	1,175	1,134
Maintenance Hours - WA	53	48	45	49	49	51	58	57	54	55	56	57	53
Maintenance Hours - NSW	84	69	73	76	80	81	89	87	83	84	86	89	80
Maintenance Hours - VIC	53	43	45	45	49	49	51	53	51	55	50	55	53
Downtime Hours - WA	15	12	12	13	14	14	16	15	16	16	14	16	15
Downtime Hours - NSW	27	23	24	24	27	25	29	29	30	30	29	28	27
Downtime Hours - VIC	11	10	10	10	11	10	12	11	12	12	11	12	11
Sales Volume - WA	24,554	25,535	26,866	23,761	21,107	20,038	23,009	20,968	21,732	22,380	22,454	24,537	23,902
Sales Volume - NSW	29,927	32,287	33,084	28,627	26,276	24,686	27,992	24,225	26,723	28,142	28,973	29,518	30,681
Sales Volume - VIC	31,287	34,240	31,819	29,298	27,322	24,876	27,541	24,880	28,335	27,566	30,612	29,809	31,755

FIGURE 15.19 Dashboard _Data Sheet—Line Charts Data

The formula in cell C47 is

```
=INDEX(C$64:C$81,MATCH($B47,$B$64:$B$81,0))
```

This formula has been copied to the ranges C47:O50 and C54:O57.

The text and values shown on the line charts are text boxes that are linked to the cells in column Q.

The formula in cell Q47 is

```
=TEXT($O$46,"mmm-yy")&"="&TEXT(O47,"#,###")&CHAR(10)&"Average  ="
  & TEXT(AVERAGE(C47:O47),"#,###")
```

The CHAR(10) function is a line feed character and causes the text "Average = " to be shown on the second line in the text box. It doesn't show in the cell itself unless you use the Wrap Text format on the cell.

The 13-month helper cells for the line chart data are in rows 63 to 81.

The formula in cell C64 is

```
=SUMIFS(s_Value,s_Month,C$63,s_Statistic,$B64)
```

This formula has been copied down and across to cell O81.

The s_ prefix range names are all on the Act_Stats_Data sheet. There are only three columns. The sheet includes the previous year's data as well as the current year's data.

Dashboard Values

The values in the report at the centre of the dashboard are based on the tables in rows 86 to 124 of Dashboard_Data. Figure 15.20 shows the rows.

The formula in cell C87 is

```
=SUMIFS(s_Value,s_Month,C$86,s_Statistic,$B87)
```

This is the same formula used in cell C64, but this table is reporting the current year. I have included all the statistics in case other charts are required.

One of the formulas is worth explaining. The formula in cell O90 is

```
=SUMPRODUCT(C87:N87,C90:N90)/SUM(C87:N87)
```

This formula calculates the total YTD defect percentage for WA. Obviously, you can't add up the percentages in the row to get the total. Using the SUMPRODUCT function in its standard form allows you to calculate the total volume based on the production volumes in row 87.

The SUMPRODUCT function multiplies the volumes by the percentages to arrive at the defect volume, which is then divided by the total volume.

The comparison report in rows 106 to 124 is based on the selection on the dashboard sheet. The choice is between Budget and Previous Year.

The formula in cell R110 is also worth analysing. It handles the YTD defect percentage calculation.

```
=SUMPRODUCT(OFFSET(C107,0,0,1,MATCH(Curr_Month,$C$106:$N$106,
  0)),OFFSET(C110,0,0,1,MATCH(Curr_Month,$C$106:$N$106,0))/
  SUM(OFFSET(C107,0,0,1,MATCH(Curr_Month,$C$106:$N$106,0))))
```

This uses the range version of the OFFSET function to create the dynamic ranges used in the SUMPRODUCT function. It works in the same way as the formula in cell O90, but the ranges are dynamic to calculate the correct YTD figure.

	A	B	C	D	E	F	G	H	I	J	K	L	M	N	O	P	Q	R
84		**Helper Cells for the Report in the Middle of the Dashboard**																
86		**Actual Statistics**	**Jul-13**	**Aug-13**	**Sep-13**	**Oct-13**	**Nov-13**	**Dec-13**	**Jan-14**	**Feb-14**	**Mar-14**	**Apr-14**	**May-14**	**Jun-14**	**Total**		**Month**	
87		Production Volume - WA	25,839	25,064	23,358	24,395	24,243	0	0	0	0	0	0	0	122,899		24,243	
88		Production Volume - NSW	29,847	30,047	28,006	31,211	30,218	0	0	0	0	0	0	0	149,329		30,218	
89		Production Volume - VIC	32,066	30,267	31,177	29,947	31,102	0	0	0	0	0	0	0	154,559		31,102	
90		Defect Perc - WA	2.8%	2.5%	2.7%	2.4%	2.6%	0.0%	0.0%	0.0%	0.0%	0.0%	0.0%	0.0%	2.6%		2.6%	
91		Defect Perc - NSW	2.6%	2.3%	2.5%	2.3%	3.1%	0.0%	0.0%	0.0%	0.0%	0.0%	0.0%	0.0%	2.5%		3.1%	
92		Defect Perc - VIC	3.0%	2.9%	3.0%	2.6%	2.8%	0.0%	0.0%	0.0%	0.0%	0.0%	0.0%	0.0%	2.9%		2.8%	
93		Machine Hours - WA	1,042	1,085	968	1,022	964	0	0	0	0	0	0	0	5,081		964	
94		Machine Hours - NSW	1,167	1,195	1,162	1,162	1,111	0	0	0	0	0	0	0	5,797		1,111	
95		Machine Hours - VIC	1,154	1,140	1,116	1,175	1,134	0	0	0	0	0	0	0	5,719		1,134	
96		Maintenance Hours - WA	54	55	56	57	53	0	0	0	0	0	0	0	275		53	
97		Maintenance Hours - NSW	83	84	86	89	80	0	0	0	0	0	0	0	422		80	
98		Maintenance Hours - VIC	51	55	50	55	53	0	0	0	0	0	0	0	264		53	
99		Downtime Hours - WA	16	16	14	16	15	0	0	0	0	0	0	0	77		15	
100		Downtime Hours - NSW	30	30	29	28	27	0	0	0	0	0	0	0	144		27	
101		Downtime Hours - VIC	12	12	11	12	11	0	0	0	0	0	0	0	58		11	
102		Sales Volume - WA	21,732	22,380	22,454	24,537	23,902	0	0	0	0	0	0	0	115,005		23,902	
103		Sales Volume - NSW	26,723	28,142	28,973	29,518	30,681	0	0	0	0	0	0	0	144,037		30,681	
104		Sales Volume - VIC	28,335	27,566	30,612	29,809	31,755	0	0	0	0	0	0	0	148,077		31,755	
106		**Comparison**	**Jul-13**	**Aug-13**	**Sep-13**	**Oct-13**	**Nov-13**	**Dec-13**	**Jan-14**	**Feb-14**	**Mar-14**	**Apr-14**	**May-14**	**Jun-14**	**Total**		**Month**	**YTD**
107		Production Volume - WA	26,097	25,377	23,727	23,910	23,635	19,179	19,804	21,014	22,139	20,990	25,997	24,415	276,284		23,635	122,746
108		Production Volume - NSW	29,439	29,405	27,397	31,617	29,831	24,089	26,110	27,120	26,080	27,592	30,344	30,446	339,470		29,831	147,689
109		Production Volume - VIC	32,693	29,405	29,977	30,260	32,055	24,729	24,794	27,208	26,868	27,078	29,633	31,115	345,815		32,055	154,390
110		Defect Perc - WA	2.7%	2.4%	2.7%	2.3%	2.6%	2.3%	2.4%	2.4%	2.2%	2.2%	2.3%	2.1%	2.4%		2.6%	2.5%
111		Defect Perc - NSW	2.6%	2.4%	2.5%	2.4%	2.4%	2.3%	2.2%	2.2%	2.1%	2.1%	2.1%	2.0%	2.3%		2.4%	2.5%
112		Defect Perc - VIC	3.0%	2.8%	3.1%	2.7%	2.9%	2.8%	2.7%	2.6%	2.5%	2.7%	2.4%	2.5%	2.7%		2.9%	2.9%
113		Machine Hours - WA	1,004	1,034	976	1,044	944	807	791	914	880	913	1,024	1,023	11,354		944	5,002
114		Machine Hours - NSW	1,186	1,139	1,199	1,130	1,077	977	967	1,016	1,031	999	1,201	1,163	13,085		1,077	5,731
115		Machine Hours - VIC	1,191	1,096	1,110	1,138	1,159	978	985	973	1,098	1,015	1,137	1,077	12,957		1,159	5,694
116		Maintenance Hours - WA	53	53	55	55	53	48	45	49	49	51	58	57	626		53	269
117		Maintenance Hours - NSW	83	80	83	89	84	69	73	76	80	81	89	87	974		84	419
118		Maintenance Hours - VIC	49	53	49	55	53	43	45	45	49	49	51	53	594		53	259
119		Downtime Hours - WA	16	15	15	17	15	12	12	13	14	14	16	15	174		15	78
120		Downtime Hours - NSW	31	30	29	28	27	23	24	24	27	25	29	29	326		27	145
121		Downtime Hours - VIC	12	12	11	12	11	10	10	10	11	10	12	11	132		11	58
122		Sales Volume - WA	21,041	21,635	22,319	23,657	24,554	25,535	26,866	23,761	21,107	20,038	23,009	20,968	274,490		24,554	113,206
123		Sales Volume - NSW	27,773	29,317	27,834	28,109	29,927	32,287	33,084	28,627	26,276	24,686	27,992	24,225	340,137		29,927	142,960
124		Sales Volume - VIC	27,609	26,852	29,933	28,369	31,287	34,240	31,819	29,298	27,322	24,876	27,541	24,880	344,026		31,287	144,050

FIGURE 15.20 Dashboard _Data Sheet—Actuals and Comparison Tables

Both sets of statistics (budget and previous year) are shown in Figure 15.21 in the helper cells in rows 129 to 167.

	A	B	C	D	E	F	G	H	I	J	K	L	M	N	O
127		**Helper Cells to Select the Comparison Figures**													
129		**Budget Statistics**	**Jul-13**	**Aug-13**	**Sep-13**	**Oct-13**	**Nov-13**	**Dec-13**	**Jan-14**	**Feb-14**	**Mar-14**	**Apr-14**	**May-14**	**Jun-14**	**Total**
130		Production Volume - WA	25,000	25,000	24,000	25,000	24,000	20,000	20,000	21,000	22,000	22,000	25,000	24,000	277,000
131		Production Volume - NSW	30,000	30,000	29,000	30,000	29,000	25,000	25,000	26,000	27,000	27,000	30,000	29,000	337,000
132		Production Volume - VIC	31,000	31,000	30,000	31,000	30,000	26,000	26,000	27,000	28,000	28,000	31,000	30,000	349,000
133		Defect Perc - WA	2.7%	2.6%	2.6%	2.5%	2.5%	2.4%	2.4%	2.4%	2.3%	2.3%	2.2%	2.2%	2.4%
134		Defect Perc - NSW	2.6%	2.5%	2.5%	2.4%	2.4%	2.3%	2.3%	2.3%	2.2%	2.2%	2.1%	2.1%	2.3%
135		Defect Perc - VIC	3.0%	2.9%	2.9%	2.8%	2.8%	2.7%	2.7%	2.7%	2.6%	2.6%	2.5%	2.5%	2.7%
136		Machine Hours - WA	1,042	1,042	1,000	1,042	1,000	833	833	875	917	917	1,042	1,000	11,543
137		Machine Hours - NSW	1,154	1,154	1,115	1,154	1,115	962	962	1,000	1,038	1,038	1,154	1,115	12,961
138		Machine Hours - VIC	1,170	1,170	1,132	1,170	1,132	981	981	1,019	1,057	1,057	1,170	1,132	13,171
139		Maintenance Hours - WA	57	57	55	57	55	46	46	48	50	50	57	55	633
140		Maintenance Hours - NSW	87	87	84	87	84	72	72	75	78	78	87	84	975
141		Maintenance Hours - VIC	53	53	51	53	51	44	44	46	48	48	53	51	595
142		Downtime Hours - WA	16	16	15	16	15	12	12	13	14	14	16	15	174
143		Downtime Hours - NSW	29	29	28	29	28	24	24	25	26	26	29	28	325
144		Downtime Hours - VIC	12	12	11	12	11	10	10	10	11	11	12	11	133
145		Sales Volume - WA	22,000	22,500	23,500	24,000	25,000	26,000	26,000	24,000	22,000	20,000	22,000	20,000	277,000
146		Sales Volume - NSW	26,800	27,400	28,600	29,200	30,400	31,600	31,600	29,200	26,800	24,300	26,800	24,300	337,000
147		Sales Volume - VIC	27,800	28,400	29,600	30,200	31,500	32,700	32,700	30,200	27,800	25,200	27,800	25,100	349,000
149		**Actual Statistics- Prev Year**	**Jul-12**	**Aug-12**	**Sep-12**	**Oct-12**	**Nov-12**	**Dec-12**	**Jan-13**	**Feb-13**	**Mar-13**	**Apr-13**	**May-13**	**Jun-13**	**Total**
150		Production Volume - WA	26,097	25,377	23,727	23,910	23,635	19,179	19,804	21,014	22,139	20,990	25,997	24,415	276,284
151		Production Volume - NSW	29,439	29,405	27,397	31,617	29,831	24,089	26,110	27,120	26,080	27,592	30,344	30,446	339,470
152		Production Volume - VIC	32,693	29,405	29,977	30,260	32,055	24,729	24,794	27,208	26,868	27,078	29,633	31,115	345,815
153		Defect Perc - WA	2.7%	2.4%	2.7%	2.3%	2.6%	2.3%	2.4%	2.4%	2.2%	2.2%	2.3%	2.1%	2.4%
154		Defect Perc - NSW	2.6%	2.4%	2.5%	2.4%	2.4%	2.3%	2.2%	2.2%	2.1%	2.1%	2.1%	2.0%	2.3%
155		Defect Perc - VIC	3.0%	2.8%	3.1%	2.7%	2.9%	2.8%	2.7%	2.6%	2.5%	2.7%	2.4%	2.5%	2.7%
156		Machine Hours - WA	1,004	1,034	976	1,044	944	807	791	914	880	913	1,024	1,023	11,354
157		Machine Hours - NSW	1,186	1,139	1,199	1,130	1,077	977	967	1,016	1,031	999	1,201	1,163	13,085
158		Machine Hours - VIC	1,191	1,096	1,110	1,138	1,159	978	985	973	1,098	1,015	1,137	1,077	12,957
159		Maintenance Hours - WA	53	53	55	55	53	48	45	49	49	51	58	57	626
160		Maintenance Hours - NSW	83	80	83	89	84	69	73	76	80	81	89	87	974
161		Maintenance Hours - VIC	49	53	49	55	53	43	45	45	49	49	51	53	594
162		Downtime Hours - WA	16	15	15	17	15	12	12	13	14	14	16	15	174
163		Downtime Hours - NSW	31	30	29	28	27	23	24	24	27	25	29	29	326
164		Downtime Hours - VIC	12	12	11	12	11	10	10	10	11	10	12	11	132
165		Sales Volume - WA	21,041	21,635	22,319	23,657	24,554	25,535	26,866	23,761	21,107	20,038	23,009	20,968	274,490
166		Sales Volume - NSW	27,773	29,317	27,834	28,109	29,927	32,287	33,084	28,627	26,276	24,686	27,992	24,225	340,137
167		Sales Volume - VIC	27,609	26,852	29,933	28,369	31,287	34,240	31,819	29,298	27,322	24,876	27,541	24,880	344,026

FIGURE 15.21 Dashboard_Data Sheet—Budget and Previous-Year Tables

The budget figure in cell C130 has a direct link to the Bud_Stats_Data sheet.

```
=Bud_Stats_Data!B2
```

This is copied across and down.

The previous year formula in cell C150 is

```
=SUMIFS(s_Value,s_Month,C$149,s_Statistic,$B150)
```

Again, the formula is the same as cells C64 and C87.

Dashboard Layout

Using a single legend at the top of the sheet saves having to repeat legends in all the charts. See Figure 15.15.

On the dashboard sheet, cells are used to hold the titles for some of the charts. Controlling the display of chart titles can be problematic in small charts. A cell can provide more flexibility in terms of layout and format.

Rows 3 and 13 of the dashboard report all have links to the Dashboard_Data sheet for the chart headings.

Cell borders have been used to group the charts. In many cases the chart borders have been removed.

The charts were all developed on the Dashboard_Data sheet to make it easy to copy and change the source data. They were then moved to the dashboard sheet.

The line charts at the bottom of the dashboard all include a text box to provide the current month's value plus the average. You need to group the text box with the chart using the instructions from Chapter 12 so that when you move the chart, the text box moves with it.

The charts have been pared down to the point where they display only the minimum requirements.

When working with multiple charts, you often need to have them be as follows:

- Identically sized
- Evenly distributed across the sheet
- All aligned

The easiest way to achieve that is to select the charts first. There are two ways to select multiple charts. You can hold down the Ctrl key and use the mouse to select multiple charts one after the other, or you can use the Select Objects icon (see Figure 15.22). This appears on the Find and Select icon drop-down list on the far right of the Home Ribbon tab.

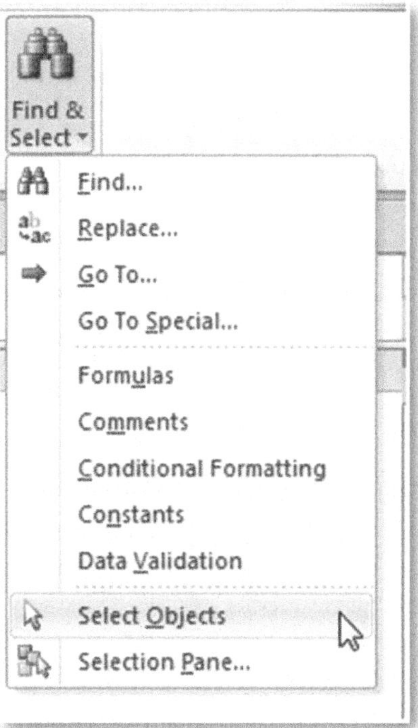

FIGURE 15.22 Select Objects Icon

I recommend adding this icon to your Quick Access Toolbar. Once you click the icon, you can select charts by clicking, holding, and dragging the mouse around the outside of all the charts.

Once the charts are selected, the Format Ribbon tab is displayed (see Figure 15.23). The right side of that tab has all the options you should need. The Align drop-down list has the options you need to align your charts.

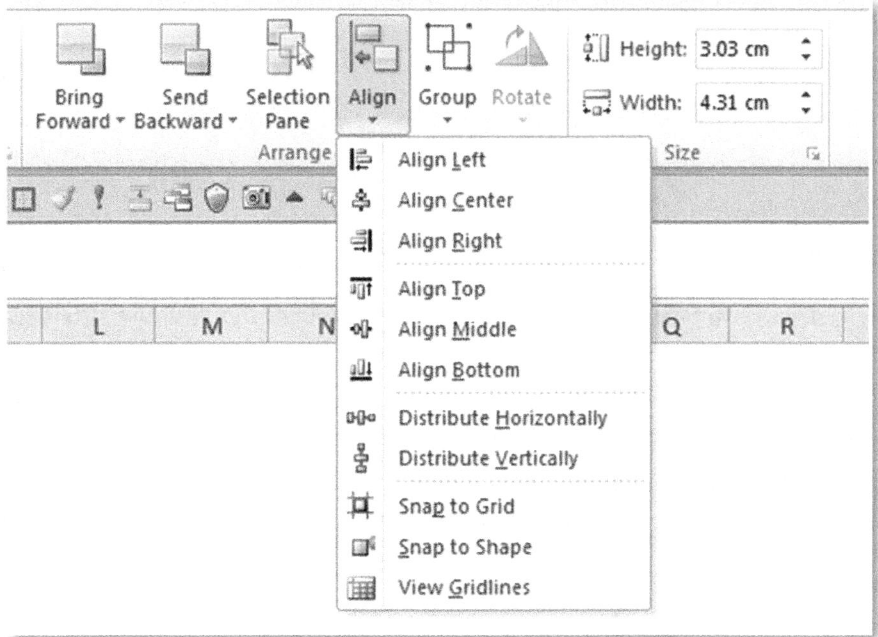

FIGURE 15.23 Format Ribbon Tab

Height and Width on the far right allows you to change all the chart sizes at once.

After you have finished, press the Esc key or click the Select Object icon again to return the cursor to its normal operation.

The State Report

The State_Report sheet, shown in Figure 15.24, lets the user choose a state (cell E4) to report on. All the statistics and averages automatically update. Combining financial and nonfinancial data provides more insights into operations than just the financial values themselves.

This report could be used as the basis for a dashboard for the state.

The report at the top of the sheet uses the GETPIVOTDATA function to extract just the state data from the PT_Stats sheet. The PT_Stats sheet has a pivot table that lists all the entries from the Act_Stats_Data sheet.

Cell D8 creates the statistic name based on the state chosen in cell E4. The formula is

	A	B	C	D	E
1				WXYZ Corporation	
3			Refresh All to ensure latest data is included.	13 Month Report	Input
4				State	WA
5				Start Month	1/11/2012

	A	B	D	Nov-12	Dec-12	Jan-13	Feb-13	Mar-13	Apr-13	May-13	Jun-13	Jul-13	Aug-13	Sep-13	Oct-13	Nov-13	Total	Average
7		Statistics	Statistics - Actuals															
8	1	Production Volume	Production Volume - WA	23,635	19,179	19,804	21,014	22,139	20,990	25,997	24,415	25,839	25,064	23,358	24,395	24,243	300,072	23,082
9	2	Defect Perc	Defect Perc - WA	2.6%	2.3%	2.4%	2.4%	2.2%	2.2%	2.3%	2.1%	2.8%	2.5%	2.7%	2.4%	2.6%	2.4%	2.4%
10	3	Machine Hours	Machine Hours - WA	944	807	791	914	880	913	1,024	1,023	1,042	1,085	968	1,022	964	12,377	952
11	4	Maintenance Hours	Maintenance Hours - WA	53	48	45	49	49	51	58	57	54	55	56	57	53	685	53
12	5	Downtime Hours	Downtime Hours - WA	15	12	12	13	14	14	16	15	16	16	14	16	15	188	14
13	6	Sales Volume	Sales Volume - WA	24,554	25,535	26,866	23,761	21,107	20,038	23,009	20,968	21,732	22,380	22,454	24,537	23,902	300,843	23,142

	Sign		Dept Actuals $ per Unit	Statistic	Nov-12	Dec-12	Jan-13	Feb-13	Mar-13	Apr-13	May-13	Jun-13	Jul-13	Aug-13	Sep-13	Oct-13	Nov-13	Total
16	-1	WA	TRADING	Sales Volume	55.04	55.41	57.51	59.92	60.94	59.29	57.13	57.03	61.37	58.69	63.61	58.22	60.70	58.75
17	1	WA	PRODUCTION	Production Volume	44.37	56.92	58.84	50.67	43.13	40.53	35.67	35.18	37.10	38.79	44.35	43.50	43.82	43.50
18	1	WA	SALES	Sales Volume	2.27	2.17	2.11	2.38	2.67	2.80	2.45	2.70	2.60	2.56	2.52	2.33	2.39	2.44
19	1	WA	ADMIN	Sales Volume	2.88	2.76	2.60	2.97	3.34	3.47	3.07	3.33	3.27	3.15	3.16	2.88	2.98	3.05

	Sign		Category Actuals $ per Unit	Statistic	Nov-12	Dec-12	Jan-13	Feb-13	Mar-13	Apr-13	May-13	Jun-13	Jul-13	Aug-13	Sep-13	Oct-13	Nov-13	Total
22	-1	WA	Revenue	Sales Volume	55.04	55.41	57.51	59.92	60.94	59.29	57.13	57.03	61.37	58.69	63.61	58.22	60.70	58.75
23	1	WA	Direct Costs	Production Volume	44.37	56.92	58.84	50.67	43.13	40.53	35.67	35.18	37.10	38.79	44.35	43.50	43.82	43.50
24	1	WA	Indirect Costs	Sales Volume	5.16	4.93	4.71	5.35	6.01	6.27	5.52	6.03	5.88	5.71	5.69	5.22	5.37	5.49

		Dept Budget $ per Unit	Statistic	Nov-12	Dec-12	Jan-13	Feb-13	Mar-13	Apr-13	May-13	Jun-13	Jul-13	Aug-13	Sep-13	Oct-13	Nov-13
27	WA	TRADING	Sales Volume	0.00	0.00	0.00	0.00	0.00	0.00	0.00	0.00	60.02	60.01	59.99	59.98	59.96
28	WA	PRODUCTION	Production Volume	0.00	0.00	0.00	0.00	0.00	0.00	0.00	0.00	38.05	39.05	43.01	42.05	46.13
29	WA	SALES	Sales Volume	0.00	0.00	0.00	0.00	0.00	0.00	0.00	0.00	2.59	2.53	2.42	2.37	2.28
30	WA	ADMIN	Sales Volume	0.00	0.00	0.00	0.00	0.00	0.00	0.00	0.00	3.22	3.15	3.02	2.95	2.83

	A	B	Statistics - Budget	Nov-12	Dec-12	Jan-13	Feb-13	Mar-13	Apr-13	May-13	Jun-13	Jul-13	Aug-13	Sep-13	Oct-13	Nov-13
33	1	Production Volume	Production Volume - WA	0	0	0	0	0	0	0	0	25,000	25,000	24,000	25,000	24,000
34	2	Defect Perc	Defect Perc - WA	0.0%	0.0%	0.0%	0.0%	0.0%	0.0%	0.0%	0.0%	2.7%	2.6%	2.6%	2.5%	2.5%
35	3	Machine Hours	Machine Hours - WA	0	0	0	0	0	0	0	0	1,042	1,042	1,000	1,042	1,000
36	4	Maintenance Hours	Maintenance Hours - WA	0	0	0	0	0	0	0	0	57	57	55	57	55
37	5	Downtime Hours	Downtime Hours - WA	0	0	0	0	0	0	0	0	16	16	15	16	15
38	6	Sales Volume	Sales Volume - WA	0	0	0	0	0	0	0	0	22,000	22,500	23,500	24,000	25,000

FIGURE 15.24 State Report Sheet

```
=B8&"—"&$E$4
```

Cell B8 extracts the statistic name from the list on the tables sheet. Its formula is

```
=INDEX(Statistics,A8)
```

The statistics range name uses a table name to define the list of statistics.

The formula in cell E8 is

```
=IFERROR(GETPIVOTDATA("Value",PT_Stats!$A$3,"Month",E$7,
  "Statistic",$D8),0)
```

Remember that the GETPIVOTDATA function requires that the pivot table be updated. This has to be done just once, after all the statistics data have been loaded.

When calculating $ per unit averages for departments, you might need to use different statistics (drivers) for different departments. Defining a statistic per department in a table provides that flexibility. Figure 15.10 showed the department table, including the statistic names.

In rows 15 to 19, in Figure 15.24, the departments' total values have been divided by a statistic. The statistic name shown in cell D16 is calculated by the formula

```
=VLOOKUP(C16,tblDepts,2,0)
```

The formula in cell E16 is

```
=SUMIFS(a_Amt,a_Date,E$15,a_Dept,$C16,a_State,$B16)/
  INDEX(E$8:E$13,MATCH($D16,$B$8:$B$13,0))*$A16
```

The $ per unit costs for categories have also been calculated in rows 22 to 24. The formula in cell E22 is

```
=SUMIFS(a_Amt,a_Date,E$15,a_Cat,$C22,a_State,$B22)/
  INDEX(E$8:E$13,MATCH($D22,$B$8:$B$13,0))*$A22
```

Column A holds the sign to convert negative values into positive values.

The budget averages have been included at the bottom of the sheet. The formula in cell E27 is

```
=IFERROR(SUMIFS(OFFSET(b_Account,0,
  MATCH(E$26,Bud_GL_Data!$D$1:$O$1,0)),
  b_Dept,$C27,b_State,$B27)/INDEX(E$33:E$38,
 MATCH($D27,$B$33:$B$38,0)),0)
```

This uses OFFSET to move the range to sum across the sheet. Note that because this is a 13-month report layout, the month might not appear in the Bud_GL_Data sheet; hence the use of the IFERROR function.

The formula in cell E33 is

```
=IFERROR(INDEX(Bud_Stats_Data!$B$2:$M$19,
  MATCH($D33,Bud_Stats_Data!$A$2:$A$19,0),
  MATCH(E$32,Bud_Stats_Data!$B$1:$M$1,0)),0)
```

This extracts the statistics from the Bud_Stats_Data sheet. As above, the month might not appear because of the 13-month layout, so the IFERROR function is used.

CHAPTER SIXTEEN

Final Thoughts

IN THIS BOOK I HAVE shared many techniques that I've applied over the years to improve my Excel reporting. There is only one way to master these techniques and that is to use them regularly. Don't be overwhelmed by the quantity; hopefully, you have already noted the techniques that you can apply immediately. You may need to return to the book when you encounter new reporting issues.

You may be surprised how quickly you can master some of these techniques and how easily they become second nature, once you have used them a few times.

Structure is the key to creating well-built spreadsheets. In most cases you need to provide that structure. With the right structures in place, the solutions, as shown in this book, become easy.

The case studies were designed to demonstrate how you can combine many of the techniques into a standalone reporting solution. Using Excel's functions and features in combination is where you achieve the most effective solutions. You may need to read some of the sections a few times to gain a better understanding of how powerful combining techniques can be.

Many Excel books show you how to use certain functions and features in isolation. I hope this book has shown you how you can use them together to achieve results you never thought possible. Along the way I am optimistic that I have also provided solutions to some of the problems that may have limited your reports in the past, as well as opening up opportunities for better reports in the future.

If this book has made you experiment and attempt new methods, then it was worth the effort, both yours and mine. Excel is an incredibly powerful package, and most people only scratch the surface. If you've starting digging a little deeper, you will soon start to see the benefits.

There are few skills as portable for accountants as Excel skills. Improving those skills is a worthwhile goal. I wish you well on your Excel journey.

FEEDBACK

I'd appreciate any feedback you can provide, both good and bad. Please e-mail your comments to me at a4@iinet.net.au.

LAST WORDS

I'd like to leave you with something my father used to say, and it's helped me immensely over the years: "People rarely ask how long it took to build, but if it's built well, they'll always ask, who built it?"

About the Author

NEALE BLACKWOOD HAS BEEN USING spreadsheets since the late 1980s, starting with Lotus and moving to Excel in the mid-1990s. He graduated with a bachelor of business degree in accounting in 1983 and took his first accounting job at the University of Western Australia the next year. He achieved his certified practising accountant (CPA) status in 1992.

Neale's job roles have included accountant, project accountant, financial controller, management accountant, and senior consultant. He has worked in many industries, including resources, building and construction products, government, and electrical and engineering services. His most recent experience has been in Excel consulting and training with organisations. He now runs his own business, A4 Accounting, which he established in 2001.

Neale achieved the Microsoft Office Specialist Expert certification in Excel in 2006. Since 2002 he has written for CPA Australia's monthly magazine, *INTHEBLACK*, to which he has contributed more than 120 "Excel Yourself" articles and 8 feature articles. He has freely answered Excel questions for Australian CPAs from many different countries for over nine years.

Neale has presented at numerous CPA Australia events around Australia, from one-hour sessions to half-day master classes. He writes and presents his own XL@Lunch Excel webinars to people from around the world.

Neale lives in Perth, Western Australia, with Jan, his wife of 28 years. He has two children and spends his spare time with his family, playing sports, ballroom dancing, and reading and writing.

About the Companion Website

THIS BOOK INCLUDES A COMPANION website that contains many of the Excel spreadsheets used as examples throughout the book. The files are named to match their corresponding chapters. These examples will help you better understand and apply the techniques demonstrated in this book.

An Excel file containing all the macros, mentioned in the book, is also included.

The two case study files have before and after versions. This enables the reader to follow along with the instructions in the two case studies to create the final reporting models. The completed versions will assist if you encounter difficulties.

To access the site, go to www.wiley.com/go/advancedexcel and enter the password blackwood123.

Index

Made in the USA
Columbia, SC
06 December 2020

26492055R00246